THE LEAST EXAMINED BRANCH

Unlike most works in constitutional theory, which focus on the role of the courts, this book addresses the role of legislatures in a regime of constitutional democracy. Bringing together some of the world's leading constitutional scholars and political scientists, the book addresses legislatures in democratic theory, legislating and deliberating in the constitutional state, constitution making by legislatures, legislative and popular constitutionalism, and the dialogic role of legislatures, both domestically with other institutions and internationally with other legislatures. The book offers theoretical perspectives as well as case studies of several types of legislation from the United States and Canada. It also addresses the role of legislatures under both the Westminster model and a separation of powers system.

Richard W. Bauman is Professor of Law at the University of Alberta, where he is also Chair of the Management Board of the Centre for Constitutional Studies. He was educated at the University of Alberta, Dalhousie University, and Oxford University. His most recent book is *Ideology and Community in the First Wave of Critical Legal Studies*. He has published in law journals in Canada, the United States, and South Africa.

Tsvi Kahana is an Assistant Professor of Law at Queen's University, Ontario, Canada. He has taught courses at the University of Alberta, the University of Toronto, and Tel-Aviv University. His work has been published in *The University of Toronto Law Journal, The Journal of Canadian Public Administration, Queen's Law Journal*, and *The Supreme Court Law Review*.

THE LEAST EXAMINED BRANCH

The Role of Legislatures in the Constitutional State

Edited by

RICHARD W. BAUMAN
University of Alberta

TSVI KAHANA
Queen's University, Canada

CAMBRIDGE UNIVERSITY PRESS
Cambridge, New York, Melbourne, Madrid, Cape Town, Singapore, São Paulo

Cambridge University Press
32 Avenue of the Americas, New York, NY 10013–2473, USA

www.cambridge.org
Information on this title: www.cambridge.org/9780521859547

First published 2006

Printed in the United States of America

A catalog record for this publication is available from the British Library.

Library of Congress Cataloging in Publication Data

The least examined branch : the role of legislatures in the constitutional state / edited
by Richard W. Bauman, Tsvi Kahana.
p. cm.
Includes bibliographical references and index.
ISBN-13: 978-0-521-85954-7 (hbk.)
ISBN-10: 0-521-85954-9 (hbk.)
ISBN-13: 978-0-521-67682-3 (pbk.)
ISBN-10: 0-521-67682-7 (pbk.)
1. Legislation. 2. Legislative bodies. 3. Constitutional law. I. Bauman, Richard W.
II. Kahana, Tsvi, 1967– III. Title.
K3316.L44 2006
328 – dc22 2006002830

ISBN-13 978-0-521-85954-7 hardback
ISBN-10 0-521-85954-9 hardback

ISBN-13 978-0-521-67682-3 paperback
ISBN-10 0-521-67682-7 paperback

Contents

Foreword: Legislatures in the Constitutional State

The distinctive role of legislatures in expressing and pursuing the goals of constitutional democracies is the subject of this volume, and it could not be more important, timely, or wide-ranging. The contributors are prominent scholars who have helped to frame some of the most original perspectives on this subject.[1]

Constitutional democracies form and express their ideals through two mechanisms. First, they contain broadly representative political bodies, which we call legislatures. Second, they are constituted by a constitution (written or unwritten) whose laws support a set of democratic procedures and substantive rights that are more basic than the ordinary statutes routinely passed by legislatures.

This volume considers how legislatures can support both the procedural and substantive goals of a constitutional democracy. Contributors consider the principles that should govern legislation; the ways in which legislatures can serve as lawmakers, law followers, and codeterminers with courts of constitutional law; and how legislatures can engage in productive dialogue with citizens and courts at home and peer institutions in other countries.

The primary reason why this subject is so timely and important is that constitutional democracies have been multiplying throughout the world; yet, theorists and practitioners of constitutional democracy alike have yet to fully grasp just how legislatures and courts should divide up the labor of furthering democratic and constitutional values. The virtue of this volume is that it does not pretend to settle this extremely complex issue, but rather it intelligently explores almost every plausible permutation of an answer.

The contributors present many different answers ranging from legislatures working democratically within constitutional boundaries (typically set by judicial authority) to legislatures being the democratic authority over courts in determining the judiciary's constitutional powers.

A less conventional view explored and defended by many contributors is that democratic legislatures act as partners with courts in an ongoing dialogue that codetermines constitutional boundaries over time. On this view, both legislatures and courts have distinct roles to play in shaping constitutional law, but their roles are interactive rather than exclusive.

[1] I wish to thank Tsvi Kahana for organizing the conference on which this volume is based, and Sigal Ben-Porath and Dennis Thompson for their insightful comments on an earlier draft of my foreword.

As constitutional democracies spread around the world, the diverse ways in which they are structured raises the question of whether there is a single optimal role for legislatures in a constitutional state. More likely, there are diverse roles for legislatures in diverse constitutional states due to historical, socioeconomic, and cultural variations among states. If we are attuned to such variations, we are likely to arrive at different answers to how legislatures can best function in varying societal contexts even as we hold constant the high-level goal of furthering constitutionally democratic values.

Constitutional democracies are different in kind from undemocratic and non-constitutional states, but there are also significant differences among constitutional states. Some have written, others unwritten, constitutions. Some have multiparty, others two-party, systems. Some contain unicameral, others bicameral, legislatures. There are also vast differences in electoral laws as well as important variations in the substance of constitutional law itself. The actual role of legislatures in different constitutional democracies varies significantly by societal context. Their optimal role is also likely to vary, again depending on context.

Examining the many plausible variations in the division of legislative and judicial labor among constitutional democracies can help us understand when legislators and judges act in ways that are inconsistent with a productive division of labor. Consider the way the two sets of institutions are designed in the United States, a nonexceptional example. Legislatures are designed to be broadly representative and to make general laws. Courts in the United States, as in many other constitutional democracies, are designed to be more insulated from electoral pressures and to hear individual cases, and therefore most often do well when they rule narrowly on the legal (or constitutional) merits of the case. The converse is true for legislatures. Legislatures, being far more representative institutions, are far better designed than courts to determine policies that affect many people. Even if their competence to foresee the consequences of complex legislation is necessarily limited, at least their broadly representative nature offers legislatures the legitimacy to act in the name of the majority when it makes general laws.

This distinction between judicial and legislative roles is not therefore between principle and policy, because both institutions can and should act in principled ways. It is rather between ruling narrowly and legislating broadly, whether the rulings are a matter of principle or policy. This distinction is fundamental to understanding the difference between how courts and legislatures are typically designed to work and how they work best in supporting a constitutional democracy. Legislatures most often make egregious mistakes when they try to rule on single, high-visibility cases for politically expedient purposes. Courts correspondingly most often make egregious mistakes when they rule in ways that go far beyond what can be confidently inferred from the merits of the actual case or cases at hand.

When this distinction between making general policy and ruling on particular cases is ignored, democratic government ties itself up in knots, as illustrated by what happened in the widely publicized and highly contentious case of Terri Schiavo in the United States. To quickly summarize the facts: Terri Schiavo suffered massive brain damage after heart failure in 1990. For fifteen years, she had been unconscious. Prior to becoming unconscious, she had not prepared a living will.

Her husband and her parents disagreed on whether she would have wanted to be kept alive under such circumstances (and they also disagreed about whether there was reasonable hope of her recovery). Who was to decide?

Her husband, Michael, was her legal guardian. Based on conversations before her heart attack, Michael insisted that Terri would not have wanted to continue living in her unconscious state. Florida courts had jurisdiction over the case, and for years heard and rejected appeals by Terri's parents and siblings, who wanted to keep her alive. Based on well-established legal precedent, the courts repeatedly sided with Michael's right to order removal of the feeding tube. The United States Supreme Court declined to hear appeals of the court rulings.

Starting in February 2000, the local executive and legislative bodies in Florida issued orders to keep her alive each time that the courts affirmed her legal guardian's right to have her feeding tube removed. In October 2003, the Florida legislature passed a bill called "Terri's law" allowing the governor to intervene in her case (to order the reinsertion of her feeding tube). This bill was struck down as unconstitutional by Florida's Supreme Court.

In March 2005, the United States Congress blocked attempts to let Terri Schiavo die. In addition, Congress passed a bill giving the federal courts jurisdiction only in this particular case, and President Bush interrupted his vacation to sign it at 1:11 A.M. on March 21. The law passed the Senate with no debate and with only three members present. The Senate Majority Leader, who led passage of the measure, called it "a unique bill" that "should not serve as a precedent for future legislation."[2] In the midst of this acrimonious partisan struggle, just about everyone could agree that legislating for one person is bad precedent and generally inconsistent with the legislative role. The bill that Congress passed even had a "sense of Congress" resolution at the end, stating that Congress should address this issue as a matter of policy in the future. Congress recognized, in the breach, its responsibility to pass general laws, not ones tailor-made for an individual case.

Not one but four mistakes were made by Congress when it ruled in the Schiavo case. First and foremost, it passed a piece of essentially private legislation, a law that applies to only one case. Second, congressional intervention was ad hoc and untimely. The courts had already taken jurisdiction of the case and for many years had heard and decided many appeals. Third, representatives in Congress who took the lead in intervening appeared to be motivated by the sheer politics of appeasing a vocal and powerful ideological (minority) base. The same representatives had shown no interest in this case or anything like it earlier. Finally, Congress was mistaken on the merits of the case just as the courts would have been had they decided to keep Terri Schiavo alive in the absence of any knowledge of Terri's prior wishes and despite her legal guardian's wishes. Being wrong in this substantive sense, however, is consistent with an institution acting in a procedurally correct way in asserting its authority to decide a case. It is important that we recognize that there is no democratic procedure so perfect as to yield correct substantive results in every case. But when legislatures (or courts) act procedurally in ad hoc ways, which depart from their clear procedural mandate, they increase their odds

[2] This and the next quotations from political actors are from the *Washington Post*, March 21, 2005, http://www.washingtonpost.com/wp-dyn/ articles/ A51402-2005Mar20.html.

of making substantive mistakes. The wrongness of legislative intervention in the Schiavo case therefore was overdetermined.

Even if Congress had not been wrong on the last three grounds, it still would be subject to criticism for passing private legislation. But that it was wrong on all these grounds is not pure coincidence. The many ways in which Congress was wrong reveal the many risks incurred by legislatures when they rule in very particular cases, rather than for the sake of making general legislation. It is a warning sign when a legislature takes up a very particular case – little or no good is likely to come of it, and damage is likely to be done to the legitimacy of the institution. Legislatures have very broad latitude in what they can do, but passing private legislation strains their institutional legitimacy.

This volume does not settle the question of what the precise role of legislatures should be, because it admirably represents a wide range of well-reasoned perspectives that are still in play, in both theory and practice. But, it does give readers good reason to criticize legislatures when they pass laws that apply to only one case, or legislation – such as earmarking, tax code amendments for particular individuals or corporations, and pork barrel bills – that defy a general justification. Historically, private legislation has been closely associated with legislative corruption, often by individual legislators who were beholden more to the interests of a few powerful individuals than to a majority of their constituents.

Yet, it is important to recognize that no single legislator who passes private legislation must be corrupt for the institution to be acting in a self-corrupting way. Even if no legislator has done anything that is individually corrupt, private legislation and laws that defy a general justification may be considered a form of institutional corruption. By acting in a way inconsistent with a general justification or defensible division of labor between legislatures and courts, the legislature contributes to its own corruption as a democratic institution and weakens its otherwise legitimate authority in society.

Fortunately for the future of constitutional democracy, examples of legislatures acting in ways consistent with their productive and essential role in a constitutional democracy abound. The United States Congress typically passes general laws, which is why the Schiavo case seems so exceptional. It is. Legislatures far more typically pass general laws that guarantee civil rights, balance budgets, reform welfare, raise or lower taxes, and establish trade agreements between countries. Of course, when legislatures pass general laws, there is no guarantee that we will find the content of those laws defensible, which is yet another reason why knowing what we should expect of legislatures at their best is so important. Laws that on their face lay claim to defending civil rights and to balancing state budgets can actually (on further analysis and evidence) violate individual rights and imbalance budgets.

When courts adjudicate individual cases, they too may or may not arrive at the right results. Those results may reside in the realm of basic constitutional rights or interpretations of more routine (and common) legislative mandates. Reasonable people disagree over when legislatures and courts actually get matters right. And so it is in every democracy that a host of challenges is brought to the doorstep of legislatures as well as courts, many of which are not clear-cut in either theory or practice.

Perhaps the greatest virtue of legislative processes – and the deepest source of ongoing frustration with them – is that they are designed to respond to gray areas of interests and expectations of complex constituencies. Often, when a tax or welfare reform is under legislative consideration, it is impossible to know without careful probing whether the legislative majority would be acting in a majority's or minority's interests in supporting the reform. And, which majority or minority is the legislature representing? It is often also impossible to know simply on the face (or by the text) of proposed legislation who the relevant constituents are whose interests should be represented. It typically takes careful deliberation for even its most avid proponents to understand the consequences (and therefore effects on the interests of individuals) of a free trade bill, a balanced budget amendment, or a welfare reform proposal.

Legislatures therefore generally do well when – rather than passing legislation without debate – they act deliberatively, bringing to bear the best evidence, reasoning, and perspectives of the widest range of representatives. A still broader aspiration is to deliberate across institutional and geopolitical boundaries. Such aspirations are crucial for keeping constitutional democratic ideals alive in practice as well as in theory. Nothing less is at stake than the well-being of present and future generations and the future of constitutional democracy.

Amy Gutmann

Contributors

Harry Arthurs is University Professor Emeritus and President Emeritus, York University.

Daphne Barak-Erez is Professor, Faculty of Law, Tel-Aviv University.

Cécile Bergada is a Ph.D. candidate at the Faculty of Law, University of Montreal.

Richard W. Bauman is Professor of Law and Chair of the Management Board, Centre for Constitutional Studies, University of Alberta.

Sujit Choudhry is Associate Professor of Law and Political Science, University of Toronto.

Neal Devins is Goodrich Professor of Law; Professor of Government; and Director, Institute of Bill of Rights Law, Marshall-Wythe School of Law, College of William & Mary.

David Dyzenhaus is Professor of Law and Philosophy, University of Toronto.

Jon Elster is Robert K. Merton Professor of Social Sciences, Columbia University.

William N. Eskridge, Jr., is John A. Garver Professor of Jurisprudence, Yale Law School.

Daniel A. Farber is Sho Sato Professor of Law, University of California at Berkeley.

John Ferejohn is a senior fellow at the Hoover Institution and Carolyn S. G. Munro Professor of Political Science, Stanford University.

Owen Fiss is Sterling Professor of Law, Yale University.

Elizabeth Garrett is Sydney M. Irmas Professor of Public Interest Law, Legal Ethics, and Political Science, University of Southern California, and Director, U.S.C.–Caltech Center for the Study of Law and Politics.

Ruth Gavison is Haim H. Cohn Professor of Human Rights, Faculty of Law, Hebrew University, Jerusalem.

Éric Gélineau is a Ph.D. candidate at the Faculty of Law, University of Montreal.

Heather K. Gerken is Professor of Law, Harvard Law School.

Amy Gutmann is President and Professor of Political Science, University of Pennsylvania.

Russell Hardin is Professor of Politics, New York University.

Hutch Hicken is an attorney with Litchford and Christopher, Orlando, Florida.

Patricia Hughes is Dean and Professor of Law, University of Calgary.

Tsvi Kahana is Assistant Professor of Law, Queen's University, Kingston, Ontario.

Andrée Lajoie is Professor of Law, Centre for Research in Public Law, University of Montreal.

Sanford Levinson is W. St. John Garwood and W. St. John Garwood, Jr. Centennial Chair in Law and Professor of Government, University of Texas.

Andrei Marmor is Professor of Law and Professor of Philosophy, University of Southern California.

Frank I. Michelman is Robert Walmsley University Professor, Harvard University.

Jennifer Nedelsky is Professor of Law and Political Science, University of Toronto.

Andrew Petter is Dean and Professor of Law, University of Victoria.

Jane S. Schacter is James E. and Ruth B. Doyle-Bascom Professor of Law, University of Wisconsin.

Frederick Schauer is Frank Stanton Professor of the First Amendment, John F. Kennedy School of Government, Harvard University.

Cass R. Sunstein is Karl N. Llewellyn Distinguished Service Professor of Jurisprudence, Law School and Department of Political Science, University of Chicago.

Chantal Thomas is Professor of Law, Fordham University.

Mark Tushnet is Carmack Waterhouse Professor of Constitutional Law, Georgetown University.

Adrian Vermeule is Bernard D. Meltzer Professor of Law, University of Chicago.

Jeremy Waldron is University Professor in the School of Law, Columbia University.

Jeremy Webber is Canada Research Chair in Law and Society, Faculty of Law, University of Victoria; Director, Consortium on Democratic Constitutionalism; and Visiting Professor of Law, University of New South Wales.

Keith E. Whittington is Professor of Politics, Princeton University.

New Ways of Looking at Old Institutions

Richard W. Bauman and Tsvi Kahana

This book seeks to redress an imbalance. Over the past few generations, scholars who study processes of constitutional lawmaking – including modes of creation, interpretation, and application – have focused largely on how courts work with constitutions. Rival theories of adjudication, whether dealing with how power is allocated in a modern state or with how rights are to be protected in light of constitutional guarantees, have been intricately constructed. Just as theories along this line have proliferated, so too have empirical studies of the performance of judges as constitutional oracles and referees.

Less attention has been paid to how legislatures, executive officials, or administrative agencies have interpreted their responsibilities to make or revise or implement constitutions. Of these branches, legislatures are the prime focus of this book. How do they respect (or occasionally overstep) constitutional boundaries? When and for what ends do they reverse the constitutional decisions of courts? How do legislatures create new forms of constitution-like instruments, doctrines, and principles? Moreover, how do they realize or make concrete the ideals that underpin a constitutional democracy? Are there discrepancies between what a constitution envisions by way of democratic processes or values and how legislatures operate in fact? In response to such questions, this book offers theoretical perspectives from a multidisciplinary group of authors. The work of legislatures, illustrated by examples derived predominantly from North America, is described as well as normatively assessed.

The systematic neglect of legislatures by legal and political philosophers has been noted by, among others, Jeremy Waldron. The work of legislatures has a bad reputation for being rife with "deal-making, horse-trading, log-rolling, interest-pandering, and pork-barrelling."[1] The rumbustious process of enacting or defeating statutes, issuing regulations, holding committee inquiries, engaging in debates over government policy, and making appointments has traditionally not earned the same respect as the development of common law. The latter is viewed as aspiring to a principled basis, whereas lawyers and political scientists have long doubted whether legislators are primarily motivated by anything other than self-interestedly maintaining power or else lusting after it. As Waldron points out, legislatures as legitimate and authoritative sources of law have been "under-theorized."[2] To embark

[1] Jeremy Waldron, *The Dignity of Legislation* (Cambridge: Cambridge University Press, 1999) at 2.

[2] Ibid. at 3.

now on such a theoretical project requires legal and political philosophers to turn their attention away from judicial reasoning or the role of courts as guardians of rights that majorities will be prone to trample, and to become more comfortable with, and informed about, democratic structures involving a plurality of political agents and the types of lawmaking that arise in practical settings that prize disagreement and diversity.[3]

Alongside the plea for a better and more accurate conception of the legislative process, doubts have been expressed about whether courts in constitutional democracies should have the exclusive or final word on what the constitution means. Mark Tushnet, for example, has written on the contingent nature of judicial review.[4] He doubts whether courts need to perform this task and, even if they do, whether they are so uniquely suited to the job of interpreting the constitution as some theorists claim. In his assessment of constitutional litigation, what often appear to be victories by rights-claimants have an underside that masks a lack of social progress on important policy issues.[5] Tushnet has offered instead a theory of "populist constitutional law" that takes to heart the ideals of dialogue and democratic self-government and that gives the constitution back to the citizens.[6] More recently, Larry Kramer has pointed out how judicial supremacy in the United States was not part of the original scheme of government but only became the rule later.[7] On the palimpsest of U.S. history is still written an older tradition, according to which citizens consider the meaning of the Constitution to be their prerogative: They refuse to recognize a judicial monopoly on constitutional interpretation. Kramer deplores the efforts to efface this tradition and treat U.S. constitutional history as "a story of judicial triumphalism" and Supreme Court doctrine.[8] To restore control of the Constitution in the hands of the people, without necessarily abolishing judicial review altogether, Kramer has floated such ideas as limiting the Supreme Court's jurisdiction, changing the appointments process, revising the constitutional amending procedure, and setting age or term limits for Supreme Court justices.[9]

This more positive and populist conception of self-government, according to which the Constitution should not be viewed as primarily constraining political choice, but rather as creating opportunities for citizens to fashion new arrangements in the future, also informs the work of scholars like Christopher Eisgruber. Unlike Tushnet, however, Eisgruber defends judicial review, not as an institution that counters democracy but as an institution that can help democracy flourish.[10] Eisgruber is more sanguine than Tushnet about the possibility that judges, when interpreting the Constitution, act as representatives of the people and therefore can

[3] See Jeremy Waldron, *Law and Disagreement* (Oxford: Clarendon Press, 1999) at 10–11.

[4] See Mark Tushnet, *Taking the Constitution Away from the Courts* (Princeton: Princeton University Press, 1999) ch. 7.

[5] See ibid. at 141–52.

[6] See ibid. ch. 8.

[7] See Larry D. Kramer, *The People Themselves: Popular Constitutionalism and Judicial Review* (Oxford: Oxford University Press, 2004) at 170ff.

[8] Ibid. at 229.

[9] Ibid. at 250–2.

[10] Christopher L. Eisgruber, *Constitutional Self-Government* (Cambridge, Mass.: Harvard University Press, 2001).

speak on their behalf about controversial questions of political or moral principle. Constitutional judgments, instead of foreclosing debate, often stimulate public argument.[11] And, overall, Eisgruber (following in the footsteps of Ronald Dworkin and Owen Fiss) believes that judicial review has worked well in the United States.[12] It works best as a practical device, according to Eisgruber, when it reinforces other democratic institutions. In a similar vein, Lawrence Sager has recently emphasized the successes resulting from judicial review as a constitutional practice.[13] On his theory, the judiciary is in league with popular political institutions – they form a "contemporary partnership" – that "promises a more complete constitutional justice than could be realized by the courts alone."[14]

Whether one prefers the populist mode of thinking espoused by Tushnet and Kramer or the type of defense of judicial review offered by Eisgruber and Sager, it is clear that legislatures are a main player in the constitutional state. Thus, we need to explore the ways in which these representative institutions act democratically vis-à-vis the interpretation and application of a constitution. The challenge is to explain the role of the legislature as an institution that both is constrained by constitutionalism and that promotes the democratic values that lie at the core of constitutionalism.

The book is organized along these lines: The first two parts address democratic theory, the ways in which constitutionalism interacts with democracy and the role of the legislature within these interactions. Part I examines legislatures from the standpoint of democratic theory. Part II looks at legislating and deliberating in a constitutional democracy. The themes then shift from democratic theory to constitutionalism. Parts III and IV examine constitution making by legislatures, whether explicitly through constitutional amendments or implicitly through enacting certain types of legislation. The succeeding two parts discuss legislatures' engagement with the constitution, once adopted. Part V focuses on how legislatures interpret and apply a constitution. Part VI is devoted to recent debates about legislative constitutionalism, or the notion that legislatures, not the courts, should have the final word on constitutional issues. The final section of the book, Part VII, includes chapters that explore how modern legislatures take part in conversation or dialogues, with both courts and with other legislatures, that might be domestic or foreign.

In this book's first part, several authors take aim at traditional accounts of political action and how legislatures ought best to function. They all reject as simplistic the idea that judges and legislators form two quite different categories of public officials. On this view, judges are guided by reason, whereas legislatures are necessarily moved by political passions and rational self-interest. Nor is it accurate to portray courts as domains of principle and legislatures as forums of policy. By contrast with these conventional accounts, Jeremy Waldron in Chapter 1 emphasizes the need for legislators in a constitutional regime to act in a principled way. He invokes some of the values associated with theories of deliberative democracy.

11 Ibid. at 96.
12 Ibid. at 210.
13 Lawrence G. Sager, *Justice in Plainclothes: A Theory of American Constitutional Practice* (New Haven: Yale University Press, 2004).
14 Ibid. at 7.

This means that, in making laws, legislators should carefully weigh and argue about a proposed law's purposes and possible consequences. Legislators, as much as judges, are bound to act reasonably and with integrity. The lawmakers bear a heavy responsibility to ensure that their actions are legitimate. Legislators are not simply delegates of electors and therefore they should make their decisions after proper deliberation.

To constrain legislators in their ability to make laws is one (though not the only) function of a constitution. It will also typically provide the institutional design under which legislators (usually by majority rule) engage in specific acts of lawmaking. Thus in the United States as Russell Hardin points out in Chapter 2, the constitutional scheme provides a separation of powers for the national government as a way to protect individual rights. Hardin does not doubt that sometimes legislators are tempted to make decisions while influenced by factors that are not purely deliberative: For example, the legislator will consider political ramifications (such as reelection or future campaign financing) in sponsoring legislation or casting a particular vote. Or, the process of law making might involve political log-rolling, compromise, or bowing to the pressure of lobbyists. Hardin emphasizes the problems for democracy created by lack of knowledge on the part of citizens. They often have little idea what the legislature is doing. With a backward look at the growth of the U.S. republic, Hardin also argues that democracy, on its best account, requires legislators continually to monitor the needs, interests, and values of a nation's citizens.

As her point of departure, Jane Schacter notes in Chapter 3 the minimalist conception of democracy relied on by previous theorists, such as Alexander Bickel or Joseph Schumpeter, who attempted to stipulate the respective spheres of legislatures and courts. Legislators are elected and judges largely are not. This makes all the difference: The popularly chosen legislature is treated as a more legitimate institution for lawmaking because it is more accountable. But this validation of the legislature as the most legitimate makes sense, according to Schacter, only if accountability – indeed, if democracy – is understood in an anemic sense. She offers instead an empirical discussion that identifies problems with different models of accountability. And she turns to a robust conception of democracy that goes beyond mere voting: It includes also conditions requiring an active citizenry, serious deliberation of proposed laws by their representatives, and adherence to norms of equality and justice. In support of her conclusions, Schacter (like Waldron) refers to Condorcet's so-called jury theorem, a principle of political philosophy that holds that decisions made by larger bodies of decision makers are likely to be more rational than smaller ones. Hardin challenges this principle.

In Chapter 4, Chantal Thomas considers one of the contemporary modes by which a legislature can arguably reduce democratic involvement in lawmaking. Her example is the fast-track procedure used in the United States that entitles the executive branch of government to negotiate international trade agreements and then provides an expeditious route for Congress to approve those agreements. This mechanism is difficult to square with such desirable democratic values as widespread public participation in lawmaking, transparency of the political process, and opportunities to revise proposed laws during the process of deliberation. The resultant debates over trade legislation tend to be poorly informed and amount to pure formalities. After criticizing these processes on grounds similar to those, Thomas questions whether the fast-track procedure violates the separation of powers contained in the U.S. Constitution. In particular, she probes the issue whether the procedure offends the nondelegation doctrine formulated in the past by the U.S. Supreme Court. She concludes that, though it is unlikely to be invalidated on judicial review, the use of the fast-track mechanism presents opportunities to debate and test different democratic theories.

In Part II of this book, which focuses on legislating and deliberating in the constitutional state, contributors peer closely into how legislators ought to conduct their business, as they operate under the shadow of a constitution in a pluralistic society. In Chapter 5, Jennifer Nedelsky articulates and defends a deliberative approach that should be used by legislatures as well as courts in a constitutional democracy. She emphasizes that good government involves a search for the public good, which Nedelsky (as does Schacter in Chapter 3) differentiates from public opinion. In her conception of democracy, Nedelsky also disputes the idea that reaching agreement on the public good is a matter of aggregating individuals' interests or preferences. Instead, what is required of legislators is an enlarged mentality or judgment, so that they sedulously take into account moral views different from their own. Her primary example of an alternative standpoint that ought to be given weight is the diverse body of religious views held by citizens. Though at first blush Nedelsky's suggestion seems to contradict the liberal foundations of democratic theory, which ordinarily treat religious convictions as irrelevant to an elaboration of constitutional values, she argues that the meaning of core values, such as equality, is best assessed by taking into account multiple perspectives, including nonsecular ones.

Andrei Marmor echoes Nedelsky's claims in favor of plurality and of a legislature's considering all moral views held by citizens, though his account features ideological, rather than religious, diversity. In Chapter 6, he argues that in a constitutional democracy, it would be anathema for the state to enact a particular set of moral doctrines. Democracies are supposed to be marked by value fragmentation and incoherence: In such a crucible, democratic disagreements can thrive. On this ground, Marmor criticizes the work of Ronald Dworkin, who attempts to set up an ideal standard of univocal political morality that should animate both legislators and judges. Marmor doubts (*pace* Waldron, in Chapter 1) whether legislators should be held to a rigorous standard of integrity. The virtue of democratic pluralism is that legislatures should be free to make laws that do not cohere with one another: This is to be expected in systems that permit political compromise, change in governments, and (as in federal states) divisions of legislative power among different levels of government.

To this point in the collection, the authors unite behind the idea that legislatures, as much as the courts, must be capable of applying the constitution in both its federalism and its rights-protection aspects. Very often, the executive branch of government and administrative agencies will also be required to do this. In Chapter 7, Cass Sunstein offers a portrait of the nondelegation doctrine (already referred to earlier by Thomas in Chapter 4), reputedly found in the U.S. Constitution. It prohibits the national government from delegating its power to make law to another body. Sunstein is doubtful about the current status of the doctrine: In the decades since it was announced, it might have fallen by the wayside. Despite this, Sunstein contends that important principles or canons of administrative law can usefully be deployed to block attempted improper delegations of power. The upshot of this is constitutional; that is, individual rights are protected because they are not left to the whim of the executive branch or administrative agencies. From his examination of U.S. jurisprudence, Sunstein concludes that these canons are alive, even if the nondelegation doctrine's viability is in question.

In Chapter 8, Harry Arthurs explores the meaning of populist challenges to the institutions of representative democracy. Partly out of a distrust of such indirect democracy, and also many of the features associated with a parliament on the Westminster model, there has been in Canada a steady use of mechanisms such as referenda and plebiscites, the effect of which is to alter constitutional arrangements, even if, as with the case of recent political initiatives, formal constitutional documents do not mention these mechanisms at all. Arthurs analyzes the initiatives used and proposed by populist movements – paying close attention to their rhetoric – and concludes that their common goal is to change structures and processes of government in a way analogous to formal constitutional reform. The impetus behind this phenomenon has not only been from the grass roots up. He traces the extent to which some governments themselves have used populist rhetoric to justify their own particular neoliberal agendas. And, thus, in the end he arrives at a paradox: Much of the impact of populism has been to entrench private power to a degree that will make it difficult for populists of the future to undo. In seeking to enhance citizens' voice and direct influence over lawmaking, populism can also exacerbate parliamentary factionalism and private-interest group lobbying.

Parts III and IV of the book shift the focus from democracy to constitutionalism, starting with the process by which a constitution is made. Jon Elster opens Part III by addressing, in Chapter 9, those junctures in history when legislatures or national political bodies are called on to create new constitutions. He identifies the problems and perplexities about how best to organize this process. After reviewing numerous mechanisms used in different countries, in different eras, and under varying social and historical conditions, Elster concludes that, on balance, it is preferable to use a special constitutional convention, called together for the purpose of designing and approving a new constitution, rather than to rely on a legislature or parliament sitting as a constituent assembly. The former process is more likely to promote unconstrained deliberation among the participants and to avoid certain biases that might creep into the process. Elster also suggests why, at certain stages, some *in camera* deliberations contribute to a better process.

In Chapter 10, Ruth Gavison also assesses the importance of a constituent assembly as a popular institution for creating a constitution. Moreover, she directly challenges the idea that courts, rather than legislatures, are the most important part of a constitutional regime and thus most susceptible to blame for constitutional results. She is especially concerned with allowing the judiciary too much involvement in the process of constitution making. She concedes that judges play a central role, but on her conception legislatures also have a critical duty to understand and adopt clear positions on constitutional issues. She addresses the traditional counter-majoritarian problem arising out of giving courts an unreviewable say over how constitutions should be enforced. Judicial power in this area is not a necessary requirement of democratic constitutions and, furthermore, the design by which courts have this power might derive from a legislative decision in the first place. She disagrees with those theorists (such as Elster) who claim that constitutional conventions, made up of people who are not primarily politicians, provide the best process of constitution making.

Like Gavison, Patricia Hughes understands how legitimacy is a bedrock requirement of a country governed under a constitution. In Chapter 11, Hughes discusses those moments or phases in a country's constitutional evolution when, for various reasons, an impasse might have been reached and legislatures follow a pragmatic course of departing from strict constitutional requirements, in service of the larger goal of maintaining political stability and avoiding crisis. Her term for this condition of reluctance to engage in constitutional definition or reform is "constitutional agnosticism." To illustrate her discussion, she draws on modern political developments in Canada, Israel, South Africa, and Germany. Her study concludes that constitutional agnosticism can sometimes be useful in staving off potentially explosive national debates or delaying full-fledged constitutional debate until more propitious circumstances arise. On the other hand, such agnosticism can also be used unscrupulously, so that legislatures can aggrandize power in ways that would not pass constitutional muster.

Which is the preferable mode for constitutional change: formal constitutional amendment, generally done by legislatures, or periodic common-law updating, generally done by courts? In Chapter 12, Adrian Vermeule argues against those who think that the latter is generally better. He disputes the view that courts are the best institution for change and, to bolster his conclusions, he analyzes those conditions under which each method of change functions best. He also notes the comparative advantages and drawbacks of each process.

Legislatures can change the constitution not only through explicit means, but also implicitly, through ordinary lawmaking. This is the subject of Part IV of the book. Frank Michelman provides a theoretical foundation to the possibility for this type of statutory constitutionalism. In Chapter 13, Michelman draws on contemporary positivist legal theory and analytically attempts to identify the essential differences between constitutions and statutes. He argues that, even though written constitutions are often considered the basic law of a legal system, this is not a necessary characteristic. Moreover, he concludes that ordinary laws enacted by legislatures can perform all the same functions that are thought usually to attach to written constitutions. Michelman's chapter is thus highly relevant to debates over the fetishization of constitutions: They might not have the extraordinary qualities often attributed to them.

In Chapter 14, Elizabeth Garrett considers the phenomenon of framework laws generally. The "framework legislation" that she describes channels the making of future laws and involves substantial delegations of authority. Garrett's aim is to identify and explore the conditions under which a legislature adopts such a scheme for regulating lawmaking on a specific matter (e.g., the budget process) into the future. This kind of statutory regime has quasi-constitutional effects and can enhance the power of party leaders or strategically important committees. It can be used to centralize power and to change the ordinary legislative rules. In that sense, Garrett demonstrates that unlike the case of the fast-track procedure for implementing trade agreements, discussed by Thomas in Chapter 4, allowing legislatures to set the self-regulatory mechanism might have a democratic benefit.

A further example of an emerging, new constitutional context in which legislatures operate is under the aegis of a "super-statute," discussed by William Eskridge, Jr., and John Ferejohn in Chapter 15. Such a broad statute can be created without a formal constitutional amendment; it is made by legislators and bureaucrats, rather than by judges; and it can lead to a process of constant change in fundamental legal norms. The authors view this new type of constitutionalism as normatively superior to the traditional account of constitution making that depends on treating a constitution as a basic document to be interpreted primarily by judges. Eskridge and Ferejohn also point to historical instances, such as the civil rights era in the United States, when judges followed legislative leads rather than anticipated them. In support of their normative arguments, the authors emphasize and defend the deliberative aspects required to enact and interpret super-statutes, with publicly accountable reasoning.

Are courts indeed better at interpreting constitutions than legislatures, as conventional wisdom would indicate? Do judges really have many professional or institutional advantages to do a better job of constitutional interpretation? Can legislatures be entrusted with this task? Parts V and VI of the book provide responses to these questions. In Part V, various authors explore constitutional interpretation and application by legislatures both in theory and through looking at modern experiences in the United States and Canada. In Chapter 16, Mark Tushnet discredits arguments that legislators are less competent than judges at interpreting a constitution. In particular, he would dispense with the usual standard for measuring legislative competence – the court-based standard – and substitute for it a better one, which he calls the constitution-based standard. Under the latter standard, one can identify the incentives that legislatures will have to interpret the constitution in compliance with the constitution's provisions. In analyzing the effect of these incentives, Tushnet concludes that legislators might justifiably be expected to interpret the constitution reasonably and that, moreover, judges might have fewer incentives than ordinarily thought. On this basis, the traditional difficulty raised by unelected courts as the final arbiter of constitutional law can be studied and debated in a new light.

In Chapter 17, Sanford Levinson reminds us of the degree to which debates over the meaning of constitutional provisions take place outside courts. He invokes examples from U.S. constitutional history where legislators who were not legally trained reached their own conclusions about what the Constitution compelled. Levinson connects this legitimate capacity on the part of legislators to a theory of constitutional protestantism (similar to that referred to earlier by Hughes in Chapter 11) that entitles each citizen to engage in constitutional interpretation without having to defer to a professional authority. Levinson's discussion thus lends support to the idea of popular, as opposed to privileged, constitutionalism.

Andrée Lajoie offers a corrective to several misapprehensions about the role of legislatures in a constitutional democracy such as Canada's. In Chapter 18, she challenges the widespread notion that courts frequently overturn legislation made by legislators and that this diminishes the elected lawmaker's role. First, she notes that, long before the Canadian constitution was amended in 1982, courts were involved in striking down legislation on constitutional grounds. Second, this exercise of judicial power is not capricious – judges must provide valid reasons consonant with what Lajoie sees as dominant Canadian values. Furthermore, by reference to a hermeneutic theory of interpretation, Lajoie concludes that legislators are constantly involved in construing constitutional norms when they make new laws. Lajoie thus might be proposing a type of implicit constitutional interpretation by legislatures, much like the implicit form of constitution making that was discussed in Part IV of the book. In her view, it is important to realize that legislators must engage with the constitution, and in the vast majority of instances, the legislative interpretation of those provisions becomes the operative one.

To deepen our understanding of the frequency with which legislatures, not only during debates of the whole membership but also through the work of specialized committees, have become involved with interpreting and applying the constitution, the chapter by Keith Whittington, Neal Devins, and Hutch Hicken provides elaborate detail about three decades' worth of committee hearings in the U.S. Congress. Their findings in Chapter 19 indicate that committees in conducting normal business have regularly paid attention to issues of federalism, separation of powers, and constitutional rights of citizens. During this period, a new trend has emerged. Increasingly, the Senate judiciary committee has become the dominant forum in Congress where constitutional issues are discussed. The authors explain this trend by considering the backgrounds and skills of the judiciary committee's members, the kinds of social issues frequently encountered, and the appetite of this committee to devote time to debating conflicting constitutional visions.

Part VI of the book deals directly with what we call "legislative constitutionalism." By this we mean that although where there is a constitution, courts play an important role in interpreting it, the final word on constitutional issues belongs to the legislature.[15] Here we ask where one might look for indications that judicial supremacy does not have to be the norm. Is there more than one type of legislative constitutionalism? What are the assumptions of each? The first two chapters of Part VI are sympathetic to legislative constitutionalism. In Chapter 20, Jeremy Webber defines the purpose of a constitution as about more than limiting the exercise of power (and, therefore, it is also about more than the power of courts to oversee the work of legislatures). He reminds us that constitutions also importantly create the institutions of government and provide the design by which democratic decisions can be made. Through the mechanism of the constitution, the public – who

[15] We use this term differently from the way it is used in Robert C. Post and Reva B. Siegel, "Legislative Constitutionalism and Section Five Power: Polycentric Interpretation of the Family and Medical Leave Act" (2003) 112 *Yale L.J.* 1943. Post and Siegel do not have in mind the notion that the legislature's interpretation of the constitution should always prevail over the court's, but rather they propose a "polycentric model" of constitutional interpretation. We prefer to contrast "legislative" as opposed to "judicial" constitutionalism, instead of "legal" versus "popular" constitutionalism, for two reasons. First, under both types of constitutionalism, institutions rather than the polity itself are engaged with interpretation. So the type of constitutionalism should terminologically reflect the institution that does the interpretation. More importantly, calling judicial constitutionalism "legal" and contrasting it with "popular" constitutionalism implies that the people do not care to view their constitution through the prism of legality.

can be expected to disagree over which position to take – is able nevertheless to voice a coherent will. Webber emphasizes the ideal of democratic participation and treats it as the fundamental principle of constitutional normativity. The upshot is that judges should be relatively modest in reviewing decisions fashioned by democratic means. Moreover, constitutions should be not drafted to provide substantive goals. Instead, they should provide only a framework within which democracy can flourish by heightening the opportunities for citizens to debate the ends of public policy.

Even though conventional wisdom has it that the United States embodies a system of judicial, rather than legislative, constitutionalism, Daniel Farber shows in Chapter 21 that there were few figures in U.S. history who favored legislative supremacy (as opposed to judicial supremacy) over the meaning of the Constitution. In addition, the structure of U.S. government makes it unlikely that the legislative branch could reasonably claim supremacy in this context. Nevertheless, Farber lists ten significant areas that still present opportunities for legislative action by the U.S. Congress to shape an understanding of the Constitution and, if necessary, to overrule judicial doctrine. He also notes that legislators have historically been partly responsible for creating the system of judicial review, and they have demurred from taking all steps they could have to rein in courts on constitutional issues.

The next two chapters are skeptical about legislative constitutionalism. Faithfully holding a torch for judicial supremacy, Owen Fiss rejects the view that legislatures and courts should simply be coordinate bodies of constitutional interpreters. In Chapter 22, he argues that the contemporary movement to retrieve some ground for legislatures, as against courts, so that the former should not have to defer to the latter on constitutional issues, arises out of a disenchantment with the performance of the U.S. Supreme Court over the past four decades. The rise of legislative constitutionalism represents for Fiss a reincarnation of the Critical Legal Studies movement. He agrees that courts should not be the exclusive interpreters of a constitution, but he would defend judicial supremacy against the strong version of legislative constitutionalism. He characterizes proponents of the stronger version as denying that the judicial interpretation of the Constitution should bind the legislature. Fiss thinks that relinquishing judicial supremacy would do some harm. Among other things, it would wreck central constitutional traditions in the United States, including those flowing from the leading decision by the Warren Court that sparked the Second Reconstruction. If judicial precedents of this type were not accorded authority, then the civil rights era could not have happened. Fiss also defends the role of judges as authoritative constitutional interpreters by pointing out that, though not elected, they are part of an overall democratic scheme of governance.

Similarly, Frederick Schauer articulates a case for why judicial review is necessary to constrain legislators in going about their ordinary business of making laws. The central difficulty, as he explains it in Chapter 23, is that governments, even when well-intentioned, will be inclined periodically to circumvent the regulative ideals that they set up or that were set up by a preceding administration. These second-order constraints, as Schauer calls them, can take various forms. They also can be enforced in different ways, as enumerated by Schauer. The sixth constraint in his list is external enforcement, and on this score again different options might be suggested. But Schauer concludes that the use of the courts for this purpose is both common and realistic. In making the case for judicial supremacy, Schauer clarifies that he does not presume that legislators are inclined to be roguish or that judges are somehow more virtuous. The key elements that require judicial supremacy are simply that courts are external to the process; that the constitutional norms are themselves external; and that legislators must be held accountable to following the law, just like everyone else.

In Chapter 24, Sujit Choudhry offers a middle ground between judicial constitutionalism and legislative constitutionalism. He contends that Schauer too quickly concludes that constitutionalism (as Schauer defines it) requires constitutional precommitments, compliance with which by the legislature is best supervised by courts. Though this might be true in some contexts, there are moments in a nation's history when the institutional design should be different. In particular, Choudhry focuses on constitutional crises, or threatened crises, involving existential legal change, illustrated by the prospect of Quebec's secession from the rest of Canada. He traces the delicate reasoning of the Supreme Court of Canada, which had been asked to identify the rules under which secession might validly occur. The judges made it clear that, having articulated the principles that create binding constitutional obligations, certain events could give rise to political obligations to negotiate. These would have to be carried out in good faith. But, importantly, the Court declared that these constitutional rules – though creating duties – would not be enforceable in the courts. Instead, the enforcement would be left to political devices and forces. In Choudhry's view, this is an example of a court preferring a type of popular (as opposed to legal) constitutionalism and it is a counterexample to Schauer's general scheme. Overall, Choudhry argues for a choice between judicial constitutionalism and legislative constitutionalism that is sensitive to the particular political circumstances.

The final part of the book shifts the discussion from inside the legislature (and questions about its ability to engage with the constitution) to outside: How do legislatures interact with other institutions, both domestically and internationally? The first two chapters focus on the domestic aspect and examine the interplay among different institutions within political society, including the legislative and executive branches, to see what forms democracy actually takes. These chapters offer new perspectives on the suggestion that courts and legislatures participate in a dialogue, a subject of extensive discussion in Canada during the past decade.[16] In Chapter 25, David Dyzenhaus examines the tensions created when statute makers include a privative clause for the purpose of protecting public officials against judicial review of their decisions. This gives rise to a conceptual conundrum, for (depending on the wording of the privative clause) it would appear that this licenses public officials to act as a law unto themselves. Dyzenhaus unearths the roots of academic and judicial disquiet with privative clauses: They appear to violate

[16] The most influential sources on this topic are P. W. Hogg and A. A. Bushell, "The *Charter* Dialogue between Courts and Legislatures (Or Perhaps The *Charter of Rights* Isn't Such a Bad Thing After All)" (1997) 35 *Osgoode Hall L.J.* 75 and Kent Roach, *The Supreme Court on Trial: Judicial Activism or Democratic Dialogue* (Toronto: Irwin Law, 2001).

some constitutional or quasi-constitutional norms. He also surveys the different approaches that U.K., Australian, and Canadian courts have taken in the face of such clauses. These contrasting approaches provide background to Dyzenhaus's argument that, whatever the institutional arrangements that carve up responsibility among the legislative, executive, and judicial branches of government, they should all be viewed as engaged in a common project of realizing the values of legality. So long as decisions by public officials are justifiable, fairly reached, and supported by reasons, then the courts might well defer – not because the privative clause requires them to submit, but because deference in this context should be interpreted as a form of respect.

In Chapter 26, Andrew Petter appraises the argument that, in Canada at least, the legislature retains the final word on lawmaking because of the presence in the Canadian Charter of Rights and Freedoms of section 1 (that provides a basis for justifying violations of certain Charter rights) and section 33 (the override or notwithstanding clause that allows a government to declare the Charter inapplicable to a particular law for a limited period). He also takes note of the suggestion that, through judicial review, legislatures engage in dialogue with the courts, and that this process reestablishes the democratic foundation for constitutional lawmaking by the courts. Petter identifies several deficiencies with this conception of a dialogue, the most serious of which is that Canada's political institutions are hardly democratic. He describes them as generally unrepresentative, unaccountable, and obsolete. In addition, Canadian citizens are woefully apathetic and cynical about politics. To remedy the defects in Canadian democracy, Petter proposes various far-reaching reforms.

The final two chapters move the focus from domestic dialogue to a level of international conversation. In Chapter 27, Daphne Barak-Erez tries to answer the question whether, during the process of legislatures borrowing from one another, they can be said to engage in a process of dialogue. Her answer is that this happens only to a certain degree. Her survey of instances where legislation in one jurisdiction has influenced or shaped the legislation adopted elsewhere turns up several patterns. Some states seem relatively immune to borrowing ideas or legislative regimes: The legal-political culture is generally unreceptive. In other countries, the drafting of laws is typically preceded by extensive comparative research. In addition, Barak-Erez points out the need for institutional support to be taken into account and identifies other factors that determine the migration of legislative ideas or models. Personal and professional linkages across borders also promote the transfer of legislative ideas and model laws. On occasion, a legislature in one jurisdiction will adopt as its own principle something enunciated by a court in another jurisdiction. And, finally, Barak-Erez notes that in many cases the traffic is one way, so what would otherwise be a dialogue is really just a monologue.

Heather Gerken also explores, in Chapter 28, the prospects for productive international dialogue among legislatures. Her method is not empirical, but hypothetical. She makes use of the suggestion that there is already a global polity, within which individual states are following one another's examples in making laws. She then proposes the hypothesis that the decisions within the legislatures would be better if they could be encouraged to practice dissent – that is, to borrow the metaphor of John Stuart Mill, out of a collision with error the truth more vividly appears.

The advantage of legislatures acting within a global polity is that they can dissent by making decisions. Gerken thinks this is more powerful than simply making an abstract argument. She concludes by speculating about how decision making by deliberative bodies could be improved if there were institutionalized ways of ensuring dissent within them.

Gerken's chapter, which concludes the book, brings us full circle. We return to the themes elaborated in the early chapters of this book. The importance she attaches to diversity of opinion and contrasting models in interlegislative relations reflects the picture painted by Waldron, Hardin, and Schacter of legislatures as important forums of principled disagreement. Indeed, the contributions to this volume exhibit the value of treating legislatures as actively involved in constitutional creation, interpretation, and implementation. Democratic activity is not invariably about majorities seeking ways to oppress minorities, despite constitutional constraints. Nor are legislatures simply passive recipients of judicial wisdom on the meaning of constitutional structures or guarantees. Contributors to this book show how legislators frequently take the initiative – indeed, they must take the lead – in deciding how to use their constitutional powers responsibly.

One theme emerging from this book involves the perennial question of the institutional division of labor in a constitutional democracy. The degree to which judicial review is a useful constraint in this context is a matter of sharp dispute. Many authors in this book refuse to paint a pretty picture of how legislatures make laws or policies. Other authors have serious qualms about judicial capacities. Another, more positive theme is the notion that legislatures can be held to articulable standards of justice. Having them meet those standards might require rethinking and redesigning democratic procedures. Several chapters refer to important empirical data on the work of legislatures, not only domestically but as part of a larger polity. A third theme of the book is comparative. Several chapters focus on descriptive analysis of particular legal systems. Other authors discuss the theory of legislatures in a universalistic and noncontextual way. Yet others combine the two by arguing about the role of legislatures in constitutional states and by examining these arguments in a specific political context. The book thus contains plenty of material to fuel further research.

Perhaps the most important theme of the book is the notion that legislatures ought to be a central, if not the main, institution to realize the polity's constitutional vision. Implicit in this theme is the recognition that most democratic states in the modern era have indeed chosen to organize their political life about a constitutional document, and that "for all practical purposes, the Westminster model had been withdrawn from sale."[17] This might mean that all democracies are now constitutional democracies and that the distinction between democratic theory and constitutional theory is slowly blurring. But the fact that virtually across the globe judicial review is now practiced on the constitutionality of legislation does not mean that legislatures can shirk the burden of thinking about the constitution. To the contrary, it means that they must reexamine they way they view both democracy and constitutionalism. The old institutions of legislatures must adjust to this

[17] Mark Tushnet, "Symposium Article: New Forms of Judicial Review and the Persistence of Rights- and Democracy-Based Worries" (2003) 38 *Wake Forest L. Rev.* 813 at 814.

new reality and must ensure that they become – or remain – constitutionally relevant, even if not politically supreme. We hope that this book will assist legislatures and those who think about them in this important mission.

The chapters in this volume arose primarily out of a conference held in Banff, Alberta, in July 2004. The participants included an outstanding array of academics, with backgrounds in law, social sciences, philosophy, and history, drawn together to address significant issues that stem from recent work on how legislatures function in constitutional democracies. The editors would like to acknowledge the support of the Alberta Law Foundation, which through a special projects grant provided the funds to host the 2004 conference. We are also grateful for the encouragement of David Aucoin, the Foundation's executive director. The University of Alberta's Centre for Constitutional Studies, of which Tsvi Kahana was formerly executive director, took responsibility for this project from the beginning and sustained it through the period when Tsvi moved to Queen's University. The Centre's Board of Management and Centre employees were unfailingly helpful, and in particular we are grateful to Jennine Foulds. The original conception of both conference and book depended importantly on advice received from Owen Fiss, David Schneiderman, and Mark Tushnet. Joseph Raz and Sanford Levinson served as conference rapporteurs, and their insights offered during the conference's final session contributed significantly to the shape of the book. For invaluable assistance with organizing the conference and making the arrangements that kept the participants happy and focused, we thank Adina Preda, Robin Penker, and Melodie Hope. The conference proceedings were enlivened by the presence of three judicial colleagues: Justice Michel Bastarache of the Supreme Court of Canada, Chief Justice Catherine A. Fraser of the Alberta Court of Appeal, and Justice Antonin Scalia of the U.S. Supreme Court. The preparation of this hefty book, which required intense editorial application, benefited enormously from the diligent efforts of Sarah Weingarten, a law student at the University of Alberta.

1 Principles of Legislation

Jeremy Waldron

A legislature is a place for making law, and because law is a serious matter affecting the freedom and interests of all the members of the community, legislating is an activity we ought to take seriously. It is like marriage in the *Book of Common Prayer*[1] – not to be enterprised nor taken in hand carelessly, lightly or wantonly, but discreetly, advisedly and soberly, duly considering the purposes for which legislatures have been instituted and considering also the harm and injustice that poorly conceived or hastily enacted legislation may do. In this chapter, I want to consider some principles that I believe ought to govern the activities that take place in and around legislative institutions.

My topic – "Principles of Legislation" – is a common one. But the sense in which I am using it may be unfamiliar. I want to distinguish the principles of legislation that I will be talking about from two other sorts of legislative principles – the principles of a utilitarian like Jeremy Bentham and the principles of a theorist of justice like John Rawls.

The year 1802 saw the publication of a work by Jeremy Bentham, whose first volume was called "Principles of Legislation."[2] Chapter 1 opened with the following ringing words, less familiar then than they are now:

> THE PUBLIC GOOD ought to be the object of the legislator; GENERAL UTILITY ought to be the foundation of his reasonings. To know the true good of the community is what constitutes the science of legislation; the art consists in finding the means to realize that good.[3]

For Bentham the pursuit of the general good was the key principle of legislation. His volume continued in a utilitarian vein, telling us how to determine the general good and instructing us to measure pleasure and pain in terms of their intensity, duration, certainty, proximity, productiveness, purity, extent, and so on. His account culminated in the startling claim that provided we keep the principle of utility in view and apply our minds rigorously to these measurements, "legislation . . . becomes a matter of arithmetic" and "[e]rrors . . . in legislation . . . may be always accounted for by a mistake, a forgetfulness, or a false estimate . . . in the calculation of good and evil."[4] Actually, there is much more to Bentham's "Principles of Legislation"

[1] *The Book of Common Prayer* (Cambridge: Cambridge University Press, 1928) at 391.

[2] Jeremy Bentham, *The Theory of Legislation* (London: Kegan Paul, Trench, Trubner & Co., 1931). This work was published originally in French as part of a larger work, *Traités de Legislation.*

[3] Ibid. at 1.

[4] Ibid. at 32.

than this: There are also excellent discussions of the difference between law and morals, the reasons for making or not making something an offense, the issues of liberty that are almost always at stake when legislation is contemplated, and the compromises that the legislative imposition of sanctions necessarily involves. The volume ends with a critique in Chapter 13 of principles that were actually used to evaluate legislation by Englishmen in Bentham's time. The headings of this critique are a delight: "Antiquity is not a Reason," says Bentham, "The Authority of Religion is not a Reason," "Reproach of Innovation is not a Reason," "Metaphors are not Reasons," "An Imaginary Law is not a Reason," and so on.[5] This chapter reminds us that although Bentham's principles were set out as principles for legislators, they were not only for legislators. They were also principles for those who call for and oppose legislation. Bentham recognized that in the evaluation of proposed laws there is always a back-and-forth relation between the prejudices of the people and the fallacies of their representatives.[6] In the new world of law dominated by statute that Bentham helped usher in, the education of the public was as much an imperative as the education of the legislators themselves.[7]

We owe a tremendous debt to Jeremy Bentham for embarking as he did on the science of legislation. But we are not comfortable these days with the character of his contribution. The arithmetic calculus of the general good seems one dimensional, and we object to the aggregative logic of general utility. It seems to us that by adding everything up, Benthamite utilitarianism does not properly address issues of the distribution of the goods and evils that are the currency of legislation: It "does not take seriously the distinction between persons."[8] To put it another way, we think principles of legislation should include principles of justice.

The emphasis on justice has been characteristic of much recent political philosophy. In John Rawls's theory, for example, the basic work of evaluation is done by egalitarian principles. Rawls tells us that legislators ought to be particularly preoccupied with what he calls the Difference Principle and the Principle of Equal Opportunity:

> Social and economic inequalities are to be arranged so that they are both: (a) to the greatest benefit of the least advantaged, consistent with the just savings principle, and (b) attached to offices and positions open to all under conditions of fair equality of opportunity.... The second principle of justice is lexically prior to the principle of efficiency and to that of maximizing the sum of advantages.[9]

Rawls acknowledges that implementing this principle at the legislative stage will often involve disagreement and indeterminacy: "judgment frequently depends upon speculative political and economic doctrines and upon social theory generally."[10] But the task of the legislator – and, again, of those in the public who call for or oppose legislation – is to do the best they can from this perspective. Also, Rawls's principles of justice as fairness are not just recipes for statesmen to use.

[5] Ibid. at 66ff.

[6] Ibid. at 77–8.

[7] See David Lieberman, *The Province of Legislation Determined: Legal Theory in Eighteenth Century Britain* (Cambridge: Cambridge University Press, 1989), Parts III and IV.

[8] John Rawls, *A Theory of Justice* (Cambridge, MA: Harvard University Press, 1971) at 27.

[9] Ibid. at 302.

[10] Ibid. at 199.

They help define a well-ordered society in which "everyone accepts, and knows that everyone else accepts, the very same principles of justice" (even if they disagree about their application) and in which this provides a common ground from which the claims that people make on their political institutions can be considered and debated.[11]

Rawls's opponents include modern-day Benthamites,[12] but he also has opponents who espouse alternative theories of justice (i.e., alternative accounts, rival to his, of why Benthamite utilitarianism is wrong).[13] I guess very few real-world legislators think of their tasks as being guided explicitly by either Rawlsian or Benthamite principles, or indeed by any principles stated at that level of abstraction. Legislators approach their tasks with much a less rigorously formulated approach to public policy and social justice than that. Still, they disagree with one another in rather the way in which Rawls disagrees with Bentham or in a very loose and informal version of the disagreement between Rawls and his other philosophical competitors. Legislation is a controversial business. The inevitability of disagreement, which I have tried to emphasize in all my work on the subject,[14] leads to the question: "Are there any principles of legislation that can be shared by the adherents of rival theories of justice or among rival agendas for public policy?"

One well-known answer looks to principles that govern certain abstract characteristics of legislation – Rule-of-Law principles or the principles of Lon Fuller's "internal morality of law."[15] In *The Morality of Law*, Fuller tells a story of how a legislator went wrong by failing to respond properly to the need for generality, stability, intelligibility, consistency, practicability, and publicity in the statutes he enacted. Quite apart from Rawlsian, utilitarian, or other "external" principles that compete to govern their content, Fuller argued that laws need to be enacted *in a certain form* to be effective, to be fair, and to respect the dignity and free agency of those to whom they are addressed. In regard to these principles, Fuller says:

> What I have called the internal morality of law is in this sense a procedural version of natural law.... The term "procedural" is... broadly appropriate as indicating that we are concerned, not with the substantive aims of legal rules, but with the ways in which a system of rules for governing human conduct must be constructed and administered if it is to be efficacious and at the same time remain what it purports to be.[16]

I think this is a mischaracterization, born of the assumption that anything which is not substantive must be procedural. In fact, there are three kinds of principles that might be relevant to the legislative task: (1) substantive principles, like Rawls's or Bentham's; (2) formal principles, that is, principles having to do with the form of legislation, like Fuller's; and (3) procedural principles, having to do with the

[11] John Rawls, *Political Liberalism*, New Edition (New York: Columbia University Press, 1993) at 35.

[12] See, e.g., Louis Kaplow and Steven Shavell, *Fairness Versus Welfare* (Cambridge, MA: Harvard University Press, 2002).

[13] See, e.g., Robert Nozick, *Anarchy, State and Utopia* (Oxford: Basil Blackwell, 1974); Bruce Ackerman, *Social Justice in the Liberal State* (New Haven: Yale University Press, 1980); and Ronald Dworkin, *Sovereign Virtue: The Theory and Practice of Equality* (Cambridge, MA: Harvard University Press, 2000).

[14] Jeremy Waldron, *The Dignity of Legislation* (Cambridge: Cambridge University Press, 1999) and Jeremy Waldron, *Law and Disagreement* (Oxford: Clarendon Press, 1999) at 1–10 and 105–6.

[15] Lon L. Fuller, *The Morality of Law*, Revised Edition (New Haven: Yale University Press, 1969) at 33–8.

[16] Ibid. at 96–7.

institutions and processes we use for legislation. Principles of all three kinds are important, but in this chapter I shall focus mainly on (3) – procedural principles, having to do with the institutions and processes we use for legislation. Just as Fuller argued that his formal principles were not just instrumental but in an important sense moral, so I shall argue something similar for my seven procedural principles. Though they do not go to substantive moral justifications of law, they address important moral issues of legitimacy. And just as Bentham and Rawls argued that their principles of legislation were principles to govern action and debate among members of the public as well as among those in power, so I shall argue that my procedural principles should discipline the kinds of demands we place on our legislators and the choices we make about the lawmaking we clamor for.

There is a temptation to think that procedural and formal principles are unimportant, compared with substantive ones. Certainly substantive principles are important because they go to the heart of the matter. But it has been the great achievement of modern Rule-of-Law jurisprudence to emphasize the importance of formal principles, and I think the importance of procedural principles needs to be understood as well. Procedures in politics are not just ceremonies or red tape or mindless bureaucratic hoops to jump through. They relate specifically to issues of legitimacy, particularly in circumstances where there is deep-seated disagreement as to what substantive principles should be observed. I mentioned legitimacy a moment ago, and I want to say that the importance of addressing issues of legitimacy cannot be overestimated. Suppose a citizen asks: "Why should I comply with or support this law, when I think its content is wrong?" Appealing in response to a substantive principle may be reassuring for the sponsors of the law, but it will carry no weight for this citizen. For this citizen, one has to appeal to something about the way the law was enacted in the circumstances of disagreement, so that he can see its enactment as fair even if he does not see its substance as just. The procedural principles of legislation that I shall identify are all related to that burden of legitimacy in various ways. They concern the processes by which laws should be enacted, the question of who should participate in those processes, the spirit in which they should participate, and the various forms of care that should be taken with a process this important.

In summary, the principles I shall consider are the following:

1. The principle of explicit lawmaking, that is, the principle that holds that when law is made or changed, it should be made or changed explicitly.
2. The duty to take care when legislating, in view of both the inherent importance of law and the interests and liberties that are at stake.
3. The principle of representation, which requires that law should be made in a forum that gives voice to and gathers information about all important opinions and interests in the society.
4. The principle of respect for disagreement, and concomitant requirements like the principle of loyal opposition.
5. The principle of deliberation and the duty of responsiveness to deliberation.
6. The principle of legislative formality, including structured debate and a focus on the texts of the legislative proposals under consideration.
7. The principle of political equality and the decision-procedure it supports in an elective legislature, for example, the rule of majority decision.

There is not supposed to be anything sacred about this list of seven principles. Others may come up with different principles, organized in a different way.[17] But I hope this way of setting them out is illuminating.

Before proceeding to the detail of my seven principles, there are some general points to be made. Procedural considerations seldom stand on their own: They are usually predicated on some sense of the importance of what the procedures are used for or what they are supposed to produce. We do not argue for democracy, for example, because participation is valued as an end in itself. We argue for democracy in the light of what political systems do: They exercise power; they have an impact on people's lives; they bind whole communities; they impose costs and demand sacrifices. It is because of all this that we make demands about voting and enfranchisement: We say that each person is entitled to a vote, for example, because of the potential momentousness for him or her of the decisions that are being made. Apart from these considerations, an insistence on democratic enfranchisement would be frivolous. Something similar is true of legislation. It would not be worth taking so much care with legislation, paying attention in the various ways that I shall consider to the processes by which laws were made, if *law* were not an important mode of governance. If law were just a game, or if the realities of political power or political impacts had little to do with law, then principles of legislation would matter less and their content might be different. I shall begin my discussion therefore with an account of why law as such is important. If we understand *that*, then we will better understand why the making of law is important, and we will understand too why it is important to have a place dedicated to the making of law in the way that legislatures are dedicated.

The concept of law is not the same as the concept of governance, and a people do not enjoy the Rule of Law just because they are ruled. Of course, any ruling or being ruled is a serious matter: When people are ruled, freedom is limited, penalties are threatened, force is used, sacrifices are demanded, costs and benefits are allocated, people are elevated or degraded, and actions reputable and disreputable are undertaken in the name of the whole community. To be ruled by law, however, is to be ruled in a particular way. It is to be ruled under the auspices of what John Locke referred to as "settled standing Rules, indifferent and the same to all Parties,"[18] that is, general rules laid down, promulgated, and then applied impartially to particular cases. The function of these rules is, in the first instance, to guide and govern the conduct of members of the community in various regards for the sake of justice and the general good, and, secondly, to direct and govern official interventions, particularly official responses (like sanctions) to the situations to which the norms are directed in the first instance. The positing and promulgation of these rules establishes them as a sort of publicly recognized morality, laying down duties and creating rights. Citizens no doubt differ in their personal moral views, including their personal views about justice and the general good; but the promulgated rules of law are supposed to constitute a code to which we can all orient ourselves despite our differences. The sheer fact of law's public presence gives it salience for us in our dealings with one another, and it stands as a focal point of our allegiance and

[17] See Jeremy Waldron, "Legislating with Integrity" (2003) 72 *Fordham L. Rev.* 373, for a slightly different list.

[18] John Locke, *Two Treatises of Government*, ed. by Peter Laslett (Cambridge: Cambridge University Press, 1988) at 324 (II, sect. 87).

obligation to the political community. Our primary political obligation is to obey the law, and the primary basis of legitimacy, in a society ruled by law, for any power that is exercised upon us is its being authorized and governed by these "settled standing Rules."

I do not mean that the claims of law *are* absolute or that their legitimating effect is unlimited: I mean that they offer themselves as the primary basis of obligation and legitimacy, and the claim they purport to make on us and our rulers is that they are to be treated with the greatest respect by those who have the well-being of the community in mind. Law, as we know, claims finality and supremacy in social affairs. What is settled in lawmaking is what finally is to prevail in our society, and that means that our laws present themselves as already taking account of everything that might be important about the matters they govern. Again, this does not mean that they always succeed in doing so: A law may be criticized for imposing a prohibition or establishing a distribution that fails to take this or that into account. My point is that making law represents a particularly comprehensive exercise of power, one that seeks to transform and redirect in quite a broad and permanent way people's sense of what is required of them in society. In view of the sort of intervention it claims to be, lawmaking ought to be taken seriously.

Edward Rubin has argued that the image of law set out in the previous paragraph is obsolete.[19] Most law, he says, is not like this; certainly most legislation is not. Much of it does not aim to govern the conduct of ordinary citizens at all, at least not directly. It does not impose obligations or establish rights. Instead, it gives directions to officials and agencies, indicating goals to be pursued and the broad types of rule-making that *they* should engage in. Rubin observes:

> We speak of legislative enactments as laws, as in the high school civics phrase about "how a bill becomes a law," and we refer to legislators as lawmakers. But this usage is quite old and bears the imprint of the pre-administrative state.... At present, a large proportion of legislation does things other than regulate human conduct, and many direct regulations of conduct are enacted by other governmental institutions, most often administrative agencies.[20]

Rubin thinks we need to "desanctify" the notion of law and not assume it has the sort of normative force or "metaphysical kick" that it seems traditionally to have had. If we do this, we will be in a position to develop realistic principles to apply to lawmaking.[21] We should evaluate laws as mere instrumentalities, as policy initiatives, Rubin says, and understand lawmaking as nothing much more than the initial stage of the mobilization of public resources. It does not follow that law is unimportant. But if we take Rubin's advice, we will see lawmaking as less of a big deal from the moral point of view and attribute less importance to grand-sounding principles regarding its form or the procedures by which it is enacted.

Rubin has a point about much modern legislation. But I think he underestimates the traditional character of much modern law. Though much of it is directed in the first instance to officials, this aspect of it does not necessarily detract from its

[19] Edward Rubin, "Law and Legislation in the Administrative State" (1989) 89 *Colum. L. Rev.* 369 at 370–1.

[20] Ibid. at 377, n. 25.

[21] Much of Rubin's critique (ibid. at 397 ff.) is directed at Fuller's "internal morality of law."

effective public normativity. If a legislature increases the penalties for marijuana use or directs that officials shall no longer regard assisted suicide as an offense in certain circumstances, a literal reading will tell us that its primary addressees are prosecutors and judges; no one is literally being told not to smoke marijuana, nor is anyone actually being given permission to help their loved ones end their lives. *Still,* people will read the directions to officials as part of a code of publicly recognized morality on drug use and end-of-life issues. And they will be right to do so. They will debate the measures solemnly as though they were norms for citizens and they will treat them, once enacted, as settled standing rules on these matters, despite the point about their literal addressees. These are examples from criminal law, but the same is true of private law: People are aware that major changes in private law doctrine – a new set of rules on class actions or punitive damages, for example – have broad normative implications for the arrangements that structure our lives together.

Earlier, I quoted the Lockean formula: "settled standing Rules, indifferent and the same to all Parties." The last phrase is particularly important. Governance by law is governance on the basis of general rules, and that is what gives it its moralistic flavor. Jurists sometimes write as though the generality of law were simply a pragmatic advantage so far as administrability is concerned.[22] But it is more than that. Generalization across acts and across persons is a token or assurance that legal decisions are made and imposed for reasons (and that those reasons are being followed where they lead), rather than arbitrarily or on a whim. It is important, moreover, for its promise of impartiality and as an intimation of justice;[23] H. L. A. Hart observed that both law and justice embody the formal idea of "treating like cases alike."[24] Generality connotes reciprocity, and this may be valued as expressive of what Ronald Dworkin has called the *integrity* of a system of governance.[25] In all these ways, law presents itself in the image of morality. Though positive law can be morally misguided and though it is undeniable that unjust laws can also be general in form, there is something morally, not just pragmatically attractive about a determination to govern according to this form even when that is inconvenient for the purposes of those in power. To make law is not just to exercise power; it is (so to speak) to make a public morality for a particular community, something which purports to have the status among a people that moral principles have in their individual consciences.

What I have said so far is true of all law, common-law doctrine and customary law as well as statutes, treaties, and constitutions. We now need to consider the more particular question of what it is for law to be *legislated,* that is, created explicitly by an institution formally dedicated to that purpose. Bearing in mind all that has been said as to the general significance of law, it is time to turn to the principles that should inform our understanding of legislation, as a particular form that law may take.

[22] H. L. A. Hart, *The Concept of Law,* 2nd ed. (Oxford: Clarendon Press, 1994) at 21: "[N]o society could support the number of officials necessary to secure that every member of the society was officially and separately informed of every act which he was required to do."

[23] See also Jeremy Waldron, "Does Law Promise Justice?" (2001) 17 *Ga. St. U.L. Rev.* 759.

[24] Hart, *supra* note 22 at 157–67.

[25] Ronald Dworkin, *Law's Empire* (Cambridge, MA: Harvard University Press, 1986), chap. 6.

1. THE VERY IDEA OF LEGISLATION

My first principle refers to the very idea of legislation. The idea of legislation is not the same as the idea of law. Others have drawn this distinction ideologically;[26] here I am drawing an institutional distinction. The idea of legislation is the idea of making or changing law *explicitly, through a process and in an institution publicly dedicated to that task.* The distinction takes notice of the fact that legislation is not the only means by which law is made or changed. Law is also made and changed by the decisions of judges as they interpret existing legal materials, including the work of other judges. This is unavoidable and no doubt in some cases it is also desirable. But it has drawbacks. Although the lawmaking role of the courts is well known to legal professionals, judicial decision making does not present itself in public as a process for changing or creating law. Quite the contrary: Any widespread impression that judges were acting as lawmakers, rather than as law-appliers, would detract from the legitimacy of their decisions in the eyes of the public. And this popular perception is not groundless. Courts are not set up in a way that is calculated to make lawmaking legitimate. Legislatures, by contrast, exist explicitly for the purpose of lawmaking, and they are known to exist for that purpose. Sure, they also have other functions. But lawmaking is their official *raison d'être,* and when we evaluate the structures, procedures, and membership of legislatures, we do so with this function very much in mind.

So our first principle embodies a commitment to explicit lawmaking. Underlying any theory of legislation is the idea that on the whole it is good, if law is to be changed, that it should be changed openly in a transparent process publicly dedicated to that task. When courts change the law, this transparency is often lacking. Courts perform their lawmaking function under partial cover of a pretense that the law is not changing at all. The English positivists put this rather well, when they distinguished between oblique and direct lawmaking. Judge-made law, according to John Austin, is an "oblique" form of lawmaking. The judge's "direct and proper purpose is not the establishment of the rule, but the decision of the specific case. He legislates *as properly judging,* and not *as properly legislating.*"[27]

How important is this principle commanding explicit rather than oblique lawmaking? It is not just a matter of giving notice to those who are to be bound by a given law. Publicity is important for the whole community, for it indicates what is being done in their name and gives them information regarding the appropriate deployment of their political energies. It is also a matter of the general liberal principle of publicity: People should not be under any misapprehension about how their society is organized, and the legitimacy of our legal and political institutions should not depend on such misapprehensions.[28] This has particular importance in the case of law, because of the connection between law and a certain ideal of political autonomy. The law of a people is often presented as something to which

[26] F. A. Hayek, *Law, Legislation and Liberty – Volume I: Rules and Order* (Chicago: University of Chicago Press, 1983).

[27] John Austin, *Lectures on Jurisprudence,* 5th ed., ed. by R. Campbell (Edinburgh: John Murray, 1885) at 266–7 and 315.

[28] Rawls, *Political Liberalism, supra* note 11 at 66ff.

they have committed themselves, rather than as something thrust upon them.[29] No doubt this is partly mythology. But the demand for explicit lawmaking, along with the demand that legislation be a democratically representative process, pays tribute to the importance of these ideas.

I noted at the outset that principles of legislation are for citizens and not just for legislators. This is particularly true of my first principle, which is *primarily* a principle for citizens. Those who advocate changes in the law have a responsibility to orient that advocacy to a forum where their proposal can be explicitly discussed for what it is, rather than to other forums where it will be presented under the guise of a matter of interpretation. A forum such as a constitutional court may be politically more promising for a given group, but that is only because less care has been taken with the legitimacy conditions of lawmaking in that forum (precisely because it has not been thought to be a forum for lawmaking). There is a responsibility not to try and "steal a march" on one's political opponents in this way but to submit one's proposals for honest debate and evaluation in a forum that everyone knows as the place to go to reach decisions about whether and how the law should be changed.

2. THE DUTY OF CARE

In view of the inherent importance of law and the interests and liberties that are at stake in their decision making, lawmakers have a duty to take care when they are legislating. We want our laws to be efficient devices for promoting the general good and we want them to be fair in the burdens they impose and solicitous of the rights as well as the interests of all whom they affect. Reckless or hasty lawmaking may impose oppressive constraints or unfair or unnecessary burdens on people. Lawmaking is not a game: The consequences of failure to satisfy this second principle are real harms and injustices to real people.

This principle has a number of implications. The general duty of care in this regard means that those who in a position to modify the law have a responsibility to arrive at a sound view about what makes a legal change a good change or a bad change. They need principles of legislation in the very first sense I identified – a theory of the sort that Rawls offered or a theory of the sort that Bentham offered; or, if those theories are thought inadequate, a better alternative theory of justice and of the general good.

Beyond that, responsible lawmakers ought to pay careful attention to the relation between their own individual decisions and the eventual effects, on citizens and on society, of the law that they make (or fail to make). Laws are seldom made by a single Solon or Pericles: Lawmaking is collective action, in two dimensions. First, laws are often made and changed by a collectivity, so individual lawmakers have to consider the relation between their participation – their proposals, their speeches, their votes – and the eventual outcome of the lawmaking process. Second,

[29] This idea has deep roots in Rousseau's political theory and in Kant's ethics. See Jean-Jacques Rousseau, *The Social Contract*, trans. by Maurice Cranston (Harmondsworth: Penguin Books, 1968) and Immanuel Kant, *Groundwork of the Metaphysics of Morals*, ed. by Mary Gregor (Cambridge: Cambridge University Press, 1997).

the making or unmaking of any particular law affects the whole body of laws, so attention needs to be paid not just to the particular measure under consideration but also to the way in which that measure will affect the broad impact of the legal system on the interests and rights of citizens.[30]

In principle this applies to all lawmaking, not just legislating. But aspects of it are worth particular emphasis in the legislative context. Unlike judges, legislators are not necessarily versed in the background law that they are changing or adding to. And legislators also have other distractions that perhaps judges do not have. After all, lawmaking is just one among many activities performed in legislatures, and, from the point of view of political power or prestige, it may not necessarily be the most important. Members of the legislature may be preoccupied with other functions such as the mobilization of support for the executive, the venting of grievances, the discussion of national policy, processes of budgetary negotiation, the ratification of appointments, and so on. It is easy for them to regard lawmaking as a distraction. Legislatures have hundreds of members, but often you would be hard put to find ten or twenty on the floor of the chamber during the middle stages of an average legislative debate. For these reasons, we need to place particular emphasis on the duty of care that is associated with the lawmaking part of a legislator's business.

Many of the structural and procedural attributes of legislatures embody a sense of the need for care in making law. Proposals for new laws are not just introduced and voted on in the legislative assembly. Usually they are debated and voted on several times – sometimes on their general character, sometimes clause by clause. Often there are public hearings; almost always there is consideration by a dedicated committee of the legislature. Many legislatures, moreover, are bicameral. They comprise different assemblies, in some cases appointed as well as elective, in others cases elected on different schedules from one another. Usually a bill must satisfy majorities in both houses. Now, we may see all this simply as an opportunity for politicking and delay, and citizens sometimes call for a more efficient legislative procedure that would eliminate these features. Such proposals, however, are almost always reckless to the duty of care that I have been talking about.

3. THE PRINCIPLE OF REPRESENTATION

A new law may be *formulated* and *drafted* by an elite – by the political executive, for example, or a Law Reform Commission, or by specialist parliamentary counsel. However, we expect these officials will not try simply to impose their ideas in virtue of their own expert assessment. However important the innovation is perceived to be, and however well-drafted the measure, we expect it to be submitted for scrutiny, debate, and decision by a large representative assembly, comprising hundreds of representatives drawn from all sectors of society.

This is partly a reflection of our commitment to democracy: We want lawmaking to be democratic, and accordingly, we expect it to take place in an institution

[30] See John Stuart Mill, *Considerations on Representative Government* (Buffalo: Prometheus Books, 1991) at 109. See also Rawls, *Theory of Justice*, supra note 8 at 7–11, on the importance of considering, from the point of view of justice, the basic social structure as a whole.

whose members have been elected by the people. I shall consider the democracy aspect under principle 7. But the principle of representation in lawmaking is older than democracy.[31] Elsewhere I have written on the sheer *numbers* of persons that deliberate lawmaking involves. Supreme courts have eight or nine voting members; legislatures have hundreds. I think these numbers are valued not just because more is better for, say, the reasons elaborated in Condorcet's jury theorem,[32] but because more gives us the opportunity to diversify the membership, to have legislators from a variety of places, representing a diversity of interests and opinions. Legislatures are formally structured to ensure diversity, and the modern idea of legislation rests philosophically on an insistence that society, being pluralistic, is in essence incapable of representation by a single voice or by reference to a single set of interests. Of course, there are disputes about what the axes of legislative diversity should be. In almost all countries, geographical diversity is represented; sometimes there are formal structures to ensure ethnic or religious diversity; but increasingly political diversity is valued in a sense that seeks some sort of rough comparability between the proportion of a given body of opinion in the legislature and the proportion of people who support that opinion in the community.

Why is this diversity so important for *lawmaking*? Partly it is informational. We hope that representatives will come from different parts of the country, bringing with them knowledge of the special needs and circumstances of different groups. We want to ensure an adequate representation of the diversity of *interests* in society. (Even if the legislature is passing general laws, universalizable in form and applicable to all, it may not need information about particularities although it will need information about how particular provisions affect different sectors of the society, in order to determine a fair allocation of benefits and burdens.) But the value of diversity also has to do with heterogeneity of opinions. The legislature is a place where we argue and debate, and we want to ensure a hearing for the largest possible variety of opinions concerning the issues that are raised when a change in the law is being contemplated. The idea is that new law emerging from this institution cannot claim its authority on the basis of any cozy consensus among like-minded people (whether in the community or in the legislature). Instead, its claim to authority must make reference to the controversies surrounding its enactment. If a citizen, who disagrees with the new law, asks why she should obey it, we want to be able to say to her that disagreements (along the lines that she is expressing) were aired as fiercely and as forcefully as possible at the time the law was considered and that it was enacted nevertheless in a fair process of deliberation and decision.

4. RESPECT FOR DISAGREEMENT AND THE PRINCIPLE OF LOYAL OPPOSITION

Few legislative proposals are likely to meet with unanimous agreement. John Rawls wrote about "the many hazards involved in the correct (and conscientious) exercise

[31] See Waldron, *Law and Disagreement, supra* note 14, Ch. 3, esp. pp. 56–67.

[32] Marquis de Condorcet, "Essay on the Application of Mathematics to the Theory of Decision-Making," in Keith Michel Baker, ed., *Condorcet: Selected Writings* (Indianapolis: Bobbs-Merrill, 1976) 33 at 48–9.

of our powers of reason and judgment in the ordinary course of political life," which make it likely that we will disagree with one another on important issues.[33]

> Different conceptions of the world can reasonably be elaborated from different standpoints and diversity arises in part from our distinct perspectives. It is unrealistic ... to suppose that all our differences are rooted solely in ignorance and perversity, or else in the rivalries for power, status, or economic gain.[34]

Rawls used this account to characterize ethical and religious disagreements. But the idea of the burdens of judgment might characterize disagreements about justice and public policy as well.[35] Of course, what distinguishes justice and public policy is that we need settlement on these issues, whereas we do not need settlement on all the ethical and religious issues that Rawls associates with the burdens of judgment. But the need for settlement does not make disagreement evaporate; instead, it means that settlements have to be forged in the heat of disagreement and not on a basis that wishes disagreement away.

Real-world legislatures differ in the extent of disagreement that is aired in their debates. Whenever any large group of people gather together to perform a civic function, there will be pressures of various sorts to conform, to refrain from rocking the boat, and to show solidarity with widely accepted ideas. For example, American legislatures are often overwhelmed by enthusiastic consensus of one sort or another, and dissenting views are often informally suppressed so that law can be made quickly before the public face of the consensus dissolves. My fourth principle, the principle of respect for disagreement, aims to combat those tendencies. It conceives of legislatures as institutions set up specifically to enable rival views to come together and confront one another in debate, so that all of those involved in lawmaking hear all that is to be said against, as well as all that is to be said in favor of the legislative proposals in front of them. Various things can facilitate expressions of dissent. In some circumstances strong party structures can help, by giving dissenting views a solid presence in politics that is not simply identified with the conscience or opinion of particular individuals. Even with minority status, a socialist party is much less vulnerable to the pressures of national consensus than one or two members each of whom happens to hold socialist views. (On the other hand, where parties are few – e.g., where there is a simple two-party [or worse, a one-party] system – then some other basis needs to be found whereby dissident members can give voice to their views without fear of intraparty retaliation.)

Above all, what is indicated under this fourth principle is the need for a pervasive doctrine of *loyal opposition*. A person is not to be regarded as a subversive or as disloyal to the society merely on account of his or her public disagreement with some social consensus. A party is not necessarily to be regarded as a threat, because it establishes and makes solidly present in the society, views on public policy that most people regard as undesirable. Loyal opposition is not just a matter of free speech guarantees. There are all sorts of ways in which legislative structures can give the principle some real embodiment, including the establishment of an officially recognized "Opposition" (say, in a Westminster-style system) with established

33 Rawls, *Political Liberalism, supra* note 11 at 56.

34 Ibid. at 58.

35 See Waldron, *Law and Disagreement, supra* note 14 at 151–3.

and paid posts like "Leader of the Opposition" and "Shadow Minister," as well as the official majority/minority arrangements that are associated with American legislatures. These are structural embodiments of the principle I have been discussing, establishing the legislature as a place where dissenting voices must be heard and given an opportunity to test their persuasiveness and the extent of their support.

5. THE PRINCIPLE OF RESPONSIVE DELIBERATION

In a well-known article, Lon Fuller argued that courts are distinguished from other political institutions as forums of reason, not because reasoning does not go on in other institutions, but because courts are set up specifically to ensure that the reasoned argument of advocates are heard and responded to. A judge has not only a duty to let each side present its case; he or she also has a duty, which (on Fuller's account) a legislator does not have, to stay awake and listen and respond to the presentation.[36] I am not sure whether Fuller is right about the formal structures: The debating rules of legislatures often allow members to put questions to one another in debate and elicit a response. But assuming he is mostly right, then it is all the more important that the *ethos* of legislation be suffused with a principle of responsiveness in deliberation. It is not enough that voice be given to a variety of conflicting views. The legislature is a place for debate not just display, and as recent theories of "deliberative democracy" have emphasized, debate requires an openness to others' views and a willingness to be persuaded.

It is important therefore that the views voiced in the legislature not be held as frozen positions, with no possibility of change or compromise. Opinions must be held as opinions, and therefore open to elaboration, arguments, correction, and modification. If (as I have been arguing) the basic argument for the legitimacy of an enacted statute is that all the alternatives had the opportunity to put their case and failed to win majority support, then we are presupposing at least in principle the possibility that people might have their minds changed through argument. This does not mean that people must be willing to change their interests or give up their principles.[37] They might be persuaded to take a different view of the respect required for their interests in relation to the interests of others, or a different view of what follows from their fundamental principles insofar as particular legislative proposals are concerned. But I am not saying that political opinion must be fickle for deliberation to work. The point is that opinions should be held and defended in a spirit of openness to argument and consideration. Sometimes this will mean that individuals must be prepared to abandon positions they have taken; other times it will mean that parties of legislators must be willing to reconsider positions to which they have committed themselves.[38]

The requirement of responsiveness is directed in the first instance to the legislators themselves. But Edmund Burke is famous for having directed it also to the people who elect the legislators, reminding the electors of Bristol that they ought

[36] Lon Fuller, "Forms and Limits of Adjudication" (1978) 92 *Harv. L. Rev.* 353 at 366.

[37] Cf. Cass R. Sunstein, "Beyond the Republican Revival" (1988) 97 *Yale L.J.* 1539 at 1548–51.

[38] The principle of responsiveness does not condemn that second, more ponderous and collective mode of reconsideration. On the contrary, reconsideration by a party may take the reevaluation of a public political position more seriously than the faltering uncertainty of an individual member.

not to demand that their representative sacrifice "his unbiased opinion, his mature judgment, his enlightened conscience" to the views of his constituents:

> Parliament is not a congress of ambassadors from different and hostile interests; which interests each must maintain, as an agent and advocate, against other agents and advocates; but . . . a deliberative assembly of one nation, with one interest, that of the whole; where, not local purposes, not local prejudices, ought to guide, but the general good, resulting from the general reason of the whole.[39]

Certainly, it is reasonable for electors to expect their representative to communicate to the legislative body important facts about their interests, especially if those would otherwise be overlooked. And it is also important that if there are opinions peculiar to a particular constituency, then the system of representation should be such that these are heard. But Burke is right too that the whole point of those demands is to allow for a process of deliberation in which views may be formed about the merits of legislative proposals that would not have been formed apart from the *bringing together* in the legislature of all this peculiar information and all these distinctive voices.

6. THE PRINCIPLE OF LEGISLATIVE FORMALITY

At the end of my discussion of principle 2, I referred to those large structural features of legislatures like bicameralism that respond to the duty of care incumbent on any group that takes it upon itself to make law. My sixth principle is concerned less with structures and more with the microfeatures of legislative debate and with their sometimes exasperating formality.

Legislation is not supposed to be an informal process, and under the heading of this sixth principle I want to explain why.

One of the reasons we take such care with the electoral system, the composition of legislative chambers, the rules about parties, and the debating- and decision-procedures, is that these features enable a political system to make use of the diversity represented in the legislature. Legislatures are large gatherings of disparate individuals who do not understand one another particularly well. This is a normative and not just a factual observation. It follows partly from what we said about principle 3: Whatever differences of ideology, value, culture, opinion, and interests are found in the community are also supposed to be represented in the legislature. If this normative expectation is fulfilled in a diverse society, it follows that the potential for mutual misunderstanding in any interaction among legislators is great. No doubt it is mitigated to some degree by the collegiality of the legislators as they go about their business and their common experience of a life in politics. But if there is too much of that, we start to lose exactly what we value about diversity.

How then is it possible for legislators to interact in the institutional mechanics of legislation? The answer lies in the highly stylized rules of procedure that govern the formal details of their interaction: *These are rules for people who have very*

[39] Edmund Burke, "Speech to the Electors of Bristol" (Nov. 3, 1774) in *The Works of the Right Honourable Edmund Burke*, vol. II (Boston: Little Brown, 1865) at 95–6.

little else in common. Unless it is structured by tight rules of order, deliberation is always liable to fall into futility, as people misunderstand one another, talk past one another, or lose the thread of the discussion. Formal rules of procedural order go a long way toward mitigating these dangers, and I believe they are therefore entitled to respect, not just as any old formalities might be, but as formalities that make possible precisely the debate-among-diversity we value among our lawmakers.

I have argued elsewhere that there is an important connection between procedural formality and the formal respect that is accorded to a legislative text. In any deliberative context, the key to rules of procedural order is a tight focus on a particular resolution under discussion – a resolution formulated clearly and publicly, established as a criterion of relevance in a particular debate, amended only in a carefully controlled way, and subject in the end to formal voting. Without that reference to a given form of words, a disparate body of representatives of the sort we have postulated would find it difficult to share a view about exactly what they have been debating, exactly what they have voted on, exactly what they have done, as a collective body, acting in the name of the community.[40]

This principle should make a difference not only to the way legislators behave, but also to the way in which legislative outcomes are received and understood. In the United States, lawyers sometimes look behind the text to what was said in debate for evidence as to how a statute is to be interpreted. When legislative history is used in this way, certain interventions in debate are given authority even though the procedural rules of debate never made them the focus of deliberation. So we see lobbyists urging representatives to insert language into the debate that will be useful for later interpretation,[41] and we see judges and lawyers according interpretive authority to speeches in debate even though that authority has not been acquired through voting or deliberation focused on those speeches. Now these practices depend for manageability on the text of the statute remaining the formal focus of deliberation and voting; they depend on legislators proceeding in debate as though the text of the bill were all that mattered. For if it were openly acknowledged that speeches given in debate were potentially authoritative also, and if an attempt were made – through deliberation and voting – to determine which of them should *be* authoritative, the whole process of deliberation would degenerate into something unwieldy. Those who use legislative history in this way need to think about the procedural implications of what they are doing (and about the extent of their free-riding on conventions that formally facilitate debate on a different basis altogether).

7. POLITICAL EQUALITY AND THE PRINCIPLE OF MAJORITY DECISION

My seventh principle is ultimately the most important, for it governs the procedures by which binding decisions are finally made concerning controversial legislative proposals. Sometimes we need law in an area even though we disagree what that law should be; in these circumstances, we need a decision-procedure, one that will

[40] See Waldron, *Law and Disagreement,* supra note 14 at 69–87 for a more detailed version of this argument.

[41] See the account of this practice in Antonin Scalia, *A Matter of Interpretation: Federal Courts and the Law* (Princeton: Princeton University Press, 1997) at 34.

involve a mode of participation like voting and a decision-rule such as the rule of majority-decision (RMD). Of course, voting in a legislature should not be sharply separated from debate. But, equally, the importance of deliberation should not obscure or sideline the need on most occasions for voting.[42] Deliberation does not always eliminate disagreement and eventually decisions need to be made.

Legislatures, I have already said, are not the only lawmaking entities in a modern state. Courts also make law. But modern legislatures, much more than courts, organize their decision-procedures around the ideal of fairness and political equality. The legislature is set up to respect the fact that, in principle, each permanent member of the community likely to be bound by its laws is entitled to participate, directly or indirectly, in the processes by which the laws are made. It is the respecting of this entitlement that gives legislation its special claim to legitimacy in modern democratic societies.

RMD is used in most legislatures for determining whether a bill is adopted finally as law or not.[43] Political theorists have posited alternatives to it,[44] but a plausible alternative would have to satisfy a number of important constraints that seem to be satisfied by the rule of majority-decision: It is neutral between outcomes, it gives equal weight to each participant's input, and it gives each participant's input as much weight as possible in the direction that their input indicates as is compatible with equality.[45] It seems fundamentally fair; it satisfies the principle of political equality. The point of my seventh principle is not to defend RMD in particular but to insist that some such rule, satisfying conditions like these, must be used in order to respect the principle of political equality in regard to legislation.

The application of RMD in legislation needs to be understood carefully. Legislatures, we know, are far from fully inclusive. Though, as I have said, they are large bodies compared (say) to courts, they are still minuscule compared to the populations of the societies they govern. A few hundred participate directly in the actual business of lawmaking; the other tens of millions do not. So when we are talking about the application of political equality in legislature, we must not talk as though the equality *of the representatives* was ultimately what mattered. The representatives have a derivative claim to be treated as one another's equals, but that arises only because their individual constituents – the millions of them – have an *ultimate* claim to be treated as one another's equals, and only because their own status as legislators rests on the votes of their constituents in a certain way. We design the representative structure, the system of elections, and the procedures of the legislature so that *as a package* they satisfy political equality. Neither RMD among the electors nor RMD among the legislators does it by itself; it is the package that works.

[42] See the discussion in Jeremy Waldron, "Deliberation, Disagreement and Voting," *Deliberative Democracy and Human Rights*, ed. by Harold Koh and Ron Slye (New Haven: Yale University Press, 1999) 210, at 211–14.

[43] The matter is complicated by bicameralism and by occasional supermajority-requirements for terminating debate or moving from one legislative stage to another.

[44] See, e.g., Matthias Riesse, "Arguing for Majority Rule" (2004) 12 *Journal of Political Philosophy* 41.

[45] For the theorem (in social choice theory) that majority-decision alone satisfies elementary conditions of fairness and rationality, see Kenneth May, "A Set of Independent Necessary and Sufficient Conditions for Simple Majority Decision" (1952) 20 *Econometrica* 680.

People will say that even conceived in this complicated way, political equality is a utopian ideal. I admit that it is an ideal, but it has undoubted real-world influence. It is what we appeal to when we worry that campaign finances or first-past-the-post electoral systems undermine one-person-one-vote. We need the idea of fair representation in a legislative assembly, along with the ideas about democratic enfranchisement and basic political equality that go with it, in order to think sensibly about the apportionment of legislative constituencies, about redistricting, about the electoral system itself, and about the rules, particularly the voting rules of the legislative process. We need all of this in order to relate what happens in the legislature to the fair conditions of decision for a society whose ordinary members disagree with one another about the laws that they should be governed by.

❧

In all of this, I have talked about *principles* of legislation rather than *rules*. Of course, legislation is a minutely rule-governed enterprise, and there is a dense procedural thicket of rules on all sorts of things that go on in the legislature. Elsewhere I have discussed the theoretical relation between this thicket of rules and principles of legislation of the sort I have been talking about.[46] Briefly, the principles underlie the detailed rules and explain why the detailed rules are important. An analogy with the rules that govern criminal trial proceedings may help here. What happens in the courtroom is minutely governed by rules of evidence and rules of procedure. These rules do not just constitute a game. They serve deep and complex principles about truth-seeking, fairness, and respect for persons, and they are supposed to be imbued with a suitable awareness of what the parties have at stake in the matter. As we frame the rules of courtroom procedure, we have these underlying principles in mind; they determine the way in which we evaluate the rules and urge changes in them; and they should also inform the spirit in which we conform our behavior, and demand that others conform their behavior, to the rules. The same – I want to suggest – is true of legislation. The principles I have mentioned may not be mentioned in the detailed rulebooks that govern the legislative process. But they help explain the point of the rulebook; they provide a basis for evaluating and criticizing the rulebook; and they offer an account of why holding ourselves and others to the requirements of the legislative rulebook should be regarded as something more than mindless proceduralism.

It is worth mentioning, finally, an even deeper value that underlies not just the rules but also the principles I have mentioned and that pervades them all. That is the value of legitimacy – the importance of the political legitimacy of the final output of the legislature, the laws that it enacts. By legitimacy, I mean the laws' claim to acceptance and compliance even by those who oppose them so far as their contents are concerned.[47] Of all the modes of making law – the emergence of custom, the development of doctrine by courts, the framing of a constitution, the enactment of statutes – it seems to me that legislation is the one that takes legitimacy most seriously. This is evident not just in the pains that are taken to establish

[46] See Waldron, "Legislating with Integrity," *supra* note 17.

[47] Legitimacy in this sense contrasts with substantive justification, but it is still a normative concept.

decision-procedures that respect political equality. It is evident also in our principle of explicitness in lawmaking and our insistence on the representation in the legislature of all substantial competing opinions. We cannot understand the work that these principles do or the detailed rules that they support without understanding the importance of legitimacy. Any laws that we enact must do their work in a community of people who do not necessarily agree with them and who will therefore demand that something other than the merits of their content – something about the way they were enacted – be cited in order to give them an entitlement to respect. The explicit and articulate process of legislation in the modern state responds to that demand and takes seriously the demand for legitimacy. And it is with an eye to that demand – as well as to the general norm of fair and responsible conduct in the discharge of this most important civic function – that I have developed my suggestions about principles of legislation and about the distinctive features of this way of making law.

ACKNOWLEDGMENTS

This chapter is a revised version of a lecture I gave at the University of Alberta in 2003 (The McDonald Lecture) entitled "Legislating with Integrity." I am grateful to Tsvi Kahana, Richard Bauman, and other members of the audience for their comments on that occasion.

2 An Exact Epitome of the People*

Russell Hardin

The core of liberalism is the decentralization of initiative. This is its great value if knowledge and creativity are diffused through the population and not subject to aggregation in some central authority. On this view, the compelling fact about liberalism is that, as Friedrich Hayek and others in the Austrian school of economics might say, it fits the epistemology of a creative social order. It does this because it gives autonomy to individuals and their own spontaneous, changing organizations. One might take such autonomy to be the central value of liberalism, or one might take the autonomy to be a means to other things, such as, especially, welfare. Nevertheless, as virtually all agree, we need government to secure our liberty. This generally means democratic government, and in the modern era of large states, it means representative democracy. Indeed, already in the days of the colony of Massachusetts, representation was necessary because the whole community could not possibly have met to govern. Each Massachusetts community of at least 120 citizens had one representative, and an additional representative was added for each additional 100 citizens.[1] Today, the people of Massachusetts have one representative in the U.S. House of Representatives for roughly 640,000 citizens.

The Austrian vision of distributed knowledge is consistent with John Stuart Mill's grounding for his principle of liberty[2] – that individuals have the best knowledge of what their interests are.[3] This claim can be qualified, of course, in ways that the individual would allow. For example, you would likely defer to judgment by medical professionals on some things that might be in your interest but that you could not understand adequately without professional advice. The Austrian, Millian vision coupled with the seeming fact that people place very high value on welfare, often especially their own welfare, yields a welfarist political theory that is essentially a mutual advantage theory. Mutual advantage is not imposed or assumed, however, as it is in ordinal utilitarian theory[4] or in contractarianism. Rather, it results from the aggregation of individual values.

* This phrase is supposed to describe any acceptable form of democratic representation. See Gordon S. Wood, *The Creation of the American Republic: 1776–1787* (New York: Norton, 1972) at 172.

1 Gordon S. Wood, *The Creation of the American Republic: 1776–1787* (New York: Norton, 1972) at 186.

2 John Stuart Mill, "On Liberty" (1859) in J. M. Robson, ed., *Collected Works of John Stuart Mill*, vol. 18 (Toronto: University of Toronto Press, 1977) at 213.

3 This discussion is drawn from Russell Hardin, "Rational Choice Political Philosophy" in Irwin Morris, Joe Oppenheimer, and Karol Soltan, eds., *From Anarchy to Democracy* (Stanford, CA: Stanford University Press, 2005) 95–109.

4 Russell Hardin, *Morality within the Limits of Reason* (Chicago: University of Chicago Press, 1988).

A major element of the mutual advantage theory is that we all want stable government. We coordinate on a constitution, including its design of a legislative body. But we do not always or even usually coordinate in the passage of specific pieces of legislation. We have a two-stage structure of government and therefore we need a two-stage theory of it, with different justificatory arguments in the two stages: coordination for mutual advantage in the first stage of constitutional design and adoption, and majority rule in the second stage of ongoing politics. In general, the legislature does not simply aggregate our interests, although on some issues – those for which there is a mutual advantage choice, such as defending our nation from attack – it can. Most of the time, we benefit from a division of labor in which we the citizens do not know what our legislators are doing or even what they, as relative experts, know.

Substantial knowledge of what individual citizens' interests are commends having a legislative body to defend them. Substantial ignorance on the part of citizens argues against the value of a democratically elected legislative body. Most citizens in modern advanced democracies are clearly deeply ignorant of many of the most important policy issues their nations face. National leaders, such as prime ministers and presidents, can lead their citizens into holding clearer views, although we can wonder whether that is a good or a bad effect of such leadership, which can grossly mislead. Traditional arguments for the separation of powers do not evoke this distinctive difference between the two institutional powers: legislature and executive.

There are two distinctively different ways to aggregate from the individual to the social level to achieve social order. A cultural theorist who supposes we are more or less all alike in that we have extensive common or shared values can simply impute individual values to the society. One who supposes we are substantially different in our values must decentralize into complementary but different groups or even all the way to individuals. In essence, Talcott Parsons[5] holds the first view and Hayek[6] the second (see further, Hardin[7]). Liberalism works in the second of these ways. If Parsons were pervasively right, we would not need a legislative body to deal with political conflict but only to determine what are our common values and to discover what policies would secure those values.

SEPARATION OF POWERS

In part because we the citizens are unable to oversee what government does, we may generally agree with James Madison on being wary of or distrusting our government.[8] Madison supposes that we should protect ourselves from government by making sure that it is weak. In particular, he supposes that the U.S. government should have power enough to prevent the individual states from interfering in commerce but that it should not have power to intervene in our lives in other ways.

[5] Talcott Parsons, *The Structure of Social Action* (New York: Free Press, 1968).

[6] F. A. Hayek, *The Road to Serfdom* (Chicago: University of Chicago Press, 1944).

[7] Russell Hardin, *Liberalism, Constitutionalism, and Democracy* (Oxford: Oxford University Press, 1999) at 9–12.

[8] Russell Hardin, "Liberal Distrust" (2002) 10:1 *European Review* 73.

If we wish to coordinate on weaker rather than stronger democratic government, then we want institutional devices that restrain government action, perhaps more in certain areas than in others. A principal reason for having separation of powers, especially of the legislative, executive, and judicial powers, is to reduce the likelihood of extreme actions by government. Having at least three institutions playing a role in what government does means at least some degree of regression toward the mean. This is heightened if the different institutions have different terms and lengths of tenure in office. For example, within the U.S. Senate there is some chance of regression toward the mean over time because one-third of the members are elected in each two-year election cycle, and they then serve for six years. Justices in many systems are appointed to very long or even life terms. Hence, the judiciary can reflect the political persuasions of different eras, and the different eras imply some regression toward the mean.

We can see how important separation is in the recent violations of the principle of separation in the Bush Administration's actions against suspected terrorists. These people are dealt with almost entirely and only by the Administration, especially under either the military or the attorney general. The indeterminate lengths of "arrest" and detainment, without right of habeas corpus, have extended well beyond the period of seeming emergency when the policies were put into place. By almost any criteria, the handling of these people has been extreme in comparison to how any other people have been treated under American law since the adoption of the Constitution in 1788. Japanese-Americans were detained in camps in the western deserts during World War II, many potential activists were detained by administrative order during the presidency of Abraham Lincoln, and many Americans of German background were treated abusively during World War I. Apart from detainment, however, the extreme measures in the current regime go much further in putting the detainees through virtual torture – torture that may be more nearly psychological than brutally physical, but still brutal.

Liberalism essentially exalts local knowledge and values insofar as these are the values of individuals and, of course, it stands implacably against totalitarian control, which is often directed at redesigning not merely society and the economy but also the individual. James Scott argues that when state capacity to monitor its populace, to make the populace legible, is joined with high modernism in social design, totalitarian or immediately postrevolutionary government, and the absence of intermediary social structures, the state can take its population into disaster. The chain of argument is that "the legibility of a society provides the capacity for large-scale social engineering, high-modernist ideology provides the desire, the authoritarian state provides the determination to act on that desire, and an incapacitated civil society provides the leveled social terrain on which to build."[9] One can add that this chain results in centralized designs that take little account of and even thwart local knowledge, and that often fail largely for that reason.

Most of Scott's discussions are about state abuses of its knowledge of and controls over a legible populace. His perspective is usually that of the poor under the control of a state that is autocratic and that massively manipulates them, ostensibly for their

[9] James Scott, *Seeing Like a State: How Certain Schemes to Improve the Human Condition Have Failed* (New Haven, Conn.: Yale University Press, 1998) at 5, 89.

own good or the good of future generations. There is, of course, also a benign side of legibility because the devices for legibility can also be used for good purposes, such as monitoring and preventing diseases.[10] Indeed, if a state is to have any policies that benefit the populace, it most likely can achieve its purposes better if it has knowledge about the populace. The devices that produce legibility enable the state to make readier, better-targeted interventions, whatever the state's purpose. The devices are neutral in the sense that they do not determine the direction of the interventions. A Nazi government can use the devices to track down those to be exterminated,[11] and a welfare state can use them to distribute social security payments. For reasons of democracy and fairness, the U.S. Constitution mandates a decennial census to allocate seats in the Congress according to population and to make tax collections equitable (the taxes were to be head taxes levied by the states and turned over to the federal government). Without the facts from such a census, democracy must be less representative and the politics of redistricting or reallocating seats in legislative bodies must be far more capricious. Representative democracy and the census go together.

If one values democracy, political fairness, mass education, and egalitarian policies, then one must accept the need for making a populace substantially legible to the state.[12] Otherwise, the state cannot intervene to make sure those who are qualified can vote or to equalize opportunities and even welfares. All of these are part of the technological capacity to mobilize large populations, a capacity that developed over the past three centuries and that has produced representative democracy, revolution, and nationalism, all of which are essentially modern phenomena. Without the capacity for mass mobilization, the state could not control its "citizens" very well (and the very idea of citizenship itself is essentially modern).

Before it had adequate measures of landholdings and other forms of wealth, the state was effectively blinded, and it could not levy taxes without sometimes grim caprice that would bankrupt some while leaving others untouched.[13] Egalitarianism can be achieved by reducing all to abject poverty in an anarchic subsistence economy, or it can be approached by elevating a state to manage at least some of the distribution of the benefits of a highly productive economy. Without access to education, the idea of equal opportunity is a farce, as suggested by the awful 1972 Supreme Court decision in *Wisconsin v. Yoder*[14] that allows the Amish of Wisconsin to end their children's education at age fourteen to protect them from the blandishments of the larger society. That decision also "protects" those children against any opportunity to enter the larger economy.

PROBLEMS OF COLLECTIVE ACTION

The logic of many defenders of legislatures and of democracy itself is often profoundly flawed. In a typical statement, in his lectures at Princeton, John Witherspoon claims that "the multitude collectively always are true in intention

[10] Ibid. at 77.
[11] Ibid. at 78.
[12] Ibid. at 339–40.
[13] Ibid. at 2.
[14] 406 U.S. 205, 92 S. Ct. 1526, L. Ed. 2d 15 (Lexis).

to the interest of the public, because it is their own. They are the public."[15] Marchmont Nedham argues that the people "are the best keepers of their own liberties... because they never think of usurping other men's rights." John Adams contemptuously retorts:

> But who are the people?... If by *the people* is meant the whole body of a great nation, it should never be forgotten, that they can never act, consult, or reason together, because they cannot march five hundred miles, nor spare the time, nor find a space to meet; and, therefore, the proposition, that they are the best keepers of their own liberties, is not true. They are the worst conceivable; they are no keepers at all.[16]

Adams is concerned to defend the need for separation of powers specifically to protect individual liberties, with each branch of government constraining the other two.

A legislature is a compromise. Sometimes, it is a perverse compromise, as when the individual legislators use their offices substantially to ensconce themselves in the offices. For example, recently the U.S. Congress voted funds to help communities guard against terrorist attacks. In legislation voted by the House of Representatives, the funds go very disproportionately to rural and small communities and to states such as thinly populated Wyoming, where the threat of terrorism is virtually nil, rather than to the far more likely targets of terrorism, which are large cities, most especially New York. The legislation allocates $5.47 per person to New York and $38 per person to Wyoming.[17] New York's Mayor Michael Bloomberg angrily commented that he had never yet heard of a terrorist who carried a map of a cornfield.[18] But better resources will be devoted to protecting Iowa cornfields than New York.

If this legislation were the product of a single author actually concerned to guard against terrorism, we would rightly say that the design of the legislation is stupid – deeply stupid – and we would wonder about the competence and intelligence of the author. But the legislation was "crafted" by 435 members of the House of Representatives (only 408 actually voted against a final effort to increase funding to likely targets of terrorism). Every one of them may have acted rationally. A legislator from Wyoming could use funds to Wyoming to help generate support for the legislator's reelection. The Wyoming allocation amounts to more than fifty dollars per potential voter. The individual legislators may have acted rationally and self-interestedly, but the body of legislators acted stupidly on behalf of the nation.

REPRESENTATION

The idea of a legislature fits oddly with Austrian social theory. First, it may be true that a representative legislature is a better aggregator of *private knowledge* in general than an executive government. But, as the case of the congressional act

[15] Quoted in Wood, *supra* note 1 at 164.

[16] John Adams, "Defence of the Constitution of the United States" (1787) in Philip Kurland and Ralph Lerner, eds., *The Founders' Constitution*, vol. 1 (Chicago: University of Chicago Press, 1987) at 59.

[17] The House action is not final because the Senate voted more generous support to high-risk cities. The final legislation will have to be hammered out in a conference committee.

[18] Raymond Hernandez, "House Rejects Increased Aid to Secure Cities at High Risk," *New York Times* (June 19, 2004) at B2.

on prevention of domestic terrorism illustrates, knowledge of the distribution of private interests in various contexts need not entail that the knowledgeable legislators will be motivated to act on *the interests* of relevant publics. In very many contexts, there is also great doubt that a legislature can adequately aggregate such knowledge for the simple reason that representatives of substantial communities of people cannot generally represent all of their community members' views. On this divisive issue, the Anti-Federalist opponents of creating a strong national government in the United States were analytically right. For representation to work according to the ideal of its substituting for full participation, the representatives must share the interests and not only the knowledge of those they represent.

In a later debate over staffing of administrative agencies beginning at about the end of the nineteenth century, some advocate passive representation of those being served. You passively represent blacks or workers if you are black or a worker. You actively represent them if you simply set their interests as your goal. For example, Massachusetts Senator Edward Kennedy actively represents workers and the poor, although he has experience neither being a worker nor being poor. The Anti-Federalists essentially held that only passive representation can be trusted. Small farmers must be represented by small farmers. Mechanics (workers) must be represented by mechanics. And wealthy estate farmers in upstate New York must be represented by wealthy estate farmers in upstate New York. Such farmers were particularly eloquent among the Anti-Federalists. This is the clear meaning of the statement by Robert Yates and John Lansing, two of the three New York delegates to the Philadelphia Constitutional Convention, explaining why they had chosen not to sign the final constitution. They say that

> if the general legislature was composed of so numerous a body of men, as to represent the interests of all the inhabitants of the United States, in the usual and true ideas of representation, the expence would [be intolerable; and] if a few only were vested with a power of legislation, the interests of a great majority of the inhabitants of the United States, must necessarily be unknown; or if known . . . unattended to.[19]

Debates over the nature of and need for representation were quite lively from colonial times through the constitutional period in the United States. And they were quite lively from well before and well after that period in England, where, in the face of a lack of genuine representation for large fractions of the population, Thomas Whately, writing in 1775, and other defenders of the status quo in that era assert that these populations enjoyed "virtual representation."[20] Whately himself, as a Catholic barred from voting, was only virtually represented. Virtual representation in his case cannot have been passive representation but could only have been active. In particular, passive representation in defense of his religious freedom was clearly not possible. One doubts that he could honorably claim to be represented with respect to much other than the national defense, provision of various infrastructures, and other such universally beneficial things, which serve the mutual advantage and must therefore be supported by everyone.

[19] Robert Yates and John Lansing, "Reasons of Dissent" (1787) in Herbert J. Storing, ed., *The Complete Anti-Federalist*, vol. 2 (Chicago: University of Chicago Press, 1981) 16 at 18.

[20] Wood, *supra* note 1 at 173–81. Also see Hardin, *supra* note 7 at 178–81.

REPRESENTATION AND MUTUAL ADVANTAGE

Representation can be credible as a device for aggregating knowledge if the representative shares the views of an entire constituency. This is apt to be true only when the constituency is quite homogeneous in its interests. Historically, this condition has been met by societies in which agriculture is still by far the largest sector of the economy. The early liberal, almost Hayekist, societies – England, the Netherlands, Scotland, and the United States – somehow insulated nascent liberalism from rural domination. In particular, they all created democratic institutions at the center of political and governmental life while largely excluding rural populations from participating. It is a perverse fact of the history of modern democracy that it could succeed only through massive exclusion of much of the population.

In the United States, of course, slaves were deliberately excluded. The Southern states with their slaves participated in the new government but were not Hayekist. They were an anomaly.

Exclusion of citizen farmers, however, happened without design in part, because rural citizens did not vote on the new constitution of 1787.[21] Most of them were subsistence farmers who may have assumed that politics at the national level would be irrelevant to their lives, as it probably was, although James Madison and many other constitutionalists feared that these people would mobilize to take control of the government and would dispossess the wealthier classes.

Other industrializing nations followed the pattern of England to a large extent. They excluded rural peasants and others who did not own property from political participation through most of the nineteenth century. England also de facto excluded many industrial cities, which had no representation in Parliament except through virtual representation. Virtual representation is what the vast bulk of subsistence farmers could enjoy from every representative of small farming interests, especially when the latter passively share the interests of farmers.

At the time of the U.S. Constitution, roughly 85 percent of the adult male population were small farmers, most of them likely subsistence farmers. Had they mobilized to obtain benefits from the new government, they would largely have shared interests enough to be represented well. Policies favoring such farmers would have been mutually advantageous for the majority of the then extant population. Farmers' ignorance of government and its possibilities enabled wealthier groups in the society to dominate politically. Indeed, dominance by wealthier citizens continued long after universal white male adult suffrage would have allowed rural interests to gain control of the government, as they did to a limited extent during the presidency of Andrew Jackson (1833–1841).

To democratize a nation that is still dominated by agriculture is a high-risk venture today, because the exclusion of rural citizens from the vote is not possible. Madison's fears of expropriation by the poor through democratic means might be fulfilled in many cases today. In the early United States and in many other nations that democratized early, communications were poor and subsistence farmers were likely woefully ignorant. Clinton Rossiter writes, "Where men farmed largely for

[21] Evelyn C. Fink and William H. Riker, "The Strategy of Ratification" in Bernard Grofman and Donald Wittman, eds., *The Federalist Papers and the New Institutionalism* (New York: Agathon, 1989) 220 at 221.

subsistence, where the printed word penetrated laboriously, where life was hard and horizons limited..., one found apathy, lethargy, and suspicion."[22] Karl Marx sharply characterizes the French peasants who, in his view, stupidly voted against their own interests in support of Louis Bonaparte in the election of 1848.[23] There might be apathy, lethargy, suspicion, and stupidity in many rural areas of the world today, but the spoken word now penetrates readily everywhere, and mobilization is far easier than it was a century or two ago.

CREATIVE DESTRUCTION

An implication of economic development has been what Joseph Schumpeter calls creative destruction, which he says "is the essential fact about capitalism."[24] Old industries and forms of production are displaced by new forms that are more efficient. The steel industry is substantially replaced by the aluminum and plastics industries. The plow pulled by a mule is replaced by a tractor. In *The Eighteenth Brumaire*,[25] Marx basically agreed with this vision. For Marx, and historically, the most important instance of such creative destruction has been destruction of the massive, stultifying investment of human labor in agriculture through the introduction of mechanized production and, later, through inputs of fertilizer and higher-yielding seed, plant, and animal varieties.

The isolating existence of peasants likely contributes to their hostility to change, particularly the destruction of subsistence farming as a way of life. Freeing 85 percent of the total workforce from farming has been the chief motor for increasing the industrial and service workforces. It has been driven by the opportunities offered by these job sectors, and it has been almost entirely voluntary – in the sense, of course, that greater prosperity seemed available off the farm than in small farming. In general, the shift out of farming was not deliberately managed by government but merely happened as a result of technological and demographic developments, although the Soviet Union was commonly accused of forcing farm laborers into urban industrial work.

Late in the nineteenth century in the United States, agricultural interests finally mobilized to capture the Democratic Party, which was one of the two major parties at the time. That party, under the leadership of William Jennings Bryan (1860–1925), who was retrograde in other important ways as well,[26] sought to wipe out farm indebtedness with "easy money" and to maintain farmers and miners in their

[22] Clinton Rossiter, *1787: The Grand Convention* (New York: Macmillan, 1966) at 296.

[23] Karl Marx, *The 18th Brumaire of Louis Bonaparte* (New York: World Publishing, 1963).

[24] Joseph A. Schumpeter, *Capitalism, Socialism and Democracy* (New York: Harper, [1942] 1950, 3rd ed.) 83–6 at 83.

[25] *Supra* note 23.

[26] Bryan is perhaps best remembered today for his fundamentalist, antievolution views, as trumpeted in his being a lawyer for the state of Tennessee in the infamous Scopes monkey trial, in which a school teacher was convicted of the blasphemy of teaching the Darwinian theory of evolution. Ironically, Bryan's politics was also based on an antiscientific view of the economy and society. After decades of the steady decline of agriculture until it employed less than a majority of the American workforce, he wanted to stop the decline as though it were the result of simple governmental decisions rather than of agricultural science and technological developments. His political career was founded on brilliant rhetoric and grand ignorance – his own and his followers' ignorance.

relatively inefficient and fast-disappearing way of life. For more than twenty years, the platforms of the party were economically retrograde. The mock-Falangist party of Juan Perón in Argentina was also economically antiprogressive in its effort to protect what was already passing. Both these parties focused on current income and its distribution, not on its increase over time, and on the then current structure of the economy, as though to fix it in that form forever. Progress in both nations likely depended on the creative destruction of those parties, which is not quite what Schumpeter had in mind.

In other nations, similar moves have nearly succeeded, sometimes with democratic backing. For example, the Algerian military intervened to block the democratic accession to power of a fundamentalist religious party that would have blocked economic progress in many ways and that would have given rural interests a strong grip on national politics. Other religious movements, such as the Taliban in Afghanistan and the Ayatollahs in Iran, have attempted similarly to block economic progress, partly in the name of religious values.

Adam Przeworski, Michael Alvarez, Jose Antonio Cheibub, and Fernando Limongi[27] argue that once GDP in a democracy passes a level of a little over $6,000 per capita, a democratic society is safe against backsliding into autocracy. Note that this level of per capita GDP virtually assures that the rural vote is relatively small. Hence, there can be no *Eighteenth-Brumaire* distortion from the agricultural sector and no mass movement to block the creative destruction of farm life. A major factor in the success of democracy has been the increasing productivity of labor, especially in the agricultural sector, because such increased productivity breaks the tight definition of particular groups that could vote in their own mutual advantage to constrain or even block economic innovation and change.

One might suppose therefore that the former fear of Madison and others that those with little or no wealth would be seen as a democratic threat to those with great wealth would have waned or even passed. In gross terms, this supposition seems to be correct, but perversely there is now an analytically analogous form of legislative capture that distorts economic performance and growth. On analogy with farmers, those most strongly motivated to seek special treatment from government are likely to be economic groups threatened with creative destruction. As has been true of agriculture in modern times, those whose dominance in some economic realm is threatened by innovation can shore up their position by legal and political devices when economic performance fails. Seeking government intervention is a sign of economic failure; getting such intervention trumps economic forces. In the United States, Ronald Reagan perhaps did more to overcome such politics than any other president; and his fellow Republican George Bush may already have done more to bring it back into play than any prior president did to initiate such intervention on behalf of failure.

Reagan's efforts were bits of creative destruction of often very clever kinds. For example, he ended the collection of data on divorce in California while he was governor, and he ended many series of data on business activities while he was

[27] Adam Przeworski, Michael Alvarez, Jose Antonio Cheibub, and Fernando Limongi, "What Makes Democracies Endure?" (1996) 7 *Journal of Democracy* 39.

president. He did most of this by simple executive order. A clear result is to make it very hard even to know enough to design any policies to benefit certain interests. In a sense, Reagan forced the Austrian social theory of distributed knowledge to be even truer than it might have been. Whereas individuals can know many things that government agencies cannot credibly claim to know, those agencies can, somewhat metaphorically speaking, know many aggregate and statistical facts that few individuals could ever know except from summary reports by those agencies. Reagan undercut that advantage of government agencies and destroyed much of the knowledge they are especially capable of mastering.

CORPORATE DEMOCRACY

Adolf Berle and Gardner Means note that the rise of the corporate form of organization of private firms breaks the link between ownership and management, thus opening the possibility of conflict of interest between owners and professional managers.[28] Among the legal forms that property in the corporate form might take as a result of such separation is an analog to what we have seen in many corporations historically, including many in recent years during the extraordinary stock bubble of the 1990s. This form creates "a new set of relationships, giving to the groups in control powers which are absolute and not limited by any implied obligation with respect to their use."[29] Through their absolute control of a corporation, the managers "can operate it in their own interests, and can divert a portion of the [corporation's income and assets] to their own uses," and we face the potential for "corporate plundering."[30]

Alternatively, they supposed that the corporate form would develop into what would now be called a socially conscious institution. This wildly optimistic expectation is at odds with their hard-headed analysis of what had already developed in corporate governance. They quote Walter Rathenau's 1918 view that the private "enterprise becomes transformed into an institution which resembles the state in character."[31] The reverse seems to have happened. The state has been transformed to resemble loosely controlled corporations. Elected officials act as "professional" managers on behalf of the citizenry who "own" the nation. The officials are co-owners along with the citizens, but their rewards from management often far transcend anything they can gain as their share of the general good produced by government, just as the corporate managers of Tyco, WorldCom, and Enron gained far more from looting these firms than from the genuine increase in value of the stock they owned. Indeed, they manipulated the market valuation of that stock through accounting misrepresentations in order to enrich themselves, as Berle and Means virtually predict.[32]

[28] Adolf A. Berle and Gardner C. Means, *The Modern Corporation and Private Property* (New York: Macmillan, 1932) at 119–25. This discussion follows Russell Hardin, "Transition to Corporate Democracy?" in Janos Kornai and Susan Rose-Ackerman, eds., *Problems of Post-Socialist Transition, vol. 1: Building a Trustworthy State* (New York: Palgrave-Macmillan, 2004) 175 at 178–82.

[29] Berle and Means, *supra* note 28 at 354–5.

[30] Ibid.

[31] Ibid. at 352.

[32] Ibid. at 296–7.

In some sense, it is not the individual elected officials but the class of them that is problematic. As John C. Calhoun says, "The advantages of possessing the control of the powers of the government, and thereby of its honors and emoluments, are, of themselves, exclusive of all other considerations, ample to divide . . . a community into two great hostile parties."[33] The political class are parasitic on the society that they ostensibly serve and that has the power of election over them. Although some representatives may be very well grounded in their constituencies, the reference group for many representatives is far more likely to be their fellow "aristocrats" than their electorates so long as they attend to certain issues of great salience to their constituencies. The supposedly powerful citizenry with its power of election over officials does not have the power to refuse to elect all of them; it can only turn out the occasional overtly bad apple. In the United States, it seldom has the temerity to overcome incumbents' advantage.[34]

Calhoun spent the last two decades of his life defending slavery and the prerogative of the Southern states to maintain slavery. The minority that his writings generally defend was the minority of Southern states and their representatives in the national government against the majority of antislavery states and their representatives. Some of his central arguments, however, are more generally compelling in the abstract and when applied to many other issues. He argued the case that officials use their offices to serve their private interests nearly a century before Berle and Means made the analogous case for the governance of the modern corporation.

Although the corporate form of organization had precedents in the seventeenth century, the first important manufacturing firm organized that way – with a significant number of stock-holders, all of them minority stockholders – was the first of the large New England textile mills, organized in Waltham, Massachusetts, in 1813.[35] This company followed the virtual invention of modern representative government in the U.S. Constitution of 1787 by a quarter century so that, in a sense, the corporate form of control with few managers and large numbers of owners was pioneered by representative government.

The possibility of perversion into corporate democracy was clearly recognized in 1776 by James Iredell, who says that the English House of Commons had become so unrepresentative that it was "separated from, and converted into a different interest from the collective."[36] He sees this perversion as an example not to be emulated. The House of Commons was a body that represented communities, originally mostly rural communities. One might suppose therefore that it was a model for what many Anti-Federalists wanted. Its distortion into the corporate form was, however, not clearly a result of its communal structure.

[33] John C. Calhoun, "A Disquisition on Government" (1853) in Ross M. Lence, ed., *Union and Liberty: The Political Philosophy of John C. Calhoun* (Indianapolis: Liberty Fund, 1992) at 5.

[34] Consider the 2002 congressional elections in the United States. Only four incumbents in the House of Representatives (which has 435 members, all of whom are elected at two-year intervals) lost to nonincumbent challengers (a few incumbents lost to other incumbents because their districts were changed to reflect demographic changes). Overall, 90% of all candidates won by margins of more than 10% of the votes cast. When districts are redrawn by a state government after each decennial census (as for the 2002 election), they are often gerrymandered to ensure election of the candidates in the state's dominant party. For data, see Rob Richie, *Fair Elections Update: Election 2002 and the Case for Reform* (Washington: Center for Voting and Democracy, November 14, 2002).

[35] Berle and Means, *supra* note 28 at 10–11.

[36] Quoted in Wood, *supra* note 1 at 165.

CONCLUDING REMARKS

Note two ironic implications of seeing like Hayek. First, seeing this way means, in theory, seeing from the bottom up, from local circumstances, although Austrian economic theorizing is as much from top down as any high-modernist theorizing is. Hayek and the Austrians have a very general theory about how knowledge works and where it resides. They may have come to this theory from particular instances that gave them a deeper understanding. But they then go on to apply this theory to many new circumstances and even to the issues of national economic and social policy. Hayek's most widely read book, *The Road to Serfdom*, was written as a general criticism of the effort to centralize the management of a socialist economy.[37] His critique followed directly from his theory of distributed knowledge and hence of the importance of entrepreneurial creativity. He did not need to know anything in particular about the Soviet economy to write that book.

Second, the Hayek vision says that there are very many things, even whole classes of things, that the state cannot know. Therefore, any defense or expectations of the state must be built on what it can know, which is more or less the simplified facts of legibility and so forth that Scott notes. As noted earlier, big institutions can amass aggregate data on a population and on their activities, as do, for example, the Centers for Disease Control in Atlanta. In the end, it is the institution that knows these things, although some of them might be put in an annual report or other document where, in summary form, the facts could be digested by individuals. For the most part, however, few individuals will come to know these data despite their importance in policy design and implementation. Even those who do come to "know" them will at most take the data on faith.

Finally, note that any Austrian economist supposes that we know some fairly general things about people, such as what motivations or kinds of motivations they are likely to have. It is partly their sense of the basically economic motivation of people who are involved in economic enterprises that led the Austrians to deplore Sovietization of the economy and of agriculture. If we switch from individual farms to collective farms, we de facto make the production of the farm a collective provision, the rewards from which must then be allocated among the collective farmers. This makes your contribution to the general product virtually irrelevant to you so that you must now be motivated not by what you gain from your efforts but by what we all collectively gain from our collective effort. To my knowledge, the Austrians did not fully articulate the logic of collective action that runs against the hope of managing and even increasing production by making it collective. Yet if one wishes to say that local knowledge was the crucial problem with collective farms, one must explain why after nearly three generations the requisite local knowledge had still not arisen to run those farms collectively. What had happened, of course, was the rise of local knowledge to subvert the collective effort by capitalizing on standard individualistic economic incentives. The failure of collectivization was therefore an Austrian failure, a failure of incentives, not a failure to rely on local knowledge.

[37] Hayek, *supra* note 6.

3 Political Accountability, Proxy Accountability, and the Democratic Legitimacy of Legislatures

Jane S. Schacter

The story of democratic legitimacy that has long dominated American legal discourse is familiar and very simple: Legislators are politically answerable to voters and appointed judges are not. This accountability is conventionally said to supply the dispositive factor in allocating institutional roles. The idea that policymaking and political accountability must travel together forms the intellectual core of this idea and gives meaning to the derisive references to "legislation from the bench" that are so common in contemporary politics. To put the idea on a loftier academic plane, consider the words of Alexander Bickel, the patron saint of the so-called countermajoritarian difficulty:

> Representative democracies – that is to say all working democracies – function by electing certain men for certain periods of time, then passing judgment periodically on their conduct of public office. It is a matter of laying on of hands, followed in time by a process of holding to account – all through the exercise of the franchise.[1]

Notice some significant characteristics of this approach. One is a single-minded democratic focus on periodic elections. This is characteristic of an approach that some have called "democratic minimalism," which requires only "choosing rulers by elections,"[2] and no more. Echoing in some respects theories associated with Joseph Schumpeter,[3] this conception of democracy rejects theories that demand robust concepts of deliberation, participation, equality, or justice as aspects of democracy itself. The minimalist emphasis is an emphatically pragmatic one: Democracies can actually deliver regular elections, but too often cannot make good on these more demanding aspirations. As long as elections are sufficient to permit the peaceful transfer of power, the democratic minimalist would say, that is sufficient.

Notice as well that, in Bickel's famous formulation, legislative accountability is not merely posited or argued to exist, but rather asserted as fact, as if irrefutable. For this reason, I call it the accountability axiom. Given the centrality of this axiom to the countermajoritarian difficulty and the traditional view of democratic legitimacy, it

[1] Alexander M. Bickel, *The Least Dangerous Branch* (Indianapolis: Bobbs-Merrill, 1962).

[2] Adam Przeworski, "Minimalist Conception of Democracy: A Defense" in Ian Shapiro and Casiano Hacker-Cordón, eds., *Democracy's Value* (New York: Cambridge University Press, 1999) 23 at 43–4.

[3] Joseph A. Schumpeter, *Capitalism, Socialism and Democracy*, 5th ed. (Boston: Allen and Unwin, 1981).

strikes me as odd that legal scholars have not taken much of a critical look at the assumption that legislators are politically accountable in a strong enough sense to warrant the potent institutional consequences that are routinely attached to that accountability.[4]

In previous work concerning both constitutional[5] and statutory interpretation,[6] I have challenged the conventional accountability axiom, arguing that it has two characteristic sorts of problems. The first is a *deficit* in accountability that arises because voters are so poorly informed about politics and legislation, and the second is an *asymmetry* in accountability that flourishes because of the disparities that characterize the contemporary American political process. Prompted by these deep and difficult problems with accountability, the main focus of this chapter is to consider what we might learn about legislative accountability from recent work in the political science literature. I address here three strands of that literature – one focused on the significance of legislators' anticipation of voter preferences, a second on voters' use of informational shortcuts in navigating political choices, and a third on how aggregating and disaggregating the electorate might ameliorate the shortcomings of individual voters.

My task here is to consider whether scholarship in these areas might offer a way around the problems of deficit and asymmetry that plague the idea of legislative accountability. I examine, more specifically, the ways in which this work might be read to supply a theory of accountability by proxy – that is, a theory by which the democratic accountability of legislators to their constituents might be achieved through certain substitute devices, notwithstanding the sorts of problems that I have mentioned. Ultimately, I conclude that, although much of this work sheds significant light on the dynamics of contemporary mass democracy, it does not cure the accountability axiom of what ails it, nor does it support the degree or quality of legislative accountability necessary to revive Bickel's animating notion.

First, I briefly summarize the critique I have made of the accountability axiom. Next, I introduce the work from political science that I engage here. Finally, I consider whether these strands of scholarship can be convincingly read to support proxy theories of accountability, and explain why I conclude that they do not.

4 Exceptions include Erwin Chemerinsky, "Foreword: The Vanishing Constitution" (1989) 103 *Harv. L. Rev.* 43 at 80–1; Barry Friedman, "Dialogue and Judicial Review" (1993) 91 *Mich. L. Rev.* 577 at 609–14, 629–42; Elizabeth Garrett, "Accountability and Restraint: The Federal Budget Process and the Line Item Veto Act" (1999) 20 *Cardozo L. Rev.* 871 at 925–36; cf. Ilya Somin, "Political Ignorance and the Countermajoritarian Difficulty: A New Perspective on the Central Obsession of Constitutional Theory" (2004) 89 *Iowa L. Rev.* 1287 (not focusing on accountability per se but arguing that voter ignorance undermines majoritarian democracy). For a thoughtful, wide-ranging look at accountability from within political science, see Adam Przeworski, Susan C. Stokes, and Bernard Manin, eds., *Democracy, Accountability and Representation* (New York: Cambridge University Press, 1999).

5 Jane S. Schacter, "Ely and the Idea of Democracy" (2004) 57 *Stan. L. Rev.* 737 at 755–60 ("Schacter, *Ely*"); Jane S. Schacter, "*Lawrence v. Texas* and the Fourteenth Amendment's Democratic Aspirations" (2004) 13 *Temp. Pol. & Civ. Rts. L. Rev.* 733 ("Schacter, *Lawrence*").

6 Jane S. Schacter, *Accounting for Accountability in Dynamic Statutory Interpretation and Beyond* in Issues in Legal Scholarship: Dynamic Statutory Interpretation (2002), available at http:www.bepress.com/isl/iss3/art5 ("Schacter, *Accounting for Accountability*").

ACCOUNTABILITY AS UNREALIZED ASPIRATION

Without rehearsing my past critique of accountability in detail, let me briefly summarize the problems of deficit and asymmetry that, I argue, weaken the accountability axiom.[7]

A core problem here is an informational deficit: Voters cannot hold legislators responsible without sufficient information about what legislators have, in fact, done. Yet that sort of information consistently eludes the electorate. It is an article of faith among political scientists that citizens are woefully uninformed about politics, and scholars have rarely resorted to understatement in characterizing the public's knowledge gaps. Consider these examples, from leading studies:

> "[t]here now seems to be a consensus that by anything approaching elite standards most citizens know jaw-droppingly little about politics."[8]

> "[t]he political ignorance of the American voter is one of the best-documented features of contemporary politics."[9]

> "Decades of behavioral research have shown that most people know little about their elected officeholders, less about their opponents, and virtually nothing about the public issues that occupy officials from Washington to city hall."[10]

> "Americans are indifferent to much that transpires in the political world, hazy about many of the principal players, lackadaisical regarding debates on policies that preoccupy Washington, ignorant of facts that experts take for granted, and unsure about the policies advanced by the candidates for the highest public offices."[11]

There are undoubtedly many complex reasons for this state of affairs, including that much legislative activity takes place behind closed doors; that the media does not cover large swaths of the legislative agenda; that even politically salient issues are often covered by the press in a sporadic or unhelpful way; that politicians and contending interests frequently spin, label, and characterize laws in ways that make it hard for the public to decipher what was actually done; and that sorting out who is responsible for particular public policies is formidably difficult in the context of a multimember legislature, multibranch government, and federal system. Perhaps the more difficult problem is simply a lack of interest: Many voters do not choose to avail themselves of the copious amount of information about policy and politics that is, in theory, available to them.[12]

[7] I draw on my previous work in this section and leave both the details and the citations to underlying sources to that work, cited in notes 5 and 6.

[8] Robert Luskin, "From Denial to Extenuation (and Finally Beyond): Political Sophistication and Citizen Performance" in James H. Kuklinski, ed., *Thinking About Political Psychology* (New York: Cambridge University Press, 2002) at 282.

[9] Larry M. Bartels, "Uninformed Votes: Information Effects in Presidential Elections" (1996) 40 *Amer. J. of Pol. Sci.* 194.

[10] John A. Ferejohn, "Information and the Electoral Process" in John A. Ferejohn and James H. Kuklinski, eds., *Information and Democratic Processes* (Urbana: University of Illinois Press, 1990) at 3.

[11] Donald R. Kinder and David O. Sears, "Public Opinion and Political Action" in Gardner Lindzey and Elliot Aronson, eds., *Handbook of Social Psychology, Volume II* (New York: Random House, 1985).

[12] On these points, see the sources cited in Schacter, *Ely, supra* note 5 at 755–6.

The accountability axiom is also undermined because elections cannot sustain the heavy institutional burden that Bickel and others place on them to deliver accountability. Congressional elections are rarely issue-driven affairs. Moreover, incumbents vote on far too many matters to make even any significant fraction of them plausible bases for accountability. This does not even include the many decisions that are not reflected in any recorded vote. Questions of volume aside, voters cannot always readily hold an individual legislator accountable for the work of a multimember body. And, legislation that is enacted into law is often deliberately crafted to avoid responsibility for the most controversial aspects of policy by using ambiguous language or by delegating to a federal agency. Extraordinarily high incumbent reelection rates, the frequent lack of credible challengers, and ever-more strategic partisan gerrymandering all make it even less likely that elections can be the accountability forcing devices Bickel assumed them to be.[13]

Notice as well that the very idea of accountability assumes that voters view elections as an occasion for retrospective assessment of the incumbent's performance – that is, for holding legislators to account. There is surely classic work that supports this idea, and it may, at a minimum, capture part of the electoral dynamic. But this construct does not deal with the possibility that voters may make their choices ex ante (the so-called selection or mandate view), not ex post (the so-called sanctions or accountability view). In fact, there may be no clearly defined distinction in the minds of voters, but this uncertainty alone undermines categorical claims about elections as tools of legislative accountability. Moreover, it is reasonable to suppose that large gaps in voter information would negatively affect voting decisions, whether such decisions are characterized as ex ante or ex post.[14]

Although all of this suggests that it is an informational deficit that weakens claims about accountability, there are good grounds to worry as much or more about asymmetries in accountability. Because of familiar collective action problems, well-organized groups, who monitor legislative activity closely, are much better situated than the mass electorate to secure real accountability from incumbent legislators. And these groups have more resources for demanding accountability; they have not just individual votes with which to threaten lawmakers, but the ability to aggregate many votes and to withhold or deploy resources like lobbyist assistance, contributions, and the threat of independent spending. Unorganized groups do not enjoy these advantages and often lack the ability even to push their issues on to the agenda. All of this suggests that the rhetoric of widespread accountability may obscure the reality of too much accountability for some and not enough for many.[15]

13 On these points, see the sources cited in Schacter, *Ely, supra* note 5 at 758. See also David Schoenbrod, *Power Without Responsibility: How Congress Abuses the People Through Delegation* (New Haven, Conn.: Yale University Press, 1993); Theodore Lowi, *The End of Liberalism: The Second Republic of the United States*, 2nd ed. (New York: Norton, 1979) at 92–126.

14 On these points, see the sources cited in Schacter, *Ely, supra* note 5 at 758–9.

15 On these points, see the sources cited in Schacter, *Ely, supra* note 5 at 759. In addition, for early perspectives on political asymmetries, see E. E. Schattschneider, *The Semi-Sovereign People: A Realist's View of Democracy in America* (New York: Holt, Rinehart and Winston, 1960); C. Wright Mills, *The Power Elite* (New York: Oxford University Press, 1956).

POTENTIAL THEORIES OF ACCOUNTABILITY BY PROXY

What can we learn from the contemporary political science literature about these weaknesses in the accountability axiom and, more importantly, about the salvageability of that axiom? There are good reasons to expect that we might learn something important. Although this scholarship does not explicitly concern itself with accountability as it may relate to the countermajoritarian difficulty and constitutionalism, it does engage squarely with many of the factors that, I argue, undermine the accountability axiom, especially the electorate's large knowledge gaps. It is thus a potentially fertile source of insights. It is also an important body of work with which to reckon because it suggests that there are grounds to be more sanguine about modern mass democracy than skeptics might believe.

For example, in his leading book, *The Logic of Congressional Action*, Douglas Arnold addresses both the deficit and asymmetry problems. As I describe in detail below, he argues that voters can play a significant role in contemporary democracy, even if they know little about politics and policy, and even if organized interest groups carry the day most of the time. His account focuses on legislators' politically driven need to anticipate uncrystallized voter preferences. Two other significant streams of work are more focused on the deficit problem in particular. One is concerned with political heuristics and argues that voters do not know much, but also do not *need* to know much, to make reasoned democratic choices, as long as good cues are available to guide voting choices. Another is concerned with how aggregating voters can yield a more rational electorate than one analyzed in terms of individual voters, and how *dis*aggregating the electorate can allow us to see that politically aware groups of voters can compensate for the deficiencies of their poorly informed peers.

These streams of scholarship have done a great deal to produce a more nuanced understanding of contemporary mass democracy. In exploring the inevitable political calculations that legislators make about roll-call voting, for example, Arnold reveals important dynamics in the legislative process, including by exploring the circumstances in which organized interest groups might not hold sway because legislators fear that the broad voting public will punish them at election time for particular votes. Similarly, the burgeoning literature on political heuristics is surely on to something significant in saying that voters eschew encyclopedic knowledge in search of efficient bits of information to guide voting decisions. And work on aggregation and disaggregation allows us to move beyond simplistic images of the polity, both by focusing on the collective performance of the electorate (rather than the properties of individual voters) and – if somewhat paradoxically – by insisting that the electorate cannot be viewed as a monolith and must, instead, be seen as multiple electorates (or "publics").

Scholarship of this sort is descriptively rich. In this chapter, however, I look to the work with a different set of questions in mind, questions that are both specifically focused on accountability and are more normative in nature: What, if anything, can these theories do to revive the accountability axiom in particular? What do they suggest about the concept of democracy that does and should inform our thinking about legislative and judicial legitimacy in the context of constitutionalism?

Read aggressively, these bodies of work can arguably supply *proxy* theories of accountability by identifying substitutes for the kind of informational environment that might make actual accountability possible. Proxy theories of this kind might be capable of reviving the idea that elections do, in fact, provide a sufficiently robust and consistent process for holding legislators accountable, and thus capable of reviving Bickel's central principle of institutional analysis. I call these potential proxy theories accountability through prediction, accountability through heuristics, and accountability through aggregation and disaggregation. I first sketch out a reading of these bodies of work that lays the basis for each proxy theory. I then explore how successful they are, once read in this way, at salvaging Bickel's premise.

ACCOUNTABILITY THROUGH PREDICTION

This idea is a culmination of several important accounts in the literature on Congress and is perhaps best represented in the work of Douglas Arnold, whose influential book, *The Logic of Congressional Action,*[16] emphasized that members of Congress attempt to anticipate how a potential challenger or other instigator might use roll-call votes against the incumbent in the next election. Arnold posits a survival-driven need to anticipate how even a mostly dormant and inattentive electorate might respond, if roused by an enterprising political opponent or reporter. This need arguably generates a form of predictive accountability that can operate even if voters do not know very much about most of the issues on which a member may vote or voice an opinion. This theory posits, in essence, a *phantom* electorate, alive in the minds of reelection oriented legislators, who fear that an issue might be used to galvanize future political opposition.

In setting out this idea, Arnold built on several important theories, such as David Mayhew's argument that members of Congress perpetually calculate the electoral consequences of their actions,[17] John Kingdon's rich empirical picture of congressional roll-call voting pointing up similar tendencies,[18] Morris Fiorina's early theory arguing that it is rational for legislators to act as if their constituents were paying attention,[19] and, especially, V. O. Key's identification of the powerful, yet elusive concept of "latent public opinion."[20] Arnold's work is particularly relevant for our purposes, however, because of his operative concept that "citizens who have no opinions about a policy at the time it is being considered may still have a large impact on legislators' decisions as long as legislators anticipate and respond to these citizens' potential preferences."[21] On this view, politicians' steady contemplation of potential voter preferences might support a version of accountability, even if voters themselves never assert or even perceive those preferences.

[16] R. Douglas Arnold, *The Logic of Congressional Action* (New Haven: Yale University Press, 1990).

[17] David R. Mayhew, *Congress: The Electoral Connection* (New Haven: Yale University Press, 1975).

[18] John W. Kingdon, *Congressmen's Voting Decisions*, 3rd ed. (Ann Arbor: University of Michigan Press, 1989). Kingdon argued that voters would typically forgive an incumbent for a few undesirable votes, but that a controversial string of votes might prove sufficient to jeopardize reelection.

[19] Morris P. Fiorina, *Representatives, Roll Calls and Constituencies* (Lexington, Mass.: Lexington Books, 1974).

[20] V. O. Key, Jr., *Public Opinion and American Democracy* (New York: Knopf, 1961).

[21] Arnold, *supra* note 16 at 11.

ACCOUNTABILITY THROUGH HEURISTICS

Like Arnold, scholars of political heuristics do not dispute the empirical picture of an electorate composed of poorly informed voters, but they argue that individuals can make rational voting decisions based on admittedly meager information. Central to this theory is the idea that cues and heuristics offer shortcuts that allow voters to function well enough, even in the absence of complex information. Theories of this kind might be traced as far back as Herbert Simon's early work on "satisficing,"[22] and have roots in Anthony Downs' well-known arguments about the high costs of political information and the consequent rationality of individual voter ignorance.[23]

This approach has picked up steam, however, through a range of contemporary accounts that paint a concept of voter rationality that does not depend on voter acquisition of extensive information and that draws as much from cognitive psychology as from economics.[24] In his introduction to an influential early volume pursuing this theme, John Ferejohn notes that, in this body of work, citizens are believed to employ "sensible decision rules, or heuristics, in acquiring and storing information about politics," such that they can make reasonable inferences based on a "relatively sparse set of signals about governmental activity."[25] Arthur Lupia and Matthew McCubbins, leading contemporary expositors of this idea, suggest that a range of limited yet efficient sources of information can guide rational, reasonably informed voting choices. Examples of such cues include party identification, the expressed views of opinion leaders, interest group endorsements, the view of people with similar interests, newspaper editorials, opinion polls, and information supplied by campaigns or by media. Lupia and McCubbins argue that, as long as the context allows voters to make judgments about the trustworthiness of the speakers they rely on, voters can, in fact, make reasoned voting decisions based on limited information. Indeed, these authors appear to go beyond grudging tolerance to show an acceptance of such cues, arguing that it makes sense for voters to ignore information that exceeds what is required to make a reasoned choice. Just as it is rational for drivers to rely on a traffic signal in lieu of collecting comprehensive information "about the intentions of other drivers and the speed, acceleration, direction, and mass of their cars,"[26] so, they suggest, voters might liberate themselves from the mass of political information theoretically available to them.

[22] See Herbert A. Simon, *Administrative Behavior: A Study of Decision-Making Processes in Administrative Organization* (New York: Macmillan, 1947) (using term "satisficing" to refer to the pursuit of a "good enough" solution rather than an optimal one, on the theory that there is too much complexity and uncertainty to make optimization realistic).

[23] Anthony Downs, *An Economic Theory of Democracy* (New York: Harper, 1957).

[24] See, e.g., Richard D. McKelvey and Peter C. Ordeshook, "Elections with Limited Information: A Fulfilled Expectations Model Using Contemporaneous Poll and Endorsement Data as Information Sources" (1985) 36 *Journal of Economic Theory* 55–85; Arthur Lupia and Matthew D. McCubbins, *The Democratic Dilemma: Can Citizens Learn What They Need to Know?* (New York: Cambridge University Press, 1998); Samuel L. Popkin, *The Reasoning Voter: Communication and Persuasion in Political Campaigns*, 2nd ed. (Chicago: University of Chicago Press, 1994); Paul Sniderman, Richard Brody, and Philip Tetlock, *Reasoning and Choice: Explorations in Political Psychology* (New York: Cambridge University Press, 1991).

[25] Ferejohn, *supra* note 10 at 5.

[26] Lupia and McCubbins, *supra* note 24 at 6.

There also is an explanatory strain within this literature, in which some (but not all) heuristics scholars point to processes of social cognition to explain *how* people acquire and assimilate political information. The gist of the idea is that voters do not use a memory-based system in which one would expect the voter to recall – and be able to rehash – political facts learned, but rather a "running tally" or mode of "online processing" in which voters integrate new facts and adjust their evaluations of public officials and candidates in an ongoing way.[27] On this view, voters need not recall much information as long as they maintain a "summary affective evaluation" of the candidates that can be tapped at election time. That running tally is offered to support the conclusion that voters have a reasonable basis for exercising democratic control over elected officials. Like the larger literature on cues as efficient ways to navigate the complexities of democracy, the idea of a running tally might offer a conceptual route to some reconceived form of legislative accountability.

ACCOUNTABILITY THROUGH AGGREGATION/DISAGGREGATION

The pivotal idea here is a familiar one in the political science literature and is captured by the venerable "miracle of aggregation." The proffered "miracle" is that the electorate as a whole may compensate for the infirmities of individual voters.[28] Although most voters may, indeed, be woefully uninformed about the issues and policies at stake in an election, the electorate as a whole can nevertheless be seen as collectively "rational" because confused voters on both sides will cancel each other out, and so cancel out the noise that seems to characterize public opinion. Grounded in Condorcet's Jury Theorem, which posits that rationality increases along with the number of decision makers, this idea suggests that "the law of large numbers applied to public opinion" can effectively save citizens from their individual deficiencies.[29]

In many renderings, however, this idea of aggregation is paired with a companion idea of *dis*aggregation, and I think it is important to isolate, name, and join both pieces of this process. On this view, not only do uninformed citizens cancel each other out, but a "small set of voters" can also guide their poorly informed peers in the electorate to a reasoned choice.[30] Sometimes, this heroic subgroup appears

[27] See, e.g., Milton Lodge, Marco R. Steenbergen, and Shawn Brau, "The Responsive Voter: Campaign Information and the Dynamics of Candidate Evaluation" (1995) 89 *Amer. Pol. Sci. Rev.* 309.

[28] See Philip E. Converse, *Popular Representation and the Distribution of Information* [*Popular Representation*] in Ferejohn and Kuklinski, *supra* note 10 at 369–88 ("Converse, *Popular Representation*") ("Thus, it is quite possible, thanks to the hidden power of aggregation, to arrive at a highly rational system performance on the backs of voters, most of whom are remarkably ill-informed much of the time"); Philip E. Converse, "The Nature of Belief Systems in Mass Publics" in D. Apter, ed., *Ideology and Discontent* (New York: Free Press of Glencoe, 1964); Benjamin I. Page and Robert Y. Shapiro, *The Rational Public* (New York: Free Press of Glencoe, 1992).

[29] Donald R. Kinder and Don Herzog, "Democratic Discussion" in George E. Marcus and Russell Hanson, eds., *Reconsidering the Democratic Public* (University Park: Pennsylvania State University Press, 1993) at 369.

[30] Vincent L. Hutchings, *Public Opinion and Democratic Accountability: How Citizens Learn About Politics* (Princeton, NJ: Princeton University Press, 2003) at 15; see also Michael X. Delli Carpini and Scott Keeter, *What Americans Don't Know About Politics and Why It Matters* (New Haven, Conn.: Yale University Press, 1996) at 44; Converse, *Popular Representation*, *supra* note 28.

as the "attentive public," the stratum of the electorate that consistently pays close attention to politics and can be expected to have a store of general information on which to draw in making vote choices. In other iterations, the key group emerges from a shifting set of "issue publics" who are knowledgeable only on matters of special interest or import to that group. Vincent Hutchings, for example, links the role of issue publics to accountability, arguing that "voters need not be generally attentive to political issues in order to ensure accountability. As long as voters are informed about the issues they care about, they are likely to hold members of Congress accountable when they are not responsive."[31] Whether the focus is on a consistently attentive public or on a shifting set of issue publics, the operative dynamic of disaggregation is to isolate a small, better-informed subgroup that compensates for the ignorance of wider swaths of the electorate. In sum, if the collective public is more rational by virtue of its collective properties, and is aided by an informed subgroup in making more reasoned political decisions, then perhaps a form of accountability can be identified.

WHY PROXY THEORIES DO NOT SOLVE THE PROBLEM

In this section, I suggest that none of the three proxy theories can salvage a meaningful form of legislative accountability from the realities of contemporary politics. I review each theory in turn and find that all of them have three attributes that prevent them from successfully rehabilitating the Bickelian notion of accountability at the heart of the countermajoritarian difficulty. First, each of the proxy theories is built on some questionable empirical assumptions. Their capacity to offer a surrogate path to accountability is undermined by these problematic assumptions. Second, the proxy theories incorporate structural inequalities and create significant risks of voter manipulation. In some ways, this is not all that surprising because the theories are, for the most part, more squarely aimed at addressing the deficit problem than the asymmetry problem with respect to accountability.[32] Legislators' predictions about future constituent opinion, citizens' use of efficient cues, and the collective dynamics of voter knowledge are each offered up to fill what is conceded to be the electorate's yawning informational gap. This will become significant as we proceed, for a case can be made that these theories at least preserve – and may, in fact, aggravate – the asymmetry problem even as they attempt to solve the deficit problem.

The third characteristic problem is a normative one: Each theory is grounded in an impoverished understanding of democracy. Taken independently and together, they amount to a kind of minimalism in pursuit of democratic minimalism. That is, each sets the bar low for democracy and then seeks only a form of plausible rationality, rather than any significantly participatory or democratically engaged enterprise. In essence, each downsizes democracy to accommodate the severe limitations

[31] See Hutchings, *supra* note 30 at 13; see also Converse, *Popular Representation*, *supra* note 28 at 375 (1990).

[32] More so than the other proxy theories, Arnold's work on prediction also addresses itself to the asymmetry problem by attempting to explain why legislators might ever decline to follow the political wishes of organized interest groups in order to make voting choices deemed more palatable to the broad public.

of the electorate rather than seeking to strengthen voter competence or engagement in pursuit of a more vigorous concept of democracy.

ASSESSING ACCOUNTABILITY THROUGH PREDICTION

As I have indicated, Douglas Arnold's *The Logic of Congressional Action* is perhaps the leading example of the predictive accountability approach, and the book owes a major debt to many leading works in political science. But perhaps no intellectual debt is more clearly owed than to V. O. Key's *Public Opinion and American Democracy*,[33] for Arnold builds on Key's work in two important ways. First, Arnold's central idea of "potential preferences" is, as he himself notes, traceable to the concept of "latent public opinion" famously offered by Key. Second, Arnold, like Key, disaggregates the public into the "attentive" and "inattentive" publics and recognizes that there are often multiple, parallel publics, including multiple attentive publics.[34] Both scholars conceive of public opinion as forged, in part, through the dynamic interaction between these multiple publics. Because Key provided critical pieces of Arnold's conceptual infrastructure, it is useful in assessing the idea of accountability through prediction to view Arnold's theory through the lens of Key's ideas.

One point of contrast between the books is immediately apparent, and it helps to suggest one reason that the idea of potential preferences may not go all that far in salvaging the concept of accountability at the heart of the countermajoritarian difficulty. Key was influential in identifying and elaborating the idea of latent public opinion that animates Arnold's account, but he was far less sanguine than Arnold about the ability of legislators to read or exploit this latent public opinion. Indeed, Key was openly skeptical that latent public opinion did or could operate on a practical level.[35] He began with the idea that "public opinion" is itself inherently murky: "[t]o speak with precision of public opinion is a task not unlike coming to grips with the Holy Ghost."[36] Beyond the general ambiguity and elusiveness of public opinion, Key spoke at some length about why, as a practical matter, legislators who might rationally seek to predict the political consequences of a vote based on latent voter opinion would likely be frustrated by their difficulty in doing so:

> We know that the factors that determine how people vote are so varied and the actions of government so numerous that the estimation of the electoral consequences of most specific actions is beyond the wit or skill of man. . . . Anxieties about electoral reprisal doubtless condition the operations of democratic governments. Their gauge of that possibility, though, is apt to be rather the momentary complaints that actions arouse than any trustworthy forecast of the translation of latent opinion into popular votes.[37]

[33] Key, *supra* note 20.

[34] Arnold, *supra* note 16 at 64–71.

[35] Despite the practical limitations he saw in latent public opinion, it is important to note that Key expressed optimism about the reasonableness of voters and thought that it was mistake to treat voters as fools. See V. O. Key, Jr., *The Responsible Electorate: Rationality in Presidential Voting, 1936–1960* (Cambridge: Belknap Press of Harvard University Press, 1966).

[36] Key, *supra* note 20 at 8.

[37] Ibid. at 268.

Key pursued this line of argument further:

> Our explorations into the nature and form of mass opinion leave no doubt that its directives tend toward generality rather than specificity.... Furthermore, translation of opinion into actions of electoral punishment or reward is a tortuous and uncertain procedure. The predictability of electoral response to a particular action remains so uncertain that the avoidance of a sensible decision because it will lose votes is usually the work of a man whose anxieties outweigh his capacities of prediction.[38]

The significant point suggested by these excerpts is that Key, who can fairly be considered the architect of the operative concept in the predictive accountability thesis, expressed substantial practical misgivings about the ability of elected officials to harness it in meaningful ways.

The fact that Key was less optimistic than Arnold about the ability of legislators to predict the course and content of future public opinion ought not itself resolve the question whether Arnold's theory supports meaningful accountability. Viewed through a temporal frame, perhaps Key's skepticism is not all that surprising. After all, the apparatus of politics has changed substantially in the years since Key wrote. Phenomena like twenty-four-hour cable television news, political Web sites and blogs, mass e-mailing, talk radio, and much more sophisticated direct mail methods all present political challengers and interest groups with ways to mobilize political opinion more swiftly and effectively than was possible with the relatively crude tools of political communication available in Key's day. Yet, the improved technology of political communications notwithstanding, there are still reasons to believe that Key's skepticism retains its intellectual force.

First, legislators operate with their own sort of informational deficit. Unlike the voters, legislators have ready access to information about the policy choices that confront them, and the ability to get into the proverbial weeds to educate themselves about those choices. But they frequently do not have – and I would suggest often *cannot* have – solid information about what issues will resonate and "stick" with the voting public at the time of a future election.[39] Even if there are groups ready to try to galvanize public reaction quickly with respect to particular votes, that does not answer the question whether such mobilized opinion will gel or be sufficiently resilient to persist until the next election. Moreover, it is reasonable to suppose that opinion that can be marshaled almost instantaneously is the opinion of one or more highly engaged and attentive publics, and the relation of that sort of opinion to future mass opinion will often be uncertain. A blistering e-mail campaign to support or stop a particular bill may or may not have lasting political consequences. Because the future fate of current public sentiment thus remains in question, despite the changing apparatus of political communication, Key's skepticism about the ability of incumbents to "read" latent opinion remains conceptually relevant.

38 Ibid. at 557–8.

39 In his review of Arnold, Steven Croley frames this question in terms of how "*imperfect information* affects legislators' decisions." Steven P. Croley, "Imperfect Information and the Electoral Connection" (1994) 47 *Political Research Quarterly* 509 (emphasis in original).

Arnold is well aware of the formidable problem with operationalizing future public opinion. He attempts to tame the problem by laying out principles that he believes legislators can use to assess whether a particular vote is likely to trigger tomorrow's electoral wrath. Drawing on principles of political economy, Arnold points to four criteria to guide legislators in assessing whether a particular issue is likely to generate public opinion that can be mobilized against the incumbent in the next election: the magnitude of the specific costs and benefits associated with a particular piece of legislation, the timing of the cost or benefit in relation to the policy involved, the proximity of a citizen to other citizens likely to be similarly affected by a cost or benefit, and the availability of an "instigator" to bring to public light the cost or benefit involved. Offering yet more specificity, Arnold proposes a five-part inquiry to guide legislators:

> To reach a decision, then, a legislator needs to (1) identify all the attentive and inattentive publics who might care about a policy issue, (2) estimate the direction and intensity of their preferences, (3) estimate the probability that the potential preferences will be transformed into real preferences, (4) weight all these preferences according to the size of the various attentive and inattentive publics, and (5) give special weight to the preferences of the legislator's consistent supporters.[40]

At the threshold, there is a question about whether we can safely assume that legislators are engaging in such a sophisticated and complex exercise as to any significant number of roll-call votes. Might they reasonably be expected to do so? Perhaps it is fair enough to think that members of Congress, with the staff and resources available to them, do embark on an inquiry roughly like this for some subset of votes deemed important by the press or by the relevant congressional leadership. In his classic study of roll-call voting, John Kingdon reported that many legislators do, in fact, consider the potential political ramifications of their votes, and Arnold explicitly offers his inquiry to channel "political intuitions" of this sort.[41] It is far less clear that state legislators, who lack the staff and political support available to their federal counterparts, are situated to do anything this sophisticated.

Moreover, even if we assume that something like this inquiry is done frequently enough to matter, substantial questions persist. Arnold's suggestion is that legislators who conduct his inquiry can accurately divine potential preferences so as to create a way for voters to control legislators, in democratically attractive terms, even if voters are unaware that a particular policy actually exists. But the ability of a legislator to carry out Arnold's proposed inquiry can easily founder at every one of his five steps, which construct an imposing chain of uncertainties.

There are surely some issues as to which a legislator can, quickly and with some confidence, run through something like Arnold's proposed method. To pick a relatively straightforward example, take a legislator who is formulating a position on

[40] Arnold, *supra* note 16 at 84.

[41] Like Kingdon, Arnold makes the point that incumbent politicians are by nature cautious. Risk aversion, one might argue, would dispose a rational legislator to undertake this inquiry more rather than less, and to fear future mass electoral wrath more than might be realistic. But as Steven Croley points out, legislators' risk aversion might just as easily cut in the other direction: Perhaps the cautious legislator should, rationally, fear crossing powerful interest groups more than he or she fears the relatively unlikely event of an awakened mass public at the next election. See Croley, *supra* note 39 at 519.

a stringent new gun control measure in a culturally conservative district where either many people own guns and like to hunt, or a vocal, well-organized minority does and the rest of the district is either tolerant or indifferent to guns. Or consider a legislator mulling a decision to authorize a controversial use of military force abroad where the legislator's district has historically had a strong antiwar majority. A legislator facing either of these circumstances could probably skip the five-point inquiry altogether.

But as we move away from simple cases like these, it can quickly become much more difficult to gauge future public opinion. For example, the predictive enterprise will become considerably more problematic as we move to less salient, symbolic, and/or familiar issues to voters. The same will be true, as Arnold himself concedes, as we move from issues with a short to a long causal chain connecting a policy to its effects,[42] or as we move away from general and simple legislative positions to actual laws that are specific, complex, nuanced, and often ambiguous.

Imagine, for example, that the legislator must vote on a behemoth communications bill affecting consumers by regulating wireless and cable communications, but doing so in complex and numerous ways not readily observable by the public; or on a drug regulation bill establishing new drug safety standards that are characterized as demanding by some but are believed by drug industry insiders to create a hospitable drug approval process. These measures contrast with the gun control and war authorization laws, where, on the facts stipulated, future public opinion seems fairly obvious, the possibility of the broad public being activated seems likely enough to warrant an embrace of the perceived public view, and an assessment of the intensity and value of electoral subgroups can be reasonably made. In contrast, the communications and drug bills present too many unknowns and contingencies to permit a reliable prediction.

It is, in other words, often very difficult to say, a priori, both how preferences might form on an issue and whether mass preferences will form at all. These are generic problems, common to a wide variety of laws. Consider some of the things that a conscientious, prediction-oriented legislator cannot know at the time of a vote: What events will unfold between the time of the vote and the next campaign? What events will command public attention? For example, will there be a series of drugs dramatically pulled off the market after having been approved through the process supported by our hypothetical legislator? What events and which people will frame the politics of this particular issue? How about 527 groups and PACs? These uncertainties raise basic questions about the efficacy of the predictive enterprise itself.

The key point to appreciate is that Arnold's theory, once cast as a surrogate route to accountability, does not really call upon *actual* public opinion or public policy preferences at all. It is, in fact, two steps removed from actual public opinion because it relies, first, on legislators' *perceptions* of public opinion, and second, on their perceptions of *future* opinion that may or may not develop. Not only is this rife with contingency, but it also does not even purport to be a method to capture actual public opinion, nor to bring such actual opinion to bear directly on legislative decisions. Arnold is instead betting on legislators' adherence to what they believe

[42] Arnold, *supra* note 16 at 271.

the public will believe in the future if, indeed, the legislator thinks that the broad public will come to believe anything at all on a particular issue.

This really is the phantom electorate and, once we view it as such, we can see the limited concept of democracy that lies beneath the approach. Like so much in politics, the operative dynamic here is more about perceptions than about reality, but here we see an interesting inversion. The familiar point about politics is that what voters come to believe about government policy, based on spin and strategic communications, may be quite different from the actual provisions of the policy. Here, the point is that what legislators come to believe about public opinion may be quite different from what public opinion (if any) comes to be. Thus, although Arnold's theory undoubtedly captures important aspects of legislators' political calculus, it is a different question whether we can harness the theory to deliver meaningful legislative accountability.

Moreover, just as it is important to see that what is proposed is significantly removed from actual public opinion because it relies on fallible beliefs about possible future opinion, it is equally important to see something else about what is – and is not – on offer here. Arnold freely acknowledges that, most of the time, the congealed, current preferences of organized interest groups will prevail over the predicted future opinion of the broad electorate. Indeed, the research question that Arnold self-consciously tries to answer with his book is why the latent opinion of the many *ever* trumps the articulated wishes of the few.[43] The idea that the broad electorate will, in fact, come to have crystallized preferences on an issue is viewed by Arnold himself as the exception, not the rule. In this vein, consider what Arnold says about his five-point inquiry:

> Many of these estimates will be zero for *most issues*, either because many people are genuinely indifferent or because it will be hard to imagine how the inattentive publics could ever be activated. When this is true, the net scores many [sic] be dominated by a few estimates – perhaps the intense preferences of a few attentive publics. If these preferences all point in the same direction, then a legislator's decision is clear. If the preferences in favor are roughly balanced by an equal number opposed, then a legislator is free to vote as he or she pleases.[44]

Arnold's candid reckoning demonstrates that he is hardly oblivious to the problem of asymmetry. Quite the contrary. As the clever title of his book suggests,[45] he needs no convincing about the power or effects of collective action problems in legislative politics.[46] Read in the light of Arnold's candid expectation, the predictive enterprise would appear to have significant asymmetry built into its very architecture.

[43] Ibid. at 3, 4 ("Political scientists can explain with ease why concentrated interests so often triumph.... [They] have had less success in explaining why Congress enacts proposals that serve more diffuse or general interests").

[44] Ibid. at 84–5 (emphasis added).

[45] Arnold's title nods toward Mancur Olson, *The Logic of Collective Action* (Cambridge, Mass.: Harvard University Press, 1965).

[46] In acknowledging that the extant preferences of the organized will frequently trump the amorphous, potential future preferences of the unorganized, Arnold echoes Key, who anticipated this theme in his own treatment of latent public opinion and who also went on to conclude that "governments enjoy, insofar as mass opinion is concerned, a high degree of discretion in the determination of what action they will take and which sector of the attentive public they will heed." Key, *supra* note 20, at 284; ibid. at 265.

This qualification is significant in assessing the capacity of Arnold's thesis to revive Bickel's idea of political accountability, and it cuts against the salvage effort. If, by Arnold's own account, the mass public will simply not be mobilized as to "most" issues, then the theory is not a good candidate to be a strong form of proxy accountability. It is, at a minimum, likely to preserve the asymmetries in accountability observed earlier. And, save for a small group of highly potent or explosive issues that meet Arnold's criteria for cost/benefit allocation, timing, and proximity to others affected, the theory would not predict that voters will often hold a legislator answerable for a vote – even if there is an instigator at the ready in the form of a political opponent or enterprising reporter.

As to this idea that accountability to the mass electorate seems to be exceptional under Arnold's own formulation, one might say in response: Arnold sketches a path toward accountability for the issues that voters are likely to care about most, and that is the only sort of accountability that democratic theory, properly understood, should demand. If voters do not feel strongly enough about an issue to be roused from their political slumber, the argument would go, then no accountability is needed. The problem I see with that argument, however, is a problem that goes to the heart of the proposition that legislators' anticipation of future public preferences can be a good proxy form of accountability: It assumes that voters are well-situated to sort those issues they care about from those they do not, and to demand accountability for issues deemed important. Yet, significant dynamics that shape contemporary politics call that assumption into question.

At the outset, recall the imposing structural problem noted in the critique of the accountability axiom that I set out earlier: Legislatures vote on hundreds, if not thousands of issues between elections; yet, only a tiny fraction of those issues have any chance of becoming election fodder. That same structural limitation undercuts the idea of predictive accountability, for if the opponent can only hope to make a legitimate election issue out of a handful of votes, the electorate is ill-equipped to decide if those issues are, in fact, the only ones for which it will demand accountability. The sheer numbers, in other words, do not support the notion that we can necessarily rely on opponents to meaningfully draw attention to any and all votes that might be deemed significant by voters. And that does not even account for strategic misfires, where opponents might concentrate some of their limited energies on pressing issues that do not end up resonating with voters at election time.

Moreover, there is a larger problem here, and it relates to the ability of political actors and the broad voting public to communicate in meaningful ways about policy. We have looked at one side of that would-be dialogue by observing that voters are not exposed to, or immersed in, a sufficient number of issues to allow them confidently to decide which issues require accountability. But there are also problems running in the other direction – that is, problems with the ability of candidates (be they challengers or incumbents) to reliably identify the content or strength of public attitudes on key issues.

One problem is suggested by John Zaller's influential analysis.[47] Zaller focuses on opinion polls and suggests that the mass public rarely *has* fixed opinions that can be

[47] John Zaller, *The Nature and Origins of Mass Opinion* (New York: Cambridge University Press, 1992).

reliably captured by polls. He argues that, instead, poll responses are frequently the artifacts of how poll questions are constructed and framed, and that respondents generate answers "on the fly" because they often have no preexisting opinions about matters of public policy.[48] Zaller also points out that, although pollsters may not consciously choose or want to exert the power of framing through the construction of their poll questions, they typically adopt frames already generated by "politicians, issue activists, interest group leaders, journalists and media consultants."[49] Zaller's skepticism about the existence of public views may be extreme, and some have taken him to task for failing to account for the role of social networks and other nonelite influences on citizens' views.[50] Yet, there are a host of reasons to wonder whether even public views that do exist can be readily or reliably ascertained.

To start with, polls are often cited by elected officials and interest groups that support the poll's results as purported quantitative proof of the public's position on a given issue.[51] This can set the contours of public debate in ways that may thwart or distort the development of public opinion. Polls offered in this way might, for instance, create an opinion bandwagon that helps to move public opinion toward the results of the particular poll offered.[52] Even short of a full-fledged bandwagon effect, which is still a matter of debate among social scientists, polls can have a potent effect on public opinion simply by shaping media coverage and public perceptions of issues.[53] And, because poll results can vary based on such considerations as the framing of questions, the construction of the sample, and the nonresponse rate, it may well be that some polls being strategically hawked by politicians or interest groups do not reflect extant public sentiment with any reliable degree of accuracy.[54] True, both incumbents and challengers may strategically hawk dubious polls, but dueling polls do not eliminate so much as complicate the problem by injecting confusion into the process.

There is, moreover, a deeper and more fundamental question about the idea of polling as an important source of information to legislators about the public's values and attitudes. It is both naive and anachronistic to assume uncritically that politicians either can or do treat broad public opinion as something passively to discern from polls and then straightforwardly to obey. Instead, there is much to suggest that politicians use polls and what they reflect about public opinion to *shape* public opinion in the direction of their own preferred policy choices.

[48] Ibid. at 1.

[49] Ibid. at 95.

[50] See, e.g., Taeku Lee, *Mobilizing Public Opinion: Black Insurgency and Racial Attitudes in the Civil Rights Era* (Chicago: University of Chicago Press) at 17–70.

[51] Susan Herbst, *Numbered Voices* (Chicago: University of Chicago Press, 1993) ("Herbst, *Voices*") at 166.

[52] On the idea that election polls can have a bandwagon effect that pushes poll consumers toward the apparent winner, see Stephen Ansolabahere and Shanto Iyengar, "Of Horseshoes and Horse Races" (1994) 11 *Political Communication* 413; Jack M. Balkin, "What Is a Postmodern Constitution?" (1992) 90:7 *Mich. L. Rev.* 1966; Herbst, *Voices*, supra note 51 at 166; Vicki Morwitz and Carol Pluzinski, "Do Polls Reflect Opinions or Do Opinions Reflect Polls" (1996) 23 *J. Consumer Research* 53.

[53] Herbst, *Voices, supra* note 51 at 166.

[54] See, e.g., Scott Althaus, *Collective Preferences in Democratic Politics* (New York: Cambridge University Press, 2003) at 3 ("Slight changes in the wording of a question can sometimes lead to drastically different response patterns. Sampling problems and non-response error are well-known pitfalls to survey researchers, and the questions that are used in surveys may fail to capture the public's real concerns").

In a provocative book, Lawrence Jacobs and Robert Shapiro highlight one important dynamic: the extent to which elected officials use polling not to identify public opinion, which is then to be followed, but, instead, to test rhetoric and frames in order to prime the public to see an issue in a particular way.[55] Based on a study of the Clinton presidency and Republican Congress of the 1990s, Jacobs and Shapiro argue that elected officials

> use research on public opinion to pinpoint the most alluring words, symbols, and arguments in an attempt to move public opinion to support their desired policies. Public opinion research is used by politicians to manipulate public opinion, that is, to move Americans to "hold opinions that they would not hold if aware of the best available information and analysis." Their effort is to *simulate* responsiveness. Their words and presentations are crafted to change public opinion and create the *appearance* of responsiveness as they pursue their desired policy goals. Intent on lowering the potential electoral costs of subordinating voters' preferences to their policy goals, politicians use polls and focus groups not to move their positions closer to the public's but just the opposite: to find the most effective means to move public opinion closer to their own desired policies.[56]

Jacobs and Shapiro wisely recognize that politicians do not have an unlimited ability to shape or change public opinion, but they argue that strategic communications can, at a minimum, cause the public to focus on the "uncertainties and risks" of policies opposed by those who are doing the strategic communicating.[57] The manipulative possibilities are readily apparent.

The picture of public opinion suggested by Jacobs and Shapiro undercuts the predictive accountability thesis in several ways. It highlights the instability and unpredictability of public opinion, vulnerable as it is to the cross-pressures of what these authors call "crafted talk" from opposing political forces. In addition, the very use of such crafted talk weakens the ability of elections to test the popular acceptability of policy choices because it allows the choices that were actually made to be obscured in a rhetorical miasma.[58] Whereas Arnold assumes that an enterprising instigator will often be able to reveal unpopular positions to the detriment of an unresponsive incumbent, Jacobs and Shapiro's perspective suggests that the very content and meaning of a particular vote or position is *itself* likely to be contested in ways that undermine the very idea of predictive accountability.[59] And this problem is not neatly solved by the fact that challengers can deploy crafted talk of their own or try to reveal the incumbent's characterizations as the strategic efforts that they may be. Counter-crafted talk, and the associated need for ill-informed voters to arbitrate between conflicting rhetorical formulations, seem as likely to confound as to clarify matters for the electorate.

[55] Lawrence R. Jacobs and Robert Y. Shapiro, *Politicians Don't Pander: Political Manipulation and the Loss of Democratic Responsiveness* (Chicago: University of Chicago Press, 2000).

[56] Ibid. at xv (emphasis in original) (quoting Zaller, *supra* note 47).

[57] Ibid. at 63.

[58] Ibid. at xvii.

[59] On the related phenomenon of laws drafted with deliberate ambiguity to facilitate the political needs of legislators, see Murray Edelman, *The Symbolic Uses of Politics*, 2nd ed. (Urbana: University of Illinois Press, 1985) at 22–72; John Hart Ely, *Democracy and Distrust: A Theory of Judicial Review* (Cambridge: Harvard University Press, 1980) at 131–3; Theodore J. Lowi, *The End of Liberalism*, 2nd ed. (New York: Norton, 1979) at 92–126.

There is a final point to be made about polling as a window on public opinion, and here again the issue of asymmetry presents itself. While polling has become virtually synonymous with public opinion in the eyes of many, Arnold notes that it is often too expensive for individual legislators to launch their own polls on any consistent basis.[60] Moreover, there is another reason to question whether polls are the dominant source of public opinion for legislators and legislative staffers. In an intriguing study of state legislative politics, Susan Herbst found that public opinion means different things to different actors. Whereas low-level party activists tend to think of polling as constitutive of public opinion, legislative staffers do not. Rejecting the idea that aggregated individual opinion is the same as public opinion, the staffers studied by Herbst were far more likely to see "public opinion and interest group opinion as nearly interchangeable."[61]

If Herbst's finding can be generalized to legislative staffers beyond the context of her study, it would be highly relevant to assessing predictive accountability, for it would suggest that legislative insiders seeking a grip on future public sentiment look to interest groups for their assessments. On this view, organized interests become the conduit for public opinion. This conduit role, in turn, takes us quickly back to the problem of asymmetrical accountability. The problem is that those to whom legislators look to divine public opinion are, precisely, the self-interested, organized groups who already command a heavy share of legislative attention and responsiveness.

This sort of legislative preference for using interest groups as the basis for judging public sentiment – and, by extension, for hypothesizing future public opinion – is strongly reminiscent of Herbert Blumer's critique of opinion polling, which argued that polls are misleading because they portray a phony kind of egalitarianism in public opinion. Blumer rejected this notion and argued, instead, that polls fatally fail to account for group activity, which is where the action is in our legislative democracy.[62] Blumer's point underscores the problem of asymmetry that is concealed by the traditional rhetoric of accountability by calling attention to the deep linkages between interest groups and perceptions of public opinion, whether we are focused on polling or on Herbst-style use of interest groups to measure public opinion.

These multiple ways in which elected officials and/or interest groups (among others) try to shape, communicate, and characterize public opinion – whether through interest group activity à la Herbst or through polling – go to the heart of a conceptual difficulty with the idea of predictive accountability: Its normative (as opposed to descriptive) force would seem to depend on the notion that the public has extant views that are tapped into by challengers or reporters who draw attention to incumbents' votes. That is, predictive accountability could be normatively attractive if we assume, first, that incumbents are genuinely interested in predicting what they think their constituents would want them to do and doing that, and, second, that these citizen preferences are in some sense "out there"

60 Arnold, *supra* note 16 at 11–12.

61 Susan Herbst, *Reading Public Opinion* (Chicago: University of Chicago Press, 1998) at 64 ("Herbst, *Reading*").

62 Herbert Blumer, "Public Opinion and Public Opinion Polling" (1948) 13 *Amer. Soc. Rev.* at 242–9; Herbst, *Reading, supra* note 61 at 55–7.

waiting to be tapped by some issue entrepreneur down the line. But the picture of public opinion developed here suggests that public opinion may be a considerably more top-down affair, one in which politicians (among others) actively try to shape and sway public opinion.[63] Politicians may often find fertile ground for doing so, given Zaller's suggestion that individual views are either nonexistent or, at best, ephemeral on many topics, and given the fact most citizens do not attend legislative hearings, read bills, or personally deliberate about public policy in the commons. The information they receive comes largely from the media and, as Zaller argues, what the media covers necessarily comes, at least in part, from content supplied by those with a clear stake in the outcome.[64] Arnold periodically brushes up against this phenomenon, as when he notes that the development of public opinion can be affected by which issue entrepreneur is successful in framing a question for the public. But although the malleability of public opinion to competing issue entrepreneurs may add descriptive purchase to Arnold's account, it does not reassure on the accountability-enhancing possibility of his theory.

Seeing public opinion as subject to elite influence is not in and of itself a bad thing. As Zaller points out, elites can bring expertise to bear on public opinion. The problem I want to emphasize is, more precisely, the way that legislative accountability can be corroded by the efforts of incumbents and forces like interest groups to exploit the public's knowledge gaps and strategically manipulate public opinion. As Jacobs and Shapiro assert, the manipulative possibilities are not unlimited. But they are nevertheless troublesome.

Along these lines, it is important to acknowledge that there are some bottom-up dynamics in the formulation of public opinion, as when views are shaped by grassroots movements, by interpersonal communications,[65] by strongly held individual views on some issues, and, increasingly, by Internet sources. But it is hard to deny that those with a strong interest in particular legislative outcomes shape many of the political constructs that then become the grist for watercooler and Web site discussion. It is, therefore, at the very least empirically problematic for a theory of predictive accountability implicitly to conceive of public opinion as an autonomous constraint on politicians that the populace imposes, if indirectly, on legislators.

ASSESSING HEURISTICS THEORY

The work on political shortcuts through cues and heuristics responds to the informational deficits that most voters unquestionably suffer. The proposition that voters do not have comprehensive political information, but also do not need it, is

[63] See generally Edward G. Carmines and James H. Kuklinski, "Incentives, Opportunities, and the Logic of Public Opinion in American Political Representation" in Ferejohn and Kuklinski, *supra* note 10 at 240–68 (arguing that American politics and public opinion are "elite-driven").

[64] On this point, see also Timothy E. Cook, *Governing with the News: The News Media as a Political Institution* (Chicago: University of Chicago Press, 1998) (arguing that media functions as a kind of political institution, and that it has come to occupy an increasingly central place in politicians' political strategy).

[65] See Katherine Cramer Walsh, *Talking About Politics* (Chicago: University of Chicago Press, 2004).

an attractive response because it lifts from the electorate the seemingly unsustainable educational burden that democratic theory would appear to impose. It is also attractive because it seems intuitively correct that voters do, in fact, eschew comprehensive information in favor of efficient, readily available guides for their voting decisions. Some key empirical questions nevertheless remain.

One question is about the extent to which ill-informed voters do, in fact, use cues and heuristics like party identification, endorsements, campaign messages, polls, and media content. It is notable that the literature on cues, though burgeoning, is not principally empirical in nature.[66] With a few exceptions,[67] it is mainly composed of work that is theoretical (mostly within the rational choice tradition) and experimental. Perhaps that is to be expected, for, as James Kuklinski and Paul Quirk point out, it is not obvious how one would systematically gather reliable data about which heuristics, if any, influenced voter decision making.[68] Still, there are unresolved questions about the role of heuristics in the real world.

It does seem logical enough to suppose that ill-informed voters would seek out informational shortcuts to guide their voting decisions. Perhaps the more significant empirical questions here concern not whether but *how* heuristics are used. The assumption of the emerging body of work on these shortcuts is that they are a positive thing because they allow voters to make rational decisions in the absence of comprehensive information. But are heuristics really so benign after all? There are reasons to wonder. Various scholars make the basic point that it is difficult for voters to use shortcuts well when they lack the necessary background knowledge to make sense of the shortcuts themselves.[69] Indeed, Samuel Popkin, one of the foremost scholars of heuristics, has explored and lamented the consequences of inequality in this arena, particularly with respect to accountability. Popkin argues that when unknowledgeable voters attempt to assess incumbent performance, they will be disadvantaged in relation to voters with better institutional knowledge of politics and will rely on less substantive information in their voting choice:

> Voters with institutional knowledge of politics can better sort through the posturing of candidates and use partisan and issue cues as shortcuts to evaluate the performance of their elected agent. Voters less able to use these political cues will rely on estimates of personal character instead of attitudes about parties and issues.[70]

[66] See Larry M. Bartels, "Information Effects in Presidential Elections" (1996) 40 *Amer. J. Pol. Sci.* 194 at 198 ("The obvious question is whether these 'appropriate assumptions' reflect real political conditions. It is easier to assume than to demonstrate that cues and shortcuts do, in fact, allow relatively uninformed voters to behave *as if* they were fully informed"); ibid. at 200 ("what seems most remarkable about the whole resurgence of interest in cues, information shortcuts, and information aggregation is how little concrete effort has been made to investigate the extent to which they actually facilitate informed choices by voters"); James H. Kuklinski and Paul J. Quirk, "Reconsidering the Rational Public: Cognition, Heuristics, and Mass Opinion" in Arthur Lupia, Matthew D. McCubbins, and Samuel L. Popkin, eds., *Elements of Reason: Cognition, Choice and the Bounds of Rationality* (New York: Cambridge University Press, 2000) at 153 (noting lack of empirical evidence).

[67] See Bartels, *supra* note 66 at 200–2 (discussing three empirical studies, one involving the 1980 presidential election and two concerning California ballot propositions).

[68] Kuklinski and Quirk, *supra* note 66 at 156.

[69] Ibid.; Delli Carpini and Keeter, *supra* note 30 at 51–3; Somin, *supra* note 4 at 1320–1.

[70] Samuel L. Popkin and Michael A. Dimock, "Political Knowledge and Citizen Competence" in Stephen L. Elkin and Karol Edward Soltan, eds., *Citizen Competence and Democratic Institutions* (University Park: Pennsylvania State University Press, 1999) 117 at 126–7.

Therein lies the paradox: The voters arguably most in need of cues are also those least able to make good use of them.

For example, if a legislator is depicted as "soft on crime" by an opinion leader or interest group, a voter deciding whether to act based on that cue ought to know, at the very least, something about the legislator's votes on crime, what crimes the relevant legislature has jurisdiction to regulate, and what has happened to the crime rate during the legislator's term. But let's face it: The point of the cue is that it either obviates the need for that sort of study or is precisely attractive to those voters who are least interested in gathering that information.

Consider as an example of this problem the venerable cue in presidential elections to vote based on the performance of the economy.[71] Kuklinski and Quirk, for example, point out that this rule of thumb is based on an assumption that is "mostly false" because a "commonplace of informed commentary is that the president's ability to influence short-term economic performance is exceedingly modest," such that use of this heuristic "merely rewards good economic luck and punishes bad."[72] Cues that are powerful may also be unsupported. Thus, whereas Lupia and McCubbins, for example, wisely specify conditions of trustworthiness and verifiability for cues, it is hard to implement those conditions in the context of election appeals that are sound-bite driven and carefully crafted.

To some degree, this problem suggests only that not all heuristics are created equal. A voter influenced by a candidate's political party may, for example, be on far firmer ground than one who uses a slogan or reductive characterization to decide how to vote. Even those openly skeptical about heuristics sometimes offer up party identification as a desirable cue.[73] And, indeed, the party affiliation of a candidate will surely be an informative cue in many circumstances. But there are some reasons for caution here as well.

Perhaps the most important thing to say about the party cue for voting is to recall that we are asking *not* whether it is a helpful cue – it undoubtedly is for many voters in many circumstances – but whether it is a good proxy device for legislative accountability. The problem here, it seems to me, goes back to one of the points central to the accountability critique itself: The American system does not maximize legislative accountability. Unlike, say, the British parliamentary system, in which the voters place one party in control and know, at least in theory, whom to hold responsible for the action of the government, our system's diffusion of power between multiple branches, and between federal and state sovereigns, can make it difficult to fix political responsibility. When one American political party holds both the executive and legislative branches, more of this kind of accountability is theoretically possible, but much of the time, we do not have one-party control.

A different question about the party cue is what, if anything, party-based voting in our system would imply about legislative accountability. Here I see a possible double bind, a sort of tightrope that the party cue must walk if it is to promote accountability. From the standpoint of promoting accountability, we might say

[71] See Morris P. Fiorina, *Retrospective Voting in American National Elections* (New Haven: Yale University Press, 1981); Popkin, *supra* note 24; V. O. Key, Jr., *The Responsible Electorate* (Cambridge: Belknap Press of Harvard University Press,1966).

[72] Kuklinski and Quirk, *supra* note 66 at 158 (citations omitted); see also Somin, *supra* note 4 at 1320–1.

[73] See, e.g., Kuklinski and Quirk, *supra* note 66.

we would want a system marked by very strong party loyalty. But pushed to its limit, such a system might actually be one in which voters *cease* to be interested in holding legislators accountable for policy choices. If voters believe that they have conclusively resolved the political debate in favor of one party, they may rationally eschew or even resist the idea of accountability and simply vote the party line without any meaningful inquiry.[74] On the other hand, if the conventional wisdom is correct and partisan loyalty has declined in the United States, that might suggest for a different reason that the party cue cannot do as much work for voters as might be thought.[75] Perhaps if the electorate, following Goldilocks, has it "just right" in terms of partisanship, the cue may be useful in promoting accountability, but even then, there are some grounds for doubt.

For example, whatever the ultimate verdict on the ebbs and flows of partisanship, the party cue will be of little utility in primary elections which, given the prevalence of safe seats in Congress,[76] may be the more important elections in contemporary politics. In addition, there are significant issues on which the major parties largely agree (for example, trade policy and welfare reform in contemporary politics) and on which there is disagreement inside one or both parties (for example, the war in Iraq for Democrats, the priority of deficit reduction and the federal same- sex marriage amendment for Republicans). Here again, the party cue cannot necessarily promote accountability.

Moving beyond specific cues, there are reasons to worry that there are systematic problems with heuristics. Kuklinski and Quick point out that political scientists have embarked on a somewhat puzzling romance with heuristics:

> Ironically, political scientists have borrowed the concept of heuristics from psychology while overlooking its main significance within that literature.... For the most part, cognitive psychologists look at heuristics differently. They see the use of heuristics as automatic, unconscious, and frequently dysfunctional.... Research has shown that people use arbitrary starting points to anchor estimates, use accessibility in memory to estimate frequency; use a source's attractiveness to judge her credibility; and draw inferences from predetermined scripts and stereotypes. In cases that do not fit their implicit assumptions, heuristic judgments produce serious departures from rationality.[77]

All of this suggests that cues may enable or even facilitate decisions that are efficient, yet normatively problematic because they produce low-quality decisions.

Kuklinski and Quick argue that there are, in fact, systematic biases in political thinking that may be fueled by cues. These include the use of unfounded policy

[74] Bernard Berelson, Paul Lazarsfeld, and William McPhee, *Voting: A Study of Opinion Formation in a Presidential Campaign* (Chicago: University of Chicago Press, 1954) at 17; Popkin and Dimock, *supra* note 70 at 121.

[75] That conventional assumption is increasingly a matter of lively debate. For competing views, compare Martin P. Wattenberg, *The Decline of American Political Parties, 1952–1996* (Cambridge, Mass: Harvard University Press, 1998) with Larry M. Bartels, "Partisanship and Voting Behavior, 1952–1996" (2000) 44 *Amer. J. Pol. Sci.* 35. For an argument that the party cue has "declined in vitality," see Richard L. Hasen, "Do the Parties or the People Own the Electoral Process?" (2001) 149 *U. Penn. L. Rev.* 815 at 824.

[76] See, e.g., Sam Hirsch, "The U.S. House of Unrepresentatives: What Went Wrong in the Latest Round of Congressional Redistricting" (2003) 2 *Election L.J.* 179.

[77] Kuklinski and Quirk, *supra* note 66 at 166.

stereotypes[78] and a greater susceptibility to what they call "easy" versus "hard" arguments, where "easy" arguments are defined as "simple and symbolic, making strong assertions without providing support," and "hard" arguments are defined as those that "use reasoning or evidence to support claims about the consequences of a proposal. They take some mental work to understand and likely evoke little emotional response."[79] Experimental work by Cobb and Kuklinski showed that easy arguments generally were more influential than hard ones, and that "[p]ure assertion, which can evoke emotion and is easily represented in memory, is what most readily changes opinion."[80]

This critical perspective on cues is reminiscent of the separate problem we saw with respect to the use of "crafted talk" by incumbents and other elites to persuade the public to see issues in a particular way. Accountability as an aspiration is frustrated by the fact that many of those who supply or frame information for voters are by no means neutral or disinterested with respect to political outcomes. This suggests a flow of information that is both top-down and frequently strategically shaped, and that combination can undermine accountability. For example, cues, when shaped and provided by incumbents, challengers, or other regular players in the political process (e.g., political campaigns, PACs, interest groups, 527s), can be hard to distinguish from what we often call "spin." And although no one ought to suggest that we turn our political arena into a "no-spin zone," we do need to think about this problem in assessing the capacity of various cues to deliver significant accountability. If, as discussed earlier, ill-informed voters are not well situated to use cues, it is reasonable to suppose that these voters are also not well situated to ascertain when a cue is being strategically manipulated by self-interested political actors.

Indeed, the potentially problematic top-down character of heuristics is not limited to instances of rank, self-interested manipulation. Even cues that come from less obviously self-interested sources, such as the mass media, can be a perilous basis for voting decisions. For example, newspaper editorials may often (if not always) be distinguished from the overtly strategic efforts of political actors and their advocates. Nevertheless, media-generated cues like these do not necessarily solve the basic problems. For one thing, the point about the difficulty of voters making informed use of cues when they lack the necessary background knowledge would hold irrespective of how self-interested the source of the cue might be. For another thing, as we have already seen, political actors are among the elites who have a significant role in shaping what the media covers and how the issues are framed. This makes problematic any effort to categorically distinguish between

[78] One experiment showed that people who were asked to estimate the number of persons on welfare, the average length for which a recipient received benefits, and a set of related questions consistently made errors that fit their preexisting perceptions of welfare. James H. Kuklinski, Paul J. Quirk, David W. Schwieder, and Robert Rich, "Misinformation and the Currency of Citizenship" discussed in Kuklinski and Quirk, *supra* note 66 at 170.

[79] Kuklinski and Quirk, *supra* note 66 at 173–4. The authors use as an example the debate over the Lani Guinier nomination, where one side charged "quota queen" and the other responded by attempting to explain the relationship between cumulative voting systems and more nearly proportional representation.

[80] Michael Cobb and James H. Kuklinski, "Changing Minds: Political Arguments and Political Persuasion" (1997) 41 *Amer. J. Pol. Sci.* 88.

self-interested cues propounded by political actors and their allies on the one hand, and assertedly more reliable sources on the other hand.

And here is where the link to structural inequalities begins to appear most clearly. We can think of these inequalities as falling into three categories. One flows from the dynamics discussed above, where the worry is that certain heuristics can be manipulated because of the self-interested influences that help shape them. A second source of inequality flows from the earlier point about some heuristics tapping into stereotypes. This may be especially pernicious and quite literally facilitative of inequality when arising in the context of volatile issues relating to, say, race, poverty, or sexual orientation.[81]

The third point about heuristics and inequality is in some ways more straightforward and does not depend on the quality or context of a particular cue. If, in fact, the mass of voters use thin cues but better-educated voters and groups use more extensive data, there is a troubling imbalance from the start. Cues can begin to look pretty paltry when juxtaposed with rich information, and their disproportionate use by less educated voters raises normative concerns about democratic equality.

This imbalance is also suggestive of the extent to which the heuristics approach is rooted in a threadbare concept of democracy. That quality is not particularly subtle here. The cues available to voters are unabashedly reductionist. That is the whole point. The very notion of a cue is that it economically expresses an idea of relevance to voter decision making. Yet that property is itself likely to sharply limit the quality and quantity of any accountability that a cue might produce. Heuristics at their best, therefore, might support a wholesale rather than retail version of accountability, and a pretty crude one at that.[82]

AGGREGATION/DISAGGREGATION THEORIES

Recall how the aggregation/disaggregation process might offer a third proxy form of accountability. The aggregation piece of the story suggests that the process of cumulating individual voters drives out the errors that individual voters make which, according to this theory, are randomly distributed throughout the electorate.[83] The disaggregation piece suggests that select, well-informed electoral subgroups can lead the mass electorate to more informed decisions.[84]

[81] On the use of inflammatory frames and rhetoric in contexts like these, see David O. Sears, "Self-Interest vs. Symbolic Politics in Policy Attitudes and Presidential Voting" (1980) 74 *Amer. Pol. Sci. Rev.* 670; Jane S. Schacter, "The Gay Civil Rights Debate in the States: Decoding the Discourse of Equivalents" (1993) 29 *Harv.C.R.-C.L. L. Rev.* 283.

[82] Cf. Jesse Choper, *Judicial Review and the National Political Process: A Functional Reconsideration of the Role of the Supreme Court* (Chicago: University of Chicago Press, 1980) at 13 (observing that "the electorate must buy its political representation in bulk form").

[83] Page and Shapiro, *supra* note 28 at 16; Robert S. Erickson and Gerald C. Wright, "Voters, Candidates, and Issues in Congressional Elections" in Lawrence C. Dodd and Bruce I. Oppenheimer, eds., *Congress Reconsidered*, 4th ed. (Washington, DC: CQ Press,1989) 91 at 114.

[84] Philip Converse, *Popular Representation, supra* note 28 at 382 ("The signal extracted from this noise is very recognizable because it is undoubtedly shaped in large measure by the small minority of the electorate that is nearly as well informed about these matters as are our elite informants"); Page and Shapiro, *supra* note 28 at 16; Hutchings, *supra* note 30 at 15.

Looking to aggregation to salvage accountability is problematic for a number of reasons. One reason traces back to Zaller's work questioning whether the mass public actually has fixed opinions. Zaller argues that:

> what gets measured as public opinion is always dependent on the way questions have been framed and ordered. If different frames or different question orders produce different results, it is not because one or the other has distorted the public's true feelings; it is, rather, because the public, having no fixed true opinion, implicitly relies on the particular question it has been asked [so as] to determine what exactly the issue is and what considerations are relevant to settling it.[85]

If Zaller is right, then aggregation only aggregates ephemeral pseudo-opinions and does not in any significant way solve the underlying informational deficit that plagues the accountability axiom.[86]

Moreover, problems persist even if, contrary to Zaller's assertion, many voters do have "real" attitudes about a range of public policy matters. For the reasons already discussed in this chapter, there remain serious questions about whether such opinions are informed and free from manipulation. That problem is, indeed, acknowledged by Robert Shapiro, a leading aggregation scholar.[87]

Aggregation theory is also limited in its ability to ameliorate the problems with accountability because one of its operative assumptions is questionable: the notion that errors are randomly distributed throughout the voting public. This is a keystone of the aggregation story that is emphasized in leading arguments pressing the power of aggregation.[88] It is pivotal because it suggests that poorly informed voters on one side of an election will be canceled out by a roughly equal number of uninformed voters on the other side.

Many scholars have criticized this core assumption and pointed out that errors made by voters are more likely to be systematic than random. These critiques have been launched from various disciplinary perspectives. Based on research in cognition, for example, Kuklinski and Quick have questioned the logic of aggregation for some of the same reasons that led them to question theories about the democracy-restoring properties of heuristics:

> it is far from clear that the errors in citizens' political judgments are largely random. Modern research in cognitive psychology has shown that bias and distortion are systematic properties of human cognition.... People process information in similar, imperfect ways; so in dealing with the same information, they tend to make the same mistakes.[89]

Drawing on the dynamics of politics, Kinder and Herzog have noted that:

> Put in terms of signal and noise, the essential problem is that the noise we want to drown out may not be random; it may instead be systematic, structured by cynical television advertisements, appeals to racism, and the like. There's no reason a priori to expect that these various forces will neatly cancel themselves out. In fact, the noise may add up to a tightly unified

85 Zaller, *supra* note 47 at 95.

86 See Robert Y. Shapiro, "Public Opinion, Elites and Democracy" (1998) 12 *Crit. Rev.* 501 at 505 (1998); see also Somin, *supra* note 4 on this point.

87 Shapiro, *supra* note 86 at 524–5.

88 See Page and Shapiro, *supra* note 28; Converse, *Popular Representation*, *supra* note 28.

89 Kuklinski and Quirk, *supra* note 66 at 11–12 (citations omitted).

signal that will drown the signal we're interested in. It is – no surprise here – an empirical question how often aggregation produces miracles.[90]

Using data from six presidential elections and deploying statistical analysis and simulations designed to produce estimated deviations from "fully informed" voting, Bartels also found that individual errors are not likely to cancel out in large electorates. He found, instead, identifiable aggregate biases:

> The aggregate deviations from "fully informed" voting shown [in a table] do not appear to be idiosyncratic deviations that advantage or disadvantage particular candidates in random, unpredictable ways. Rather, the aggregate deviations display two clear and politically consequential patterns: relatively uninformed voters are more likely, other things being equal, to support incumbents and Democrats.[91]

Also using simulated models, but in the context of polling (as opposed to voting), Althaus made a similar finding in his study of political knowledge. He concluded:

> Correcting for the low levels and uneven social distribution of political knowledge reveals that many collective policy preferences would look quite different if all respondents were equally well informed about politics. The biases in collective preferences brought about by information effects are most clearly revealed by simulating measures of fully informed opinion based on the actual opinions that respondents provide, although the degree of divergence in the opinions of ill- and well-informed respondents can also be used as a rough gauge of information effects. An analysis of these biases suggests that citizen disinterest in politics leads collective preferences to become more approving of politicians and political institutions, more isolationist in foreign policy, more accepting of governmental intervention in the economy, more desiring of a larger and more powerful federal government, and more conservative on social policy issues than they might appear if citizens were better acquainted with the realm of public affairs.[92]

This multidisciplinary set of studies suggests that it is perilous to assume that the errors made or knowledge gaps suffered by uninformed voters neatly or automatically cancel out.[93] And if the errors do not, in fact cancel out, then processes of aggregation can embody troublesome biases that shape electoral outcomes.

The idea that aggregation and disaggregation can combine to create a surrogate form of legislative accountability is also problematic because it reproduces – so explicitly and so starkly – the problem of asymmetrical accountability. The problem of asymmetry that plagues this theory arises most clearly with respect to the role of better informed subgroups in rationalizing electoral outcomes. As we have seen, these groups are often enlisted by aggregation enthusiasts, without apology, to support the idea of collective rationality. But whether these groups are conceived as the politically sophisticated and engaged stratum of the electorate known as the "attentive public" or as the shifting "issues publics" who spring to life when issues of importance to them are salient in a particular election, there is a disquieting dynamic that goes right to the heart of democratic equality. The active role of

90 Kinder and Herzog, *supra* note 29 at 372.

91 Bartels, *supra* note 66 at 218.

92 Althaus, *supra* note 54 at 279.

93 For cites to other work pursuing this theme, see the sources cited at Somin, *supra* note 4 at 1291, n. 11; 1323, n. 169.

these groups may well improve the knowledge base of the electorate, but from a normative standpoint, it hardly salvages broad-based democratic accountability to have the mass electorate essentially delegate its collective power to a subgroup. This only recasts the *functional* electorate – the real decision makers – in much smaller terms.

Moreover, there is no necessary reason to believe that this functional mini-electorate is descriptively representative of the larger electorate.[94] As I have argued elsewhere in the context of the accountability critique, "political knowledge is not equally distributed among social groups."[95] To the contrary, the lack of political knowledge is correlated with low voting rates,[96] and there is substantial evidence that more knowledgeable voters are disproportionately drawn from the ranks of more socially advantaged citizens. In their comprehensive analysis of the distribution of political knowledge, Delli Carpini and Keeter concluded:

> We find that citizens tend to be generalists in their knowledge of politics, though there are important exceptions to this pattern, especially when considering different levels of government. There is great variability in what Americans know about politics, making it nearly impossible to characterize the public as informed or uninformed. There is, however, a disconcerting correspondence between the distribution of political knowledge across the public and the distribution of other valuable resources that are both the source of political power and consequence of it . . . political ignorance is not randomly distributed but is most likely to be found among those who arguably have the most to gain from effective political participation: women, blacks, the poor, and the young . . . to paraphrase Orwell, while all citizens are equal, some citizens are more equal than others.[97]

Pursuing and updating these findings, Somin offers an extended analysis of inter-group differences in political knowledge.[98] And Althaus reached a similar conclusion in his study of polling, noting that:

> Knowledgeable [survey] respondents – who tend to be more affluent, educated, male, white, and partisan than ill-informed respondents – usually are over-represented in the ranks of opinion givers. As a result, the voices of relatively knowledgeable demographic groups may carry a disproportionate weight in surveyed opinion measures.[99]

There is another dimension to the inequality. Recall that Hutchings places great weight on the role of subgroups within the electorate in promoting accountability by monitoring legislators closely on issues of special concern to that group, even if the group is not otherwise politically alert or engaged. But Hutchings himself seems to concede that something like a collective action problem may well arise here, even if we are talking about what are conventionally conceived of as issue publics, not interest groups:

> an unfortunate implication of this study is that democratic responsiveness merely requires the presence of relatively small, discrete groups that care intensely about particular issues. While there is no shortage of such groups in American society, there are also many important

[94] See Somin, *supra* note 4.
[95] Schacter, *Accounting for Accountability*, *supra* note 6 at 11.
[96] Popkin and Dimock, *supra* note 70 at 137.
[97] Delli Carpini and Keeter, *supra* note 30 at 174, 177.
[98] Somin, *supra* note 4 at 1323–4, 1352–70.
[99] Althaus, *supra* note 54 at 92–3.

issues that do not easily lend themselves to groups of this type. For example, issues affecting consumers in general, or issues such as campaign finance, do not appeal primarily to a recognizable segment of the electorate.[100]

The strain of inequality that runs through these findings suggests that aggregation and disaggregation do not, in the end, offer a robust response to either the deficit or the asymmetry problems that weaken the accountability axiom.

Finally, like the other proxy theories, the aggregation/disaggregation approach is grounded in a diluted concept of democracy. The reasons closely track the reasons cited earlier in linking heuristics to a thin theory of democracy. Aggregation enthusiasts aspire to what Page and Shapiro call a "rational public." Though undoubtedly better than an irrational public, it might not be saying all that much to call the public "rational," as indeed we have seen in the related body of work on heuristics. A rational democratic public, in these terms, may mean a public that clears the bar of minimum competence, but that is still a long conceptual distance from either an engaged or educated democratic public and, more to the point, from a public that is able to hold elected officials accountable in convincing or systematic way.

CONCLUSION

I have argued that the accountability axiom is empirically flawed, and that, if we read recent scholarship in political science to supply theories of proxy accountability, those proxies do not revive Bickelian accountability as a critical ordering principle in democratic legitimacy. I have focused on three problems with such proxy theories, certain questionable assumptions that undergird these theories, the ways in which the theories reproduce inequalities associated with accountability itself, and the thin and normatively undesirable ideas about democracy on which the proxy theories rest.

It is notable that, to a great extent, these theories simply take as a given the public's lack of knowledge about, and engagement in, public affairs. Although that may be wise as a matter of *describing* our present politics, these theories do seem, lamentably, to accept rather than resist the status quo. That stance is consistent with democratic minimalism but also shares what I regard as one of minimalism's most troubling traits: its accommodationist bent, which discourages attention to institutional mechanisms that might ameliorate the somewhat sorry state of contemporary affairs, such as a careful, pragmatic exploration of which cultural and educational initiatives work to encourage more civic engagement and active citizenship.[101]

What does all of this mean for the organizing topic of this book – namely, the role of legislatures in the context of constitutionalism? The questions raised here relate to the meaning, contours, and implications of democratic legitimacy, and to

[100] Hutchings, *supra* note 30 at 141.

[101] See, e.g., Benjamin R. Barber and Richard M. Battistoni, *Education for Democracy* (Dubuque, Iowa, Kendall/Hunt Publishing Company, 1999) (revised printing); Harry Boyte, *Everyday Politics: Reconnecting Citizens and Public Life* (Philadelphia: University of Pennsylvania Press, 2004); Elkin and Soltan, *supra* note 66; William A. Galston, "Political Knowledge, Political Engagement, and Civic Education" (2001) 4 *Ann. Rev. Pol. Sci.* 217.

the idea that such legitimacy flows, both definitively and exclusively, from Bickel's animating idea of political recourse. My goal has been to suggest that legislative accountability is far too thin, sporadic, and unequal to do the fundamental normative work that Bickel asks of it.

One might accept much of my critique of accountability yet argue that legislators are still politically legitimate in ways that courts cannot be because legislatures can credibly claim to act with the consent of the governed. That is, one might say that accountability offers one route, but not the *only* route, to satisfying the core democratic norm requiring popular consent.[102] To recall a point made earlier in my critique of accountability, one might say that accountability is an ex post device for securing such consent, while representation is an ex ante variant. On this view, the fact that voters can choose legislators at elections ensures some measure of consensual collective choice, even if voters are not well situated to hold legislators accountable, after the fact, for votes previously cast. This is different from Bickel's notion, which underscores recourse, but can be said to pivot – as accountability itself does – on the underlying idea of consent. If citizens can at least make a crude choice between representatives from the left or right, one might argue, that still allows for more consent than appointed judges can receive from citizens.[103] The idea of representation is a famously complex one[104] and surely deserves more extensive conceptual analysis than I can offer here. But several points lead me to suspect that shifting the focus in this way is not likely to obviate the kinds of problems I have been discussing.

First, the two major underlying problems I have associated with accountability – the problems of deficit and asymmetry – are likely to recur and wreak similar havoc on ideas about representation. Voters with sharply limited knowledge about government, whose influence and access are dwarfed by the influence and access of organized groups or select strata of the electorate, are likely to suffer unequal representation in ways that undermine democratic legitimacy.[105] Whether we look ex ante or ex post, in other words, the consent that voters are positioned to give legislators through elections is likely to be far more attenuated and unequal than is conventionally supposed. And, if there are, in fact, normatively significant disparities in the degree and quality of representation that citizens enjoy, it is not necessarily persuasive, from the standpoint of democratic theory, to say that some

[102] Alternatively, one can say the consent norm is, at base, about ensuring democratic responsiveness, and that accountability and representation are two different procedural paths toward responsiveness. I have argued in previous work that the concepts of responsiveness, accountability, and representation are often used interchangeably, but have distinct meanings and should be conceptually disaggregated. *Responsiveness* "refers to the state of affairs in which a government 'adopts policies that are signaled as preferred by citizens'"; *representation* entails a "structural set of relationships" that make it possible to say that "'the people really do act through government, and are not merely passive recipients of its action'"; and *accountability* is a procedural mechanism that makes government answerable for its actions by allowing voters to sanction incumbents. Schacter, *Accounting for Accountability, supra* note 6 at 6 (quotations omitted). For more on this question, see Schacter, *Ely, supra* note 5 at 757–8.

[103] Elected judges raise separate, complex questions that are not addressed here.

[104] For a canonical source on this point, see Hanna Pitkin, *The Concept of Representation* (Berkeley: University of California Press, 1967).

[105] For a variant on this point, see Somin, *supra* note 4, who argues that the broad idea of popular will is undermined by the gaps in voter knowledge and is not rehabilitated by work stressing cues or aggregation.

degree of representation through election is always and necessarily better than none.[106]

Second, because of declining political competition and the rising number of safe districts discussed earlier, as well as the dominance of two-party politics, it is far from obvious that voters always, or even often, have meaningful choices to make in selecting representatives. That fact weakens the notion of consent that can be inferred based on elections alone and suggests that refocusing from accountability to representation does not solve all the problems.

Third, we ought to be skeptical about categorical claims that elected officials alone can lay claim to popular consent. This is true whether we are talking about accountability or representation. If we see consent in historical terms, then the constitutional provision for unelected judges might be understood to evidence a form of consent.[107] More pertinent, perhaps, federal judges can be said to enjoy at least some form of derivative consent: They are appointed and confirmed by elected officials, through a politicized appointments process, after campaigns that sometimes stress judicial themes.[108] Appointed judges are, of course, not directly accountable to voters for their decisions, but the system – in theory at least – affords a measure of political accountability by allowing voters unhappy (or, for that matter, happy) with the perceived judicial status quo to choose legislative and presidential candidates based in part on their views about what sort of judges should fill future vacancies.[109] Or, if we switch from accountability to representation, we might say that the system allows voters to choose representatives based on, among other things, their attitudes about the role and future composition of courts.[110] This idea has been captured most recently by Sen. John McCain's pithy comment that "elections have consequences," a comment meant to support the prerogative of a Republican president and Republican Senate to choose a more conservative Supreme Court Justice, based on the outcome of the 2004 elections.[111] The relationship between voters and judges reflected in this idea is, of course, mediated by elected officials,

[106] For a provocative argument that judges can sometimes not only represent the public, but also *better* represent the public than legislatures can, see William N. Eskridge, Jr., *Dynamic Statutory Interpretation* (Cambridge, Mass: Harvard University Press, 1994) at 1524, 1529–33.

[107] See generally Jed Rubenfeld, *Freedom and Time: A Theory of Constitutional Self-Government* (New Haven: Yale University Press, 2001) .

[108] On the political dynamics of the judicial appointments process, see Charles G. Geyh, "Judicial Independence, Judicial Accountability and the Role of Constitutional Norms in Congressional Regulation of the Courts" (2003) 78 *Ind. L.J.* 153 at 211–21. For an exploration of presidential campaigns in which controversies about the courts have figured prominently, see William G. Ross, "The Role of Judicial Issues in Presidential Campaigns" (2002) 42 *Santa Clara L. Rev.* 391; William G. Ross, *Muted Fury: Populists, Progressives, and Labor Unions Confront the Courts, 1890–1937* (Princeton, NJ: Princeton University Press, 1994); Donald Grier Stephenson, Jr., *Campaigns and the Court: The United States Supreme Court in Presidential Elections* (New York: Columbia University Press, 1999).

[109] There is a large literature on different mechanisms of judicial accountability, such as impeachment, removal, funding restrictions, and court-stripping measures, but I do not intend to explore those sorts of accountability in this chapter, nor to engage here the debate about the norm of judicial independence. See generally "Symposium, Perspectives on Judicial Independence" (2003) 64 *Ohio St. L.J.* 3; "Symposium, Judicial Independence and Accountability" (1999) 72 *S. Cal. L. Rev.* 311.

[110] Pursuing a different aspect of this question, I have argued that courts might be understood to conform to some norm of responsiveness, depending on how that term is conceptualized. See Schacter, *Ely, supra* note 5, at 758 and n. 98.

[111] See Ronald Brownstein, "Vacancy on the Supreme Court; Legal, Political Landscapes Could be Realigned," *Los Angeles Times* (July 2, 2005) A 28.

but the relationship between legislators and voters is itself mediated, for example, by things like political parties and nominating systems.

True enough, everything I have argued in this chapter would suggest that any such indirect legislative accountability for judicial decisions is not likely to be robust or meaningful. It is highly doubtful that voters who know little about policy will know any more about law and courts. But the point I mean to stress is that the comparison should be a consistent one and should recognize that the nature and degree of democratic consent to legislative action is highly attenuated for all the reasons explored in this chapter. Perhaps the important point is that it is, in the end, more realistic to array legislatures and courts along a continuum of consent than to cede the idea of consent categorically to elected officials. And once we move from an on/off switch to a continuum, it is possible to reengage the question of democratic legitimacy with a different perspective.

Reframing consent in terms of a continuum might also lead us to see a final point: reliance on consent as the only democratic norm that matters not only has to grapple with the empirical frailties of, and inequalities in, such consent, but also with the normative limits of the democratic minimalist's insistence on prizing elections alone. Approaches that ignore the larger context in which self-government operates offer us only a partial and sharply limited look at democracy. I have argued elsewhere that democratic theory ought also to be concerned with questions of democratic citizenship and culture, and that courts, along with legislatures and others, can and should promote democracy by expanding civic participation and equal, engaged citizenship.[112] My analysis suggests that we ought to take a fresh look at the democratic legitimacy of legislatures in a system of constitutionalism. It suggests more particularly that we ought to subject to critical empirical and normative analysis the range of ideas that structure our concept of legitimacy, much as we have done here with respect to accountability. The hope is that such analysis might allow us to move beyond easy institutional truisms to engage the large questions surrounding democracy and democratic legitimacy with new insights.

ACKNOWLEDGMENTS

I am grateful for the helpful comments I received from Juliet Brodie, David Canon, Anuj Desai, Don Herzog, Heinz Klug, Victoria Nourse, Kathy Cramer Walsh, and the participants in faculty workshops at Cornell Law School and the University of Wisconsin Law School.

[112] See Schacter, *Lawrence*, *supra* note 5; Jane S. Schacter, "*Romer v. Evans* and Democracy's Domain" (1997) 50 *Vand. L. Rev.* 361.

4 Constitutionalism, Trade Legislation, and "Democracy"

Chantal Thomas

Under the legislative procedure – the so-called *fast track* – that the Trade Act of 1974 established to expedite the process of negotiating and implementing international trade agreements,[1] trade legislation occurs in two phases. First, Congress statutorily authorizes the president to negotiate an international trade agreement and articulates what the president's general negotiating objectives should be.[2] Second, Congress considers, within an expedited time frame and without the option of amendment, whether to accept or reject legislation proposed by the president to implement these agreements.[3] The fast-track procedure was used to enact legislation implementing the North American Free Trade Agreement (NAFTA)[4] and the World Trade Organization (WTO).[5] This chapter places trade legislation within a broader discourse on foreign affairs as it relates to democratic and constitutional theory – a connection rarely made in existing literature.[6]

Critics mounting a "democratic deficit" objection against the fast-track procedure have argued that, in the name of free trade, citizens are asked to agree not just to liberalization of trade policies protecting particular industries, but to changes in their broader way of life[7] relating to employment security and health, safety, and

[1] See *Trade and Tariff Act of 1974*, Pub. L. No. 93-618, 88 Stat. (1978) (codified as amended at 19 U.S.C. §2112 et seq.).

[2] See 19 U.S.C. §§ 2191–2193. Congress also authorizes the president to "proclaim into law any tariff reductions negotiated as part of the agreement." The second step applies only to "nontariff" concessions.

[3] Both houses of Congress must take an up-or-down vote within sixty legislature days of introducing the bill. Ibid. This is a highly simplified description of the procedure. For a more detailed exposition, see Harold H. Koh, "The Fast Track and United States Trade Policy" (1992) 18 *Brook. J. Int'l L.* 143 at 145–53. The president must fulfill several notification requirements prior to submission of the bill, including notice to Congress ninety days before signature, notice to the *Federal Register*, and notification of the International Trade Commission as to tariffs that might be modified. See 19 U.S.C §§ 102(e)(1); 102(e)(2)(A); 131(a).

[4] See *North American Free Trade Agreement Implementation Act*, Pub. L. No. 103-182, 107 Stat. 2057 (1993). The statute implemented the *North American Free Trade Agreement*, Canada, Mexico, and the United States Dec. 8, 1992, 32 *I.L.M.* 289.

[5] See *Uruguay Round Agreements Act*, Pub. L. 103-465, Dec. 8, 1994, 108 Stat. 4809. The statute implemented the *Final Act Embodying the Results of the Uruguay Round of Trade Negotiations*, Apr. 15, 1994, reprinted in 33 *I.L.M.* 1125 (1994).

[6] In doing so, this chapter revisits themes addressed in Chantal Thomas, "Constitutional Change and International Government" (2000) 52 *Hastings L.J.* 1 and further elaborated in Chantal Thomas, "Challenges to Democracy and Trade: The Case of the United States" (2004) 42 *Harv. J. Legis.* 1.

[7] See, e.g., Letter from Rep. Richard Gephardt to Carla Hills, United States Trade Representative, Oct. 25, 1991, quoted in Michael Gregory, "Environment, Sustainable Development, Public Participation and the NAFTA: A Retrospective" (1992) 7 *Envit'l L. & Litig.* 99 at 108.

environmental regulation.[8] The fast track, the objection goes, exacerbates this corrosive dynamic by imposing constraints on the trade legislation process, through reductions in participation in and the transparency of the process, and through its prohibition against legislative amendment. These constraints have led to regulatory outcomes contradictory of popular concerns the conventional legislative process would have recognized.[9]

The general argument for why the fast track could be said to be unconstitutional, as well as antidemocratic, forges a link between separation of powers doctrine and social contract theory.[10] Contractarian constitutional theory[11] posits that the federal Constitution receives its status as "higher law" by virtue of popular consent to this status.[12] To enact "ordinary" law that contradicts the constitutional plan, in this case by violating the separation-of-powers doctrine, would be to undermine popular will.[13] This general argument, somewhat paradoxically, applies both to constitutional measures designed to facilitate the expression of popular will through government and those designed to limit it.[14]

THE AMBIGUITY OF DEMOCRATIC THEORY: THE PRINCIPLES OF TRANSPARENCY AND PUBLIC PARTICIPATION

Tensions in democratic theory

Democratic theory reflects the precise division that we see among arguments deployed in the trade legislation debate: That is, democratic theory is split between conceptualizing "rule by the people" as, on the one hand, reflecting the aggregate actual *preferences* of the electorate,[15] and even more specifically, of a majority of the electorate;[16] and, on the other hand, requiring a determination of the public

[8] See, e.g., "North American Trade Barriers Arising from Differences in National Law" (1992) 86 *Am. Soc'y Int'l L. Proc.* 141. Traditionally, trade liberalization was understood as the elimination of trade barriers designed to protect particular sectors. Such barriers included both tariffs and "nontariff barriers" such as import quotas and subsidies.

[9] See, e.g., "The Internationalization of Domestic Law: The Shrinking Domaine Reserve" (1993) 87 *Am. Soc'y Int'l L. Proc.* 553 at 566 (remarks by Professor Joel R. Paul: "One of the things that troubles me about the GATT is that if you could put it to a vote in the U.S. Congress, it would be rejected. In fact, there is no domestic political support for the GATT in this country.... It is difficult to see how we can build a structure of international trade on an agreement that itself does not represent a democratic consensus.").

[10] The most influential exposition of social contract theory in American discourse is John Locke, *Two Treatises on Government*, Peter Laslett, ed. (Cambridge: Cambridge University Press, 1988).

[11] For examples of "contractarian" constitutional theory, see John Patrick Diggins, *The Lost Soul of American Politics: Virtue, Self-Interest and the Foundations of Liberalism* (New York: Basic Books, 1984).

[12] See, e.g., Bruce Ackerman, *We the People: Foundations* (Cambridge, Mass.: Belknap Press of Harvard University Press, 1991) at 6–7.

[13] Contractarian theory can derive popular consent to the Constitution either from its initial ratification or from the ongoing "tacit consent" of the electorate.

[14] See Stephen Holmes, "Precommitment and the Paradox of Democracy" in *Constitutionalism and Democracy*, Jon Elster and Rune Slagstad, eds. (Cambridge: Cambridge University Press, 1988) 195.

[15] Robert A. Dahl, *A Preface to Democratic Theory* (Chicago: University of Chicago Press, 1956) [hereinafter Dahl, *Preface*].

[16] Alexis de Toqueville, *Democracy in America*, vol. 1, ed. by Francis Bowen, trans. by Henry Reeve, orig. pub. 1862 (New York: Vintage Books Edition, Alfred A. Knopf, 1990) at 220 ("[T]he majority governs in the name of the people... in all countries in which the people are supreme.").

interest,[17] often as reached through the deliberations of a governing elite.[18] That democratic theory would embrace the notion of a governing elite at such a fundamental level seems counterintuitive. It follows quite easily, however, from an elemental tension, pervasive in modern Western theory, between what might be called the "is" and the "ought."[19] In the case of conceptualizing democracy, this tension poses the question whether government should reflect what the popular will is – that is, public *preferences* – or what the popular will *ought to be* – the public *interest.*

The conceptual tension between public preferences and the public interest is exemplified in the equivocal treatment by American democratic theory of the principles of openness and public participation.[20] On the one hand, such values are manifestly necessary to ensure democratic government, as they help to effectuate the public's expression of its preferences. These principles are, as such, foundational to American democratic theory. The notion of a self-governing population (restrictively defined, of course) prevailed in the political theory of the American Revolution.[21] In contemporary democratic theory, both pluralism[22] and its rival, often described as "civic republicanism," value the principles of openness and public participation, albeit for different reasons.

American democratic theory is characterized by a general orientation toward the "is" side of the equation – that is, toward a conceptualization of democracy that privileges the expression by the electorate of its actual preferences, rather than one which seeks to determine the public will through some other means. At the same time, however, American democratic theory, including contemporary pluralism and civic republicanism, recognizes the importance of countervailing values in governance, such as "efficiency," and "expertise" or "enlightenment."[23] Its orientation

[17] John Stuart Mill, *Considerations on Representative Government*, ed. Currin V. Shields, 3rd ed. (New York: The Liberal Arts Press, 1958) [hereinafter Mill, *Representative Government*]; Jean-Jacques Rousseau, *The Social Contract and Discourses*, ed. and trans. G. D. H. Cole (New York: E.P. Dutton, 1950).

[18] Of course, that an elite *will* rule in the public interest is a normative assumption. See Currin Shields, "Introduction" to Mill, *Representative Government, supra* note 17 at xxxi–xxxii.

[19] The best-known conceptualization of the relationship between "is" and "ought" is Hume's "naturalistic fallacy," which posits that "ought" cannot be derived from "is." David Hume, *A Treatise of Human Nature*, ed. L. A. Selby-Bigge (Oxford: Oxford University Press, 1980).

[20] See William Kelso, *Pluralism and Its Critics* (Westport, Conn.: Greenwood Press, 1978) at 7 (describing these values as common to rival political theories such as pluralism, "populism," and "participatory democracy"). The theory of civic republicanism also stresses these values: see Frank I. Michelman, "Law's Republic" (1988) 97 *Yale L.J.* 1493; Cass R. Sunstein, "Beyond the Republican Revival" (1988) 97 *Yale L.J.* 1539; Cass Sunstein, "Interest Groups in American Public Law" (1985) 38 *Stan. L. Rev.* 29; Suzanna Sherry, "Civic Virtue and the Feminine Voice in Constitutional Adjudication" (1986) 72 *Va. L. Rev.* 543. The civic republican tradition has generally been opposed to contemporary pluralist theory because it does not envision public preferences as existing prior to the lawmaking process (with the lawmaking process merely aggregating them), but rather sees them as a result of deliberation on the public good among the citizenry. See, e.g., Cass R. Sunstein, "Interest Groups in American Public Law" (1985) 38 *Stan. L. Rev.* 29 at 31.

[21] Scholars of this era locate these principles within a "republican" early American political culture, stressing civic virtue and citizen deliberation. Gordon S. Wood, *The Creation of the American Republic, 1776–1787* (Chapel Hill: University of North Carolina Press, 1969); Herbert Storing, *What the Ant-Federalists Were For* (Chicago: University of Chicago Press, 1981).

[22] See Edward C. Banfield, *Political Influence* (New Brunswick, NJ: Transaction Publishers, 2003); James Buchanan and Gordon Tullock, *The Calculus of Consent* (Ann Arbor: University of Michigan Press, 1962); Dahl, *Preface, supra* note 10.

[23] "Expertise" describes situations in which that superior decision-making capacity stems from particular empirical knowledge. "Enlightenment" describes situations in which the capacity stems not from any greater empirical knowledge but from a disinterested ability to create policy that opposes current

toward openness and public participation, consequently, is incomplete. Indeed, significant portions of American democratic theory concern themselves precisely with the question of the extent to which public preferences should be tempered by the public interest in government.[24] This tension can be demonstrated by looking to developments of American democratic theory that concern themselves with governmental structure such as American constitutional theory and theories of legislation. The tension can also be seen in substantive areas such as, particularly in the era of globalization, trade policy.

As related to trade policy

Trade policy exemplifies the tension between actual public preferences and the public interest, because the very basis of trade-liberalization policy lies in the self-consciously "counterintuitive" principle of comparative advantage.[25] The gist of comparative advantage is that by increasing vulnerability to extranational market competition, societies increase their benefits from trade even if they are less competitive in overall terms than other societies. That this proposition is "counter-intuitive" is borne out by the fact that generally used measures – opinion polls, for instance – consistently show a majority position against lowering national trade barriers.[26] Presidents are arguably elected despite, rather than because of, their positions on trade.[27] And, of course, Congress generally favors more rather than less protection against international market competition.[28] Indeed, the brand of American politics that emerged in the late nineteenth century under the rubric of "populism" is known primarily for its advocacy of antiliberalization economic policy. Thus, Jagdish Bhagwati has remarked of comparative advantage and free trade: "This fundamental intuition of Economics has never been plausible to the general public."[29]

The more straightforward advocates of free trade respond to this majoritarian stance against trade liberalization by arguing that it is nonetheless in the public interest (because it increases national wealth and consumer choice). Such an

majority will but that, it is believed, will further the long-term interests of society as a whole. The values of democracy and efficiency are not always viewed as contrary, however; see, e.g., Cass Sunstein, "Democratizing America Through Law" (1991) 25 *Suffolk L. Rev.* 949 at 950.

24 The Federalist view "willingly abandoned the classical republican understanding that citizens should participate directly in the processes of government." See Cass Sunstein, "Interest Groups in American Public Law," *supra* note 15 at 42 and n. 58. Rather, the Federalists viewed all potential rulers, whether the general citizenry or a ruling elite, as corruptible. Hence the famous statement that "ambition must be made to counteract ambition." Federalist No. 51 (J. Madison). Thus, the Federalists, while assuming the dominance of the electorate, sought to ensure that governmental structure would protect not only individual rights but also the "permanent... interests of the community." The Federalists therefore favored structure as a limit on democracy; and part of this structure included a means "to obtain for rulers men who possess most wisdom to discern, and most virtue to pursue the common good of the society." Federalist No. 57 (Hamilton).

25 To wit, the following recollection of Jagdish Bhagwati: "Paul Samuelson, my old teacher at MIT and the celebrated Nobel laureate in Economics, recalls being asked... which proposition is both true and counterintuitive. He scratched his head for a while and then came up with the law of comparative advantage." Jagdish Bhagwati, "Challenges to the Doctrine of Free Trade" (1993) 25 *N.Y.U. J. Int'l L. & Pol.* 219 at 219.

26 See, e.g., American Political Network, The Hotline, Volume 10 No. 9 (2005) (showing roughly 25% in favor of, and 40% against, the North American Free Trade Agreement).

27 Ibid.

28 Ibid.

29 Bhagwati, *supra* note 20 at 219.

argument falls squarely within a well-established tradition of privileging a vision of the public interest over public preferences.[30] If free trade is in the public interest despite being contrary to public preference, then a governmental structure that delegates the task of trade policy formulation to entities more capable of acting in a countermajoritarian fashion is preferred over one in which actors are more closely beholden to direct expression of public preferences. Consequently, trade policy is one of the more prominent areas,[31] where the strategy of delegation finds ample justification in democratic theory.

THE AMBIGUITY OF CONSTITUTIONAL INTERPRETATION: THE SEPARATION-OF-POWERS CHALLENGE

The foregoing section described the theoretical tension that problematizes the claim that the fast-track procedure can be condemned as antidemocratic because it reduces transparency and public participation in government. The discussion has proceeded, however, without explicitly addressing the fact, potentially disastrous to fast-track opponents, that the fast-track procedure was approved via the conventional legislative process. There are two potential conclusions that follow.

First, one might conclude that if the fast-track procedure has been approved according to the conventional political process, then it is a legitimate qualification of democratic principles. Fast-track opponents, according to this response, cannot decry the procedure as antidemocratic as long as it has been democratically approved; the most they can do is mobilize to persuade the polity to change its mind. On the other hand, one might conclude that the fast track creates undue aggrandizement of executive power at the expense of legislative power as established in Article I of the Constitution. In particular, this construction would argue that the fast-track procedure offends the constitutional principle of separation of powers.

This separation-of-powers challenge requires, first, a consideration of doctrine that has developed with respect to the Article I legislative power; and, second, a consideration of the doctrine that has developed with respect to foreign affairs. Constitutional doctrine is ambiguous on both points; yet, it has been deployed in both areas to support a particular structural outcome – the shift of power to the executive branch. As is more fully discussed below, a constitutional challenge to the fast-track procedure is unlikely to result in its judicial invalidation, given contemporary separation of powers and foreign affairs jurisprudence. The likelihood of this outcome despite theoretical ambiguity suggests an extradoctrinal impetus: In the context of U.S. lawmaking on international economic issues, it is the impetus of

30 For example, a majority of the Federalists were pro free trade, with some notable exceptions such as Alexander Hamilton.

31 Civil rights is another prominent area. It is interesting to note that in economic discourse the countermajoritarian stance falls on the opposite end of the political spectrum from the countermajoritarian stance in rights discourse. That is, strong pro–free trade positions are generally associated with political conservatism, whereas strong pro-rights positions are generally associated with political liberalism or progressivism. Conversely, weaker rights positions are associated with political conservatism, whereas weaker free trade positions are associated with political liberalism or progressivism.

globalization. In this context, the values of efficiency and expertise have supported what Joel Paul has called a "discourse of executive expediency."[32]

The relationship between constitutionality and the democratic objection

The separation of powers argument asserts that the incorporation of the separation-of-powers principle into the Constitution was designed specifically to facilitate and preserve popular control over government. The design was to realize these ends by "fractur[ing]" governmental power and therefore preventing tyranny, and by multiplying channels of popular communication with government.[33] It is not surprising, in this light, that many commentators have argued that the rise of the federal administrative state, resulting from massive delegations by Congress of its constitutionally allocated powers, has significantly compromised democracy in the federal government.[34] So the democratic objection incorporates into itself a structural objection to the shift of power from Congress to the president – an objection that contemporary governmental structure deviates unacceptably from the constitutional plan. This structural objection is far from new – it has been perennial at least since the rise of the administrative state.[35] The particular argument here would be that the fast-track procedure deprives Congress of the power of amending the legislation it is considering.

These arguments provide a basis on which fast-track opponents can mount a democratic objection alternative to the one described in the first section. The rest of this section observes, however, that neither the constitutional text nor any theory of constitutional interpretation, without more, can definitively resolve these claims; although folding in considerations of political context yields a prediction that, as currently applied, available theories of constitutional interpretation would endorse rather than uphold fast track.

[32] See Joel Paul, "The Geopolitical Constitution: Executive Expediency and Executive Agreements" (1998) 86 *Cal. L. Rev.* 671.

[33] See, e.g., *Bowsher v. Synar*, 478 U.S. 714 at 722 (1986) (stating that the constitutional "system of division and separation of powers . . . was deliberately so structured to assure full, vigorous, and open debate on the great issues affecting the people and to provide avenues for the operation of checks on the exercise of government power"); see also Federalist No. 47 ("The accumulation of all powers, legislative, executive, and judiciary, in the same hands, . . . may justly be pronounced the very definition of tyranny").

[34] David Schoenbrod, *Power Without Responsibility: How Congress Abuses the People Through Delegation* (New Haven, Conn.: Yale University Press, 1993). It is worth noting that the modern administrative state originated in no small measure to prevent the federal judiciary from overturning "New Deal" statutes that were viewed as embodying the popular will. See Cass Sunstein, "Constitutionalism After the New Deal" (1987) 101 *Harv. L. Rev.* 421. Moreover, the New Deal unquestionably sought to improve *economic* democracy, that is, to ensure a relatively egalitarian distribution of wealth.

[35] The objection specifically to the delegation of lawmaking power to the executive branch is known as the nondelegation doctrine. The nondelegation doctrine was originated by the Court in the cases of *A.L.A. Schechter Poultry Corp. v. United States*, 295 U.S. 555 (1935) and *Panama Refining Co. v. Ryan*, 293 U.S. 388 (1935). "Though *Panama* and *Schechter* technically continue to be good law, the Court has never again struck down an act of Congress as violative of the nondelegation doctrine." Alfred C. Aman, Jr., "Symposium: *Bowsher v. Synar*: Introduction" (1987) 72 *Stan. L. Rev.* 421 at 425. Although the judiciary has been reluctant to enforce the nondelegation doctrine, commentators have kept the doctrine alive. See, e.g., John Hart Ely, *Democracy and Distrust: A Theory of Judicial Review* (Cambridge, Mass.: Harvard University Press, 1980) at 131–4; David Schoenbrod, *Power Without Responsibility: How Congress Abuses the People Through Delegation, supra* note 34; "The Phoenix Rises Again: The Nondelegation Doctrine from Constitutional and Policy Perspectives" (Symposium presented to Benjamin N. Cardozo School of Law, March 19, 1998).

Ambiguity in constitutional theory

If deep tensions in democratic theory problematized the attempt to expose the fast-track procedure as antidemocratic, a constitutional objection, to be explored in this section, might at first blush appear more promising for fast-track opponents. This apparent promise is generated not only by the Constitution's status as the law of the land, but also by the perception that claims rooted in text are more certain than those rooted in principle alone. But interpretation of the constitutional *text* is impossible without reference to some *con*text. Notwithstanding the existence of a writing, the Constitution turns out to be subject to the same multiplicity as democratic theory standing alone – hence the long-standing suggestion that the U.S. Constitution is an *unwritten* one.[36]

In the specific case of the applicability of the separation-of-powers doctrine to the fast-track procedure, ambiguities appear in several key constitutional provisions. First, the term "separation of powers" appears nowhere in the text of the Constitution.[37] The Constitution does, however, explicitly allocate specific powers to the respective branches of the federal government, so that this silence might be resolved by looking to see whether the text allocates the power to make trade legislation to Congress, the president, or both. This, however, leads one to Article I, Section 8, which allocates to Congress the ability to "regulate Commerce with foreign Nations." The language fails to specify whether this power includes or excludes (thereby leaving to the president) the power to make international commercial agreements.[38] Moreover, the only explicit allocation of the ability to make

[36] The legal realists were the first to identify the Constitution as unwritten. Take, for example, Karl Llewellyn's statements: "I am not arguing that the United States ought to have the sort of constitution loosely designated as 'unwritten.' I am arguing that they *have* such a constitution, and that nobody can stop their having such a constitution, and that whether anyone likes that fact or not, the fact has been there for decades, and must be dealt with by any theory that purports to do a theory's work." Karl Llewellyn, "The Constitution as an Institution" (1934) 34 *Colum. L. Rev.* 1 at 2 n. 5 (emphasis added). Thomas Grey relaunched the concept with respect to the individual rights; see Thomas C. Grey, "Do We Have an Unwritten Constitution" (1975) 27 *Stan. L. Rev.* 703.

[37] Nonetheless, the relevance of the principle to constitutional interpretation is undisputed, though the *degree* of relevance is. See Thomas O. Sargentich, "The Contemporary Debate About Legislative–Executive Separation of Powers" (1987) 72 *Cornell L. Rev.* 430. The doctrine has received such acceptance, of course, because of its prominence in the political writings of the Federalists, and of the Constitution's framers more generally, and its consonance with the format of the Constitution. See *Buckley v. Valeo*, 424 U.S. 1, 124 (1976) ("The principle of separation of powers was not simply... in the minds of the Framers; it was woven into the document that they drafted..."); 1 *Annals of Cong.* 581 (J. Gales, ed., 1834) (statement of James Madison during the first Congress) ("[I]f there is a principle in our Constitution... more sacred than another, it is that which separates the Legislative, Executive and Judicial powers.") (quoted in Sargentich, ibid. at 438 n.34).

[38] Indeed, the executive branch has suggested that the president is endowed with the constitutional authority to make such agreements free from congressional oversight. The extreme unpopularity of this view, however, has prevented presidents from pressing it, at least since the 1960s. Prior to that period, however, there were marked struggles between president and Congress on this issue, many of which related to the GATT. To begin with, the text of the GATT was never congressionally ratified, either as a treaty or as a congressional–executive agreement (that is, not until the Uruguay Round). Congress resented this oversight for some time. Another well-known example of this tension comes from the so-called Kennedy Round of negotiations among members of the GATT. Congress had enacted a statute authorizing President Kennedy to make only tariff concessions. The president returned from the negotiations, however, with agreements regulating the "nontariff" matters of antidumping law and customs valuation. Congress responded by refusing to adopt the agreements, causing some international comment. The fast-track procedure was devised largely as a response to this and other incidents of congressional recalcitrance.

international agreements lies in Article II's allocation to the president of the power to make treaties. The text therefore offers no definitive answer to the question of whether the fast-track procedure accords with or contravenes the constitutional allocation of powers between Congress and the president. Thus, the argument that the fast-track procedure, and specifically its no-amendment rule, unconstitutionally constrain Congress's foreign commerce power is problematized by the fact that the fast-track procedure is intended to allow the president to increase his efficacy in exercising powers that *are* deemed to be constitutionally his – the powers to negotiate and enter into international agreements.[39]

This textual ambiguity, of course, is hardly novel in the area of separation of powers.[40] The standard response to such ambiguity is to turn for resolution to theories of textual interpretation. The multiple plausibility thesis contends, however, that theories of constitutional interpretation by themselves cannot resolve the matter, and that arguments for and against fast track can be sketched out with respect to both the legislative power and the "foreign affairs" power. The source of multiple plausibility differs with respect to these two powers. In the case of the legislative power, the question is precisely the need to determine what is meant by the phrase in Article I, Section 1 that "[a]ll legislative Powers . . . shall be vested in a Congress of the United States." Do these "Powers" entail only the enactment of statutes within enumerated substantive areas? Or, do they include all aspects of the process that ultimately lead to enactment, including the power to amend proposed legislation? In the case of the "foreign affairs" power, there is even less instruction. Here, the interpretive dilemma arises not because it is unclear what a part of the constitutional text means, but because the activity in question – regulating international trade by virtue of participation in an international trade organization – is neither mentioned by nor implicit in the constitutional text.

Ambiguity in the legislative power

The primary issue of constitutional interpretation with respect to separation-of-powers jurisprudence concerns whether the text should be understood according to a "formalist" or a "functionalist" approach.[41] I note here that my focus is

[39] The power to enter into international agreements derives from Article II treaty power. The power to negotiate international agreements is not allocated in the text but was established in *United States v. Curtiss-Wright Export Corp.*, 299 U.S. 304 (1936).

[40] In addition to the example of trade given here, there are many other similar dilemmas within the separation-of-powers doctrine, such as the removal power and the meaning of the constitutional requirements of Senate "advice and consent."

[41] The first, more general level is what source of meaning to use in interpreting the text. There are many different positions, but I will focus here on the methods of "originalism," "translation," and "justice." Originalism seeks to read the text in a way that enforces the literal and original understanding of the framers as determined through the text and historical sources. For examples of originalist theory, see *Harmelin v. Michigan*, 501 U.S. 957 (1991) (Scalia, J.); Robert Bork, *The Tempting of America: The Political Seduction of the Law* (New York: Free Press, 1990). Translation explicitly seeks to adapt this original understanding to contemporary *norms*. See Lawrence Lessig, "Fidelity in Translation" (1993) 71 *Tex. L. Rev.* 1165; Paul Brest, "The Misconceived Quest for Original Understanding" (1980) 60 *B. U. L. Rev.* 204. In the jurisprudence of the Supreme Court Justices, this approach can be seen in *INS v. Chadha*, 462 U.S. 919 (1983) at 977 (White, J., dissenting) (arguing that "our Federal Government was intentionally chartered with the flexibility to respond to contemporary needs without losing sight of fundamental democratic principles"). "Justice" seeks to ensure the consonance of textual interpretation with prior values, as in Dworkin and Rawls.

on the power to enact law at the domestic level, rather than the power to make international agreements. Whether the president is or is not authorized to enter into agreements is a separate question from whether the President is allowed to control the process at the domestic level. The constitutional challenge here lies in the fact that the only opportunities for congressional and public participation to result in legislative amendment are tightly circumscribed and controlled by the executive branch rather than the legislature.

"Formalism" holds as the central premise of the separation-of-powers doctrine "[t]he fundamental necessity of maintaining each of the three general departments of government entirely free from the control or coercive influence, direct or indirect, of either of the others."[42] Current formalist jurisprudence progresses from this premise to the conclusion that, in the context of the Article I legislative power, the separation-of-powers doctrine must be enforced through strict and exclusive attention to the procedural requirements in Article I, Section 7 of bicameralism and presentment. On this view, the fast-track procedure is unproblematic, as the law resulting from it meets these requirements, even though under it the executive branch is responsible not only for drafting legislation but also for managing the debate and amendment process.

The formalist position on separation of powers would, according to this rendition, seem to be unassailably determinate. But there is an earlier – and now (somewhat) discredited – rendition: the nondelegation doctrine.[43] Under this interpretation, the separation-of-powers doctrine requires more than enforcement of the procedural requirements of Article I, Section 7; it requires, as the above quotation suggests, that the courts guard against the exercise by any branch of power naturally residing within another branch, unless the constitutional text explicitly approved such exercise. That is, although in recent years the "formality" of the formalist approach has been thought to vest in the technical requirements of the Constitution, one can argue that it instead rests on the preservation of complete distinctness and control within the branches. While the procedural requirements of Article I, Section 7 have more recently been applied as though they are the independent variable,[44] the earlier application viewed the actual distinctness of control as the real predicate. Consequently, whereas the current version allows any legislative

[42] *Humphrey's Executor*, 295 U.S. 602 (1935) at 629. This passage, from an early functionalist case discussing formalism, has been repeatedly quoted in other formalist analyses in Supreme Court cases. See, e.g., *Bowsher v. Synar*, *supra* note 33. Alfred Aman quotes a typical modern-day understanding of formalist separation-of-powers doctrine: "The Founding Fathers ... created a federal government of *three* well-defined branches. And they carefully enumerated the powers and responsibilities of each. With a few exceptions, such as the veto and impeachment powers, they vested the legislative power *solely* in the Congress, the executive power *solely* in the President, and the judicial power *solely* in the courts." Aman, "Symposium: *Bowsher v. Synar*: Introduction," *supra* note 35 at 425, and 428. See also Martin Flaherty, "The Most Dangerous Branch" (1996) 105 *Yale L.J.* 1725 at 1734. ("Formalist catechism posits three discrete branches, each exercising one of three distinct powers. The legislative, executive and judicial branches, with certain carefully crafted exceptions [explicit in the constitutional text], each controls its own domain, unconstrained by its counterparts.")

[43] See Richard Stewart, "Beyond Delegation Doctrine" (1987) 36 *Am. U. L. Rev.* 323 at 324–5 (describing the nondelegation doctrine as formalistic "fundamentalism").

[44] Thus, in *Chadha*, *supra* note 41 and *Bowsher*, *supra* note 33, focusing on explicit requirements maintained a clear separation of the branches.

delegation as long as it passes scrutiny for accordance with the procedural requirements of Article I, Section 7, the earlier version reversed the scrutiny, disallowing legislative delegations that were not explicitly sanctioned by the constitutional text.[45]

The earlier formalist analysis would therefore argue that, since the functions delegated to the executive branch under the fast-track procedure could in no way be characterized as executive in nature, they must be legislative, and violate the separation-of-powers mandate. The Supreme Court's present formalism is a retreat from this position. The original establishment and subsequent retreat from the nondelegation doctrine exemplify both textual and interpretive ambiguity.[46]

The same ambiguity can be attributed to the theory of functionalism. A functionalist theory of interpretation would seek to preserve for each of the branches its "core" functions, understanding that there would be overlap and integration at the margins.[47] This would, of course, raise the question as to whether the congressional power to amend trade legislation proposed by the executive branch was a "core" function of the legislature. How might we answer this question? On the one hand, amendment would seem to be an integral part of the legislative process. On the other, one could take a narrow view and argue that legislative power means only the power to enact a statute. Would there be any clear way to decide the issue? While the functional approach tends to approve of structures worked out through

[45] Even using formal markers, the fast-track procedure is unlike other types of legislative delegation in that it does not delegate a power to make law that could be characterized as implementing the dictates of the Congress. Rather, it delegates the authority to engage in process of lawmaking that is prior to the enactment of the statute. It is true that many if not most bills introduced into Congress have been drafted by some part of the executive branch. However, those bills are then subject to the conventional legislative process of debate and amendment, as controlled by Congress. In the case of fast track, those conventionally legislative powers have been delegated to the executive and, indeed, are controlled by the executive branch. Thus, if formalism is said to depend on external evaluative criteria, then it seems plausible to argue that one of the criteria for defining the legislative power is that it is the activity that occurs after the introduction of a bill and before its rejection or enactment. For legislative activities to occur before or after that – in the case of *Chadha*, with a legislative veto; in the case of fast track, with congressional consultation – may be to offend this formalist conception of legislation.

[46] This point can be made clear in comparing the Court's disposition in *Buckley v. Valeo, supra* note 37 of the two separation-of-powers challenges to the Federal Election Campaign Act of 1971. The Court rejected the argument that the statute unconstitutionally delegated legislative power, finding that the separation-of-powers doctrine did not require "a hermetic sealing off of the three branches of Government from one another": 424 U.S. at 121. Yet the Court upheld the argument that the statute unconstitutionally breached the separation-of-powers doctrine because it gave Congress the power to appoint some members of a commission whose mandate included "executive" duties of law implementation and law enforcement: 424 U.S. at 124–37. The Supreme Court's dual retreat from the structural doctrine of *Panama* and *Schechter* and from the rights doctrine of *Lochner* are of course *susceptible* to identification as the crudest manifestation of ambiguity in which political exigencies external to the interpreter dictate interpretive flux. Cf. Michael Ariens, "A Thrice-Told Tale, Or Felix the Cat" (1994) 107 *Harv. L. Rev.* 620 at 622–3 and 631–3.

[47] Examples of functionalist jurisprudence in Supreme Court separation-of-powers cases are *Commodity Futures Trading Comm'n v. Schor*, 478 U.S. 833 at 851 (1986) (eschewing a "formalistic and unbending" approach); *Nixon v. Administrator*, 433 U.S. 425 at 443 (1977) (looking to "the extent to which [the measure in question] prevents the Executive Branch from accomplishing its constitutionally assigned functions"); *United States v. Nixon*, 418 U.S. 683 at 713 (1984). For examples of functionalist approaches on the Supreme Court, see the opinions of Justice White in *Bowsher v. Synar, supra* note 33 at 759, 762 (White, J., dissenting) (lamenting the majority's "distressingly formalistic view of separation of powers"); *Northern Pipeline Construction Co. v. Marathon Pipe Line Co.*, 458 U.S. 59 at 92–118 (1982) (White, J., dissenting); *INS v. Chadha, supra* note 41 at 967–1003 (White, J., dissenting).

the legislative process,[48] the point here is that a plausible functional argument can be made to support a disapproving stance.[49]

Ambiguity in the foreign affairs power

If applying the separation of powers doctrine to the legislative power shows how complicated the question of interpreting the Constitution with respect to the fast-track procedure is, considering the significance of foreign affairs under the Constitution makes it even more so. Although, as Louis Henkin has noted, the term "foreign affairs" is not to be found in the constitutional text, it has long been used to apply to the power to conduct affairs – both diplomatic and legal – of the United States in the international realm.[50]

As I noted above, the focus of this chapter is on the power to make law at the national rather than the international level. Yet in the procedure we are talking about, legislation at the national level accompanies and implements legislation at the international level. The question of what U.S. law and policy should be with respect to international trade requires a consideration of constitutional doctrine on foreign affairs. If the foreign affairs power accrues exclusively to the executive branch, for example, then the president's exercise of that power in making international trade arguments should arguably preempt the accouterments of legislative power (such as the power to amend a bill). If, on the other hand, Congress and the president share the foreign affairs power, especially with respect to trade, Congress arguably has a stronger claim.

The interpretive difficulty posed here differs somewhat from the one discussed just above. There, the question was whether the power of amendment was or was not necessarily a part of the legislative power. Here, the difficulty is that the process of making international trade agreements simply is not expressly addressed by the Constitution. Article I, Section 8 allocates the power to regulate commerce with foreign nations to Congress. Article II allocates the power to make international agreements to the president.[51] The placement of these clauses suggests that not only is

48 See Peter Strauss, "The Place of Agencies in Government, Separation of Powers and the Fourth Branch" (1984) 84 *Colum. L. Rev.* 573. This has certainly been true of the functionalist approach as employed on the Supreme Court. See *Commodity Futures Trading Comm'n v. Schor, supra* note 47 at 851 (1986) (favoring functionalism over formalism on grounds that it does not "unduly constrict Congress' ability to take needed and innovative action pursuant to its Article I powers"); *Bowsher v. Synar, supra* note 33 at 759 (1986) (criticizing the "formalistic view of separation of powers as a bar to the attainment of governmental objectives through the means chosen by the Congress and the President in the legislative process established by the Constitution").

49 Under Martin Flaherty's version of functionalism, the goal is to preserve the "functions – for example, balance among the branches of government – for which [the Constitution and in this case] the doctrine of separation of power was developed." See Flaherty, *supra* note 42 at 1734 n. 34. Again, however, this only raises the question of proper balance among the branches, which can be resolved only by resort to one of these secondary theories.

50 Louis Henkin, *Constitutionalism, Democracy and Foreign Affairs* (New York: Columbia University Press, 1990).

51 An additional interpretive difficulty arises from the fact that the text of Article II describes these agreements as "treaties" and says they can be made only with the advice and consent of the Senate. Earlier in this century, the difficulty was the increasing number of international agreements and the lack of desirability of Senate control. Whereas it seemed appropriate for the president to be able to make sole executive agreements in limited areas relating to diplomacy and other areas traditionally within the executive branch, sole executive agreements seemed inappropriate with respect to international agreements that actually impacted domestic issues.

the prospect of international commercial agreement not explicitly contemplated in the Constitution, but it is also not *implicitly* contemplated. This conclusion is supported by the complete absence of such agreements at the time the Constitution was framed. As in the case of the legislative power, there are arguments both for and against construing the "foreign affairs power" to legitimate the fast-track procedure.

The pro–fast-track argument would be that concerns ordinarily accompanying delegations of legislative power must take a back seat to overriding priorities of international effectiveness – "expediency" – in foreign affairs.[52] This argument could point to the fact that the Supreme Court, even in the brief era of its allegiance to the nondelegation doctrine, upheld statutes in which Congress authorized the president to act in foreign affairs.

One variation of this argument relates to the president's "inherent" foreign affairs power and asserts that legislative delegations otherwise constitutionally insupportable are bolstered by this inherent power. This was the view espoused by the Supreme Court in *United States v. Curtiss-Wright Export Corp.*, a 1930s case involving a congressional authorization of the president to prohibit arms sales to certain countries.[53] Here, the Court famously moved from the premise that "inherent" foreign affairs powers constitutionally accrue to the government to the conclusion that these powers necessarily accrue specifically to the executive branch to allow the United States to "speak with one voice" in foreign affairs. Under *Curtiss-Wright*, the fast-track procedure would be a legitimate and necessary tool to ensure efficacy in the international trade policy of the United States.

Subsequent Supreme Court cases determining the scope of the foreign affairs power, however, sharply curtailed the potential expansiveness of *Curtiss-Wright*, finding that the president's inherent power was sufficient to validate presidential action in foreign affairs only when such power proceeded by explicit or implicit authorization of the Congress. Where presidential action in the international sphere contradicted contrary policy set by Congress, the Court found it to be invalid.[54] It

The compromise was to devise the congressional-executive agreement. This was said to be more democratic. It also seemed to be a better integration of the two relevant provisions. If Congress had the power to regulate commerce with foreign nations according to the regular process in Article I, Section 7, it was argued that to allow the Senate to dominate the process with respect to international agreements was unfair. For the same reason, to allow the president to enter into sole agreements seemed unfair because the types of agreements that would otherwise be treaties did not address diplomacy but substantive areas of domestic regulation.

52 See Paul, *supra* note 9.

53 See *supra* note 39.

54 The cases striking down executive exercise of the foreign affairs power are *Youngstown Sheet & Tube Co.* and *United States v. Guy Capps.* In *Youngstown Sheet & Tube Co v. Sawyer*, 343 U.S. 579 (1952), steel companies brought suit for declaratory and injunctive relief to prevent the secretary of commerce from seizing steel mills in conjunction with an executive order that sought to take over steel mills in the middle of a work stoppage and labor dispute between companies and United Steelworkers of America. Congress had provided for seizure of real and personal property under two other statutes (the Selective Service Act of 1948 and the Defense Production Act of 1950), but the conditions for those statutes were not met in this case. In *United States v. Guy Capps*, 204 F.2d 655 (1953) (aff'd on other grounds), the Supreme Court voided the executive agreement that contradicted tariff policy set by Congress and the Tariff Commission. This case suggested that the foreign affairs power does not extend to trade issues or at least "foreign commerce"; however, it expressly leaves aside this issue (i.e., whether executive could make trade agreements where congressional silence) because here there was contradictory legislative policy – in that sense the situation was similar to *Youngstown*. But note that the Supreme Court decided

might be possible to argue that a president who negotiated agreements that made concessions running explicitly contrary to congressional instructions would be acting beyond the scope of his inherent foreign affairs power. However, since Congress would retain the power ultimately to approve or disapprove the agreement, such action would probably not be seen as constitutionally unsustainable.

Curtiss-Wright might be distinguished from the fast-track procedure in that it focused on diplomacy in the context of international war,[55] whereas the fast-track procedure looks to issues of commerce. Yet in this area as well, the Court upheld legislative delegations in its otherwise nondelegation era. In *J. W. Hampton & Co. v. United States*, the Court upheld a statute in which Congress delegated to the president the power to fix tariffs for the purpose of equalizing the prices of foreign imports and domestic goods in domestic markets.[56]

Indeed, Congress has had a long history of delegating to the president the authority to set tariffs, arguably the authority defined by the phrase "regulat[ion of] of Commerce with foreign Nations." These delegations sought not only to realize the policy at issue in the *J. W. Hampton* case of tariff "equalization" of import prices with domestic prices but also the policy of "reciprocal trade" – that is, of allowing foreign producers benefits from trade in the United States only to the extent that U.S. producers were allowed to benefit from trade in foreign countries. In the latter category, such delegations began in the form of authorizing the president to modify tariffs unilaterally in response to tariff modifications, either increases or decreases, by foreign nations.[57] In the 1930s, they became authorizations allowing the president to modify tariffs via bilateral "reciprocal trade agreements."[58]

the case on other grounds and may have thought that the executive in fact did possess an inherent power to sign trade agreements. See John H. Jackson, William J. Davey, and Alan O. Sykes, *Legal Problems of International Economic Relations* (St. Paul, Minn.: West, 1995) at 105–6, citing Bernard Schwartz, *Super Chief: Earl Warren and His Supreme Court* (New York: New York University Press, 1983) at 165–6 (which quotes a memo from Frankfurter).

[55] See *Curtiss-Wright, supra* note 39 at 315 and 318 arguing that powers that fall "within the category of foreign affairs" as "powers of external sovereignty" are the "powers to declare and wage war [notwithstanding Art. I, sec 8, cl.11], to conclude peace, to make treaties, to maintain diplomatic relations with other sovereignties. . . . "

[56] 276 U.S. 394 (1928). The *Tariff Act* of September 21, 1922 (the "flexible tariff provision") provided that "in order to regulate the foreign commerce of the United States and to put into force and effect the policy of Congress by this Act intended, whenever the President, upon investigation of the differences in costs of production of articles wholly or in part the growth or product of the United States and of like or similar articles wholly or in part the growth or product of competing foreign countries" shall find that tariffs do not equalize the cost of production between that in the United States and that in other countries, he shall raise or decrease the rate in order to "equalize the same."

[57] See *Field v. Clark* and *The Brig Aurora.* In *The Brig Aurora,* 7 U.S. 382 (Cranch) (1809), the Supreme Court upheld the Act of March 1, 1809, expiring on May 1, 1810, forbidding importation of goods from Great Britain and France provided that the president, by proclamation, is authorized to revoke or modify these restrictions with these countries if they "revoke[d] or modifi[ed]" their trade laws "as that they shall cease to violate the neutral commerce of the United States." On May 10, 1810, Congress passed another law declaring that if Great Britain or France revoked or modified their trade laws "as that they shall cease to violate the neutral commerce of the United States, which fact the President of the United States shall declare by proclamation, and if the other nation shall not" then certain restrictions in the 1809 Act would be revived. In *Field v. Clark,* 143 U.S. 649 (1892), the Supreme Court upheld the *Tariff Act* approved Oct. 1, 1890, 26 Stat. 567. The Act imposed tariffs on woolen dress goods, apparel, silk embroideries and laces, and colored cotton cloth but provided that the president could suspend provisions of the Act allowing duty-free entry of certain goods and levy duties on such goods as provided by statute, if he finds that the exporting country has imposed duties on U.S.-made like goods that "he may deem reciprocally unequal and unreasonable."

[58] See the *Reciprocal Trade Agreements Act* of 1934, 73 Stat. 943 (1934), and subsequent renewals.

These cases all suggest an interpretation of the "foreign affairs power" that would look upon the coordination of Congress and president in the international sphere with utmost priority and uphold any arrangements worked out between the two branches to realize such coordination. In other words, this interpretation of the foreign affairs power would privilege efficiency and expertise over transparency and openness. And yet, there is certainly a potential strain of jurisprudence that is less passive toward areas implicating foreign affairs when they also implicate issues of domestic law. This strain would follow *Youngstown Sheet & Tube Co.*, which prohibited executive intrusion for purposes of international expediency into a domestic labor relations dispute. Justice Frankfurter expressed this sentiment in his concurrence to *Youngstown*:

> A scheme of government like ours no doubt at times feels the lack of power to act with complete, all-embracing, swiftly moving authority. No doubt a government with distributed authority . . . labors under restrictions from which other governments are free. It has not been our tradition to envy such governments. In any event our government was designed to have such restrictions. The price was deemed not too high in view of the safeguards which these restrictions afford.[59]

Youngstown involved an executive order that exceeded and therefore defied the instructions of Congress as laid out in other statutory delegations. It could be argued that a president who exceeded the bounds of congressional instructions in the initial grant of trading authority and then attempted to use the fast-track procedure to implement the final agreement would have exceeded his authority in a similar way. There is, of course, the fact that in the fast-track procedure, the retention by Congress of the ultimate power to approve or disapprove implementing legislation would seem to resolve any possible question of presidential excess. Congress could simply refuse to ratify such a transgressive proposal.

The counterargument might begin with the observation that, at least according to some commentators, this is easier said than done. Members of congress are under a great deal of pressure to ratify agreements,[60] as even fast-track proponents have recognized.[61] Moreover, the sheer volume and complexity of the proposed agreements, seen by the majority of Congress for the first time when presented for ratification, arguably make it difficult for Congress to determine whether, in fact, the agreements exceed congressional instructions, due to the short period of time before the vote that the agreement becomes available to congressional review.[62] There is, therefore, at least an argument to be made that the fast-track procedure unduly constricts Congress's ability to hold the president to its initial instructions.

[59] See *Youngstown, supra* note 54 at 613.

[60] See 137 Cong. Rec. S6550-01, Proceedings and Debates of the 102nd Congress, First Session, Thursday, May 23, 1991, Extension of Fast-Track Procedures, at S6558 (Remarks of Sen. Packwood) (describing fast track as a "gun at our heads"); 137 Cong. Rec. S6777-01, Proceedings and Debates of the 102nd Congress, First Session, Friday, May 24, 1991, Extension of Fast-Track Procedures, at S6778 (Remarks of Sen. Hollings) (also describing fast track as a "gun at our heads").

[61] See Koh, *supra* note 3 at 168 ("The Fast Track critics' most persuasive critique is of the President's tactic of *bundling* disparate trade proposals . . . and placing them before Congress for a single vote. Taken to the extremes, they argue, bundling makes it too painful for Congress to vote against a completed trade accord.")

[62] See Patti Goldman, "The Democratization of the Development of United States Trade Policy" (1994) 27 *Cornell Int'l L.J.* 631 (attributing reduced requirements in meat regulation following NAFTA to constraints on congressional review of implementation legislation).

There is also the fact that the contemporary delegations of trade legislation authority are quite different from those of *J. W. Hampton* and the Reciprocal Trade Agreements statutes. Modern trade agreements require legislation in areas that have historically been understood as domestic rather than international. They explicitly mandate, for example, modifications of intellectual property rights for domestic property rights holders,[63] government procurement law,[64] environmental protection law relating to domestic environmental regulation,[65] and health and safety regulation relating to domestic consumption.[66] One could move from this fact to the argument that, at least with respect to these areas, the fast-track procedure cannot only be understood as an exercise of the foreign affairs power but also as a delegation of *domestic* legislative power and, consequently, properly subject to higher levels of congressional participation.

While these doctrinal questions cannot be resolved through theories of constitutional interpretation standing alone, the question of how the courts would likely apply the doctrine is probably easier to resolve. The fast-track procedure is unlikely ever to come before the Supreme Court. If it did, it is entirely conceivable that the Court would refuse to adjudicate it, on the basis of the "political question" doctrine.[67] The Court has been notoriously unwilling to adjudicate questions relating to foreign affairs, to the dismay of many international legal theorists.[68]

CONCLUSION

There seem to be arguments available from constitutional theory both to support and reject the fast-track procedure. The primary difficulty underlying this question is that the process of making international trade agreements simply is not expressly

[63] For example, under the Uruguay Round, the patent term was extended to twenty years from seventeen years but made to start from date of filing rather than date of grant. Domestic interest groups were bitterly critical of this measure, arguing that it reduced their actual term of protection significantly.

[64] See *Uruguay Round Agreement on Government Procurement.* Agreement on Government Procurement, Apr. 15, 1994, Marrakesh Agreement Establishing the World Trade Organization, Annex 4B, Legal Instruments – Results of the Uruguay Round, vol. 31, 1915 U.N.T.S. 103 (1994), available at http://www.wto.org/English/docs_e/legal_e/52-dproc.pdf.

[65] An example is the gasoline case finding EPA standards in violation of Article II. See World Trade Organization, Report of the Appellate Body, United States – Standards for Reformulated and Conventional Gasoline, WT/DS2/AB/R (April 29, 1996). This is distinct from "extraterritorial" environmental measures that disallow imports not produced in accordance with U.S. standards, such as those addressed by the "Tuna–Dolphin" (World Trade Organization, Report of the Panel, United States – Import Prohibition of Certain Shrimp and Shrimp Products, WT/DS58/R (May 15, 1998), 37 *I.L.M.* 832 (1998); World Trade Organization, Report of the Appellate Body, United States – Import Prohibition of Certain Shrimp and Shrimp Products, WT/DS58/AB/R (Oct. 12, 1998), 38 *I.L.M.* 118 (1999) and "Shrimp–Turtle" decisions (World Trade Organization, Report of the Appellate Body, United States – Import Prohibition of Certain Shrimp and Shrimp Products; Recourse to Article 21.5 of the DSU by Malaysia, WT/DS58/AB/RW (Oct. 22, 2001); see also World Trade Organization, Report of the Panel, United States – Restrictions on Imports of Tuna, GATT Doc. DS29/R (May 20, 1994), 33 *I.L.M.* 839 (1994); Report of the Panel, United States – Restrictions on Imports of Tuna, GATT Doc. DS21/R (Aug. 16, 1991), GATT B.I.S.D. (39th Supp.) at 155 (1993)).

[66] See harmonization measures resulting from NAFTA and reducing domestic requirements for ensuring disease-free meat. Some argue that, in addition to such explicit modifications, trade agreements eventually impact the regulatory scheme in a much more fundamental way, by increasing international pressure to liberalize.

[67] See, e.g., *Made in the USA v. United States,* 242 F.3d 1300 (2001).

[68] See, e.g., Henkin, *Constitutionalism, Democracy and Foreign Affairs, supra* note 50.

addressed by the Constitution. This difficulty is strikingly similar to the difficulties posed by the rise of the administrative state earlier in the century. Now, as with the administrative state, a new form of government arises to respond to modern-day exigencies that were not contemplated, either explicitly or implicitly, at the time the Constitution was framed. Now, as with the administrative state, the consequence is that the question of the constitutionality of the new governmental structure must be determined with minimal assistance from the constitutional text. Now, as with the administrative state, principles of constitutionalism and democracy clash with modern-day exigencies in the struggle to resolve the issue. What emerged then was a fourth branch of government: administrative government. What emerges now is a fifth branch of government: "*internationalized*" government.

The above discussion shows that theories of constitutional interpretation rather than resolving the tensions within American democratic theory, simply reproduce them. Rather than stifling discourse on important political and constitutional questions, however, this conclusion of ambiguity encourages it in a way that is deeply democratic. If political and constitutional arguments cannot be objectively confirmed, then resolution of the fast-track debate can come only from straightforward and explicit political choice. This realization encourages rather than discourages – indeed, it necessitates – political debate and persuasion. Indeed, it opens for discussion a question whose honest confrontation has been too long avoided: How do we *want* the "fifth branch" of American government – "internationalized" government – to look?

5 Legislative Judgment and the Enlarged Mentality: Taking Religious Perspectives

Jennifer Nedelsky

Hannah Arendt outlined a preliminary theory of judgment in her lectures at the New School and in various essays. But she did not live to write the volume she had planned on judgment as the final volume to her work on thinking and willing.[1] In my earlier work, I have built upon her theory of judgment, primarily by looking at its implications for judgment in the judicial context.[2] Here, I return to her own primary interest, political judgment. In this chapter, I look at the importance of judgment for two of the central functions of the legislature in a constitutional state: the legislature as a locus of collective deliberation about the common good and the legislature as a participant in the ongoing, dynamic, and contested definition of core constitutional values. These functions are, in turn, linked to a third issue: the link between the ordinary practices of citizens and what we can hope for from a legislature.

The central concept in Arendt's theory, which she borrowed from Kant, is the enlarged mentality. Briefly put, what distinguishes judgment from both subjective preference and provable truth claims is that judgment involves reflection on the question at hand from the standpoint or perspective of others. Judgment as such remains subjective; it cannot compel the assent of others as truth claims can. But it can claim validity with respect to other judging subjects. It is the use of the enlarged mentality, the consideration of others' perspectives, that makes this validity possible. It is this exercise that distinguishes mere private opinion from valid judgment.

There are many unresolved questions about what this taking of others' perspectives entails, how exactly it works, whether it is possible at all. Here, I am going to bypass most of these questions and focus on one dimension of the question of

1 Arendt died just before beginning the volume on judgment, which was to be the third volume of *The Life of the Mind* (New York: Harcourt Brace Jovanovich, 1977). Her notes for lectures on judgment at the New School were published posthumously by Ronald Beiner as Hannah Arendt, *Lectures on Kant's Political Philosophy* (Chicago: University of Chicago Press, 1982) [Kant Lectures]. There is also an important early discussion of judgment in Hannah Arendt, "The Crisis in Culture" in *Between Past and Future* (New York: Meridian Books, 1963) section II, pp. 211–26 [Arendt, *Crisis in Culture*].

2 "Law, Judgment, and Relational Autonomy" in *Judgment, Imagination and Politics: Themes from Kant and Arendt*, Ronald Beiner and Jennifer Nedelsky, eds. (Lanham, MD: Rowman and Littlefield, 2001) 103; "Embodied Diversity: Challenges to Law" (1997) 42 *McGill Law Journal* 91. Also reprinted in *Judgment Imagination and Politics*; "Communities of Judgment and Human Rights" (2000) 1 *Theoretical Inquiries in Law* 245–82.

whose perspectives one should try to take. In particular, my project is to see how this approach to judgment helps in thinking about the optimal role of spiritually or religiously based argument in the exercise of two legislative functions: (1) deliberation on the common good and (2) the articulation and evolution of constitutional values. My argument will be that both of these require the exercise of judgment by legislators (and by citizens) and that the optimal use of the enlarged mentality in these contexts will include trying to take the perspective of those who see their engagement with public policy issues in religious terms.

Before I begin my argument, let me offer a brief clarification. In making this argument, I am under no illusions that religion is always a force for the good. If one looks at history since the beginning of the Christian era, I would say that organized religion has probably done more harm than good.[3] And even religiously based argument need hardly be benign. Any feminist in the twenty-first century knows that. Throughout the world, there have been religiously based policies and rhetoric that have been terrible for women. Currently in both the United States and Canada, the religious interventions that one hears most about do not promote policies I would support. Moreover, these interventions are often not made in ways that promote respectful public deliberation and mutual understanding. But part of my point is that if the norms of public discourse were to change to invite religious argument from a wide variety of perspectives, this distortion might shift. What I think of as negative voices are heard anyway. If they became one among many diverse examples of religious argument, they would not have the disproportionate volume they now do. In any case, I believe my argument stands even though some of the voices that will be heard will not be making arguments with the constructive potential that I point to here. That is true of all norms that foster open democratic dialogue.

Finally, a caveat that I will return to briefly at the end of the chapter: My argument is situated in a particular historical context; I do not claim its validity for all times and places. In Canada and the United States, we come out of a history (whose details I do not claim to know) in which religion was once an obvious and dominant force in society and politics. These forces coexisted with the development of constitutional traditions in both countries with strong (but different) norms of separation of church and state. At the beginning of the twenty-first century, we find ourselves at a juncture in which there are strong norms of secularism around public discourse at the same time that religion plays, in certain locations and contexts, an increasingly powerful and contested role in public debate. My view is that neither the secularist norms nor the most vocal of the religious voices provide us with a good model for reflecting on optimal contemporary norms for religiously based argument in the public sphere. I believe that finding such norms is important and pressing because religiously based policy positions are of increasing importance both in North America and around the world. My claim here is that thinking

3 My emphasis here is on *organized* religion. I have in mind such things as the Crusades, the Inquisition, witch-burning, the religious wars of Europe, and destructive missionary practices such as the residential schools that aboriginal children were forced to attend in North America. Although a real calculation of harms and benefits is probably impossible, I think it is plausible that such widespread harms outweigh the salutary interventions of organized religion in such areas as the antislavery movement.

about legislative functions in terms of judgment and the enlarged mentality will contribute to the development of such norms.

I. LEGISLATIVE FUNCTIONS: FORMULATING CONSTITUIONAL VALUES AND COLLECTIVE DELIBERATION ON THE PUBLIC GOOD

Let me begin by briefly sketching what I have in mind when I refer to these two legislative functions. Let me begin with the ongoing formulation of constitutional values. I take as my starting point that core constitutional values, such as equality, dignity, security of the person, or liberty, are broad concepts that require ongoing formulation both at a level of high abstraction – such as formal versus substantive equality – and in terms of general categories – say, whether economic equality is part of the constitutional mandate – and in terms of concrete application in particular cases, such as whether the absence of sign language interpreters in hospitals is a violation of equal access to health care. In both Canada and the United States the practical, legal meaning of equality has changed over time at all these levels. That is as it should be, indeed as it must be given the nature of language, of conceptual frameworks, and the dynamic nature of human societies. Although legal scholars tend to focus on the role of the courts in this process of articulation and evolution of the meaning of core values, the legislatures have a role to play as well. Indeed, the whole political system, including the casual public discussions and deliberations of citizens, plays a role in this process. Legislatures, and legislators, should be in ongoing interaction not just with the courts but with all the other forums of public deliberation about the meaning of the core values. Sometimes the debate focuses around big changes, such as the role of women and the meaning and value of gender equality, or the rights of racialized peoples to be free from discrimination, or whether access to marriage is entailed in true equality for gays and lesbians. At other times, the changes are smaller, subtler, such as the rights of welfare recipients to be free of certain kinds of surveillance and invasions of privacy. Some, like this last example, shift back and forth as government policies come and go, are challenged, come back in different forms.

At whatever level the debate and transformation is taking place, legislators should be making law and policy with at least intermittent conscious reflection on constitutional values and what they think the best understanding of them is, in both abstract and concrete terms. Of course, one of their central tasks is to think about how to translate constitutional values into concrete policy. Because of the focus on courts that judicial review gives rise to, this thinking is often focused (when it exists at all) on the question of whether a given law can withstand constitutional scrutiny, that is, whether it violates constitutional values. But, in fact, the legislative task is a broader one. The big constitutional values of equality, dignity, liberty, security need to be given realization through policies designed to promote these values, not just to refrain from violating them.

I shall shortly be arguing that this task involves judgment and thus attending to the perspectives of others, including those whose "standpoint" is religious or spiritual. But to prefigure part of this argument, I want to note at this point that I think one needs to be open-minded about what might be useful perspectives to take, what might be useful sources in the ongoing consideration of the best meaning and implementation of, say, equality. Even views or frameworks that do not seem consistent with the existing conceptions of liberal democracy may have something important to offer. Thus, Stephen Macedo's glib confidence that nothing will be lost if certain nonliberal communities of belief wither under the constraints of the liberal state seems (at the least) shortsighted.[4] Many different traditions treat dignity and equality as core values. The fact that they have not signed onto a particular conception of liberalism does not mean that they have nothing important to offer to the ongoing reflection about the optimal meaning and implementation of these values. In addition, because legislatures are not restricted to the implementation of constitutional values, reflection on the ways in which a value such as compassion may contribute to the optimal realization of equality and dignity may be assisted by considering spiritual traditions not firmly rooted in liberalism.

My primary focus will be on the second legislative function, collective deliberation on the common good or the public interest. Of course, some might dispute this as a reasonable objective for legislatures. If the marketplace of ideas coupled with bargaining over competing interests is itself supposed to yield the public good, then my argument would not work. The issue is whether one thinks that the public good *is* what emerges from fair bargaining, or whether it has an independent meaning that requires deliberation and discernment on its own terms – and whether the term "fair" here also simply takes its meaning from bargaining and negotiation. (I might note that in the American context, James Madison was ambivalent on this question, sometimes arguing for a system that would optimize bargaining through representatives and sometimes arguing for a system that would return the kind of representatives capable of discerning and advancing the public good. Canada has a clearer tradition of the public good as an objective of government.)

I think it is likely that any legislative system will involve ongoing bargaining over interest and advantage. Perhaps that will even dominate some of the time. But, in my view, good government requires attention to and serious deliberation about the public good. If a system relies on bargaining alone, those with greater bargaining power will prevail. And because no existing system of democratic constitutionalism has yet solved the problem of the interpenetration of economic and political power, bargaining alone will lead to skewed results. But even aside from that consideration, the public good is a conception that requires a different kind of reflection than bargaining over competing interests. It requires the articulation of (contested) visions of an optimal society, of optimal relations among citizens, optimal relations with other nations, and an optimal relation with the natural environment.[5] Particular policies and laws must be considered in the context of such a larger vision. And, conversely, it is the task of legislators to figure out how to translate their vision of the public good into concrete, workable policies. (It is also part of their task to figure out how to effectively engage with the bargaining process to gain backing for

[4] Stephen Macedo, "Transformative Constitutionalism and the Case of Religion: Defending the Moderate Hegemony of Liberalism" (1998) 26:1 *Political Theory* 56.

[5] Danielle Allen makes a persuasive case that polities often require sacrifice from some subset of their population. Part of what is important is that, over time, the call for sacrifice is distributed fairly, that one group is not repeatedly called on to sacrifice for the rest. I think this is another arena in which the enlarged mentality is important for judgment about the collective good. One needs to be able to take the perspective of others in order even to recognize their sacrifice. *Talking to Strangers: Anxieties of Citizenship since Brown v. Board of Education* (Chicago: University of Chicago Press, 2004).

their preferred policies. But I will not be addressing the kind of strategic judgment involved in that skill.) Even outside of the bargaining mode, the inevitability of limited resources means there will be difficult choices among different ways of promoting the public good. And, of course, the kinds of resources the government can command through taxation are themselves a key part of a conception of the public good and the role of government in promoting it. Each dimension of this reflection and deliberation on the public good requires judgment.

There is one other dimension of the public good that requires emphasis here. The core constitutional values that I mentioned as part of the first legislative function have in the Anglo-American tradition been conceptualized primarily in terms of individual rights. Although this is less true in Canada than in the United States, an individualistic conception of rights is powerful in Canada as well. Seeing the role of the legislature in a constitutional state as a primary locus for collective deliberation about the public good is an important counter to this individualism. Of course, one could define the public good exclusively in terms of the protection of individual rights. But even in the United States, such common dimensions of the public good as prosperity and national security can only be recast in terms of individual rights with considerable distortion. Generally, and appropriately, the idea of the public good is itself a collective rather than an individual value. Optimal legislative deliberation will thus be in the context of attention to the interactive process of fashioning a vision of the public good and considering policies to implement it. That means that the (periodically) simultaneous consideration of the meaning and implementation of core constitutional values will take place in a context, unlike that of the courts, in which the public good is a regular (if not completely routine) part of the discourse.

I do not mean to sound either naïve or overly optimistic about what the actual practices of legislative decision making look like or could look like under existing institutions. But for my purposes here, I think it is useful to think about what the role of the legislature *should* be, as long as it not impossible within existing institutions. The kinds of reflections on core values and the common good that I have in mind here seem to me to be entirely possible and occasionally practiced. (Such reflections might also provide guidance about changes in institutions and practices that could facilitate the exercise of these functions, but that is not my focus here.)

As I have already noted, reflecting on the meaning of core constitutional values and on the public good both require judgment. In Arendtian terms, these functions meet the criteria of the kind of issue that involves reflective judgment: The truth or rightness of answers to these questions cannot be proven, but neither are they merely a matter of subjective preference. Those who argue that equality should, say, be interpreted in a substantive rather than merely formal way make a claim of validity for their position. They believe that this position is not merely their preference, but a position that would be shared by those who exercise their judgment well. That is the mark of true judgment.

I think it is also helpful to note that in more colloquial terms judgment is seen as necessary for these functions. For example, in Stephen Elkin's article about what fosters public spiritedness in citizens and legislators, he repeatedly invokes the role of judgment.[6] His arguments are interesting in our context here because he

[6] "Citizen and City: Locality, Public-Spiritedness, and the American Regime" in Martha Derthick, ed., *Dilemmas of Scale in America's Federal Democracy* (Cambridge: Cambridge University Press, 1999) 37.

reminds us that some dimension of public spiritedness is entailed in the capacity to deliberate about the public good. And although he is not using Arendt's approach to judgment, he notes that the capacity to consider an issue from another's perspective, to recognize that one's own interests and perspectives are not the only relevant considerations, are essential to public spiritedness and deliberation on the public good. (Elkin is particularly interested in the ways in which legislators' capacity to deliberate on the public good is dependent on citizens' capacity for public spiritedness – a connection I will touch on later in my argument.) In this article Elkin does not address the legislative role in the articulation of constitutional values, but I think that a similar argument applies. The capacity to reflect on optimal conceptions of core value requires an ability to think in terms larger than self-interest. Although one might say that human rights are ultimately in everyone's interest, the importance – and validity – of a substantive conception of equality, or more particularly of, say, the availability of sign language or of access to legal marriage may be clear to some only by virtue of their capacity to think from the perspective of others.

II. THE ENLARGED MENTALITY: TAKING OTHERS' PERSPECTIVES

As I noted above, there are many puzzles involved in what it means to take the perspectives of others in the exercise of the enlarged mentality. For example, Arendt (in the existing articles and lectures) says virtually nothing about what actually enables one to do this. She does make clear that she does not mean canvassing the opinions of others. Indeed, it is not even the judgments of others that one should take into account. The task is to think about what one's own judgment would be from the standpoint of another. And she is clear that it is the particularities of another's standpoint that matter. She says that each person has their own standpoint, "actually, the place where they stand, the conditions they are subject to, which always differ from one individual to the next, from one class or group as compared to another."[7] The enlarged mentality relies on our imaginative capacity to put ourselves in the position of another. And most of what she has to say is about the use of imagination in this context.

It seems clear to me, however, that each person's ability to so use their imagination depends on the extent to which they have informed themselves about the standpoint they want to consider. As Elizabeth Spelman warns us, simply trying to imagine how things are for another is a dangerous exercise.[8] We are far too likely to project our own experiences, assumptions, values, and preferences onto others. There is, of course, an irreducible danger of some of this. But the better informed we are, the more experience we have of actual conversations with those whose perspectives we want to take into account, the more likely we can use our imaginations well when we reflect on multiple perspectives. Although Arendt said one wants to avoid simply replacing one's own prejudice and limited perspective with the limitations of someone else,[9] it seems likely to me that one can gain some

[7] Kant Lectures, *supra* note 1 at 43.

[8] *Inessential Woman* (Boston: Beacon Press, 1988) at 178–82.

[9] "To accept what goes on in the minds of those whose 'standpoint'... is not my own would mean no more than passively to accept their thought, that is, to exchange their prejudices for the prejudices proper to my own station." Kant Lectures, *supra* note 1 at 43.

important information even from becoming informed about the biases and undigested opinions of others. That is, even those who do not exercise the enlarged mentality themselves, who do not make true judgments as such, may have perspectives about which it is important to be informed in order to optimally exercise the enlarged mentality.

Arendt's description of standpoint quoted above might suggest external conditions. But she says, quoting Kant, that "'enlarged thought' is the result of first 'abstracting from the limitations which contingently attach to our own judgment,' of disregarding its 'subjective private conditions... by which so many are limited,' that is disregarding what we usually call self-interest.... " We enlarge our thought by "comparing our judgment with the possible rather than the actual judgments of others, and by putting ourselves in the place" of others.[10] The project is to ask oneself how one would judge from another's standpoint. Again, it seems clear to me that part of what constitutes our limiting, subjective private conditions is what might be called our mental standpoint, including our ideologies, assumed frames of reference, and core values. For many people, a key component of their mental standpoint is their religion or spiritual commitments. It would follow then, that in many instances the exercise of the enlarged mentality, essential for true judgment, would require considering this dimension of the standpoints of others. Presumably, different dimensions of others' standpoints are relevant to different kinds of judgment. But when it is the case either that one's own judgment or that of another is strongly influenced by their religious standpoint (which might include hostility to religion), then one's thought will not be adequately enlarged if one neglects trying to take account of this standpoint.

Of course, this claim about enlarging one's thought begs my central question here of how this approach is helpful in thinking about *legislators'* responsibilities to consider religious arguments and perspectives. If one starts with a version of the meaning of the secular state that stipulates that religion has no place in public, political discourse, then one might think that whatever limitation its absence places on the judgment of legislators is all to the good.

My purpose is to challenge such a stipulation by taking seriously both the Arendtian claim that judgment requires an enlarged mentality and the more colloquial claim that deliberation on the public interest requires a capacity to move beyond self-interest to the consideration of not just the interests, but the perspectives of others. (Here I am blending Elkin's argument with Arendt's.) But the question remains, whose perspectives should be considered and the particular question, whose perspectives should legislators consider.

III. THE BENEFITS OF TAKING RELIGIOUS PERSPECTIVES

I want to look at what some of the benefits might be of considering religious perspectives as well as what might be lost if legislators fail to do so. In asking these questions, one might want to distinguish between paying attention to the concerns of those who see issues in religious terms and the question of *how* one ought to engage their concerns. In particular, should trying to consider their standpoint include listening, in public contexts, to their own understanding of the issue in

[10] Ibid.

religious terms, that is, considering the religious basis for their positions? This would mean, for example, inviting explicitly religious arguments into public hearings or into the repertoire of positions considered through submissions to parliamentary committees, and perhaps even into parliamentary debate. Ultimately, I will argue that the benefits of considering religiously based positions are linked to the mode in which those holding these positions are encouraged to bring them forth. (Of course, nothing in this argument is about subjecting any form of argument to criminal sanction.[11] It is about optimal norms of public discourse, in light of the optimal functions of a legislature in a constitutional state.)

My argument is that in many instances, the religious content of arguments can benefit our collective capacity to deliberate about the public good for two reasons: (1) this content offers substantive arguments for considering the public good and (2) because the failure to engage with this content would preclude taking seriously the perspective of those who see their positions in religious terms. In a democracy, no group should be excluded from the range of perspectives legislators try to consider. Indeed, Arendt says (though she does not elaborate) that judgments are only valid for those whose perspectives one has taken into account.[12] The kind of judgment necessary for deliberation about the public good requires taking the perspectives of all the relevant groups into account, and this includes, in many instances, their "mental standpoint."

A. Taking the public good seriously

Let me begin with some of the substantive benefits that would follow from norms of public discourse that encouraged the articulation of arguments in the religious terms that were the chosen formulation of their authors. I take as my opening example *Lives in the Balance*, a "social audit" of people living on various forms of social assistance in Ontario, done under the auspices of a multifaith organization called the Interfaith Social Assistance Reform Coalition (ISARC).[13] I will then briefly consider "Guidelines for Christian political service and Charter of social rights and responsibilities" produced by Citizens for Public Justice (CPJ), "a Christian association seeking to hear and obey what God requires politically... [and] committed to honouring God and serving our neighbors in responsible cooperation with others through struggling to establish just relations."[14]

As I have said, Elkin correctly argues that deliberation on the public good requires a capacity to see that one's own interests or perspective are insufficient for the task. One has to recognize that trying to take others' interests and perspectives into account are an integral part of the public spiritedness that discerning and advancing the public interest requires. There are, however, powerful norms in virtually all areas of contemporary life that suggest that rational self-interest is the only thing

[11] I am not addressing here the contentious issue of whether there could be examples of religiously based argument – say, about homosexuality – that could amount to hate speech in Canada. This is something that some evangelical Christian groups are concerned about.

[12] "Hence judgment is endowed with a certain specific validity but is never universally valid. Its claim to validity can never extend further than the others in whose place the judging person has put himself for his considerations." Arendt, *Crisis in Culture, supra* note 1 at 221.

[13] Murray MacAdam and Interfaith Social Assistance Reform Coalition, Murray MacAdam, ed., *Lives in the Balance: Ontario's Social Audit* (Kitchener, ON: Pandora Press, 2004) [*Lives in the Balance*].

[14] Online: Citizens for Public Justice, www.cpj.ca/about/g_polserv.html.

anyone need consider in judging policy or life plans or individual choice. One can repeatedly see rational self-interest treated as the organizing concept for inquiry into all social relations, whether the economy, family, or politics. And this is true both in the academy and in popular discourse. It is not just that the focus on rational self-interest is pervasive; in the tenor of much of this discourse there is the implication that acting to advance the well-being of others, or the public good, or the social fabric of one's neighborhood or school is naïve or romantic, if not just a cynical play to disguise self-interest. Sophisticated adults should know better than to jeopardize their own interests by such naïve objectives, and they should certainly know better than to try to plan effective policy on the basis of anything other than a model of bargaining about self-interest.

Religiously based argument can provide an important countervailing norm. Such argument taps into a language of common good and responsibility for others that is familiar to many from their diverse religious backgrounds. In their religious contexts, the language does not sound foolish or naïve. It seems possible to me that this language, familiar to many from religious contexts, can serve to reinvigorate a political language of collective responsibility that still has a strong, if threatened and eroding, secular tradition in Canada.[15]

A closely related point is that religiously based argument frequently is moral argument. Public engagement with such argument would promote the idea that ethics should be taken seriously in public policy making.[16] The idea that ethical purposes should be central to many areas of policymaking is tacitly belittled by the prevalent language of politics as bargaining about self-interest using whatever power each person or group has available. By inviting religiously based argument into public forums, those advocating in these terms become not just another interest group to be bargained with, but a challenge to how to think about collective deliberation about policymaking.

For example, the debates around health care in Canada seem to me to take a variety of forms. Some of it is about efficient, cost-effective delivery of services. But the distinction that matters for my purposes here is between discussions that focus on whether Canadians feel confident that *they* will be able to have fast access to high-quality care when they need it and the discussion about whether we have a system that will provide quality health care to *all*. It is my sense that much of the public debate has shifted over the past ten years from the latter to the former, that is, from what I see as arguments addressed to a collective vision of equality to individual self-interest. It is interesting to note that both forms of argument can invoke the language of rights: the right of *all* Canadians to health care, on the one hand, and, on the other, the invocation of the fear that one's right to high-quality health care is being jeopardized by a public system that does not have the resources

[15] There can, of course, be dangers in policies guided by a notion of the public good. But my context is a constitutional state, in which core constitutional values take a strong institutional form in individual rights. The presence of these rights provides an important check to collective norms and pursuits. Optimally, legislatures engage in deliberation that addresses both, including potential tensions as well as complementarity between the two.

[16] Of course, there are also problems with the project of legislating morality. I will not be addressing the question of where to draw the line between the appropriate scope for ethical purposes of legislation and illegitimate, or even unadvisable, legislation of morality.

to ensure excellent, timely care. Thus, the claim that Canadians are committed to a right to health care is somewhat ambiguous.

I think the increased use of the language of self-interest reflects the relative impoverishment of the public language of collective responsibility and collective ethical commitments. *Lives in the Balance* offers an example of the use of religiously grounded argument to enrich this language. In its opening section on "Mandate and Mission," ISARC explains that it "has expanded its mandate beyond welfare to include the broader issues of poverty, hunger and homelessness," and that it "has met with political leaders and MPPs [members of the provincial parliament] from all parties, hosted hearings to give low-income people a voice . . . organized Queens Park [the Ontario legislature] forums for religious leaders and MPPs. . . . "[17] It says that it has taken up this cause because "faith communities believe that the moral core of faith traditions inspires a response. It is a message of compassion and love for our neighbour, and a call for justice. To be a person of faith is to understand that each human being has value and dignity that far transcends what society deems to be useful, practical, or affordable."[18]

They elaborate, offering the slightly different formulations of this commitment from the Christian, Jewish, Muslim, and Buddhist traditions.[19] Each is an invocation of individual and collective responsibility for the well-being of all:

> As Christians, our belief in community leads us to put aside selfish goals and private interests for the sake of the common good. We are to "love your neighbour as yourself" (*Matthew 22:24–40*), and take seriously Christ's command: "Whatever you did for the least of these you did it unto me." (*Matthew 25:40*)
>
> As Jews, we understand the pursuit of social justice to be the responsibility of every person and of the social institutions and government structures which we develop as part of living in community. We are to "Do unto others as you would have them do unto you." (*Leviticus 19:17*)
>
> As Muslims, the Qur'an affirms that the socio-economic welfare of the individual and of society depends upon the degree of justice and equity in the distribution patterns of income and wealth. The poor, too, have a right to the wealth of the nation and the community. (*The Qur'an 51:19*)
>
> As Buddhists, it is our duty and responsibility to educate and protect future generations, since we want to come back to a more enlightened society. "Hurt not others, in ways that you yourself would find hurtful." (*Udana-Varga 5:18*)

Part of what makes their arguments such important contributions is that they ground their position in claims about the fundamental interconnectedness of human beings: "We carried out our community-based social audit for all of us. Because what happens to those who are impoverished and marginalized affects us all. We are all affected and implicated in the deepening crisis of hunger, poverty, and homelessness in our communities and our province."[20] They suggest that if people listen to the stories of people in need, they will experience a sense of that

[17] *Lives in the Balance, supra* note 13 at 4–5.
[18] Ibid. at 6
[19] Ibid. at 6.
[20] Ibid. at 7.

implication: "It's difficult to read these accounts of how so many people are living on the edge of survival in our wealthy province without a sense of shame. What kind of society have we become when we allow this to occur? What values do we live by?"[21]

These claims and questions are posed in secular language. Indeed, part of the book's effectiveness is that it connects secular language recognizable by all with references to the spiritual basis for the moral commitments of the coalition. Faith traditions are invoked to account for their motivation, and they are offered as a way of understanding or seeing the interconnectedness that is the underpinning of their position. For example,

> It takes no philosopher to understand, however, that our very survival makes us critically dependent on each other.
> What stories and metaphors can help us clarify our vision? Most of our faith traditions are replete with stories about our relatedness to one another, to creation, to the Creator.
> In my tradition, one of the most helpful metaphors to describe how we are connected to one another comes from the Bible, in 1 Corinthians, chapter 12 . . . [the body] is not, we are told, in and of itself one part but many. . . . When one part of the body (society) suffers, every part suffers. When one part rejoices, so do all.

The author then returns to secular language, continuing with the metaphor:

> As those who get left out become more ill, it is not just as individuals that they find themselves deteriorating. This disease contributes to the dis-ease of the whole body politics, with a growing part of it becoming stressed, disabled, potentially malfunctioning and ineffective.[22]

While she says that it does not take a philosopher to understand our interdependence, she also says that it is "disheartening to see how easily interconnectedness is dismissed."[23] As a theorist who spends a lot of time trying to articulate the nature of this interdependence and its implications for law, I would not dismiss the contributions of philosophy. But the invocation of spiritual tradition allows for a vital shortcut. The authors do not have to try to spell out all the details of their vision of interconnection. They hope that the stories and metaphors that their various readers are familiar with from their different faith traditions will resonate with the short references they provide. Even more importantly, they hope that their own faith-based vision of interdependence and the mutual responsibility it entails will resonate with widespread, if submerged, values that Canadians hold:

> As poll after poll shows us, Canadians remain unwavering about the things we want to achieve together: reduce poverty, shelter the homeless, and deal with the degradation of the environment. These are the things we owe one another, the challenges we need to grapple with as a society. They are the determinants of health (tacitly invoking both the literal and metaphoric health of the body politic).[24]

Thus, the faith-based language is never offered as authority. The authors use it as a kind of spur to remind Canadians of their shared commitments, of what they know about the realities of interdependence, of their sense that they do care about

[21] Ibid. at 9.
[22] Ibid. at 13.
[23] Ibid.
[24] Ibid. at 16.

the kinds of values that we live by, about the kinds of values that our public policy reflects. For some it will remind them of their own faith-based values; for others it will resonate with similar values understood in secular terms. I take the project to be to use their faith-based values to help cut through a pattern of indifference and ignorance, to cut through the superficial self-evidence of self-interest as an adequate language of politics. It is a reminder that moral commitments entail collective responsibilities for the well-being of society, which requires particular attention to those least well off. The authors do not need or want to use their faith traditions as authority, because they assume that their readers (and Canadians generally) already share their core moral commitments. What is needed is a reminder that those commitments need to be translated into public policy, and, therefore, that ethical concerns with the well-being of others is an appropriate, indeed essential, component of deliberation about public policy. Although such reminders increasingly sound awkward or naïve in conventional public discourse, the invocation of a multifaith perspective allows a relatively easy avenue into the wider shared commitments of Canadians. By making increased public space for such arguments, the norms around all forms of arguments about collective responsibility and moral commitments may shift away from the dominant language of bargaining around self-interest.

Let me now briefly offer another example from the Citizens for Public Justice Guidelines for Christian Political Service. Under the heading of "Economic Enterprises," they offer the following:

> Although economic enterprises may seek reasonable profits and responsible returns to shareholders, they may never forget that their task is not to maximize such profits and returns. Enterprises are called by God to provide needed goods and services in a stewardly way, by means of creative, responsible and rewarding work, respecting the social and natural environment. Governments should by means of legislation, taxation, and regulation and advice guide and encourage economic enterprises to behave this way and protect their freedom and ability to do so.[25]

This seems to me another example of religiously based argument that both reinforces and offers additional credence to a view which polls suggest is widely shared by Canadians and yet not implemented in the law. There is a sharp disjuncture between the wider notion of responsibility that Canadians say they want corporations to assume and the law, which still privileges profit maximization in its conception of duty to shareholders.[26] As I see it, among the many obstacles to changing the law is the power of the notion of profit and rational self-interest as the only really viable tools of analysis for economic and social policy. If religious voices such as that of the CPJ were more widely heard, they would offer an alternative, which, like the examples in *Lives in the Balance*, would resonate with widely shared but underarticulated values.

[25] Online: Citizens for Public Justice, sss.cpj.ca/about/g_polserv.html.

[26] See Ronald Davis, *In Whose Interests? Democracy and Accountability for Pension Fund Corporate Governance Activity* (S. J. D. Thesis, University of Toronto, Faculty of Law, 2004). A summary of his argument is available in "The Enron Pension Jigsaw: Assembling Accountable Corporate Governance by Fiduciaries" (2003) 36 *U. B. C. L. Rev.* 541 at 574. He offers creative, practical arguments for changes in the laws outlining corporate responsibility as well as a system of giving the beneficiaries rather than corporate managers effective control of the vast pension funds corporations generate.

This particular example is linked to broader implications of the enlarged mentality for the public good. Arendt's understanding of political judgment is itself a challenge to a vision of politics as the forum for bargaining about interests. Judgment is distinct from preference and truly operates only when self-interest does not influence it.[27] The essence of reflective judgment is that it requires taking others' perspectives into account in order not to be limited by one's own interests and idiosyncrasies. It has an intrinsically social, public dimension to it, even though it is carried out in private via one's imagination. There is thus a reciprocally supporting relationship between genuine deliberation about the public good and the exercise of the enlarged mentality for the purposes of true judgment: The more politics is understood as about the public good, the more people will see the need to consider the perspectives of others; and the more adept people are in exercising the enlarged mentality, the better equipped they will be to deliberate about the public good. In light of this, I want to return to the issue of why the enlarged mentality requires taking account of religiously based public argument.

B. The enlarged mentality and collective deliberation: Understanding the issues

The first reason this is required is the one I pointed to earlier: If one truly wants to see something from the perspective of another, and that perspective is heavily shaped by religious commitment or belief, then it will not be possible to take their perspective seriously without trying to understand it in those terms. And, as I argued earlier, taking account of another's perspective as one forms one's judgments, requires that one has acquired the relevant experience or information about that perspective. Hence one requires the experience of hearing, and trying to understand, another's position *in the religious terms in which they understand it.*[28] Thus, it will not be sufficient, in many cases, for people to translate their spiritually based ethical commitments into secular ones, even if it may be helpful for them to try to do so *in addition to* articulating their views on their own terms. Part of the usefulness of this additional exercise in translation is for both speaker and listener to notice where the translation is difficult or inadequate. In my example above of ISARC's *Lives in the Balance*, the translation seemed quite smooth and, indeed, it seemed part of their point to highlight the similarities between faith-based and secular moral commitments to the well-being of others and the "health" of society. What the standpoint in their faith traditions seemed to add was motivation and confidence about invoking moral commitments as part of public policy.

In the case of same-sex marriage, strictly secular conceptions of equality do not fully capture why many gay and lesbian couples believe that full equality requires access to marriage, not just some legal form of civil union that would provide the same legal benefits and obligations. Similarly, those opposed on religious grounds cannot fully capture the depth of their opposition in secular language. Both arguments reveal the complexity of an issue that has merged state and religious status

[27] I do not think the usefulness of this idea depends on believing that it is ever possible to free oneself of all influence of self-interest.

[28] I will later discuss the some of the special problems of doing this across religious beliefs, as discussed by James Boyd White.

for centuries. Both sides agree that to try to separate them now will not be fully satisfactory.

For some (certainly not all) of the gays and lesbians seeking access to marriage, part of what they want is access to a social institution that combines religious and legal meaning. For those who are members of religious communities, they want to have their vows recognized and celebrated within those communities in the same way as heterosexual couples. The reason is the religious meaning of marriage celebrated in their communities is important to them. This meaning cannot be provided either by an exchange of vows before the community that is not marriage, or by "marriage" within a religious community that is not recognized as marriage by the state. Marriage has a social, legal, and religious meaning that (for many) must be combined in order for them to enjoy equal status with heterosexual couples who can marry. Those who do not take seriously the religious meaning of marriage will not understand why "marriage" as such is important to this group of equality seekers.

One might say that this is just another way in which separate but equal can never be equal. But to understand why this is so requires not only a full understanding of the social significance of "marriage" (which a civil union is unlikely to replicate), but also the significance of the religious component for some. Thus, one cannot really take their perspective into account without trying to understand how it matters to them. And I think my abbreviated argument above will be insufficient for those to whom it does not automatically convey a sense of understanding of the significance of being excluded from an important religious ceremony or sacrament. I think it is important to read or hear the arguments of those who see the issue in these terms.

Something similar is true for those who oppose same-sex marriage on religious grounds. I think the opponents are particularly articulate about the depth of the social transformation this legal change would bring about – though, of course, it is in large part because of this transformation that many gays and lesbians feel strongly in favor of the change. The opponents understand and articulate the way the social significance of marriage is built upon its joint legal and religious meaning. To say that every religious community is free to define marriage as they see fit, but that the legal definition will include same-sex couples, is for some entirely unsatisfactory. Their definition (which they take to be God-given) would no longer be identical with the state definition (though theirs would be recognized legally).

In my view, an important part of what one gains from "listening" (from written text in my case) to the arguments of the opponents is the depth of their sense of loss and anger. At the same time, one can gain a clearer sense of how persuasive one finds their arguments – and thus how one will take account of their perspective. For example, David Novak makes an argument from an Orthodox Jewish perspective that I find internally inconsistent.[29] He insists that the meaning of marriage is inseparable from the potential for procreation. But he is unable to reconcile that view with his recognition that men and women past the age of childbearing marry, or that men and women who know that one of them is not capable of childbearing marry.

[29] David Novak, "Religious Communities, Secular Society, and Sexuality: One Jewish Opinion," in Saul M. Olyan and Martha Craven Nussbaum, eds., *Sexual Orientation and Human Rights in American Religious Discourse* (New York: Oxford University Press, 1998) 10.

He does not suggest that these are not "real" marriages. Of course, not long ago one could read similar arguments about marriage and procreation from Canada's judges. But they have since been discredited as inconsistent and unpersuasive. Novak also argues both that the meaning of marriage is God-given and thus cannot properly be changed by legislation and that (on the basis of sociological research) the meaning of marriage universally refers to a union of a man and a woman and thus cannot properly be given a different meaning. But the argument about why a state committed to equality should be bound in its legal definition of marriage by a religious meaning (even if one accepted that that particular meaning was God-given) is weak. The implication of claims about universal norms for law is treated as self-evident. I found far more persuasive the claim that adherents to orthodox religions that reject the idea of same-sex marriage will find themselves even further marginalized in society if there comes to be a disjuncture between their conceptions of marriage and that recognized by the state. (He also offers the implausible suggestion that Orthodox rabbis may refuse to perform marriages because they would not want anything to do with the tainted state version.)

By actually listening to the content of the religiously based argument, one can make better judgments about how to take account of it in one's own decision making, even when one is not part of that faith tradition. But even if one discounts Novak's position because it is unpersuasive and internally inconsistent, that does not mean one should discount the sense of loss and anger that he conveys. When legislators undertake reforms that involve deep social transformation, I think they are likely to do a better job overall if they take account of the sense of loss some will experience. This loss is not itself an argument against change. Most changes that advance equality by shifting long-standing patterns of advantage and exclusion will involve some real loss for those who once enjoyed unjust advantage. But the fact that the advantage was unjust does not mean that there is no need to attend to the depth of the loss, and thus pain and anger. And in the case of same-sex marriage, I do not think one can fully understand that loss and anger without listening to the religiously based objections.

In this case, it is not clear to me what exactly one should do with such understanding.[30] In Canada, I think the time for compromise via civil union is past. Perhaps the hardest question, which the Anglican Church in Canada is struggling with, is whether deep social change should go slowly when that means allowing inequality and exclusion to continue. I think that in some instances there can be ways of responding to the loss entailed in the ending of unjust practices. For example, in South Africa, the means provided for sustaining the Afrikaans language may be a way of responding to the loss of a way of life built on injustice. It remains to be seen whether the Supreme Court of Canada's decision in the "spanking case"[31]

[30] It might be part of an argument for getting the state out of marriage altogether. The state would provide civil unions for everyone (thus requiring good arguments about which forms of intimate relationship the state should support), and marriage would be left to religious and perhaps other nongovernmental organizations, none of whom would be state licensed or otherwise regulated or supported by government. One such argument has been made by Joel Marks, "Sacral rites and civil rights: A modest proposal (of non-marriage)," *New Haven Register* (*Milford Weekly* section) (March 11, 2004).

[31] *Canadian Foundation for Children, Youth and the Law v. Attorney General in Right of Canada*, [2004] 1 S.C.R. 76.

is an example of a compromise with unjust practices that allows for more gradual social transformation than an outright ban on corporal punishment of children (as an exception to the assault provisions of the Criminal Code). As in the South Africa example, the implication of taking loss seriously is not always the compromise of the rights of the disadvantaged. Sometimes one can find a response or compensation that does not compromise those rights. The point is that the potential for creative paths to social transformation is maximized if one does what one can to understand how all parties, including the opponents of changes proposed in the name of equality, see the issue. That potential is fostered by listening to religiously based argument.

C. The enlarged mentality and mutual respect

The central point above has been that optimal judgment is fostered by the exercise of the enlarged mentality, which, in turn, requires understanding how others see things. In the case of the religiously based policy positions, this usually entails listening to the argument in religious terms. There are also other related benefits for public deliberation. Listening to the arguments of those who see their positions as religiously grounded will often overcome prejudice and stereotypes. This was certainly my experience in my course on Law, Religion and Public Discourse, which includes students from law, political science, theology, and religious studies. The first year I taught the course, there were several evangelical Christians in the course. For example, in the very first weekly "comment on the readings" circulated to the class, one of the students said that her mission was to re-Christianize Canada and that she agreed with a statement in one of the readings that all religions worth their salt make universal and exclusive truth claims. When I had read that statement, I had experienced it as a direct affront to my own beliefs. An aboriginal student in the class noted that in her training in her community's spiritual tradition the first lesson taught is that all creation stories are true. I was worried about how we were all going to manage to talk to one another. But then that was the subject of the course. Over the course of the three months together, I think all the students not only treated each other with great civility and care but also came to respect each other. In my own case, I came to like, respect, and appreciate the woman who had so forthrightly and courageously stated her views in that first comment. I saw how important honesty and openness are in facilitating mutual understanding and that sometimes the great circumspection the class displayed slowed our capacity to engage with the hard issues. I think many found that they had had a set of unexamined assumptions about those with fundamentalist religious views that did not hold up after three months of sustained conversation. I also think (though I am less sure about this) that those with more orthodox or fundamentalist beliefs came to respect the spiritual and ethical commitment of those with different beliefs.

Public deliberation about the common good requires some basic level of mutual respect. I think a tacit policy of "don't ask, don't tell" with respect to the religious basis for one's views may foster a superficial respect born of avoidance of divisive issues. But generating norms of public discourse that include space for the respectful articulation of religious argument, met with respectful listening, will foster a deeper respect that is an important foundation for all the dimensions of constitutional democracy. There is surely a reciprocal influence between wider norms of public discourse and those of the legislature and its hearings. Citizens who are adept at this sort of exchange would foster that capacity in government and vice versa. This is just a particular example of the more general claim that Elkin elaborates, that if one wants legislators who are able to make good judgments about the collective good, then one needs citizens with a basic capacity to do so. And this capacity is closely tied to the ability to take others' perspectives into account.

D. Religious perspectives and cross-cutting values

An additional benefit of engaging religious argument is finding cross-cutting values, interests, and policy preferences. This is, of course, a version of James Madison's famous argument in *Federalist* 10. Part of what keeps a democracy from dangerously cleaving along major lines of conflict is the many cross-cutting interests that actually characterize a large polity. Governments have to be organized in ways that facilitate cooperation along these crosscutting lines. Providing public forums for religiously based argument would offer such facilitation. Of course, one often hears that inviting religiously based views into the public forum just invites deep divisiveness, irreconcilable conflict, and the inability to compromise because such deeply held values are at stake. But my own experiences arising out of my course suggest the opposite. Students were asked to provide what they thought were good examples of using religious argument in public debate. The same student who wanted to re-Christianize Canada offered a position paper from the Evangelical Fellowship of Canada (EFC) (a conservative Christian group) on reproductive technologies. What I was most struck by was their statement of the values they thought should guide the inquiry and their choice of language, rejecting the "reproductive material" phrase that is common in academic discourse on the topic. Some years back, I had written an article evaluating the usefulness of a property law framework for dealing with the myriad of legal conflicts that arise from the existence of frozen zygotes. I outlined very similar values and opted for the term "potential life" to describe the contested substances. Both they and I also felt compelled to add to our commentary on reproductive technology a brief statement of our views on abortion. Here we parted company completely. And we each argued that our views on abortion were consistent with the other positions we had outlined and that our position on abortion was important.

The new experience for me was that although we differed fundamentally on one key issue, abortion, we not only agreed on a variety of other policy positions, but we also agreed on the values that were at stake and how to express them. I discovered a hitherto completely unexpected ally on issues of importance to me. All I had known about (or anticipated) earlier was the point of our disagreement. As it turned out, there were both crosscutting shared values and interests and the possibility of more fruitful discussion about the point of disagreement.

I then had the same experience when I was researching religiously based argument about economic and social justice issues. I looked on the EFC Web site. Although the material about these issues is a little harder to find than the hot topics of same-sex marriage and the definition of hate speech (to include antihomosexual hate speech), it is there. I found a lot of invocations of Christian duty to help the poor, but I found it harder to pinpoint what I was looking for: their position on state responsibility for aiding the poor, the homeless, the disabled. For more detail, they recommended a Charter of Social Rights and Responsibilities produced by the Centre for Public Justice. This document, along with Guidelines for Christian Political Service, offers a very clear position on these issues, linking individual Christian responsibility to collective responsibility to state responsibility. I still do not know exactly where the EFC stands on these issues. Perhaps it is a point about which their members disagree. But in any case, they provided a path to another point of crosscutting interests. As the churches themselves found out some time ago in Canada,[32] strong disagreements on issues such as abortion do not preclude effective alliances around shared commitments to economic and social justice.[33]

As I just noted, it is not that members of religious communities do not know about the value of these cross-cutting interests. But open public forums for religiously based arguments would make these potential opportunities for alliance clear to the public at large. It would also make clear (what is also obvious within religious communities), that there is virtually no major contested issue about which there is consensus within or across religious groups. Thus, there is no issue, including same-sex marriage or abortion, that can properly be characterized as presenting a conflict between religious beliefs on the one hand and secular values, such as equality, on the other. There are disagreements within religions on all major issues.[34] And virtually no religious group would be willing to cede concern with equality to the secular realm. But these complexities are often obscured when there is only a very limited range of religious voices heard debating public policy.

Public debate open to religious argument would then dispel prejudice, open up awareness of crosscutting interests, and avoid false characterization of issues around a secular-religious dichotomy. Shifting the norms of public discourse would also have the effect of making space for a wider variety of religious voices than are currently widely heard in Canada (and I think in the United States). At present, I would say that those who suffer no hesitance, no anxiety about the complexity of mixing religion and politics, who feel comfortable proclaiming their deepest personal commitments in election speeches are those who make their voices heard. They come to stand for what it means to invite religious speech into the public forum.

[32] Roger Hutchinson, "Ecumenical Witness in Canada: Social Action Coalitions" (1982) LXXI:3 *International Review of Mission* 344–53. See also "Christian Social Action: The Coalition Model," 1988, presentation at Canadian Political Science Association, on file with author.

[33] For example, the *Toronto Star* reported that "Unlike their American neighbors, Canadian evangelical Christians vote across the political spectrum, from right to left. Conservative Protestants supported former NDP leader and social reformer Tommy Douglas for decades." They also note that contrary to what many might expect, polls show that "child poverty tops the list of issues of concern to evangelicals. But there is a splintering in how they should address the problem – some support government programs, others support more private solutions." They close the article with a quote by Bruce Clemenger, president of the Evangelical Fellowship of Canada (who provided the information on child poverty): "Clemenger says that church and state should be separate, but he says faith and politics cannot be. 'People of faith engage in public life from their world view which is invariably shaped by something deeper, a philosophy rooted in some vision of life.'" The same article notes that the head of the Islamic congress says, "Most Muslims don't consider gay or abortion rights the top issue in the campaign and are more concerned about housing and poverty." *Toronto Star* (June 26, 2004) A29.

[34] Of course, this raises the complicated issue of the differences between the views of adherents to a religion and the positions espoused by the official spokespeople for the religion. Madhavi Sunder offers a very thoughtful commentary on the question of who the law recognizes as speaking for a religion. "Piercing the Veil" (2003) 112:6 *Yale L.J.* 1399.

IV. THE DIFFICULTIES OF RELIGIOUS DISCOURSE

Here I want to return to the issue of the enlarged mentality from a different angle, to consider the difficulties of applying it in the ways I propose. James Boyd White has offered a thoughtful commentary on what it takes to have good dialogue among those of different faiths.[35] Although his concern is not about bringing religious dialogue into the public realm of the legislature, his discussion turns out to address the core issue of the enlarged mentality: the possibility of understanding another's perspective on religious belief when one does not share those beliefs. He argues that at some level words alone cannot communicate one's perspective in this context. And yet, using an example of poetry, he very poetically and effectively suggests that important verbal communication is possible. In thinking about the project of understanding a different faith perspective, it is important both to acknowledge a kind of impossibility of the enterprise and the value of the effort if undertaken in the right way. I think one might say the same thing about all versions of the attempt to understand another's perspective. That is part of what makes White's commentary so useful.

A. Intimate beliefs, truth claims, and pluralism

There are particular aspects of religious belief that make the communication difficult. White says that religious beliefs are difficult to talk about. Certainly, that is both my own experience and an observation one often sees.[36] Yet part of the puzzle of thinking about optimal norms of public discourse – both in the legislature and more generally, as they are mutually sustaining – is that there seems to be some kind of radical disjuncture between this common experience of awkwardness and difficulty on the one hand, and, on the other, the willingness of some to proclaim their religiously based positions on public policy loudly and apparently confidently. Envisioning optimal norms requires taking account not only of the difficulty for many, but also the ease for some.

White points to another issue in what it takes to understand another's religious perspective that is relevant in trying to use the idea of judgment and the enlarged mentality in the context of optimal legislative discourse. He discusses the deep tension that can exist between commitment to one's own beliefs and the interest in engaging respectfully with the beliefs of others. He says that for many their religion is "the absolute, unique and eternal truth. All other religious are false." Initially, he says that "this position is, I think, impossible for the person who engages seriously with the religious life of others." But he goes on to offer an example of someone who finds a way of sustaining the tension. Of course, he is talking about a deeper kind of communication than what I think is required in a legislative context. But his point remains an important one. Too many people would be excluded from the dialogue

[35] "How Should We talk About Religion? Inwardness, Particularity, and Translation," Occasional Papers of the Erasmus Institute, 2001 series, Number 1.

[36] For example, Tom Levinson, author of *All That's Holy: A Young Guy, an Old Car, and the Search for God in America* (San Francisco: Jossey-Bass, 2003), comments, "It's ironic: our faith is of bedrock importance to most of us, yet often we feel skittish publicly broaching the subject. Given our differences, our sensitivities, as a culture we're uncertain how to engage others in a discussion about it." "Road to Religion," Chicago Journal, Q&A, *University of Chicago Magazine* 96:4 (April 2004), also online, University of Chicago Magazine, online: http://magazine.uchicago.edu/0404/campus-news/qa.shtml.

if the requirement for respectful communication were that it was available only to those who did not see their religious beliefs in universal and exclusive terms. Both those who should exercise their enlarged mentality and people whose perspectives are to be taken into account must include those whose beliefs are exclusive and universalistic in ways that are offensive to others or simply incompatible with their beliefs.

All spiritual traditions make some kind of truth claims, though, of course, there are traditions that do not presuppose that their understanding of the divine or the transcendent is the only valid one. The Dalai Lama, for example, commented that he thought that the plurality of religious beliefs in the world was a good thing.[37] Others argue for respect for the plurality, but not because it is a good thing that there are many different approaches to spiritual truth (as the Dalai Lama suggested), but because respectful norms will ultimately enable their own one truth to be recognized and prevail.[38] The problem that universalistic religious truth claims pose for my argument is that they often seem in tension with the mutual respect that underlies the use of the enlarged mentality. Sometimes this tension is of the kind that White points to: It is deep and difficult, but resolvable in respectful practice. Other times, the claims of exclusive hold on the truth– with consequences, for example, of eternal bliss or damnation – are, or will be heard to be, incompatible with real mutual respect. This dimension of religiously based argument must be acknowledged in any effort to include such argument in the norms of public discourse.

I find this the hardest issue in thinking about an optimal role for religion in public discourse. Because the understanding of the nature of truth claims and their relation to religious plurality are themselves so central to many people's theology, no particular stance toward those truth claims can be a condition for participation in the public discourse. Those whose stance toward pluralism is closer to the Dalai Lama's will fit more easily into a model of democratic deliberation that makes space for religiously based argument. But the model must also accommodate those who make explicit, implicit, or covert claims of exclusive grasp of universal truths.

Although the norms of public discourse cannot require a pluralism like the Dalai Lama's, I think there is hope for civil conversation about religiously founded policy commitments because the kinds of policy debates relevant to legislative functions will rarely, if ever, require delving into deep theological foundations for people's positions. The norms of public discourse can encourage people to recognize the difference between evangelism and the opportunity to articulate one's position, including its religious basis. The purpose of the latter is to allow one's perspective to be adequately heard – for all the reasons outlined above – and not to convert others to one's faith. Thus, one need not, and should not, elaborate on one's beliefs beyond what is necessary to explain one's view. And prudence and mutual respect might also foster norms of using as general a theological foundation as remains

[37] Honorary degree address presented to the University of Toronto, June 2004 [unpublished].

[38] Jonathon Chapman, "Faith in the State: The Peril and Promise of Chritian Politics" (1999: Institute for Christian Studies, Toronto), footnote 34 at 32: "I am not suggesting that 'religious pluralism'– the fact of a diversity of radically incompatible religious viewpoints – is itself a normative state of affairs. Such a situation of spiritual fragmentation must, from a Christian point of view, be seen as a consequence of the fall."

true to one's understanding of one's position. *Lives in the Balance*,[39] for example, used very little contentious theological argument to ground their recommendations. This was much less true of Novak's argument against same-sex marriage.[40] Although my strongest ground for rejecting it was internal inconsistency, it also posed the problem of why a particular theological understanding of God's purpose for marriage should be legally imposed on everyone. The more specific and contentious the foundation for a position, the less persuasive it is likely to be. This does not, however, mean that such arguments breach the norms of public discourse. Novak's argument required that particular theological foundation, and so it was appropriate. Indeed, part of the virtue of bringing religious arguments into the public realm is to enable everyone to differentiate between different kinds of religious foundations for positions – some of which will resonate with a wide variety of beliefs and some of which will not.

B. Unreason and divisiveness

The question of the nature and scope of religious foundations for public policy positions brings up another dimension of the problem of mutual respect in deliberations that include religiously based argument. While I said earlier that ideological differences can yield plenty of mutual contempt, I think the view of religion as the antithesis of reason can bring out a particularly naked form of hostility and contempt. Perhaps this is more common among academics (many of whom revere reason as something akin to sacred) than in the population at large. In any case, both the substance of their objections and their affect need to be addressed if we are to envision a respectful public discourse that includes religiously based argument. I take it that the core of the objection is that no one should take seriously an argument whose premises are not open to debate. And, furthermore, that one should doubt the likelihood of any argument based on faith rather than reason yielding anything useful or persuasive. (I shall return to this issue below.)

First, I think it is fair to say that generally when people offer a religiously based position, they are not inviting a debate about their underlying religious commitments. But it is also generally the case that when people make arguments about the requirements of equality, they are not inviting a debate about the equal moral worth of all human beings. More generally still, most people reason from core premises rather than debate them – whether those premises are secular or religious. Indeed, I think it is open to reasonable debate whether one can reason across premises, whether reason can change core premises or enable one to communicate when core premises are not shared. It is true that there are some academics (and others, I suppose) who are interested in debating all the premises that ground their own and others' intellectual frameworks. But in the ordinary course of debates about public policy, this is neither necessary nor useful. In that sense, the fact that people are not holding their foundational religious beliefs out for debate when they ground their policy views on them does not distinguish them from those who causally rely on the liberal commitment to equal moral worth. Most of what is up for debate is about

39 *Supra* note 13.

40 Novak, *supra* note 29.

what flows from a commitment to, say, equality, not the underlying commitment itself, whether secular or spiritual.

There can, of course, be debates about the appropriateness of a special commitment to, say, the least well off or most vulnerable in a community, and there can be a variety of justifications for it such as that offered by Rawls or the spiritually based organic community arguments of *Lives in the Balance*.[41] In part because *Lives in the Balance* was a multifaith project, it does not rely on one (inevitably contested) scriptural source, and it offers a metaphor of organic community that can make sense even to those who share none of the faith commitments of its authors. I think it does make itself open to debate about the value of the idea of a community where the "ill health" of any will affect/infect the whole. The multiple possible starting points for this idea of community may not matter. It is true that those who think this idea is not open to debate because there is scriptural authority for it will not be able to participate in the fullest possible debates on the subject. But I doubt whether this failure to engage will actually interfere with constructive legislative debate about, say, optimal welfare systems any more than the nonmeeting of the minds of Rawlsians and Nozickians. In sum, I think the fact that those who offer religiously based argument are generally not prepared to engage in debate about the deep religious foundations of their arguments does not radically distinguish them from either a general unwillingness to question core premises or from the difficulty people experience in communicating effectively when they do not share the same secular premises or theoretical or ideological frameworks. It is not therefore good grounds to dismiss their arguments.

C. Religion as authority

The issue of scriptural authority mentioned above is one of the most common concerns about including religiously based argument in democratic deliberation. Of course, some such argument will invoke the authoritative commands of scripture as the (usually nonnegotiable) basis for their position. I take Novak's argument to be an example of this. (He tries to support his position by anthropological claims that marriage everywhere has always meant a union of man and a woman, but the heart of the argument is his claim about God's intention.) But the existence of such claims seems to lead to a vast overstatement or misunderstanding of the *necessary* role of authority in religiously based argument and sometimes with a further confusion between a claim about the nature of the argument and a concern about particular arrangements of political power.

As I see it, there are two problems of authority-based argument. The first is a political problem that this chapter does not address: when authority-based arguments are backed by significant political power, such as the power of the Catholic Church in some Latin American countries.[42] Such combinations of authority and power may really foreclose democratic debate. And the effective enforcement of authority positions via political power may become a form of coercion. I can certainly see why some would want to exclude religious argument from public debate in these contexts. (Remember that I am not making universal claims for the

[41] *Supra* note 13.

[42] I would like to thank the graduate students who attended the Yale Legal Theory Workshop for helping me to see this issue.

usefulness of my arguments here.) But, in Canada and the United States, whatever the political power of the Christian right[43] it does not have the concentrated institutional power that would justify norms of exclusion of religious argument from public debate.

It is important to distinguish this political problem from the second issue: a more general misunderstanding about the nature of religious argument. There is a fairly widespread and firmly held view that religiously based arguments are inherently authority based. (I have most often heard this position from people who are not religious but have firm views about the nature of religion.) As I will argue below, that is factually incorrect. Even those who see some of their views as authority based will not see all of their religiously informed positions in authority terms, or the authority – for example, humans should be stewards of God-given creation – is so broad that it does not dictate policy in any simple way. For many, the effort to discern what actions or policies their spiritual commitments direct them to is not an effort to apprehend an authoritative command.

As we have seen in *Lives in the Balance*, not all people who understand their positions to be grounded in spiritual commitment make arguments from authority. For example, one of the authors suggests that faith traditions offer stories and metaphors about "our relatedness to one another, to creation, to the Creator" that can help us to clarify our understanding of human interdependence and the responsibilities that flow from it.[44] She treats the interdependence itself as a fact that needs neither philosophy nor scriptural authority to ground it. And she does not suggest that the details of how that responsibility should be undertaken and implemented are to be found in divine command. As she puts it, the "central teachings of compassion and love for neighbor, shared among Ontario's religious communities, form the moral imperative that inspires people of faith to respond to our neighbours in need."[45] It is the sense of moral imperative and not divine command that they want to contribute to collective deliberation:

> The moral dimension of this issue [homelessness] is so important. There are plenty of economic arguments that it's cheaper to build housing than put people in shelters. Yet it's cruel to reduce people to economic units. I believe that the vast majority of Canadians feel a fundamental moral repugnance when they see people forced to live and die on the streets of Canada. The faith community can continue to play a prophetic role by emphasizing the ethical issues at stake.[46]

The authors of *Lives in the Balance* do not need or want to use their faith traditions as authority, because they assume that their readers (and Canadians generally) share their core moral concerns. What is needed is a reminder that those moral commitments need to be transformed into public policy, and therefore that ethical concerns with the well-being of others is an appropriate, indeed essential component of deliberation about public policy. Although such reminders sound somewhat awkward (or naïve) in conventional public discourse, the invocation of a multifaith perspective allows a relatively easy avenue into the wider social commitments of Canadians.

[43] And the "unholy alliances" with minority religions in ethnic communities; see Saeed Rahnema, "Unholy alliance on the right," *Toronto Star* (May 11, 2005) A18, Editorials and Opinions.

[44] *Lives in the Balance, supra* note 13 at 12.

[45] Ibid. at 6.

[46] Ibid. at 71.

Of course, it is difficult to assess how many people would express their religiously based political views in authority-based terms if they felt these views were welcome in public debate and how many would make use of spiritual commitments in ways more like the authors of *Lives in the Balance.* What matters here is to reject the claim that all religious argument is authority based. At the same time, I do not suggest that authority-based claims should be seen as violating the norms of public discourse. These claims will, of course, need an additional argument about why the state should enforce a particular interpretation of God's command. Arguments based on scriptural authority (or the authority of a particular religious spokesperson) are not likely to have wide appeal or persuasive power outside the community that accepts that authority. Nevertheless, I think it is useful for the deliberating public to know how their fellow citizens see the issue.

D. The purpose of religion and politics: Radically distinct?

Finally, White indirectly reminds us of another difficulty. This is perhaps at the heart of the deepest opposition to my project here: the idea that there is a great difference in the purpose and scope of religion and politics. For example, at one point White refers to the task of the preacher as addressed to "transformations at the center of the self." Some might say that is clearly not the task of politics. I think that some important political projects like achieving gender equality will ultimately involve such transformations, so one cannot simply say that the state need never concern itself with the way it is implicated in such matters.[47] Sorting out the relation between the proper objectives of the state and those of religion is a complex task. Nevertheless, most people in North America would agree that there are some clear divisions. For example, most would agree that for the state to directly take up the objective of encouraging people's openness to spiritual reflection would be unwise and often dangerous. But even for those who accept some such clear division, there is often a dimension of their understanding of religion that creates another tension for the optimal role of religious argument in legislative deliberation. That is that for many, the project of living one's faith in daily life is a central part of their religious commitment. And that project involves taking up the sort of responsibility for the welfare of others and the health of their societies and states that *Lives in the Balance* invoked. And that, in turn, means advocating for the enactment of certain kinds of public policy. For many people, their religious beliefs have both the intimate nature White points to and a commitment to enact them in the world in both personal and political ways.

V. RESPECTING TENSIONS IN THE MODE OF DISCOURSE: TOWARD THE OPTIMAL TENOR OF DEBATE

If we take seriously the idea that taking account of the perspectives of others is a crucial part of the judgment that legislators must engage in, then religious argument must become a welcome part of the debates that engage legislators (in hearings,

[47] I make a version of this argument in "Violence Against Women: Challenges to the Liberal State and Relational Feminism" (1998) *NOMOS*, XXXVIII *Political Order*, Ian Shapiro and Russell Hardin, eds., pp. 454–497.

submissions to parliamentary committees, and perhaps on the floor of parliament). But to serve these purposes (as well as the substantive contributions to deliberation about the public good and core constitutional values), the nature of the discourse has to address all the issues raised above: the tension between the difficulty for many versus the ease of some in speaking publicly about religious beliefs, the tension between commitment to one's beliefs and respectful engagement with others, possible differences in scope and purpose between politics and religion, and the need to respect both the intimacy of religious beliefs and the importance of living one's faith in the world. I want to suggest, following the hints offered by White, that although none of these tensions can actually be resolved, the apparently insurmountable puzzles they pose can be overcome in the right kind of practice. Optimal forms of dialogue can shift the nature of the difficulties.

On the first point, I think the difficulty that many experience in talking about their beliefs would change significantly if the norms of public conversation – in playgrounds, schools, universities, and media commentary – were such that religious beliefs were regularly discussed *with* a respectful stance toward pluralism.[48] This is, in turn, connected to the issue of the intimacy of religious beliefs. The kinds of invocations of religious commitment that appear in the examples I have discussed are, I believe, serious, not merely superficial. But at the same time, they do involve the deepest exploration of people's understanding of the nature of the divine and its relation to their understanding of the universe and their place in it. To articulate the kinds of commitment to the poor they want to express, they do have to give some sense of their understanding of the relation between the divine and human nature and purpose. But they do not have to delve into the most complex and intimate dimensions of this understanding. They explain why and how their religious commitment informs their political commitments in a way that I think adds to others' understanding of how they see the issues. But it does not involve engagement that would require the level of trust and respect that White suggests is required for deep conversation among people of different faiths. I think it is possible for the public culture to transform so that serious, mutually respectful discussion of religiously grounded views could become a norm – at the level necessary for the constructive use of religious argument in collective deliberation about the public good. I believe that as we approach that norm, the gap will narrow between the difficulty so many people feel about expressing their religious beliefs and the ease of a very vocal minority. This is possible in part because what for some is the inherently difficult dimension of such expression, the engagement with the ineffable, can be avoided or handled with shorthand for the purposes of public policy deliberation.

I should add that I think that changes at the general level of casual conversation and media coverage are essential to achieve the shift in norms of public discourse I am advocating. In Canada, religious groups already do submit briefs to legislative hearings and to high-profile court cases. But this sort of intervention

[48] I recognize, of course, that the norms around public discussion of religiously based views vary from locality to locality. But the mere presence of comfort around discussion of religion does not advance the norms I am talking about, unless it is also characterized by a deep respect for, and attention to, pluralism.

receives relatively little publicity. At this point, there seems to be a kind of disjunction between the existence of many of the practices I advocate and the general public norms that still seem to make room only for an unabashed minority. It is probably a good thing that many contemporary experiments with introducing religion into legislative debate have taken place in the relative obscurity of hearings and submissions to committees.[49] But for the mutually sustaining interaction of general conversation and legislative deliberation to work to generate optimal norms, a greater degree of publicity and self-consciousness about the project of norm creation will be necessary.

Although it is fortunate that the extent of mutual trust and respect that I think White has in mind for his purposes are not necessary in the legislative context, some degree of both is necessary. But this is true across other divides than religion. Ideological differences, what some perceive as ethical differences, are equally capable of generating intemperance, mutual contempt, close-mindedness, and prejudice. And yet good politicians learn some version of what is called for in terms of the tension between deep commitment to one's own religious beliefs and respectful engagement with others. They learn that reasonable people of good faith can disagree deeply about issues such as the proper role of the state. Such disagreement can generate irreconcilable disagreement over policies that some see as required by collective responsibility for the least well off. Good politicians learn to engage in divisive debate with a core of mutual respect (while presumably also differentiating between principled ideological disagreement and what really seems like callous indifference). This capacity for mutual respect does not undermine their own core commitments, though their routine exercise of the enlarged mentality will presumably generate a capacity for critical reflection even on core beliefs. Thus, I think the personal skills and norms of mutual respect that characterize the best politicians will be sufficient to handle the tensions around personal belief and respectful engagement with the religiously based beliefs of others. Although it may be true that it is more common for religious belief to go to the core of one's sense of self – and thus raise the degree of the tension and difficulty of accommodation – I think for some their core, identity-shaping beliefs are experienced in secular, ethical, and what might be sometimes called ideological terms. Thus, I do not think the challenge of creating respectful dialogue that includes religious language is fundamentally different from the general demands of optimal public deliberation.

This is also the answer to the question of whether inviting religious argument into the public forum is inherently divisive. But I do not want to deny that there are any differences in how people react to religious and political arguments they disagree with. While I welcome the kind of shift in norms of discourse that I am advocating, I have also been angered and offended by some forms of religion in politics. For example, I was appalled by a *USA Today* ad a couple of months after 9/11 whose large print ran (words to the effect of): Why isn't God on our side? Find out what to do to get Him back. I was even a little shocked, certainly put off,

[49] I am conscious, of course, that from a historical perspective, bringing religious argument into legislative debates is not in fact new. I am referring to the project of finding norms of public deliberation suitable to a secular state.

by the EFC home page of their Web site: get current information so you can pray and act effectively.[50] (It was the pray effectively part that disturbed me.) Both the intimacy and the centrality of religious beliefs to people's sense of themselves are part of why reactions to beliefs contrary to their own can elicit powerful emotional responses. In my own case, I am more often *offended* by the public use of religion I disapprove of and *angered* by ideological positions (or cynical manipulation of fear) I disapprove of. Maybe the sense of offense goes deeper. But overall, the real project is the development of shared norms of discourse that will enable people to reveal the religious grounds for their positions in the context of mutual respect. Of course, as with all dimensions of politics, not everyone will respect the norms. But in the current situation, we do not even have a good venue for debating what the norms should be. Aspiring simply to exclude religious argument is not only a bad idea for the reasons I have offered, but it also will not reach those who persist and will not help generate collective understanding about how to talk about religion and public policy in mutually respectful ways.

In this context, I want to return to a point I raised earlier in the discussion of the view that religion is antithetical to reason. The view that it is unlikely that religiously based positions would have anything useful to offer to collective deliberation was captured at the conference for which this chapter was written by a comment from Jon Elster. I had replied to a question of his by saying that even if one could not debate the premises of a religiously based position, it might still have something substantively useful to offer. He replied, yes, by accident, like astrology might. I want to comment first on the substance of this remark and then on its affective quality. This seems an odd claim to make about many of the world's oldest ethical systems of thought. Even if one views a belief in any form of the divine as superstition – and thus as an affront to reason that should be challenged wherever possible – one might still be able to recognize religions as long-standing systems of ethics which have a better than random chance of making a contribution to collective deliberation about issues which have an ethical component and to the recognition of that ethical component. I say this despite my earlier caveat that institutionalized religion has historically probably done more harm than good. There is no system of thought, including liberalism and its entanglement with colonialism, that has anything like a clean record when one examines the uses made of it by those in power. The view that religion can make no constructive contribution may also be fostered by the fact that in the United States, and to some extent in Canada, it is largely the fundamentalist, conservative voices that make the news. As I said above, one of the virtues of changing the norms of public discourse to make more space for religiously based argument would be that a wider range of such arguments would be heard.

Elster's comment also captures the hostility some feel for religion and the problem that poses for mutually respectful deliberation. Over the many years that I have spent at academic conferences, I have heard my fair share of dismissive remarks about different methodologies, about feminist theory and women's studies, about self-satisfied liberalism. (I have even been guilty of some myself.) But I have never

[50] http://www.evangelicalfellowship.ca/.

heard any of them compared to astrology.[51] As I suggested above, I take it that the reason for such a comparison is that if religion is seen as fundamentally irrational, then it can be seen as not only having no proper place in collective deliberation, but also as undermining the foundation of that deliberation, namely reason. I would say that this view is misguided at least with respect to the role reason plays in much religiously based argument. As I noted earlier, most of what matters in public policy debate is not the core premises, but what is seen to flow from them. Reason plays a similar role whether the premises are secular or religious. But the issue I want to take up here is what to do about the existence of strongly felt hostility to religion as contrary to the foundational norm of democratic dialogue. Even if this hostility is, in my view, unreasonable, it exists and my confidence in the power of reason is not such that I believe that it will prevail against all that is unreasonable.

What can one reasonably ask of those who view religion as destructive superstition? One cannot, of course, ask them not to articulate that view. One might ask them to listen to see if the underlying religious premises about equality or human dignity or the nature of human community and interdependence, or the human capacity for creation and for individual responsibility, are similar to views they hold for other reasons. Precisely because there is such significant overlap between religiously grounded ethical views and their contemporary secular counterparts, such overlap is likely to be common. Of course, because both secular and religious positions are contested, different people will find shared views in different places. When it is the very fact of a religious foundation to the position that is repugnant, I think one can ask for the same kind of civility that would be optimal for mutually respectful deliberation when one encounters a secular position one finds normatively repugnant. Perhaps one can also ask for prudence in judging when a challenge to underlying premises is likely to further mutual understanding and effective deliberation.

The real issue is what norms of public discourse will best foster legislators' capacity to fulfill their functions. Mutual respect and civility seem essential components. This is, of course, a challenge when the views of one's interlocutor do not seem worthy of respect, whether because one sees them as, say, racist or as fundamentally irrational because they are religious (whether substantively pernicious or benign). I think I would settle for the option of as civil a declaration as possible of one's (perhaps inevitably offensive) view that religion is irrational superstition together with an effort to see if there are any shared values from which to proceed to rational deliberation. Strong differences about core values, whether understood in secular or religious terms, will inevitably give rise to conflict and offense. What one can ask of those hostile to religion on principled grounds of their understanding of reason (or on any grounds) is that their behavior be guided by norms that will foster the mutual respect and tolerance necessary for democratic deliberation in a society characterized by deep divisions.

Overt expressions of contempt can undermine this respect. But it is nevertheless useful for everyone to know the beliefs that matter deeply to the judgments of one's fellow citizens, including the belief that religion is antithetical to reason. Indeed,

[51] I should perhaps add that I have no views on whether astrology has only a random chance of contributing anything valuable to a discussion. I am responding to the clear intent of the comment.

I found it very useful to be reminded by Elster's remark of the kind of contempt religion can generate. An earlier conversation with another colleague about his puzzlement over why one should engage in deliberation with someone unable (or unwilling) to debate the foundation for their position failed to convey to me the depth of suspicion and hostility toward religion that some members of the polity feel. And that is important information for the project of envisioning norms of public discourse that include religiously based argument. Moreover, from my perspective, Elster's comment succeeded in doing what is often advocated, but which I had always thought was so difficult as to be impossible: As I experienced it, he conveyed contempt for the argument I was making, but not contempt for me. To the extent that it is possible for that to become a norm of public discourse, it seems optimal for the project of taking one another's perspectives into account. One can then learn both the content of others' views and the affect associated with it. Both are valuable in the ongoing task of deliberation about core values and the common good. But it will requite considerable attention to the norms of civility and mutual respect to work. An easier, and generally safer, path would be to avoid expressions of contempt.

VI. CONSTITUTIONAL VALUES AND THE CONTRIBUTION OF RELIGIOUSLY BASED ARGUMENT

Let me close by briefly connecting these arguments to the legislative function of participating in the definition of core constitutional values. My argument takes as its starting point that the practical meaning of core constitutional values such as equality evolve and that the legislature should play a role in the deliberation about their meaning. One of the advantages of focusing on the legislature's role in this task of constitutional governance is that legislatures can, in contrast to courts, focus on how to implement these values rather than on how these values place limits on what government can do. Constitutional values such as equality, dignity, and security should guide the formulation of policy, and in order to do that, legislators need to reflect on the meaning of these values in an ongoing way.

Another virtue of such reflection is that the courts' tendency to think about these values in individualistic terms is countered by the legislators' capacity to think about them in the wider context of their connection to community, of the ways in which values such as equality and dignity are fundamentally about structures of social relations that legislative policy cannot help but shape. These advantages are connected, for legislatures can think about rights such as equality in terms that can be given practical meaning only when communities take responsibility for ensuring social structures that foster equality. Equality is a value that must characterize a community in order for an individual to enjoy it. It is not that courts cannot analyze issues in these terms; to some extent they should and must. But in many ways legislatures are a better forum for reflection on the social meaning of rights and what it takes to implement them.

What then is the contribution of religiously based argument to this legislative function? First, there is the same general point that I have made above. The kind of judgment involved in deliberation and action on the meaning of rights requires the use of the enlarged mentality, and in order to include those who understand their perspectives in religious terms, legislators must engage with those terms. But, in addition, we have reason to believe that such engagement will make important contributions. Spiritual communities are places where people spend time reflecting on core values and what it means to live in accordance with them. In my own case, for example, where do I participate in ongoing reflection as well as reminders to take my commitments seriously, to put them into action? By far more often in my church community than in my academic encounters. This is true despite the facts that I am a politically engaged citizen (I follow the news, participate in electoral campaigns, and virtually never fail to vote[52]) and that my academic specialties are law and political science, where one might expect the deep questions of public policy to be discussed. Yet my church is the place where I most often encounter discussion of individual and collective obligation to the public good, to the poor, to those suffering throughout the world from violence, hunger, lack of shelter or education – from things political action could change. And my church is a context not just for discussion but for action. The framework for both discussion and action is living one's faith commitments, with biblical authority playing virtually no role. Not all of the values faith communities are concerned with have analogues in secular, constitutional values. But many of them do. Dignity, equality, respect, and the nature of mutual obligation are some that come to mind.

Legislators can best learn from the potential contributions of the sustained reflection in spiritual communities when they listen to those reflections in their own terms.[53] The nuances of the understanding of equality or of the optimal role of compassion, which may inform the evolution and implementation of constitutional values, are best captured without the potential distortion that all translation entails. As I noted earlier, I think there are some virtues to the exercise of translating spiritual understandings of core values and their implications for action into, secular language of, say, legal rights and liberal values. One of those virtues, noticing where the translation is difficult or imperfect, may itself help to highlight the nuances of the spiritually based understanding. But notwithstanding those virtues, it cannot be a requirement for participation in the public forum that one engage in such translation. Not everyone will want to, and the work (related to the exercise of the enlarged mentality) that is required to try to engage with another's spiritual perspective will advance the enterprise of reflecting on different ways of understanding the core values a society has enshrined in its constitution. This reflection will be aided by considering not only the conceptual nuances of different understandings, but also the nature of the motivation, commitment, perhaps even passion of those advocating a particular policy in light of their core spiritual values.

Finally, let me note that the precise norms for public debate are likely to vary with the context. It seems likely to me that the ways in which religiously based argument should be used in factums (or briefs) in courts may be different from those appropriate to legislative hearings, and these in turn from arguments in Parliament. I am prepared to partially agree with John Rawls by saying that when judges deliver

[52] With the exception of rarely using my right to vote via absentee ballot in the United States, where I am a citizen but not a resident.

[53] The importance of multiple communities in which the core values of a society are developed (in ways that may both feed into and conflict with the norms articulated in "law") was eloquently articulated by Robert Cover in "Forward: Nomos and Narrative" (1983–84) 97 *Harv. L. Rev.* 4. My thanks to Judith Resnick for drawing my attention to this connection.

opinions and legislators make public arguments for their positions, they should make an effort to translate their spiritually based arguments into widely shared secular language.[54] But I would add my own provisos to this agreement by saying first that I do not share Rawls's confidence in the existence of an unproblematically shared "public reason." Even my phrase "widely shared secular language" can obscure deep differences that may exist around such core concepts as "public" and "private" or the meaning or relevance of the terms "property" or "title" or, indeed, "religion" in disputes between aboriginal peoples and provincial or federal governments. Such differences can go to the heart of what counts as the kind of argument that everyone should be able to respect. My second proviso is that public officials should be encouraged to articulate the ways in which they think they can most fully capture how they see an issue and why. And they should be encouraged to articulate the ways (if any) in which the effort to translate these terms fails or is imperfect. Such public articulation of the nuances of difference will be as important to good public deliberation (and accountability) as the effort at translation. In addition, as I noted above, I see it as desirable for diverse norms for religiously based public argument to develop for playgrounds, schools, classrooms (perhaps different for teachers and for students), public debate on television and radio. In short, I am advocating a flourishing public conversation, with somewhat different norms in different contexts, using religiously based argument. I take this to be rather different from Rawls's welcoming of religious argument in the "background culture."[55]

CONCLUSION

In sum, two of the most important tasks of the legislature in a constitutional state are collective deliberation on the common good and participation in the ongoing evolution of core constitutional values, such as equality. These functions require judgment, which in turn requires the exercise of the enlarged mentality: taking the perspective of others into account in the formation of one's judgment. These perspectives must include those who see policy issues in religious terms, and to truly take their perspective into account requires understanding it in their terms, that is, in religious terms. As a result, religiously based argument must be invited into the public forum of legislative deliberation. An additional contribution of doing so will be an aid in articulating the value of norms of collective responsibility and the role of ethics in public policy. Similarly, there are likely to be substantive contributions to reflecting on the meaning of core constitutional values, as this is a project that overlaps with the central concerns of many spiritual communities.

There are deep tensions involved in engaging with religiously based argument in public forums. But these tensions can be worked through, though not overcome, in practice. The process of developing shared norms for exchanging such views is crucial to good governance in a constitutional state. The solution of simply trying to keep them at bay, sequestered in the private realm, was never optimal and is no longer viable. It may be that in developing these new norms, both citizens and legislators need to develop new skills, such as being able to discern the nature and

[54] "The Idea of Public Reason Revisited" in *The Law of Peoples* (Cambridge: Harvard University Press, 1999) at 152–6.

[55] Ibid. at 134.

level of their disagreement. When, for example, is the dispute really about deep disagreement over fundamental principle and when is it about how to implement those principles?[56]

Finally, I return to my opening caveat. While I have used very broad language here about what will foster optimal legislative functions in a constitutional democracy, I am most confident about its application in Canada. I expect that the arguments apply to the United States, but of course the nuances of what it would take to generate the optimal shared norms would differ. Similarly, I expect that it would apply to Europe with appropriate attention to local context. Much greater accommodation in the argument might be necessary where the relation between religion and state is quite different, as in a constitutional state such as Israel or where particular religious institutions wield great political power. Similarly, states that do not have a well-established tradition of a separation between "church" and state may have different requirements.

ACKNOWLEDGMENT

I would like to thank the participants in the conference on Legislatures in the Constitutional State and the Yale Legal Theory workshop for stimulating questions and conversation.

[56] Roger Hutchison has articulated a framework for facilitating debate by making such distinctions. See, for example, *Prophets, Pastors and Public Choices: Canadian Churches and the Mackenzie Valley Pipeline Debate* (Waterloo, ON: Wilfrid Laurier University Press, 1992).

6 Should We Value Legislative Integrity?

Andrei Marmor

"We have two principles of political integrity:" – Dworkin suggests in *Law's Empire* – "a legislative principle, which asks lawmakers to try to make the total set of laws morally coherent, and an adjudicative principle, which instructs that the law be seen as coherent in that way, as far as possible."[1] In this chapter, I will be concerned with only the first of these two principles. My arguments here aim to show that legislative integrity is not an ideal, certainly not an important one.

A. THE MEANING OF LEGISLATIVE INTEGRITY

Before we can proceed to the main arguments, a few clarifications about the meaning of legislative integrity are necessary, and some assumptions must be rendered explicit.

1. Two applications of coherence to the law

Legal theorists have applied the idea of coherence to the law in at least two distinct ways: as part of an explanation of what the law is, and as a value of political morality that the law should strive to adhere to. Dworkin has employed the idea of coherence in both of these ways,[2] but this should not confuse us into thinking that they are the same thing. In the former sense, coherence performs an explanatory function in a theory about the nature of law. In this sense, coherence constitutes part of the conditions for the legal validity of norms: A norm is legally valid if it forms part of, or is entailed by, the most coherent account of other norms that we take to be part of the law.[3] This is not what Dworkin has in mind, however, when he discusses political integrity. The latter is not part of an explanation of what the law is but a distinct value of political morality.

Coherence can be a value of political morality (either in the legislative or adjudicative contexts) even if coherence does not play a constitutive role in determining what the law is. In other words, you can reject a coherence theory of law (in its explanatory sense) but still maintain that coherence is a valuable objective that the

[1] Ronald Dworkin, *Law's Empire* (London: Fontana Press, 1986) at 176.

[2] For a detailed account of Dworkin's use of coherence in legal theory, see Andrei Marmor, *Interpretation and Legal Theory*, 2nd ed. (Oxford: Hart Publishing, 2005) at ch. 4.

[3] For a possible distinction between an epistemic and a constitutive version of coherence theories of law, see Joseph Raz, "The Relevance of Coherence" in his *Ethics in the Public Domain: Essays in the Morality of Law and Politics* (Oxford: Clarendon Press, 1994) 261.

law should strive to instantiate. And vice versa: A coherence theory of law does not entail that legislative integrity is a value or a moral-political ideal. Even if coherence forms part of the conditions of legal validity, it does not follow that coherence is a good thing or that we should want more of it rather than less. Thus, I will assume that we can discuss the value of integrity without taking a stance on the role coherence can play in a theory about the nature of law.[4]

2. Coherence and truth

Another important clarification is in place here. Some people tend to think that we should value coherence simply because an incoherent theory cannot be true. Whatever coherence is, at the very least, it involves the avoidance of contradictions. Not every consistent set of propositions is necessarily coherent, but every inconsistent set is necessarily incoherent. If this is correct, one might conclude that the lack of coherence entails a contradiction, and because it cannot be the case that contradictory propositions are both true, it follows that an incoherent theory must be false. But this is a non sequitur. The lack of coherence does not necessarily entail a contradiction, although the opposite is true: An inconsistent set of propositions is, ipso facto, incoherent. The reason for this is very simple: Coherence must mean something more than just the lack of consistency. When we talk about coherence, we have in mind a set of propositions that are somehow mutually supportive; they somehow fit together in the overall scheme of things.[5] I am not sure that I can explain what this means precisely, but the point here does not require much more. It only requires the realization that a theory, or a set of propositions, can fail to be coherent even if it does not involve straightforward contradictions. Therefore, it does not follow that an incoherent set of propositions is necessarily false.[6]

3. The scope of integrity

Another clarification is appropriate here. Suppose that we espouse the ideal of legislative integrity: How far can it be carried? Whose obligation would it be to implement it? Should individual legislators actually be guided by it? Would legislators have a reason to vote for a law because it would be required by the principle of legislative integrity? Should it also extend to voters when they consider who to vote for, or when they participate in lawmaking through referenda and initiatives? I am not sure how far Dworkin would take this principle, but it is quite clear that the main implication of legislative integrity Dworkin had in mind concerns the theory of adjudication. He has certainly maintained that judges should interpret statutory law following the principle of legislative integrity.[7] Judges should assume

[4] I am quite confident that Dworkin would share this assumption. I do not think that Dworkin has sought to derive his conclusions about legislative integrity from his coherence theory of law.

[5] An indefinite number of logically consistent but incoherent sets of propositions can be constructed. For example, consider the following set: "John is a law professor," "2 + 2 = 4," and "All swans are white." This set is logically consistent but hardly coherent. Coherence requires some notion of connectedness and mutual support between the propositions that constitute the relevant set.

[6] I do not intend to imply that incoherence has no epistemic implications. Even a coherence theory of knowledge, however, is not committed to maintaining that any incoherent theory is, ipso facto, necessarily false.

[7] Dworkin, *supra* note 1 at ch. 7.

that laws are enacted with this ideal in mind, as it were, so that even if the legislature fails to achieve it, greater coherence can be imposed on legislation through judicial interpretation. Suffice it to say that none of these implications of the ideal of legislative integrity are logically entailed by it, though each one of them may be supported by other reasons. And vice versa; it should not be assumed that the rejection of legislative integrity as a distinct political ideal necessarily entails that judges need not be guided by a similar principle. The reasons for endorsing a coherence approach in adjudication might be different, independently justified on other grounds.

4. The meaning of legislative integrity

Still, a crucial question remains unanswered: Is there anything more to political integrity than the requirement that laws be made coherent? If I understand Dworkin correctly, then the answer actually is that there is less to political integrity than coherence, not more. Political integrity is the requirement to make the law in a way that is *morally* coherent. The law can probably fail to be coherent in other ways, which have nothing, or perhaps just very little, to do with morality. For instance, the law can be pragmatically incoherent in that it actually creates incentives for behavior which are, from a certain pragmatic point of view (e.g., economic, environmental policy, etc.), somehow incoherent. If this is a possibility, then it is possible for the law to be incoherent without violating the principle of political integrity. It may thus violate some other principle or ideal but not necessarily the one of integrity.

Let us assume, then, that the law is morally incoherent if its various prescriptions and their underlying justifications cannot be subsumed under one coherent moral theory. Or, we could say that in such cases there is not a conceivable single rational moral agent whose moral point of view could justify the entire set of prescriptions under consideration. I think that this is basically what Dworkin means by the value of integrity in law.

Unfortunately, however, Dworkin's famous example of what constitutes a violation of integrity in legislation does not actually support the meaning of integrity as he defines it.[8] Dworkin asks us to envisage what he calls a "checkerboard" type of legislation which would prescribe, for instance, that abortions are legally permitted for women who were born on even days of the month and forbidden for women who were born on uneven days. The reason we would find such checkerboard laws unacceptable, Dworkin claims, is because they would violate the integrity of the law.[9] No single moral agent, Dworkin claims, could justify such a checkerboard solution as a coherent compromise of conflicting considerations with respect to the permissibility of abortions. But this is a bad example. We do not need the requirement of integrity, or coherence, in order to explain what is wrong with such checkerboard laws. What is wrong with them is that they are not supported by a good reason. When the law makes a distinction, as it does here on the basis of women's birthdays, it must be a distinction that is somehow supported by reason.

[8] I have made this point in Andrei Marmor, "The Rule of Law and Its Limits" (2003) 23 *Law and Phil.* 1.
[9] Dworkin, *supra* note 1 at 178–84.

If there is no good reason for the different treatment, then the law is a bad one, simply because it is not supported by reason.[10]

One may wonder, however, how we would distinguish such checkerboard laws from many other cases in which the law makes distinctions that seem to be rather arbitrary, but nevertheless are understandable and justified. For instance, the law can stipulate that only people who were born after a certain date are allowed to vote in the forthcoming elections. Surely, the particular date chosen is not supported by any particular reasons; it is just an arbitrary cutoff point. But this is precisely the point: In numerous cases, such as in solving coordination problems and other similar situations, we do have a good reason to use arbitrary cutoff points. In such cases, the cutoff point itself is arbitrary, that is, not supported by any particular reason, but there are good reasons to have it as some sort of an arbitrarily chosen cutoff point.[11] The problem with the abortion example is precisely that it is the kind of situation where there is no good reason to have an arbitrarily chosen cutoff point.

None of this means, however, that legislative integrity is a vacuous concept. Far from it. There are countless ways in which the legislature can enact laws that are morally incoherent. My point simply was that "checkerboard legislation," as Dworkin describes it, is not one of them. Legislation that is not supported by a good reason is wrong just because it is not supported by a good reason. The law is morally incoherent, and thus violates the ideal of integrity, when the various norms or prescriptions it embodies are somehow morally contradictory. But here we have to be very cautious. Surely not every tension or potential conflict between moral principles amounts to an incoherence. Every comprehensive moral doctrine involves countless tensions and conflicts in the application of its principles and ideals. As we all know, the values of equality and freedom may often come into conflict. Liberalism endorses both ideals, but surely that does not render liberalism incoherent.

5. Conflict and contradiction

It may be tempting to think that a moral theory is incoherent only when its principles are contradictory. There is, after all, a pretty clear distinction between a conflict of principles and a contradiction.[12] In a world of limited resources, a stringent protection of the environment may come into conflict with creating new jobs for the poorer segment of society. But surely these two types of concerns are not contradictory. A rational moral person can easily aspire for both. On the other hand, maintaining that the state should guarantee equal rights to homosexuals and heterosexuals, but at the same time deny gays the right to get married, for instance, looks very much like a contradiction. So there is a sense in which moral contradiction is quite distinct from conflict or tension between morally sound principles. It

[10] At some point, Dworkin admits that "this is in the right neighborhood" (*supra* note 1 at 180), but then fails to acknowledge that it undermines the force of his example.

[11] See, for example, David K. Lewis, *Convention: A Philosophical Study* (Cambridge: Harvard University Press, 1969). On the definition of arbitrariness, see also Andrei Marmor, "On Convention" (1996) 107 *Synthese* 349.

[12] Dworkin makes this point drawing on the distinction between conflict and contradiction of principles in Dworkin, *supra* note 1 at 268–75.

is also quite clear that a contradiction of principles does violate the requirement of coherence. The question remains whether moral principles or ideals can be incoherent even if they do not quite amount to a contradiction. Presumably, the answer is yes. As we have noted earlier, coherence must mean something more than mere logical consistency. So it must be the case that there are moral conceptions or worldviews that just cannot be subsumed under one coherent doctrine, even if it is the case that the overall set of propositions one believes in are not logically inconsistent.

6. The background of value pluralism

Be this as it may, there are two types of moral incoherence that are relevant to the ideal of legislative integrity: One stems from the fragmentation of values within any given comprehensive moral doctrine and the other from the fact of reasonable pluralism (I use these Rawlsian terms advisedly). Let me call them *internal* and *external* incoherence, respectively. Internal incoherence stems from the complexity of the sources of moral thought. With the possible exception of a single-minded, monistic utilitarianism,[13] every comprehensive moral doctrine is bound to be incoherent, to some extent. Our moral and ethical concerns do not form a response to a single question; they reflect a myriad of human concerns, some of them private and individual, others public and social. As many moral philosophers have noted, it seems extremely unlikely that we can ever construct a comprehensive moral and ethical worldview that would subsume all these divergent concerns under a coherent set of principles.[14]

The idea of external incoherence stems from a different fact about the moral complexity of our world: the fact of reasonable pluralism.[15] In most contemporary societies there is a whole range of comprehensive moral doctrines that are, on the one hand, mutually inconsistent, but on the other hand, also within the bounds of reasonable disagreement. It is important to keep in mind that there is a difference between a plurality of moral doctrines and value pluralism. Not every plurality of moral doctrines involves a deep form of conflict, even if the doctrines are mutually exclusive. There are many forms of life and moral worldviews that are mutually exclusive in the sense that a person cannot possibly entertain, or strive to instantiate, both. But this does not necessarily entail a deep conflict. It may simply reflect a choice between sets of incommensurable values or mixed goods.[16] On the other hand, when we talk about value pluralism, we refer to a deep moral or ethical

[13] Arguably, however, monistic utilitarianism can only maintain its moral coherence at the expense of a huge simplification of morality. This lack of subtlety is partly what makes a monistic utilitarianism so suspect.

[14] See, for example, Raz, *supra* note 3; Thomas Nagel, "The Fragmentation of Value" in his *Mortal Questions* (Cambridge: Cambridge University Press, 1979) 128; and Bernard Williams, "Conflict of Values" in his *Moral Luck* (Cambridge: Cambridge University Press, 1981) 71. It was probably Isaiah Berlin who most famously insisted on this fragmentation of values as being part of the foundation of liberalism. See his collected essays in Isaiah Berlin, *Concepts and Categories* (Harmondsworth, UK: Penguin Books, 1978). I think it is fair to say that Rawls has also maintained such a position in John Rawls, *A Theory of Justice* (Cambridge, Mass.: Harvard University Press, 1971).

[15] Reasonable pluralism is a moral fact, not merely a social one. See John Rawls, *Political Liberalism* (New York: Columbia University Press, 1993).

[16] By pointing to the fact that in such cases the various options are incommensurable, I mean only that no ranking between the options is morally determinable.

conflict. There are many comprehensive moral doctrines or forms of life that are morally at odds with each other, in the simple sense that if the one is true, the other must be false, and vice versa.[17]

Pluralism stems from the fact that comprehensive moral doctrines are potentially in deep conflict, entailing straightforward moral contradictions between different doctrines people adhere to and live by. Nevertheless, it has been the benchmark of liberalism for centuries that there is a sense in which value pluralism (and not just plurality) is reasonable. I cannot hope to explain the philosophical underpinning of the idea of reasonable pluralism here. But I will make two assumptions. First, that rational people can have reasonable disagreements about fundamental moral and ethical values.[18] Second, I will assume that the idea of reasonable pluralism does not necessarily derive from, nor does it necessarily entail, moral skepticism. I may disagree with your moral views and believe them to be wrong or mistaken, but still acknowledge your right to live by your mistakes. In other words, reasonable pluralism may be as much a view about politics as it is about meta-ethics. Even if you are profoundly wrong, the assumption we make here is that the state should not be in the business of correcting your mistakes (up to a point, of course.) So there are at least two possible grounds for acknowledging reasonable pluralism, and they are not mutually exclusive: It may reflect a view about the nature of morality and the limits of moral knowledge, and it may be a political view about the limits on the coercive authority of the state. Either way, the argument about legislative integrity that I will explore now assumes that pluralism of comprehensive moral doctrines is reasonable and, as such, ought to be respected by a liberal state.[19]

B. THE ARGUMENT FROM PLURALISM

So now at long last we come to the main issue. There are two ways in which we can explore the value of legislative integrity. First, and this is probably the more important argument, I will try to show that the ideal of legislative integrity is directly at odds with the value of pluralism and the commitment of a liberal state to respect reasonable pluralism. Second, I will explore the main causes of the failure of legislative integrity in democratic legislatures, arguing that there is nothing regrettable about those causes and often there is something to commend them.

Let me admit from the outset, however, that none of these arguments can be conclusive. It is generally very difficult to prove that something is not a value. I can

[17] Moral doctrines inevitably make certain claims to truth. Even a moral skeptic makes certain claims to truth, at the very least, to the truth of his meta-ethical stance and the practical implications following from it. Thus, it should not be surprising if many of these various claims to truth turn out to be mutually contradictory.

[18] This is certainly not tantamount to saying that *any* fundamental moral principle is subject to reasonable disagreement.

[19] There is a very difficult question about the scope of this principle: Does it apply to societies that are not, as a matter of fact, pluralistic? Is there anything inherently wrong in a political society that happens to be homogeneous in terms of people's conception of the good, all, say, adhering to the same moral or religious comprehensive doctrine? At least in his later writings, Rawls certainly thought that the answer is yes; he called it the fact of oppression. See Rawls, *supra* note 15 at 36–7. I do not take a stance on this complex issue here.

only hope to show that there are important reasons to forgo legislative integrity. I cannot prove that legislative integrity is not valuable when those reasons are not present. I do hope to show, however, that we have no reason to maintain that *ideally*, the law should be morally coherent, or as coherent as possible.[20]

The main argument against the ideal of legislative integrity relies on two points: A moral-political ideal, very much inspired by John Rawls, and an observation, which actually rejects part of Rawls's stance on the matter. The moral-political ideal, which I can only assume here, is the requirement that in a well-ordered society the state should try to refrain, as far as possible, from enacting into laws comprehensive moral doctrines that are potentially contentious and subject to reasonable disagreement between various segments of the population. Note that this is not the ideal of neutrality that Rawls himself advocated, but a much more modest principle. I do not believe that the state can, by and large, remain neutral between conceptions of the good or comprehensive moralities. Partly because this is just not possible, practically speaking, and partly because often it is inherently unclear what neutrality would require, or that there is, indeed, any morally acceptable neutral stance with respect to the relevant conflict. (It is not part of my argument here to deny the plausibility of Rawls's conception of neutrality. I am just pointing out the fact that I do not intend to rely on it.[21]) Nevertheless, Rawls's insight that there is something very objectionable to an attempt by the state to impose any particular comprehensive morality on its subjects is, I believe, a powerful insight that liberal conceptions of the state have in one way or another always endorsed.[22]

Rawls believed that the stronger principle of neutrality is possible partly because he thought that it is possible to delineate a sphere of public debate and state action – a sphere of *public reason*, as he called it – that can remain above the fray. As he put it, "a liberal view removes from the political agenda the most divisive issues."[23] This means that "in discussing constitutional essentials and matters of basic justice we are not to appeal to comprehensive religious and philosophical doctrine."[24] Shortly thereafter, Rawls clarifies what he means by "constitutional essentials" and it becomes clear that he means quite a lot: "Constitutional essentials" include "fundamental principles that specify the general structure of government and political process" as well as "basic rights and liberties."[25] Of course, a lot depends here on what we would regard as "basic" and what as not so basic, but this is just one

[20] I do not want to put too much weight on the distinction between a value and an ideal. However, there is a sense in which an ideal is something that we aspire to achieve as much of as possible or, at least, (all other things being equal) we would normally want to have more of it rather than less. This is not necessarily, or even typically, true of values in general.

[21] For a comprehensive and powerful criticism of neutrality, see Joseph Raz, *The Morality of Freedom* (Oxford: Oxford University Press, 1986) at ch. 5. For some of his replies, see Rawls, *supra* note 15 at 190–200. See also Andrei Marmor, *Positive Law and Objective Values* (Oxford: Oxford University Press, 2001) at 147–52.

[22] As Rawls himself suggests, and I think rightly so, this is a natural extension of the traditional principle of toleration. See Rawls, *supra* note 15, introduction.

[23] Rawls, *supra* note 15 at 157.

[24] Ibid. at 224.

[25] Ibid. at 228. Another crucial sense in which it is notable that Rawls assumes quite a lot here concerns the fact that for him even Kantian morality or utilitarianism are "comprehensive moralities" and therefore should be excluded from the realm of public reason. See Charles Larmore, "Public Reason" in Samuel Freeman, ed., *The Cambridge Companion to Rawls* (Cambridge: Cambridge University Press) 368.

aspect of a deeper problem. Any attempt to draw a sharp line between constitutional essentials, which ought to be free from appeal to comprehensive doctrines, and other matters of law and legislation that need not be, is questionable at best. First, it is often controversial just what is, and what is not, a matter of "constitutional essentials" and, moreover, such controversies often lie at the core of the relevant public debate.[26] Second, the law, as such, recognizes no inherent limits on its reach. The law cannot recognize such limits mostly because its quintessential function is to regulate and resolve conflicts, and there is no limit on which conflicts actually arise and need a resolution.

A brief illustration of the first point should suffice here. Consider, for example, the current controversy in U.S. politics and jurisprudence about gay marriages. Those who advocate the right of gays and lesbians to marry do so on the grounds that this is an issue of basic constitutional rights, whereas those who oppose this social change may claim the exact opposite. Opponents may not see the issue as one of basic rights but as a matter of tradition that should be left out of the constitutional domain.[27] In other words, many of the legal/political controversies are partly, but crucially, about the very question of what is, and what is not, a matter of "constitutional essentials."

The second point is perhaps even clearer, and it is much more important: There is no practical way in which issues can be removed from the legal/political agenda just because they are divisive or deeply controversial. Even if we grant (generously, I would say) that certain aspects of constitutional law can be confined within the constraints of public reason, those constraints cannot possibly apply to legislation as a whole.[28] This should not be surprising. The law is essentially comprehensive in its reach because it must claim the authority to regulate any type of behavior in every sphere of life. Because the law must resolve conflicts that actually arise, it cannot abstain from judgment. Even when the law decides not to intervene in a given conflict, it is a decision that reflects judgment, namely, a judgment to refrain from taking a certain legal action or granting a certain remedy. Once again, we must keep in mind that an essential function of the law is to resolve conflicts in society, and there is no inherent limit on the kinds of conflict that may arise and need some sort of legal regulation. I think that in this respect, Dworkin's vision of the law as an all-encompassing "empire" that potentially reaches into every aspect of our lives is much more realistic than Rawls's ideal of a secluded sphere of public reason. Even if we can theoretically delineate such a sphere of public reason (and I actually doubt that we can), there is just no hope of enclosing the law within that realm.

But then, taken with the previous point about the need to respect reasonable pluralism, this is precisely the reason to refrain from espousing an ideal of legislative integrity. Any attempt to impose strict moral integrity on the law would

[26] Larmore, *supra* note 25 at 384–390.

[27] I am not suggesting that these are the only two positions available. For example, many see the issue as one about state versus federal jurisdiction, which is a different type of a constitutional debate.

[28] This is not meant to be a direct criticism of Rawls, as Rawls himself believed that public reason should be confined to the basic constitutional domain and some other, limited, aspects of the "public political forum," as opposed to what he called the "background culture" or the media, and such. Whether any of these distinctions makes sense is questionable, but the argument in the text is more limited. It only purports to claim that even if public reason makes sense in some aspects of law and politics, it cannot be extended to encompass legislation as a whole.

undermine the essential and, we assumed, reasonable, moral fragmentation of a pluralist society. The more we wish to have moral integrity implemented by the law, the more we would have to expect it to implement a single comprehensive moral view. It is inconceivable that an entirely coherent legal regime could be endorsed by opposing (reasonable) comprehensive moralities. Therefore, integrity basically entails a "winner takes all" strategy, which is directly at odds with respect for reasonable value pluralism. A certain moral fragmentation of values and incoherence is inescapable if we are to respect pluralism as such. The whole point of respect for value pluralism is that we do not want to have a legal/political system, whereby the winner (be it the ruling majority or the Supreme Court, for that matter) imposes its comprehensive moral views on the rest of the population. Furthermore, as we have seen, even within a single comprehensive moral doctrine it is far from clear that coherence can be somehow imposed without a considerable loss to the subtlety and complexity of the relevant moral concerns. (But my point here can be made even if we ignore the problem of internal incoherence, so I will not strive to defend this stronger claim.)

One interesting way in which Rawls expressed a very similar worry is by emphasizing that a well-ordered society governed by principles of justice "is neither a community nor . . . an association."[29] A democratic society does not have final ends or aims in the way that communities or associations do: "A well ordered democratic society is not an association, it is not a community either, if we mean by a community a society governed by shared comprehensive religious, philosophical, or moral doctrine."[30] Now this is particularly interesting in light of Dworkin's argument in favor of political integrity, which is premised on the duty of loyalty to one's community. Dworkin has argued that such a duty of loyalty entails an obligation to obey the law, and that the latter must be seen as the organized voice of the community, taken as a whole. From this Dworkin strove to derive the need to assume a personification of the law, as if it should be taken to speak with one voice, manifesting the community's collective decision.[31]

It is not my purpose here to offer a detailed critic of this complex argument. That has been done by others cogently enough.[32] My observation here is confined to one aspect of this argument, namely, its underlying assumption that a well-ordered democratic society can, and should, be seen as a community, and its laws perceived as the community's collective decision. I think that Rawls was right to argue that such a view of a political society, that is, of a liberal state, is quite straightforwardly at odds with the need to respect reasonable pluralism. A political society cannot speak with one moral voice because its moral voice is essentially fragmented and, taken as a whole, profoundly incoherent. An attempt to impose coherence on it can only mean that some comprehensive doctrines will win the day while others will be suppressed. This cannot be a liberal ideal.

Let me summarize the argument. I began with the Rawlsian insight that a well-ordered liberal society should respect value pluralism. One clear implication of this

[29] Rawls, *supra* note 15 at 40.
[30] Ibid. at 42.
[31] Dworkin, *supra* note 1 at 195–214.
[32] In particular, see Raz, *supra* note 3 at 291–8.

ideal is an aspiration to try to avoid, as far as possible, using the state and its legal coercive institutions to implement any particular comprehensive moral or religious doctrine. Contra Rawls, however, I do not think that such an ideal can (or should) be carried as far as to recommend a principle of neutrality. More importantly, I have argued that this principle cannot be implemented by designating a sphere of public reason that would enclose legislation within strict neutral boundaries. The law is inevitably comprehensive, and there is no hope of actually preventing the law from regulating aspects of our lives that are clearly, but reasonably, controversial morally, ethically, and otherwise. Therefore, I concluded, it would be wrong to insist on the ideal of legislative integrity. The law should not be expected to speak with one voice because there is no single voice that could possibly encompass the range of reasonable comprehensive moral doctrines held by various segments of the society.

There are two possible rejoinders to this argument. First, it can be argued that I have not quite proven what I promised: At best I have shown that the ideal of integrity just happens to conflict with the value of respect for pluralism, and thus may need to succumb to the latter, but I have not shown that integrity is not valuable at all. Second, it could be argued that integrity can incorporate the value of pluralism as one of the ingredients in a complex moral view that comprises a set of first-order values, *and* the second-order value of respect for value pluralism. So that when we expect the law to speak with one voice, as it were, it is a voice that already takes into account the need to respect the views of others who may disagree. Let me take up these two points in turn.

It is certainly possible that the conflict between integrity and pluralism is just that, a conflict between opposing (second-order) moral principles. I have not shown that we have no reason to value integrity at all. But I am not sure that it is important to show that. The argument purported to show that there are important reasons to forgo legislative integrity, whether the latter is valuable or not. Furthermore, I am willing to assume that those reasons are not always present. Partly because the value of pluralism has its own limits, of course, and partly because there may be cases in which pluralism is not at stake. As I have indicated from the start, it is generally very difficult to show that something is not a value under any circumstances. But again, such a proof is not really needed. We have seen that the need to respect value pluralism strongly counts against an ideal of legislative integrity, and this should be sufficient to show that even if integrity is valuable, we have no reason to regard legislative integrity as an ideal, that is, to expect the law to be as morally coherent as possible. Now it is true, of course, that if you feel that we should regret the need to respect pluralism, you may also regret the fact that we must forgo legislative integrity. Because I do not think that pluralism is regrettable, I would not share this sentiment, but a detailed argument about this would exceed the scope of this chapter.

Let us now consider the second counterargument. It suggests that even if we take into account the need to respect pluralism, we should still expect the law to speak with one voice, given that this "one voice" already incorporates the need to respect pluralism. This is a tricky argument, but its appeal dissipates as soon as we realize that it only adds a new label to the same package. It is like suggesting that the conflict between equality and utility can be solved by recognizing that there is some more complex value of equality that already contains a need to constrain equality when it stands in the way of greater utility. If there is a genuine conflict between the ideal of legislative integrity and the need to respect pluralism, the conflict cannot be resolved by relabeling integrity to incorporate respect for pluralism. In other words, I have argued for the need to respect value pluralism as an external constraint on the unqualified pursuit of any comprehensive morality. You do not gain anything of substance by incorporating this constraint into, say, a liberal comprehensive morality. The same constraint is there; it just has a different label now.

Finally, it can be argued that even if legislative integrity is not a distinct political ideal, the actual mechanisms that tend to engender moral incoherence in legislation are morally troubling or regrettable. In the next section, I will try to show that the opposite is true. The main circumstances that bring about a failure in legislative integrity actually manifest morally commendable aspects of democratic practices and institutions.

C. THE CAUSES OF LEGISLATIVE INCOHERENCE

As we want to focus on legislative, as opposed to judicial, integrity, let us stipulate a class of legal norms, call them *statutory law*, which would comprise all those legal norms that are enacted by legislative institutions, such as Congress, state legislatures, administrative agencies, and such. Now, if nothing else, at least the sheer number of such legislative institutions and their political diversity make it very unlikely that the entire body of statutory law at any given time would be morally coherent. Legislative integrity takes considerable effort to achieve and, often enough, it clearly fails. One of the ways in which we can examine the value of legislative integrity is by looking at the causes of its failure and asking ourselves whether those causes involve morally disturbing or regrettable aspects of our political institutions. Or, if we prefer to put it in a slightly different way: If legislative integrity is an ideal, what would it take to achieve it?

There are, presumably, many causes for the failure of legislative integrity. For example, the legislature can simply make a mistake. Needless to say, mistakes are always regrettable. Mostly, however, legislative integrity fails for much better reasons. Let me consider, in what follows, three of the main causes for the failure of legislative integrity.

1. Division of legislative power

First, as we have already mentioned, incoherence of statutory law often results from the great number of legislative institutions and the limited means by which their various legislative actions can be coordinated by a central authority. In fact, this results not just from the number of legislative agencies but also from their divergent social and political roles. For example, an administrative agency entrusted with the protection of the environment, like the EPA, is inherently biased in favor of certain social political goals it is there to advance, and those objectives might be at odds with the social and political goals of a different legislative agency. Similarly, a state legislature is naturally expected to promote the welfare of the state's residents and their local interests, and such aims may be at odds with those of the federal government or some other state. So there is a division of legislative power here that is both numerical and substantive. A well-functioning democracy purposefully creates a complex division of legislative power by entrusting legislation to different institutions, some of them with relatively special and limited authority. There are, of course, very good reasons for creating such divisions of legislative power. First, any division of legal/political power is a safeguard against tyranny. Second, such division of power typically aims to achieve a deliberate diversity of legislative goals by establishing legislative institutions that would be inherently motivated to advance a certain type of political agenda. By the creation of relatively specialized legislative institutions, alongside general ones, we aim to promote a diversity of interests that we think of as worthy of special care or concern.

There is no reason to assume that division of legislative power is purposefully designed to undermine the integrity of legislation. But it is certainly the case that the more legislative power is divided between different, and often competing, legislative institutions, the less likely it is that integrity will prevail. However, to the extent that division of legislative power tends to undermine the integrity of legislation, it is, as we have seen, for good reasons. The failure of integrity here derives from aspects of our political institutions that are based on sound moral-political principles.

Needless to say, there is a certain level of legislative coordination and coherence that is essential for the efficient functioning of any legal system. Too much incoherence and confusion make it very difficult for people to follow the law. But this only means that a certain *minimal* level of coherence is necessary for the functioning of a legal system. It does not come close to substantiating *an ideal* of legislative integrity. This is very much like the stability of law: A minimal level of stability over time is essential for the functioning of law, but again, this does not entail that stability is an ideal or that, ideally, the law should be as stable as possible.

2. Logrolling and compromise

In the case of division of legislative power, as we have seen, the lack of integrity in legislation is a result of the multiplicity of legislative institutions and their diverse goals. However, even within a single legislative body, especially one as politically diverse as a parliament or Congress, there are familiar legislative strategies that tend to undermine the integrity of legislation. Bargaining and compromise which are so often necessary to achieve an act of legislation may certainly result in laws that are morally incoherent. To be sure, not every legislative compromise undermines integrity. Roughly, there are two main types of compromise: Either you have to retract some of what you wanted to achieve, or else you get it all, but then you also have to give the other party some of what he or she wants (which may or may not be related to what you get). In both of these cases, the question of whether the resulting compromise is morally coherent or not depends on many specific details that we need not explore here. Suffice it to say that compromise and logrolling *may* result in legislation that falls far short of the ideal of legislative integrity. Does it make the necessity of compromise a regrettable aspect of democratic decision procedures? Surely that depends on the alternatives, and the relevant alternative is much worse. Political parties that do not have to compromise have too much power: They have the power to implement their comprehensive moral and political agenda without having to pay sufficient attention to the needs and interests of those who oppose their doctrines or whose interests are at odd with theirs. Once again, there is a delicate balance that needs to be maintained between too much and too little partisan political power. If the ruling majority is very flimsy and the government needs to compromise on every step it wants to take, governing itself might be seriously compromised. But this truism does not entail that the opposite is a political ideal: It does not follow that a good government is one which does not have to compromise with minority parties. In other words, in a pluralistic society compromise is not a regrettable necessity, but an important virtue of democratic decision procedures.[33]

3. Partisan realignment and the continuity of law

In a well-functioning democracy, control of the government periodically changes hands among various political parties. Naturally, every government wants to implement its political and ideological agenda, inter alia, by enacting new laws that purport to implement its views or repealing old ones that stand in its way.[34] This is certainly not an anomaly; it is what elections are held for. On the other hand, no government or legislature can start from a clean slate. Previous governments have had their own moral and political agenda enacted into laws that are still in force, and those old laws can be at odds with the moral-political views of the new government. These are the circumstances of partisan realignment, and these circumstances are bound to engender legislative changes that are morally incoherent. New laws and policies may coexist rather uneasily with the laws and policies still in force from the previous regimes.[35]

The failure of legislative integrity here stems from both practical and principled reasons. Even if the new government wanted to wipe the slate clean and change or repeal all those laws and policies that are inconsistent with its new ones, it would normally fail. The vast amount and complexity of legislation make such a task dauntingly difficult to carry out. But it is noteworthy that governments should not even attempt the task, and for principled reasons. Two of those reasons are very important: First, there is a principle of legal stability and continuity. Legislation typically creates an expectation that it will be relatively durable. People normally adjust their behavior and expectations to the legal regime currently in force. Changes of the normative environment often require an adaptation phase, which may be costly or otherwise disruptive. To be sure, none of this means that laws ought not be changed or that any legal change is, ipso facto, costly or disruptive. But as we all know, some level of stability over time is essential for the law to achieve its purposes, whatever they are.

Second, and more important in the present context, a general recognition that partisan realignment should not involve an attempt to wipe the previous legislative

[33] Jeremy Waldron, "The Circumstances of Integrity" in his *Law and Disagreement* (Oxford: Oxford University Press, 1999) 187.

[34] Of course, in the United States this is somewhat more complicated due to the separation between control of Congress and the presidency. For simplicity's sake, however, I will not dwell on this complexity and speak of "control of government" according to the parliamentary models in which the government is composed of the ruling majority in the legislature. Nothing in my substantive arguments should be affected by this difference.

[35] See Waldron, *supra* note 33 at 188–9 and Raz, *supra* note 3 at 280–1.

slate clean also stems from a principle of respect for pluralism. If elections result in partisan realignment, it is because the minority party has become the majority, and vice versa. But the previous majority-turned-minority has not vanished; it is still there, often representing a considerable segment of the population. It is widely acknowledged in well-functioning democracies that it would be wrong for the new majority to eradicate all the legislative achievements of the previous majority, even if they were partisan and ideological, because such an attempt would manifest disrespect for the views and moral convictions of the majority-turned-minority segment of the population. There is a delicate balance that needs to be respected here. On the one hand, an electoral victory resulting in partisan realignment is certainly a mandate for change, but it is not normally conceived of as a license to ignore the moral political convictions of those who lost, and this is as it should be.

To conclude, the circumstances of partisan realignment engender a considerable amount of legislative incoherence. The new government is typically forced to introduce legislative changes amid a tight network of previous laws and policies that may conflict with the new ones. These circumstances are likely to produce a patchwork of statutory law that cannot possibly reflect the moral and ethical views of a single, morally coherent, legislature. But this is not a regrettable aspect of democracy. On the contrary. As we have seen, the resulting legislative incoherence reflects moral political considerations that are supported by principled reasons. Those reasons derive from the need to maintain a certain level of legal stability as well as the need to respect value pluralism. Partisan realignment requires a delicate compromise between competing considerations. Not every compromise is regrettable. This is the kind of compromise that manifests respect for the moral complexity of our social and political realities. The best solution to social problems often consists in doing without the best.

ACKNOWLEDGMENTS

I am indebted to Scott Altman, David Dolinko, David Enoch, Elizabeth Garrett, Alon Harel, Joseph Raz, Jeremy Waldron, and Gideon Yaffe for very helpful comments.

7 Nondelegation Principles

Cass R. Sunstein

The American Constitution, like many other constitutions, is said to contain an interesting doctrine specifically designed to ensure democratic self-government. According to this doctrine, sometimes called "the nondelegation doctrine," the national legislature is not permitted to give, or to delegate, its lawmaking powers to any other body.

Many people say that the nondelegation doctrine is dead.[1] According to the refrain, the doctrine was once used to require Congress to legislate with some clarity, so as to ensure that law is made by the national legislature rather than by the executive. But the nondelegation doctrine – the refrain continues – is now merely a bit of rhetoric, as the United States Code has become littered with provisions asking one or another administrative agency to do whatever it thinks best. Although this is an overstatement, it captures an important truth: Since 1935, the Supreme Court has not struck down an act of Congress on nondelegation grounds, notwithstanding the existence of a number of plausible occasions.

Is the nondelegation doctrine really dead? To the extent that it is not flourishing, is there a way to promote its essential purposes, in a way that requires legislative deliberation on the most fundamental issues? I believe that the doctrine is actually alive and well. It has been relocated rather than abandoned. Federal courts commonly vindicate not a general nondelegation doctrine, which would raise serious problems, but a series of more specific and smaller, though quite important, nondelegation doctrines. Rather than invalidating federal legislation as excessively vague and open-ended, courts say that executive agencies may not engage in certain controversial activities unless and until Congress has expressly authorized them to do so. When fundamental rights and interests are at stake, the choices must be made legislatively. As a technical matter, the key holdings are based not on the nondelegation doctrine but on certain "canons" of construction.

What I mean to identify here are the *nondelegation canons*, not organized or recognized as such, but central to the operation of modern public law and designed to ensure clear legislative authorization for certain decisions. These are nondelegation canons for the simple reason that they forbid the executive, including administrative agencies, from making decisions on its own.

[1] See John Hart Ely, *Democracy and Distrust: A Theory of Judicial Review* (Cambridge: Harvard University Press, 1980) at 132–3.

Although my emphasis will be on nondelegation canons in American law, the basic idea has analogues in numerous legal systems and indeed plays an important role in many democratic orders. In Israel, for example, the Supreme Court's invalidation of torture was based on a judgment that if it is to occur, torture must be affirmatively authorized by the Knesset; it cannot be a product of the executive branch alone. Or in Britain, consider the *Human Rights Act* of 1998, which governs interpretation of statutes that may conflict with the *European Convention on Human Rights*. Section 3 declares: "So far as it is possible to do so, primary legislation and subordinate legislation must be read and given effect in a way which is compatible with the Convention rights." In this sense, the *Human Rights Act* creates a kind of nondelegation canon, requiring express legislative deliberation on behalf of any abridgement of Convention rights.

Consider a few examples from the United States. Most important, executive agencies are not permitted to construe federal statutes in such a way as to raise serious constitutional questions. If the constitutional question is substantial, Congress must clearly assert its desire to venture into the disputed terrain.[2] This principle means that without clear congressional permission, courts will not permit the executive to intrude on liberty or equality in a way that might compromise the Constitution. Here is a clear effort to link institutional protections with individual rights: It is difficult to get specific language through Congress, and hence a requirement of congressional specificity helps protect rights by ensuring that any interference with them must be clearly authorized and supported by both Congress and the executive.

In addition, Congress must affirmatively and specifically authorize the extraterritorial application of federal law. Agencies cannot exercise their ordinary discretion, under an ambiguous statutory provision, so as to apply national law outside of American borders. A clear congressional statement to this effect is required. When treaties and statutes are ambiguous, they must be construed favorably to Native American tribes; the agency's own judgment, if it is an exercise of discretion, is irrelevant.[3]

One of my central purposes here is to show that these canons should be understood as entirely legitimate and that they should be used even more than they now are. The nondelegation canons represent a salutary kind of *democracy-forcing judicial minimalism*, designed to ensure that certain choices are made by an institution with a superior democratic pedigree. Indeed, the nondelegation canons turn out to be a contemporary incarnation of the founding effort to link protection of individual rights, and other important interests, with appropriate institutional design. In certain cases, Congress must decide the key questions on its own. This is the enduring function of the nondelegation doctrine, and it is endorsed, not repudiated, by current law.

[2] See, for example, *Bowen v. Georgetown University Hospital*, 488 U.S. 204, 208–9 (1988) (stating that a congressional delegation of authority will be understood as granting the power to make retroactive rules only if the Congress specifically said so).

[3] See, for example, *Muscogee (Creek) Nation v. Hodel*, 851 F.2d 1439, 1444–5 (D.C. Cir. 1988) (stating that "canons of construction applicable in Indian law" require that "[s]tatutes are to be construed liberally in favor of the Indians, with ambiguous provisions interpreted to their benefit").

I. THE CONVENTIONAL DOCTRINE: PROMISES, DIFFICULTIES, AND DOUBTS

Let us begin with the conventional nondelegation doctrine. My conclusion is that in general, courts should not understand Article I, section 1 of the Constitution to require Congress to legislate with specificity, by sharply limiting the discretion of administrators. The most convincing claim on behalf of the conventional doctrine is far narrower and more modest: that certain highly sensitive decisions should be made by Congress, and not by the executive under open-ended legislative instructions.

A. Intelligible principles (?)

As the Supreme Court has long said, the conventional doctrine requires Congress to supply something like an "intelligible principle"[4] to guide and limit executive discretion.[5] According to its supporters, the nondelegation doctrine was a central part of the original constitutional plan but fell into disuse in the aftermath of the New Deal. Indeed, it is true that the Court referred to the nondelegation principle on a number of occasions in the pre–New Deal period.[6] Moreover, the Court invoked the doctrine to invalidate two acts of Congress in 1935, most famously in the *Schechter Poultry* case.[7] There the Court struck down a quite open-ended grant of authority, to the president, to develop "codes of fair competition"; a particular problem with the underlying statute was that it combined a high degree of vagueness with a grant of power, in practice, to private groups to develop such codes as they chose.[8] But it is also true that the Court has not used the doctrine to invalidate any statute since that time, notwithstanding many occasions when it might have found an absence of the requisite "intelligible principle."[9] Focusing on what they see as a plain breach of constitutional requirements, many observers have argued on behalf of a large-scale revival of the nondelegation doctrine in its conventional form.

For those who are committed to the conventional doctrine, there are a number of underlying concerns.[10] Many of those concerns are connected with deliberative

4 The specific term is used and discussed in *Amalgamated Meat Cutters v. Connally*, 337 F. Supp. 737, 745–7 (D. D.C. 1971).

5 *The Brig Aurora*, 11 U.S. (7 Cranch) 382, 387–8 (1813) (recognizing the nondelegation principle but upholding a disputed legislative Act because it was a revival of a legislative Act and not merely a presidential proclamation); *Field v. Clark*, 143 U.S. 649, 692 (1892) (noting the "universally recognized" principle that "Congress cannot delegate legislative power to the President"); *United States v. Grimaud*, 220 U.S. 506 at 521 (1911) (quoting *Field*); *J. W. Hampton, Jr., & Co. v. United States*, 276 U.S. 394 at 406–7 (1928) (collecting cases discussing delegation).

6 See *Field*, 143 U.S. at 692–3; *The Brig Aurora*, 11 U.S. at 388; *Grimaud*, 220 U.S. at 510.

7 *A.L.A. Schechter Poultry Corp. v. U.S.*, 295 U.S. 495 (1935) [*Schecter Poultry*]. The only other decision invalidating agency action on nondelegation grounds is *Panama Refining Co. v. Ryan*, 293 U.S. 388 (1935).

8 *Schechter Poultry*, ibid. at 537.

9 See *Mistretta v. U.S.*, 488 U.S. 361 (1989); *U.S. v. Southwestern Cable Co.*, 392 U.S. 157 (1968); *Lichter v. U.S.*, 334 U.S. 742 (1948); *Yakus v. US*, 321 U.S. 414 (1944).

10 See Gary Lawson, "The Rise and Rise of the Administrative State" (1994) 107 *Harv. L. Rev.* 1231, at 1240–1; Ely, *Democracy and Distrust*, *supra* note 1 at 132; Ernest Gellhorn, "Returning to First Principles: *A Symposium on Administrative Law – The Uneasy Constitutional Status of the Administrative Agencies: Part I – Delegation of Powers to Administrative Agencies: Commentary*" (1987) 36:2 *Am. U. L. Rev.* 345 at 347–8. A helpful symposium is "The Phoenix Rises Again: The Nondelegation Doctrine from

democracy, but perhaps the most basic are textual and historical. The Constitution's textual grant of lawmaking power to Congress might well be taken to mean that Congress, and no one else, has lawmaking authority; a delegation of "legislative" power to anyone else might seem inconsistent with the constitutional plan. In addition, the conceptual background of the whole system of checks and balances seems to provide historical support for this view – suggesting that the original understanding would have condemned open-ended grants of power to the executive. Even if there is no direct support in the founding era for the view that delegations are prohibited (a point to which I will return),[11] the principle of nondelegation might seem such an inevitable implication of the division of powers that it went without saying.

To the textual and historical points, enthusiasts for the conventional doctrine are able to add a series of claims about constitutional purpose and structure. The most important involves political accountability – and in particular that form of accountability that comes from the distinctive composition of Congress and the system of bicameralism. In light of the particular design of the central lawmaking institution, any delegation threatens to eliminate the special kind of accountability embodied in that institution (not incidentally including, in the Senate, the representation of states as such). It is worth underlining the role of bicameralism here. The evident obstacles to the enactment of federal law – a point of great relevance to the nondelegation canons – might be overcome if Congress could ask another institution, not subject to those obstacles, to enact law as it chooses. Outside of the United States, related points might be made, with suitable adjustments for differences in the design of lawmaking institutions.

This point is closely related to another. Simply by virtue of requiring legislators to agree on a relatively specific form of words, the nondelegation principle raises the burdens and costs associated with the enactment of national law[12] – in a way that ensures against a situation in which like-minded people are pressing one another in the direction of an unjustifiable position. Those burdens and costs can be seen as an important guarantor of individual liberty, because they ensure that national governmental power may not be brought to bear against individuals without a real consensus, established by legislative agreement on relatively specific words, that this step is desirable. To those who believe that the original institutional design was founded partly on the belief that the central government was a potential threat to freedom, open-ended delegations might seem to be a core violation of constitutional commitments.

In various ways, the nondelegation doctrine also promotes values connected with the rule of law, above all insofar as it ensures that government power must be bounded by clear limitations laid down in advance. Indeed, the ban on open-ended

Constitutional and Policy Perspectives" (1999) *20 Cardozo L. Rev.* 731, as is "A Symposium on Administrative Law, the Uneasy Constitutional Status of the Administrative Agencies" (1987) *36 Am. U. L. Rev.* 277.

11 See Eric Posner and Adrian Vermeule, "Interring the Nondelegation Doctrine" (2002) 69 *U. Chi. L. Rev.* 1721.

12 Some questions emerge about this conventional view from David Epstein and Sharyn O'Halloran, *Delegating Powers: A Transactions Cost Politics Approach to Policy Making Under Separate Powers* (New York: Cambridge University Press, 1999) at 237–9; the analysis there emphasizes the role of committees in fashioning specific terms when delegation is unavailable.

delegations appears to be closely connected to the void for vagueness doctrine, requiring that certain laws be clear rather than open-ended. The two key purposes of the latter doctrine are to provide fair notice to affected citizens and also to discipline the enforcement discretion of unelected administrators and bureaucrats. By ensuring that those asked to implement the law be bound by intelligible principles, the nondelegation doctrine serves the same purposes. Quite apart from promoting accountability, the conventional doctrine thus seems to promote goals typically associated with the rule of law.

Finally, the requirement of legislative clarity might also seem to be a check on the problems of factional power and self-interested representation, two of the problems most feared by the American framers.[13] Indeed, the nondelegation doctrine might be taken as a central means of reducing the risk that legislation will be a product of efforts by well-organized private groups to redistribute wealth or opportunities in their favor. The institutional design of Congress was intended to limit the power of well-organized private groups over government, and the requirement of general approval, from various legislators, seems to reduce the risk that self-interested representatives, with narrow agendas of their own, would use the lawmaking process to promote their parochial interests. These points might be summarized by linking the nondelegation principle with the general constitutional goal of providing a deliberative democracy.

B. Problems, institutional and otherwise

As arguments for a large-scale revival of the conventional doctrine, these points raise many questions. The most serious problems are twofold. First, judicial enforcement of the nondelegation doctrine would raise serious problems of judicial competence and would greatly magnify the role of the judiciary in overseeing the operation of modern government. Because the relevant questions are ones of degree, the nondelegation doctrine could not be administered in anything like a rulebound way, and hence the nondelegation doctrine is likely, in practice, to violate its own aspirations to discretion-free law. Second, it is far from clear that a large-scale judicial revival of the nondelegation doctrine would do anything to improve the operation of the regulatory state. It might well make things worse, possibly much worse.

1. QUESTIONS ABOUT PEDIGREE. In American law, does the conventional doctrine really have a good constitutional pedigree? It turns out that this question does not have a simple affirmative answer, from the standpoint of judicial practice, text, or history.[14] (I will return shortly to the place of the nondelegation doctrine in constitutional doctrine generally.)

[13] James Madison referred to both but spoke of the former as the more serious danger: "[I]n our Governments the real power lies in the majority of the Community, and the invasion of private rights is chiefly to be apprehended, not from acts of government contrary to the sense of its constituents, but from acts in which the Government is the mere instrument of the major number of the constituents." Letter from Madison to Jefferson (Oct. 17, 1788), in R. Rutland and C. Hobson, eds., *The Papers of James Madison* (Charlottesville: University Press of Virginia, 1977) at 298. This point bears on the defense of the nondelegation canons as requirements of clear legislative authorization for certain actions, as we will see.

[14] See Posner and Vermeule, *supra* note 11.

It is true that the Supreme Court *last* invalidated a statute on nondelegation grounds in 1935. But it is also true the Court *first* invalidated a statute on nondelegation grounds in exactly the same year, notwithstanding a number of previous opportunities. It is therefore misleading to suggest that the nondelegation doctrine was a well-entrenched aspect of constitutional doctrine, suddenly abandoned as part of some post–New Deal capitulation, by the Supreme Court, to the emerging administrative state. Indeed, it is more accurate, speaking purely descriptively, to see 1935 as the real anomaly. We might say that the conventional doctrine has had one good year, and 211 bad ones (and counting).

Nor do the Constitution's text and history provide unambiguous support for the conventional doctrine. The Constitution does grant legislative power to Congress, but it does not in terms forbid delegations of that power. Perhaps silence on the point can be taken to show that the ban on delegations was so obvious that it need not have been discussed. But the practice of early congresses strongly suggests that broad grants of authority to the executive were not thought to be problematic. The first Congress granted military pensions, not pursuant to legislative guidelines, but "under such regulations as the President of the United States may direct."[15] The second Congress gave the president the authority to grant licenses to trade with the Indian tribes, not with limitations, but under "such rules and regulations as the President shall prescribe."[16] There appears to be no evidence, in these or other cases, that members of Congress thought that such grants of authority violated a general nondelegation principle, notwithstanding extensive discussion of constitutional requirements within Congress in the early years of the nation.

These points do not demonstrate that the conventional nondelegation doctrine has no foundation in the original document. But the text and history must be counted ambiguous rather than plain on the point, and the fact of ambiguity raises questions about any large-scale judicial enforcement of a nondelegation principle.

2. QUESTIONS ABOUT STRUCTURE, LIBERTY, AND WELFARE. Turn now from text and history to some broader issues. Despite initial appearances, democratic considerations do not provide obvious support for the conventional nondelegation doctrine.[17] Executive agencies are themselves democratically accountable via the president. In addition, any delegation must itself have come from democracy, as an exercise of lawmaking authority. Congress may face electoral pressure merely by virtue of delegating broad authority to the executive; this is a perfectly legitimate issue to raise in an election, and "passing the buck" to bureaucrats is unlikely, in most circumstances, to be the most popular electoral strategy. If Congress has delegated such authority, maybe that is what voters want.

To be sure, these points are not decisive. We have seen that Congress has a distinctive form of accountability, through the mechanisms for representation and the system of bicameralism, and it is that form of accountability, not accountability

[15] 1 Stat. 95 (1789).

[16] 1 Stat. 137 (1790).

[17] See the excellent treatment in Jerry L. Mashaw, *Greed, Chaos, and Governance: Using Public Choice to Improve Public Law* (New Haven, Conn.: Yale University Press, 1997) at 131–57.

in the abstract, that justifies a nondelegation doctrine. But the democratic case for sharp limits on agency discretion is not clear-cut. In fact, congressional specificity often seems to produce outcomes that reflect the power of self-interested private groups – as, for example, where legislation reflects a capitulation to organizations using public-spirited rhetoric for their own parochial ends. And delegations often stem not from a desire to evade accountability but from a problem of lack of relevant information,[18] a pervasive and far from illegitimate basis for delegation in law or even life.[19]

Indeed, there is no evidence that from any point of view, the old nondelegation doctrine would make the operation of federal law better rather than worse. Clear statutory language, especially on details, is often a product not of some deliberative judgment by Congress, but of the influence of well-organized private groups. It is hard to come up with any abstract reason why decisions by agencies under vague language would be worse, from the standpoint of promoting social well-being, than decisions by agencies under more specific language from Congress. And in practice, respect for regulatory agencies, and evidence that agencies do more good than harm, cannot easily be connected to the narrowness of statutory delegations. There is no evidence that executive agencies operating pursuant to open-ended authority do better, on any dimension, than agencies operating pursuant to statutes that sharply limit their discretion; nothing appears to link agency performance with clear statutory language.

It is also highly speculative – an unacceptably crude generalization – to suggest that social welfare is, on any view of that contested ideal, likely to be promoted by reducing the total volume of law. What precedes any new legislative enactment is always some body of law, whether legislatively or judicially created. Why is there any reason to think that the preceding law systematically promotes social welfare? Consider in this regard the conclusions of the most systematic and detailed empirical analysis of the sources of delegations of authority.[20] The authors emphasize that the idea of wholesale delegation is a myth; in many areas, "some of which, like the budget and tax policy, require considerable time and expertise – Congress takes a major role in specifying the details of policy."[21] Nor is Congress oblivious to executive performance. On the contrary, "legislators carefully adjust and readjust discretion over time and across issue areas."[22] Most important for present purposes, the authors conclude that delegation operates not as an alternative to *congressional* judgment, but instead as a check on domination of lawmaking processes by legislative *committees*. In those committees, well-organized groups can often dominate. Indeed, delegation is "a necessary counterbalance to the concentration of power in the hands of committees," or to the surrender of "policy to a narrow subset of" members.[23] In these circumstances, the authors conclude that limits on delegation "would threaten the very individual liberties they purport to protect."[24]

[18] See Epstein and O'Halloran, *Delegating Powers, supra* note 12 at 206–31.
[19] See Cass R. Sunstein and Edna Ullmann-Margalit, "Second-Order Decisions" (1999) 110 *Ethics* 5 at 16.
[20] See Epstein and O'Halloran, *Delegating Powers, supra* note 12.
[21] Ibid. at 237.
[22] Ibid.
[23] Ibid.
[24] Ibid.

There is a final point here. Why should it be thought that any particular status quo, itself pervaded by law, embodies freedom, and that the new law at issue would threaten to abridge freedom? Is a law forbidding discrimination on the basis of disability, or sex, something that threatens liberty, so that it is crucial to obtain legislative agreement about the details, lest liberty be overridden? Or might the discriminatory status quo, the one that precedes the new law, be the real threat to freedom? Questions of this kind raise serious doubts about the idea that the conventional doctrine would promote liberty, properly conceived. As we shall see, there are contexts in which requirements of legislative specificity would indeed operate as liberty-enhancing safeguards; but the conventional doctrine is too broad and crude to be defensible on this ground.

3. QUESTIONS ABOUT JUDICIAL COMPETENCE. For the conventional doctrine, an especially serious problem stems from problems of judicial competence. Under that doctrine, the line between a permitted and a prohibited delegation is one of degree, and inevitably so. The distinction between "executive" and "legislative" power cannot depend on anything qualitative; the issue is a quantitative one. The real question is: How much executive discretion is too much to count as "executive"? No metric is easily available to answer that question.

In these circumstances, the overwhelming likelihood is that judicial enforcement of the doctrine would produce ad hoc, highly discretionary rulings, giving little guidance to lower courts or to Congress itself. The matter is even worse than that. Because the underlying issue is one of degree, decisions invalidating statutes as unduly open-ended are likely to suffer from the appearance, and perhaps the reality, of judicial hostility to the particular program at issue. For this reason, those concerned about rule-free law are especially likely to be uncomfortable with any large-scale revival of the conventional doctrine. Without much exaggeration, and with tongue only slightly in cheek, we might say that judicial enforcement of the conventional doctrine would violate the conventional doctrine – because it could not be enforced without delegating, without clear standards, a high degree of discretionary lawmaking authority to the judiciary. These points are all the more troubling in light of the simple fact that judicial enforcement of the conventional doctrine would grant massive new authority to the federal judiciary, authority to second-guess legislative judgments about how much discretion is too much, without clear constitutional standards for answering that question. As we shall now see, there are alternatives that do the good work of the old doctrine, but without presenting these problems.

II. HIDDEN NONDELEGATION PRINCIPLES

I am going to argue that in order to protect important rights and interests, courts do not allow the executive branch to make certain choices unless Congress has specifically decided that those choices are appropriate. But let us begin with a somewhat technical question, one that bears directly on the current status of the nondelegation doctrine: What is the authority of executive agencies to interpret the law?

When Congress has spoken clearly, everyone agrees that agencies are bound by what Congress has said. The disputed question has to do with the authority of agencies to act when Congress has not spoken clearly. Of course, a very strong version of the conventional nondelegation doctrine would suggest that agencies can, in such cases, do nothing, because the underlying grant of power is effectively void. But short of this radical conclusion, what is the allocation of authority to agencies?

A. *Chevron* as canon: aggravating the delegation problem?

In American law, the place to start is of course *Chevron USA v. Natural Resources Defense Council, Inc.*,[25] the decision that dominates modern administrative law. Seemingly technical and abstruse, the Court's decision in this case has had large implications for the American public – much larger, in fact, than many other cases receiving much more publicity.

In *Chevron*, the Supreme Court held that unless Congress has decided the "precise question at issue,"[26] agencies are authorized to interpret ambiguous terms as they see fit, so long as the interpretation is reasonable. *Chevron* creates a two-step inquiry. The first question is whether Congress has directly decided the precise question at issue. The second question is whether the agency interpretation is reasonable. Indeed, *Chevron* establishes a novel canon of construction: In the face of ambiguity, statutes mean what the relevant agency takes them to mean.

This is an emphatically "prodelegation" canon; indeed, it is the quintessential prodelegation canon, and it is possible to argue that *Chevron* is highly objectionable precisely on nondelegation grounds – that it is objectionable precisely because it increases executive discretion. On this view, the problem is that under *Chevron*, agencies are not merely given authority that is often open-ended; they are also permitted to interpret the scope of their own authority, at least in the face of ambiguity. A system in which agencies lacked this authority would – it might be claimed – better promote nondelegation principles, for under such a regime, agencies would lack the power to construe statutory terms on their own.

The weakness of this objection stems from the fact that when statutory terms are ambiguous, there is no escaping delegation. By hypothesis Congress has not been clear – perhaps because it has been unable to resolve the issue, perhaps because it did not foresee it. The recipient of the delegation will be either agencies or courts. *Chevron* does increase the discretionary authority of agencies – this is the sense in which it creates a prodelegation canon – but only in relation to courts. With respect to the question whether the national legislature will actually legislate, it is neither here nor there.

B. Trumping *Chevron*: three categories of nondelegation canons

It is plain, however, that a variety of canons of construction – what I am calling nondelegation canons – trump *Chevron* itself.[27] In other words, the agency's

[25] 467 U.S. 837 (1984).

[26] Ibid. at 842, 843.

[27] See, for example, *Bowen v. Georgetown University Hospital*, 488 U.S. 204 at 208–9, 212–13 (1988) (noting a canon against interpreting a statute to be retroactive and denying judicial deference to an agency

interpretation of law does not, under current doctrine, prevail if one of the nondelegation canons is at work. These canons impose important constraints on executive authority, for agencies are not permitted to understand ambiguous provisions to give them authority to venture in certain directions; a clear congressional statement is necessary.

The nondelegation canons fall into three principal categories. Some are inspired by the Constitution; others involve issues of sovereignty; still others have their foundations in public policy. The unifying theme is that the executive is not permitted to intrude on important rights or interests in its own. The national legislature, with its diverse membership and multiplicity of voices, must explicitly authorize any such intrusions. In this sense, the torture case in Israel is a classic case of a nondelegation canon – exemplifying how requirements of legislative clarity can trigger political safeguards in the service of individual rights.

1. CONSTITUTIONALLY INSPIRED NONDELEGATION CANONS. A number of nondelegation canons have constitutional origins; they are explicit efforts to promote democracy's constitution. They are designed to promote some goal, often involving rights, with a constitutional foundation.

Consider, as the most familiar example, the idea that executive agencies will not be permitted to construe statutes in such a way as to raise serious constitutional doubts.[28] Notice that this principle goes well beyond the (uncontroversial) notion that agencies should not be allowed to construe statutes so as to be unconstitutional. The principle appears to say that constitutionally sensitive questions will not be permitted to arise unless the constitutionally designated lawmaker has deliberately and expressly chosen to raise them. For example, a law will not ordinarily be taken to allow the executive branch to intrude on the right to travel, violate the right to free speech, interfere with religious liberty, or constitute a taking of private property without compensation.

The only limitations on the principle are that the constitutional doubts must be serious and substantial, and that the statute must be fairly capable of an interpretation contrary to the agency's own.[29] So long as the statute is unclear, and the constitutional question serious, Congress must decide to raise that question via explicit statement. This idea trumps *Chevron* for that very reason. Executive interpretation of a vague statute is not enough when the purpose of the canon is to require Congress to make its instructions clear.

Belonging in the same category is the idea that the executive agencies will not be allowed to interpret ambiguous provisions so as to preempt state law.[30] The constitutional source of this principle is the evident constitutional commitment to a federal structure, a commitment that may not be compromised without a

counsel's interpretation of a statute when the agency itself has articulated no position on the question). This is the tendency of current law with respect to all of the nondelegation canons discussed here, but the tendency is, in some cases, little more than that, and on the conflict of the canons with *Chevron*, there are some conflicts in the lower courts. See, for example, Peter S. Heinecke, "Comment, *Chevron* and the Canon Favoring Indians" (1993) 60 *U. Chi. L. Rev.* 1015. I do not discuss these conflicts here.

28 See *supra* note 2.

29 See *Rust v. Sullivan*, 500 U.S. 173, 191 (1991).

30 See *National Association of Regulatory Utility Commissioners v. FCC*, 880 F.2d 422 (D.C. Cir. 1989).

congressional decision to do so – an important requirement in light of the various safeguards against cavalier disregard of state interests created by the system of state representation in Congress.[31] Notice that there is no constitutional obstacle to national preemption; Congress is entitled to preempt state law if it chooses. But there is a constitutional obstacle of a sort: The preemption decision must be made legislatively, not bureaucratically.[32]

As a third example, consider the notion that unless Congress has spoken with clarity, agencies are not allowed to apply statutes retroactively, even if the relevant terms are quite unclear.[33] Because retroactivity is disfavored in the law,[34] Congress will not be taken to have delegated to administrative agencies the authority to decide the question. The best way to understand this idea is as an institutional echo of the notion that the due process clause (Fifth Amendment) forbids retroactive application of law.[35] Of course, the constitutional constraints on retroactivity are now modest; while the ex post facto clause (Article I, section 9) in the American Constitution forbids retroactive application of the criminal law, the clause is narrowly construed, and Congress is generally permitted to impose civil legislation retroactively if it chooses.[36] But there is an institutional requirement here. Congress must make that choice explicitly and take the political heat for deciding to do so. It will not be taken to have attempted the same result via delegation, and regulatory agencies will not be taken to have the authority to choose retroactivity on their own. Perhaps part of the courts' motivation here is ambivalence about judicial refusal to apply the ex post facto clause, or the due process clause, so as to call into constitutional question some retroactive applications of civil law. The nondelegation canon is a more cautious way of promoting the relevant concerns.

Consider, finally, the extremely important *rule of lenity*, which says that in the face of ambiguity, criminal statutes will be construed favorably to criminal defendants. One function of the lenity principle is to ensure against delegations, to courts or to anyone else. Criminal law must be a product of a clear judgment on Congress's part. Where no clear judgment has been made, the statute will not apply merely because it is plausibly interpreted, by courts or enforcement authorities, to fit the case at hand. The rule of lenity is inspired by the due process constraint – central to democracy's constitution – on convicting people of crimes under open-ended or vague statutes. Although it is not itself a constitutional mandate, the idea is rooted in a constitutional principle and serves as a time-honored nondelegation canon.

[31] See Herbert Wechsler, "The Political Safeguards of Federalism" (1954) 54 *Colum. L. Rev.* 543, for the classic discussion of these safeguards.

[32] It is not entirely clear whether an agency might be able to decide the question if Congress expressly said that the agency is permitted to do so. This raises a general point about the nondelegation canons: What would happen if Congress attempted to bypass them by a clear statement of delegation? I take up this question below.

[33] *Bowen v. Georgetown University Hospital, supra* note 2 at 208.

[34] Ibid.

[35] The notion is defended in Richard A. Epstein, *Takings: Private Property and the Power of Eminent Domain* (Cambridge, Mass.: Harvard University Press, 1985) at 255–9.

[36] See, for example, *Usery v. Turner Elkhorn Mining*, 438 U.S. 1 at 14–20 (1976) (holding that the Black Lung Benefits Act of 1972 does not violate the Fifth Amendment due process clause by requiring employers to provide retrospective compensation for former employees' death or disability due to employment in mines).

2. SOVEREIGNTY-INSPIRED NONDELEGATION CANONS. The second category of nondelegation canons contains principles that lack a constitutional source but that have a foundation in widespread understandings about the nature of governmental authority – more particularly, in widespread understandings about sovereignty. Consider here the fact that the executive is not permitted to apply statutes outside of the territorial borders of the United States.[37] If statutes are to receive extraterritorial application, it must be as a result of a deliberate congressional judgment to this effect. The central notion here is that extraterritorial application calls for extremely sensitive judgments involving international relations; such judgments must be made via the ordinary lawmaking process (in which the president, of course, participates). The executive may not make this decision on its own.[38] One of the evident purposes of this requirement is now familiar: to ensure deliberation among diverse people, and not merely within the executive branch, before an American law will be applied abroad.

For broadly related reasons, agencies cannot interpret statutes and treaties unfavorably to Native Americans.[39] Where statutory provisions are ambiguous, the government will not prevail. This idea is plainly an outgrowth of the complex history of relations between the United States and Native American tribes, which have semi-sovereign status; it is an effort to ensure that any unfavorable outcome will be a product of an explicit judgment from the national legislature. The institutional checks created by congressional structure must be navigated before an adverse decision may be made.

Consider, as a final if more controversial illustration, the fact that agencies are not permitted to waive the sovereign immunity of the United States, and indeed statutory ambiguity cannot be used by agencies as a basis for waiver, which must be explicit in legislation.[40] Sovereign immunity is a background structural understanding, defeasible only on the basis of a judgment to that effect by the national legislature.

3. NONDELEGATION CANONS INSPIRED BY PERCEIVED PUBLIC POLICY. The final set of nondelegation canons is designed to implement perceived public policy, by, among other things, giving sense and rationality the benefit of the doubt – and by requiring Congress itself to speak if it wants to compromise policy that is perceived as generally held. The most sympathetic understanding of these canons rests on

[37] *EEOC v. Arabian American Oil Co,* 499 U.S. 244, 248 (1991).

[38] Of course, the executive is permitted to make a large number of quite sensitive decisions involving foreign relations, partly because of express constitutional commitments, partly because of perceived contemporary necessities. And it would not be impossible to imagine a legal system in which the executive was permitted, in the event of ambiguity, to resolve the issue of extraterritoriality. Recall that my goal here is descriptive, not normative. The best defense of this particular nondelegation canon would be that the question whether the enacted law should be applied outside of the nation's borders is a large and essentially legislative one, which cannot be made by the executive on its own.

[39] See *Ramah Navajo Chapter v. Lujan,* 112 F.3d 1455 at 1461–2 (10th Cir. 1997) (grounding a canon of statutory construction favoring Native Americans in "the unique trust relationship between the United States and the Indians"); *Williams v. Babbitt,* 115 F.2d 657 at 660 (9th Cir. 1997) (noting in dicta that courts "are required to construe statutes favoring Native Americans liberally in their favor"); *Tyonek Native Corp v. Secretary of Interior,* 836 F.2d 1237 at 1239 (9th Cir. 1988) (noting in dicta that "statutes benefiting Native Americans should be construed liberally in their favor").

[40] *United States Department of Energy v. Ohio,* 503 U.S. 607 at 615 (1992).

the view that the relevant policies are not the judges' own but have a source in widely held, and properly held, social commitments.

There are many examples. Exemptions from taxation are narrowly construed;[41] if Congress wants to exempt a group from federal income tax, it must express its will clearly. A central idea here may be that such exemptions are often the product of lobbying efforts by well-organized private groups and thus a reflection of factional influence; hence agencies may not create such exemptions on their own. At the same time, there is a general federal policy against anticompetitive practices, and agencies will not be permitted to seize on ambiguous statutory language so as to defeat that policy.[42] If Congress wants to make an exception to the policy in favor of competition, it is certainly permitted to do so. But agencies may not do so without congressional instruction. So, too, it is presumed that statutes providing veterans' benefits will be construed generously for veterans, and agencies cannot conclude otherwise.[43] This idea is an analogue to the notion that statutes will be construed favorably to Native Americans; both require a congressional judgment if a group perceived as weak or deserving is going to be treated harshly.

In decisions of particular importance for the modern regulatory state, agencies are sometimes forbidden to require very large expenditures for trivial or de minimis gains.[44] If Congress wants to be "absolutist" about safety, in a way that might well compromise social well-being, it is permitted to do so by explicit statement. But agencies will not be allowed to take ambiguous language in this direction. This is a genuinely novel nondelegation principle, a creation of the late twentieth century. It is an evident response to perceived problems in modern regulatory policy.

4. BARRIERS, CATALYSTS, AND MINIMALISM. How intrusive are the nondelegation canons? What kind of judicial role do they contemplate? Consider the view that these canons are best understood not as barriers but as catalysts, allowing government to act so long as it does so through certain channels. The effort is to trigger democratic (in the sense of legislative) processes and to ensure the forms of deliberation, and bargaining, that are likely to occur in the proper arenas.

In a sense this understanding – of nondelegation canons as catalysts – is correct. So long as government is permitted to act when Congress has spoken clearly, no

[41] *United States v. Wells Fargo Bank*, 485 U.S. 351 at 354 (1988).

[42] *Michigan Citizens for an Independent Press v. Thornburgh*, 868 F.2d 1285 at 1299 (D.C. Cir. 1989) (Ginsburg, dissenting) (noting the "accepted rule" that antitrust exemptions must be narrowly construed); *Group Life & Health Insurance v. Royal Drug Co.*, 440 U.S. 205 at 231 (1979) (noting the "well settled" rule that antitrust exceptions "are to be narrowly construed").

[43] *King v. St. Vincent's Hospital*, 502 U.S. 215 at 220 n. 9 (1991).

[44] See *Industrial Union Department, AFL-CIO v. American Petroleum Institute*, 448 U.S. 607 at 644 (1980) (plurality) (holding that in promulgating OSHA, Congress "intended, at a bare minimum, that the Secretary [of Labor] find a significant risk of harm and therefore a probability of significant benefits before establishing a new standard"); *Corrosion Proof Fittings v. EPA*, 947 F.2d 1201 at 1222–3 (5th Cir. 1991) (vacating the EPA's proposed rulemaking under the Toxic Substances Control Act and its ban on asbestos, partially on the grounds that the agency's own figures suggested that enforcing the regulation might cost as much as $74 million per life saved); *Alabama Power Co v. Costle*, 636 F.2d 323 at 360–1 (D.C. Cir. 1979) (stating that "[u]nless Congress has been extraordinarily rigid, there is likely a basis for an implication of de minimis authority to provide exemption when the burdens of regulation yield a gain of trivial or no value"); *Monsanto Co. v. Kennedy*, 613 F.2d 947 at 954–5 (D.C. Cir. 1979) (allowing the Commissioner of Food and Drugs not to apply the strictly literal terms of the statute and to make de minimis exceptions).

judicial barrier is in place.[45] In this way, the nondelegation canons are properly understood as a species of judicial minimalism, indeed democracy-forcing minimalism, designed to ensure that judgments are made by the democratically preferable institution.[46] As compared with more rigid barriers to government action, the conventional nondelegation doctrine itself is a form of minimalism insofar as it requires Congress to speak with clarity and does not disable the government entirely. And because the nondelegation canons are narrower and more specifically targeted – requiring particular rather than general legislative clarity – they are more minimalist still.

But this understanding misses an important point. Nondelegation canons are barriers, and not merely catalysts, with respect to purely administrative (or executive) judgment on the matters in question. They erect a decisive barrier to certain discretionary decisions by the executive. In this respect, at least, the relevant institutions are blocked.

III. CANONS RECONCEIVED AND REDEEMED

A. Judicial administrability and congressional lawmaking

Canons of the sort I have outlined here are highly controversial. Judge Richard Posner, for example, fears that some of them create a "penumbral Constitution," authorizing judges to bend statutes in particular directions even though there may in fact be no constitutional violation.[47] But if the analysis here is correct, there is a simple answer to these concerns: The relevant canons operate as nondelegation principles, and they are designed to ensure that Congress decides certain contested questions on its own. If this idea is a core structural commitment of the Constitution, and if it ensures broad rather than narrow deliberation on sensitive issues, there can be no problem with its judicial enforcement.

We can go further. As noted above, there are serious problems with judicial enforcement of the conventional nondelegation doctrine. Compare, along the relevant dimensions, judicial use of the nondelegation canons. Here the institutional problem is far less severe. Courts do not ask the hard-to-manage question whether the legislature has exceeded the permissible level of discretion, but pose instead the far more manageable question whether the agency has been given the discretion to decide something that (under the appropriate canon) only legislatures may decide. In other words, courts ask a question about subject matter, not a question about degree.

Putting the competence of courts to one side, the nondelegation canons have the salutary function of ensuring that certain important rights and interests will not be compromised unless Congress has expressly decided to compromise them. Thus, the nondelegation canons lack a central defect of the conventional doctrine:

[45] Consider *Hampton v. Mow Sun Wong*, 426 U.S. 88, 114–17 (1976) (holding that the Civil Service Commission could not decide to exclude aliens from the civil service, but leaving open the question whether Congress or the president could do so).

[46] On minimalism generally, see Cass Sunstein, *One Case at a Time* (Cambridge, Mass.: Harvard University Press, 1999).

[47] See Richard A. Posner, *The Federal Courts: Crisis and Reform* (Cambridge, Mass.: Harvard University Press, 1985) at 285.

Although there is no good reason to think that a reinvigorated nondelegation doctrine would improve the operation of modern regulation, it is entirely reasonable to think that for certain kinds of decisions, merely executive decisions are not enough.

If, for example, an agency is attempting on its own to apply domestic law extraterritorially, we might believe that whatever its expertise, it is inappropriate, as a matter of democratic theory and international relations, for this to happen unless Congress has decided that it should. Or courts might reasonably believe that retroactive application of regulatory law is acceptable not simply because the executive believes that an ambiguous law should be so construed, but if and only if Congress has reached this conclusion. This judgment might be founded on the idea that political safeguards will ensure that Congress will so decide only if there is very good reason for that decision. For those who believe that retroactivity is constitutionally unacceptable, this may be insufficient consolation. But a requirement that Congress make the decision on its own is certainly likely to make abuses less common, if they are legitimately characterized as abuses at all.

These points have the considerable advantage of understanding the nondelegation canons as a modern incarnation of the framers' basic project of linking individual rights and interests with institutional design. The link comes from protecting certain rights and interests not through a flat judicial ban on governmental action, but through a requirement that certain controversial or unusual actions will occur only with respect for the institutional safeguards introduced through the design of Congress. There is thus a close connection between the nondelegation canons and a central aspiration of the constitutional structure.

B. Qualifications and futures

I have not suggested that the nondelegation canons accomplish precisely the same goals as the old nondelegation doctrine, or for that matter vice versa. There are several differences. For its defenders, the nondelegation doctrine is supposed to operate as a general or global requirement that Congress make the basic judgments of value. The nondelegation canons have a conspicuously more limited office. Consider, for example, the authority of the Federal Communications Commission (FCC) to give out broadcasting licenses in accordance with "public convenience, interest, or necessity." Those who are enthusiastic about the nondelegation doctrine would want to invalidate this authority altogether. By contrast, a nondelegation canon would operate to forbid the FCC from exercising its authority in such a way as to create serious First Amendment questions, by, for example, requiring broadcasters to provide free airtime for candidates for public office. A ruling to this effect limits FCC discretion, but only in a narrow, targeted way.

My basic response to this objection is that even for those who believe the nondelegation doctrine is great, the nondelegation canons are good. In any case I have offered reasons to believe that the nondelegation doctrine is far from great; the nondelegation canons seem to me far preferable, because they are easily administrable, impose a much less serious strain on judicial capacities, and promise to do more good while also producing less harm.

The most important future debates will involve not the existence or legitimacy of nondelegation canons, but their particular content. Of course, the category changes over time. As noted, a core nondelegation canon of the early twentieth century required a clear legislative statement to authorize an interference with common-law rights. For the most part, this canon is no longer reflected in current law. By contrast, the idea that statutes will be construed so as to require de minimis exceptions is relatively new, a creation of the late twentieth century, a self-conscious judicial response to certain problems in regulatory law. It would be easy to imagine the introduction of new canons and the repudiation of current ones. I have attempted to sketch defenses of existing nondelegation canons, in order to understand the basis for the view that the relevant issues may not be resolved bureaucratically. But nothing in the general account depends on whether any particular canons are defensible.

As a class, the nondelegation canons are best defended on the ground that certain decisions are ordinarily expected to be made by the national legislature, with its various institutional safeguards, and not via the executive alone. A central goal of those safeguards is to ensure against the problems that occur when like-minded people are deliberating with one another, and failing to confront alternative views. In this way the nondelegation canons take their place as one of the most prominent domains in which protection of individual rights, and of other important interests, occurs not through blanket prohibitions on governmental action, but through channeling decisions to particular governmental institutions, in this case Congress itself.

ACKNOWLEDGMENTS

This is a substantially revised and updated version of Cass R. Sunstein, "Nondelegation Canons" (2000) 67 *U. Chi. L. Rev.* 315.

8 Vox Populi: Populism, the Legislative Process, and the Canadian Constitution

Harry Arthurs

This chapter is concerned with the constitutional implications of populism for Canadian parliamentary democracy. It begins with working definitions of two crucial concepts – "populism" and "the constitution." It then offers an account of how contemporary Canadian populism has attempted to reshape the constitution and identifies the possible effects of populism on legislative powers, processes, functions, and actors; on relations between citizens and their elected representatives; and on relations amongst the legislature, the executive, and the judiciary. A brief conclusion explores the possible long-term constitutional significance of these populist initiatives.

I. POPULISM AND THE CONSTITUTION: WORKING DEFINITIONS

Neither "populism" nor "the constitution" is a term of art; they are words whose meanings shift over time and across space. "Populism" in contemporary America is quite different from Australian or Austrian populism, but also from its Canadian cousin, though populists and populisms have often wandered back and forth across the 49th parallel. Likewise "constitution," a term whose technical and vernacular meanings have evolved as they migrated across the Atlantic and from Canada's colonial period to the present.

Populism

As a recent study of populism notes, the term "has an essential impalpability, an awkward conceptual slipperiness."[1] However, like the other "p-word" – pornography – even if we cannot define populism, we can usually recognize it when we see it. And we have been seeing it for much of our history – arguably as far back as the 1837 uprisings in Upper and Lower Canada and the Riel rebellion of 1885.[2] Often closely associated with regional alienation,[3] in the interwar years it inspired movements

[1] P. Taggart, *Populism* (Buckingham/Philadelphia: Open University Press, 2000) at 1. Taggart lists six recurring themes that appear throughout his comparative study of populists: "populists as hostile to representative politics; populists identifying themselves with an idealized heartland within the community they favour; populism as an ideology lacking core values; populism as a powerful reaction to a sense of extreme crisis; populism as containing fundamental dilemmas that make it self-limiting; populism as a chameleon, adopting the colours of its environment" (at 2).

[2] Tom Flanagan, "From Riel to Reform: Understanding Western Canada" (Montreal: McGill Institute for the Study of Canada, Fourth Annual Seagram Lecture 1999).

[3] Ibid.

of the left such as the Progressive Party, the United Farmers, and the CCF; similar tendencies persist today.[4] However, contemporary populism has often inclined to the right, resulting sometimes in ephemeral, sectarian, or quixotic movements (the Bloc Populaire, Confederation of Regions, and Family Values parties); sometimes in effective new political formations (the Social Credit, Creditiste, Reform, and Alliance parties); sometimes in the reinvention of existing parties (the Alberta and Ontario Progressive Conservatives and the B.C. Liberals); sometimes in a mixture of these (the new Conservative Party of Canada).[5] Sometimes too, it has turned out to be no more than a stylistic affectation by politicians who in fact lead fairly conventional parliamentary parties or governments.

What, if anything, do these very different manifestations of populism have in common? They are all recognizable to some extent in the following imagined populist account of Canadian politics today.

Government – populists will say – is remote and unresponsive; it is run by and for the benefit of politicians and bureaucrats and/or their own friends and supporters and/or "powerful" or "special" interests; the ideas that shape public policy are not those of "ordinary people" but of liberals (or the left, the right, separatists, intellectuals, civil servants, farmers, the business community, minority groups); within the Canadian federation the interests of the peripheral (or central) provinces are ignored, and within each province the interests of large cities (or suburbs or rural communities) are given undue attention. Government is not accountable for what it chooses to do with "your tax dollars": It takes, more than it needs, spends more than it takes, and wastes large sums on foolish projects designed only to improve its own electoral fortunes and the interests of its supporters. It squanders money on overpaid and underworked teachers or civil servants (or farm subsidies, corporate welfare, highbrow culture, lowbrow entertainment, state ceremonials, or foreign adventures), but it denies help to those who need or are entitled to it by reason of their personal virtue (or inescapable misfortune, historic claims, economic contributions, or faithful support of the governing party). Incumbent governments in particular are "out of touch," autocratic, undemocratic, and corrupt; but politicians are all the same: They make reckless promises to get your vote; but then once elected, your wishes no longer matter to them.

For each of these shortcomings of governments, politicians, and civil servants (some of them real enough), populists propose a single, simple remedy: Heed the people; listen to their wisdom; respond to their concerns; respect their interests; let them make the choices. From one perspective, then,

> populism is . . . not an ideology but a methodology, not a doctrine or a set of positions but a process for discovering "the will of the people" and thereby overcoming superficial divisions amongst the people.[6]

[4] David Laycock, *Populism and Democratic Thought in the Canadian Prairies, 1910–1945* (Toronto: University of Toronto Press, 1990).

[5] See, e.g., Tom Flanagan *supra* note 2; Trevor Harrison, *Of Passionate Intensity: Right Wing Populism and the Reform Party of Canada* (Toronto: University of Toronto Press, 1995); D. Laycock, *The New Right and Democracy in Canada – Understanding Reform and the Canadian Alliance* (Don Mills: Oxford University Press, 2002).

[6] Tom Flanagan, *Waiting for the Wave: The Reform Party and Preston Manning* (Toronto: Stoddart, 1995).

But this methodology can produce variable outcomes. Sometimes, it is used cynically to win support for particular policies, parties, and politicians, and once it has achieved its purposes, this methodology is discarded in favor of politics-as-usual. Sometimes it inspires true believers, alienated from electoral politics and parliamentary institutions, to discover and express "the will of the people" in millenarian cults, street protests, civic disobedience, or even, in extreme cases, violence. Sometimes, it is highly cerebral and principled, a kind of populism-from-above. Originating in academic institutions or think tanks, this populism-without-the-people begins with a diagnosis of the democratic deficit of parliamentary institutions, federalism, or public administration and concludes by prescribing their reinvention. In one version, information technologies enable a digital democracy in which elected representatives are informed in real time of "the people's" preferences. In another, voters are reincarnated as consumers, forums for public policy debate as markets that offer competition and choice, and the general welfare as the sum of individual transactions.

However, Canadian populism has generally concentrated on more modest proposals to reform legislative institutions and processes: Important public policy decisions should involve referenda or plebiscites; politicians should be kept on a short leash by the threat of recall elections, fixed terms and modest salaries, pensions, and perquisites; checks and balances should ensure that no level or branch of government can act unilaterally; particular constituencies – regions, communities, occupations, or viewpoints – should be assured an "equal" voice so that others do not exercise "disproportionate" influence; openness, transparency, and accountability should be engineered into government so that the bright light of public opinion can cleanse corruption and punish cynicism; and above all, the power, influence, and financial resources of the state should be reduced so that the power, influence, and wealth of the people can be enlarged.

What binds together these very diverse tendencies within populism is their shared premise that the institutions of government must be changed so that they better reflect the people's will. But what divides them – from each other and from nonpopulist approaches – is neither "methodology" nor "ideology"; it is in the most profound sense, issues of constitutional form and substance.

Critiques of populism are also various. The first is that populism tends, paradoxically, to be undemocratic; it ignores the fundamental democratic principle of majority rule. Unlike majoritarian democrats, populists tend to believe that "ordinary people" (rural, white, francophone, god-fearing, working class, etc.) deserve to exercise control not so much because of their numbers as because of their inherent virtue and/or intuitive "common sense," because they are uncorrupted by effete lifestyles or excessive, educations, or because they have earned that right through heroic achievement (migration, military service), community contribution (business, moral leadership), or sacrifice (surviving drought, recession, crime). A related critique is that populism is exclusionary and divisive. "Ordinary people" tend to be assigned, in populist discourse, specific regional, ethnic, class, or other adjectival identities (alienated westerners, humiliated Quebeckers, angry workers) that make them responsive to specific symbolic behaviors – either positive (vernacular speech; unpretentious manner; constant invocation of the values, lifestyle, and mental world of "ordinary Canadians") or negative (antistate, antielite, antiintellectual, or anti-"other" rhetoric). Whether positive or negative – the critique proceeds – this kind of populist rhetoric diverts attention from substance to style, lowers the tone of political debate, encourages the development of false consciousness, divides the country, and, at its worst, descends into xenophobia or racism.

A third critique is practical: Most citizens realistically cannot and do not want to participate in making significant public decisions; they lack knowledge, understanding, time, motivation, and means. A fourth is political: Many so-called populist movements are inauthentic and cynical attempts by lobbyists, ideologues, powerful business interests, and conventional politicians to manipulate genuine populist sentiment for their own political purposes, with no intention of ever allowing the people to govern. A fifth focuses on outcomes: If the steadying influence of elected representatives and civil servants is reduced, and if the legislative process is made to more immediately and accurately reflect transient popular sentiments, foolish or repressive measures are likely to be adopted. And a sixth rests on principle: Some features of a democratic society are so sacrosanct that they must be protected even from the will of "the people" themselves.

Like the various strands of populism, these critiques have something in common: a less idealized view of how "the people" might rule, and a more idealized view of how "the system" might work better if it were reformed from within. But they diverge on issues of constitutional significance.

The constitution

A constitution – in my lexicon – is not simply a canonical text glossed by judges and scholars. It is the sum of all those influences that over time shape the fundamental character of the state, the configuration of its institutions and the behavior of its agents, that motivate or constrain the exercise of national sovereignty and that define the meaning of citizenship. Thus, constitutions – properly understood – include conventions of political, legal, and administrative behavior and discourse; established cultural understandings and social practices; and the deep structures of domestic and international political economy.[7] Nor given the peculiar permeability of Canada's fundamental law, does my own idiosyncratic definition diverge much from the technical, legal definition of "constitution."

The *British North America Act 1867* – not itself styled as a "Constitution" until 1982[8] – begins with a preamble reciting Canada's desire to have a "constitution similar in principle to that of the United Kingdom." The British constitution was generally understood to embrace the fundamental values, norms, institutions, and processes of state whose provenance included ancient and contemporary statutes,

[7] Trading regimes are often referred to metaphorically as "constitutions" and function as such juridically and politically. See, e.g., David Schneiderman, "NAFTA's Takings Rule: American Constitutionalism Comes to Canada" (1996) 46 *U.T.L.J.* 499; Jane Kelsey, "Global Economic Policy-Making: A New Constitutionalism?" (1999) 9 *Otago L. Rev.* 535; S. Clarkson, *Uncle Sam and US: Globalization, Neoconservatism and the Canadian State* (Toronto: University of Toronto Press, 2002) ch. 4, "NAFTA and the WTO as Superconstitution."

[8] Arguably, the failure to formally entitle the 1867 Act a "Constitution" takes on some significance given contemporary imperial and/or Canadian usage: cf. *The Constitutional Act* (1791) 31 Geo. III c. 31 (dividing Quebec into Upper and Lower Canada); *An Act to grant a Representative Constitution to the colony of New Zealand*, 1852 (U.K.), 15 & 16 Vic., c. 72; *An Act to Confer a Constitution on New South Wales* (1855) 18 & 19 Vict. c. 183; *Queensland Constitution Act* (1867) 31 Vict. c. 38.

common-law decisions and extrajudicial musings by respected jurists, political and parliamentary conventions, and (in Hobsbawm's phrase) "invented traditions" of judicial, executive, and royal behavior. However, it was neither entrenched nor legally supersessive; parliament enjoyed plenary powers, and judges could only interpret, not strike down, legislation.[9] More to the point, the 1867 usage of "constitution" – the older British usage referring to the "composition" or "arrangement" of the institutions of state[10] – was left untouched by the 1982 repatriation process: The original preamble, the original textual references, the original link to British parliamentary practice all survived.[11] Thus, the present-day "constitution" of the United Kingdom – unentrenched, unwritten, unascertainable – remains a relevant if elusive point of reference for Canada.

However, a new layer of complexity was added by the *Constitution Act 1982.* Section 52(1) proclaims "the Constitution of Canada" as "the supreme law of Canada," dismisses any "inconsistent" law as "of no force and effect," and implicitly confirms the Supreme Court's right to invalidate legislation. Section 52(2) "includes" as part of the Constitution of Canada the *Constitution Acts* of 1867 and 1982, and thirty other "acts or orders" specified in a schedule. However, as the courts have held, it also "includes" other historic texts not specified in the schedule as well as common-law principles governing, for example, the royal prerogative.[12] Indeed, some diligent judges and ambitious academics maintain that Canada's "Constitution" also "includes" unwritten norms derived from conventions, from the "foundational principles" of the Canadian federation, and from Canada's "organic," "common-law," or *ur*-constitution.[13] Many of these unwritten norms relate to the architecture, procedures, and powers of legislative bodies and their relationship to the Crown, the courts, and the executive. The text, to reiterate, is not canonical.

Nor is it comprehensively entrenched. The written texts – the 1867 and 1982 Acts and the thirty scheduled "acts and orders" – can only be amended in accordance with a complex amending formula.[14] However, statutes, common-law doctrine, and conventions that are "included" but not "scheduled" can presumably be changed in the same way they were initially established – by legislation, judicial rulings, or new political understandings. This is especially important with regard to conventions

9 A. V. Dicey, *Introduction to the Study of the Law of the Constitution,* 10th ed. (Toronto: Macmillan, 1965) at 91.

10 The 1867 Act refers to the "Constitution of Parliament" and other legislative institutions as well as "the Constitution of the Province."

11 For example, section 18 of the *Constitution Act 1867* defines the powers and privileges of Canada's parliament by reference to those at Westminster.

12 See W. Newman, "Grand Entrance Hall, Back Door or Foundation Stone? The Role of Constitutional Principles in Construing and Applying the Constitution of Canada" (2001) 14 *Supreme Court L.R.* (2d) 197 and "Defining the Constitution of Canada since 1982: The Scope of the Legislative Powers of Constitutional Amendment Under Sections 44 and 45 of the *Constitution Act,* 1982" (2003) 22 *Supreme Court L.R.* (2d) 423.

13 See, e.g., R. Elliot, "References, Structural Argumentation and the Organizing Principles of Canada's Constitution" (2001) 80 *Can. Bar Rev.* 67; M. Walters, "The Common Law Constitution in Canada: Return of *Lex non scripta* as Fundamental Law" (2001) 51 *U.T.L.J.* 51; J. Cameron, "The Written Word and the Constitution's Vital Unstated Assumptions" in P. Thibault, B. Pelletier, and L. Perret, eds., *Essays in Honour of Gérald-A. Beaudoin: The Challenges of Constitutionalism* (Cowansville: Editions Yvon Blais, 2002) at 89; J. Leclair, "Canada's Unfathomable Unwritten Constitutional Principles" (2002) 27 *Queen's L.J.* 27.

14 *Constitution Act* 1982, being Schedule B to the *Canada Act 1982* (U.K.), 1982, c.11, part V.

governing the legislative process, which have evolved from centuries of royal, parliamentary, and executive practice and which acquired their normative force by being actively acknowledged or passively acquiesced in by the relevant political actors. Of course, if formal constitutional amendments change or ratify "included" texts or unwritten constitutional norms, these too would become entrenched as provisions of the Constitution of Canada. But at the provincial level, entrenchment seems impossible as provincial "constitutions" (not defined in the 1982 Act, but clearly "constitutions" in British sense) are amendable by a simple act of the legislature.[15]

Thus, the Canadian constitution (and consequently the Constitution of Canada) can be described as highly permeable, even in the technical legal sense. It may absorb new values and meanings that originate in the deep structures of economy, culture, society, and polity and that percolate slowly and imperceptibly (but occasionally suddenly and dramatically) into the consciousness and conduct of political and juridical actors. Ultimately, these new and tentative norms win sufficient acceptance to be accorded formal recognition as elements of the constitution, either through the accumulation of parliamentary practices and precedents, acknowledgment by the courts as established conventions, or, occasionally, enactment as statutes or adoption as constitutional amendments. But note: In each case formal recognition implies that these norms were for some time, or perhaps always, part of the bedrock of rules, procedures, and institutions that we call "the constitution" even though not yet recognized as such.

In the "*Persons*" case, for example, the constitution was characterized as a "living tree capable of growth and expansion" without formal amendment.[16] In the *Patriation Reference*, patterns of behavior by the provincial, federal, and Westminster governments were found to have hardened into a "constitutional convention" cognizable in law, even if not enforceable.[17] In the *Québec Secession Reference*, the Court, relying on a "brief historical review" and/or "an historical lineage stretching back through the ages" identified the "general," "underlying," "foundational," or "defining" principles that "operate in symbiosis" to "inform and sustain the constitutional text"[18] and then used those principles to pencil in a framework for dissolution of the Canadian federation.

In each case, by necessary implication, there must have been an earlier but unspecified moment – before the "living tree" grew or expanded, before patterns or practices governing constitutional amendments became evident, before the "foundational principles" emerged or their symbiosis commenced – when a court could not yet have concluded that the constitution meant what it was ultimately held to mean. Thus, taking official accounts of constitutional change at face value, even judges seem to acknowledge that the Canadian constitution is by no means juridical bedrock. Rather, it is highly permeable, even unstable, easily eroded by the drip-drip of evolving political, social, and administrative practice, capable of being radically reconfigured by the glacial mass of passing historical forces, frequently

[15] *Constitution Act* 1982, ibid., section 45.
[16] *Edwards v. Attorney General of* Canada, [1930] 1 D.L.R. 98 (PC).
[17] *Re Resolution to Amend the Constitution of Canada*, [1981] 1 S.C.R. 753.
[18] *Reference re Secession of Québec*, [1998] 2 S.C.R. 217 at paras. 48–49.

reinterpreted by academic geologists and consigned without much historical evidence or analytical ado to this constitutional category or that by the judicial office of claims and assays.

To all these familiar sources of constitutional permeability and instability, I propose to add yet another: "the people's" views about how public policy and law ought to be made, and their proper role in the legislative process. That source – that populist source – is the main focus of this chapter.

II. THE POPULIST REINVENTION OF THE LEGISLATURE

Populist parties have had limited local, and perhaps transient, success in winning elections, holding office, and implementing their programs. However, confronted by the passionate intensity of populist movements, their political opponents have often found it prudent to appropriate populist rhetoric and adopt as their own populist proposals for institutional reform. Thus, while the populist project remains a work-in-progress, and while much of it may never acquire a "constitutional" character, populism has precipitated a series of transformations in how the Canadian state is perceived, governed, and ultimately, "constituted."

The recent experience of two right-wing populist parties illustrates my point. The first, Ontario's Progressive Conservative Party, swept to power in 1995 under the leadership of Mike Harris, whose neoliberal and populist "common sense revolution" dominated provincial politics for the next eight years. Harris's "common sense revolution" ended in 2003 with the defeat of his successor, Ernie Eves, who was in turn replaced in 2004 by a more centrist, less populist, Conservative leader. The second, the federal Reform Party, was founded in 1987. Initially a right-wing populist party based in Alberta and British Columbia, Reform also attracted widely dispersed, but significant, support in Saskatchewan, Manitoba, and Ontario. Having crucially failed to enlist support among nonwestern, nonpopulist Progressive Conservative voters, Reform reinvented itself as the Canadian Alliance, which in 2003, through merger or acquisition, finally metamorphosed into the new, integrated (but no longer Progressive) Conservative Party of Canada. How right-wing and how populist the Conservatives will remain is still unclear; but they have become the government-in-waiting.

Despite the electoral vicissitudes of the Harris Conservatives and of Reform/Alliance, their neoliberal and populist legacies live on in their successor parties, in the entrenched Conservative government of Ralph Klein in Alberta (1993–), in the Liberal government of Gordon Campbell in British Columbia (2001–), and in the Saskatchewan Party (1997–), which twice narrowly missed winning office in that province. Moreover, their strategies and policies have been borrowed by nonpopulist and non-neoliberal parties engaged in the sincerest form of flattery. And most important for present purposes, their populist principles have influenced constitutional legislation and helped to shape parliamentary and administrative practices that are en route to becoming constitutional conventions.

Of course, legislation can be repealed, practices altered, and conventions repudiated. But neoliberal populism – for all its past or future failures – has already left its mark on the constitution, especially as regards Canada's legislative institutions and processes.

a. THE LEGISLATURE'S ROLE IN THE AMENDMENT OF THE WRITTEN CONSTITUTION. Under part V of the *Constitution Act, 1982* amendments to the Constitution of Canada must be authorized by resolutions of the federal parliament and/or the provincial legislatures, depending on the subject matter. Provincial constitutions, by contrast, may be amended by a simple statute.[19] No provision is made for popular participation of any sort at any stage. Nonetheless, during Canada's recent prolonged constitutional negotiations, populist politics not only determined the fate of proposed constitutional amendments but also led to the adoption of new procedures ensuring citizens a dominant role in the amending process.

During the Meech-Charlottetown round of constitutional negotiations, from 1987 to 1992, the incumbent federal Progressive Conservative government, heavily dependent on western populist voters, pledged not to allow the traditional "men in suits" – the first ministers – to determine the outcome behind closed doors. Instead, it launched an ambitious program of citizen consultations and convened Canada's first constitutional referendum.[20] The ensuing rejection of the proposed amendments, it is widely believed, constituted a defeat for Canada's elites who largely favored them and an historic victory for "ordinary Canadians" and populist politicians who were largely opposed.[21]

At the provincial level, constitutional referenda have been relatively common. In 1948 Newfoundland conducted a constitutional convention, and subsequently a referendum, on whether to join Canada or remain independent, and two more referenda in 1995 and 1997 on changes to its constitutionally entrenched denominational school system.[22] Québec – which was considering leaving Canada rather than joining it – first convened an Estates-General in 1994 to hear the views of important communities and constituencies,[23] and then conducted a constitutional referendum in 1995 (its second in two decades).[24] This approach was subsequently endorsed by the Supreme Court in the *Québec Secession Reference*, which held that a referendum – though not binding – might legitimate efforts to dissolve the federation.[25] Nunavut, after extensive grassroots consultation, held two plebiscites before establishing its new government.[26] Prince Edward Island conducted a referendum on whether to exchange its constitutionally guaranteed ferry service to the mainland for a fixed link.[27] It is hard to imagine that the formal amending procedures in the *Constitution Act 1982* – which give legislatures the sole and definitive say – can ever again be invoked unless the people have spoken first. Indeed, recent legislation in British Columbia and Alberta requires that all amendments to the

[19] The sole exception relates to the office of the lieutenant governor; see *Constitution Act* 1982, ss. 41, 45.

[20] See generally P. Russell, *Constitutional Odyssey: Can Canadians Become a Sovereign People?*, 2nd ed. (Toronto: University of Toronto Press, 1993).

[21] See, e.g., Brooke Jeffrey, *Strange Bedfellows, Trying Times: October 1992 and the Defeat of the Powerbrokers* (Toronto: Key Porter Books, 1993).

[22] *Newfoundland Act*, 1949 (U.K.), 12 & 13 Geo. VI., c. 22; *Constitution Amendment*, 1997 (*Newfoundland Act*), S.I./97-55, C. Gaz.1997.II.1 (Extra No. 4, May 2, 1997); *Constitution Amendment*, 1998 (*Newfoundland Act*), S.I./98-25, C. Gaz.1998.II.1 (Extra No. 1, January 14, 1998).

[23] "Sovereignty Hearings Launched," *Globe & Mail* (February 4, 1995) A4.

[24] The referendum sought approval for *An Act Respecting the Future of Quebec*, Bill 1, 1st Sess., 35th Leg., Quebec, 1995.

[25] *Reference re Secession of Quebec, supra* note 18 at para. 87.

[26] The *Nunavut Act*, S.C. 1993, c. 28 was enacted by Parliament after two plebiscites, in 1982 and 1992.

[27] *Constitution Amendment*, 1993 (Prince Edward Island), S.I./94-45, C.Gaz.1994.II.2021.

Constitution of Canada which require approval by the provincial legislature must first be approved in a referendum.[28]

No populist experiment in constitution making, however, is more daring than British Columbia's where a Citizens' Assembly was charged with drafting a new electoral system. Apart from its independent chair, chosen by unanimous vote of the provincial legislature, the Assembly comprised one male and one female member, chosen by lot, from each of the province's seventy-nine constituencies. It had no structural or reporting connection to the government and no designated representatives of civil society, ethnocultural, socioeconomic, political, or other groups (although two aboriginal members, selected by lot, were added after the Assembly was formed). After a year of public hearings and private discussions, constrained only by the need to respect the Constitution of Canada and the Westminster parliamentary system, the Assembly proposed a new electoral system that was submitted on May 17, 2005 – unaltered – to a provincial referendum in which voters were asked to choose between its proposal and the status quo.[29]

The populist credentials of this project are impeccable. As a newspaper editorial noted:

> This "bold and courageous" experiment in democracy is unprecedented in Canada and has rarely been attempted anywhere in the world – other than in ancient Greece, though the "randomly chosen" citizens there were all men.... While some might question the wisdom of placing an important decision in the hands of people who aren't likely to have much political knowledge or experience, assembly members will have experts at their disposal to answer any questions. Further, you need only look at provincial or federal politics to see that some of the most ill-advised decisions are made by those with political expertise. And juries have proven time and again that "average" people with no specialized knowledge are capable of assimilating vast amounts of material and making sound decisions.[30]

British Columbia's "bold and courageous" populist experiment may fail: The Assembly's proposals for a new system of proportional representation (PR) are complex; a high threshold of support is required for ratification; and the referendum coincides with a hotly contested general election. However, Québec, Prince Edward Island, Ontario, Saskatchewan, and New Brunswick are all committed to or engaged in a process of consulting their voters on PR.[31] Thus, whatever the immediate results, "ordinary citizens" are likely to become accustomed to playing a meaningful role in the redesign of the institutions and processes of representative democracy – a constitutional task of the highest order and a significant advance for populism.

PR itself may not be. Populists favor PR because it ensures that the legislature will more accurately reflect the wishes of the electorate than the present

[28] *Constitutional Amendment Approval Act,* R.S.B.C. 1996, c. 67; *Constitutional Referendum Act,* R.S.A. 2000, c. C-25.

[29] Premier's announcement, April 28, 2003, "Citizens' Assembly to Strengthen Public Confidence" (April 28, 2003) online: Office of the Premier, http://www2.news.gov.bc.ca/nrm_news_releases/2003OTP0031-000400.htm. The proposal to change the electoral system in British Columbia failed to pass. A majority of at least sixty percent of voters was needed to approve the proposal. Only 57.7 percent voted in favor. The results of that referendum can be found online at: http://www.elections.bc.ca/elections/sov05/refSOV05/electionsBC_ReferendumOverview

[30] "Everyone Gets a Chance to Influence Democracy," *Vancouver Sun* (August 2, 2003) C6.

[31] Law Commission of Canada, *Voting Counts: Electoral Reform for Canada* (Ottawa: LCC, 2004) ch. 6, "The Process of Electoral Reform: Engaging Citizens in Democratic Change."

first-past-the-post system. However, the populist appeal of PR is likely to be spent once the votes are counted. It will neither make legislators more accountable between elections, nor convert them into the faithful agents of their constituents, nor insulate them from the discipline of the political parties that fund them and, under the Westminster system, offer them their only chance of advancement. Indeed, because PR will almost certainly lead to a proliferation of parties and prevent the formation of single-party governments, it may well encourage unstable, multiparty coalitions, in which policies will be shaped through continuous backroom political dealmaking rather than by open legislative debate or public consultation. Nonetheless, although no clear national consensus has so far emerged in favor of PR, the idea seems, to be gaining political traction.

Reform of the membership and powers of the Senate is another populist project. At present, Senators are appointed by the prime minister to serve until age seventy-five, with membership allocated on a regional formula that somewhat favors the small Maritime provinces and Québec and disfavors Ontario and the western provinces. Populists, at least those associated with Reform/Alliance, advocate a so-called triple-E Senate – elected, effective, and with equal representation from each province. However, this proposal has limited appeal elsewhere. A triple-E Senate might increase Alberta's influence in national politics – and thereby the influence of populist parties – but it would correspondingly diminish the influence of voters in Québec and Ontario, which account for about half of Canada's population. Moreover, whereas now citizens are able to focus on influencing their MPs, if the Senate were "elected" and "effective" they would have to divide their efforts between two equally powerful legislative bodies whose differently constituted majorities might produce policy stalemate. Finally, the Senate's composition and powers can only be changed by a formal constitutional amendment that is unlikely to pass.[32] For all of these reasons, "the people" remain divided over whether the Senate should be reformed or simply abolished.

b. DIRECT LEGISLATION. No reform of parliamentary institutions could be more radical than bypassing them altogether, an idea that enjoyed considerable support in western Canada in the early twentieth century. Four provinces passed "direct legislation" statutes providing for laws to be enacted by "initiative and referendum," rather than by the legislature itself.[33] These statutes – clearly amendments to the provincial constitution – represented populism in its purest form, but they were found constitutionally suspect and were either never declared in force or repealed.[34]

[32] Alberta's Conservatives, closely aligned with Reform/Alliance, held elections under its *Senatorial Selection Act,* R.S.A. 2000, c. S-5 to fill Alberta Senate vacancies. However, the prime minister refused to appoint the successful candidates.

[33] See Saskatchewan: *Direct Legislation Act,* S.S. 1913, c. 2; *An Act to Submit to the Electors the Question of the Adoption of the Direct Legislation Act,* S.S. 1913, c. 3. The second Act authorized a referendum on the first; when it failed to gain the requisite support, it was immediately repealed. Alberta: *Direct Legislation Act,* S.A. 1913, c. 3. (repealed S.A. 1958, c. 72). Manitoba: *Initiative and Referendum Act,* S.M. 1916, c. 59 This Act was declared invalid in *Re Initiative and Referendum Act,* [1919] A.C. 935, 48 D.L.R. 18 (P.C.). British Columbia: *Direct Legislation Act,* S.B.C. 1919, c. 21. This Act was never proclaimed and apparently never repealed; see Patrick Boyer, *Direct Democracy in Canada: The History and Future of Referendums* (Toronto: Dundurn Press, 1992) at 93.

[34] A principal concern was that the power of the provinces to amend their own constitution by statute was subject to an exception under the *Constitution Act* 1867: Such amendments must not interfere with

British Columbia reintroduced initiative legislation in 1994, but its stringent procedural requirements make its successful use unlikely;[35] no other province has yet followed suit. Consequently, Canada does not presently experience the recurring policy traumas triggered by initiatives in some American states.[36] However, the federal government and most provinces have enacted laws enabling them to conduct nonbinding referenda or plebiscites on any matter,[37] and several provinces now require majority support in a referendum for proposed increases in taxation.[38]

These developments may presage renewed support for the old populist dream of direct democracy. Moreover, some obstacles and objections to direct democracy have been removed: The constitution has been changed, new limits on corporate spending and public subsidies for both "yes" and "no" committees have diminished the campaign advantages enjoyed by wealthy proponents,[39] and new communications technologies may reduce the logistical difficulties and cost of referenda.[40] Perhaps, then, Canadians' current alienation from electoral politics will translate into renewed interest in alternative forms of democratic participation. If this happens, we will have compelling evidence that populism can in fact alter the constitution by transforming our sensibilities.

c. TRANSFORMATION OF PARLIAMENTARY PROCEDURES AND PRACTICES. Flanagan remarks that populist parties

> are not wholly opposed to parliamentary government because they believe it can be reformed; but their populist reforms, if ever thoroughly implemented, would change the parliamentary system almost beyond recognition.[41]

Changing the parliamentary system "almost beyond recognition" is nothing if not a constitutional project.

It is widely agreed that Canada's parliamentary system is in serious difficulty. However, populist prescriptions are more radical than most. The first step, populists believe, is to liberate individual legislators from the control of their party, leader, caucus, and (presumably) conscience, so that they can become more reliable and

the powers of the lieutenant governor, who in theory had the right (long since fallen into desuetude) to disallow legislation or to reserve it for consideration by the federal cabinet. See generally P. Hogg, *Constitutional Law of Canada*, 4th ed. (Scarborough: Carswell, 1997) at 14–15.

35 *Recall and Initiative Act*, S.B.C. 1994, c. 56 requires that on petition signed by 10% of the voters from each constituency, proposed laws must be submitted to an initiative ballot. If the measure wins majority support in 75% of the electoral districts and 50% overall, a bill must be introduced into the legislature, which is under no legal obligation to enact it. This requirement apparently avoids the holding in *Re Initiative and Referendum Act*, *supra* note 33.

36 See generally Richard J. Ellis, *Democratic Delusions: The Initiative Process in America* (Lawrence: University Press of Kansas, 2002).

37 See, e.g., *Referendum Act* Stat. Can. 1992, c. 30; *Election Act* Rev. Stat. Alta. C. 398 s. 128 ff; *Referendum Act*, Stat. Que. 1978 c. 6; *Plebiscites Act* Rev. Stat. P.E.I. 1988 c. P-10; *Elections Act* Rev. Stat. N.B. c. E3 s. 129; *Referendum and Plebiscite Act* Stat. S. 1990–91 c. R-8.01; *Referendum Act* R.S.B.C. c. 400.

38 See below: *Legislative control of the fisc.*

39 Federal, Quebec, and British Columbia statutes impose limits on campaign contributions and expenditures, on the participation of parties other than the proponents and opponents, and on advertising.

40 See, e.g., David Zussman, "Electronic Democracy: Challenging Our Traditional Notions of Governance" (1996) 1:3 *Insights* (Public Management Research Centre) http://www.ppforum.ca/ow/ow_fn_win_1997; Cynthia Alexander and Leslie Alexander Pal, eds., *Digital Democracy: Policy and Politics in the Wired World* (Toronto: Oxford University Press, 1998).

41 Flanagan, *supra* note 2 at 4.

accountable spokespersons for their constituents. This is to be accomplished by permitting more "free" votes in the legislature; by subjecting legislators to the ultimate discipline of recall petitions and special elections; by ensuring greater transparency and frugality in regard to their pay, pension, and expenses; and, finally, by conferring greater power on committees dominated by backbenchers, including the power to investigate government actions, to recommend legislation, and to vet important executive and judicial appointments. In general, however, populist parties have exhibited somewhat less enthusiasm for such measures once in office, although many governments have revised compensation and pension schemes for legislators that were deemed too generous or rules governing their expenses that were deemed too lax.

The second populist prescription is to liberate the electorate from the control of the legislature. On important issues the people must retain for themselves the ultimate right to decide: to have the last word on constitutional change, to bring forward legislation by initiative and referendum (both described above), and to approve or reject tax increases (described below). When the people are unable, for practical reasons, to participate in such important decisions directly, when they are forced to rely on their representatives, they must have the means to hold those representatives to account. Thus, the people should have the right to know: freedom of information legislation, careful financial and performance audits of government departments and agencies, registration of lobbyists, disclosure by legislators and cabinet members of their significant financial or property holdings. The people should have the right to be heard: plain language drafting and a new legislative semiotics so that everyone can grasp what is being proposed, posting for public comment of white papers and draft legislation, open and extensive legislative committee hearings where everyone's views can be aired, and actual or virtual town-hall meetings and doorstep or e-mail polls conducted by their legislative representatives. And, finally, the people should have the right to make their displeasure felt: Nonperformance of election promises should be grounds for voiding either the election or legislation passed in breach of promise;[42] unfaithful representatives should be subject to recall;[43] and governments which have lost the confidence of the people – not of the legislature, as at present – should be required to resign.

The rights to be informed, to be heard, to register discontent, and to decide important matters belong – in populist terms – to "the people." But "the people" – in the sense of all Canadians – is too amorphous a group to mobilize effectively, too diffuse a group to exercise power or even oversight, too physically remote from the centers of power to be heard loudly even if it shouted with one voice. Hence the third item on the populist agenda for the reform of parliamentary institutions: "The people" must exercise power not as undifferentiated aggregations of individual citizens, but as collectivities with essentialized identities. Hence Québec's militant defense of *pur laine* Québecois against the depredations of the federal government and the rest of Canada. Hence the 1970s Conservative vision of Canada as a "community

[42] Unsuccessful actions have been brought to unseat government members for campaign statements misrepresenting the state of the provincial budget, *Friesen v. Hammell*, [2000] B.C.J. No. 1618, and to prevent introduction of a health levy in violation of an election pledge not to increase taxes. *Canadian Taxpayers Federation v. Ontario (Minister of Finance)*, [2004] O.J. No. 5239.

[43] Only one such statute exists: *Recall and Initiative Act*, R.S.B.C. 1996, c. 398.

of communities" – a decentralized federation whose members share responsibility for national affairs. Hence the Reform Party slogan of the mid-1980s, "the West wants in," an appeal to regional identity. Hence Reform/Alliance attempts in the 1990s to return decision making and resources to provincial governments that – in populist perception – are most easily held accountable to taxpayers. Hence the tendency of provincial populists of all stripes to emphasize that they alone speak for Ontarians or British Columbians, Newfoundlanders or Albertans.

Thus, populists – especially the Reform/Alliance and Conservative parties – propose to end federal spending in areas of provincial jurisdiction, to terminate the existing federal-provincial tax agreements that underpin equalization transfers from the richer to the poorer provinces, to create new institutions with the prestige and power to forestall unilateral federal initiatives in areas of shared competence, and to institutionalize discussions between the federal and provincial first ministers (most recently through the "Council of the Federation").[44] These strategies are designed to "protect" local taxpayers from a "tax grab" by Ottawa (and neoliberal provincial governments from having to support unwanted and expensive programs emanating from the same source). For similar reasons, populist provincial premiers want to displace exclusive federal control over the appointment of judges of the Supreme Court (and, presumably, of the provincial superior courts). Provincial involvement would ensure that judges are both less beholden to the federal government that appoints them and better attuned to the unique social and political sensibilities of the provinces from which they came.

These attempts by populists to redefine "the people" by emphasizing the rights of specific communities and identities reveal considerable ambivalence about who "the people" really are. Thus, in a Senate with equal provincial representation, "ordinary" – more rural and/or Anglo-Celtic – citizens of the smaller provinces would enjoy a share of political power commensurate with their virtues rather than their numbers, thus happily reducing the influence of provinces with more urbanized, francophone, or polyglot populations. And, in an effective Senate, powers of investigation, review, and veto would allow those same "ordinary people," through their provincial Senate delegations, to protect themselves against the egregious tendencies of the House of Commons, which is notoriously dominated by metropolitan elites in league with the Ottawa mandarins (or vice versa).

Of course, provincial identities are not the only identities on offer. Oddly, some populists (while tolerant of religious identities) deprecate gender-, language-, ethnicity-, aboriginality-, or class-based identities. Indeed, one of the hallmarks of populism has been its dismissal of "others": of legislated bilingualism and French-language labeling on packages, of official multiculturalism, of the wearing of turbans by policemen or veils by schoolchildren, of legally enforceable equality rights for gays and lesbians, of distinctive forms of law and government for first nations. While more mature populist parties and governments have generally eschewed such sentiments, and have grudgingly or willingly accommodated within their ranks a wide variety of identities, a degree of xenophobia and intolerance of difference can still be found closer to their grass roots. This intolerance surfaces as well in populist complaints about "judicial activism," a euphemism used to describe the

[44] See online: http://www.councilofthefederation.ca/.

enlargement and enforcement of equality rights under the Charter, which, in populist perspective, constitutes an intrusion not so much on legislative prerogatives as on the sense and sensibilities of ordinary folk.[45]

d. THE CHANGING SEMIOTICS OF LEGISLATION. The raison d'être of legislatures is legislation. The form of legislation – I will argue next – is almost as significant for populists as its content. Indeed, for two hundred years, the form of legislation has been the subject of debate. Statutory drafting preoccupied the Benthamite lawyers of Victorian England.[46] Numerous treatises stipulated that statutes should be drafted in a "logical" manner in "plain language," that unity of subject matter should be maintained, that sections and subsections should adhere to a particular syntax, that statutes should be systematically collected, amendments periodically consolidated, and methods of citation and numbering standardized. As Rod Macdonald has noted:

> The . . . nineteenth century statute and its compendious presentation, the nineteenth-century statute book (both of which really achieved their apotheosis only in the mid-twentieth century) were remarkable social, intellectual, political and technical achievements.[47]

Perhaps this movement was an expression of Victorian devotion to order, logic, and "science." Perhaps it symbolically conveyed the omnipotence of the legislature or the unimpeachable excellence of the Crown law officers. Perhaps it reflected concerns that people should know their rights and duties under legislation; that vague laws would be difficult to enforce; that over- or under zealous officials and tribunals would take advantage of loosely worded provisions.

Whatever the reason, Anglo-Canadian statutes came to be drafted in an austere, anodyne, and syntactically rigorous style. However, as Macdonald notes, statutory drafting is being transformed by broader cultural changes in communication. The function of statutes has shifted, he says, "from the semantic to the semiotic."[48] This shift has been cleverly exploited by populists who feel no particular loyalty to "scientific" drafting, prefer "common sense" to the dry logic of parliamentary lawyers, and instinctively understand that evocative language can sometimes accomplish what juridical precision cannot. Hence the introduction of a new populist semiotic to celebrate the arrival of "ordinary people" in power and to signal the overthrow of the old, technocratic mandarin class.

By way of example only, I have examined statutes enacted in Ontario under successive Liberal, New Democratic, and Progressive Conservative governments between 1985 and 2002. In some thirty-five instances after 1995, the populist

[45] During the 2004 federal election campaign, a prominent Conservative candidate (and former Alliance Justice critic) conveyed his strong distaste for various Charter rulings ("to heck with the courts") and proposed greater use of the legislative override power to avoid their effect. "White harsh critic of justice, immigration systems," *Globe & Mail* (June 26, 2004) A10. The ensuing controversy allegedly cost his party a significant number of votes, though the candidate in question was handily elected in his own riding.

[46] See generally H. Arthurs, *"Without the Law": Administrative Justice and Legal Pluralism in Nineteenth Century England* (Toronto: University of Toronto Press, 1985) esp. ch. 4, "The New Administrative Technology."

[47] Rod Macdonald, "The Fridge-Door Statute" (2001) 47 *McGill Law Journal* 13 at 16.

[48] Ibid. at 31.

Conservatives departed from the drafting conventions followed by predecessor governments. Compare, for example, *An Act to amend Certain Acts Concerning Collective Bargaining and Employment*[49] – the newly elected NDP government's updating of the province's Labour Relations Act – with *An Act to Restore Balance and Stability to Labour Relations and to Promote Economic Prosperity and to make Consequential Changes to Statutes Concerning Labour Relations* – which repealed the NDP legislation in its entirety.[50] Or compare the NDP's *Employment Equity Act*[51] with the Conservative statute that repealed it, *The Job Quotas Repeal Act*[52] – a comparison made all the more poignant by the fact that the *Employment Equity Act* mandated adoption by employers of employment equity plans but did not establish job quotas.

During the populist Conservative's "common sense revolution," the Ontario statute books were festooned with titles such as the *Better Local Government Act* (abolishing a number of municipal governments and creating the Toronto mega-city),[53] the *Fewer Politicians Act* (reducing the size of the provincial legislature),[54] the *Prevention of Unionization (Ontario Works) Act* (preventing unionization of workfare recipients),[55] the *Fairness is a Two-Way Street Act* (banning Quebec construction workers from working in Ontario),[56] the *Red Tape Reduction Act* (enacted in annual versions from 1997–2000),[57] the *Sergeant Rick McDonald Memorial Act* (increasing penalties for suspects triggering car chase by police),[58] *Brian's Law* (permitting community release for institutionalized psychiatric patients),[59] and *Christopher's Law* (creating a sex offenders registry).[60] Quite apart from their content, these and other statutes represented a calculated decision to exchange semantics, for semiotics, and professionalism for populism.

This new populist semiotic celebrates the marriage of style and substance, as becomes clear in any examination of the Conservative's strategy for permanently reducing taxation and public expenditure. Evocatively named statutes such as *The Tax Cut and Economic Growth Act*,[61] *the Taxpayer Protection and Balanced Budget Act*,[62] and *The Balanced Budget for A Brighter Futures Act*[63] were complemented by another spectacular populist gesture. The government announced its 2003 budget

49 Bill 40, 2d Sess., 35th Leg., Ontario, 1992 (assented to November 5, 1992).

50 Bill 7, 1st Sess., 35th Leg., Ontario, 1995 (assented to November 10, 1995).

51 *An Act to provide for Employment Equity for Aboriginal People, People with Disabilities, Members of Racial Minorities and Women* (long title) / *Employment Equity Act* (short title) Bill 79, 3d Sess., 35th Leg., Ontario, 1993 (assented to December 14, 1993).

52 *An Act to repeal job quotas and to restore merit-based employment practices in Ontario* (long title) / *Job Quotas Repeal Act* (short title) Bill 8, 1st Sess., 36th Leg., Ontario, 1995 (assented to December 14, 1995).

53 S.O. 1996, c. 32.

54 S.O. 1996, c. 28.

55 S.O. 1998, c. 17.

56 S.O. 1999, c. 4.

57 *Red Tape Reduction Act (Ministry of Finance)* S.O. 1997, c. 19; *Red Tape Reduction Act (Ministry of Northern Development and Mines) Red Tape Reduction Act (Ministry of Finance)* S.O. 1997, c. 19; *Red Tape Reduction Act (Ministry of Northern Development and Mines)* S.O. 1997, c. 40; *Red Tape Reduction Act* S.O. 1998, c. 18; S.O. 1999, c. 12; S.O. 2000, c. 26.

58 *Sergeant Rick McDonald Memorial Act (Suspect Apprehensions Pursuits)* S.O. 1999, c. 13.

59 *Brian's Law (Mental Health Legislative Reform)* S.O. 2000, c. 9.

60 *Christopher's Law (Sex Offender Registry)* S.O. 2000, c. 1.

61 S.O. 1996, c. 18.

62 S.O. 1999, c. 7.

63 S.O. 2000, c. 42.

(*Keeping the Promise for Growth and Prosperity Act*)[64] not in the Legislature, but in a training facility owned by an auto parts manufacturer who also happened to be both a significant employer (of nonunion labor) and a generous political donor (to the Conservative Party). The intended message – that the government's sound fiscal policies were generating investment and jobs – failed to impress Ontarians. Instead, the government's "photo-op" provoked universally hostile editorial comment; it alienated even Conservative voters; and it prompted the Speaker of the Legislature to secure a legal opinion that condemned the move as a clear violation of long-established parliamentary practice and constitutional convention.[65] Perhaps populism generates its own antibodies.

e. LEGISLATIVE CONTROL OF THE FISC: THE PEOPLE'S REVOLT AGAINST PAYING TAXES AND RUNNING DEFICITS. A defining characteristic of contemporary Canadian populism is its antipathy to "high" levels of taxation, government expenditure, and (though this is less clear) public debt. Aggressive tax cuts – and commensurate expenditure reductions – fueled Ontario's "common sense revolution," much as it did similar movements elsewhere. Most Canadians claim to be willing to pay taxes in order to maintain a high level of public goods and services.[66] Nonetheless, populist neoliberal parties draw considerable electoral strength from grassroots small business and antitax organizations and intellectual respectability from neoliberal think tanks, mainstream business leaders, and finance ministries. Consequently, politicians of all persuasions routinely pledge to reduce (or at least not increase) taxes, cut government spending, and balance budgets while virtually no party has campaigned for office recently on a platform of higher taxes – none, at least, with any hope of success.

However, what distinguishes populist parties is their attempt to constitutionalize "fiscal responsibility" and small government by imposing permanent legal constraints on backsliding by future governments, regardless of their circumstances or convictions. The most extreme restraints were introduced by Ontario's Conservatives, whose *Taxpayers Protection and Balanced Budget Act 1999* provided that no provincial tax increase could be instituted without first being approved by a majority of voters either in a general election or in a special provincial referendum. It also provided that in any year in which a government failed to balance expenditures and revenues (unless it inherited a deficit from its predecessor or encountered one of several strictly defined emergencies), cabinet ministers would forfeit in the first year 25 percent of their ministerial salaries, and in subsequent years, 50 percent.[67]

[64] S.O. 2002, c. 8.

[65] Opinion of Neil Finkelstein, Blake, Cassels and Graydon LLP, March 24, 2003, Legislative Library of Ontario, CA2ON, X600, 2003 C53. In response to a question of privilege raised by an opposition member, the Speaker ruled that he could not address issues of constitutionality (only courts could do so) but found that the budget procedure adopted by the government raised a *prima facie* case of contempt of the Legislature. Ontario, Legislative Assembly, Official Reports of Debates (Hansard), 6 (May 8, 2003) at 230–4 (Hon. Gary Carr).

[66] In a recent EKOS poll (May 30, 2004) respondents identified as their top electoral concerns health care/education (53%), ethics/accountability (17%), economy/jobs (15%), and taxes/debt (15%). "Federal Election Part II: A Look at What Is Driving Federal Voting Intentions," online: EKOS Research Associates, http://www.ekos.com/admin/articles/30May2004PressRelease.pdf.

[67] *Supra* note 62.

As Premier Harris said in introducing the Act:

The Act... will provide permanent protection to Ontario taxpayers, protection from unfair and unwanted tax hikes, protection from reckless deficit spending.... This money belongs to the taxpayers and we are requiring future governments to recognize this reality. This bill also contains a balanced budget law that would prevent governments from running budget deficits. It is my hope... that the era of deficit financing in Ontario is over once and for all.[68]

For one government member, the issue was not just fiscal orthodoxy but populist principle:

How can it be that a democratically elected government can raise taxes and spend money it doesn't have without answering to the people? How can it be that a government can pretend it doesn't need to justify its actions when it flies in the face of the democratic will? This act begins the process of empowering citizens, giving them the opportunity on a regular basis to have a real say on issues like taxation.... The... Act will ensure that all future governments will have to seek voter approval if they ever begin to feel the temptation of taxation.[69]

For another:

[T]oo often politicians think it's their money and they have the right to be spending it however they think it should be spent.... [I]t is in fact the taxpayers' money.... [I]f there's no consumer choice and it's just, "We know what's best for you" as we've heard from the other side of the House, then taking those taxes is just like expropriation.[70]

The NDP, which alone opposed the legislation, did so glumly and with dire predictions for the future:

If you pass balanced budget legislation, I think it would be fairly difficult for any government to stand up and try to counter that after another election.... I don't quite know what our party would do... if we ended up in that situation, because... this whole balanced budget legislation... is quite appealing to many voters across party lines.... This government, by way of balanced budget legislation, is moving to enshrine changes in government. They're trying to handcuff future governments in dealing with policies they have created.[71]

Constraints on legislative control over taxation clearly have constitutional significance. The struggle for control over taxation and expenditure was a recurring theme in parliament's historic contestations with the monarchy and legislative primacy remains a core value of the Anglo-Canadian parliamentary system. Several early decisions cast doubt on the constitutionality of legislation that conditions tax increases on the outcome of a binding referendum.[72] More recently, the Supreme Court has held that legislators cannot deprive their successors of the right to make

[68] Ontario, Legislative Assembly, *Official Reports of Debates (Hansard)*, 4A (October 26, 1999) at 76; Ontario, Legislative Assembly, *Official Reports of Debates (Hansard)*, 8 (November 2, 1999) at 301 (Hon. Michael Harris).

[69] Ontario, Legislative Assembly, *Official Reports of Debates (Hansard)*, 10 (November 4, 1999) at 409–10 (Brad Clark).

[70] Ontario, Legislative Assembly, *Official Reports of Debates (Hansard)*, 11B (November 15, 1999) at 474 (Doug Galt).

[71] Ontario, Legislative Assembly, *Official Reports of Debates (Hansard)*, 11B (November 15, 1999) at 467–70 (Gilles Bisson).

[72] *Re Initiative and Referendum Act*, *supra* note 33; *R. v. Nat Bell Liquors*, [1922] 2 A.C. 128, 65 D.L.R. 1 (Privy Council) and see Hogg, *supra* note 34.

fiscal decisions,[73] nor can the executive preempt that right.[74] And, finally, as the controversy over Ontario's 2003 budget announcement revealed, constitutional convention requires that the budget must first be presented to the legislature, not to "the people." Thus, the Conservative attempt to entrench low taxes and budgetary discipline may be open to constitutional challenge. Ironically, the Conservatives themselves resorted to a "technical amendment" to the *Taxpayers Protection Act* to rescue their ill-starred 2003 budget from the indignity of a referendum,[75] while their successors, the Liberals, did likewise in 2004.[76]

The Conservative's *Balanced Budget for a Brighter Futures Act, 2000*[77] advanced another neoliberal and populist project, mentioned earlier, of shifting money and power from the federal government to the provinces. As Finance Minister (later Premier) Eves stated:

> We firmly believe that all provinces should have the ability to develop taxation policies that meet the specific needs of their economies and their taxpayers. A made-for-Ontario personal income tax system will allow us the flexibility we require to meet the needs of Ontarians.[78]

Another Conservative enlarged on Mr. Eves' statement:

> If the Liberals in Ottawa choose to hike rates to pay for their cradle-to-grave guaranteed annual income scheme . . . then Ontario taxpayers could be pulled right along. A made-in-Ontario tax system will allow this government to make changes based on Ontario's needs. Ontario can protect its tax system from increases by Ottawa, as well as targeting credits, exemptions and deductions to areas that really deserve assistance.[79]

The *Brighter Futures Act*, which facilitates Ontario's withdrawal from long-standing federal-provincial tax-sharing arrangements, undermines the principle – enshrined in the *Constitution Act 1982*, section 36 – that all Canadians, wherever they reside, should have access to a reasonable standard of public services. And, by denying the federal government access to the fiscal tools it uses to maintain its leading role in social and economic policymaking, it alters the balance of power within the federation.

Thus, although populist-inspired statutes designed to enforce balanced budgets, low taxes, and small governments are not entrenched, they remain in force in many provinces,[80] form part of their provincial constitutions, and impose

[73] *Re Canada Assistance Plan*, [1991] 2 S.C.R. 525 at 569. See also *Interpretation Act*, R.S.C. 1985, c. I-21 s. 42(1), "Every Act shall be so construed as to reserve to Parliament the power of repealing or amending it, and of revoking it, restricting or modifying any power, privilege, or advantage thereby vested in or granted to any person."

[74] *Re Eurig Estate*, [1998] 2 S.C.R. 565, [1998] S.C.J. No. 72.

[75] *Taxpayers Protection Act* S. O. 1999 c. 7 as amended by S. O. 2002, c. 8, s 2(6) Schedule L.

[76] *An Act to Implement Budget Measures*, Bill 83, 1st Sess., 38th Leg., Ontario, 2004 (introduced May 18, 2004).

[77] S.O. 2000, c. 42.

[78] Ontario, Legislative Assembly, *Official Reports of Debates (Hansard)*, 111 (November 30, 2000) at 5997 (Hon. Ernie Eves).

[79] Ontario, Legislative Assembly, *Official Reports of Debates (Hansard)*, 119 (December 14, 2000) at 6372–3 (Raminder Gill).

[80] See generally Lisa C. Philipps, "The Rise of Balanced Budget Laws in Canada: Legislating Fiscal (Ir)Responsibility" (1996) 34 *Osgoode Hall L.J.* 681. Legislation closely resembling Ontario's has been enacted in British Columbia, Alberta, and Manitoba and less draconian versions in four other provinces.

significant limits on national legislative action. They are, in short, a constitutional constraint. How and when will these statutes cease to constrain? Not when they are struck down by the courts (unlikely) nor when millennial populism has run its course (likely, but not imminent), but only when governments are prepared to risk the electoral consequences of making fiscal policy without either conducting a referendum or propitiating the Janus god of balanced budgets. When that happens, we will have witnessed another constitutional change.

f. THE LEGISLATURE'S RELATIONS WITH THE EXECUTIVE BRANCH. The power of the prime minister to control not only the executive but the legislature has been termed a "friendly dictatorship."[81] In reaction, populists propose to eliminate key prime ministerial prerogatives: to choose the date of elections (a device for enforcing caucus discipline), to appoint Senators (a useful patronage tool), to control the budgets and chairs of parliamentary committees (a means of forestalling criticism), and to appoint judges and senior public officials (a long-term strategy to immunize government policies against regime change). Such proposals – whatever their merits – would alter constitutional conventions and parliamentary practice. However, populist governments are likely to be leery of such changes. After all, they are elected to office precisely because they claim to be innovative, determined, and willing to be held accountable. But to innovate, they must dominate the legislature and therefore enforce caucus discipline. To achieve fiscal restraint, they must force line departments to meet centrally determined spending targets. To avoid being undermined by backsliding civil servants, they must centralize policymaking.

Consequently, just as they tolerated domineering leaders while in opposition,[82] populists in government in Alberta, Ontario, and British Columbia accepted the need for the minister of finance, and especially the premier, to control the legislative agenda rather than leave its development to legislative committees, individual members or grassroots party structures, to impose discipline on their caucus and party rather than the other way around, to narrow the discretion customarily accorded civil servants, and to bend the public service to its will not by formal legislative or executive direction, but by political means. Each of these developments has constitutional significance – especially the last.

The independence of the professional civil service is a long-established, if somewhat vague, principle of parliamentary government.[83] Arguably, public servants have themselves weakened the principle by lobbying and litigating to secure the right to engage in political activity,[84] and by overtly aligning their unions with the NDP.[85] Arguably too, by reducing public expenditure – and the pay, tenure, and job satisfaction of civil servants – governments have violated the "implicit bargain"

[81] See, e.g., Jeffrey Simpson, *The Friendly Dictatorship* (Toronto: McClelland & Stewart, 2001).

[82] See Flanagan's assessment of the founding leader of the Reform Party, *supra* note 6 at 27–32.

[83] Lorne Sossin, "Speaking Truth to Power? The Search for Bureaucratic Independence" (2005) 55 *U. T. L. J.* 1.

[84] *Delisle v. Canada (Deputy Attorney General)*, [1999] 2 S.C.R. 989, [1999] S.C.J. No. 43.

[85] However, public sector unions have often disagreed violently with NDP governments and worked to overthrow them. See Patrick J. Monahan, *Storming the Pink Palace: The NDP in Power: A Cautionary Tale* (Toronto: Lester Publishing, 1995) ch. 6, 7.

whereby their impartiality and professionalism earned them a degree of autonomy and respect.[86]

Populist governments – in fairness, all governments – use subtle strategies to avoid directly confronting the issue of independence. Political staff edge into policy domains once controlled by civil servants; unsympathetic senior bureaucrats are gradually culled; more malleable candidates are recruited to leadership roles. But populists sometimes use unsubtle strategies. Political operatives are inserted into key civil service posts and even appointed to independent administrative tribunals.[87] Incumbent members are illegally purged both individually[88] and en masse[89] or paid off and sent packing.[90] And most successfully and egregiously, right-wing populist governments have used funding cuts, cancellation of programs, and abusive rhetoric to demoralize civil servants, to goad them into passive and active resistance, including illegal protests and strikes, and to encourage resignations and retirements. The predictable result has been a deterioration of public services, which in turn lends credence to the populist claim that civil servants care only about their own interests, not that of "the people" they are meant to serve. In this way, populist governments have been reshaping the constitutional convention that civil servants are expected to take successive governments as they find them, to serve them loyally within the limits of law and custom, and that governments are expected to treat public servants as competent professionals, to respect their integrity and autonomy, and to give them political direction without demanding their political affinity or loyalty.

The implications are especially serious in relation to the police. Police officers are, by virtue of their status, not mere civil servants but holders of an office under the Crown.[91] Moreover, because the police wield coercive powers, there is an especially strong argument for ensuring their operational autonomy, at least from elected politicians. However, the independence of the police has been compromised by their close alignment with right-wing populist governments committed to a "law and order" agenda. Such governments have also not only proposed draconian penal legislation; they have also insulated the police against complaints of brutality, racism, or corruption[92] and, occasionally, mobilized them for partisan political ends.[93] In return, militant police unions have sometimes endorsed

[86] See Donald J. Savoie, *Breaking the Bargain: Public Servants, Ministers, and Parliaments* (Toronto: University of Toronto Press, 2003) ch. 2, "Creating a Non-partisan Civil Service."

[87] See, e.g., S.R. Ellis, "An Administrative System in Jeopardy: Ontario's Appointments Process" (1998) 6 *C.L.E.L.J.* 53.

[88] *Hewat v. Ontario* (1998), 37 O.R. (3d) 161, [1998] O.J. No. 802 (Ont. Court of Appeal).

[89] *Canadian Union of Public Employees (CUPE) v. Ontario (Minister of Labour)*, [2003] 1 S.C.R. 539, [2003] S.C.J. No. 28.

[90] See, e.g., "Campbell Vows to Purge NDP Patronage Appointments: Provincial Liberal Leader Tells Board of Trade He Will Restore 'Professional, Non-Partisan, Public Service,'" *Vancouver Sun* (April 2, 1999) D1; "Firing NDP Appointees Costs B.C. Liberal Government $9 Million in Severance." *Canadian Press* (July 26, 2001).

[91] *Nicholson v. Haldiman Norfolk (Regional) Police Commissioners*, [1979] 1 S.C.R. 311.

[92] Ontario's Conservatives abolished the independent Ontario Police Complaints Commission and assigned primary responsibility for investigating complaints to police forces themselves (subject to appeal to the Ontario Police Commission). See *Ontario Police Services Act* RSO 1990 c. P15 as amended SO 1995 c. 4, SO 1997 c. 8.

[93] Peter Edwards, *One Dead Indian: The Premier, the Police, and the Ipperwash Crisis* (Toronto: Stoddart, 2001); Bryan Palmer and David McNally, "The Riot Act: Reviving Protest in Ontario" (2000) 34:5 *Canadian Dimension* 28.

(or blacklisted) candidates for public office based on their support for (or opposition to) tougher laws, bigger police budgets, and police immunity from civilian oversight. If populism indeed compromises the constitutional convention of police neutrality, the long-term consequences both for democratic electoral politics and for open public debate on the criminal justice system are potentially grave.

Finally, populists have sought to liberate government from the supposed grip of elites, intellectuals, and "special interests" such as women's groups, racial minorities, and unions by preemptive strikes at consultative bodies that offer such groups the opportunity to influence governments. For example, in Ontario, the government simply announced in the legislature[94] that it was accepting the recommendations of a task force on "red tape" to abolish over thirty advisory and expert bodies, including the women's secretariat and the antiracism secretariat, both established by order-in-council and – a potential constitutional innovation – the Law Reform Commission, which was established by statute.[95]

g. THE JUDICIARY AND ITS RELATIONS WITH THE LEGISLATIVE BRANCH. The advent of the Charter is disturbing to populists in two respects. First, appointed judges now decide matters over which elected legislatures used to have exclusive, or at least ultimate, authority. Second, they are reaching decisions which are unpalatable to "the people" – especially to social and religious conservatives who make up an important right-wing populist constituency. Such decisions include more stringent rules governing the behavior of the police and crown prosecutors; expanded rights for gays, lesbians, sex offenders, and refugee claimants; and enhanced protection for freedom of expression and association.

Although these controversies are accurately characterized as a clash of fundamental constitutional principles – the right of the people to rule directly or through their representatives *versus* the rule of law as administered and applied by independent judges – the populist critique is often less about principles than about outcomes. Consequently, judges find themselves embroiled in a culture war in that they are perceived to be leading proponents of changes in Canadian society that offend the moral sense of "ordinary people" and their populist champions. This is ironic given that judges are at the same time accused by nonpopulists of failing to exploit the full emancipatory potential of the Charter, or, more generally, of political, intellectual, and social conservatism.

Controversy over the Charter at least partly explains intense populist criticism of the procedures whereby federal judges are effectively appointed by the justice minister or, in the case of the Supreme Court, by the prime minister.[96] This criticism is unlikely to be deflected by evidence that nonstatutory procedures have been developed to vet candidates or that appointees are generally able and

[94] Statement of Hon. David Johnson, Chair of Management Board, Ontario Legislative Assembly Debates (Hansard) 36th Parliament, 1st session at 3145–7 (May 29, 1966).

[95] The government did not repeal the statute that established the Commission but advised its members and employees that it would no longer be funded after a certain date. (Information provided to the author by the former Chair of the Commission.)

[96] But there are other concerns: See Bibliography and Conference Proceedings, *Judicial Appointment in a Free and Democratic Society: The Supreme Court of Canada* (University of Toronto, Faculty of Law, April 19, 2004), http://www.law-lib.utoronto.ca.

well-reputed. Until these procedures are legislated or harden into constitutional conventions, they can be bypassed or manipulated. Moreover, professional reputation does not count for much when the crucial issue, for many populists, is the judge's position on controversial issues. Furthermore, judges, however appointed, are likely to be regarded with suspicion by populists: They are members of a technocratic elite who enjoy considerable salaries, privileges, and power but are "accountable" only for egregious misconduct. Still, populist criticism has had an effect, and there is now widespread agreement on the need to reform judicial appointments procedures. Current controversy focuses on whether judicial appointments should be subject to parliamentary review and approval, as in the United States, in order to expose the views of candidates on controversial issues, or whether they ought to be scrutinized on grounds of merit by an independent appointments commission.

Finally, because even judges appointed in a more acceptable fashion may make decisions that violate "common sense" principles, populists argue that governments should find ways to overcome such decisions. This they can do in various ways: by invoking section 33 to override Charter rulings,[97] by amending existing legislation[98] or enacting new laws to reduce the risk of unconstitutionality,[99] by ignoring adverse decisions and forcing litigants to go back to court for further relief,[100] or (as was proposed in Ontario) by reducing the scope of judicial discretion – in sentencing, for example – and making its exercise subject to oversight by elected officials.[101] As these proposals make clear, in the end, populists are focused on securing "common sense" outcomes by means that clearly have constitutional implications.

CONCLUSION: POPULISM, GOVERNANCE, AND THE CONSTITUTION

Contemporary Canadian populism has many names, many faces, many manifestations in movements, parties, and governments. However, a common thread unites them: Populists are concerned to enlarge the role of citizens in the governance of the Canadian state. This concern almost inevitably takes on a constitutional dimension, whether its focus is on the design of state institutions, on how they function, on the practical outcomes they produce, or on symbolic dimensions of governance. Moreover, populism may become embroiled in arenas beyond the state – in the global economy, for example, or in the domains of faith, community, or culture – many of which also have constitutional implications, in the broad sense in which I have used that term. Finally, populism is so pervasive, if ill-defined, that (as used to be said about socialism) "we are all populists nowadays." Many nonpopulist parties

[97] See, e.g., Lynk Byfield "When will Martin live up to the Charter and protect majority rights?" (Weekly Commentary "Just between us," January 17, 2005), http://www.citizenscentre.com/comment/05-01-07.pdf.

[98] Peter Hogg and Allison Bushell, "The Charter Dialogue between Courts and Legislatures (Or Perhaps the Charter of Rights Isn't Such a Bad Thing After All)" (1997) 35 *Osgoode Hall L.J.* 75.

[99] *Agricultural Workers Protection Act*, S.O. 2002 c. 16.

[100] *Doucet-Boudreau v. Nova Scotia (Minister of Education)* [2003] 3 S.C.R. 3, [2003] S.C.J. No. 63.

[101] Bill 66, *An Act to make Ontario judges more accountable and to provide for recommendations from the Legislative Assembly for appointments to the Supreme Court of Canada*, 1st Sess., 37th Leg., Ontario, 2000 (Private member's bill, introduced April 18, 2000; not enacted).

and politicians have adopted populist rhetoric or appropriated populist projects for their own purposes. In this way, populism has become part of the "new normal" of government – itself a fact of potential constitutional significance.

This last point, concerning the "new normal," requires explanation. By way of historical analogy, during the postwar period Canada's social democratic parties not only advocated new public policies and introduced innovative legislative programs to implement those policies, when they occasionally formed governments. They also changed the discourse of politics and governance and, in so doing, created new expectations concerning the role of the state. Fifty or sixty years ago, no one could imagine that Medicare might come to be viewed as the institution which binds Canadians together, much as the transcontinental railway did in the nineteenth century, that it might exemplify the qualities of compassion and social equity which are said to distinguish Canada from the United States, or that it might lead to the invention of new institutions to enable the provincial and federal governments to discharge their shared responsibilities in the field. However, the commitment in the Charter of Rights and Freedoms to provide "essential public services of reasonable quality to all Canadians" suggests that at least by 1982 Medicare had become an implicit assumption of our polity and society.[102] Ten years later, the implicit almost became explicit when a "Social Charter" was included in the proposed Charlottetown Accord.[103] But its rejection in the 1992 constitutional referendum[104] not only marked the end of the postwar social democratic impulse in Canadian constitutionalism; it also coincided with – and was causally related to – the rise of Reform and the transformation of the Alberta and Ontario Conservatives. In short, the assumptions of the Canadian welfare state, once our constitutional "normal," were displaced by a populist-inspired neoliberal "new normal."

Thus, neoliberal populism has shaped constitutional reforms and fiscal policy; its discourse is being assimilated into the vernacular of politics, the media, and government; its prescriptions for the reform of legislative institutions and procedures are being debated and, to an extent, adopted and implemented. Clearly, neoliberal populism is becoming inscribed – if not entrenched – in Canada's political system, legislative institutions, and constitution.

Already it is possible to identify some populist reforms that are strong candidates to become permanent features of Canada's constitution in a more explicit sense: Referenda and popular consultations will almost certainly be mandatory in any future attempts to amend the *Constitution Acts*; new electoral arrangements, parliamentary procedures, and legislative semiotics are likely to take hold; new norms governing relations amongst politicians, the public, and civil service are

[102] This does not mean that it is a right enforceable by individual citizens, any more than individual citizens can effectively enforce other constitutional rights of which they are beneficiaries. Attempts to read a right to Medicare into s. 7 of the Charter (the "right to life, liberty and security of the person") have failed.

[103] Section 4 of the final text of the Charlottetown Accord, *The Consensus Report on the Constitution* (Charlottetown, August 28, 1992) provided that nonjusticiable constitutional language should ensure for all Canadians health care, adequate social services, reasonable access to housing, food and other basic necessities, high-quality primary and secondary education, and access to postsecondary education, as well as protection for workers' rights and the environment.

[104] See *supra*, *The Legislature's role in the amendment of the written constitution.*

emerging; and "fiscal responsibility" statutes inhibit legislatures in the exercise of their historically plenary power to tax and spend. All of these reforms have been undertaken in the name of guaranteeing "ordinary citizens" greater influence over government but with the ultimate intent that this influence should be deployed to deter governments from pursuing activist constitutional or legislative agendas. The result of a "new populist normal" will be the constitutional entrenchment not of an idealized form of populism but of the particular variant of populism that, at the end of the twentieth century, aligned itself with neoliberalism.

This is but one of many contradictions that lie at the heart of populism. Whereas populists propose many institutional reforms to remedy Canada's democratic deficit – referenda, initiatives, recall elections, the triple-E Senate, the decentralization of power within and among governments – they tend to overlook the dangers to democracy posed by concentrations of private power. Whereas populists tend to view guarantees of low taxes as a central pillar of their constitutional program, they view entrenchment of other substantive rights – of first nations, women or the poor – as impermissible derogations from the people's will. Whereas, populists insist that governments should act in accordance with the wishes of the people, many reforms they propose and, when in office, actually institute are likely to make government more responsive to parliamentary factions and power brokers. Whereas populists believe in repatriating programs from the federal level to provincial governments because they are closer to their voters, they have been assiduous in reducing the powers and resources of local governments.[105]

Even on substantive issues, populist positions sometimes seem to be at odds with majority sentiment and, for that matter, with electoral democracy. For example, general social attitudes toward abortion, gay rights, and women's equality seem more liberal than those espoused by populist politicians, parties, and voters.[106] Or, to take another example: The populist vision of a Canada in which all provinces enjoy equal influence within the national government denies the reality that most Canadians now live in large provinces, and especially in metropolitan areas that, so far at least, have been relatively immune to the charms of populism. Or a final example: While the majority of voters obviously will (and should) prevail in a budget referendum or recall election, that majority may be manufactured by expensive campaigns financed by corporate contributions.

It seems therefore that populists are somewhat conflicted over the extent to which "the people" ought to be trusted. And with reason: The views of ordinary citizens, experts, officials, and politicians may change over time; neoliberalism may fall into disfavor; populists themselves may regret their embrace of particular institutional arrangements. But even differently minded populists or postpopulists may find it difficult in the future to strike out in new directions, to repeal the constitutional norms enacted by today's neoliberal populists, or to revise or abandon the constitutional conventions they have initiated.

[105] The Harris Conservatives, for example, consolidated municipalities into larger regional units, reduced the size of municipal councils, curtailed the taxing power of municipalities, reduced the stipends of members of education authorities to derisory levels, stripped them of power over budgets and curricula, and, for violation of provincial guidelines, suspended them from office altogether.

[106] To cite one example, a recent poll found that 57% favor gay marriage and 38% are opposed; see "Canadians tolerant – well, mostly," *Globe & Mail* (July 1, 2004) A9.

On the other hand, it is also possible that Canadians will do what they have always done: circumvent, reinterpret, and reimagine the constitution, to accord with their own perception of what is required for the long-term good of the country or for their own short-term advantage. If so, a new postpopulist constitution may emerge. Whether, in what sense, by what means, and to what effect it will contribute both to a more robust democracy and to more efficacious lawmaking remains to be seen. As constitutions always do.

ACKNOWLEDGMENTS

I have benefited from the research assistance of Michael Rutherford, the financial support of the SSHRC and Osgoode Hall Law School, the reactions of participants at the Banff Conference from which this publication arose, and especially from conversations with Andrew Petter, Allan Hutchinson, and Tsvi Kahana.

9 Legislatures as Constituent Assemblies

Jon Elster

Constitutions regulate legislatures, and legislatures sometimes create constitutions. Does it follow that in such cases, legislatures engage in acts of self-binding? Or that they use the constitutions to bind *others*, to enhance their own freedom of action? Although neither of these simplistic propositions is adequate, each of them captures an aspect of the relation between the institution of the legislature and the text of the constitution.

The idea of viewing constitutions as acts of self-binding is one for which I have to take some responsibility.[1] For various reasons, I have come to be skeptical of its normative and explanatory value.[2] For one thing, the "binding" effect of constitutions is much less constraining than in such paradigm cases of individual self-binding as saving your money in a scheme under which you cannot take it out before Christmas.[3] For another, the "self" that is supposed to bind "itself" is much more elusive in the collective than in the individual case. Concerning the second point, the idea of self-binding makes somewhat more sense when the constitution is written by the legislature than when it is the work of a special convention. A legislature that writes the ground rules under which future legislatures will operate does at least have the *capacity* to bind "itself," in a loose sense of that term. By contrast, a convention that is convened for the sole purpose of writing the constitution and that is disbanded once that task is done, has no enduring "self" to bind. To say that the act of binding later legislatures (and other political actors) is an act of self-binding borders on the meaningless.

At the same time, however, we might question the *motivation* of constituent legislatures to bind themselves. We might rather expect these assemblies to try to limit the power of the other branches of government, so as to leave themselves with maximal freedom of action. Needless to say, this is not inevitably the case. Constituent legislatures may be concerned with the common good and not merely with their own power, and in fact be quite willing to constrain themselves. I give

[1] Jon Elster, *Ulysses and the Sirens: Studies in Rationality and Irrationality*, rev. ed. (Cambridge: Cambridge University Press, 1984) at ch. II.7.

[2] Jon Elster, *Ulysses Unbound* (Cambridge: Cambridge University Press, 2000) at ch. II; Jon Elster, "Don't burn your bridge before you come to it: Some ambiguities and complexities of precommitment" (2003) 81 *University of Texas Law Review* 1751.

[3] Richard H. Thaler and Hersh M. Shefrin, "An economic theory of self-control" in Richard H. Thaler, ed., *Quasi-Rational Economics* (New York: Russell Sage Foundation, 2001) 77.

some examples later. Yet on general Humean grounds, the danger of allowing one branch of government to determine its own future power should be obvious. In fact, this danger exists with regard to the executive no less than to the legislative branch. When the task of writing the constitution is entrusted to the head of the executive, we should not be surprised if it creates a strong executive, as in the French constitution of 1958.

In the rest of this chapter, however, I shall avoid the somewhat metaphysical language of a collective body "binding itself." Instead, I shall try to make out a normative argument for the view that constitutions ought to be written by assemblies called into being exclusively for that purpose and devoting themselves exclusively to that task. I shall refer to these as *constitutional conventions* or, more briefly, as *conventions*. A striking fact, however, is that only a small fraction of constitutions have actually been written in this way. The large majority of them have been written by *constituent legislatures*, that is, by bodies that have combined constituent and legislative functions. At the end, I shall address, very briefly, the question why the normatively desirable mode of constitution making has not been more widely adopted. My main concern, however, is to make the case for the superiority of conventions over other assemblies.

Let me first make a few conceptual observations and then briefly cite some important examples of the two types of constituent assemblies. In addition to the distinction between conventions and constituent legislatures, we can distinguish between *mandated* constituent assemblies and *self-created* assemblies. All constitutional conventions are elected with the mandate of writing a constitution. Some constituent legislatures also have a clear mandate. A clear case of the latter was the election of the first French parliament after 1945, where the voters were asked, "Do you want the assembly elected today to be a constituent assembly?" Ninety-six percent of the voters answered yes.

Some constituent legislatures, however, are self-created. Although originally created for other purposes, they arrogate to themselves the right to adopt a constitution. This was a very common pattern among the American states during the revolutionary years.[4] Among the constituent assemblies convened in this period, eight were self-created legislatures, nine were mandated legislatures, and three were constitutional conventions. The Second Continental Congress, too, was a self-appointed constituent body when it enacted the Articles of Confederation. The Hungarian parliament of 1989–1990 was also self-appointed. It had been created under Communist rule, but took it upon itself to destroy that regime by piecewise constitutional amendments that amounted to a wholly new constitution.

Conversely, some assemblies begin as constitutional conventions and then assume legislative powers, following the principle that "He who can do more can do less,"[5] or, perhaps, "He who can *create* a power can also *exercise* it."[6] For lack of a better term, I shall refer to these as *self-created legislating assemblies*. An example

[4] The following draws on the data presented in Roger S. Hoar, *Constitutional Conventions* (Boston: Little, Brown & Co., 1917).

[5] Arnaud Le Pillouer, *Les pouvoirs non-constituants des assemblées constituantes* (Paris: Dalloz, 2005) at 103, 106. As he notes, the French Constituante of 1789–1791 broke with this principle when it allowed the king a veto over ordinary legislation but not over the constitution.

[6] Ibid. at 114.

is the Frankfurt parliament of 1848, which dissolved the Assembly of the German Confederation and arrogated its powers to itself.[7] In the nineteenth century, a number of American states called conventions that authorized themselves to legislate.[8]

Altogether, therefore, we need to distinguish among four types of constituent assemblies:

- constitutional conventions
- mandated constituent legislatures
- self-created constituent legislatures
- self-created legislating assemblies

To repeat, the last three are all constituent legislatures. Whereas mandated constituent legislatures are elected with the dual task from the beginning, this is not true of the two types of self-created assemblies. The self-created constituent legislatures begin as legislatures and turn themselves into constituent assemblies. In self-created legislating assemblies, the opposite transformation occurs.

Let me proceed to a selective historical overview. The best-known constitutional conventions are those that adopted the American constitution and the German Basic Law. These are federal constitutions, and not surprisingly the delegates were appointed by the states rather than chosen in popular elections. A nonfederal example is provided by the Norwegian constitutional convention in 1814, where delegates were chosen by popular vote cast in the local churches. In addition, as I mentioned earlier, there are three examples from the early American period: Massachusetts in 1780, and New Hampshire in 1778 and in 1783. In a moment I shall discuss some recent Latin American conventions.

Typically, constitutional conventions have to be supplemented by some other political authority to manage current affairs. An apparent exception is the current Bulgarian constitution, which allows parliament to call for elections to a Grand Constituent Assembly, whose possible tasks include that of creating a new constitution. The relevant provisions are poorly thought out, however. On the one hand, "the mandate of the National Assembly shall expire with the holding of the elections for a Grand National Assembly." On the other hand, it is only "in an emergency [that] the Grand National Assembly shall further perform the functions of a National Assembly." It follows that if there is no emergency, ordinary parliamentary functions, including the vote of the budget, must come to a standstill during the work of the Grand National Assembly. As there is no time limit on the duration of the Grand National Assembly, the ensuing political paralysis might create the very emergency that would justify its assumption of legislative powers.

The Bulgarian case is a mere possibility. If we look at actual conventions, they always operate in tandem with other authorities. The Federal Convention operated concurrently with the Continental Congress, which adopted the momentous Northwestern Ordinance on July 13, 1787, whereas on the same day the delegates to the Convention were debating matters of taxation. In Germany after World War II, the Allies were firmly in charge of national policy matters. In Italy, the decree-law of March 16, 1946, assigned most legislative powers to the government. A solution of

[7] Frank Eyck, *The Frankfurt Parliament 1848–1849* (London: Macmillan, 1968) at 196 and ch. 5.

[8] Hoar, *supra* note 4 at ch. XI.8.

this kind was also what de Gaulle had wanted for the constituent assembly in 1945, but it was rejected by the provisional consultative assembly that had been established in Alger in 1943 and transferred to Paris in 1944.[9] The Indian constituent assembly that met on December 9, 1946, was supposed to deal with constitutional matters only, while current affairs were to be handled by an interim government. When the assembly began to function after the partition of the country the following year, it turned itself into a constituent legislature.

Conventions may thus either be supplemented by a strong executive or exist side by side with an ordinary legislature. The latter constellation, which was observed in the United States in 1787, also occurred in Colombia in 1991 and in Venezuela in 1999. In both cases, a president essentially declared war on his legislature by calling elections to a constituent assembly in ways not provided for by the existing constitution. The "cohabitation" of the two assemblies proved to be highly unstable. In Colombia, the constitutional convention ordered the dissolution of the legislature and elected an interim legislature from within its own body. In Venezuela, the constitutional convention took it upon itself to "assume the functions of the legislators [...] when these do not [...] carry out their tasks or delay their execution."[10]

From the beginning, nevertheless, constituent legislatures have been the most common kind of constituent assembly. The Virginia Convention that in 1776 adopted what is arguably the first constitution in the modern sense of the term, had originally been elected, in Jefferson's words, as "agents for the management of the war."[11] The first French assembly, the Assemblée Constituante that deliberated from 1789 to 1791, was elected both to write a constitution and to vote taxes. Once in place, it exercised extensive legislative and executive functions in addition to its constituent task. While spelling out the separation of powers for future legislative assemblies, the Constituante did not apply that principle to itself.[12] Similarly, even those who argued for a bicameral constitution insisted that the Constituante itself had to be unicameral.

Let me briefly mention some other constituent legislatures. Many of them are *transitional* assemblies, which mark the demise of an autocratic regime and the beginning of a democratic one. Examples include the German and French assemblies of 1848, the Spanish parliaments of 1931 and of 1977, the East European assemblies after 1989, and the South African assembly of 1994. Others are created under the impetus of *defeat in war*, such as the French assembly of 1871, the German assembly of 1919, and the Italian assembly of 1946, or at the *end of a war*, as in France in 1945–1946. Still others are established as part of the creation of a

[9] As noted by Le Pillouer, *supra* note 5 at 235, the solution proposed in France and adopted in Italy amounted to "avoiding the confusion of constituent and legislative powers by creating the cumulation of executive and legislative powers."

[10] *Le Monde* (September 1, 1999); see also *Le Monde* (September 11, 1999).

[11] As cited later by Edmund Randolph in Irving Brant, *James Madison*, vol. II (Indianapolis: Bobbs-Merrill, 1941) at 252. In Jefferson's opinion (ibid.), as well as in Madison's (ibid. at 251), the self-created nature of the Convention undermined its legitimacy.

[12] This is at least the traditional view. For objections, see Le Pillouer, *supra* note 5 at 124–8. Although he appeals to André Castaldo for support, the latter is actually quite unambiguous in his assertions that the Constituante violated the principle of separation of powers. See A. Castaldo, *Les méthodes de travail de la constituante* (Paris: Presses Universitaires de France, 1989) at 35, 235, 253. The focus in these discussions, however, is on the cumulation of constituent and executive powers, and only marginally on that of constituent and legislative powers.

new state, as in Czechoslovakia after World War I, or the restoration of an old one, as in Poland at the same time. In 1992, constituent legislatures were created in the two new successor states to Czechoslovakia. A special case is that of constituent legislatures in colonial countries acceding to *independence*, such as the Continental Congress after 1776.

In all these cases, the process of constitution making was induced by a political or military rupture. This, in fact, seems almost invariably to be the case. There are very few instances of either constitutional conventions or constituent legislatures deliberating "*à froid*," in the absence of any internal or external crisis. One relatively clear-cut example is the Swedish constitution that was adopted in 1974, after nearly two decades of debates and partial reforms. Other Nordic constitutions have also been modernized after World War II, but not as radically as the Swedish one. A more ambiguous instance is the 1997 Polish constitution, which may also be seen as the last stage in a protracted transitional process that began with the transition in 1989.

The "hot" nature of constitution making also extends to constitutional conventions. In 1787, the American states were widely seen as being in a state of crisis, with several scenarios of internal breakdown and external conflict being seriously entertained. The Norwegian constitution of 1814 was made in the middle of an armed conflict, and the German one of 1949 under the still devastating impact of defeat in war. Thus, it seems to be a near-universal rule that constitutions are written in times of crisis and turbulence. Nothing could be further from reality than the idea that "Constitutions are chains with which men bind themselves in their sane moments that they may not die by a suicidal hand in the day of their frenzy."[13] Yet passion may not be the worst enemy of reason: Interest can be even more dangerous.[14]

I now want to build a normative argument that a constitutional convention is a more desirable arrangement than a constituent legislature. It is not an open-and-shut case. In some respects, constituent legislatures may be preferable. Yet, on balance, conventions are better. We may note that arguments for conventions vary with the alternative to which they are contrasted. Some reasons why conventions are superior to self-created constituent legislatures do not apply to mandated assemblies or to self-created legislating assemblies. These latter may also be inferior to conventions, but for different reasons.

I shall not make the claim, which would be hard to make precise and even harder to prove, that conventions tend to produce better constitutions. Instead, I shall argue in procedural terms that conventions are more likely to embody the process value of free and unconstrained deliberation among all concerned parties. More abstractly, I claim that conventions promote the predominance of *reason* over *interest*. I shall also claim that they make it more likely that reason will gain the upper hand in the contest with *passion*. Although the turbulence of constitution-making periods makes it unlikely that framers in either kind of assembly will act as "Peter when sober legislating for Peter when drunk," I shall argue that the format

[13] John Potter Stockton in debates over the Ku Klux Klan Act of 1871, as cited in John E. Finn, *Constitutions in Crisis: Political Violence and the Rule of Law* (New York: Oxford University Press, 1991) at 5.

[14] Elster, *supra* note 2.

of the convention will at least insulate them against certain kinds of passion. In addition, I shall argue that constitutions produced by conventions tend to have greater *legitimacy* and hence tend to enjoy greater stability. As a constitution produces many of its desirable effects by virtue of its stability alone,[15] somewhat independently of its substantive features, a legitimacy-conferring process will also be desirable.

Let me begin with the last issue. The proper contrast here is between self-created constituent legislatures on the one hand, and the other three kinds of assembly on the other hand.[16] An assembly that takes it upon itself to write a constitution when its members were not elected for the task, will inevitably invite criticism. The Hungarian parliament of 1989, for instance, was a self-created constituent legislature. For this reason, and even more because of its Communist pedigree, the legitimacy of the new constitution was initially questioned. Earlier, the constitution-making power of the 1871 French legislature was called into doubt by those who argued, perhaps disingenuously, that it had been elected only to deal with the aftermath of the Franco-Prussian war.[17] Even earlier, in 1776, John Scott argued that the existing Provincial Congress in the state of New York "had the power to [frame] a government, or at least, that it is doubtful whether they have not that power." Gouverneur Morris argued strongly, however, for the calling of a constitutional convention, and a compromise was reached in the form of the election of a mandated constituent legislature, which took care of Morris's concern for the legitimacy of the new constitution.[18]

Self-created constituent legislatures are also normatively inferior in another, related respect. In modern societies, an important function of the legislature is to provide the basis for an effective government. It is widely agreed that for that purpose, one wants an electoral system that limits the number of parties represented in the assembly. Majority voting or proportional voting with a high threshold are generally agreed to promote this end.[19] To the extent, however, that the task of a

[15] Jon Elster, "The impact of constitutions on economic performance" in *Proceedings from the Annual Bank Conference on Economic Development* (Washington, DC: The World Bank, 1995) 209 at 209–26.

[16] The issue of legitimacy can also arise in the case of constitutional conventions. The two best-known constitutional conventions – Philadelphia in 1787 and Bonn in 1949 – were both criticized for lack of legitimacy. In Philadelphia, some claimed that the Federal Convention went beyond its mandate when it recommended a wholesale replacement of the Articles of Confederation and proposed a mode of ratification different from the one stipulated in those articles; see, for instance, the dissents by Yates and Lansing in Herbert J. Storing, *The Complete Anti-Federalist*, vol. 2 (Chicago: University of Chicago Press, 1981). In Bonn, objections arose from the fact that the Basic Law was written under the tutelage of the Allies; see, for instance, Carlo Schmid, as cited in John Ford Golay, *The Founding of the Federal Republic of Germany* (Chicago: University of Chicago Press, 1958) at 94. If, contrary to fact, the Germans had preferred a strong unitary government, the occupying powers would not have allowed them to adopt it. Needless to say, in the end the American and German constitutions gained uncontested legitimacy.

[17] Le Pillouer, *supra* note 5 at 78; Paul Bastid, *Le gouvernement d'assemblée* (Paris: Editions Cujas, 1956) at 216.

[18] Mary-Jo Kline, *Gouverneur Morris and the New Nation, 1775–1788* (New York: Arno Press, 1978) at 54–6. In Delaware, by contrast, the need for a special convention was seen as more important than the need for a mandate; see Mark W. Kruman, *Between Authority and Liberty: State Constitution Making in Revolutionary America* (Chapel Hill: University of North Carolina Press, 1997) at 28–9.

[19] This is not the place to summarize the large literature on the relation between electoral systems and party formation. It is of some interest to note, however, that in the French debates in 1946 over the possible constitutionalization of proportional voting it was assumed, contrary to what the experience of the Fourth Republic would show, that this system would lead to the emergence of a "coherent and

constituent assembly is to promote free and unconstrained deliberation among all concerned parties, with a large variety of interests being represented, proportional voting with no threshold or a low threshold is more desirable. A self-created constituent legislature elected for the purpose of effective governance might not, therefore, enjoy the legitimacy of a body with a broader basis.

The argument also applies to the extent of the suffrage. Thus, after the Declaration of Independence, the general court (lower house) of Massachusetts "enfranchised all free adult male town inhabitants for the duration of the constitution-making process,"[20] from the election of delegates to a constituent legislature up to (but not beyond) the ratification of the document. When the proposed constitution was turned down, partly because of a perception that the legislators had "Preposesssions in their own Favor,"[21] the house called for a convention whose proposal was then ratified. We may note, however, that in other cases where delegates to a constituent assembly have been elected by universal or wide suffrage, the assembly has found it difficult to write a more restricted suffrage into the constitution. In France in 1791, the framers managed to do so by subterfuge.[22] In Frankfurt in 1848, the unease of the framers at the prospect of discarding the mode of election by which they themselves had been chosen caused them to retain universal male suffrage in the constitution.[23]

The choice of a mode of election to a constituent assembly can indeed be a decisive moment. Those who can influence or constrain the choice of delegates may also, at one remove, be able to shape the constitution. If the assembly is at the same time to serve as a legislature, they may also be able to affect current affairs, and in particular to ensure that their party will form the government. These considerations, notably the second, may induce the choice of majority voting. The composition of the 1931 Spanish constituent legislature owed a great deal to the adoption by the interim Republican government of a strongly majoritarian electoral system that favored Republican forces. The subsequent constitution making was deeply nonconsensual. The 1990 elections to the Bulgarian constituent legislature "caused a deep legitimation crisis"[24] because they took place within a mixed majoritarian-proportional system that was heavily shaped by the greater bargaining power of the Communists.

Even proportional voting may be adopted for such tactical reasons. The choice by de Gaulle of proportional voting for the elections to the constituent legislature in 1945 has been explained on a number of grounds. According to one account, the decisive reason was the need for a variety of opinions to be represented.[25]

stable majority." See Jeannette Bougrab, *Aux origines de la Constitution de la IVe République* (Paris: Dalloz, 2002) at 362.

20 Kruman, *supra* note 18 at 30–1.

21 Ibid. at 32.

22 See, for instance, Brissot, as quoted by Patrice Guennifey, *Le nombre et la raison: La révolution française et les élections* (Paris: Editions de l'Ecole des Hautes Etudes, 1993) at 61.

23 Eyck, *supra* note 7 at 44–5, 367–8, 382.

24 Rumyana Kolarova and Dimitr Dimitrov, "The Round Table Talks in Bulgaria" in Jon Elster, ed., *The Round Table Talks and the Breakdown of Communism* (Chicago: University of Chicago Press, 1996) 178 at 200.

25 Odile Rudelle, "Le rôle du Général de Gaulle et de Michel Debré" in Didier Maus, Louis Favoreu, and Jean-Luc Parodi, eds., *L'Écriture de la Constitution de 1958* (Paris: Economica, 1992) 749 at 759.

According to another, PR was chosen in conformity with the justice-based ideology of the Resistance.[26] We know today, however, that he chose this mode of voting to minimize Communist representation in the assembly. As he explained in conversations with Alain Peyrefitte: "In [1945], the communists represented one vote out of three, the other two thirds being dispersed among numerous formations. If I had adopted majority voting, the assembly would automatically have been three quarters Communist. This could only be avoided by the proportional vote."[27]

At the same time, it would be inaccurate to assume that the choice of the mode of election to constituent assemblies is never governed by the desire to assure a broad representation. In four cases that I shall now briefly survey, the conveners of the assembly were in fact guided by this desire. In each but the last of these episodes, the result of this choice was arguably disastrous, for the conveners, for the country, or for both.

In 1789 Louis XVI made a choice that turned out to be unfortunate for him, when he devised electoral rules that made the parish priests rather than the bishops the main representatives of the clergy to the Estates-General. He did so, he asserted in the electoral rules announced on January 24, 1789, because "the good and useful pastors, who assist the people in their needs on a close and daily basis, [. . .] know their sufferings and apprehensions most intimately."[28] The lower clergy "thus were to represent the peasantry as well as the clerical assemblies that had elected them."[29] It should not have come as a surprise, therefore, when in May–June 1789 the priests allied themselves with the Third Estate to undermine the estate system itself and ultimately the royal power.

In the election of delegates to the 1919 Weimar assembly, the provisional Socialist government deliberately adopted proportional voting, together with female suffrage, in spite of the fact that both features were against their electoral interests.[30] It is at least arguable that a more self-serving choice of electoral system would, by enhancing the stability of the government, have prevented the disasters that followed.

In 1990, Vaclav Havel imposed a similarly *counter-interested* proportional system, to allow a place for his former Communist enemies in the constituent assembly.[31] As Louis XVI before him, he paid a high price for his impartiality. The Communists, notably the deputies from Slovakia, ended up as constitution wreckers

[26] Bougrab, *supra* note 19 at 266. Her discussion is confused, however, as she first asserts that PR "privileges the large parties" and then that the alternative system, majority voting, "brutally eliminates the small" parties.

[27] Alain Peyrefitte, *C'était de Gaulle*, vol. I (Paris: Fayard, 1994) at 451.

[28] *Réimpression de l'Ancien Moniteur* (Paris, 1840) at 558, Introduction Historique [AM]. We may note the important idea that the deputies were to represent *knowledge* of interests rather than the interests themselves. Similarly, Charles Beard stated that "The purpose of [his] inquiry is not [. . .] to show that the Constitution was made for the personal benefit of the members of the Convention. [. . .] The only point considered here is: Did they represent distinct groups whose economic interests they understood and felt in concrete, definite form through their own personal experience with identical property rights?" *An Economic Interpretation of the Constitution of the United States* (New York: The Free Press, 1986) at 73.

[29] Ruth F. Necheles, "The Curés in the Estates General of 1789" (1974) 46 *J. Mod. Hist.* 425 at 427.

[30] Ernst R. Huber, *Deutsche Verfassungsgeschichte seit 1789*, vol. 5 (Stuttgart: Kohlhammer, 1978) at 1067. A third reform, the lowering of the voting age, may have worked to the advantage of the socialists (ibid.).

[31] Jon Elster, "Transition, constitution-making and separation in Czechoslovakia" (1995) 36 *Archives Européennes de Sociologie* 105.

rather than as constitution makers. One of Havel's close associates told me in 1993 that "this decision will be seen either as the glory or the weakness of the November [1989] revolution: we were winners that accepted a degree of self-limitation."

The making of the 1919 Czechoslovak constitution does not fall into this depressing pattern. As a general election to the constituent assembly was out of the question, with a large proportion of the male population still out of reach and unable to vote due to war circumstances, the provisional government assigned seats to the parties according to their representation in the prewar Reichsrat of the Habsburg empire, which had been elected by universal suffrage under a majoritarian system. When the 1919 municipal elections, held under a proportional system, gave a very different outcome, seats in the constituent assembly were reallocated to reflect the more recent results.

Let me conclude on this point. In *mandated constituent legislatures*, the conveners may find themselves torn among three desires: to maximize the representation of their own group in the assembly, to ensure stable and effective governance, and to produce a set of deputies that represent a large variety of groups and interests. Although the last goal sometimes dominates, at other times it does not. Those who organize elections to *constitutional conventions* or to *self-created legislating assemblies* would tend to give greater weight to the third desideratum. By contrast, there is no intrinsic reason why conveners of *self-created constituent legislatures* should accord much importance to the desire for representativeness.

Next, I turn to the role of private interests and of techniques for reducing their importance in the constitution-making process. It is a truism that many decisions made by an ordinary legislature have a strong short-term impact on legislator interests. If the decision-making process is shielded from the public eye, arguing about the common interest will easily degenerate into naked interest bargaining. The effect of and perhaps the intention behind the practice of allowing the public to follow the proceedings and observe the votes, is to limit such self-serving scheming and, as a by-product, promote the public good. As Bentham wrote, "The greater the number of temptations to which the exercise of political power is exposed, the more necessary is it to give to those who possess it, the most powerful reasons to resist it. But there is no reason more constant and more universal than the superintendence of the public."[32] Yet if publicity is useful to prevent the intrusion of private interest into public affairs, it may also have adverse effects, to be described shortly.

By contrast, constitutional provisions usually do not have a strong short-term impact on the constitution makers themselves. The American constitution, to be sure, is an exception. Many framers had extensive economic interests in a number of matters that were to be or might have been regulated by the constitution. For instance, "Given the existence of debtor relief statutes in many states and the potential for debtor relief measures in other states, it is not surprising that delegates with private security holdings tended to favor national veto over state laws."[33] In

[32] Jeremy Bentham, Michael James, et al., eds., *Political Tactics* (Oxford: Oxford University Press, 1999) at 29.

[33] Robert A. McGuire and Robert L. Ohsfeldt, "An economic model of voting behavior over specific issues at the constitutional convention of 1787" (1986) 46 *J. Econ. Hist.* 79 at 102. See also generally Forrest McDonald, *We the People: The Economic Origins of the Constitution* (New Brunswick, NJ: Transaction Books, 1992).

the Assemblée Constituante, too, the opposition of Abbé Sieyes to the abolition of the tithe may have had something to do with the fact that it would affect him personally.[34] Art. 41.7 of the Romanian constitution of 1991 says that "Property is presumed to have been acquired legally," which is an unusual sort of provision. To make sense of it, we might look to a decision made by the Czechoslovak government on September 26, 1991, that in the future successful bidders for state-owned business would have to prove where their money comes from. The measure was intended to block the use of "dirty money" that had been illegally accumulated by members of the former nomenklatura or black marketeers. There was a presumption of guilt: The government is under no obligation to show that the funds have an illegal pedigree. Instead, citizens will have to prove that their money is clean. The Romanian clause may have been intended to preempt similar measures.

I believe, nevertheless, that the scope for self-serving behavior is in general much smaller in constitutional contexts than in ordinary legislation.[35] Framers do not benefit personally from a system of checks and balances or from a ban on arbitrary search and seizure. It does not matter to them personally whether the majority to overrule a presidential veto shall be two-thirds or three-fourths, or whether elections shall be every third or every fourth year. Moreover, the long time horizon for constitution making may create a "veil of ignorance" behind which personal interest and the general interest tend to coincide.[36] Even framers who represent a strong *group interest* usually have few opportunities to write it into the constitution. An important systematic exception is the tendency in the establishment of federal systems for small states to propose an equal or close-to-equal representation of the states in the upper house, and for large states to propose strictly proportional representation. Although (contrary to their claims) small states would have little to *fear* in a proportional system,[37] their *interest* (as that of any state) is obviously to have as many senators as possible. Another frequently observed exception is the imposition by economic elites of economic restrictions on the suffrage, to prevent

[34] Georges Lefebvre, *Etudes sur la Révolution Française* (Paris: Presses Universitaires de France, 1963) at 151. Castaldo claims that "personal and familial interest" was of minor importance in the votes of the *constituants* (*supra* note 12 at 174).

[35] Calvin Jillson asserts that whereas at the Federal Convention ideas governed the "'higher' level questions of constitutional design," economic and geographic interest dictated the "'lower' level choices among specific decision rules, each of which represented an alternative distribution of authority within and over the institutions of government." *Constitution Making: Conflict and Consensus in the Federal Convention of 1787* (New York: Agathon Press, 1987) at 17. Referring to the interest of individual framers rather than to those of the states, Robert McGuire reaches a similar conclusion in "Constitution-making: A rational choice model of the Federal Convention of 1787" (1988) 32 *Am. J. of Pol.* Sci. 483. This very convergence – explaining the same outcomes twice over – ought perhaps to induce some skepticism.

[36] For three examples of veil-of-ignorance reasoning at the Federal Convention, see Jon Elster, "Mimicking impartiality" in Keith Dowding, Robert Goodin, and Carole Pateman, eds., *Justice and Democracy* (Cambridge: Cambridge University Press, 2004) 112 at 119–20. This case, in which framers base their *own* decisions on ignorance about their future consequences, differs from that in which they try to shape the decisions of *future* legislators by subjecting them "to uncertainty about the distribution of benefits and burdens that will result from a decision." Adrian Vermeule, "Veil of ignorance rules in constitutional law" (2001) 111 *Yale L.J.* 399.

[37] For rebuttals of this small-state claim at the Federal Convention, see Madison in Max Farrand, ed., *Records of the Federal Convention* (New Haven: Yale University Press, 1966) at vol. 1, pp. 446–9 and Brian Barry, "Is it better to be powerful than lucky?" in his *Democracy, Power and Justice* (Oxford: Oxford University Press, 1989) 270 at 293–4. In two-state federations such as Czechoslovakia before the breakup, the fear can obviously be more justified.

the poor from using their vote to confiscate their wealth or to protect the interests of large landed property holders. Important as these cases are, I do not think they invalidate the claim that *overall*, individual and group interest are substantially less important in constitution making than in ordinary legislation. Below, I make a similar claim for the role of "institutional interest."

The relative unimportance of interest in the outcome reduces the benefits to be obtained from publicity, but does not provide an argument for secrecy. It is possible to provide an argument for closed proceedings, however, by pointing to the negative effects of publicity. Debates in front of an audience tend to generate rhetorical overbidding and heated passions that are incompatible with the kind of close and calm scrutiny that ought to be the rule when one is adopting provisions for the indefinite future. By denying the public admission to the proceedings and by keeping the debates secret until the final document has been adopted, one creates conditions for rational discussion that are less likely to prevail in the presence of an audience. As Madison wrote many years after the Convention, "had the members committed themselves publicly at first, they would have afterwards supposed consistency required them to maintain their ground, whereas by secret discussion no man felt himself obliged to retain his opinions any longer than he was satisfied of their propriety and truth, and was open to the force of argument."[38]

To be sure, secrecy also facilitates bargaining, by removing the opprobrium on displays of self-interest. Bentham's point was indeed that the creation of that opprobrium is one of the great benefits of publicity. But since the purchase of self-interest on constitutional provisions is likely to be relatively small, the benefits of secrecy will tend to outweigh the costs.[39] On this score, therefore, we have a stark incompatibility between the two aspects of a constituent legislature. If the proceedings are secret, the members can strike private deals in the legislative sessions. If they are public, the quality of the constitutional debates will suffer.

There are other reasons why a dual assembly might perform its constitutional tasks poorly. For one thing, constitutional provisions might be shaped indirectly by private interest through the mechanism of logrolling. One deputy might offer to vote for another's favored constitutional provision in exchange for support on a legislative issue in which he or she has a personal interest. For another, the dividing line between statute and constitutional provisions might be blurred. As soon as the Assemblée Constituante had imposed the principle that statutes but not constitutional provisions were subject to the royal veto, the deputies had a clear incentive to present each of their decisions as a constitutional one.[40] In the Hungarian constituent legislature in 1989 it sometimes happened (I have been told) that a conflict between a statute and a constitutional provision was resolved by modifying the latter rather than the former.

Two episodes from the Assemblée Constituante illustrate the perils of duality. In each case, it is likely that a decision by the assembly to prevent its members from seeking executive or legislative office had the effect of creating a precedent for the

[38] Farrand, *supra* note 37 at vol. III, p. 479.

[39] I overlooked this point in Jon Elster, "Strategic uses of argument" in K. Arrow et al., eds., *Barriers to the Negotiated Resolution of Conflict* (New York: Norton, 1995) 236 at 251–2.

[40] Mme de Staël, *Considérations sur la Révolution Française* (Paris: Tallandier, 2000) at 243.

constitution. In the fall of 1789, Mirabeau twice addressed the issue of the relation between the king's minister and the assembly. In September, his proposal that ministers chosen from the assembly might retain their seat (or stand for reelection) might have been adopted had it been put to a vote, which for technical reasons it was not.[41] When the issue came up again in November, he argued for the more limited proposal that the ministers be allowed to have a "consultative voice" in the assembly until "the constitution shall have fixed the rules which shall be followed with regard to them."[42] Had the vote not been postponed until the next day, the proposal might have been adopted. As the delay gave Mirabeau's enemies time to gather their forces, it was defeated. Among the arguments offered against it, the most relevant for my purposes was made by Pierre-François Blin, a deputy of the Third Estate: "The issue may seem detached from the constitution and to be merely provisional; but the authority of the past on the future binds the facts at all times."[43] Although the appeal to the danger of precedent-setting was probably a pretext for excluding Mirabeau from the ministry, the argument itself is plausible and, in fact, applies directly to Blin's own successful motion that "No member of the National Assembly shall from now on be able to enter the ministry during the term of the present session." It is likely although not rigorously provable that the article in the constitution of 1791 banning members of any assembly from the ministry during their tenure and in the two years following it, can be traced back to his motion. Although mainly adopted for the purely tactical purpose of stopping the ascent of Mirabeau, the assembly could hardly disavow the lofty principle on which it pretended to rest.

The even more momentous adoption of Robespierre's self-denying ordinance on May 16, 1791, making members of the current legislature ineligible for the next one, also set a precedent for the constitution. His professed motive was that since "we are going to vote on the [...] organization of the legislative body and on the constitutional principles of the elections, let us make sure that we are not involved in these great questions (*que ces grandes questions nous soient étrangères*); let us rid ourselves of all the passions that might cloud our reason."[44] His real motive, although shrouded in the hypocritical and intimidating appeal to the public interest of which he was a master, was dictated by his interest in a weak legislature, which would remove his political enemies from power and allow the Jacobin clubs to dominate.[45] The motives of the deputies in their near-unanimous adoption of the proposal were complex.[46] Some may have been "drunk with disinterestedness," in the words of the biographer of the deputy Thouret, who unsuccessfully tried to stem the tide of enthusiasm.[47] Others may have voted for the motion because they

[41] AM, *supra* note 28 at vol. 1, pp. 532–3. See also R. K. Gooch, *Parliamentary Government in France: Revolutionary Origins, 1789–1791* (Ithaca, NY: Cornell University Press, 1960) at 104–6.

[42] AM, *supra* note 28 at vol. 2, p. 152. See also Gooch, *supra* note 41 at 108–17.

[43] AM, *supra* note 28 at vol. 2, p. 153. As a French proverb has it, "*Rien ne dure comme le provisoire.*"

[44] AM, *supra* note 28 at vol. 8, p. 418. The speech as a whole makes it clear that the danger to be protected against was the *interest* of the constituants in being elected to the first legislature rather than their passions.

[45] Gerald Walter, *Maximilien de Robespierre* (Paris: Gallimard Walter, 1989) at 107.

[46] Barry Shapiro, "Self-sacrifice, self-interest, or self-defense? The constituent assembly and the 'self-denying ordinance' of May 1791" (2002) 25 *French Historical Studies* 625.

[47] E. Lebèque, *Thouret* (Paris: Felix Alcan, 1911) at 261.

feared to be stigmatized as self-interested, and perhaps persecuted if they opposed it. Using the routine scare tactic of the left, the noble deputy Custine said, "It is easy to see that the opponents want to be reelected."[48] Many right-wing deputies voted for the measure because they thought it would destabilize the regime by ensuring that the new legislature would be made up of inexperienced novices.[49] Whatever the mix of motives, it is plausible that this episode set a crucial precedent for the limitations on reeligibility adopted in the 1791 constitution.[50]

These examples (and others that might have been cited) reflect a mechanism of *path-dependency*.[51] The constitution that is finally adopted may depend in accidental or irrelevant ways on decisions made by the framers when wearing their legislative hats. As an analogy, in courts that combine the functions of a supreme court and of a constitutional court, decisions made in the former capacity might contribute to shaping those made in the latter capacity.[52] Unlike courts with a dual function, one-purpose or "pure" constitutional courts have the invalidation of statute as their only raison d'être. Thus, if "a constitutional court is not 'pure', but has additional functions apart from reviewing legislation [...], the more easily a court can exercise deference towards parliament, if other factors push in that direction."[53] This is *not* an argument for pure constitutional courts, since in order to affirm their autonomy they may display insufficient rather than excessive deference. By contrast, it is hard to see that any analogous dangers would be created by having an assembly that devoted itself exclusively to constitution making.

Robespierre's self-denying ordinance was proposed for bad reasons and turned out to have bad effects, but this should not prevent us from acknowledging that an arrangement of this kind might be a possible response to a genuine problem. A constituent legislature might be subject to a self-enhancing bias, in the sense that it might create an excessively strong legislative branch with correspondingly weak executive and judicial branches. The bias might stem from one of two sources. First, if the framers expect or hope to be elected to the first postconstitutional assembly, they have a direct interest in being able to promote their interest – or just to exercise power – at that later stage. Second, as members of the legislature they might naturally come to think that the institution to which they belong is a particularly important one, partly because they have more intimate knowledge about it than about the other branches and partly because there is a natural human tendency to enhance one's own importance in the scheme of things.[54] A similar

[48] AM, *supra* note 28 at vol. 8, p. 420.

[49] C. E. Ferrières, "Mémoires" in M. de Lescure, ed., *Bibliothèque des mémoires, t. XXXV* (Paris: Firmin-Didot, 1932) 344.

[50] Although Robespierre wanted to exclude reeligibility for the next legislature, the constitution allows reeligibility for one legislature.

[51] For a general discussion of such lock-in effects in constituent legislatures, see Le Pillouer, *supra* note 5 at 293–314.

[52] I am indebted to Patricia Hughes for drawing my attention to this parallel.

[53] V. Ferreres Comella, "The consequences of specializing constitutional review in a special court" (2004) 82 *Texas L. R.* 1705 at 1732.

[54] For an analogy, when each of a pair of spouses claims to be doing more than 50% of the housework, it may be because each is in a position to note all the work he or she does but not all that the other does (a "cold" or unmotivated error) or because each wants to present himself or herself in a favorable light (a "hot" error). For the first mechanism, see M. Ross and F. Sicoly, "Egocentric biases in availability and attribution" in D. Kahneman, P. Slovic, and A. Tversky, eds., *Judgment under Uncertainty* (Cambridge:

bias, stemming from the same two sources, may apply to members of the executive branch, to the extent that they, too, are involved in the constitution-making process.[55]

To be sure, members of constitutional conventions might also be subject to a self-enhancing bias. If they expect that they will play a prominent role in one of the branches of government, they might tend to write an important place for that branch into the constitution. This bias could only arise, however, from the first of the two sources mentioned in the previous paragraph. It is rooted in simple individual interest. Bias rooted in the second source reflects what we might call "institutional interest," not because an institution can have interests (it cannot), but because this bias is shaped by the current place of the deputies in the institutional structure rather than by the place to which they aspire.[56]

In general, it is hard to tell when and by how much one of these biases might be more important than the other.[57] Yet, recognizing the difficulty of distinguishing between them, let me cite some historical examples. I believe many French *constituants* were subject to a bias of the second kind when they voted against bicameralism and an absolute royal veto in September 1789. A vote for bicameralism and absolute veto would have been an implicit recognition that an unchecked popular assembly, such as the one to which they belonged, might not possess infallible wisdom. In the enthusiasm of the day, this idea was unthinkable.[58]

The French constituent legislature of 1848 created a document that was essentially legislative-centric. The assembly could bring down the government by refusing to vote the budget, but the president could not dismiss parliament or veto its decisions. Yet the assembly refrained, for reasons that remain obscure, from having the president elected by the assembly so that he could be its creature. Instead, the framers opted for popular election, thus producing an outcome that few of them wanted, that of Louis Napoleon being chosen as the first president. The outcome was disastrous, as might be expected when a formally omnipotent assembly

Cambridge University Press, 1993) 179–89; for the second, G. Loewenstein et al., "Self-Serving Assessments of Fairness and Pretrial Bargaining" (1993) 22 *J. Legal Stud.* 135.

55 As president of Czechoslovakia, Vaclav Havel repeatedly asked parliament to increase the powers of the presidency in the new federal constitution. His constitutional draft of March 5, 1991, for instance, gave the president the right to declare a state of emergency, to dissolve parliament, and to call a referendum (*Report on Eastern Europe*, March 22, 1991). In November 1991, President Walesa of Poland produced a constitutional draft that replaced the parliamentary supremacy adopted in the 1989 Round Table Talks with the supremacy of the presidency (ibid., December 12, 1991). The constitutions proposed (in 1946) or imposed (in 1958) by General de Gaulle were similarly executive-centered. As I argue in Jon Elster, "Beyond Rational self-Interest in Ian Shapiro, ed., *The Crafting and Operation of Institutions* (New York: New York University Press, 2006), however, it would be simplistic to assume that de Gaulle created the constitution of the Fifth Republic merely to enhance his own power. Rather, he wanted to create a strong presidency for the sake of future heads of state who would not be able to rely, as he could, on personal charisma and authority.

56 Mark Kruman refers to the distrust of "institutional interest" to explain the preference for conventions over constituent legislatures in revolutionary America, but it is unclear which of these biases he has in mind. His phrasing is consistent with either or with both. See Kruman, *supra* note 18 at 7, 22, 25, 31.

57 I suspect but cannot prove that Havel was subject to institutional bias and Walesa to a simple self-interested bias.

58 A. Duquesnoy offers an explicit statement by a deputy that in the passions of the moment, the assembly was incapable of taking precautions against the passions of the future. See *Journal sur l'Assemblée Constituante*, vol. I (Paris: Alphonse Picard, 1894) at 324 (diary entry from September 9, 1789).

confronts an executive endowed with few formal powers but with the legitimacy of popular election and a magical name.[59]

A hundred years later, the French constituent legislature elected in 1945 proposed a pure "régime d'Assemblée" that was rejected in a popular referendum, mainly because the voters feared it might facilitate a Communist bid for power. The constitution adopted the following year by a new constituent legislature was slightly modified in favor of the executive but remained highly legislative-centric, with the president as well as the prime minister being elected by the assembly.[60] The constitution-making process is best characterized as a deal among politicians regulating their future deals. Again, the outcome was disastrous, not because the constitutional machinery was smashed, as on December 10, 1851, but because it ultimately wore itself down.

These three episodes display the self-serving tendency of constituent legislatures. There are also episodes that point in the opposite direction, a striking case being the Hungarian one from 1989. By adopting the constructive vote of no-confidence, the constituent legislature endowed the government with greater independence from parliament. By creating a very strong constitutional court, it severely limited its own future legislative powers. One might seek the explanation for these self-limiting enactments in the general spirit of euphoria that was reigning in much of Eastern Europe at the time. Perhaps the Hungarian framers, like the French *constituants* in 1791, were "drunk with disinterestedness." In the case of the Constitutional Court, however, a more mundane explanation is also available, since there is considerable evidence[61] that the Hungarian Communists wanted a strong constitutional court that could be expected to strike down vindictive legislation once the democrats got into power. A more clear-cut counterexample is provided by the German constituent legislature of 1919, which created an executive that was intended to be strong and turned out to be disastrously so.

As with the other arguments I have adduced for the normative superiority of conventions, their lesser vulnerability to self-serving biases is only a tendency, not an invariant feature. The arguments have some support in first principles, and the preponderance of the empirical evidence seems to be in their favor. On balance, I believe they suggest that conventions are superior to any of the three alternatives. Before concluding, however, we should also consider some arguments that might favor one of the latter. At the end of the day, I do not think they outweigh the considerations I have offered, but they do make the case more complicated.

It has been argued that constituent legislatures are superior because the framers can be held accountable at the next election.[62] It is certainly desirable that self-created constituent legislatures be held accountable in some way, either by election or by downstream ratification of the constitution. To arrogate the constituent

[59] Already in 1848, three years before the coup d'état of Louis Napoleon, clear-headed minds were in no doubt on this issue. F. Luchaire, *Naissance d'une Constitution: 1848* (Paris: Fayard, 1998) at 12.

[60] Paul Bastid, *Le gouvernement d'assemblée* (Paris: Editions Cujas, 1956) at Part II, ch. III.

[61] Summarized in Jon Elster, *Closing the Books* (Cambridge: Cambridge University Press, 2004) at 194.

[62] Dale Kreibig (personal communication) informs me that this argument was made in the report by the Canadian Special Joint Committee of 1991 known as the Beaudoin-Edwards Special Joint Committee. See Government of Canada, Special Joint Committee on the Process for Amending the Constitution of Canada, *The Process of Amending the Constitution of Canada: The Report of the Special Joint Committee* (Ottawa: Supply and Services, 1991) 47–51.

power to themselves without being accountable to anyone would amount to a legislative coup d'état. It is less clear why conventions or constituent legislatures with an upstream mandate would also need a downstream approval. If this should be thought desirable, ratification can obviate the need to hold the ax of reelection over the head of the framers.

One might argue, furthermore, that constituent legislatures are desirable because of the scarcity of competent legislators. If a country opts for the concurrent operation of a legislature and a constitutional convention, the quality of debates and decisions in one or both will suffer. The "Bulgarian" alternative of shutting down current affairs until after the convention is finished, is equally undesirable. The force of this argument will depend on institutional detail. It is stronger if there is an existing legislature in place and its members are ineligible to the convention, as when in 1991 President Gaviria of Colombia issued a decree, upheld by the Supreme Court, that made sitting congressmen ineligible for the Assembly. In that case there is indeed a risk, at least in the abstract, that the most competent politicians will end up devoting themselves to the less important tasks. By contrast, delegates to the Continental Congress were eligible to the Federal Convention. Ten were in fact elected, out of whom eight showed up, including Madison. We may also consider the frequent coexistence of two elite bodies in the lower and upper houses of parliament. There are many objections to bicameralism, but the scarcity of competent legislators is not one I have ever seen cited.[63]

A third objection rests on the dangers, rather than merely the inefficiency, of having two concurrent assemblies. As I noted earlier, the two-track systems of Colombia and Venezuela created an acute conflict between the two assemblies in which the conventions, supported by the presidents, won the upper hand. This outcome corresponds to the analysis of Robespierre in a speech from 1793, in which he said that "A double representation contains the germ of civil war. [...] One assembly would appeal to the existing constitution and the other to the keener interest that a people takes in new representatives; the struggle would be engaged and the rivalry would excite hatred."[64] One might imagine a civil war occurring in 1787, if Congress had insisted on the constitution being ratified by the state legislatures. Yet an eventuality that did not materialize cannot provide an empirical basis for the objection. Nor does the experience of two unstable Latin American countries provide a very telling argument. The theoretical basis for the objection is essentially a warning by Robespierre, who is hardly a credible authority in these matters.[65]

Finally, some might object to the condition of secrecy that I used as a premise in part of my argument for the superiority of conventions. In the modern world, they

[63] We may also cite the claim by Bryce that "Experience has shown [...] in the United States, the country in which this method [conventions] has been largely used for redrafting, or preparing amendments to, the Constitutions of the several States, that a set of men can be found for the work of a Convention better than those who form the ordinary legislature of the State." J. Bryce, *Constitutions* (Oxford: Oxford University Press, 1905) at 62.

[64] Cited by Le Pillouer, *supra* note 5 at 101–2.

[65] As further evidence, one may also cite the paucity of expressed feelings of envy and jealousy in the relations between the two legislative branches in the United States. See L. Little, "Envy and jealousy: A study of separation of powers and judicial review" (2000) 52 *Hastings L.J.* 47 at 75.

might say, an elite forum of this kind will inevitably lack legitimacy.[66] Upstream legitimacy, if necessary supplemented by downstream legitimacy through ratification, will not be enough: Process legitimacy is also required. The constitution will not appear as legitimate unless it has been hammered out in public, through public hearings, public debates, and public voting. My response is that these public processes can take place at the upstream stage and perhaps also at the downstream stage, but that between these two stages the writing of the constitution should be shielded from the public. The process as a whole, that is, should be hourglass-shaped.[67] If the people have a self-destructive desire for full and constant illumination of the proceedings, it will of course have its way. The best-known popular rejections of secret constitution making, following the Meech Lake and Charlottetown accords in Canada, do not provide any evidence of this desire. These accords emerged from the ultimate "smoke-filled back-room" processes, with very little upstream legitimacy.[68]

Why, then, are constitutional conventions rare? I suspect it is because conveners choose the path of least resistance. When a legislature is in place, why not use it? If a legislature is not yet in place, there is a need to establish one to deal with current affairs. Again, why not use it to write the constitution rather than elect two separate bodies? As my discussion should have made clear, the superiority of conventions is not blindingly overwhelming. The claim that they are better shielded from the play of interest and the empire of passion is mainly a theoretical one, given the rarity of this arrangement in the history of constitution making. The risk that role confusion might lead to an inappropriate influence of the legislative process on the constituent one will also, if perceived at all, be seen as remote or abstract. Constituent legislatures, therefore, are chosen because they are doubly capable of serving as focal points. On the one hand, by virtue of being the most common type of constituent assembly they offer a natural model. On the other hand, the fact that a legislature already exists or will have to be created makes it the obvious first choice, in the absence of compelling arguments for another option. In the United States in 1787, in Colombia in 1991, and in Venezuela in 1999, the flaws of the existing legislature were so obvious that steps were taken to bypass it. This outcome is rare, however. It requires not only the perceived deficiency of the existing body but also the presence of individuals capable of creating an alternative one without triggering a civil war.

ACKNOWLEDGMENTS

I am grateful to Dale Kreibig, Arnaud Le Pillouer, and Pasquale Pasquino for comments on an earlier draft.

[66] I am indebted to Dale Kreibig for pressing this point on me.

[67] Peter Russell, *Constitutional Odyssey: Can Canadians Become a Sovereign People?* rev. ed. (Toronto: University of Toronto Press, 1993) at 191.

[68] Ibid. at 134–45, 191, 219–27.

10 Legislatures and the Phases and Components of Constitutionalism

Ruth Gavison

All constitutions seek to enable government, structure its powers, and limit them. To do this effectively, constitutions must enjoy a legitimacy which is broader and deeper than that enjoyed by any specific organ of government or any specific policy or piece of legislation. A constitution's fundamental nature is supposed to provide elements of the "civil religion" that binds all members of society and all major groups within it to the constitutional system. Obtaining the legitimacy needed for fulfilling such a major role in any society depends, to a great extent, on the different roles various organs play in framing and adopting constitutional regimes, and on the roles they play within these regimes.

The roles played by various organs in the constitutional process should also differ in accordance to the three distinct elements of a constitution in terms of structure and functions: credos, rules of the game, and bills of rights. Thus, the roles played by various organs should depend on a complicated interrelationship of both the phase of the constitutional process and the part of the constitution under discussion.

In this chapter, I argue that legislatures and courts have different roles in the phases of constitutionalism. The role played by legislatures (or, more accurately, by the people's representatives) is almost exclusive during constitution making, central when amending the constitution, and then diminishes during the application/interpretation of the constitution. The role played by courts is marginal during constitution making, small when amending the constitution, and central during the application/interpretation of the constitution.

In addition, I argue that institutional roles differ when we look at different parts of constitutions. We can derive empirical and normative guidelines for the various organs of government from the combination between the phase of constitutionalism and the part of the constitution in question. Thus, the central features of the constitutional framework should be decided at the initial constitution making stage. This is particularly true when dealing with the "rules-of-the-game" part, which should be comprehensive and provide a coherent system of checks and balances, and that should be negotiated and adopted with broad consensus. The natural candidates for performing these tasks are constituent assemblies or legislatures. Application and interpretation of the constitution are routine activities, in which all powers partake, with a special role granted to an independent judiciary. Constitutional amendments should be more celebratory and broadly discussed than regular legislation, but they do not have to have the features of constitution making itself. The primary organ of amendments is the legislature itself, using a special mode of legislation, and possibly aided by built-in guarantees of popular involvement. Usually, the legitimacy of the constitution is enhanced if the institutional implications of these distinctions are adhered to.

Effective constitutionalism does require enforcement of constitutional norms and finality in such decisions. As a part of a comprehensive system of checks and balances established by the constitution in its "rules-of-the-game" part, courts may serve as the final arbiters of disputes concerning the separation of powers and federalism. Courts do have a special role to play in protecting individuals and groups when their constitutional rights are violated by legislative majorities. However, effective protection of rights requires a partnership between all organs of government. Sweeping rights-based or credo-based court supremacy, resulting in the courts imposing values that are deeply controversial in their societies and outside the core of blatant violations of human rights, may in fact weaken constitutional regimes instead of enhancing them.

In the normative dimension, I argue that the roles played by legislatures and courts in the three phases in the "life cycle" of a constitution and in relation to the different parts of the constitution should be such that the functions of structuring and legitimating government in its broad sense are achieved in the best way. In the empirical dimension, I suggest that a constitution is more likely to gain legitimacy if legislatures and courts adhere to these guidelines.

This line of argument helps in reviewing the popular claim that courts, especially supreme or constitutional courts, are the guardians of constitutions. Courts are thus presented as the most critical organ of a constitutional regime. By examining the role the courts play in the life cycle of a constitution and in relation to different parts of the constitution, I hope to show that this presentation is misleading and may have pernicious results.

Because my argument addresses the entire life cycle of a constitution, it is relevant to all constitutional systems. In most constitutional regimes, legislatures as well as other constitutional powers operate under and within an agreed-upon constitution. Often, they are established by it and gain their legitimacy and stability, to a large extent, from it. The constitution is taken as a given. In rare cases it may itself be amended, but the idea is that the constitution sets the framework of activity of the other organs of government, including the legislature itself. This situation permits intense discussions of the roles of the various powers under the constitution, and systems may have constitutional crises when one of these powers challenges the limits of the power of another. But these discussions all take place within the constitutional framework. Indeed, one of its main functions is to make such debates more structured and "safer" than they would have been had all the rules of the game been vulnerable to "normal" political exigencies. This explains why stable constitutional regimes can usually contain heated and persistent debates about constitutionalism and its implications.

My argument – and its institutional implications – gains special importance in dealing with constitutional systems in which the status and the basic contours of the constitutional regime itself are quite controversial.[1] I argue that this fact does weaken the legitimacy and stability of the constitutional arrangements, and that in order to resolve controversies relating to the constitutional contours of a legal system itself, what is necessary is for the legislature to take a clear and firm position on constitutional issues, rather than letting the court be the driving agent of the process.

I. INSTITUTIONAL IMPLICATIONS OF PHASES OF CONSTITUTION MAKING AND OF COMPONENTS OF CONSTITUTIONS

A. Three phases of constitutionalism

A prime function of constitutions is to structure and legitimate the political system it regulates. Legitimacy may come from the process through which the constitution was made and is implemented (formal legitimacy), from the content of its arrangements (material legitimacy), or from both. I will argue that there are important institutional implications to these aspects of gaining legitimacy. There should be a distinction in institutional competence between the three phases of constitutionalism – initial constitution making, amendment of constitutions, and their routine application and interpretation. Similarly, the competence of different institutions depends on the parts of the constitution they deal with – rules of the game, credos, or bills of rights.

Constitutions are metalaws in the sense that they structure lawmaking itself as well as the general contours of government and its constraints. This structuring and entrenchment of the framework rules create a special legitimacy for the constitutional order and its actors, so that it increases the stability of government in its broad sense. The legitimacy of the constitutional order is supposed to be sufficient to command obedience to laws and authorized decisions that would have otherwise lacked this legitimacy because they do not enjoy majority support on their merits. This legitimacy and stability is of special importance in divided societies, where there is deep controversy about the good life and the identity of the state. Agreement about policies is likely to be fragile or nonexistent. In such societies, the stability and legitimacy of the constitutional order may be critical to the ability to negotiate serious political crises, which without that stability and legitimacy might have led to the collapse of the regime itself.[2]

The health and robustness of society may depend on the commitment of all members and groups to the shared framework rules included in the constitution. These framework rules provide the secure realm within which each of the groups

[1] Israel is a good example of such a system. For an application of the thesis developed here to the Israeli context, see Ruth Gavison, "The Israeli Constitutional Process: Legislative Ambivalence and Judicial Resolute Drive" (2005–2006) 11 *Rev. Const. Stud.* (forthcoming).

[2] The French fourth republic created a constitutional structure that could not have handled the Algerian crisis. De Gaulle indeed succeeded in getting France out of Algeria based on the new constitution he demanded, which established the fifth republic. In part, his success was based on the fact that he could have presented his policies as required to save the republic, not simply to implement his (deeply resisted) policy – see Jean Foyer's "The Drafting of the French Constitution of 1958," the following "Commentary" by François Luchaire, and the "Discussion" afterwards in Robert A. Goldwin and Art Kaufman, eds., *Constitution Makers on Constitution Making* (Washington, DC: American Enterprise Institute for Public Research, 1988) 7 at 10–15, 47–9, 56–62.

can fight for its vision of the good life knowing that the framework will hold the joint enterprise together. The groups may not realize their full visions every time, but the system will guarantee that their constraints, as well as those of the others, are maintained. In divided societies, the rules of the game are of special importance because often it is clear that no substantive compromise can be reached, and the only shared element may be the willingness to adhere to a fair process.[3] Under such circumstances, the question of the identity of those deciding sensitive issues may be crucial. This may affect both the rules of the game and the arrangements themselves. Indeed, deep rifts within a society are likely to be reflected in all components of the constitution, including election systems and in the structure of state organs. They may result in a lot of emphasis on the identity of lawmakers and law interpreters, and on a stronger interest in representation of the various groups and interests. The rifts may also mean that credos will be especially hard to agree on. In divided societies, therefore, constitutions may have the additional function of making otherwise disparate groups, with very different aspirations, members of the "demos" that is the source of legitimacy of the state. Equal citizenship under the constitution may be a way to bridge, in the political context, the gaps between the various groups.

The need to cater to different interests and conceptions of the good means that constitutional schemes often involve "great compromises," which permit each of the groups to subscribe to the shared framework despite the fact that it does not meet one's own ideal of governance. These great compromises need to be protected from regular partisan politics, because they are the basis for the willingness of the groups to join in the game and to see themselves as a part of the civic nation to begin with. It will undermine the agreement if the legislature or anyone else starts to erode the compromise once the moment of constitution making is over. This is true for all societies, but especially for deeply divided societies and for federal nations. In the latter, the member states would not give up any of their power if the compromise is not entrenched against unilateral actions by the central government.[4]

Moreover, as the constitution sets up the rules of the game, it should include an elaborate structure of checks and balances. It is important to see these as a whole, because the effectiveness of the system may depend on the full range of constitutional arrangements. Constitutional players should see these as interrelated and avoid an extensive use of piecemeal changes that may endanger the overall balance. Naturally, it is much easier to design that kind of a system in a comprehensive

[3] The relationships of process and substance in constitutional regimes in general, and in divided societies in particular, are very complex. They are sometimes described as the relationships between rules of the game, or formal democracy, and human rights. But this in itself may be misleading. Democracy in the thinnest meaning does entail the need to protect some rights. For a sensitive discussion, see Peter Jones, *Rights* (London: Macmillan, 1994).

[4] The enactment of the U.S. Constitution, for example, involved two such great compromises. One was on the structure of the Senate (two representatives to each state irrespective of size), which was entrenched indefinitely, the other on slavery, which gave the controversial institution a period of grace. Attacks on slavery started in Congress from the very beginning, but the political system upheld the compromise. It is quite clear that without both compromises, the "miracle" in Philadelphia would not have happened. It seems quite clear that the Union would have collapsed had Congress undermined the provisional delay in prohibiting the slave trade. See Joseph Ellis, *Founding Brothers: The Revolutionary Generation* (New York: Knopf, 2001) and Catherine Drinker Bowen, *Miracle at Philadelphia: The Story of the Constitutional Convention, May to September 1787* (Boston: Little, Brown and Co., 1986).

enactment and not in a series of piecemeal statutes or arrangements, each enacted within a background of constraints. For example, a person who is apprehensive about judicial review of social and economic policy may agree to judicial review only if the bill of rights explicitly excludes social and economic rights; or she may agree to an expansive bill of rights if courts are denied the power of judicial review over all primary legislation; she may concede some judicial review over social and economic rights if judicial review is administered by a constitutional court whose judges are appointed by the political branches for a limited term and not by a professional judiciary with life tenure. Thus, the leeway for flexibility and negotiation is greater if more of the basic arrangements are negotiable.

The need to reach great compromises and to uphold them suggests that it is good for constitution making processes to involve both broad participation and some entrenchment against simple political change. While usual legislation may pass on the basis of a simple and even narrow parliamentary majority, constitutions should be acceptable to all major sectors of the population, with a special sensitivity to "chronic" minorities. It is for them that issues of legitimacy of the system loom large. Majorities usually can rely on their political power to protect their interests.

These desiderata will usually be met by making the constitutional design comprehensive, so that the system of checks and balances is coherent, and so that the room for compromise and configuration is maximal. It is hard to change one element of government without touching on others. A comprehensive change may enable us to design institutions that can fit together and suit the powers and functions they are given. It is also healthy for constitutions to be made in a process of public debate, and to require broad participation in their enactment in the form of constitutional assemblies, ratification, or referenda. All these features, which are not essential for regular legislation, support the special legitimacy we hope the constitution will enjoy, which will in turn devolve upon elected governments and authorized organs acting within the constitution. It is almost impossible to achieve such a comprehensive set of checks and balances and "big compromises" without a deliberate, transparent and deliberative process of both drafting and ratification. Constitution making is thus an enterprise very different from regular politics.

Similarly, the phases of constitutional amendment and normal life under the constitution and within it should be distinct. Usually, constitutional amendment is much less dramatic than making a constitution, as it is aimed at a particular aspect of the constitution, leaving most of it intact. It thus may lack the elements of comprehensiveness and major compromises required by constitution making.[5] Nonetheless, it is a deliberate change of the framework rules themselves. It will enjoy the supremacy and the entrenchment levels of the constitution itself. It will share in the special symbolic and legitimating functions of the constitution. It seems reasonable to expect that the process of constitutional amendment will be more formal and celebratory, and may allow or even require more public participation, than that of regular legislation. Moreover, the more structural and comprehensive

[5] There are notable exceptions to this rule. The post–Civil War amendments to the U.S. Constitution and the amendments of the Hungarian constitution after the collapse of the U.S.S.R. are two cases in point. For the Hungarian example, see Andrew Arato, *Civil Society, Constitution, and Legitimacy* (Lanham, MD: Rowman & Littlefield, 2000).

the amendment is, the more similar it is to constitution making itself. The functions of the constitution may also suggest guidelines as to when constitutional amendments are proper and how they should be made. Thus, stability is always a virtue in the law, but its weight is higher when the arrangement to be modified belongs to the constitution. It is hard to generalize on amendments to constitutions because their background may be so varied. However, it is almost inevitable that with changing circumstances or with experience a society realizes that a constitutional arrangement does not serve it purpose and an amendment is needed. Other amendments may be the simple result of the fact that a constitution originally included material that should not have been included in it to begin with.[6] However, in all of these cases, at times the entrenchment may mean that an amendment deemed desirable by a majority cannot in fact be enacted.[7]

Once a constitutional regime is established, its test lies in the way it is applied and interpreted. No text speaks for itself. In some senses, the activity of interpretation is the same for all legal materials. The functions of the constitution, however, affect the way it should be interpreted. In a democracy, this is especially true if the interpretation results in the invalidation of a law passed by a majority of the legislature. For all practical purposes, the law is what the authoritative interpreters say it is. So the identity of interpreters and the canons of interpretation they use are of cardinal importance. It is also crucial who has the last word. It is therefore not surprising that issues of review of the constitution, and especially of the power to invalidate primary legislation and the question of its finality, are central in all constitutional designs. Again, this is of special importance in divided societies, where individuals and groups have radically different interests and visions of the good life.

The phases of constitutionalism are clearest and most distinct when constitution making is a deliberate, conscious process, resulting in a constitutional document that specifies how it should be amended and implemented. But reality is rarely very clear. We can find debates about the characterization of moments in the constitutional history of many countries. The fuzziness of the distinctions results, as it should, in both theoretical and practical controversies. The U.S. federal Constitution provides a dramatic illustration of such fuzziness with the decision to regard the Bill of Rights as the first ten amendments and not as a stage of the ratification of the Constitution itself. More often, it is hard to distinguish (informal) amendment and interpretation.[8]

Most "new" states use the constitution "literally" – the document constitutes the polity and defines it.[9] In most of these countries, a constitution is the reflection

[6] For example, even if one supports the policy of Prohibition, the idea that it should have been included in the Constitution itself is dubious.

[7] Many constitutional scholars feel that the electoral college system of presidential elections is obsolete. This idea gained some momentum after President George W. Bush won the 2000 electoral college but did not get a majority of the votes. Two other examples of failures to try to overrule judicial decision through constitutional amendments are the abortion controversy and the school prayer dispute.

[8] More rarely, as in Israel, there is a debate about whether what took place in 1992 is constitution making or legislation of constitutional import. See Gavison, *supra* note 1.

[9] The United States was a new state in this sense, because the Constitution replaced the loose union under the Articles of Confederation with a much stronger federal state. More recent examples are Poland and Czechoslovakia after World War I. For the Polish example, see Daniel H. Cole, "Symposium

of a great transformation, sometimes even a revolution.[10] Nonetheless, a constitution can never be enacted without a society and some political structure in place. Someone must have the power and the authority to prepare the document and supervise the process of its enactment and possible ratification. Even the most radical constitution making involves some social and political continuity.

Moreover, some countries use a new constitution to achieve a major change in government without a great social transformation preceding it and thus not as a reflection of a "constitutional moment." It follows that the identification of a constitution-making process (as distinct from an amendment of an existing constitution or creative interpretation of an existing one) is not necessarily connected to the establishment of a new state or even to a serious political transformation.[11] Rather, the best test of a process of constitution making is its product. A constitution-making process is completed when a country that did not have an entrenched constitution has one. Once we can say that the country does have a formal, entrenched constitution, the phase of constitution making itself is ended.[12]

Once a country has a constitution, the usual processes are application, interpretation, and amendment. All these take place within the constitutional order. In rare cases, a country with a functioning constitution chooses to deliberately replace (rather than amend) it, without a revolution. The change is a process of constitution making (even if a lot of the old constitution's content has remained unchanged).[13]

Surely, the differences between these phases are not always clear and distinctions between them may be hard to make. Nonetheless, I will argue that there are good theoretical and practical reasons for maintaining the distinctions and for checking constitutional processes in specific countries according to them.

B. Components of constitutions

In addition to constitutional phases, there is also a difference in institutional roles within the phase of application and interpretation, as state organs live under the constitution and invoke the three main parts of constitutions – rules of the game, credos, and bills of rights. These parts have somewhat different functions within

on the Constitution of the Republic of Poland – Part II – Poland's 1997 Constitution in Its Historical Context" (1998) 1998 *St. Louis-Warsaw Trans'l* 1 at 21–3; for Czechoslovakia see Lloyd Cutler and Herman Schwartz, "Constitutional Reform in Czechoslovakia: *E Duobus Unum?*" (1991) 58 *U. Chi. L. Rev.* 511 at 513–16.

[10] Both Elster and Ackerman mention the usual strong connection between transformations and new constitutions and explain how such moments create the rare incentive structure that may facilitate constitution making. See Jon Elster, "Forces and Mechanisms in the Constitution-Making Process" (1995) 45 *Duke L.J.* 364; Bruce Ackerman, *The Future of Liberal Revolutions* (New Haven: Yale University Press, 1992). See also Ruth Gavison, "Constitutions and political reconstruction: Israel's quest for a constitution" (2003) 18(1) *International Sociology* 53.

[11] A notable example of a constitution without a serious transformation is that of Sweden. See Olof Ruin, "Sweden: The New Constitution (1974) and the Tradition of Consensual Politics" in Vernon Bogdanor, ed., *Constitutions in Democratic Politics* (London: Gower, 1988) 309.

[12] Clearly, this is an ideal-type sort of analysis of social realities. Often, there are many contingent facts about constitution making. Canada and Israel are described by some as having an evolving constitution, with a permanent power of constitution making (and not of simple amendment).

[13] Thus, for example, the change in France's constitution in 1958 is seen as a process of constitution making generating the fifth republic. It is not a mere amendment, leaving the fourth republic in place. Elster, *supra* note 10, provides a catalog of circumstances in which constitution making is likely and describes this case as one of making a constitution under the threat of a regime collapse.

the constitutional regime, and the difference may affect plausible and desirable institutional roles within them.

All constitutions must have a rules-of-the-game part, which structures, legitimates, and facilitates all organs of government. Furthermore, constitutions build a system of checks and balances by using some powers to check others. Seen in this way, all empowered organs are the guardians of the constitution and all are legitimated by it. Effective government is not less important than an independent and courageous judiciary or from a conscientious and productive legislature. Constructing these different organs, each one with its own special form of legitimacy, is in fact an important part of the constitutional design itself. The details of the constitutional arrangements may differ. No real constitution adheres to a full separation of powers. Rather, legislative, executive, and judicial powers and functions are divided among organs which are structured in ways that fit their major and central function. All of them operate under the constitution, and this activity requires that they interpret the powers entrusted to them by the constitution and the limits that it imposes on them.

What is special about the rules-of-the-game part is that most of its provisions are neutral. They talk of structures and powers and decision-making procedures and about elections and terms and age limits. Interpretation of these laws does not seem to be based on any specific ideology besides the fairness of a general law. Majority rule is a decision rule that gives legitimacy to those decisions made by the majority irrespective of their content. Similarly, a principle allocating power to decide between states and central government may be neutral in respect to the actual content of the decisions made by the parties.

The neutrality of the rules of the game is, of course, not accidental. It is what makes them a strong source of legitimacy, especially in divided societies. Dividing labor and entrusting most of the power to the representative body is the best way of guaranteeing that we will have government of the people, by the people, and for the people. Moreover, it is easier to accept a decision that runs against one's convictions if it comes from an authorized body of the whole community (which includes those who do not share one's convictions) than to accept the decision as an alleged interpretation of one's convictions themselves.

Constitutions must include rules of the game, but they do not have to have either credos or bills of rights. Indeed, divided societies may be attracted by "thin" constitutions, consisting of rules of the game only; and at least some believe that a wisely designed system gives all the required protection to minorities and factions.[14] Thin constitutions permit agreement on procedures that are necessary and neutral, without talking about controversial conceptions of the good or of values. Unified societies may enjoy lofty credos that contribute a sense of nation building and cohesiveness. For divided societies, the choice is between a universalistic credo that might do this at the cost of blandness, or a more particularistic credo very critical to some but that may well alienate others.[15]

[14] It might be that this was the view of Madison, elaborated most fully in the celebrated *Federalist #10* (Rossiter, ed., New York: Mentor, 1999). However, Madison did wholeheartedly work for including the Bill of Rights in the Constitution after ratification.

[15] This is clearly the case in Israel, where some insist that the state is defined as the home of the Jewish people while others advocate a thin constitution in order not to alienate the Arab minority. But the

The picture becomes even more complicated for bills of rights. On the one hand, one could well argue that every well-ordered state, and especially deeply divided societies, should have a bill of rights with independent, effective enforcement, as this is where democracy in the sense of majority rule must give way to the substantive values of human rights that should constrain all governments. These rights are universal and do not depend on the preferences of majorities. Their function is to protect minorities and individuals from majorities. And judicial independence is given so that protection is more effective. It is true that human rights often impose substantive constraints on government and that these constraints may be controversial, but the very nature of human rights requires that they are given a status above the rules of the game. On the other hand, human rights rhetoric can become very expansive. It might mean that human rights are invoked to undermine the ability of the majority to enact its preferences where reasonable people may disagree whether a core human right was violated. In such circumstances, a bill of rights may itself become a divisive element, generating a crisis in the legitimacy of those who enforce it (if such enforcement is not left to the representative branches themselves).

As with constitutional phases, here too the dividing lines are not always clear. Are political rights a part of the rules of the game, or are they parts of the bill of rights? Is a commitment to democracy a part of the rules of the game or of the credos of society? Yet, here too, the distinctions are important, and we should attend to them when we look at the institutional implications of constitutionalism.

C. Institutional implications

In the initial stage of constitution making, the main contenders for the job are special constituent assemblies or regular legislatures, with a clear preference for the former.[16] Special assemblies can concentrate on the constitution without the need to work at the same time on current political issues. The main options and the great compromises can be negotiated without the "noise" created by regular politics. If the members of the assembly are people who are not directly involved in day-to-day politics, it is likely that their judgment will be less clouded by their own immediate political interests. This is especially true if a major purpose of the constitution is to limit the powers of the legislature. Nonetheless, at times it is impossible or undesirable to let constituent assemblies enact constitutions, for examples, when a delay in constitution making is needed for learning new social conditions and responding to them gradually.[17]

The second-best candidates for constitution making are legislatures. What these two bodies have in common, however, is crucial for the task: They are representative bodies, structured to include all or most of the major interests and views in the society to be regulated by the constitution. Furthermore, their mode of work is built on understanding political constraints and on negotiating compromises. They do

same may happen in a society divided along the lines of commitment to free markets versus welfare state.

16 This question is discussed in depth in Jon Elster, "Legislatures as Constituent Assemblies," Chapter 9 in this volume. See also his systematic analysis in Elster, *supra* note 10. This is a view widely shared in the literature, almost to the point of consensus.

17 See the evolutionary constitutional process in Hungary – see Arato, *supra* note 5 at 254–5.

not work on the basis of articulating principles set out elsewhere. They are the ones who set the rules and make the social compact. And they set the rules because they have the mandate to do so, given to them by those who have elected them for the job of creating the constitution (in the case of constituent assemblies) or representing their constituents (in the case of legislatures).

To make sure the product of their processes of deliberation enjoys the broad support of the people, it is often required that the constitution will not only be enacted in a celebratory way and with a special majority, but also be subjected to a broad public debate and possible ratification by a referendum. These processes may be based on presentations prepared by the government or by civil society groups, but the actual process of enactment and ratification should be conducted in ways that involve representatives of the people and the people themselves. The most obvious way of going to the people is ratification by a referendum.[18] The courts as such should not have a role at the stage of constitution making. In fact, some may suggest that it is best for them to stay out of these negotiations as far as possible.[19] We do not have to go into the fascinating question of whether constitutions stem from "We the People" directly (as distinct from regular legislation that is generated by the political game of representatives of various sorts). There is a consensus that this is an exercise of the powers of citizens. Courts, with their professionalism and their relative independence from government and the preferences of the majority, are not – as such – primary players in these constitution-making stages.[20]

Some systems require, or at least permit, the use of special assemblies for amendments as well. But, mostly, amendments to the constitution move on a spectrum between full flexibility (same procedure as regular legislation) and very high levels of entrenchment, using "regular" modes such as special majorities, additional vote, requirement of two consecutive parliaments, or referenda. Usually, the mode of amendment is different from, and more relaxed than, the mode of comprehensive constitution making. But in terms of the choice between citizens, via their representatives, or the courts as the primary agents, the choice of formal procedures is clearly the former. This is as it should be.

Constitutional amendments raise fascinating problems. If a constitutional amendment threatens to undermine the complex system of checks and balances or an element of a "big compromise," it may be reasonable to either make it impossible

[18] Indeed, some argue that the constitutional process leading to the U.S. federal constitution as well as the constitutional process in Hungary and Poland did not really involve the peoples concerned. The Hungarian example is of special interest because "whatever legitimacy the Hungarian constitutional settlement has been able to slowly acquire was through the ritualized and traditionalized ministry of the constitution through court interpretations." Arato, *supra* note 5 at 227–8. Nonetheless, in all these cases constitution making involved expansive public discussion. Thus, we can see the importance of visibility and transparency that permit broad participation and can rarely be attained when courts serve as major player in the process.

[19] Comparative analyses of constitution making do not usually disclose involvement by courts. Moreover, in most deliberate processes of constitution making, the constitution itself empowers and creates the constitutional court that is supposed to enforce it, so that institution does not even exist prior to the constitution.

[20] One might object that this expectation is itself unfair because the constitution will decide the limits of the power of the court, and it should be able to participate and protect its "interests" just as the legislature does. This is indeed one of the arguments in favor of making constitutions by constituent assemblies and not by legislatures. But it seems that courts fare well in constitutions even in their absence; see Elster, *supra* note 10 at 380–2.

or at least require the same procedure of constitution making itself. [21] The picture can get more complicated, however, if courts have the power to review the constitutionality of constitutional amendments as well as that of regular legislation.

Once a constitution is in place, the constitution itself governs the way the constitutional regime should operate. Through empowering the different organs, the constitution awards them public legitimacy. Concerning the rules of the game, each of the powers may and should act according to its own interpretation of the law and the constitution. No organ of government may act in a way that it itself concedes is unconstitutional. In this sense, all empowered organs are the guardians of the constitution.

Rules of procedure and justiciability will determine which of these actions by the legislature and the executive may be subject to judicial review and in what form. The legislature and the executive are considered strong branches, and the courts are often granted powers to check their activities. The fact that supreme courts' decisions are not subject to review by any other legal authority is often justified by saying that the court is "the least dangerous branch." This may be so, but it is no reason to give up on the basic insight that no power should come without some accountability. The accountability of supreme courts should thus be achieved through other forms of checks and balances. Mainly, these should take the indirect form of control over appointments and short terms.[22] More important, the centrality of courts as interpreters should not lead us to belittle the role of other organs in the interpretation and enforcement of the constitution.[23]

True, courts are seen as the authoritative interpreters of law when a provision of the law – including the constitution – comes to them. Their decision is final for the parties. The broader legal and social forces of their decision depend on the status of the constitution itself, the rules of *stare decisis*, and on future acts by the other constitutional players.[24] The constitutional design may also govern, formally or informally, the limits of the jurisdiction of courts and the nature of cases they can (and cannot) decide. Inevitably, these constitutional limitations will also be interpreted by the courts themselves. But courts do need legitimacy, and they cannot persist over time if their decisions lack a solid basis of support in society and the legal community.

There is no question that the role of the courts in the application and the interpretation of the constitution is pervasive and central, whatever the status and nature of the constitutional regime. But while there are some constitutions that explicitly grant courts the power to invalidate primary legislation, there are others under which this power is inferred by courts from the supremacy of the

[21] This was in fact done in the U.S. Constitution concerning representation in the Senate and in the German constitution concerning the commitment to human dignity. For a comprehensive discussion, see Sanford Levinson, ed., *Responding to Imperfection: The Theory and Practice of Constitutional Amendment* (Princeton: Princeton University Press, 1995).

[22] The need to supervise judicial power is naturally greater the more power the Supreme Court has under either law or convention.

[23] For a systematic argument in this direction, see Mark Tushnet, *Taking the Constitution Away from the Courts* (Princeton: Princeton University Press, 1999).

[24] The decision may result in a constitutional amendment, or a legislative override, or by a practice of ignoring the decision altogether. Any student of the fifty years of literature about the famous *Brown* decision of 1954 knows that judicial victories are not the end. They may not even be a beginning.

constitution,[25] and still others that explicitly deny courts this power.[26] Even when there is a judicial power to review primary legislation and invalidate it for inconsistency with the constitution, there are a variety of such institutions and regimes.[27] Be this as it may, most constitutions provide for legal enforcement of constitutions, and most see judicial institutions as the ones best suited to enforce them. Often, this is based on a deep reluctance to place full trust in legislatures and a wish to add an effective constraint on their power. There are a variety of ways of dealing with the countermajoritarian difficulty that may then emerge.

Judicial review of primary legislation has been the norm in a growing number of jurisdictions. It is especially salient in societies that emerge from dictatorial regimes and seek to entrench the hard-won commitment to democracy and freedom. Although there are serious political limits of various sorts to the effectiveness of courts as defenders of rights or as movers of social change,[28] judicial review over primary legislation has in general provided an important avenue to check local excesses within political systems. Against this background, countries that have struggled with these questions in recent times and decided against such judicial review are of special interest.[29] They point to the fact that although there are many powerful reasons for giving courts such powers over primary legislation, there are also reasons against this. These reasons are tied, among other things, to the distinction between different components of constitutions.

Before returning to these, let me summarize the thesis about institutional implications of the phases of constitutionalism. As I noted above, the dividing lines between the phases are often not very bright and clear. The distinction between regular or normal politics and constitutional debate may well be a matter of degree. Regular politics constantly challenge constitutional limits. One does not have to endorse Ackerman's theory of constitutional moments to claim that the U.S. Constitution has in effect been amended many times without invoking the formal process of constitutional amendment.[30] In such amendments, which are instances of constitution making rather than application and interpretation, courts naturally take an important part. At times, they may be the movers or the consolidators of such

[25] This is the case in the United States.

[26] This is the case in the Netherlands, New Zealand, and the United Kingdom. See the Netherlands *Constitution*, 1989, Article 120; the U.K. *Human Rights Act*, 1998, c. 42, s.4; and the New Zealand *Bill of Rights Act*, s.4 (1990). (The U.K. model is a novel model in that it allows only judicial *declarations* of constitutional inconsistencies, thus implicitly denying judicial power to invalidate legislation, whereas the other two explicitly deny the power of judicial review.)

[27] See Vicki C. Jackson and Mark Tushnet, *Comparative Constitutional Law* (New York: Foundation Press, 1999) at 455–91. The main differences are between regular courts (as in the United States and Canada) performing all such review and constitutional courts (as in most of the continent and South Africa), between systems allowing only prelegislative review (as in France) and those allowing only or also postlegislative ones, and between systems allowing only incidental review and those also allowing abstract review and advisory opinions.

[28] See, e.g., Gerald N. Rosenberg, *The Hollow Hope: Can Courts Bring About Social Change?* (Chicago: University of Chicago Press, 1991); Harry Arthurs, "Constitutional Courage" (2004) 49 *McGill L.J.* 1 at 8–10; William N. Eskridge, Jr., and John Ferejohn, "Super-Statutes: The New American Constitutionalism," Chapter 15 in this volume.

[29] One may say that European countries are less relevant here because they are subject to the jurisdiction of the European Court. The main non-European examples are Australia and New Zealand.

[30] Bruce Ackerman, *We the People: Foundations* (Cambridge: Harvard University Press, 1991). See also Adrian Vermeule, "Constitutional Amendments and the Constitutional Common Law," Chapter 12 in this volume.

processes. At others, they may well undermine, by their interpretation, the practical effects of enacted constitutional amendments.[31] Moreover, due to the finality of adjudication and to the prestige of courts as defenders of the rule of law, it is often politically quite difficult to use legislation to change a law or a practice or an interpretation ruled by courts as inconsistent with constitutional values.[32]

Nonetheless, with all this inevitable and immanent ambiguity, the field in processes of constitution making and in amending constitutions should mainly belong to representatives of the people. By contrast, in processes of interpretation and application of constitutions and their amendments, courts are serious and central players – seen by some as supreme. This division of responsibilities is not merely a universal description of the realities in legal systems. It is a natural outcome of the different bases of the legitimacy of the various organs of government and the different functions of constitutional frameworks, normal politics, and adjudication. One can discuss these questions either analytically or empirically. Both approaches yield similar results.

As noted above, we can better assess the institutional implications of constitutionalism in the different phases of the constitutional process when we attend to the different components of constitutions and their different rationales. Despite the complexity of various organs having different roles on the different phases of the constitutional process and with relation to the different components of constitutions, one should remember that, most of the time, the organs operate within regular politics under the constitutional regime. Our focus henceforth will be on the role of courts in this "regular politics" phase in the life cycle of a constitution.

In terms of constitutional design, credos and human rights are particularly tricky when interpreted and enforced by a court that has the power to invalidate statutes. The inevitable ideological and abstract nature of these parts of constitutions means that decisions by unelected courts may be, and appear to be, not sufficiently responsive to self-government. The fact that courts are seen as "the forum of principle" and do not engage in negotiation and compromise may mean that important social and political debates will be resolved without the give-and-take needed when a complex

[31] Indeed, some argue that courts can declare constitutional amendments themselves unconstitutional! For example, the Israeli Supreme Court President, Aharon Barak, introduced in both judicial opinions and in his scholarly writings the notion of the "unconstitutional constitutional amendment." According to this notion, a constitutional amendment that complies with the provisions relating to amendments in the constitution will be declared unconstitutional due to its contradiction to the "supraconstitutional" fundamental principles of a legal system. Barak discusses this notion as an hypothetical possibility in his, "Foreword: A Judge on Judging: The Role of a Supreme Court in a Democracy" (2002) 116 *Harv. L. Rev.* 16 at 89–90 and especially footnote 262. See Gavison, *supra* note 1 on perceiving this far-reaching doctrine in its Israeli context. Under this theory, courts are the ultimate interpreters of the constitution not only in the sense that they can invalidate laws which they hold to be inconsistent with the constitution, but also because they can undermine attempts to overrule their decisions by an amendment to the constitution itself.

[32] A dramatic illustration of these difficulties is the fact that some senior Canadian officials have declared that they see the use of the famous override clause in the Canadian Charter as improper. For example, Canadian Prime Minister Paul Martin has said that he would "never use the [override] clause to take away a right that had been enshrined in the Charter." Les Whittington and Richard Brennan, "Martin aims at Tories' Achilles' heel," *The Toronto Star* (June 16, 2004) A06. This declaration may itself be a constitutional moment because it is quite plausible that the Charter would not have been enacted in the absence of the override, so that its inclusion can be seen as a "big compromise" in the system of checks and balances.

society works out its positions. The results may be either loss of legitimacy by the courts and of the constitution they purport to invoke, or pressure to politicize them, or both.[33]

Divided societies may be tempted to use credos in order to give celebratory force to the vision of the enacting powers and to remove their vision from the contingencies of future controversy. This, of course, may be very problematic for the groups whose visions are excluded or silenced. It may well reduce the legitimacy of the constitution for them as it may appear not to include them fully.

Indeed, the privileging of particularistic credos in an entrenched constitution governing a divided society is problematic. Judicial interpretation of this credo may run one of two risks, both of which may weaken the court's standing. The first is that the court echoes the sentiments and aspirations of the majority that had entrenched the credo, and can be challenged for preferring that vision of the good life to a neutral commitment to the welfare of all citizens. The second is that the court will indeed prefer the universalist interpretation and seek to define away the controversial credo. In that case, the court may risk being perceived as an organ seeking to undermine the constitutional consensus.[34]

In the case of human rights, as we saw, the basis of the court's mandate to protect those rights even against the majority is stronger than it is in the case of most credos, because it is the essence of human rights that they have prelegal force. Nonetheless, once the courts protect rights that have not been clearly incorporated into laws, and whose scope is deeply controversial, they are likely to be seen by those whose views are different as an organ imposing its own values on the majority of its society.[35] As we saw, human rights talk tends to become very expansive with some people and groups, so that everything that one wants very badly is translated into a right. Most of the democratic discourse and debate may easily be reformulated in terms of rights.[36] So the question again becomes not "What are one's rights?" but "Who decides?"

It is to be expected that bills of rights are vague and will require interpretation. The real question to be decided here is that of the structure of the commitment to rights and its institutional implications. This question in itself may be seen as a part of the rules of the game, because it goes to the supremacy and the enforceability

[33] This fear is the basis of the judicial doctrine of self-restraint advocated by some judges and the spirit of Holmes' famous dissent in *Lochner* [*Lochner v. New York*, 198 U.S. 45 at 75–6 (1905)]. Holmes warned against judicial invalidation of laws on the basis of vague ideas like property or freedom of contract that were in fact judges enforcing their own system of values. He noted that although federalism required that there would be a final arbiter on constitutional matters between states and central government, the court could have endured well enough without the power to overrule laws of Congress on the basis of the Bill of Rights. See Ruth Gavison, "Holmes's Heritage: Living Greatly in the Law" (1998) 78 *B.U.L. Rev.* 843.

[34] For a sensitive discussion of the predicament of abolitionist federal judges who were asked to enforce the fugitive slaves laws before the Civil War in the United States, see Robert M. Cover, *Justice Accused: Antislavery and the Judicial Process* (New Haven: Yale University Press, 1975). The Israeli Supreme Court is attacked on both sides of this dilemma. Some complain that it is too "Zionist" and some see it as undermining the Jewishness of the state. See Gavison, note 1 *supra*.

[35] For elaboration of these themes, see Ruth Gavison, "The Role of Courts in Rifted Democracies" (1998) 33 *Is. L. Rev.* 216.

[36] For a critical analysis of this feature of rights discourse by a person with a strong commitment to human rights, see Mary Ann Glendon, *Rights Talk: The Impoverishment of Political Discourse* (New York: Macmillan, 1991).

of the constitution, and to the powers of courts vis-à-vis the government and the legislature. It follows that even where there is no debate about the existence of judicial review over primary legislation, courts should beware of "legislating" where the issue is not a clear violation of a core right of an individual or group.

A further guideline follows: Because judicial review, particularly over legislation, is a subject of known great controversy, it is best that the issue be explicitly addressed in all its aspects in the process of constitution making itself. A decision to give a judicial body the power of judicial review over an abstract bill of rights is known to transfer a lot of political power from the legislature to courts. This decision should therefore be made by the legislature itself, with some broad public ratification, and the nature of the judicial body and the scope of its powers of review should ideally be decided within the same phase of constitution making in which the power is conferred.[37] The court should be extra careful not to advocate legislation expanding its own powers to review primary legislation, and not to expand its own powers to do so through adjudication. Such caution should be seen as a part of the "package deal" that gives courts independence, finality, and limited accountability. A court that does not heed these limitations may overstep its own legitimacy.

These guidelines, although not mandatory, suggest important lessons, supported by both empirical and analytical insight. They suggest that a constitution is more likely to gain legitimacy if made and amended through broad participation, and that there are good reasons of political morality to take this route. But those who believe that liberal constitutions are critical for the health of good societies may prefer that such constitutions are enacted by whatever means available rather than giving them up just because legislatures will not provide them. And if the public feels that a liberal constitution is good for it, better than the rule of the political branches without the constitution, legitimacy will follow. The presumption is, however, that broad participation and big compromises by authentic representatives of all segments is a more promising route for a constitution than imposing one from above by a small elite. This is especially true when the society is deeply divided and when the small elite is anything but representative.

II. CONCLUSION

It has become very fashionable to see courts as the central players and custodians of a democratic constitution. Courts are indeed crucial partners in the maintenance of a robust constitutional regime. Yet, it is misleading to present them as the ultimate guardians of democracy and constitutionalism. It is even misleading to present them as that power most clearly identified with the protection of constitutional human rights. Legislatures and government are central constitutional actors, as

[37] One may argue that this guideline was not met by the U.S. Constitution and that this did not harm the legitimacy and importance of judicial review. True, *Marbury v. Madison*, 5 U.S. 137 (1803), went beyond the constitutional text. True, the fact of judicial review (as against its proper scope) is not challenged by anyone in the United States. But the pervasiveness of the debates over its scope suggests that this vulnerability exists in the United States as well. Besides, we do learn from experience. In current debates about enacting bills of rights into constitutions, these themes are central and often lead to decisions not to endorse judicial review (as in Australia and New Zealand) or to reach compromises (as in the U.K. and Canada). Furthermore, when the power to invalidate laws is granted, it is often relegated to special organs, with specific modes of appointment, limited terms, and serious limitations on access.

important as are courts, each in its own sphere of activity and responsibility. They all share responsibility for the continued existence of the constitutional order. Furthermore, in the critical stages of initial constitution making and of constitutional amendments, the legislature (or other bodies and processes representing the public at large) is and should be the prime actor.

A constitutional democracy is a democracy. Its most basic characteristic is that the power of government is justified by the consent of the people. No stable government can act without legitimacy. There is no substitute for the legitimacy stemming from the fact that the basic arrangements of political power are ones designed taking into considerations the actual preferences and wishes and attitudes of the people living under the constitution. Power corrupts and absolute power corrupts absolutely. At the same time, nothing much can be done without effective power. We therefore need complex systems of checks and balances to structure power, divide it, and minimize its abuses. It makes sense to anchor these systems in an entrenched constitution. This constitution limits the powers of the legislature itself. No other law could have done this. This is as it should be. But this desirable limitation of the power of the legislature should not be taken to mean that it has lost its status as the best reflection within government of the source of political power – the people.

ACKNOWLEDGMENTS

I thank Or Bassok, Yoel Cheshin, and Allan E. Shapiro for illuminating discussions and research assistance. Tsvi Kahana triggered the writing of this chapter by inviting me to the conference on which this book is based and provided excellent comments on a previous draft.

11 Legislatures and Constitutional Agnosticism

Patricia Hughes

As constitutional actors, legislatures are accustomed to asserting their understanding of the constitutionality of the legislation they enact. They are also not uncommonly engaged in constitutional disputes with other constitutional actors. At times, they appear to be avoiding their constitutional role, informally "delegating" it to another actor, and for this they are likely to be subject to criticism. But are there times legislatures – and legislators – stand back, suspend judgment, and engage in what I am calling "constitutional agnosticism"? Are there times when they *should* be?

Whether constitutions are limited to institutional organization or are aspirational, written or unwritten or a hybrid, easy or difficult to amend, one thing they must do is help maintain stability in the country, at least sufficient to allow for orderly transition of power within a recognized government structure. At a higher level, the constitution may play a much greater role in shaping common values or in allowing a regular "conversation" about identifying and defining the values that "matter." Without saying that both of these are functions the Constitution *must* fulfill, they are important functions that constitutions *do* fulfill and the first, if the country is to function at all, must be filled in some manner or under some authority.

The constitution's capacity to meet these goals of stability, orderly transition, and/or shaping of the nation's value structure depends on the extent to which it is recognized as "legitimate" by the public or by those who have been acknowledged as "speaking for" the public. Furthermore, in a system governed by constitutionalism, "all government action [must] comply with the Constitution."[1] Thus, the concept of constitutional legitimacy looms large in political and constitutional theory. Lack of legitimacy, it may be argued, absolves the populace of the duty of obedience and justifies disregarding constitutional niceties or even revolution. At the very least, it might make it difficult to govern, with much that the government does considered suspect. Lack of "objective" legitimacy – a failure to abide by constitutional rules and norms – has the potential to result in a serious constitutional crisis. Even where the situation is not clearly a deviation but more a fundamental disagreement about the proper form of the constitution or about fundamental constitutional values

[1] *Reference re Secession of Quebec* [1998] 2 S.C.R. 217 at para. 72. The principle of constitutionalism, according to the Supreme Court of Canada, is similar to the rule of law, but the Court appears to believe that the rule of law is broader than constitutionalism: "The constitutionalism principle requires that all government action comply with the Constitution. The rule of law principle requires that all government action must comply with the law, including the Constitution."

or norms, crises may occur or constitutional destabilization may result (as when a legislature regularly challenges its relationship with another duly constituted constitutional actor). The crisis may warrant wholesale constitutional change or the deviation may be so serious that it has to be addressed (a military coup overturning a civilian government, for example); but turning a constitutional deviation into a constitutional crisis is not necessarily the best approach.

A "time-out" may ultimately be the more preferable response to wholesale constitutional change or constitutional dissolution. This requires toleration of deviation from the standards that determine objective legitimacy or a willingness to treat as legitimate aspects of the constitution with which one has significant concerns. Still, toleration for deviation – or agnosticism – may seem unappealing, normatively cowardly, or, worse, an invitation for constitutional malcontents to seize the upper hand, while "all good citizens" politely refrain from pushing their own constitutional agenda in the interests of the common good. And when a "time-out" is perceived as giving the opportunity to avoid addressing an issue, constitutional agnosticism may become dysfunctional (a not unfair characterization of the ongoing dispute about Quebec and the Canadian confederation).

Constitutional agnosticism has relevance for the entire constitutional regime (constitutional creation, content, application, and interpretation and enforcement) and for all constitutional actors (obviously the executive, the legislature, judiciary, "the people," and, perhaps less obviously, others who influence constitutional developments, including bureaucrats and commentators). This chapter focuses on the interrelationship between legislatures and constitutional agnosticism. It explores two questions: From one perspective, to what extent should the legislature engage in constitutional agnosticism and to what extent, indeed, *can* it do so; and from the other perspective, to what extent should constitutional deviation by the legislature be tolerated by other constitutional actors; that is, to what extent should legislative constitutional deviation be tolerated or received with an attitude of agnosticism?

Before exploring some aspects of the legislative relationship with constitutional agnosticism that relate to these two "big" questions, a fuller appreciation of the concept of constitutional agnosticism in more general terms will provide a useful context.

I. CONSTITUTIONAL AGNOSTICISM: A BRIEF OVERVIEW

"Constitutional agnosticism" refers to toleration for constitutional ambivalence, for fundamental constitutional disagreements, or for deviation from constitutional norms. The term echoes the concepts of "protestant" and "catholic" understandings of constitutional interpretation. Those who adhere to the former believe that everyone may develop his or her own interpretation of the constitution; a "catholic" view, in (obvious) contrast, is that a particular constitutional actor, an authoritative adjudicator, such as a court, has a clear or effective monopoly on constitutional interpretation.[2] Thus, "constitutional agnosticism" means a willingness,

[2] See Jack M. Balkin, "Respect-Worthy: Frank Michelman and the Legitimate Constitution" (2004) 39 *Tulsa L. Rev.* 485 at 492 and 508, for a brief explanation of the protestant and catholic understandings of constitutional interpretation.

under certain circumstances, to suspend the need to act on one's concerns that the constitution is, for some reason, not legitimate or about which there is serious dissension.[3] It is not synonymous with "compromise," although certainly compromise might result from a period of agnosticism and the openness to alternative views that it might generate.

I do not dive here into the crowded waters of normative legitimacy or the objective criteria determining when a constitution is legitimate and therefore the source of rightful authority. Rather, I am interested in a more basic, pragmatic question: the part played by a willing suspension of the need to determine whether a constitution is legitimate or, indeed, toleration of deviation from constitutional norms by constitutional actors, especially the legislature. This question in turn raises several issues: Is periodic toleration for an ambivalent constitution – that is, with respect to whether it is in fact legitimate – *necessary* for the smooth functioning of the constitutional state? And are there states in which this toleration is unlikely or undesirable? The degree of toleration for constitutional deviation will have, I suggest, a considerable impact on the capacity of a political and legal system to navigate the rocky shoals of popular unrest or significant and potentially disruptive debate about basic values to calmer, more definitive, waters. Similarly, it will have an impact on the likelihood that less responsible navigators will use the disruption to impose a constitutional regime outside the boundaries of the usual constitutional process. It would not do if the only citizens prepared to be agnostic were the equality-seeking groups, for example. If only certain actors "give up the field" temporarily, it will not be long before their opponents dominate. Agnosticism requires goodwill on all sides, or its cost will be viewed as too high.

Nor do I argue that constitutional agnosticism is always appropriate. I *am* suggesting that it can sometimes allow progress when it otherwise might not be possible or can provide a space for developing ways of forestalling pending constitutional crises. Nor does constitutional agnosticism entail renouncing one's notions about what the proper constitutional values are; rather, its intention is to provide the space for a more thoughtful conversation about those values if debates about legitimacy do not have to be resolved at exactly the same time. Is this about postponing the inevitable time when legitimacy issues must be resolved? In some ways, this is exactly what constitutional agnosticism is about, but with the purpose of establishing a better climate for that later conversation.

Constitutional agnosticism is conditionally agnostic, indifferent under appropriate conditions, to whether there is a legitimate constitution or not, as long as there is a constitution or something that will serve the functions we usually ascribe to a constitution well enough to stave off dissolution. This agnosticism might result from indifference to whether the constitution is legitimate or from a considered appreciation of the need for tolerance of the ambivalence about legitimacy. The former, I suggest, is dangerous, although it may well be convenient, particularly to certain political actors who are up to no good (we might say), whereas the latter derives from a broader confidence in the overall political and legal systems. We do not have to go so far as to say that agnosticism defines the culture of constitutional

[3] There is a difference between acceptance (even though one *disagrees* with the particular actions, one *accepts* that they fall within constitutional parameters) and agnosticism (believing that the constitutional bounds have been exceeded or not observed, but being willing to tolerate that situation).

legitimacy as I am using it and, indeed, we would not want to, for this hiatus of engagement could have disastrous results should it go on too long or occur under the wrong circumstances.

II. LEGISLATURES AND CONSTITUTIONAL AGNOSTICISM

The notion of constitutional agnosticism relates to legislatures in several ways: the legislature's deliberate refusal to act constitutionally; somewhat related to the first way, the legislature's taking advantage of a period of constitutional agnosticism to further a constitutionally doubtful agenda; the legislature's choice not to confront another constitutional actor that may be acting unconstitutionally; and the legislature's promotion of constitutional debate or its taking steps to temper constitutional passion.

In all these instances, it must be remembered that legislatures are not homogenous bodies, but comprise representatives with different allegiances and holding different values and different mandates from their constituents. As a result, these representatives may also possess different understandings about constitutional requirements. Furthermore, as constitutional actors, legislatures may be vulnerable to the actions of other constitutional actors, including the executive (in a parliamentary system, this is particularly the case when the governing party has a clear majority in the legislature); the judiciary (their partnership may be confrontational or constructive); and the citizens of the country whom they represent but a large portion of whom may actually have quite different ideas about the appropriate constitution compared to the legislature.

Legislatures may refuse to acknowledge the constitutional constraints under which they function. ("Refusal" is the operative word here: The legislature is deliberately flouting constitutional requirements, not merely taking a different view of them.) This deviation from constitutional norms, expectations, or requirements may lead to a constitutional crisis if another constitutional actor – such as the judiciary – does not have the authority (particularly in the eyes of the legislature) to ensure that the legislature will comply. Alternatively, the force of popular will may suffice to bring the legislature back into line or compel new legislative leadership. Should the legislature enact clearly unconstitutional legislation, another actor may respond to the deviation. In Canada, for example, the governor general or a provincial lieutenant governor may refuse to proclaim the suspect bill, although this constitutionally correct maneuver may itself result in constitutional crisis.[4] In

[4] In Canada, before legislation comes into force after passing both the House of Commons and the Senate, it must be granted Royal Assent by the governor general, who may grant or decline Royal Assent or reserve the bill for the personal assent (or not) of the sovereign: s. 55 of the *Constitution Act, 1867*. On the Royal Assent powers of the governor general and the actual practice followed, see Legislative Summaries: The Royal Assent Act, online: Parliament of Canada, http://www.parl.gc.ca/common/Bills_ls.asp?Parl-37&Ses=1&ls=513. Today a convention stipulates that the governor general will not refuse assent. Similarly, the lieutenant governor of a province must grant Royal Assent to legislation enacted by the provincial legislature before it becomes law. The lieutenant governor of Alberta "reserved for the signification of the Governor General's pleasure" a number of bills enacted by the Social Credit government, which the governor general then disallowed under the federal disallowance power, also no longer exercised: *Reference re Alberta Statutes*, [1938] S.C.R. 100. The Reference by the federal government concerned three of the statutes, all of which the Court found to be *ultra vires* the Alberta legislature.

either case, the exercise of constitutional agnosticism by citizens may assist in remedying the constitutional deviation, more likely in the former case than the latter, and in restoring the proper constitutional institutional balance.

There are milder versions of this situation in which the legislature flirts with the idea of acting unconstitutionally. The legislature may take advantage of an ambivalent constitution – one about which there are doubts or concerns – to advance its own political agenda, even though it is constitutionally doubtful. In this instance, the executive may receive advice that its own agenda (or path to achieving it) is not constitutional or at least of doubtful constitutionality, but forges ahead to please its predominant voting constituency. Something of this kind occurred in Alberta, Canada in regard to same-sex marriage. Widespread judicial consensus is that the Constitution requires the recognition of same-sex marriage, but among the population, the issue is more controversial and this is reflected in the attitude and conduct of legislators. Although as a vocal dissentient on the matter, the Alberta executive, controlling the Legislative Assembly, for a time considered fighting the federal legislation[5] extending marriage to same-sex couples, it decided not to do so.[6] Rather, it will attempt to circumvent it through the exercise of its provincial power over the solemnization of marriage to allow people to refuse to perform same-sex marriage if they do not wish to do so.[7] Federally, the leader of the opposition announced he would raise this issue again were he to become prime minister.[8] Having been elected prime minister in the January 2006 federal election, it remains to be seen whether he follows upon this promise. In the Canadian context, these statements and actions are mild instances of resistance to the norms of polite constitutional discourse, grudging recognition of correctness under the constitutional regime as it exists while promising not to end the fight. The insistence in keeping this issue alive is not independent of these actors' perception that there is a constitutional imbalance between the legislatures and the judiciary that has removed "moral" issues from the control of the "the people" these legislators represent.

Constitutional interpretation and enforcement can raise ongoing challenges to constitutional legitimacy. Theoretically, no one branch of government can lay exclusive claim to the role of constitutional adjudicator. Legislatures, executives, and courts usually all have some role to play, but the prominence of each will vary with the type of constitutional regime. Legislatures must be involved in constitutional interpretation or, at least, it is a major mistake for them not to be. The extent of their involvement, however, or perhaps the extent of their *deliberation* about the constitution will depend on the role of the other branches and the

[5] Bill C-38, *The Civil Marriage Act*, received Royal Assent on July 20, 2005.

[6] "Alberta rules out notwithstanding option," online: CTV.ca: http://www.ctv.ca/servlet/ArticleNews/story/ CTVNews/1102608109348_98017309?s_name=&no_ads=.

[7] "Law to protect religious officials, places of worship and marriage commissioners," Alberta Government News Release (July 26, 2005), online: http://www.gov.ab.ca/acn/200507/184962C549349-3701-451D-BAE5BF2E13FD56D1.html.

[8] "Conservative Leader Stephen Harper says if his party forms the next government, the law will be revisited" because the vote in support of same-sex marriage was not legitimate, as it relied on the support of the Bloc Québécois: "Same sex marriage law passes 158–133" (June 29, 2005), online: CBC News: http://www.cbc.ca/story/canada/national/2005/06/28/samesex050628.html. Also see Alexander Panetta, "Harper to revisit law if he forms gov. Conservative party leader says his party will revisit the same-sex marriage law," online: National Post: Canada.com: http://www.canada.com/national/story.html?id=bcb3ce14-39a1-4c42-a8e8-91b10af59cda.

form the constitution takes and the way in which it was created (if, indeed, it was deliberately "created"). In some cases, it might be preferable to talk about recognition of existing practices, statutes, or inherited government institutions as the constitution.

As I have already hinted with respect to same-sex marriage, the Canadian example is illustrative in this regard. The *Constitution Act, 1982,* gives the courts a far greater role than they had previously enjoyed because of the introduction of the *Canadian Charter of Rights and Freedoms*[9] and the explicit power of judicial review under section 52(1) of the *Constitution Act 1982.*[10] With the advent of the Charter, it was not that the courts would actually be doing something new in checking legislative action – they had always adjudicated division of legislative power disputes – but that they would be doing so in the new and potentially highly controversial arenas of individual rights and with section 35 of the *Constitution Act, 1982,* of aboriginal rights. As a compromise, section 33 of the Charter permits legislatures to render statutes immune for a limited period from challenge under certain Charter guarantees. This may be seen as a remnant of parliamentary (or legislative) supremacy or as a check on the judiciary. Indeed, section 33 of the Charter may be characterized as a form of institutionalized agnosticism. While obviously the legislature invokes section 33 because it thinks that a provision is vulnerable to Charter challenge, if it does so at the time of passage of the legislation (rather than after a court decision), section 33 constitutes toleration of ambiguity: Is the provision unconstitutional or not? During the 2004 Canadian federal election, this clause was represented by the Conservative Party as giving (at least temporarily) the final word to the people through their legislative representatives and by the Liberal Party as being antithetical to the constitutional scheme of protecting minority rights. Underlying this debate was the broader one about the legitimacy of the constitutional regime, including the respective roles of the legislatures and the judiciary and the meaning of constitutional supremacy and its impact on legislatures.

If the courts are embedded in a full governance regime, it becomes easier for people who strongly disagree with their constitutional decisions to keep their questioning of the legitimacy of the courts within bounds. They may believe that the deviation they perceive can be remedied by other actors in the system, most likely the legislature. For this to occur, however, the legislature must be viewed as a *constitutional* actor, not merely as a *constituent* actor, one created by the constitution or whose authority derives from the constitution. Constitutional agnosticism requires a legislature capable of assuming its own responsibilities, while at the same time promoting through its own actions the legitimacy of the other actors in the regime and respect for the coherence of the constitutional regime as a whole, even where there might be some dispute about the constitutional decisions of the other actors. To the extent, for example, that there is some question about the interpretation process, a legislature that conscientiously assesses the constitutionality of its decisions may well stave off the kind of "confrontation" that might otherwise

[9] Part I of the *Constitution Act, 1982,* being Schedule B to the *Canada Act 1982* (U.K.), 1982, c. 11 [*Charter*].

[10] Section 52(1) reads: "The Constitution of Canada is the supreme law of Canada, and any law that is inconsistent with the provisions of the Constitution is, to the extent of the inconsistency, of no force or effect."

occur or be perceived to occur between two constitutional actors. In Canada, the partnership in constitutionalism between the legislatures and the courts gives rise to greater concerns when the judiciary appears to be – or is characterized as – doing the legislatures' job. Although there may be genuine debate about the constitutionality of a particular statute, as evidenced by 5–4 splits in more than a few Supreme Court of Canada cases, raising the debate to the fundamental level of questioning the legitimacy of the courts' role risks constitutional destabilization. In this situation as well as others with similar consequences, part of the debate should be whether a degree of constitutional agnosticism on the part of legislative representatives, that is, restraint in raising the constitutional temperature, would be in order.

Where passions run high and agnosticism is not a likely option, the legislature might be wary of embarking on the road to constitutionalism. Israel provides an example of when the attempt to create a constitution signifies that differences are too great for constitutional agnosticism to see it through future periods of crisis. In this case, the legislature – the Knesset – acted in a manner that avoided the dangerous controversies resulting from making determinations on crucial questions necessary to establish a constitution.

When the State of Israel was established, there already existed government bodies which had been developed under the British mandate and which the majority accepted as legitimate for the short term. In 1949, a constituent assembly was formed to create a constitution, but "the transitory legislature hastened to transmit to it all regular legislative authority" and it became the first parliament. In 1951, the Knesset decided not to enact a constitution, but rather to enact basic laws that would eventually form a constitution.[11] There may have been a number of reasons why it was decided not to create a constitution, but a major one was the fact that the nature of the State of Israel was ambiguous and the site of considerable tension, one that if anything has been exacerbated since.[12] A constitution would have forced a determination of how the new state was more accurately or appropriately defined, whereas, Gavison suggests, legislative supremacy and the absence of effective judicial review "permitted the political system, and the courts, to avoid charged political confrontations over matters of ideology. In this way, political controversies were mitigated and various *modus vivendi* arrangements were reached."[13] In today's Israel, while major parts of the community want to establish a constitution, they have divergent reasons for doing so, and significant groups do not want a constitution or are divided on whether they will support constitutional change.

Should Israel develop a system characterized by constitutionalism, the prospect that constitutional agnosticism might serve as a tool to move beyond constitutional crises is highly unlikely. There seem to be too few people prepared to be agnostic or,

[11] Ruth Gavison, "Constitutions and Political Reconstruction? Israel's Quest for a Constitution" (2003) 18 *Int'l. Soc.* 53 at 57.

[12] There was and remains serious dispute about whether Israel should be a secular or religious state; indeed, the debate has become more serious and threatening to stable government. In addition, the ethnic tensions created by a strong Arab minority claiming recognized status and a revocation of the "Jewish nature of Israel" have seriously divided the country.

[13] Gavison, *supra* note 11 at 59.

perhaps, to trust that others will be prepared to be agnostic at times of significant debate or crisis.

The conditions for creating a constitution may affect the potential for constitutional agnosticism. For example, the majority of the population of South Africa had very limited political involvement and little experience or understanding of constitutionalism prior to the establishment of a constitution following the end of apartheid.[14] The process of creating the postapartheid constitution by the legislative assembly sitting as a constitutional convention involved significant consultation, review by the Constitutional Court, and enactment by the National Assembly (née Constitutional Assembly). The resulting constitution, although a constitution for the whole population, acknowledged the many differences among them. For Simone Chambers, the importance of this seems to be less the content of the constitution (which is pluralist), important though that is, and more that the constitutional process established a culture of accountability and participation.[15] Through the shared act of participation, this process created "a people," even though the resulting "people" comprises many identities.

In South Africa, the elected representatives triumphed over the potential for enormous constitutional and actual disruption by bringing otherwise divergent groups into the process. The legislature sought to give the constitution depth and breadth, to embed it in a way that would make it less vulnerable to every twist in opinion and the vicissitudes of wholesale cultural transformation. The South African constitutional experience shows how the constitutional process can itself serve as a transformative force. In doing so, however, it may make it difficult to tolerate extended periods of constitutional agnosticism. When the constitution is a reflection of people's identities, indeed, when in many respects it has created a transcending identity, deviations might be perceived as a denial of identity. When very disparate groups transcend difference to create a common constitution, the failure to observe it may be viewed as a challenge to the process of creation, not only of the constitution, but also of the capacity of the people to remain "a people."

Yet such a context may make agnosticism even more important. One might even ask whether a constitutional regime *must* incorporate the dimension of agnosticism within its culture of legitimacy for the regime to be effective. A constitution reflective of many different "voices" is likely to be vulnerable to constant criticism and marked by ambivalence, particularly after the initial euphoria has dissipated. Its effectiveness will require a high degree of toleration for ambivalence among a sufficiently high proportion of the population that it can withstand crisis without dissolution. Such a constitution is hard work, both to create and to interpret. Even so, many different communities will have an interest in ensuring that a pluralist constitutional regime continues as long as, on balance, they benefit more than they are disadvantaged by it. Although there may be a temporary suspension of perceived legitimacy by one or a few communities at any given time, more groups will perceive it as legitimate than not. This changing dynamic of perceived legitimacy will mean that the necessary balance will be achieved to maintain the constitutional

[14] The discussion of the South African constitutional experiences relies on Simone Chambers, "Democracy, Popular Sovereignty, and Constitutional Legitimacy" (2004) 11 *Constellations* 153.

[15] Ibid. at 161 and 163–4.

regime. Where the legislature has been significantly involved in the creation of the constitution, as in South Africa, even if clothed as the constitutional convention, there is an onus on the legislature to provide room for periods of agnosticism.

The willingness to tolerate deviation in the observance or interpretation of an existing constitution is often stronger than willingness to bring agnosticism to the creation of a new (amended) constitution. Both Germany and Canada illustrate this point.

Germany's attempt to develop a constitution in response to the challenge of unification provides a useful contrast to the example of South Africa.[16] The unification necessitated the creation of a new constitution to replace the Basic Law established in 1949 as a temporary document. As Chambers explains, however, by 1989 and the fall of the Berlin Wall, "jurists and politicians alike considered the Basic Law a fully legitimate constitution" out of which had developed a body of constitutional law decided by the Federal Constitutional Court and many people did not want to embark on a constitutional project.[17] Others wanted a "constitutional debate," despite their view that the Basic Law was a "good" constitution. Instead, a small Joint Constitutional Commission was established, even though there had been a desire for a "broad Constitutional Convention representing many levels of society."[18] In a Foreword to the Basic Law, following the unification of the two Germanies, the president referred to it as a "constitution."[19] At the same time, the Basic Law is far more detailed than one would normally expect in a constitution.

Although Chambers believes that the Basic Law has not been effective because "it cannot engender the allegiance needed to keep it stable and effective," she concludes that "[i]n many ways . . . Germany is a very strong constitutional state." Yet it "has not developed a tradition of constitutional dualism in which there are periodic revitalizations of popular sovereignty and of the connection of the 'people' to the constitution."[20] Chambers brings to her analysis of both Germany and South Africa an American understanding of constitutionalism, although in doing so she reflects the predominant view of constitutions today and is certainly not alone in thinking that the German constitution is deficient because "the people" have not been involved in its creation.[21] Yet this is not the only form that a constitution can take. In Germany, a subset of the Bundestag or federal parliament and the Bundesrat (the federal Council of the States or Länder) took a more "elitist" approach, one that may be out of fashion but nevertheless appears to be working. It should also be noted that the Basic Law has been amended many times since 1949; this has been viewed both as bringing the Basic Law into conformity with its original intention and as gradually departing from its original intention and democracy.[22]

[16] This discussion is also reliant on Chambers: ibid. at 164–8.

[17] Ibid. at 165.

[18] Ibid. at 167. The JCC was "a 32-member subcommittee of the two houses and, as such, reproduced the party divisions and power differentials of parliament." Moreover, it did not engage with the public, despite the call for and response of public submissions.

[19] See the Web site for the Basic Law: http://www.iuscomp.org/gla/statutes/GG.htm.

[20] Chambers, *supra* note 14 at 168.

[21] See, for example, Andreas Busch, "The *Grundgesetz* after 50 years: Analysing changes in the German constitution," online: http://users.ox.ac.uk/~busch/papers/grundgesetz.pdf.

[22] Ibid.

Germany appears to provide an example of a state where agnosticism allows the constitution to do its basic job. The need to come to terms with its history and to bring together two distinctive economic and social cultures of the same nationality may make passionate constitutionalism risky. In this case, some citizens suspended their desire to develop an aspirational constitution in favor of toleration for a document treated as a legitimate constitution by most people, even if not the constitution they prefer, perhaps to avoid a more serious challenge to the legitimacy of a new constitution. Agnosticism (or indeed the stronger "acceptance" or "acquiescence") at the creative stage in the process may reflect the fact that a sufficient degree of agnosticism at a later stage would have been difficult to foster.

Canada is a state with a highly functioning constitution in many respects. It is built on compromise and compromise has thus far kept it stable, it carries out orderly transfers of power, and its citizens for the most part possess civil liberties and equality rights. It is gradually developing a constitutional order inclusive of First Nations, the status of whom in constitutional terms is one of serious challenge.[23] It was able to transition into a new constitutional order in 1982 with the implementation of the *Canadian Charter of Rights and Freedoms*. Although the role of the courts has become a real source of dispute in Canada, it is probably one within manageable bounds.

The most significant challenge to legitimacy in Canada has been the longtime dissatisfaction of Quebec with the existing constitutional order and the desire of at least a significant minority of people in Quebec for independence. This alienation was exacerbated by the 1982 amendments, as Quebec's exclusion from the final negotiations about the new constitution and failure to sign it did not prevent its implementation and application to Quebec. But when the opportunity to remedy Quebec's sense of constitutional isolation in 1987 through the Meech Lake Accord[24] arose, it not only failed, but also had the effect of expanding the legitimacy gap.

In part, Quebec dissension reflects the fact that one of the strongest bases of constitutional legitimacy, namely, a sense of shared history and ongoing social and cultural development, has not satisfactorily been met in Canada. Legitimacy stems from several sources, including the process under which rules are made[25] and

[23] This may take several forms, including self-government, as well as recognition of distinct First Nations practices and inclusion of aboriginal law in Canada's legal system. See, for example, the Nisga'a Treaty, which establishes an additional level of government for the Nisga'a First Nation, although it operates within the Canadian constitutional structure: Nisga'a Lisims Government Web site at http://www.nisgaalisims.ca/tl.html. See, generally, John Borrows, *Recovering Canada: The Resurgence of Indigenous Law* (Toronto: University of Toronto Press, 2002) and Alan C. Cairns, *Citizens Plus: Aboriginal Peoples and the Canadian State* (Vancouver: UBC Press, 2000).

[24] The text of the Meech Lake Accord can be found on the Government of Canada Privy Council Web site: http://www.pco-bcp.gc.ca/aia/default.asp?Language=E&page=consfile&sub= thehistoryof constitution&Doc=meech_e.htm.

[25] Randy Barnett, "Constitutional Legitimacy" (2003) 103 *Colum. L. Rev.* 111 at 113. Adherence to the process under which rules are made might be better viewed as a measure of legality, however, not legitimacy. Kay summarizes the distinction succinctly: Legality is determined "based on conformity of the constituent process with existing positive law," whereas legitimacy is "based on [the constitution's] social and political acceptability." See Richard S. Kay, "The Creation of Constitutions in Canada and the United States" (1984) 7 *Can-U.S. L.J.* 111 at 111.

whether the content meets certain goals.[26] But the constitution might also derive legitimacy from a more complex source, from general acceptance "as an ongoing social practice."[27] This view requires "the political community's collective identification with the deeds, promises, obligations, and commitments of the past as they understand them and interpret them in the present."[28] Even if the people are not enamored of the current situation, they must have faith that things will change to accord more with their own views.[29] For constitutional agnosticism to be a positive force, or at least a benign one, it probably must exist against this background of connection; it must also mean that citizens do not act precipitously on their protestant interpretations or they must be willing to trust the constitutional adjudicator in a scheme characterized by catholicism. They must at least believe that somewhere in the constitutional regime there is an actor – or a connectedness – that allows them for a short period to suspend not only the need to enact their preferences, but also their judgment about legitimacy. Under certain circumstances, this actor might be the legislature, and this has been the case in the Canada–Quebec scenario.

Amendments to the Constitution of Canada are effected by the legislatures, but will have been developed by the executive – the prime minister of Canada and the premiers of the provinces. Given the parliamentary system, the executive may have much influence on legislative behavior. It is also the case, however, that the legislature may severely restrict the scope of the exercise of its power by the executive. Although agreed to by the provincial premiers, the Meech Lake Accord failed to obtain the unanimous consent required. The Accord was effectively defeated by one legislator, Elijah Harper of the Manitoba Legislative Assembly, who filibustered until the deadline for passing the required resolution occurred. He opposed the Accord because it did not address the situation of aboriginal peoples. Clyde Wells, elected premier after the initial agreement by the premiers, then removed the Accord from consideration by the Newfoundland House of Assembly. Thus, although eight provinces and both houses of parliament approved the Accord, it failed.[30]

The period from 1982 to 1987 could be characterized as a period of constitutional agnosticism, an opportunity to remedy constitutional deviation or fundamental differences about the nature of the constitutional state. When this period

[26] Chambers, *supra* note 14 at 160: "An abstract constitution will not address injustice." Also see Rebecca L. Brown, "Accountability, Liberty, and the Constitution" (1998) 98 *Colum. L. Rev.* 531, especially at 571 where she explains the difficulty with justifying a legislature "in a government devoted to the preservation of liberty" Brown is more concerned with the structure of the constitution than with legitimacy itself, but clearly content matters.

[27] Balkin uses this phrase to describe one theory of constitutional legitimacy: See *supra* note 2 at 486.

[28] Ibid. at 493–4. Also see Hanna Fenichel Pitkin, "The Idea of a Constitution" (1987) 37 *J. Legal Educ.* 167 at 168: "To constitute, one must not merely become active at some moment but must establish something that will enlist and be carried forward by others."

[29] Balkin, *supra* note 2 at 494–5.

[30] On both the Meech Lake Accord and the Charlottetown Accord (discussed *infra*), see, for example, Kenneth McRoberts, *Misconceiving Canada: The Struggle for National Unity* (Toronto: Oxford University Press, 1997) at 190ff.; Peter H. Russell, *Constitutional Odyssey: Can Canadians Become a Sovereign People?* 2nd ed. (Toronto: University of Toronto Press, 1993) at 126ff.; and Jeremy Webber, *Reimagining Canada: Language, Culture, Community, and the Canadian Constitution* (Kingston & Montreal: McGill-Queen's University Press, 1994) at 125ff.

of agnosticism did not bear fruit, following the release of the Charest Report that sought to address the concerns of some provinces about the Meech Lake Accord in 1990, several members of parliament left the Conservative Party and Liberal Party to form the Bloc Québécois (BQ), a federal party committed to the separation of Quebec from Canada.[31] There was also a great deal of popular dissatisfaction with the Accord outside Quebec for the very reason that it would have ascribed to Quebec the status of a "distinct society," but although this might have influenced legislators, it did not prevent most legislators from supporting it. The premiers and most legislators believed that "bringing Quebec into the constitution" was significant enough a goal that they should put aside the other constitutional issues that they could have easily raised.[32] In this case, the executives in a sense exercised constitutional agnosticism by putting aside temporarily their own concerns and the vast majority of legislatures and legislators followed suit; the unwillingness of a small number to do so delivered a message to Quebec that has not yet been transcended.

The 1992 Charlottetown Accord, a far more complex mix of constitutional amendments, also failed, but this time because of its defeat in referenda not constitutionally required. The proposed amendments covered a wide range of issues, and this was the Accord's fatal flaw. Alberta, British Columbia, and Quebec had enacted legislation requiring that constitutional amendments be put to a popular vote, and it was decided that there would be a federal referendum in which all Canadians except those living in Quebec could vote and a Quebec referendum in which persons living in Quebec could vote. Initially, the mood in English Canada was that although the Accord was not perfect, it was better to support it than to risk dissolution of the country. There were strong opponents, too, however, and one argument was that rather than preventing the dissolution of the country, the Accord would actually result in dissolution. In the referenda held on October 26, 1992, the Accord was rejected in six provinces, including Quebec, and one territory and was barely approved in Ontario.[33]

From the sovereigntists' perspective, the outcome of the Accord was yet one more indication that Quebec's place in confederation was not accepted by English Canada.[34] At this point, the Quebec legislature clearly rejected the concept of constitutional agnosticism. In 1995, Quebec, under a Parti Québécois (PQ) Government, held a referendum on independence. Although the question was ambiguous

[31] On developments following the failure to ratify the Accord, see McRoberts, ibid. at 219ff. and Russell, ibid. at 154ff. These developments are also available in the CBC Archives: http://archives.cbc.ca/IDC-1-73-1180-6494/politics_economy/meech_lake/clip5.

[32] The phrase "bringing Quebec into the constitution" reflects the labeling of Meech Lake as "the Quebec Round." With its failure, negotiations leading toward the Charlottetown Accord were called "the Canada Round." On the phrase "bringing Quebec into the constitution," see McRoberts, *supra* note 30. at 190, on "distinct society"; on the "Quebec Round," see Webber, *supra* note 30 at 146 and 150; and on the "Canada Round," see Russell, *supra* note 30 at 154.

[33] The results for all provinces and territories except Quebec can be found on http://www.solon.org/Constitutions/Canada/English/Proposals/ charlottetown-res.html.

[34] See, for example, Daniel Turp, academic and BQ representative: "This episode in the political and constitutional history of Québec and Canada reveals again a struggle to reconcile irreconcilable visions of the federation." "Daniel Turp on the Future of Quebec: Forum Constitutionnel: Solutions to the Future of Canada and Québec after the October 26th Referendum: Genuine Sovereignties within a Novel Union," online: http://www.rocler.qc.ca/turp/eng/Future/Works9.htm.

and it was not clear that everyone understood it in the same way, it *was* clear that the PQ was prepared to use the legislature to move toward independence. Had there been any doubt about this, it was eliminated by the introduction of legislation that provided for a unilateral declaration of independence within one year following a successful referendum.[35] Far from legislative constitutional agnosticism, the legislature was the setting for raising the constitutional temperature with respect to the fundamental constitutional meaning of Canada.[36]

The degree of constitutional agnosticism in Canada has so far been adequate to maintain the existing constitutional regime, although not without some serious disadvantages. In the 1995 Quebec referendum on independence, with a turnout of over 90 percent, 49.42 percent voted in favor of independence or, more accurately (and possibly the reason for the result), for negotiations leading to independence.[37] In this respect, the Canadian constitutional regime is under constant, albeit sometimes dormant, threat; it is not strong enough to support constitutional amendments. At times, constitutional agnosticism appears to allow the country to engage in business other than deliberately addressing the legitimacy gap, although much of what it does is influenced by it. But it is vulnerable to being swept aside by more aggressive responses to what is seen by many Quebeckers as a fundamental constitutional deviation. While dormant for a period, including during the 2004 and for the most part the 2006 federal elections, the challenge to Canada's most fundamental constitutional legitimacy – its existence in its current form – has been raised again, although it remains to be seen how significantly.[38] In this, the Quebec legislature is a major actor, prompted by the executive. Under current Parti Québécois plans, the final decision about whether Quebec unilaterally declares independence will be that of the legislature, following a referendum. André Boisclair, elected leader of the PQ in November 2005, has promised a referendum on

[35] The proposed legislation was Bill 1, *An Act Respecting the Future of Quebec* (also known as "the Sovereignty Bill"), providing that if negotiations with the federal government following a successful referendum supporting Quebec independence failed, Quebec would declare independence unilaterally. It died on the order paper.

[36] For a brief reference to legislation enacted by the Quebec National Assembly relating to Quebec independence, and the text of the Sovereignty Bill, see online: Thomson/Nelson Publishing http://polisci.nelson.com/quebec.html. It states in part: "In 2000, the federal government enacted the Clarity Act, to stipulate the requirements for a clear question on sovereignty and a clear majority in favour before the federal government will negotiate separation with Quebec. The Quebec government responded with their own legislation, Bill 99 – An Act respecting the exercise of the fundamental rights and prerogatives of the Quebec people and the Quebec State, which declares the autonomy of the Quebec people and the National Assembly to decide their future. Note that the Quebec National Assembly also passed a unanimous resolution on October 30, 2003 which declared: 'That the National Assembly reaffirm that the people of Québec form a nation.' The National Assembly also passed a unanimous resolution on April 17, 2002, the 10th anniversary of the *Constitution Act, 1982*, which declared: 'That the National Assembly reaffirm that it never acceded to the Constitution Act, 1982, whose effect was to lessen the powers and rights of Québec without the consent of the Québec Government, of the National Assembly, and that this Act is still unacceptable for Québec.'"

[37] The results of the 1995 referendum are available on http://polisci.nelson.com/quebec.html, ibid. The actual question in English was: "Do you agree that Quebec should become sovereign after having made a formal offer to Canada for a new economic and political partnership within the scope of the bill respecting the future of Quebec and of the agreement signed on June 12, 1995?" The "agreement signed on June 12, 1995," was one reached by the leaders of the PQ, the BQ, and the Action démocratique du Québec.

[38] "Splits within PQ run deep over vision of gaining sovereignty," *Globe and Mail* (August 28, 2004) A7.

sovereignty should the PQ form the government in the next Quebec election. He is prepared to declare independence unilaterally. For Canada, this will be the supreme legislative act in a system characterized by constitutionalism and the supreme test for a legislature of the willingness and capacity to engage in constitutional agnosticism.

III. CONCLUSION

This chapter has merely introduced the concept of constitutional agnosticism and identified some of the issues it raises, particularly with respect to legislatures. Constitutional agnostism is not a stance that many constitutional scholars will find attractive because it seems to require denial of normative standpoints. It does not do that, however, so much as it asks whether the assertion of one's normative standpoint is sufficiently crucial in times of constitutional deviation that it is worth risking constitutional crisis. Agnosticism may be helpful at different stages of the constitutional regime. The challenge, however, is deciding when it will advance the constitutional conversation and when it will leave the field open to the constitutionally unscrupulous and more powerful.

The actions (or inaction) of any constitutional actor may give rise to the need to consider the appropriateness of constitutional agnosticism. By the same token, any constitutional actor can take advantage of the hiatus provided by it to transcend the constitutional dilemma. Legislatures in systems defined by constitutionalism can deviate from constitutional norms in two ways in particular. The first is that they can fail to abide by written or conventional constitutional requirements, thereby risking undermining the constitutional safeguards available to citizens or, indeed, denying citizens their constitutional rights. Depending on the circumstances, this deviation may be compensated for by the response of other constitutional actors, such as the judiciary through the process of judicial review. As long as the legislature accepts the result, this deviation will right itself. The second way is more subtle: It can simply be "lax" in being a responsible constitutional actor by leaving the constitutional work to others, again such as the judiciary (a complaint heard about Canadian legislatures). In itself, this is less dangerous than the first type of deviation, resulting more in an imbalance in the constitutional regime. Nevertheless, it can result in serious doubts among a minority of citizens about the legitimacy of the constitutional regime itself or, more likely, about the legitimacy of the constitutional actor that has been forced to exercise its authority more than at least some citizens would like. In all these cases, if the deviation becomes sufficiently serious to warrant it, a period of constitutional agnosticism may assist in providing the conditions under which the deviation can be addressed.

Should legislatures themselves engage in constitutional agnosticism? This seems to me to be a more difficult question and which, despite the examples of Israel and Germany, on the one hand, and Alberta, on the other, is probably usually or presumptively best answered with a "no." Legislatures always owe citizens an active constitutional presence, an engagement with the constitution to which the country has committed, or with attempts to develop a new constitutional regime. In this respect, far from reducing the legislature's power, constitutionalism enhances it. And from that perspective, constitutional agnosticism for legislatures may simply be too easy a position to take, contrary to the burden that a deliberate constitutional agnosticism imposes on citizens.

ACKNOWLEDGMENTS

My thanks to Sara Bagg, an LL.B. student and Ph.D. candidate in Philosophy at the University of Calgary, for her research assistance and discussion about the themes of this chapter.

12 Constitutional Amendments and the Constitutional Common Law

Adrian Vermeule

Constitutions obsolesce rapidly and must be updated over time to reflect changes in the polity's circumstances and citizens' values. What institution or process should be entrusted with the authority to do the updating? If periodic wholesale replacement of the constitution is infeasible, the realistic choices are a constitutional amendment process involving legislatures, flexible interpretation by judges under the banner of constitutional common law,[1] or some mix of the two. Here I explore the question by comparing the relative merits of formal amendments and the constitutional common law as means of constitutional updating. I attempt to dispel some prominent arguments that unjustifiably privilege constitutional common law over the amendment process and also attempt to sketch the empirical conditions under which either process proves superior to the other.

To structure the discussion, I advance two subsidiary theses about constitutional amendment.[2] The first is that constitutional amendments can and do change constitutional law, including the law in action as well as the formal constitutional text. The second is that there is no good general reason to prefer common-law updating to the amendment process; to the contrary, an evenhanded institutional comparison suggests that each process shows to best advantage under particular conditions, and in particular domains.

These theses sound banal, but each has been denied in important recent work. As to the first thesis, David Strauss has argued that constitutional amendments are "irrelevant" because an amendment is neither a necessary nor a sufficient

[1] I do not use "constitutional common law" in Henry Monaghan's sense of constitutionally inspired doctrine that might be overridden by legislation. See Henry Paul Monaghan, "The Supreme Court, 1974 Term – Foreword: Constitutional Common Law" (1975) 89 *Harv. L. Rev.* 1. Rather, I use the term to denote constitutional rules, not defeasible by ordinary legislation, that are elaborated by judges through precedent-based reasoning. See generally David A. Strauss, "Common Law Constitutional Interpretation" (1996) *U. Chi. L. Rev.* 877 [hereinafter Strauss, *Common Law*]. So constitutional common law is short for something like "judge-made constitutional law" or "common-law constitutional exegesis." Moreover, Parts I and II equate constitutional common law with judge-made law, temporarily bracketing questions about whether constitutional change outside the formal amendment process is primarily driven by judges or by nonjudicial actors. Part III examines the issue in detail.

[2] For simplicity, I shall reserve the term "amendment" to mean "formal constitutional amendment" – in America, through the Article V process. I shall describe other changes to constitutional rules, especially through judicial interpretation, as "constitutional common law," "constitutional change," or "constitutional updating." On the semantic problems surrounding "amendment," see Sanford Levinson, "How Many Times Has the United States Constitution Been Amended? (A) <26; (B) 26; (C) 27; (D) >27: Accounting for Constitutional Change" in Sanford Levinson, ed., *Responding to Imperfection: The Theory and Practice of Constitutional Amendment* (Princeton, NJ: Princeton University Press, 1995).

condition for legal change. The second thesis contradicts a standard academic view that I shall call *the generic case against constitutional amendment.* On this view, there are good general reasons to reject, or to indulge a presumption against, any proposed amendment. Among these reasons are the following claims: It is bad to "tamper" with the Constitution; the Constitution should not be "cluttered up" with amendments that will "trivialize" its majesty; constitutional amendments are "divisive" or "polarizing"; constitutional amendments may have bad unanticipated consequences; and constitutional amendments diminish the coherence of the constitutional text or of judicially developed constitutional doctrine. Something like this view has become the conventional wisdom in the legal academy, following explicit arguments by Kathleen Sullivan and others.

My critical aims are to question the view that amendments are irrelevant, contra Strauss, and to question the view that amendments are generically or presumptively suspect, contra Sullivan and others. Those two views have a common purpose and effect: They privilege constitutional updating by judges, the first by suggesting that constitutional amendment is generically futile, the second by suggesting that constitutional amendment is generically harmful. The implicit alternative is a practice that entrusts all constitutional change to common-law constitutionalism – that is, to an ongoing constitutional convention whose delegates are all judges (and hence all lawyers).

As against those views, I will attempt an evenhanded institutional comparison of the amendment process and common-law constitutionalism, as alternative means of constitutional updating.[3] I consider the strengths and weaknesses of each process: Relative to common-law constitutionalism, the amendment process is less focused on the facts of particular cases (both for good and ill); puts less weight on the views of past judges (both for good and ill); allows for the participation of decision makers from a broader range of professions and backgrounds (both for good and ill); produces more enduring constitutional settlements, albeit at higher initial cost; and trades the benefits of flexibility for the benefits of rigidity. By identifying these variables, I hope to make some tentative progress toward identifying the empirical conditions under which, or the domain in which, either process is most likely to produce valuable constitutional change.

The discussion is organized as follows. Part I critiques Strauss's thesis that constitutional amendments are systematically irrelevant. First, even if constitutional amendments are neither necessary nor sufficient to produce legal change, they may nonetheless be *causally efficacious* in producing legal change. Strauss has overlooked that the causal force of amendments is probabilistic: Even if an amendment neither guarantees a desired legal change nor is indispensable to it, the amendment may nonetheless make the change more likely than it would have been in the amendment's absence. Second, the irrelevance view slips imperceptibly from the denial that any particular amendment is relevant to the denial that the total set of amendments is relevant. But if the reason that particular amendments are irrelevant is that other amendments would have been interpreted to produce the

[3] An excellent treatment in the same spirit is John R. Vile, *Constitutional Change in the United States: A Comparative Study of Constitutional Amendments, Judicial Interpretations, and Legislative and Executive Actions* (Westport, Conn.: Praeger, 1994) [*Constitutional Change in the United States*].

same effect – and this is the form of Strauss's argument in many cases – then the irrelevance claim cannot hold true of all amendments at once. Even if every particular constitutional amendment can be shown to be irrelevant through a seriatim procedure, we cannot generalize the conclusion that all constitutional amendments might be irrelevant simultaneously.

In Part II, the core of the chapter, I argue that the generic case against constitutional amendment fails. The generic case rests on a nirvana fallacy that implicitly contrasts a jaundiced view of the amendment process with a romanticized view of constitutional common law. The real alternative to constitutional amendment is flexible judicial interpretation that updates the Constitution over time – a practice that can also be seen as tampering with or trivializing the Constitution, that is at least as polarizing or divisive as constitutional amendment, that equally risks bad unintended consequences, and so on. Moreover, a public norm of the kind embodied in the generic case against amendment would produce either a suboptimal rate of constitutional amendments or an optimal rate at excessive cost. The generic case can be reconstructed as a weak presumption, but in that form it loses its distinctive force.

Once we have dispelled the nirvana fallacy underlying the generic case against amendment, constitutional updating is seen to pose a comparative institutional question. Part III compares constitutional amendment, on the one hand, and constitutional common law, on the other, as institutional alternatives for managing the inevitable updating of constitutional law over time. Under what circumstances might one process or the other prove superior? What institutional considerations, or variables, determine their relative performance? I suggest that amendments show to best advantage, relative to common-law constitutionalism, where the constitutional changes in question involve large value choices as opposed to technical improvements in the law, where constitutional change must be systemic and simultaneous rather than piecemeal, and where irreversible change is more valuable than reversible change. A brief conclusion follows.

I. THE RELEVANCE OF CONSTITUTIONAL AMENDMENTS

The irrelevance thesis holds as follows:

> [S]ubject to only a few qualifications, [the American constitutional] system would look the same today if Article V of the Constitution had never been adopted and the Constitution contained no provision for formal amendment.[4]

The basic thesis is an extended counterfactual: In the absence of the Article V amendment mechanism, the American constitutional order would look roughly the same as it actually does today. (An important qualification to the thesis is that it does not apply to the original or "unamended" Constitution or to the Bill of Rights; I return to this domain restriction on the thesis in I.B.) For want of historical expertise, I shall not attempt to engage the irrelevance thesis to the extent that it happens to incorporate historical claims about how actual amendments actually

[4] David A. Strauss, "The Irrelevance of Constitutional Amendments" (2001) 114 *Harv. L. Rev.* 1457 at 1459 [hereinafter Strauss, *Irrelevance*].

worked out, rather than counterfactual claims about the "relevance" of the formal amendment process. I will instead confine myself to some comments on the conceptual foundations of the irrelevance thesis.

In Section A, I examine some problems that inhere in the counterfactual character of the thesis. Counterfactual claims are not the same as causal claims. The irrelevance thesis makes a general counterfactual claim, but the thesis must not be interpreted to make, nor can it support, a general causal claim. The critical point is that constitutional amendments may be causally efficacious in producing legal change, even if (as the irrelevance thesis claims) they are neither necessary nor sufficient for producing legal change. In Section B, I examine some conceptual problems that inhere in the application of the irrelevance thesis to the interaction between and among different constitutional provisions. Here the point is that, in many cases, the thesis establishes the irrelevance of particular amendments only by pointing to other amendments that would otherwise have subsumed the functions of the irrelevant amendment. This mode of analysis might work for any particular amendment, but it cannot be generalized across a whole set of amendments simultaneously.

The overall conclusion is not that the irrelevance thesis is wrong. If its conceptual foundations are infirm, much of the structure erected on those foundations retains great value. Construed in its best light – as a series of retail-level historical claims about particular amendments – Strauss's thesis makes an important contribution to constitutional legal history. But nothing more ambitious follows. In particular, we cannot, in my view, subscribe to any more general claim that amendments are intrinsically inefficacious.

A. Counterfactuals, causation, and constitutional amendment

The irrelevance thesis, although striking, says less than the casual reader might assume. There is a fundamental ambiguity in the claim that the formal amendment process is "irrelevant." Rightly understood, the thesis claims only that amendments are neither necessary nor sufficient for legal change; but the thesis is easily confused with a very different and far more ambitious claim, to the effect that amendments do not *cause* legal change. The slippage between these two claims gives the irrelevance thesis a hard rhetorical punch, but the first claim does not entail the second, or so I shall argue.

The subsidiary propositions of the irrelevance thesis are these:

> [The irrelevance thesis may be proved by] establishing four propositions. First – a relatively familiar point – sometimes matters addressed by the Constitution change even though the text of the Constitution is unchanged. Second, and more dramatically, some constitutional changes occur even though amendments that would have brought about those very changes are explicitly rejected. Third, when amendments are adopted, they often do no more than ratify changes that have already taken place in society without the help of an amendment. The changes produce the amendment, rather than the other way around. Fourth, when amendments are adopted even though society has not changed, the amendments are systematically evaded. They end up having little effect until society catches up with the ambitions of the amendment.[5]

[5] Ibid. at 1459.

We may compress the "four propositions" of the passage quoted above into two claims, as follows:

(~N) amendments are not a necessary condition for change; and
(~S) amendments are not a sufficient condition for change.

The first and second propositions in the quoted passage are variants on (~N), while the fourth proposition asserts (~S). The third proposition is ambiguous; I shall return to it below.

In my view, the basic counterfactual thesis, and its two subsidiary propositions, are entirely compatible with the following:

(C) amendments cause legal change.

The crucial point is that (C) may hold even if both (~N) and (~S) are established. In general, *causal claims cannot be straightforwardly reduced to counterfactual claims.*[6] The claim that (1) "A caused B" does not entail the claims that (2) "A is a (counterfactually) necessary condition for B, so that if A had not occurred, B would not have occurred" or that (3) "A is a sufficient condition for B, so that if B did not occur, A must not have occurred." So denying claims (2) and (3), separately or together, does not establish that claim (1) is wrong, as I shall illustrate below.

This is a material point as well as a logical one. The tempting assumption that (~N) and (~S) jointly entail denial of (C) is responsible for much of the rhetorical punch of the irrelevance thesis. But even if amendments are neither necessary nor sufficient for legal change, amendments may still be causally efficacious. Stripped of the invalid implication, the irrelevance thesis is much less arresting. To be sure, there is still a sense in which amendments are irrelevant, but it is not an impressive or even very interesting sense. If I may go from Point A to Point B by either train or plane, and would have gone by train had I not in fact gone by plane, there is a sense in which the plane was irrelevant. But it is hardly obvious that irrelevance in this sense is something anyone should care about.

Before exploring that issue, there is a threshold exegetical question. Some passages in Strauss' paper might be taken to assert that (C) does not hold in some particular cases. The third proposition quoted above (especially "the changes produce the amendment, rather than the other way around") might be construed to deny (C), but the thrust of the passage and of the whole paper is just to advance the claims (~N) and (~S). Of course, we might establish that (C) is false, in particular cases, through independent historical investigation; we might discover, for

[6] See William K. Goosens, "Causal Chains and Counterfactuals" (1979) 76 *The Journal of Philosophy* 489–90. For the latest philosophical efforts, see John Collins, Ned Hall, and L. A. Paul, eds., *Causation and Counterfactuals* (Cambridge, Mass.: MIT Press, 2004). The best-known attempt to explain causation in counterfactual terms is David Lewis, "Causation" (1973) 70 *The Journal of Philosophy* 556. Lewis, however, claims only that a relationship of "causal dependence" (B is "causally dependent" upon A) is explicable in terms of counterfactual necessitation (if A had not occurred, B would not have occurred). The relationship of causal dependence is not equivalent to, nor is it intended to capture, causation in the standard sense of "direct causation." See Daniel M. Hausman, "Causation and Counterfactual Dependence Reconsidered" (1996) 30 *NOÛS* 55. Note also that Lewis has since modified his views (in ways not material here). See David Lewis, "Causation as Influence" in *Causation and Counterfactuals*, *supra* at 75.

example, that the Twenty-Seventh Amendment[7] has changed nothing except the constitutions reprinted in the back of constitutional-law textbooks. The detailed historical discussion that makes up the bulk of Strauss's article might be read in this light; although the particular accounts are impressively argued, I cannot judge their historical merits. What I do question is the conceptual link between the retail historical arguments and the wholesale counterfactual thesis; the former do not follow from the latter. In any event, establishing the counterfactual thesis is clearly the main project of Strauss's paper. And the burden of the discussion here is that even if the counterfactual thesis is established, amendments may be and frequently are relevant in a straightforward sense.

NECESSARY CONDITIONS AND PREEMPTIVE CAUSATION. Let us begin with necessary conditions. Granting that if A had not occurred, B would have occurred in any event, can we nonetheless say that A caused B?[8] Yes, because of the possibility that *actual causes may preempt counterfactual causes.*[9] In A's absence, some third factor C might have produced B in any event; yet, in A's presence, so to speak, it is A rather than C that brings about B. The hypotheticals are familiar. Able and Charlie shoot at Baker, who is felled by Able's bullet, but who would have been felled by Charlie's bullet had Able not fired. Whatever we say about Charlie's causal role, it seems clear that Able caused Baker's death in a straightforward sense.

Although this sort of casuistic example seems abstruse, in the case of constitutional amendments the idea of preemptive causation applies straightforwardly. An amendment might very well cause legal change even if similar changes would have occurred in the amendment's absence. Many of Strauss's most striking claims and examples, it turns out, are of this sort. Consider the following passages, all of which seem to acknowledge (explicitly or implicitly) that the relevant amendment *actually brought about* the relevant legal change, but all of which argue for irrelevance by appealing from facts to counterfacts:

- The Thirteenth Amendment's only practical effect was to abolish slavery in the border states. Even without the Amendment, however, "in any event, Congress

[7] U.S. Const. Amend. XXVII ("No law, varying the compensation for the services of the Senators and Representatives, shall take effect, until an election of Representatives shall have intervened.").

[8] Two caveats are necessary. First, I am denying the validity of an inference from "it is not the case that if A had not occurred, B would not have occurred" to "A did not cause B." Denying that a given amendment (or the whole set of amendments) was counterfactually necessary for a given change in the law (or a whole set of changes in the law) does not entitle us to infer that the amendment (or set of amendments) did not *cause* the change in the law, because of the possibility of preempted causation, explained in the text. The inference whose validity is thus denied should not be confused with the converse inference, from "A did not cause B" to "it is not the case that if A had not occurred, B would not have occurred." This inference is valid. See Leo Katz, *Bad Acts and Guilty Minds: Conundrums of the Criminal Law* (Chicago: University of Chicago Press, 1987) at 235. But this is not the form of the irrelevance argument. Second, I am ignoring the philosophical complexities that arise from David Lewis's argument that whenever two events stand in a causal relationship but not a relationship of counterfactual necessity, there must at least be a chain of events, standing in counterfactually necessary relations one to another, that link the two events. See David Lewis, "Causation" in Ernest Sosa, ed., *Causation and Conditionals* (New York: Oxford University Press, 1975) at 180; Katz, *supra* at 235. Suffice it to say that it would require a thorough overhaul of the irrelevance thesis to incorporate this complex view.

[9] Goosens, *supra* note 6 at 489. For some legal examples, see Katz, *supra* note 8 at 233. For a defense of the counterfactual account of causation that dismisses the preemption problem, see David Coady, "Preempting Preemption" in *Causation and Counterfactuals, supra* note 6 at 325.

very likely would have outlawed it, and the Supreme Court might have upheld Congress' action."[10]

- "In view of [the Court's later decision in] *Harper* [*v. Virginia Board of Elections*], the net effect of the Twenty-Fourth Amendment was, at most, to abolish the poll tax in federal elections, in a few states, two years before it would have been abolished across the board anyway."[11]
- "It is difficult to believe that the Supreme Court would have ruled differently in *Brown* [*v. Board of Education*] if the Fourteenth Amendment had not been adopted.It seems more likely that the Courtwould have identified some other text in the Constitution as the formal basis for the claim of equality."[12]
- "The lack of resistance to the Twenty-Sixth Amendment suggests that inevitably most of the states, and probably all of them, would have changed their laws [respecting voting age] within a relatively short time."[13]
- Although "the amendment process [that produced the Nineteenth Amendment] nationalized the women's suffrage debate, and that may have been crucial," "[o]n the other hand,a state-by-state campaign for women's suffrage might also have succeeded."[14]

One wonders why this sort of appeal from facts to counterfacts should be permitted, however. A criminal defendant cannot excuse his acknowledged deed of homicide by showing that the victim would soon have died from other causes.[15] No *causal* sense of irrelevance can be established by showing that some other legal instrument or institutions would have produced the effect that was, in fact, produced by a constitutional amendment. To be sure, what counts as a "cause" differs in different settings, partly because of differences in normative considerations. Causal attributions in the criminal setting are very different than causal attributions in the setting of constitutional amendments. But this is a point about how causation should be defined, including preemptive causation; it assumes, rather than denying, that causal claims cannot (in any straightforward way) be reduced to counterfactual claims.

Some of the quoted passages include an explicit or implicit suggestion that, because of or in addition to the phenomenon of preemptive causation, the relevant amendments did not "matter" very much or at all.[16] This claim is only ambiguously connected to the thesis that constitutional amendments are irrelevant. The ambiguity can be brought out by an analogy to the standard distinction between statistical significance, on the one hand, and economic significance, on the other. A correlation may be statistically robust, and even capture a real causal relationship, without at all being important in a broader sense. So too the claim that a given amendment did not matter equivocates between saying that the amendment was epiphenomenal, a dependent product of underlying causes rather than

[10] Strauss, *Irrelevance*, *supra* note 4 at 1480.
[11] Ibid. at 1481.
[12] Ibid. at 1485.
[13] Ibid. at 1489.
[14] Ibid. at 1502.
[15] Leo Katz, *Ill-Gotten Gains: Evasion, Blackmail, Fraud, and Kindred Puzzles of the Law* (Chicago: University of Chicago Press, 1996) at 167–8.
[16] Strauss, *Irrelevance*, *supra* note 4 at 1462–4, 1478.

an independent causal force, and saying that the legal changes the amendment did cause were small-bore. In general, the claim that "X does not [or does] matter for Y" is riven with ambiguity. It might mean, variously, that Y would occur even in X's absence, that X is not significantly correlated with Y in a statistical sense, that X is significantly correlated with Y but has no causal effect on Y, or that X has a causal effect on Y that is not important in some broader perspective.

As I mentioned above, we may interpret some of Strauss's retail examples as making claims of the last sort, which would mean that Strauss has garnished the central counterfactual thesis with some causal arguments. Because the causal claims are incidental to the irrelevance thesis, however, Strauss's criteria of "importance" are unclear; where they can be discerned, they seem dubious. To isolate the issue in the examples above, put aside the possibility of preemptive causation and imagine a counterfactual world in which, today, a few border states still permitted slavery, in which a few (other) states still denied women the vote, and so on. In that counterfactual world, the (in turn counterfactual) failure of the Thirteenth and Nineteenth amendments would matter very much indeed.

SUFFICIENT CONDITIONS AND JOINT CAUSATION. The analysis can easily be extended to include sufficient conditions. Granting that A is not a sufficient condition for B, so that even if A occurs, B might not occur, can we nonetheless say that A is a cause of B? In the easiest case, of course, A might still be a necessary condition for B. But we need to grant the premises of the irrelevance thesis, among which is the claim that A is not a necessary condition for B either; the irrelevance thesis asserts ($\sim$S) *and* ($\sim$N). Still, A might cause B even if A is neither necessary nor sufficient to bring about B. Able and Charlie shoot at Baker. Simultaneously, Delta pushes Baker closer to Able than to Charlie; as a result, Able's shot reaches and kills Baker before Charlie's shot, even though Baker would have been killed by Charlie's bullet had Able not fired, and even though (let us suppose) had Delta not acted, Charlie rather than Able would have been the one to kill Baker. Able's action, by itself, is neither necessary nor sufficient to kill Baker, yet it caused Baker's death.

The constitutional-law parallel to this sort of case arises in the frequent situation in which (1) a constitutional amendment is adopted in order to produce a legal change; (2) the change would have been accomplished in some other way absent the amendment (although perhaps less speedily or efficiently); and (3) the enactment of the amendment is not by itself sufficient to produce the change. Usually condition (3) holds because the cooperation of legal actors not part of the amendment process – most prominently the judges – is needed to implement amendments. So amendments are typically merely one of a set of conditions that are *jointly* sufficient to produce legal change. Yet it would be odd to deny that amendments, even given their insufficiency taken in isolation, nonetheless (help to) bring about legal change.

In the case of the Fourteenth Amendment, for example, we may grant both that the Amendment was not by itself sufficient to produce change in the legal status of race, given the unwillingness of federal officials to implement the Amendment's equality guarantees until the 1950s; and that, absent the Amendment, federal judges might later have reached similar outcomes under some other constitutional provision. Still, when the judges did become willing to implement the Amendment, they in fact implemented *that* provision, and not some other one – if only for the very good practical reason that it is easiest to explain or justify an egalitarian ruling by pointing to a legal provision that contains a guarantee of "equal protection of the laws," as opposed to, say, a guarantee of a "republican form of government" or a prohibition on "titles of nobility."[17] In this straightforward sense, the Amendment helped to bring about legal change.

NECESSITY, SUFFICIENCY, AND PROBABILITY. The largest point here is that Strauss's focus on necessary and sufficient conditions is misplaced because the causal force of amendments is probabilistic.[18] Some cause C that is neither necessary nor sufficient for producing some effect E may nonetheless make E more likely, perhaps far more likely, than it would have been in C's absence. Having Babe Ruth on the team was neither necessary nor sufficient for the 1927 Yankees to win the World Series – they might have won anyway, and they might not have won even with Ruth – but it certainly helped. The same point holds as against the idea that amendments are often futile or irrelevant because amendment drafters cannot foresee all later questions and cannot control all decisions of later interpreters. Of course, initial drafters cannot settle all relevant questions; of course, subsequent enforcement is partly, but only partly, at the mercy of subsequent generations; of course, hostile judges may interpret the amendment grudgingly. But these possibilities do not make amendments systematically meaningless. Rather, passage of an amendment systematically tends to push later outcomes in the directions desired by the amendment's proponents.

Strauss has one terrific example, the Reconstruction Amendments, in which subsequent generations of judges and other officials nullified amendments for a time through grudging interpretation and sheer defiance. But even in that example, the amendments lay around waiting to be picked up and used by yet later generations, as they actually were; and most other amendments have been implemented straightforwardly. There is no reason to think that the Reconstruction example is broadly representative of amendments in general.

THE INSIGNIFICANCE OF IRRELEVANCE. The upshot is that the irrelevance thesis cannot support any suggestion that amendments lack causal force. As such, the irrelevance thesis is a distinctly less interesting claim than might be assumed. To be sure, an actually operative cause can be irrelevant in a counterfactual sense. The airline that actually takes us from Point A to Point B might be dismissed as counterfactually irrelevant, in the sense that we could have gone by rail instead. I do not deny that "irrelevance" can be given this sense, but I do deny that this strictly counterfactual sense of irrelevance holds much interest in practical affairs.

[17] Brannon P. Denning and John R. Vile, "The Relevance of Constitutional Amendments: A Response to David Strauss" (2002) 77 *Tulane L. Rev.* 247 at 260–2.

[18] I bracket here underlying philosophical controversies about whether all causation is ultimately probabilistic or deterministic. See Igal Kvart, "Causation: Probabilistic and Counterfactual Analyses" in *Causation and Counterfactuals*, *supra* note 6 at 359. Even if it is not always so, few deny that it is often so; and it seems safe to assume that legal variables, such as amendments, generally have probabilistic causal force.

Consider that, had we gone from A to B by train instead of plane, we could argue in turn that the railway was counterfactually irrelevant; after all, we could have gone by plane. Whenever there are alternative means for accomplishing an end, all such means will be irrelevant in the counterfactual sense. It would, however, be very odd to conclude that it is immaterial which means is actually used. Counterfactual irrelevance does not at all entail that the alternative means are equally costly, or legitimate, or equivalent in any other respect. So even if the constitutional rules would be the same today had Article V never existed, it might also be true that Americans are much better off because Article V did exist – if, for example, the Article V process produced the relevant constitutional rules at lower cost than judicial updating would have. To know whether (the addition of) Article V makes things better, we would have to compare the virtues and vices of formal amendments and judicial updating as alternative means of constitutional change. I undertake that inquiry in Parts II and III; here my point is that counterfactual irrelevance says nothing at all about those crucial questions.

In the end, it is entirely unclear that counterfactual irrelevance is a property anyone should care about. Imagine a counterfactual world in which Article V contained no amendment process, and all constitutional change had been accomplished by judicial updating. In that world, we may imagine a counterfactual Strauss brilliantly arguing that judicial updating is irrelevant because the Constitution could have included an amendment mechanism that would eventually have produced the same results. The response of our counterfactual selves to the counterfactual Strauss would properly be one of puzzlement; why should we care about irrelevance in that science-fictional sense, when we live in a world in which, in fact, judicial updating is the sole mechanism of constitutional change? The proper response of our actual selves to the actual Strauss should be the same, *mutatis mutandis.* We live in a world (Strauss seems to acknowledge) in which amendments have in fact been robustly causal in the production of constitutional change; it is not at all clear why we ought to care about what might have happened in other possible worlds.

B. Irrelevance and generalization

I now put aside the issue of counterfactual relevance *versus* factual causation, to focus on some problems of generalization that inhere in the irrelevance thesis. These problems arise when a claim that might hold true of any particular amendment is incautiously assumed to be generalizable to all amendments simultaneously. In some cases, the generalization does not hold *even if* the constituent claims are each plausible, taken one by one. So I will assume, contrary to I.A, that showing any particular amendment to have been counterfactually irrelevant suffices to show it to have been causally irrelevant as well. Still, however, there is a separate problem: It does not follow that all amendments can be *simultaneously* irrelevant in either sense.

To elicit the problem, consider the argument that the protracted struggles over the rejected Equal Rights Amendment, which would have constitutionalized a guarantee of gender equality, were irrelevant. "Today, it is difficult to identify any respect in which constitutional law is different from what it would have been if the ERA [the

Equal Rights Amendment] had been adopted."[19] The reason given for this, however, is that the Supreme Court subsequently read a strong presumption against gender-based law into the Fourteenth Amendment's Equal Protection Clause. The ERA was irrelevant because the work it would otherwise have done was picked up by (the Court's reading of) a different constitutional amendment.

If that is so, however, then we have established that the ERA was or would have been irrelevant only because there was some *other* amendment in the picture that picked up the slack and which must therefore have itself been relevant. To be sure, the Court's decision to interpret equal protection this way was necessary for this story; but it is equally true that the Court felt it necessary to find some text, somewhere in the picture, into which gender equality could be read. Absent the text providing for "equal protection," the Court might have used some third text altogether – say, the Privileges and Immunities Clause – but then *that* text would have been relevant in turn.

The underlying problem may be illustrated schematically by imagining a set of, say, twenty-six constitutional amendments. For any amendment A in the set, we might argue that A's functions would have been subsumed by some other member of the set, say B; B's functions would have been subsumed by C; and so on, the final claim being that the only amendment not yet shown to be irrelevant, Z, would in turn have been subsumed by A. Arguing piecemeal in this way, we can then proceed to examine each amendment seriatim and show that it is irrelevant. What results is a series of individually plausible arguments that any *particular* amendment is irrelevant; but the series cannot be generalized to claim that the whole *set* of amendments is irrelevant simultaneously. To show that any given amendment is irrelevant through the seriatim procedure, we cannot help but posit that some other amendment in the set is relevant, although the identity of the relevant amendment changes at each step in the argument. In the limiting case of a set of amendments with only two members, we can imagine an argument that, say, the due process clause is irrelevant (at least in its substantive aspect) because the Court would have generated the same results out of the Ninth Amendment – conjoined with an argument that the Ninth Amendment is irrelevant because the Court would have generated the same results out of due process.

The irrelevance argument takes a similar form in many cases, although the structure of the argument is often tacit rather than explicit. Here are some examples:

- [As previously described,] the ERA was irrelevant because its content was subsumed in the equal protection clause of the Fourteenth Amendment.[20]
- In similar vein, had the Nineteenth Amendment not been enacted, "the nation's commitment to women's suffrage would have been just as profound . . . an influence on the interpretation of the Equal Protection Clause."[21]
- An omitted provision of the Twenty-Fourth Amendment, which would have abolished poll taxes in state elections, was "adopted" by the Court through interpretation of the Equal Protection Clause.[22]

[19] Strauss, *Irrelevance, supra* note 4 at 1476–7.
[20] Ibid. at 1476–8.
[21] Ibid. at 1504.
[22] Ibid. at 1481–2.

- Absent the Fourteenth Amendment, the effects of the Equal Protection Clause on state-sponsored segregation would have been achieved through interpretation of the Due Process Clause of the Fifth Amendment, the Guaranty Clause of Article I, or some other text.[23]
- The proposed Child Labor Amendment was irrelevant because the Supreme Court expanded the Commerce Clause to achieve the same results.[24]

It is important to be clear, however, that in some of these cases there is a restriction on the irrelevance thesis that avoids the transparently invalid position I have illustrated above. The independent limitation is that the irrelevance thesis does not apply to either (1) the Bill of Rights, defined as the first twelve amendments, or (2) the text of the original Constitution. This limitation saves any irrelevance claim in which an amendment *within* the irrelevant set is placed there on the ground that its functions would have been subsumed by a Bill of Rights amendment, or a provision of the "unamended" Constitution, that lies *outside* the irrelevant set. So this restriction clearly saves the last two cases on the list above. In the first three cases, however, the irrelevance thesis is arguing, piecemeal, that some constitutional amendments in the irrelevant set are irrelevant because of their subsumption in other amendments in the irrelevant set, which are then claimed, in turn, to be irrelevant. It seems that something here must give.

We might attempt to save the first three cases as well, on the following grounds: The generalization problem I have indicated only arises when the chain of irrelevance circles back on itself. So long as there is some (one) constitutional amendment stipulated to be relevant, and so long as the chain of irrelevance can eventually be grounded in that amendment, the problem is obviated. We can, for example, argue that the Nineteenth Amendment is irrelevant because of (counterfactual) subsumption in the Fourteenth Amendment, and then say that the latter is irrelevant because of (counterfactual) subsumption in the Fifth Amendment's Due Process Clause, which itself, by virtue of the domain restriction on the irrelevance thesis, lies outside the irrelevant set.

I am not sure how much this saves, however. It seems rather to concede than to rebut the point that not all amendments can be simultaneously irrelevant; it avoids, rather than solving, the generalization problem. (This is not true if the grounding provision is part of the "unamended Constitution," rather than one of the later amendments, but I shall shortly suggest that there is no such thing as the "unamended Constitution" – that all constitutional provisions are amendments of one sort or another.) The restriction on the domain of the irrelevance thesis, moreover, can be questioned on the ground of arbitrariness. Having some amendments outside the set claimed to be irrelevant avoids the generalization problem (so long as all irrelevance claims can be linked to a chain eventually grounded in an amendment outside the set), but the price for this is a thesis that is *necessarily* truncated, and in potentially unjustifiable ways.

The domain restriction on the irrelevance thesis is justified by a claim that the text of the original Constitution, and the first twelve amendments, are products of

[23] Ibid. at 1484–6.

[24] Ibid. at 1475–6.

a "fledgling constitutional order" rather than a "mature democratic society."[25] In the fledgling phase, constitutional texts serve important functions, whereas in the mature phase, nontextual processes of change dominate. This is, in my view, a clear expression of a questionable picture of constitutions and constitutional change. To say, as Holmes did,[26] or to imply through metaphors, as this argument does, that a constitution is or is like an "organism" that has a "fledgling stage" and a "mature stage," is to fall into the trap of misleading biological analogy. Constitutions just do not have any biologically programmed stages of birth, growth, and maturation.

Strauss's position rests on substance as well as metaphor. Strauss is suggesting that, over time, societies develop institutionalized patterns of trust and cooperation that enable them to change the constitution informally. Formal processes are more important in new constitutional polities, in part because constitutional text supplies focal points for coordinating collective behavior. In ongoing polities, however, formal constitutional text and formal processes of constitutional change become less important, as ties of trust and cooperation among citizens become increasingly robust.

This is a possible view of the general trajectory of the relationship between written constitutions and political development. But it is a very optimistic view, and one that does not particularly resonate with American history. There is no general reason to think that trust, or affective ties, or tacit cooperation (not founded on formal lawmaking rules and processes) all generally increase over time in liberal democratic polities. Exogenous trends or shocks, changing political alliances, and increasing polarization within hostile economic or social camps may all reduce informal political cooperation in later periods. In the American case, the nation was quite plausibly more divided, more riven with mutual mistrust between or among competing views or factions, in 1861 (the beginning of the Civil War), 1932 (the election of Roosevelt), 1974 (the Nixon scandal), and 2000 (a contested presidential election) than it was in 1791 or 1804 (the date of the Twelfth Amendment, the latest amendment Strauss excludes from the scope of his thesis). So even given Strauss's premises, there is no real reason to think that formal lawmaking processes were systematically more valuable or necessary during the period in which the first twelve amendments were enacted than they were in later periods, when in Strauss's view all amendments were irrelevant.

Here is a different picture of the whole matter: An "original" constitution is just a *package* of amendments simultaneously adopted on a blank slate, and what we call "amendments" are simply modifications of the initial package. At some point, a new polity adopts a new constitution; at various later points, amendments occur, with complex relationships between formal legal change and political, economic, and social change; the polity changes more or less drastically at various points and over time, both in formal legal ways and in informal ways; eventually we face questions about whether the sequence of retail changes has cumulated to a wholesale change in the polity itself (as in the puzzle of the ship of Theseus, whose planks were all replaced, one by one). There is no particular reason to think that we can cut into the sequence of changes at some particular point, such that before that point formal

[25] Ibid. at 1460.

[26] *Missouri v. Holland*, 252 U.S. 416 (1920) at 433.

constitutional texts "matter" (or matter more than informal processes) while after that point formal constitutional texts do not "matter" (or matter less than informal processes). So there is no particular reason, in our own polity, to distinguish between the original-Constitution-plus-the-first-twelve-amendments, on the one hand, and later amendments, on the other. The irrelevance thesis avoids the generalization problem only by adopting a domain restriction that lacks adequate justification.

I close by emphasizing the limits of this critique. Even if the counterfactual irrelevance thesis is conceptually infirm, a series of causal theses, each addressing a particular amendment, would not be. We might decompose the wholesale irrelevance thesis into a series of retail-level claims that particular amendments did not, in fact, efficaciously cause legal change (sidestepping the critique offered in I.A), combined with the stipulation that no generalization about amendments as a class is possible (sidestepping the critique offered in I.B). In this domesticated version the irrelevance thesis would be shorn of its most arresting implications, but it would retain its impressive core of hard-won historical argumentation.

II. THE GENERIC CASE AGAINST CONSTITUTIONAL AMENDMENT

I shall introduce the generic case against constitutional amendment with the following passage, from an essay by Kathleen Sullivan:

> [R]ecent Congresses have been stricken with amendment fever. More constitutional amendment proposals have been taken seriously now than at any other recent time. Some have even come close to passing.... Many of these amendment are bad ideas. *But they are dangerous apart from their individual merits.* [The Constitution] should be amended sparingly, not used as a chip in short-run political games. This was clearly the view of the framers, who made the Constitution extraordinarily difficult to amend.[27]

The remainder of the essay elaborates this thesis. Americans have traditionally been reluctant to amend the Constitution, for good reasons. First, it is "a bad idea to politicize the Constitution," because "the more a Constitution is politicized, the less it operates as a fundamental charter of government."[28] We should particularly beware of amendments that "impose a controversial social policy," such as the Eighteenth Amendment (repealed by the Twenty-First).[29] "Amendments that embody a specific and debatable social or economic policy allow one generation to tie the hands of another, entrenching approaches that ought to be revisable in the crucible of ordinary politics."[30] Second, "writing short-term policy goals into the Constitution... nearly always turn[s] out to have bad and unintended structural

[27] Kathleen M. Sullivan, "What's Wrong with Constitutional Amendments" in *Great and Extraordinary Occasions: Developing Guidelines for Constitutional Change* (New York City: Century Foundation Press, 1999) 39–40 (emphasis added) [hereinafter Sullivan, *Constitutional Amendments*].

[28] Ibid. at 41.

[29] Ibid.

[30] Ibid. at 41.

consequences," in part because "amendments are passed piecemeal. The framers had to think about how the entire thing fit together."[31] Third, a "danger lurking in constitutional amendments is that of mutiny against the authority of the Supreme Court.... [The Court's] legitimacy is salutary, for it enables the court to settle or at least defuse society's most ideologically charged disputes."[32]

This argument is the clearest statement of a view that I take to be widespread both within and without the legal academy.[33] In the academic and popular commentaries that track Sullivan's argument, the verbal formulas vary – sometimes the injunction is against "tampering" with the Constitution, sometimes the emphasis is on the "divisiveness" of constitutional amendments, sometimes the core point is that only "structural" amendments or amendments expanding "individual rights" are permissible – but the common intellectual premise is something like Sullivan's idea: There is a generic class of reasons to believe that the amendment process is systematically or presumptively suspect.

I will claim, however, that the generic case against amendment rests on the nirvana fallacy: Generic arguments typically fail to compare amendments with the institutional alternatives for producing constitutional change, principally constitutional common law. The alternative to constitutional amendment is not, as generic arguments often imply, a stable subconstitutional order; the alternative is continual judicial updating of the Constitution through flexible common-law constitutionalism. That practice fares no better, and in many cases worse, on the margins of institutional performance the generic case takes to be valuable.

Section A examines some ambiguities in the generic case against constitutional amendment, attempting a charitable reconstruction of the position before proceeding to the business of critique. Section B considers a series of generic arguments. In each case, the infirmity in the argument is some version of the nirvana fallacy; in each case, the main alternative to formal constitutional amendment, constitutional updating by judges, is equally susceptible to the concerns that underpin the generic arguments.

Section C turns to a different critique of the generic case. When internalized by political actors, the generic case produces a presumptive public norm against amending the Constitution, one that acts as a drag on formal constitutional change. If the Article V rules produce the optimal rate of constitutional change, however, then this norm amounts to a form of pernicious double-counting. Political actors should indulge no general reluctance to amend the Constitution; instead, they should simply let the Article V rules weed out some fraction of proposals. On the other hand, if the Article V rules are too lax and allow too frequent amendment, the best response would be to amend Article V itself to increase the cost of enacting amendments, rather than to encourage a fluctuating and uncertain norm that presumes against or disfavors constitutional amendment.

[31] Ibid. at 42.

[32] Ibid.

[33] Ibid. at 3 (questioning "the wisdom of engaging in constitutional change, even to advance popular and legitimate policy outcomes") [hereinafter *Guidelines*]; Naftali Bendavid, "Group Aims to Stem Those Who Would Amend," *Chicago Tribune* (June 18, 1997) A3.

A. An ambiguity

There is a threshold ambiguity concerning the *weight* of the generic case against constitutional amendment. Should it be understood to support rejection of proposals for constitutional amendment, or a (mere) presumption against constitutional amendment? The strongest version of the generic case suggests that all amendment proposals should be rejected. Although this view is absurd on the level of theory, it is commonly encountered in practice, as in the following remarkable statement of a Massachusetts legislator: "I've always been philosophically averse to amending the State Constitution – it doesn't matter what the issue is."[34] If "averse" here means "opposed," rather than "reluctant," this is merely the hypertrophy of the common attitude that "tampering" with the Constitution is objectionable in itself.

More plausible, and also very common, is a weaker version, in which the generic case against constitutional amendment merely supports some sort of presumption against constitutional amendment. The notion of "presumption" here is ambiguous in its turn. Sometimes this is a sort of free-floating substantive rule of thumb to the effect that the Constitution should not be amended "too often," or only (in Madison's words) on "great and extraordinary occasions." In other arguments, however, the presumption takes on a procedural cast, akin to the rule that parties adversely affected by agency action must exhaust administrative remedies before invoking judicial review. Analogously, constitutional amendment should be a last resort, to occur only if subconstitutional processes have proven somehow incapable of solving a problem.

In what follows, I shall take it as understood that each of the generic arguments against amendment can be expressed in stronger or weaker versions, by means of stronger or weaker presumptions. The trade-off inherent in the generic case against amendment is that generic arguments become more plausible as they are implemented by weaker presumptions, but the price for increased plausibility is diminished bite. In the limiting case, generic arguments would become most plausible if reduced to simple tiebreakers. This sort of pallid version of the generic case does not, however, capture the force with which such arguments are typically advanced.

B. The generic arguments

Here I shall list the most prominent generic arguments against constitutional amendment, and offer remarks on each of them in turn. Each of these arguments is unsuccessful, and for similar reasons. Each of them, in different ways, rests on some version of the nirvana fallacy; each of them assumes, arbitrarily, that the objections that can be lodged against the proposed amendment do not also apply to the alternative process of common-law constitutionalism.

AMENDMENTS "POLITICIZE THE CONSTITUTION." An initial reaction is that any slogan of this sort is puzzling in the extreme. In *any* sense that "political" might be given here, the Constitution is already political, or politicized, and it always has been. As a constitution, what else could it possibly be? Whatever else it does, the

[34] Pam Belluck and Katie Zezima, "Gays' Victory Leaves Massachusetts Lawmakers Hesitant," *NY Times* (November 20, 2003) A29.

Constitution sets ground rules that govern a political association, that are politically determined, and that have political consequences.

The picture that animates this argument is a distinction between law, the sphere of constitutional rules, and politics, the sphere of action within the constitutional rules. On this picture, "[l]osers in the short run yield to the winners out of respect for the constitutional framework set up for the long run. This makes the peaceful conduct of ordinary politics possible."[35] But this is illusory, a false alternative. The alternative to formal constitutional amendment is not the placid subconstitutional state of affairs implicitly presupposed here – perhaps the jousting of interest groups for legislative benefits. The concrete alternative to constitutional amendment is judicially developed constitutional law, which itself changes over time in response to political, social, and cultural shifts, and which itself produces *constitutional* winners and losers (not merely losers and winners of the "ordinary" sort). During the decades-long political struggle over the content of constitutional abortion law that has succeeded *Roe v. Wade*,[36] a struggle waged simultaneously in legislatures, agencies, and courts and at all levels of government, proposals have been advanced at various points to amend the Constitution's text to enforce one or another view of the matter. Whatever else might be said about such proposals, it is hard to see anything meaningful in the injunction not to "politicize" the Constitution by enacting them, given the background of constitutional politics – emphatically including judicial politics – against which the proposals have arisen.

AMENDMENTS "CLUTTER UP" THE CONSTITUTION. Another idea is that amendments are objectionable because and to the extent they "clutter up" the Constitution with highly specific rules – causing the Constitution, in John Marshall's words, to "partake of the prolixity of a legal code."[37] On this view, the Constitution's text should be limited to general or high-level principles, as opposed to detailed legal rules.

But the nirvana illusion is at work here as well. The real alternative to a prolix formal constitutional code, promulgated by the amendment process, is a prolix *informal* constitutional code promulgated by judges. Whatever may be said about the value of the latter, it is not "the intelligible Constitution"[38] of general principles that the objection seems to contemplate. Shunting constitutional prolixity from the Constitution's text into the U.S. Reports puts it off the textual books but does nothing to make the overall body of constitutional law any more accessible to officials or citizens.

Consider the notoriously intricate and codelike character of judicially developed free speech law or the tangled underbrush of Fourth Amendment search-and-seizure law. Part of the reason these bodies of law are so highly reticulated is that the underlying texts ("the freedom of speech," "unreasonable searches and seizures") are so skimpy. The judges have had to fill in their content but would not have had to do so had those texts been more expansive and detailed, as other amendments are.

35 Sullivan, *Constitutional Amendments, supra* note 27 at 41.

36 410 U.S. 959 (1973).

37 *McCulloch v. Maryland*, 17 U.S. 316 (1819) at 407.

38 Joseph Goldstein, *The Intelligible Constitution: The Supreme Court's Obligation to Maintain the Constitution as Something We the People Can Understand* (New York: Oxford University Press, 1992).

A complex society will produce complex constitutional law; the only real question is whether it is good to outsource constitutional complexity from the amendment process to the adjudicative process.

AMENDMENTS ARE DIVISIVE OR POLARIZING. This is among the most popular of popular arguments against amendment, and it has gained new prominence in the debate over same-sex marriage.[39] Most charitably construed, the objection here is not to amendment proposals that are actually enacted. Article V's stringent supermajority requirements ensure that successful amendments tend to embody a broad consensus – far more so than many judicial decisions that change constitutional rules. (I discuss these points at length in Part III.) Rather, the claim often seems to be that the decision to formally *propose* an amendment itself has objectionable effects on public discourse or the polity at large.

Although I cannot fully defend the claim here, I believe, as a general matter, that injunctions not to put "polarizing" or "divisive" issues on the public agenda have repressive political, and social effects.[40] They are typically deployed by winners, or insiders, or those privileged by the status quo, to exclude from the public agenda claims of injustice on the part of the disadvantaged. This is a broad assertion, but consider that labor movements and civil rights movements and feminist movements have often been met with similar arguments.[41] Here the injunction not to "divide" or "polarize" shades into the injunction not to "politicize." Losers or outsiders, relative to some status quo ante, want precisely to politicize, to bring political decision making to bear in order to disrupt preexisting political and legal allocations that would remain entrenched absent public action, and that are (at least in the outsiders' view) unjust.[42]

In the setting of constitutional amendments, this picture reemphasizes the point I made above about the generic claim that amendments "politicize" the Constitution. To say that losers or outsiders in the constitutional status quo ante, meaning the status quo established by judge-made constitutional law, should not propose "divisive" or "polarizing" amendments, is to choke off one of the principal avenues of constitutional change. Formal amendment is not the only such channel, of course. Status quo losers can participate in presidential or senatorial politics, with the hope of influencing the selection of judges, in order to overturn the judge-made status quo. But that course of action will itself lead to charges of politicization, or polarization, or divisiveness. Shifting the forum in which the constitutional status quo is challenged does not eliminate the fact of the challenge itself.

So the nirvana illusion here is the same as in (1) above. Judge-made constitutional law is itself inherently and inescapably divisive or polarizing; and it remains

[39] See, e.g., Andrew Sullivan, "Bush and Marriage: A Middle Way?," online: http://www.andrewsullivan.com/main_article.php?artnum=20031210.

[40] A similar point holds against the claim that constitutional "gag rules" can benefit the polity by taking controversial issues off the table. See Stephen Holmes, *Passions and Constraint: On the Theory of Liberal Democracy* (Chicago: University of Chicago Press, 1995). The problem is that constitutional gag rules take issues off the table only by *resolving* them one way or the other; gag rules are never neutral.

[41] See, e.g., Bruce Miroff, "Presidential Leverage over Social Movements: The Johnson White House and Civil Rights" (1981) 43 *The Journal of Politics* 2; Nicol C. Rae, "Class and Culture: American Political Cleavages in the Twentieth Century" (1992) 45 *The Western Political Quarterly* 629 at 638.

[42] Ian Shapiro, "Elements of Democratic Justice" (1996) 24 *Political Theory* 579.

so whether the status quo losers attempt to change it ex post, through litigation seeking a change of course, or ex ante, through influence over judicial selection (that may subsequently produce overrulings). When judges decided that there was a constitutional right to burn the American flag,[43] or to own slaves,[44] the decisions sharply divided Americans who believed the courts were right from those who believed them wrong. A proposal by the latter group to amend the Constitution, over the objections of the former group, adds no additional divisiveness.

AMENDMENTS REPRESENT A "MUTINY" AGAINST THE SUPREME COURT. The "mutiny" metaphor here is Sullivan's, and it is striking. What if the Supreme Court is Captain Bligh, and we are all Fletcher Christian, to be condemned as mutineers no matter how grievous the provocation? Here is the argument behind the metaphor:

> We have lasted two centuries with only twenty-seven amendments because the Supreme Court has been given enough interpretive latitude to adapt the basic charter to changing times. Our high court enjoys a respect and legitimacy uncommon elsewhere in the world. The legitimacy is salutary, for it enables the Court to settle or at least defuse society's most ideologically charged disputes.[45]

One of the premises here is an argument about the supply and demand of constitutional change. Changing circumstances produce demand for changing constitutional law. The supply of new constitutional law is limited; although many institutions participate in its creation, the two most prominent sources are the amendment process, on the one hand, and judge-made constitutional law on the other. Those two sources are at least partial substitutes: judicial updating reduces the demand for constitutional amendment, all else equal, just as the Hughes Court's switch in time may have preempted various New Deal reform proposals.[46]

The basic intuition about comparative statics is sensible, and it is broadly confirmed by empirical work in political science.[47] But it does not at all support the conclusion offered in the remainder of the passage. We may reconstruct the argument as follows: (1) Judicial updating of the Constitution is at least a partial substitute for formal amendments; (2) formal amendments reduce judicial legitimacy; (3) maximizing judicial legitimacy is good for the polity as a whole. Of these, only (1) is explicit; and there is a further assumption, which I will not question, that "legitimacy" is to be interpreted in a purely sociological sense – as something like the Supreme Court's standing in opinion polls over time. Even if (1) is correct, and I believe that it is, the current state of the evidence gives us little reason to subscribe to (2). There is no reason to assume, a priori, or to believe, empirically, that the use of the amendment process tends to undermine the judiciary's legitimacy. [I also bracket the large question raised in (3), whether maximizing the Court's legitimacy is good for the larger polity.]

43 *Texas v. Johnson*, 491 U.S. 397 (1989).

44 *Scott v. Sanford*, 60 U.S. 393 (1857).

45 Sullivan, *Constitutional Amendments*, *supra* note 27 at 42.

46 See, e.g., Richard D. Friedman, "Switching Time and Other Thought Experiments: The Hughes Court and Constitutional Transformation" (1994) 142 *U. Penn. L. Rev.* 1891.

47 Donald S. Lutz, *Toward a Theory of Constitutional Amendment*, in Levinson, *supra* note 2 at 237.

Premise (2) embodies the nirvana illusion that afflicts generic arguments against amendment. Here the illusion takes the form of the unjustified belief that the Court's (sociological) legitimacy is necessarily at a maximum so long as no outside agitators produce amendments that intrude on judicially managed change. On this assumption, the Court's public standing is diminished whenever the amendment process produces outcomes that differ from those the Court would independently choose – perhaps because the amendment effects a visible public rebuke to the judiciary. Behind this assumption doubtless lurks some sort of picture in which amendments enacted to overturn particular Supreme Court decisions (such as the Eleventh and Sixteenth) reduce the Court's public standing.[48]

There is another side to the ledger, however. Premise (1) holds that the lower the rate of amendment, the more updating that the Court must supply; and the need to update constitutional law can itself damage the Court's public standing in straightforward ways. Overrulings, switches in time, creative and novel interpretation, all the tools that judges use to change the course of constitutional adjudication, themselves may draw down the Court's political capital by fracturing the legalistic façade of constitutional interpretation. An equally plausible causal hypothesis is that increasing the rate of amendments might *increase* the Court's sociological legitimacy by reducing the need for judicial self-correction. In particular cases, legitimacy-granting publics might react poorly to judicial flip-flops, while viewing formal amendments that overturn judicial decisions as the proper legal channel for change – the very use of which could suggest that the judges have done their job well, not poorly. This is rankly speculative, but the point is that (2) is rankly speculative as well. It is hard to know about any of this in the abstract; but we cannot simply assume (2), in the faith that a world without (nonjudicial) amendments is the best of all possible worlds to inhabit.

AMENDMENTS HAVE BAD UNINTENDED CONSEQUENCES

Amendments undermine the coherence of constitutional doctrine. I will consider these arguments jointly, for reasons that will become apparent. It is, of course, an admissible argument against a proposed amendment that the proposal will have some particular bad consequences. The argument from bad unintended consequences, however, is different on two counts. First, the bad consequences are precisely those *not* foreseen[49] at the time of debating and voting on the proposal. This is the key feature that makes this a generic argument. The difference is between a caution not to cross the street lest one be hit by *that* oncoming car, and a caution not to leave the house lest something bad occur. Second, the unforeseen bad consequences are sometimes said to be "structural." As Sullivan puts it:

> A second reason to resist writing short-term policy goals into the Constitution is that they nearly always turn out to have bad and unintended structural consequences. This is in part because amendments are passed piecemeal. In contrast, the Constitution was drafted as a whole at Philadelphia. The framers had to think about how the entire thing fit together.[50]

[48] The Eleventh Amendment overturned *Chisholm v. Georgia*, 2 U.S. 419 (1793); the Sixteenth Amendment overturned *Pollock v. Farmers' Loan & Trust Co.*, 157 U.S. 429 (1895).

[49] I will treat unforeseen and unintended as synonymous, ignoring the case of effects that are foreseen but not intended, as in the casuistic doctrine of "double effect."

[50] Sullivan, *Constitutional Amendments, supra* note 27 at 42.

Below I take up the separate idea that "short-term policy goals" should not be written into the Constitution. Here I shall focus on the other main features of the argument in the passage above: (1) the concern with bad and unintended structural consequences, a concern that is underwritten by (2) a concern that amendments produce piecemeal and incoherent, as opposed to globally coherent, constitutional law, and by (3) an assumption that legal coherence is both feasible and desirable.

I shall not question (3) here, although there are institutional reasons to think that a degree of doctrinal incoherence is inevitable,[51] and there are also good reasons to praise incoherence in law, especially in constitutional law.[52] Good coherence is better than incoherence, but bad coherence is worse than incoherence; coherence raises the stakes of constitutional decision making by propagating either good or bad decisions through the legal system. Nor shall I question the dubious historical premise of the argument – that the framers designed a coherent constitutional scheme, as opposed to aggregating competing values and preferences, through horse-trading, into a patchwork document. Those issues aside, the rationale offered in (2) exemplifies the nirvana illusion that underpins the generic case against amendments. The comparison between the framers' globally coherent design, on the one hand, and piecemeal amendment, on the other, is not the right comparison to make. The principal substitute for formal amendment is not formal constitutional conventions, but judicial updating of constitutional law through flexible interpretation. The question is whether piecemeal amendment produces greater incoherence than piecemeal judicial updating, carried out in particular litigated cases, by judicial institutions whose agenda is partly set by outside actors.

There is little reason to believe the latter process more conducive to coherence than the former, and much evidence to suggest that judicial decision making produces a great deal of doctrinal incoherence. We should disavow any implicit picture of judge-made constitutional law as an intricately crafted web of principles whose extension and weight has been reciprocally adjusted. Precisely because judicial updating requires overrulings, reinterpretations, and other breaks in the web of prior doctrine, a system that relies on judicial updating to supply constitutional change – the system that the generic case tends to produce – generates internal pressures toward incoherent doctrine. Constitutional adjudication in America, let us recall, has produced both *Plessy v. Ferguson* and *Brown v. Board*,[53] both *Lochner v. New York* and *West Coast Hotel v. Parrish*,[54] both *Myers v. United States* and *Humphrey's Executor*,[55] both *Dennis v. United States* and *Brandenburg v. Ohio*,[56]

51 See Frank H. Easterbrook, "Ways of Criticizing the Court" (1982) 95 *Harv. L. Rev.* 802.

52 Cf. Andrei Marmor, "Should We Value Legislative Integrity?" Chapter 6 in this volume (suggesting that legislative integrity is not a value). Marmor does not speak to the issue of integrity in adjudicative decisions, however.

53 *Plessy*, 163 U.S. 537 (1896) (racial segregation of public railway passengers is constitutional); *Brown*, 347 U.S. 483 (1954) (racial segregation of public education facilities is unconstitutional).

54 *Lochner*, 198 U.S. 45 (1905) (state law limiting working hours violates freedom of contract); *West Coast Hotel*, 300 U.S. 379 (1937) (minimum wage law constitutional).

55 *Myers*, 272 U.S. 52 (1926) (president may remove executive officials at will); *Humphrey's Executor*, 295 U.S. 602 (1935) (president can only dismiss "quasi-executive" officers with cause).

56 *Dennis*, 341 U.S. 494 (1951) (upholding federal statute against Communists' free speech claims); *Brandenburg*, 395 U.S. 444 (1969) (striking down state statute as violating Ku Klux Klan's free speech rights).

both *Wickard v. Filburn* and *Lopez v. United States*,[57] both *Bowers v. Hardwick* and *Lawrence v. Texas*.[58] Whatever else can be said about this judicial work-product, and whatever other justifications can be given for judge-made constitutional law, deep inner coherence does not seem either a plausible description of the terrain or even a plausible regulative ideal for the system.

The collective authorship of "Great and Extraordinary Occasions," a set of "Guidelines for Constitutional Change,"[59] advances a related argument from coherence. The argument is best illustrated with the example of the proposed amendment that would have stripped free speech protection from the act of burning the American flag. The guideline authors object that the amendment would have been "[in]consistent with related constitutional doctrine that the amendment leaves intact."[60] The problem arises "when framers of amendments focus narrowly on specific outcomes without also thinking more broadly about general legal principles."[61] The Court's decision to label flag burning protected speech was derived from established background principles of judge-made free speech law, whereas a flag desecration amendment would merely have overturned a particular judicial outcome.

Here the nirvana illusion is twofold; the argument underestimates the capacity of specific positive enactments to generate broader principles in the future, and overestimates the principled, as opposed to specific, character of the background free speech doctrine, and constitutional doctrine generally. As to the first point, an argument emphasized by James Landis in the statutory setting, as against defenders of the common-law status quo, was that new statutes may themselves generate new principles when interpreted over time, in part by judges sympathetic to the aims of the new enactment.[62] So too in the constitutional setting. It is easy to imagine future courts generalizing new principles from a flag desecration amendment, principles emphasizing the authority – the right, if you will – of enduring majorities to mark out as fundamental a limited class of symbols or ideals or aspirations, and to grant those symbols immunity from the ordinary hurly-burly of free speech in an open society. The precise contour of such principles is not now apparent, but that is also true whenever courts embark on the development of new lines of constitutional doctrine. In both cases, coherentists should expect a process of mutual adjustment to occur, as new principles elbow their way into the constitutional arena and force old principles to reconcile themselves to a new, narrowed scope.

As to the second point, free speech law cannot usefully be described as a coherent web of principles that yield particular decisions. The principles that do exist underdetermine the outcomes of many cases; after all, four Justices thought that statutes banning flag burning were consistent with the central free speech injunction of content neutrality, and it requires a *great* deal of confidence to declare them

57 *Wickard*, 317 U.S. 111 (1942) (Commerce Clause authorizes the federal government to regulate wheat grown for personal consumption); *Lopez*, 514 U.S. 549 (1995) (student's possession of a firearm near a school may not be regulated under the Commerce Clause).

58 *Bowers*, 478 U.S. 186 (1986) (upholding a state law criminalizing sodomy); *Lawrence*, 539 U.S. 558 (2003) (striking down state antisodomy laws as unconstitutional).

59 Sullivan, *Constitutional Amendments, supra* note 27.

60 Ibid. at 17.

61 Ibid. at 18.

62 See James McCauley Landis, "Statutes and Sources of Law" (1934) *Harvard Legal Essays* 213.

not only wrong, but also trivially or obviously wrong.[63] Thus, much free speech law takes the form of rules, not principles – rules that in many cases have a narrow scope, highly specific content, and that are derived from background principles only with the help of supplemental empirical and institutional premises.[64] Even if a flag desecration amendment generated no broader principles, it would not have represented the intrusion of a particular outcome into a web of principle. It would merely have changed the content of one or a few highly specific rules previously established by judges.

Perhaps the concern with bad unintended consequences can be justified on other grounds even if the coherence rationale fails. An incoherent state of constitutional doctrine is just one type of bad unintended consequence that amendments might produce. Even if the particular concern is not that amendments will produce incoherent constitutional law, still we might hold a generic concern about the bad unforeseen (and possibly "structural") consequences of constitutional amendment. Indeed, the general concern may work better shorn of any connection to coherence. After all, a standard public-policy response to uncertainty about the risks of action is to counsel decision makers to proceed through small steps or piecemeal reform,[65] as opposed to more ambitious global action. Whether or not the counsel is a sound one,[66] it sits uneasily with a preference for coherence, which condemns piecemeal tinkering.

Yet the nirvana illusion occurs on this more general level as well. Here the illusion takes two related forms. The first is the belief that constitutional amendments represent risky action, while the steady state of judge-made constitutional doctrine represents safe inaction. This is a trivial mistake, akin to the crudest defenses of the so-called precautionary principle in environmental law[67] or of the Hippocratic injunction to "do no harm." Inaction may produce the medically worst outcome of all, and the status quo may itself contain dangerous environmental risks. Likewise, a persistent judicial refusal to update obsolete constitutional law can itself produce large political, social, and economic harms; this is a possible account of the mistakes of the Lochner Court.

In a second version, the alternative to formal amendment is not judicial "inaction," but affirmative judicial action to update obsolete doctrine. Here the nirvana illusion is the failure to recognize that judicial updating, as a substitute for formal amendment, can itself produce bad and unforeseen structural consequences. To the extent, for example, that *Morrison v. Olson* rested on a decision to adapt the law of executive power to the era of the imperial presidency,[68] the decision is widely

[63] But see Akhil Reed Amar, "The Case of the Missing Amendments: *R. A. V. v. City of St. Paul*" (1992) 106 *Harv. L. Rev.* 106.

[64] Frederick Schauer, "The Boundaries of the First Amendment: A Preliminary Exploration of Constitutional Salience" (2004) 117 *Harv. L. Rev.* 1765.

[65] Cass R. Sunstein, *One Case at a Time: Judicial Minimalism on the Supreme Court* (Cambridge, Mass.: Harvard University Press, 1999) at 3–6 [Sunstein, *One Case at a Time*]; Karl Popper, *The Poverty of Historicism* (London: Routledge and Kegan Paul, 1957) at 67.

[66] Robert E. Goodin, *Political Theory and Public Policy* (Chicago: University of Chicago Press, 1982) at 28–34; Jon Elster, "Consequences of Constitutional Choice: Reflections on Tocqueville" in Jon Elster and Rune Slagsted, eds., *Constitutionalism and Democracy* (New York: Cambridge University Press, 1988) 82.

[67] Cass R. Sunstein, "Beyond the Precautionary Principle" (2003) 151 *U. Penn. L. Rev.* 1003.

[68] Abner S. Greene, "Checks and Balances in an Era of Presidential Lawmaking" (1994) *U. Chi. L. Rev.* 123 at 174–6; cf. Lawrence Lessig and Cass R. Sunstein, "The President and the Administration" (1994) 94

thought to have tampered with the deep structure of government in disastrous ways – although this may not strictly count as an unforeseen consequence, given Justice Scalia's dissent.

I conclude that there is no way to leverage a concern for disrupting coherence, or a broader concern for unforeseen consequences more generally, into a generic caution about constitutional amendment. Anything that people or institutions do or fail to do may result in bad unforeseen consequences. Statutes may produce them, but so may the failure to enact statutory reforms; judicial decisions may produce them, but so may judicial "inaction"; and so too for constitutional amendments. The worry about perverse consequences suggests nothing in particular; it yields paralysis, not safety.

Amendments should not encode "mere social policies." Usually, as in Sullivan, this argument rests on a contrast between "controversial" or "short-term" social policies, on the one hand, and "structural amendments to tie our hands against short-term sentiments," on the other.[69] Here the stock example of constitutionalized social policy is the Eighteenth Amendment, the Prohibition amendment, repealed by the Twenty-first. The Prohibition amendment has often been said to result from a passing sociopolitical frenzy, a sort of collective akrasia. And the Prohibition analogy has been invoked to condemn the gamut of amendment proposals, from the balanced budget and term limits amendments to flag desecration and same-sex marriage.

Here two points are important. The first is familiar: Judge-made constitutional rules, no less than amendments, often represent or embody "mere social policies." What else are we to call the rule that prosecutors must hold an arraignment within forty-eight hours of arrest,[70] or the quondam rule that states may not tax interstate goods that remain in their "original packages"[71]? The reason that judicial constitutionalism not infrequently operates at this strikingly low level of generality is that judges must often implement constitutional concepts through specific doctrinal conceptions,[72] such that any particular doctrinal conception might seem arbitrary even though some such conception is indispensable. There is a parallel relationship between specific amendments and the more general political commitments that underlie them. As I suggest shortly, the Prohibition and flag-burning amendments both represented policy conceptions that attempted to implement larger political concepts and commitments. In the case of both amendments and judge-made law, specific legal policies can be condemned as "mere social policies" if, but only if, one detaches the policy from the underlying commitments that animate it.

Second, the idea that "social policies" should not be encoded in the Constitution, and the accompanying prohibition analogy, are in my view both vacuous at the operational level. What produces such widespread agreement on the

Colum. L. Rev. 1 at 104. There are many historical controversies here. I mean only to offer an account of what the Justices in the majority may have believed themselves to be doing.

69 Sullivan, *Constitutional Amendments, supra* note 27 at 44.

70 See *Gerstein v. Pugh,* 420 U.S. 103 (1975).

71 See *Brown v. Maryland,* 25 U.S. 419, 441–2 (1827), repudiated by *Michelin Tire Corp. v. Wages,* 423 U.S. 276, 282–3 (1976).

72 See Richard H. Fallon, Jr., *Implementing the Constitution* (Cambridge, Mass.: Harvard University Press, 2001).

injunction against constitutionalizing "mere" social policy is that no one ever seeks to violate it. No serious constitutional movement ever describes itself as seeking to encode a mere social policy in the Constitution, as opposed to a structural or rights-protecting or otherwise fundamental sort of policy or legal rule. Any constitutional movement that becomes nationally prominent features at least a core of leaders and activists who describe themselves as engaged in structural or fundamental reform. Thus, Stephen Presser can say, quite rightly in my view, that the "social policy" criticism of the flag desecration amendment missed the main argument of the amendment's proponents:

> [O]ne person's narrowness is another person's entirety, at least where constitutional amendments are concerned. Most academics and intellectuals regard the flag as a mere piece of colored cloth, but the eighty percent of Americans who favor the amendment regard it as a unique symbol and physical expression of the self-sacrifice of loved ones who served their country. They believe that protecting the flag from desecration – as the Supreme Court no longer permits – is fundamental to national honor, and that a nation in which nothing is officially sacred is a nation in danger of moral collapse.[73]

Those who approved of the flag desecration amendment should find Presser's argument devastating as against the social policy objection. Those who opposed the amendment will think that Presser's argument rests on a category mistake. Abolition was fundamental, the civil rights movement was fundamental, reproductive choice is fundamental, but protecting the flag from desecration is not. Given their shared major premise and different minor premises, both sides are right; the debate is purely over the application of a principle held in common by all concerned. It is not that anyone disputes the injunction against constitutionalizing mere social policy; it is that no one takes *their* cherished amendment to violate the principle.

The injunction against encoding social policies in the Constitution is largely vacuous, not wholly so. It might rule out a small class of low-level policies; let us have no amendments to constitutionalize the earned income tax credit! The point, however, is that there are no serious or influential constitutional movements organized for the purpose of putting policies like that in the Constitution anyway. The Prohibitionists, of course, did not see themselves as advocating a constitutionalized social policy, in the disparaging sense. They saw temperance as the token of an essential moral and spiritual and socially progressive crusade. If we now see things differently, that gives us no help at all for the future, because we cannot now guess which of our own crusades that we now cherish as fundamental will be dismissed as akratic frenzies in the hindsight of later generations. The owl of Minerva flies at dusk, which means that the injunction against encoding social policies bites only where and when it is not needed. When it is needed, it does not bite.

Amendments debase the symbolic currency of constitutionalism. It is hard to find explicit statements of the view I want to address here, although I believe it to be implicit in the thinking of many, especially those who on other grounds hold the view that amendments are largely devoid of material significance for constitutional law – a close cousin of the irrelevance thesis discussed in Part I, or an interpretation

[73] Stephen B. Presser, "Constitutional Amendments: Dangerous Threat or Democracy in Action?" (2000) 5 *Tex. Rev. L. & Pol.* 209 at 221.

of it. So, on this implicit view, amendments are essentially constitutional symbols, akin to national holidays, and too many amendments (and perhaps too frequent a rate of amendment) would debase the symbolic currency of constitutionalism, just as making every day a national holiday would mean no holidays at all.

I will assume here, contra Part I, that the most robust versions of the irrelevance thesis are correct. Even on that premise, the symbolic-currency argument rests on the same nirvana illusion we have seen throughout. Constitutional processes other than amendment – most dramatically, judicial decisions that identify or create "new" constitutional rights through interpretation of vague texts like due process or equal protection – themselves may debase, at the margin, the symbolic currency of rights. Before and after federal and state judges and local officials moved to protect gay rights and to increase opportunities for same-sex marriage, proponents drew an analogy between the gay rights movement and the civil rights movement. The analogy has been publicly disputed by some African Americans,[74] fearing that the analogy devalues the moral credit that has accrued to civil rights groups by virtue of African American history. The debasement problem arises because any pluralist democracy contains multiple groups that compete for claims on the public conscience, for a pot of moral currency that is not infinitely expandable. Suppressing one margin of symbolic competition, for symbolic constitutional amendments perhaps, will only exacerbate competition on other margins, say judicial constitutionalism.

To say that judge-made constitutional law is also subject to the debasing effect of cumulative symbolism is not a critique of the irrelevance thesis. That thesis is compatible with the view – although it does not itself *entail* the view – that judge-made constitutional law is often irrelevant in precisely the same sense,[75] that *both* formal amendments *and* judicial decisions are often or usually no more than superstructural froth. The only point I wish to make is that the irrelevance thesis, even if established, would neither commit us to nor justify the further, independent view that constitutional amendments uniquely or distinctively threaten to debase the symbolic currency of constitutionalism, as compared to judge-made constitutional doctrine.

Amendments should not nationalize questions best left to the states. Here the nirvana illusion is the failure to recognize that federalism arguments apply to federal constitutional decisions by judges just as much as they do to amendments. Every Supreme Court decision that puts some forms of government action off-limits to all states, and perhaps to the federal government as well, nationalizes the relevant question.[76] When the flag desecration amendment was proposed, it would have been silly to say that amendments should not nationalize questions best left to the states; the Court's flag-burning decisions had already done that. The only question

[74] Dawn Turner Trice, "Blacks' opposition to gay civil rights ignores history," *Chicago Tribune* (March 29, 2004) B1.

[75] A view that finds support in Gerald N. Rosenberg, *The Hollow Hope: Can Courts Bring About Social Change?* (Chicago: University of Chicago, 1991) at 10–36; Michael I. Klarman, *From Jim Crow to Civil Rights: The Supreme Court and the Struggle for Racial Equality* (New York: Oxford University Press, 2004).

[76] Some forms of "constitutional" law bind the states but not the federal government. The dormant commerce "clause" is an example.

was whether those decisions should be left undisturbed or whether the issue should be remitted to the discretion of states and the federal government. Although the federal government might in turn have prohibited flag burning nationwide, as it had previously tried to do, that shows only that federal statutes are yet another instrument that might be objectionable on the ground that they commit questions to the wrong level of government.

A NOTE ON "RIGHTS" AND "STRUCTURE." So far we have been examining strictly generic arguments, which purport to identify bad features of amendments generally. Narrower arguments, however, sometimes identify some subcategory of disfavored amendments. Usually such arguments turn on a distinction between "rights" provisions and "structure" provisions and allow broader scope for amendments to affect structure than to affect rights. For concreteness, I will consider the following version of this view: All previous amendments can be categorized as either (1) expanding individual rights or (2) improving government structure, and amendments outside these two categories should be rejected or disfavored.[77]

This view seems untenable, on both empirical and normative grounds. The historical premise that no amendments have limited individual rights is very dubious.[78] A major purpose of the Thirteenth Amendment was to contract an individual right: the substantive due process right to own slaves, identified by the Court in *Scott v. Sandford*.[79] Section 1 of the Amendment reallocated the right to control the slaves' labor from the slaveowners to the slaves themselves, a classic taking from A to give to B – which is why the fourth section of the Fourteenth Amendment later specified that no compensation would be due to the slaveowners.

But let us suppose the historical premise true, or largely so. The hard question is what normative significance this has. Why should those categories, into which previous amendments happened to fall, be taken as exclusive? Why should not other types of amendments be added as circumstances change? In particular, we might imagine a category of amendments that

> (3) restrict judicially identified individual rights in order to protect collectively held symbols or values or aspirations.

[77] Sullivan, *Constitutional Amendments*, supra note 27; Cass R. Sunstein, "President Versus Precedent: Bush's reckless bid for an amendment defies an Oval Office tradition," *Los Angeles Times* (February 26, 2004) B13.

[78] In addition to the Thirteenth Amendment, discussed in text, there are scattered constitutional provisions that directly restrict individual rights. See, e.g., U.S. Const. Amdt. XIV, §3 (establishing lustration rules and civil disabilities for former confederates). Congress and state legislatures had previously attempted to impose similar rules by statute, but the Supreme Court invalidated the laws on civil-libertarian grounds. See *Ex Parte Garland*, 71 U.S. (4 Wall.) 333 (1866) (invalidating, on bill of attainder and ex post facto grounds, a federal statute that excluded former rebels from the Supreme Court bar); *Cummings v. Missouri*, 71 U.S. (4 Wall.) 277 (1866) (invalidating a state disqualification and loyalty-oath provision as an ex post facto law). Less directly, some provisions that improve governmental structure might be understood to do so precisely by restricting individual rights. Consider the Twenty-second Amendment, which imposes a two-term limit on the presidency, and thus harms individuals who would otherwise have the "right," guaranteed by the Qualification Clauses of Article II, to stand for election to a third presidential term. Compare U.S. Const. Amdt. XXII with Art. II, §1, cl. 5.

[79] *Supra* note 44 at 450–2.

Is there a generic argument against (3)? Burkeans may believe or hope that there is some immanent logic underlying U.S. amendment practices, a logic that might justify taking categories (1) and (2) as exhausting the set of permissible amendments. Perhaps; it is never clear what to make of Burkean claims of this sort, which by their nature resist any request to explain the theory that might justify the immanent principle.

Another possibility, however, is that our ability to sort the previous twenty-seven amendments into categories (1) and (2) is sheer curve-fitting; it is an artifact of the small number of amendments, in turn an artifact of the stringency of Article V's supermajority requirements. The list of approved amendments turns out to be exquisitely sensitive to small changes in the Article V rules. Had Article V, for example, required the approval of only a majority of states, the Constitution would contain, inter alia, the 1924 Child Labor Amendment.[80] That amendment would have been a category (3) amendment in spades: It was opposed not only on the predictable ground of federalism but also on the ground that (in the words of its chief opponent) it was "a highly socialistic measure – an assault against individual liberty,"[81] presumably the joint liberty of parents and employers to bind children to labor contracts.

I conclude that the generic case against constitutional amendment fails. There is no basis for global or presumptive skepticism of the amendment process as a means of constitutional change. The standard attempts to identify deficiencies in the amendment process fail to compare the institutional alternatives: They identify features that are common to both the amendment process and the alternative institutional process of constitutional common law.

C. Voting rules, public norms, and Article V

In this section, I will attempt to clarify the relationship between the generic case and the formal supermajoritarian voting rules governing constitutional amendment. Most charitably understood, the generic case proposes a norm of public action that increases the inertial burden facing amendment proponents, over and above the inertial burden that already exists by virtue of Article V's requirement of voting supermajorities in Congress and the states. Yet if the Article V rules already produce the optimal rate of constitutional change, this supplemental norm represents a form of pernicious double-counting, producing an excessively low rate of amendment. If Article V is too lax, permitting more change than is optimal, a public norm that disfavors amendments is not the best response. Better would simply be an amendment to change the Article V rules themselves to make amendments more difficult.

80 See Stephen Griffin, "The Nominee is . . . Article V" (1995) 12 *Const. Comm.* 171. The amendment was ratified by twenty-eight states. See Richard E. Bernstein, with Jerome Agel, *Amending America: If We Love the Constitution So Much, Why Do We Keep Trying to Change It?* (New York: Times Books, 1993) at 180.

81 David E. Kyvig, *Explicit and Authentic Acts: Amending the U.S. Constitution, 1776–1995* (Lawrence: University of Kansas Press, 1996) at 259.

What is the optimal pace of constitutional change? A familiar view is that constitutional change would occur too quickly in a legal regime that authorized constitutional amendment by a simple majority vote of the national legislative body. This view does not or need not rest on the essentialist argument that supermajoritarian amendment processes are definitional of constitutionalism. Not a few liberal democracies with written constitutions permit or have permitted national parliaments to amend the constitution by simple majorities;[82] in such regimes the constitution functions as a special type of higher-order statute. Instead, the view is a strictly consequentialist one. It is desirable, the argument runs, that the pace of constitutional change be slower than the pace of change of ordinary law. Supermajority requirements for amendment build in a status quo bias of a healthy sort, allowing the constitution to serve as a precommitment device against ill-advised constitutional change. To be sure, this sort of justification for supermajoritarian amendment requirements is famously controversial. The notion of a constitutional precommitment is conceptually obscure and normatively dubious, because of the dead hand problem,[83] because there is no agent external to society that can enforce the precommitment,[84] and because of subsequent disagreement over what the terms of the prior precommitment were.[85]

In this section, however, I propose to bracket these large questions in favor of a narrower point. I will assume that some independent theory specifies the optimal rate of constitutional change, and that in light of that theory it is desirable to build in a status quo bias through supermajority voting requirements for amendment. Even given these premises, the generic case against amendment is exposed to an objection of the following form.

When internalized by political actors, the generic case against amendment becomes a public norm that places a kind of drag on the enactment of amendments. It is hard to see how such a norm could be beneficial. Either the formal voting rule for amendment captures the optimal rate of change or it does not. Suppose first that it does. In that case, any additional public norm that causes constitutional decision makers to filter out amendments that they would otherwise favor will result in a suboptimal rate of amendment; the Constitution will be amended too rarely. On the assumption that the formal supermajoritarian voting rule is optimal, to supplement the status quo bias built into the voting rule by an internalized public norm disfavoring amendment is a form of pernicious double-counting.

To elicit the issue here, consider the following argument of Sullivan's: "[The Constitution] should be amended sparingly, not used as a chip in short-run political games. *This was clearly the view of the framers, who made the Constitution extraordinarily difficult to amend.*"[86] But this is puzzling, as the following analogy may help to illustrate: A legislature must decide a quotidian issue governed by simple

[82] See, e.g., Aust. Const. Art. 44 §1; N.Z. Const. (Constitution Act 1986) Part 3 §15.1.

[83] Louis W. Hensler III, "The Recurring Constitutional Convention: Therapy for a Democratic Constitutional Republic Paralyzed by Hypocrisy" (2003) 7 *Tex. Rev. L.* & Pol. 263 at 290–300.

[84] Jon Elster, *Ulysses Unbound: Studies in Rationality, Precommitment and Constraints* (New York: Cambridge University Press, 2000) at 157.

[85] Jeremy Waldron, "Precommitment and Disagreement" in Larry Alexander, ed., *Constitutionalism: Philosophical Foundations* (New York: Cambridge University Press, 1998) 271.

[86] Sullivan, *Constitutional Amendments, supra* note 27 at 39–40 (emphasis added).

majority voting. In this legislature, as in many others (although not the Senate), a slight status quo bias is built into majority rule by a supplemental rule that a tie vote defeats a bill. A legislator argues against the proposed bill as follows: "We should approach this proposal with a presumption against amending the code of laws. After all, the framers of our legislative rules built a status quo bias right into our voting rule itself." But *if* the background voting rule already captures the right amount of status quo bias, then the legislators should just decide whether they think the proposal is good or bad, "on the merits," and let the voting rule take care of the rest. Sullivan is quite right that the framers wanted the Constitution to be difficult to amend. But if the formal supermajority requirements of Article V already create as much difficulty as the framers desired, then the addition of a normative presumption against amendment would push the level of difficulty past the optimum.

Suppose then that the formal voting rule for amendment is too lax – that it permits a supraoptimal rate of constitutional change, as specified by our background theory. The generic case might then be defended as an informal norm of public action that supplements the voting rule, topping it up to the optimum. Against this view, however, there are two objections. The first is that the Article V supermajority voting rules for amendment are already, in global perspective, radical outliers. Very few constitutional democracies make their constitutional amendment process as difficult as the United States'.[87] Perhaps other democracies' rules are themselves *far* too lax, or perhaps their rules are optimal in their circumstances while our rules are optimal in our circumstances. The more natural suspicion, however, is just that our Constitution is too difficult to amend. At the very least, it is extremely difficult to believe that Article V is itself too lax, as the defense of the generic case we are now considering must suppose.

There is also a second objection. If the voting rule is too lax and needs to be topped up, the better course might simply be to amend Article V to increase the requisite supermajorities – say, three-fourths of each house of Congress followed by five-sixths of the states. This is a claim about rules and standards. If our background theory specifies the optimum with some precision, then an adjustment to the voting rule can hit the optimum more accurately than can an informal norm of public action. Such norms are high-variance standards: Although everyone may say that there is a "presumption" against amendments, we have seen that this is an ill-defined metaphor drawn from the rules of evidence, and different people may, predictably will, mean different things by it, and what they mean will fluctuate over time. At one extreme lies the mere tiebreaking presumption that is almost always overcome, at the other lies the nigh-irrebuttable presumption advanced by the Massachusetts legislator who proclaimed himself averse to all constitutional amendments. There is no reason to be confident that a fluctuating, high-variance public norm of this sort will usually or even predictably produce the right amount of supplemental drag on the amendment process, as specified by our background theory. Where it does do so, the success will be but a lucky coincidence.

The second objection is incomplete, for the following reason: As against the variance costs of an informal norm, we must consider that the social costs of generating

[87] Lutz, *supra* note 47 at 260.

such a norm are plausibly lower than the costs of amending the amendment rules. Generating a norm of this sort through public argument may well be easier than amending Article V through public action. This is a curious way to save the generic case against amendment, however. It rests on two premises that are in some tension with each other: on the one hand, that Article V is too lax and so needs to be topped up with a supplemental norm and, on the other hand, that Article V is so stringent as to exclude the alternative course of amending the voting rules themselves. This is not quite a contradiction, but the two premises do not leave much space through which the generic case might slip.

III. CONSTITUTIONAL UPDATING: AN INSTITUTIONAL COMPARISON

So far, I have suggested that constitutional amendments are neither systematically irrelevant nor generically suspect. Those suggestions are both negative or critical. Here I turn to constructive analysis, attempting to elaborate an affirmative view of constitutional amendment. The crucial question, on this view, is a comparative evaluation of institutional processes. The Constitution must be updated over time; which institution (or set or mix of institutions) shall be entrusted with the task? Section A clarifies the questions and considers the objection that nothing useful can be said about the institutional comparison unless we specify some substantive theory of what a good constitution would contain. Section B examines the strengths and weaknesses of the amendment process, on the one hand, and common-law constitutionalism, on the other. Section C sketches the empirical conditions under which one process or the other might prove superior.

A. Preliminaries

We want to conduct a comparative, and evenhanded, evaluation of the institutional processes that engage in constitutional updating over time. We might approach this choice at the level of constitutional design, asking how an optimal amendment process would look, given other features of the Constitution, and so on. That is a worthy project, but not the one I pursue here. I will take the current Article V rules as fixed. Instead, I assume that the constitutional rules and political constraints, even taken together, leave some freedom of action or play within the system. Political actors may choose to steer more or less constitutional change, and varying types of constitutional problems, through the Article V process, on the one hand, or the processes of constitutional common law, on the other. We are interested in the normative question which choice they should make, under what circumstances.

Taking the constitutional rules as given, I will address three preliminary questions. The first question is what, precisely, the institutional alternatives should be taken to be. I will assume away the Jeffersonian possibility of periodic constitutional conventions sitting to draft the whole constitution anew. The formal Article V amendment process is one means of constitutional updating, but the alternative of common-law constitutionalism is harder to define with precision.

On one view, constitutional change outside of Article V is *not* primarily constitutional common law, if constitutional common law is taken to mean judge-made law.[88] (Equivalently, we may say that constitutional common law is the sole alternative to Article V, but then simply define constitutional common law to include constitutional change by nonjudicial actors.) On this picture, most constitutional change outside of Article V is initiated by nonjudicial actors, and perhaps completed by those actors as well; judges often simply acquiesce in structural innovations produced by legislative and executive actors, innovations that are so large scale as to change the constitutional order.[89] Consider, for example, the large role played by nonjudicial actors in the rise of the administrative state and the development of presidential power in the twentieth century.

This picture is doubtless a valuable corrective to an exclusive focus on judge-made constitutional law. But we should also be careful not to understate the leading role of judges in producing or at least ratifying non–Article V constitutional change. Here the distinction between constitutional rights and constitutional structure is useful. As far as rights are concerned, few deny the leading role of the federal judiciary in constitutional updating. As Dennis Mueller puts it, "The U.S. Constitution contains broad definitions of rights, and the task of amending their definitions to reflect changes in the country's economic, social and political characteristics has been largely carried out by the Supreme Court."[90]

As for structure, it is more plausible to say that large-scale change occurs outside the judiciary, that the judges simply get out of the way of it, and that the outcomes are the same as those that would have occurred had the judges simply gotten out of the business of constitutional review altogether. But getting out of the way, as the judges did after the New Deal, required capacious interpretation of the national government's powers – which was itself just another type of judicial updating. It is illusory to think that structural innovations can achieve constitutional status through silent judicial acquiescence. Many such innovations have developed over generations, and seemingly become entrenched, only to be rejected by the judges when the issue was squarely posed. Consider the legislative veto, which became a ubiquitous feature of federal law between World War I and 1983, when the Supreme Court invalidated all such provisions at a stroke.[91] Many thought the legislative veto was an entrenched nonjudicial structural change, a fait accompli that the judges would have to ratify; but the judges did not think so.

The lesson of the legislative-veto episode is that structural changes developed by the political branches are always constitutionally insecure until the judges put an affirmative stamp of approval on them; judicial acquiescence in the sense of inaction will not do. In that sense, there is no such thing as nonjudicial constitutional change outside the Article V process. Unless and until change has been ratified by a formal amendment, there is always a residual risk of judicial invalidation. Despite the New Deal's transformation of American public law, the absence of a New Deal

[88] Stephen M. Griffin, "Constitutionalism in the United States: From Theory to Politics" Sanford Levinson, ed., in *Responding to Imperfection: The Theory and Practice of Constitutional Amendment* (Princeton, N.J.: Princeton University Press, 1995) 37.

[89] See, e.g., William N. Eskridge, Jr., and John Ferejohn, *Super-Statutes: The New American Constitutionalism*, Chapter 15 in this volume.

[90] Dennis C. Mueller, *Constitutional Democracy* (New York: Oxford University Press, 1996) at 223.

[91] *INS v. Chadha*, 462 U.S. 919 (1983). The legislative veto lives on as a legal tool in congressional–executive interaction, but a legally unenforceable one. See Louis Fisher, "The Legislative Veto: Invalidated, It Survives" (1993) 56 *Law & Contemp. Probs.* 273.

Amendment means that the Court can flirt with retro-restrictive interpretations of the Commerce Clause, and originalist law professors can seriously urge the judges to reinstate the pre-1937 "Constitution in Exile."[92]

So the two institutional processes for updating that I will compare here are the Article V process, on the one hand, and judge-made constitutional law, on the other. A second preliminary question is in what sense these processes are alternatives. After all, under the current rules, judicial updating of constitutional doctrine is always potentially available and occurs continuously. And even well-motivated political actors may resort to proposing and securing amendments when they believe that common-law constitutionalism has produced a bad outcome. Amendments are unlikely ever to be the exclusive means of constitutional updating, given the judges' current authority to engage in judicial review. But all this is compatible with the assumption that amendments and judicial updating are at least partial substitutes, that political actors can affect the relative mix of amendments and judicial updating, and that the mix might be better or worse as it contains more or less change produced by one institutional process or the other, and as certain types of problems are channeled through one process or the other.

We should pause to emphasize the qualifier that amendments and judicial updating are substitutes in some circumstances, but not in all. In other circumstances, amendments and judicial updating may be complements rather than substitutes; political constraints may rule out one or both means of change; or political constraints may make both inevitable if either occurs. As a practical matter, three cases are of the greatest interest: (1) Widespread consensus for a given change does not exist and cannot be generated, so that the supermajoritarian amendment process cannot be used. (2) Widespread consensus exists or is generated by the amendment process; the social forces that produce consensus are so strong that they soon force the courts to adjust the constitutional rules as well, so there is no real choice between amendment and judicial updating. This is the sort of case Strauss emphasizes when he argues that amendments are not necessary for constitutional change. (3) Widespread consensus exists or could be generated by the amendment process, but that consensus has not yet forced judicial updating. Political actors enjoy some freedom to steer change through the amendment process or through the judicial process (by means of judicial appointments and other sources of influence); there is a substitution effect between these two avenues of change.

Case (3) is the one I address here. How often that case occurs is an empirical question, but there is no reason to believe, in the abstract, that Cases (1) and (2) exhaust the possibilities; the political constraints are probably not so tight as all that. The tentative suggestion that rates of amendment vary inversely with the flexibility of judicial interpretation across polities[93] also suggests that Case (3) occurs with nontrivial frequency. The most famous example of this case is the New Deal, whose leaders faced a real choice between managing change through

[92] The literature stems from Douglas H. Ginsburg, *Delegation Running Riot*, Regulation, 1995 (Washington, DC: Cato Institute) (reviewing David Schoenbrod, *Power Without Responsibility: How Congress Abuses the People Through Delegation* [New Haven, Conn.: Yale University Press, 1993]).

[93] See Lutz, *supra* note 47.

the amendment process or through judicial updating of the Constitution.[94] Their choice of the latter course proved fateful; the judicial avenue made New Deal constitutional reforms easier to obtain but also less enduring, as I mentioned above and shall amplify below.

Finally, by what criteria are we to evaluate the institutional alternatives? A wholly substantive view would hold that it is impossible to say anything useful about an institutional comparison without a fully specified account of what rules a good constitution would contain. On this view, what we want to know is which institutional process will tend overall to produce better constitutional law; and we cannot answer that question without knowing what better constitutional law would look like.

I do not believe this, nor do I believe that anyone else really believes it either. Here as elsewhere, it is often not only reasonable but inescapable to consider institutional issues without a fully specified theory of the good constitution. Theoretical approaches might converge, from different starting points, to an overlapping consensus[95] or incompletely theorized agreement[96] on mid-level institutional ideas. The emphasis is on the conditions under which decisions are made, not on the results of decision making; disagreement about the outputs of some decision-making process can be bracketed in favor of a focus on the inputs to that process. The relevant variables are ground-level features of the alternative institutional processes that can be evaluated without recourse to a comprehensive account of constitutionalism.

B. Institutions and updating

Let us turn to a comparison of institutional processes. I suggest that the Article V process takes a relatively abstract perspective, detached from the facts of particular cases; is relatively free from the influence of past judicial decisions; incorporates a relatively wider range of professions and perspectives; produces more enduring constitutional settlements, at higher up-front cost; and emphasizes the benefits of rigidity over the benefits of flexibility.[97] All of these differences produce both costs and benefits that vary across different domains; neither process is better universally or in the abstract. After identifying the structural trade-offs, III.C sketches some empirical conditions under which either process shows to best advantage.

ABSTRACTION AND INFORMATION. A structural constraint on common-law constitutionalism is that decisions about constitutional updating are made in the setting of particular litigated cases and controversies. By virtue of the prohibition on advisory opinions in the Article III courts, judges deciding constitutional cases have before them flesh-and-blood parties whose particular circumstances are often arresting or dramatic and who often come to exemplify various claims for or against constitutional change. This focus on the particular case is sometimes

[94] See Kyvig, *supra* note 81 at ch. 13.

[95] John Rawls, *A Theory of Justice* (Cambridge, Mass.: Belknap Press of Harvard University Press, 1971).

[96] Cass R. Sunstein, *Legal Reasoning and Political Conflict* (New York: Oxford University Press, 1996) at 35–8.

[97] For a different (but partly overlapping) list of comparative considerations, see Vile, *Constitutional Change in the United States, supra* note 3 at 85–115.

said, and often assumed, to improve the quality of judicial decisions. The concrete setting of litigated cases, on this view, provides judges with information that legislators or amendment drafters lack. The contrast is just a matter of degree, of course. Participants in the amendment process may draw on vivid anecdotes, while courts may, within limits, frame their deliberations in more or less abstract ways. But matters of degree are important. The case-or-controversy requirement in courts creates an insistent structural pressure toward focus on the concrete, a pressure that has no obvious analogue in the amendment process.

There is a cost to the focus on particulars, however. Abstraction may for many reasons represent a virtue, and information a vice. It is not the case that decisions made with more information are always superior to decisions made with less information. For one thing, the information that comes from the presence of particular parties may produce a kind of inferential error: Boundedly rational judges may err by assuming that the parties at bar exemplify the average or modal case within some larger class, whereas the parties may in fact represent atypical outliers in one or another respect. Consider, as a possible example, the majority opinion in *INS v. Chadha*. As Justice White noted in dissent, the *Chadha* majority invalidated "an entire class of statutes based on . . . a somewhat atypical and more-readily indictable exemplar of the class."[98] Another possibility is that the presence of flesh-and-blood parties may induce cognitive failure on the judges' part. One mechanism here is salience, a heuristic that causes decision makers to overweight the importance of vivid, concrete foreground information and to underweight the importance of abstract, aggregated background information.[99] A risk is that judicial updating will be distorted, in various ways, because judges overreact to the parties before them, perhaps by underestimating the relatively abstract social benefits that result from governmental infliction of vivid social harms on those parties.

That the amendment process is less tightly focused on highly salient particulars is in part a good. Federal and state legislators considering amendments may draw on the particulars of prior judicial decisions, but also possess a broader range of data produced by legislative fact-finding and the submissions of competing interest groups. Although amici, expert witnesses, and judicial notice of "legislative" facts allow the adjudicative process to partially compensate for the structurally superior fact-finding capacities of legislatures, common-law adjudication is in the end lashed to a particular set of facts in a way the amendment process is not. Most importantly, abstraction produces a kind of neutrality or impartiality. Participants in the amendment process enjoy a broader, systemic perspective, one that ranges simultaneously over sets of cases and that sees the costs in one part of the system that are necessary to produce benefits in another part. That enlarged perspective plausibly improves the ability of constitutional amenders, relative to that

[98] *INS*, 462 U.S. at 974 (White, J. dissenting).

[99] See Scott Plous, *The Psychology of Judgment and Decision-Making* (New York: McGraw-Hill, 1993) (discussing the salience heuristic and the closely related heuristics of vividness and availability). Cf. Robert M. Reyes, William C. Thompson, and Gordon H. Bower, "Judgmental Biases Resulting from Differing Availabilities of Arguments" (1980) 39 *J. Personality & Soc. Psychol.* 2 at 5–12 (demonstrating that vivid, concrete information exerts greater influence on mock jury deliberations than abstract, pallid information). Chris Guthrie, Jeffrey J. Rachlinski, and Andrew J. Wistrich, "Inside the Judicial Mind" (2001) 86 *Cornell L. Rev.* 777 (discussing the impact of cognitive illusions on judges).

of constitutional judges, to make the large-scale tradeoffs, influenced by implicit or explicit cost-benefit analysis, that are indispensable to systemic constitutional policymaking.

PRECEDENT AND PATH DEPENDENCE. An important advantage of common-law constitutional adjudication is the discipline provided by precedent, and by the related common-law emphasis on analogical reasoning. Precedent and analogical reasoning conserve on the costs of information, encourage consistency over time, and ensure a kind of Burkean epistemic humility that dampens sudden or radical shifts in policy.[100]

These points, however, capture only one side of the ledger. Precedent, and the constraint that new decisions be related analogically to old decisions, effect a partial transfer of authority from today's judges to yesterday's judges. As against claims of ancestral wisdom, Bentham emphasized that prior generations necessarily possess less information than current generations.[101] If the problem is that changing circumstances make constitutional updating necessary, it is not obvious why it is good that current judges should be bound either by the specific holdings or by the intellectual premises and assumptions of the past. Weak theories of precedent may build in an escape hatch for changed circumstances, but the escape hatch in turn weakens the whole structure, diluting the decision-making benefits said to flow from precedent.

Another cost of precedent is path dependence. Path dependence is an ambiguous term, but a simple interpretation in the judicial setting is that the order in which decisions arise is an important constraint on the decisions that may be made. Judges who would, acting on a blank slate, choose the constitutional rule that is best for the polity in the changed circumstances, may be barred from reaching the rule, even though they would have reached it had the cases arisen in a different order. Precedent has the effect of making some optimal rules inaccessible to current decision makers. When technological change threatened to render the rigid trimester framework of *Roe v. Wade* obsolete, the Supreme Court faced the prospect, in *Pennsylvania v. Casey*, that precedent would block a decision revising constitutional abortion law in appropriate ways, even though a decisive fraction of the Justices would have chosen the revised rule in a case of first impression.[102] The joint opinion in *Casey* resorted to intellectual dishonesty, proclaiming adherence to precedent while discarding the trimester framework that previous cases has taken to be the core of *Roe*'s holding.[103] The lesson of *Casey* is sometimes taken to be that precedent imposes no real constraint, but absent precedent the Justices would have had no need to write a mendacious, and widely ridiculed, opinion.

The institutions that participate in the process of formal amendment, principally federal and state legislatures, are not subject to these pathologies. The drafters of constitutional amendments may write on a blank slate, drawing on society's

[100] Cass R. Sunstein, *Legal Reasoning and Political Conflict, supra* note 96; Strauss, *Common Law, supra* note 1.

[101] See Jeremy Bentham, *The Handbook of Political Fallacies*, Harold A. Larrabee, ed. (Baltimore: Johns Hopkins University Press, 1952).

[102] *Planned Parenthood of Southeastern Pennsylvania v. Casey*, 505 U.S. 833 (1992).

[103] *Ibid.* at 833–4.

best current information and deliberation about values, while ignoring precedent constraints that prevent courts from implementing current learning even if they possess it. The contrast is overdrawn, because legislatures deliberating about constitutional amendments use precedent in an informal way. But precisely because the practice of legislative precedent is relatively less formalized than the practice of judicial precedent, legislative practice may capture most of the decisional benefits of formal precedent while minimizing its costs. Legislatures may draw on their past decisions purely to conserve on decision-making costs, while shrugging off precedential constraints whenever legislators' best current information clearly suggests that the constitutional rules should be changed.

PROFESSIONALISM AND PARTICIPATION. Whatever else is true of common-law constitutional adjudication, it is clear that essentially all the participants in it are lawyers. Nonlawyers participate only indirectly, as expert witnesses or amici; their participation is always refracted through the agency of lawyers. It is striking that *no member of another profession has ever been appointed to the Supreme Court*, although no positive law prohibits such an appointment. The benefits that flow from the dominant role of lawyers in common-law constitutionalism are obvious: a kind of expertise and technical legal competence.[104]

What are the costs? Let us first dispose of a bad answer. Jeremy Bentham drew on this sort of contrast to emphasize the elitist, exclusionary character of common-law adjudication.[105] A principal evil of common-law constitutionalism, on a Benthamite view, is that Judge & Co. develop a set of practices that are elitist, jargon-ridden, and (consequently) opaque or unintelligible to the citizens affected. I do not believe, however, that this sort of point supports a general impeachment of common-law constitutionalism. Although much common-law constitutionalism undeniably savors of guild exclusivity, the indictment is fatally noncomparative. Constitutional amendment currently takes place in a world of highly professionalized legislatures, at least at the federal level and increasingly in many states. The choice between constitutional updating through adjudication, on the one hand, or through the formal amendment process, on the other, is not primarily a choice between guild constitutionalism and popular or direct constitutionalism. It is a choice between institutional processes dominated by different sets of professional and socioeconomic elites.

What is true is that the range of participating professions is far greater in the formal amendment process. Within Congress, only 40 percent of legislators are lawyers, and a potpourri of other backgrounds, skills, and experiences are represented.[106] The principal *comparative* cost of common-law constitutionalism, in this respect, is not that it is elitist, but that it draws on a remarkably narrow band

[104] See Sanford Levinson, "Constitutional Engagement 'Outside the Courts' (and 'Inside the Legislature'): Reflections on Professional Expertise and the Ability to Engage in Constitutional Interpretation," Chapter 17 in this volume.

[105] See Jeremy Bentham, *A Comment on the Commentaries*, Charles W. Everett, ed. (Oxford: The Clarendon Press, 1928); H. L. A. Hart, "The Demystification of the Law" in *Essays on Bentham: Studies in Jurisprudence and Political Theory* (New York: Oxford University Press, 1982) 21.

[106] The percentage of state legislators who are lawyers has fallen in recent years and hovers around 10% in many states. See, e.g., Randall T. Shepard, "Making Good Law Requires More Lawyers" (2002) 35 *Ind. L. Rev.* 1111.

of professional skills. We need no very elevated account of legislative deliberation to believe that a broader range of represented skills, interests, and backgrounds conduces to better policy, including better constitutional policy.

Suppose we adopt a minimalist account of deliberation as talk or discussion, to be valued primarily as a means of exchanging information, of supplying causal and instrumental arguments that take preferences as given, or of providing grounds for justifying decision to constituents or other interested publics.[107] Still, it is plausible that a broader representation of professions and backgrounds in a deliberating group will produce better discussion, in this low-level sense, than will a group composed solely of lawyers. This might not be so for the ordinary business of law; even the sample of hard constitutional cases that comes before the Supreme Court is dominated by technical lawyer's fare. Constitutional updating, however, is sometimes a matter of large-scale value choice, as to which it is hardly clear that the lawyer's characteristic technical competence is particularly relevant or helpful. I return to this point below.

DECISION COSTS AND BENEFITS. We must account for the costs of decision making as well as the quality of decisions. A simple view would be that the formal amendment process is too costly to serve as the principal means, or even as an important means, of constitutional updating, just as periodic constitutional conventions are too costly to be practical.

Dennis Mueller denies this view. He suggests instead that the decision costs of the formal amendment process are decision benefits:

> The U.S. Constitution contains broad definitions of rights, and the task of amending their definitions to reflect changes in the country's economic, social and political characteristics has been largely carried out by the Supreme Court. While this method of updating the Constitution's definition of rights has helped to prevent them from becoming hopelessly out of date, it has failed to build the kind of support for the new definitions of rights that would exist if they had arisen from a wider consensual agreement in the society. The bitter debates and clashes among citizens over civil rights, criminal rights and abortion illustrate this point.... Although [alternative procedures for constitutional amendment] may appear to involve greater decision making costs, they have the potential for building consensus over the newly formulated definitions of rights.[108]

On this view, it is an illusion that constitutional common law incurs lower decision costs in the long run, even if a given change may be more easily implemented through adjudication in the short run. Although at any given time it is less costly to persuade five Justices to adopt a proposed constitutional change than to obtain a formal amendment to the same effect, the former mode of change incurs higher decision costs over time, because common-law constitutionalism allows greater conflict in subsequent periods.

A benefit of formal amendments is to more effectively discourage subsequent efforts by constitutional losers to overturn adverse constitutional change. Precisely because the formal amendment process is more costly to invoke, formal

[107] James D. Fearon, "Deliberation as Discussion" in *Deliberative Democracy*, John Elster, ed. (New York: Cambridge University Press, 1998) 44.

[108] Mueller, *supra* note 90 at 223.

amendments are more enduring than are judicial decisions that update constitutional rules;[109] so losers in the amendment process will less frequently attempt to overturn or destabilize the new rules, in subsequent periods, than will losers in the process of common-law constitutionalism. This point does not necessarily suppose that dissenters from a given amendment come to agree with the enacting supermajority's judgment, only that they accept the new equilibrium *faute de mieux*.

Obviously more work might be done to specify these intuitions, but it is at least plausible to think that the simplest view, on which formal amendments incur decision making costs that exceed their other benefits, is untenably crude. The overall picture, rather, is a trade-off along the following lines: Relative to common-law constitutionalism, the Article V process requires a higher initial investment to secure constitutional change. If Mueller is right, however, constitutional settlements produced by the Article V process will tend to be more enduring over time than is judicial updating, which can be unsettled and refought at lower cost in subsequent periods.

FLEXIBILITY AND COMMITMENT. Finally, and related to the last point, we may contrast amendments and common-law constitutionalism in terms of the costs and benefits of flexibility. Judicial updating is less costly to reverse in subsequent periods; the common-law process thus enjoys a kind of flexibility that is beneficial where the costs of a mistaken but irreversible change would be very high. Flexibility is an ambiguous virtue, however. In some domains, costly precommitments enable policies and social bargains that would not be possible under more flexible rules. In those settings, it is a good and not a bad thing that the products of the Article V process are costlier to undo in later periods.

C. Relative superiority: Some variables

If there are structural trade-offs between the Article V process and common-law constitutionalism, it does not follow that the comparison is always a wash. In some domains the costs of one process may reach a zenith while the benefits reach a nadir, and vice versa in other domains. Here I offer some conjectures about the relevant variables – about the conditions under which one process or the other shows to best advantage.

VALUE CHOICE VERSUS TECHNICAL IMPROVEMENTS. We have seen that lawyers' expertise dominates the process of common-law constitutionalism. That expertise appears in its best light where constitutional rules of a relatively technical character must be adjusted over time. In settings of this sort, the updating is itself relatively uncontroversial, although perhaps technically tricky; judges can accomplish the change at low cost; and it is not worth incurring the higher up-front costs of the formal amendment process, because it is unlikely that any disaffected group or large-scale social movement will attempt to unsettle the new, updated rules in future periods.

[109] See Donald J. Boudreaux and A. C. Pritchard, "Rewriting the Constitution: An Economic Analysis of the Constitutional Amendment Process" (1993) 62 *Fordham L. Rev.* 111.

An example involves one of the great success stories of nineteenth- and twentieth-century constitutional adjudication, the so-called dormant or negative commerce clause. The problems in the area involve the reciprocal adjustment of competing state interests in a framework where all states benefit, in the long run, from national free trade; in which there is substantial consensus on the values to be promoted; and in which the judges have spent most of their time sorting out low-level questions about what rules can best be used to identify various de facto trade barriers. Many of these are technical lawyers' questions par excellence – if state regulation imposes differential burdens on out-of-staters, should evidence of protectionist motive on the part of state officials be admitted? – and it is very hard to imagine that an amendment or series of amendments would have produced a better body of law, overall, than has the Court. The comparison is slightly inapposite here; dormant commerce law is also constitutional "common law" in the sense that the rules may be changed by statute as well as by amendment, and Congress has occasionally intervened. But the point is that judicial updating and development has been by far the dominant means of updating and has plausibly worked best of all.

A very different problem arises when constitutional rules fall hopelessly out of step with large-scale changes in public values. It is not at all obvious that lawyers, as a professional class, enjoy any superior capacity to identify those values; as John Hart Ely remarked, lawyers' values are likely to have the "smell of the lamp" about them.[110] This is just the downside of lawyers' technical expertise. Specialization and professionalization always introduces a kind of distortion, a narrowness or like-mindedness in beliefs and commitments.

Judges' political insulation gives them some distance from current electoral politics, which might help them to sort passing political frenzies from deep changes in public values (although I shall question that premise shortly). But insulation frees judges to do anything they want, within broad limits, and there is no guarantee that what they do will correspond to *any* account of what makes for good constitutional updating. Even more importantly, judges pay a very large price for insulation, in the form of reduced information about what actual people desire and believe. What the electoral constraint does for federal and state legislators is to force them into closer contact with a broader range of views, professions, and social classes than most judges encounter. It is hard to say, in the abstract, how these considerations wash out, but there is no general reason at all to be confident that common-law adjudication can update constitutional rules in ways that track enduring changes in public values.

The crucial point here is comparative. Because the costs of constitutional change through judicial updating are much lower than the costs of amendment, common-law constitutionalism is more responsive to passing public moods, both for good and for ill. The stringency of the Article V requirements tends to ensure, by and large, that formal amendments pass only if they embody some sort of large-scale public consensus on new rules of the constitutional game. It will not do to focus only on the amendments that might represent the product of a passing political frenzy, such as the Prohibition Amendment. Such cases are few and far between, whereas

[110] John Hart Ely, *Democracy and Distrust* (Cambridge: Harvard University Press, 1980).

common-law constitutionalism is rife with examples in which the judges have bowed to political winds. Consider the Supreme Court's deferential attitude toward the excesses of anticommunism in the 1950s and its near-invariable deference to the political branches in wartime.[111]

SYSTEMIC CHANGE VERSUS PIECEMEAL CHANGE. I have suggested that actors in the amendment process have relatively greater capacity to take a systemwide perspective. Where circumstances require structural change in the polity, the systemic perspective is at a premium, and the relative virtues of the amendment process are indispensable. It is unimaginable, in my view, that the basic readjustment of power between federal and state governments embodied in the Reconstruction amendments could have emerged from a process of common-law constitutionalism; nor would it have been desirable for it to do so. The politywide scale of the necessary changes demanded that they be considered, if not all at once, then at least in much larger decisional chunks than a case-by-case process of decision making could provide. The Reconstruction Congresses saw a wide range of political actors, representing a wide range of skills, information and interests, deliberate and bargain over large packages of rules simultaneously, reciprocally adjusting the choices made on different margins.

The incremental character of common-law constitutionalism, by contrast, shows to best advantage where a series of piecemeal changes and small steps are in order.[112] Consider the Supreme Court's relatively successful efforts, moving cautiously, to update free speech and Fourth Amendment privacy rules in light of twentieth-century changes in the technology of information, such as the widespread use of telephones.[113] This sort of adjustment of rules and principles to slowly changing technical circumstances puts common-law constitutionalism in its best light. Under circumstances of this sort, it will rarely be obvious, at any particular point, that the large up-front costs of the Article V process are worth incurring to make small adjustments. Conversely, the relative flexibility of the common-law process is a benefit in this sort of setting, where it is useful to be able to undo or reverse a failed adjustment at low cost in later periods.

IRREVERSIBLE AND REVERSIBLE CHANGE. It follows from these considerations that common-law constitutionalism performs poorly where the benefits of rigid constitutional commitments are high and the benefits of flexibility in future periods are low, and vice versa. Where it is desirable that new constitutional rules be tentative and reversible, because of a rapidly changing environment or because mistaken rules will have very high costs, common-law constitutionalism shows to advantage. Where it is desirable that new constitutional rules be irreversible or very costly to reverse, the amendment process is superior, just because amendments are much harder to destabilize in future periods. This is the case where, for example, the entrenchment of constitutional property rights serves as a costly

111 See Lee Epstein et al., "The Supreme Court During Crisis: How War Affects Only Non-War Cases" (2005) 80 *N. Y. U. L. Rev.* 1.

112 See Sunstein, *One Case at a Time, supra* note 65.

113 See *Katz v. United States*, 389 U.S. 347 (1967). For an overview, see Orin S. Kerr, "The Fourth Amendment and New Technologies: Constitutional Myths and the Case for Caution" (2004) 102 *Mich. L. Rev.* 801.

signal that encourages investment,[114] or where it is desirable to commit ex ante to political ground rules that will have important and contentious distributive effects when applied ex post. An example in the latter category involves the presidential succession rules, adjusted most recently by the Twenty-fifth Amendment.

Of course, amendments will have to be interpreted by judges ex post as well, so the contrast is again just a matter of degree. But, to repeat an earlier point, the need for judicial interpretation does not make amendments otiose or meaningless. Amendments can and often do sharply constrain interpretation within certain boundaries,[115] and can function as political and legal rallying points for groups and interests skirmishing in the courts in later periods. The need for later judicial interpretation gives amendments an added degree of flexibility, but as a comparative matter they are certainly less flexible (for good and for ill) than a common-law constitutional decision with identical content.

INSTITUTIONAL VARIABLES AND INSTITUTIONAL ROLES: A CAUTIONARY NOTE. A final caveat is in order. The variables I have outlined supply institutional reasons to think that constitutional change should be channeled through either the amendment process or the processes of common-law constitutionalism. It is a different question which actual decision makers, with their distinctive roles, cognitive limitations and institutional capacities, should be charged with directly considering and implementing these considerations. That is a second-order question about the decision-rules that institutional actors, with particular roles and abilities, should use to implement first-order theories.[116] I do not take up those further implementing questions here, beyond noting the important possibility that some particular decision makers would not do best by directly applying the considerations I have sketched. It is perfectly possible, for example, that one might want legislators and executive officials to steer constitutional change through the processes of common-law constitutionalism (rather than the amendment process) in certain circumstances, yet not want judges directly to consider such matters in making their decisions. I bracket all such questions for the present.

CONCLUSION

To identify the empirical conditions under which the amendment process or common-law constitutional updating proves superior is the beginning of a full institutional analysis, not the end of it. The variables need to be filled in with actual values, which requires empirical work. The contribution I attempt to make here is just to pose the right comparative institutional questions. The two theses critiqued in Parts IV and II both attempt to privilege common-law updating over amendment,

[114] Daniel A. Farber, "Rights as Signals" (2002) 31 *J. Legal Studies* 83.

[115] The Article V process, it has been argued, implies that judges should adopt a textualist approach to constitutional interpretation. See John F. Manning, "The Eleventh Amendment and the Reading of Precise Constitutional Texts" (2004) 113 *Yale L.J.* 1663.

[116] On this sort of question, see Fallon, *Implementing the Constitution, supra* note 72; Frederick Schauer, *Playing by the Rules: A Philosophical Examination of Rule-Based Decision Making in Law and in Life* (New York: Oxford University Press, 1991); Adrian Vermeule, "Interpretive Choice" (2000) 75 *N. Y. U. L. Rev.* 74; Cass R. Sunstein and Adrian Vermeule, "Interpretation and Institutions" (2003) 101 *Mich. L. Rev.* 885.

by claiming that amendment is either generally futile or generally bad. In particular, the generic case against constitutional amendment rests on a systematic nirvana fallacy, or failure of institutional comparison. It is a prejudice that must be cleared away in order to bring the right questions into view.

ACKNOWLEDGMENTS

Thanks to Tsvi Kahana for excellent editorial assistance and thanks to Will Baude, Frank Easterbrook, Beth Garrett, Daryl Levinson, Jacob Levy, John Manning, Frank Michelman, Eric Posner, Geof Stone, Lior Strahilevitz, Cass Sunstein, John Vile, Ernie Young, and participants at a workshops at Harvard University and the University of Chicago for helpful comments. Special thanks to David Strauss for providing both detailed comments and a model of collegiality in the face of disagreement. Justin Rubin and Carli Spina provided helpful research assistance, and the Russell J. Parsons Fund provided generous support.

13 What Do Constitutions Do That Statutes Don't (Legally Speaking)?

Frank I. Michelman

I. PROLOGUE

"We know that in the relevant sense Britain does not have a written constitution."[1] So reflects Joseph Raz, hard upon his own observation that Britain's constitution is composed, in part, of "written law." By written law, Raz means statutes; he mentions, for example, the Bill of Rights of 1689 and the Act of Union (between England and Scotland) of 1706.[2] Other usual suspects in roundups of British constitutional statutes include the Magna Carta and the Act of Settlement of 1701,[3] and of course there is now also the Human Rights Act of 1998.[4] Given the existence of such material along with universal acknowledgment of its substantially constitutive character, some authors quibble with the judgment that Britain lacks a written constitution. "Uncodified," they say; "piecemeal"; "scattered"; but not unwritten.[5] But, of course, Raz is right. We do *know* that Britain lacks a written constitution – lacks it thoroughly, lacks it in some more deeply significant sense than "uncodified" or "scattered" seems prepared to allow.

What is that sense? By what mark do we know what we know? What is it about the ensemble of the Magna Carta, the Act of Settlement, and the others that makes us turn away from calling their sum a written constitution? (*Written* these laws surely are, so it must be the title "constitution" that we decline to grant them.) All of these legal monuments undoubtedly are "bedrock" law in today's United Kingdom.[6] It must therefore be some other key property that they all (or jointly) lack, their lack

[1] Joseph Raz, "On the Authority and Interpretation of Constitutions: Some Preliminaries" in *Constitutionalism: Philosophical Foundations*, Larry Alexander, ed. (Cambridge: Cambridge University Press, 1998) 152 at 154 [hereinafter *Authority of Constitutions*].

[2] See ibid.

[3] See, e.g., Eric Barendt, *An Introduction to Constitutional Law* (New York: Oxford University Press, 1998) at 27, 32.

[4] See ibid. at 32.

[5] See, e.g., Giovanni Sartori, "Constitutionalism: A Preliminary Discussion" (1962) 46 *Am. Poli. Sci. Rev.* 853 at 855 ("I would rather say that the English do not have a codified constitution, *i.e.*, that Britain has a constitution that is written only in part..., in piecemeal fashion, and scattered in a variety of sources"); accord Barendt, *supra* note 3 at 33.

[6] "Bedrock" is Michael Perry's term for premises, emanating from prior political actions that may or may not have been, in fact, legally authorized acts of constitutional law creation, that have nevertheless "achieved a virtual constitutional states; [they] have become part of our fundamental law – the law that is constitutive of ourselves as a political community of a certain sort." Michael J. Perry, "What Is 'the Constitution'? (and Other Fundamental Questions)" in *Constitutionalism*, Larry Alexander, ed. (Cambridge: Cambridge University Press, 1998) 99 at 105 [hereinafter *What Is "the Constitution"?*].

of which disqualifies them, in our eyes, from together composing Britain's written constitution. What is the missing property? Raz does not attempt to say.

In his contributions to the Banff Conference on Legislatures and Constitutionalism, Matthew Palmer has proposed what may look like an answer. What no mere collocation of statutes can ever contain, Dean Palmer says, is "constitutional conventions, in the sense of recognised practices, usages and understandings." Palmer calls these usages and understandings "meta norms of the constitution." He says that they find their existence not in enacted laws but "in the actions, understandings and inter-relationships of those who operate" the constitution.[7]

As will be evident, I agree in substance with these remarks. However, they cannot supply an answer to the precise question I mean to pose here: What is the property that we feel to be missing from the ensemble of British constitutional statutes, but find to be manifest in enactments such as the Constitution of the United States and the Constitution of the Republic of South Africa, such that we judge the latter two countries to have written constitutions while Britain has none?

To *that* question, constitutional conventions cannot be the answer. As Palmer points out, even such full-scale written charters as the U.S. and South Africa Constitutions are "inherently capable" of containing all of the "structures, processes, principles, rules, conventions and culture" that go to make up any "complete constitution."[8] Constitutional conventions are and can be no more contained in the written constitutions of countries where we affirm such things to exist than they are or can be contained in the collocation of British constitutional statutes.

Has my question, then, no answer? Try this: British enactments fail to make a *constitution*, in our eyes, because we do not remotely regard them, singly or conjointly, as being law from which other law in the legal system "derives its force."[9] They are not, in that sense, "basic" laws. Fundamental, yes; organizing, yes; "bedrock," yes; but basic, no. As I make this suggestion – that we reserve the accolade "constitution" for enacted laws that we do regard as basic in the sense I have just defined – I hope that heads will nod because I am trying to set you up. One of my aims in what follows is to cast doubt on the idea that it can possibly make any difference, for any conceivable legal purpose, whether we do or do not regard *any* enacted law – including any enacted constitution – as basic law.

II. TWO THESES

Our project is a comparison of two classes of "statutoids," as one might call them, with respect to their possible deployments and effects. First, there are mere statutes.

[7] See Matthew Palmer, "Legislative Constitutionalism Ascendant? Who Interprets an Unwritten Constitution in New Zealand" 18–19 (manuscript draft of July 2, 2004). Palmer further observes, in a spirit consistent with my argument to come, that constitutional conventions evolve through social "interactions," that their development "can be consciously led," and that the success of any given effort to lead their development is "inherently uncertain." Ibid. at 29.

[8] Ibid. at 33–4.

[9] The Constitutional Court of South Africa describes in those terms that country's enacted Constitution, Republic of South Africa Constitution Act 108 of 1996 [hereinafter *SA Const.*]. See *In re Pharmaceutical Mfrs. Ass'n of S.A.*, 2000 (3) BCLR 241 (CC) ¶ 44 [hereinafter *Pharmaceutical*]; *infra* Part III.

Second, there are constitutions, meaning enacted or "written" constitutions – statutoid constitutions. There exist nonenacted constitutions, too. Indeed, as we shall see, the presumed existence of the latter is both indispensable to legal-systemic understanding and a key to my modest argument to come. However, we cannot interestingly compare the uses of statutes with the uses of nonenacted constitutions. (What, pray, is a nonenacted statute?) Accordingly, in what follows, "constitution" unmodified means an enacted law. Whenever I mean anything else, I shall say so.

Now, here is a remark about mere statutes to place beside what I have already said about constitutions. As typically envisioned, a statute most decidedly is *not* a law from which all other law "derives its force"; it is not, in that sense, a basic law. To the contrary, a statute, as we typically conceive it, is an enactment (or, if one prefers, a product of enactment) that derives its own legal force from some prior, deeper normative base: a constitution, as we often call it, enacted or nonenacted.[10] A statute, we think, is legally forceful in virtue of its being constitutional.

By no means do I intend to challenge here the common notions of legislatures as *pouvoirs constitués* and of statutes, correspondingly, as nonbasic laws. Rather, I mean to call on these notions. No mere statute is a basic law. Enacted constitutions, by contrast, often *are* said to be basic laws – some, indeed, are *named* "the basic law"[11] – as if everything depended on their being such.[12] My first thesis here – "Thesis 1" – is that nothing of strictly legal consequence depends on it.

Lest you be concerned that this thesis contradicts my suggestion, above, that we tend to reserve the accolade "constitution" for those written laws that we do regard as basic, let me assure you that it does not.[13] Thesis 1, to repeat, is that nothing of *strictly legal consequence* depends on an enacted constitution's being regarded as a basic law. By "strictly legal consequence" (hereinafter "legal consequence" for short), I mean a consequence of producing or altering a norm of the legal system, or of altering the arrangement or structure of the system. I mean the legal system as, say, Hart would define it, that is, as a particular, going instance of an institutionalized interplay of primary and secondary rules, necessarily including at least one rule of recognition.[14] It should be obvious that the production of legal consequences is not the only conceivable kind of objective that political actors actually might have in view when seeking to introduce a written constitution into a legal environment that currently lacks one. Such an undertaking well may have – let us call them – extralegal objectives in view. For example, an enacted constitution might be designed to serve as a focal point for a sense of national unity, identity, or membership. Along similar lines, adoption of a constitution may be meant to serve the tremendously significant aim of marking the

[10] If you are thinking that statute might draw its force from a "rule of recognition" that is not itself properly regarded as a norm of any sort, bear with me; I shall get to that. See *infra* Part V.

[11] E.g., the German Grundgesetz of May 23, 1949, as from time to time amended.

[12] See Part III.

[13] There is a second reason why it does not, which I will present *infra* Part VIII.

[14] See H. L. A. Hart, *The Concept of Law* (New York: Oxford University Press, 1961), ch. V at 77–96. On rules of recognition, see *infra* Parts III and V.

In this chapter, I cite to the first edition of Hart's book, except in one instance, *infra* note 53, where my reference is to Hart's postscript to the second edition of 1994.

emergence of a country from colonial to full nation-state status in the Westphalian world.[15]

So, to be clear: The claim of Thesis 1 is not that nothing *at all* depends on a country's enacted constitution being regarded as a basic law. We have recognized that the motivation for any given undertaking of constitution enactment may be supplied by extralegal objectives. That being so, it could further be true that such objectives are better achieved by an enacted constitution that enjoys a reputation of being the country's basic law than by one that does not. A finding to that effect would not impeach Thesis 1 – which, I repeat, is that nothing of *legal* consequence depends on imputation of a basic-law character to a country's enacted constitution.

I can now introduce a second thesis – "Thesis 2" – pertaining to mere statutes. We consider mere statutes at all times *not* to be basic laws. Suppose I could show – this being Thesis 2 – that whatever of legal consequence you might hope to do by enacting something as or into a constitution, you similarly might hope to accomplish by enacting something as or into a mere statute. (Is not the case of British quasi-constitutional statutes already suggestive of such a conclusion?) Again, I wish not to overstate the claim. I think it is true that sometimes, for some legally consequential purposes, a performance recognized as constitution enactment can succeed where a performance classed as mere statute enactment would fail. Thesis 2 asserts that, when such is the case, it is the case only circumstantially and contingently, not conceptually or necessarily.

We may put the matter this way: Whatever of worthwhile legal consequence you may hope to do by writing and enacting a constitution or constitution-part, you may be able to do as well or better by writing and enacting a statute. Which type of performance is likelier to succeed depends (we will say for now) on the weather. The weather is not always conducive to a statute aimed at this or that desired legal-systemic consequence, and people cannot always wait for the wind to shift. When they cannot, resort to a performance of constitution enactment can make perfectly good sense, without contradicting Thesis 2.

If Thesis 2 is true, even as thus qualified, it helps to bolster Thesis 1; although, as we will soon see in Part III, Thesis 1 can be supported adequately in other ways. If Thesis 2 is true, and considering that we regard statutes at every step as decidedly nonbasic laws, it amounts to a showing that *lack of basicness* does not disable a law from achieving any legally consequential result one might be looking for in a constitution. It apparently would follow that Thesis 1 – that nothing of strictly legal consequence depends on an enacted constitution's being a basic law – is true.

To summarize, we have before us two theses as follows:

- Thesis 1. *Nothing of legal consequence hinges on an enacted constitution's being regarded as a basic law.*

[15] I suppose one might ask whether adoption of a constitution can possibly serve such ulterior, social purposes unless people believe the adoption will be attended by major legal-systemic consequences. See Dieter Grimm, "Integration by Constitution" (2005) 3 *I-CON* 183 at 193–5. I would assume it can, simply as a socially resonant, expressive, and performative event. But even if we assume otherwise, the ulterior purposes might explain fully and satisfyingly why resort was had to a constitution, with no need to show that practically equivalent legal-systemic results could not otherwise have been obtained.

- Thesis 2. *Whatever of legal consequence can get done through constitution enactment can also possibly, depending on the weather, get done through statute enactment.*

Before moving on, it is worth nothing that the two theses, although closely linked, are not identical. They are not semantically or logically equivalent. If Thesis 2 is true, then it does not follow necessarily that Thesis 1 is true (because we also have as a premise that no statute is a basic law). However, the converse proposition does not hold. Thesis 1 as stated could be true and yet Thesis 2 as stated could be false. Nothing we have said so far rules out the possibility that (a) there are legal consequences that only constitution enactment, and not mere statute enactment, conceivably could produce, *and* (b) this result holds regardless of whether enacted constitutions are regarded as basic laws. Note that (a) is the negation of Thesis 2 while (b) can be obtained directly from Thesis 1, of which it is an included case.

III. THESIS 1: THE SIMPLE ARGUMENT

As I have mentioned, an argument supporting Thesis 1 easily can be laid out in a form that makes no reference to what you can or cannot do using mere statutes as distinct from an enacted constitution. We do that now.

In an attention-grabbing case called *Pharmaceutical*, the Constitutional Court of South Africa declared emphatically that there exists in that country "only one system of law. It is shaped by the Constitution which is the supreme law, and all law, including the common law, derives its force from the Constitution and is subject to constitutional control."[16]

The immediate occasion for this manifesto was a jurisdictional tug-of-war between two branches of the South African judiciary. Briefly and roughly, South African common law from pre-Constitutional days is said to contain a "doctrine of legality, an incident of the rule of law," which denies the force of law to acts of executive government lacking authorization by Act of Parliament.[17] All parties to the case apparently agreed that the "legality" or ultra vires doctrine also falls among norms enacted as part and parcel of the current Constitution, at least as an "implied provision" thereof.[18] A lower court had set aside a certain presidential proclamation as ultra vires. A party sought review, and the Constitutional Court had to decide whether the matter fell within its constitutionally delimited jurisdiction.

Ostensibly, there are two pinnacle courts in the South African judicial system: the Constitutional Court (CC) and the Supreme Court of Appeal (SCA). The

[16] *Pharmaceutical, supra* note 9 at ¶ 44.

[17] Ibid. at ¶ 17. "Pre-Constitutional days" here refers to the times prior to the deep constitutional transition marked by the coming into force of the so-called interim Constitution of 1993, Republic of South Africa Constitution Act 200 of 1993. There had been indigenously enacted constitutions in South Africa for a span of more than thirty years prior to that time; the Republic Constitution (Constitution of the Republic of South Africa Act 32 of 1961) and the Tricameral Constitution (Constitution of the Republic of South Africa Act 110 of 1983) had succeeded the imperially enacted Union Constitution (South Africa Act 1909 (9 Edw. VII c9)). However, the doctrine of legality invoked by the Constitutional Court in *Pharmaceutical* had always been understood to be a part of the common law and not to have been laid down by any pre-1993 enacted constitution.

[18] See *Pharmaceutical, supra* note 9 at ¶ 17.

Constitution[19] makes the CC the court of last resort in "constitutional matters."[20] The apparent design is to divide final appellate authority between the two courts, so that the SCA has the last word in a certain set of cases (presumably not a null set), namely, those not turning on constitutional matters.[21] A clear corollary would be that the CC lacks jurisdiction in that same class of cases.

In the run-up to the CC's *Pharmaceutical* decision, the SCA twice had suggested that a party complaining of a breach of legality might frame the cause of action as one based strictly on common law, and that in such a case the SCA would be sitting in review of a common law-matter as distinct from a constitutional matter.[22] The clear implication was that the SCA's decision in such a case would be final, nonreviewable by the CC. (Forum shopping, anyone?) In *Pharmaceutical,* the CC said "no way," using the language I quoted above: "There is only one system of law. It is shaped by the Constitution which is the supreme law, and all law, including the common law, derives its force from the Constitution and is subject to constitutional control."

One can, if so minded, detect in this pronouncement three discrete attributions to the Constitution of special legal properties. The Constitution is described as *supreme* law, as *pervasive* law ("all law is subject to constitutional control" or is "shaped by the Constitution"), and as *basic* law ("all law... derives its force from the Constitution"). We easily can understand these as three distinct legal strengths or virtues.

"Supreme" means that when a constitutional norm collides irreconcilably with another norm in the legal system, the constitutional norm prevails. Note that this does not necessarily make the Constitution pervasive. "Pervasive" means that there is no case law in which the Constitution does not figure, at least potentially. It means that the Constitution demands notice on every single occasion when someone is expected to decide or to act in accordance with law. A constitution can be supreme as far as it goes, but if its norms do not go everywhere the law goes, it is not pervasive. (Do American jurists typically think our Bill of Rights goes everywhere the law goes?)[23] Conversely, a constitution can be thought pervasive without being thought supreme. Its norms can radiate through the length and breadth of the law, conversing (as it were) with the common law and the statute law they meet up with, without necessarily trumping them or demanding the last word.[24]

[19] *SA Const., supra* note 9.

[20] Ibid., s. 167(3)(a). Section 167 provides further that the CC "makes the final decision whether a matter is a constitutional matter." Ibid. S. 167(3)(c).

[21] Ibid., s. 168(3).

[22] See *Comm'r of Customs and Excise v. Container Logistics (Pty) Ltd.* (1999), 8 BCLR 833 (SCA); *Fedsure Life Assurance Ltd. v. Greater Johannesburg Transitional Metropolitan Council* (1998), 6 BCLR 671 (SCA). The CC had signaled its own doubt about the SCA's view in *Fedsure Life Assurance Ltd. v. Greater Johannesburg Transitional Metroolitan Council* (1998), 12 BCLR 1458 (CC), but without resolving the matter definitively.

[23] See *Flagg Bros., Inc. v. Brooks,* 436 U.S. 149 (1978).

[24] See, e.g., *Retail, Wholesale & Dept. Store Union v. Dolphin Delivery Ltd.,* [1986] 2 S.C.R. 573 (S.C.C.) [*Dolphin Delivery*] (refusing to subject common-law rules – in this case, a rule allowing for injunctions against secondary picketing – to direct Charter review, but adding that courts "ought" to develop common law principles to keep them consistent with "the fundamental values enshrined in the Charter"); *R.W.D.S.U. v. Pepsi-Cola Canada Beverages (West) Ltd.,* [2002] S.C.C. 8 (Jan. 24, 2002) (revising the common-law rule applied in *Dolphin Delivery* to make it accord more comfortably with Charter values, but leaving in place the barrier against direct constitutional review of the common law).

"Basic" means the constitution figures as an exclusive rule of recognition for all other purported exercises of power to affect legal content, legal positions, or legal relations within the system. A rule of recognition is a norm in the legal system that "specif[ies] some feature or features possession of which by [some other alleged norm of the system] is taken as conclusive affirmative indication that [the latter norm truly] is a rule of the [system] to be supported by the pressure [the system] exerts."[25] By an "exclusive" rule of recognition, I mean one to which an appeal ultimately *must* be had in order to satisfy any given demand for validation of a questioned, purported exercise of legal-systemic power.[26] Thus, to say that a constitution figures as an exclusive rule of recognition for all other exercises of legal-systemic authority – to call it, by my definition, a "basic law" – is to say that every purported exercise of legal-systemic authority must look ultimately to that constitution for its authorization and its validation.[27] Granted, it is hard to see how a law can be basic as I have defined that term without being both pervasive and supreme. A basic law, I have said, is one that figures as an exclusive rule of recognition for *all* other exercises of legal authority (pervasive), and an exclusive rule of recognition simply has to quash every nonconforming claim to exercise legal authority (supreme).

Can an enacted constitution be both pervasive and supreme without being basic? Certainly yes, in a quite robust sense of those terms. We can imagine law – it would be, by our definition, a basic law – having no content or function other than (1) to provide an exclusive rule of recognition for judge-made or common law, (2) to provide an exclusive rule of recognition for statutes, and (3) to provide an exclusive rule of recognition for an enacted "constitution" that, if adopted in accordance with the basic-law rule, will – for so we may take our basic law to dictate – be both supreme and pervasive in its relations with either or both statute law and common law. Any resulting, enacted constitution then will be robustly pervasive and supreme, by which I mean as fully pervasive and supreme as one could have any reason for wishing a constitution to be.

One could not call the constitution basic, however, inasmuch as it is perceived to rest on the back of another law that is force-giving with respect to it, and, moreover, is force-giving with respect to common law and statute law. A constitution enacted in accordance with this other, basic law doubtless will contain most or all of the system's express rules governing statutory enactment; that is, it will specify institutions and procedures for enacting statutes and it may impose certain demands and restraints on permissible statutory content (a bill of rights). It is quite another

[25] Hart, *supra* note 14 at 92.

[26] Consider a set of prevalent understandings in which the power of Parliament to create a law of given content can be vindicated *either* by an appeal to an enacted constitution *or* by an appeal to the common law. In such a case, the enacted constitution would not contain a relevant, *exclusive* rule of recognition. Nor would it therefore, by my definition, be a basic law.

It is not clear that every legal system contains or must contain an exclusive rule of recognition. See *infra* note 51 (describing a view of Joseph Raz). If one takes the view that some might not, then the ones that do not will not contain any basic law, by my definition of a basic law.

[27] "Ultimately," because there can be chains of authorizations. A defender of the lawfulness of a given judicial judgment might look first to an agency regulation for validation of the court's power to impose a judgment of that particular tenor; then to a statute for validation of the agency's power to promulgate as law a regulation having that effect; then to the Constitution (or something else) for validation of Parliament's power to promulgate as law a statute having *that* effect.

question, however, whether the enacted constitution can be regarded as the law from which statutes enacted in compliance with its terms "derive their force." It cannot, if we posit an unwritten law "beneath" the enacted constitution (so to speak), which by its terms as widely understood gives force to that constitution, as well as to such statutes as may be enacted in whatever manner, and subject to whatever substantive limits and constraints that constitution may prescribe – as well as to the common law. The enacted constitution fixes the terms and conditions of valid statutory enactment, but it does so under delegation (as it were) from the other, deeper law, and the legal force of compliant statutory enactments flows from the other, deeper law.[28] At first look, anyway, no reason appears why we are not free thus to envision the situation.

Suppose we do thus envision it. Would the resultant lack of basicness be in any way a defect or weakness in the enacted constitution? Why did the Constitutional Court, in the *Pharmaceutical* case, feel impelled to describe South Africa's Constitution as a law from which "all law… derives its force"? We can imagine the CC wishing to lay claim to a virtually unbounded subject-matter jurisdiction as a court of last resort. For that purpose, however, the Constitution does not have to be basic. It does not have to be supreme. All it needs is to be robustly pervasive because, if it is, then no matters can arise that categorically are not constitutional matters.[29] Of course, one can perceive practical reasons why the CC may also have wished to see the point established that the Constitution is supreme, and in any event that point is clear on the face of the instrument.[30] But to what end does the Constitution also have to be a law from which all (other) law derives its force? Was calling it that a dispensable extravagance on the CC's part, or does something of legal-systemic moment depend on it?

In considering this question, we can ask separately about the Constitution's legal-systemic relation to the common law and to statutes. Common law first. Suppose South Africans wish their enacted Constitution to be both pervasive and supreme with respect to the common law. Maybe the first thing they will do is write language saying so into the text of the Constitution. An example might be: "When construing or developing the common law, a court must promote the spirit, purport and objects of the Constitution."[31] In order for that language to do the trick, does the Constitution have to be "basic" with respect to the common law? Must it be the law from which the common law derives its force? Surely not.

"Constitution of the Republic of South Africa Act 108 of 1996" is an enacted law. The Constitutional Court's *Pharmaceutical* manifesto seems to presuppose that any enacted law must "derive its force" from some other law. If so, there must be another law from which the Constitution derives its force, which for now we just

[28] This other deeper law apparently would be what has been called an (or the) "axiom" in its country's legal system. It would be the system's "final authorizing law" for the enactment of which no further authorizing law can be identified. See Michael Steven Green, "Legal Revolutions: Six Mistakes About Discontinuity in the Legal Order" (2005) 83 *No. Car. L. Rev.* 331 at 336–8.

[29] Remember, the South African Constitution stipulates that the CC "makes the final decision whether a matter is a constitutional matter." *SA Const., supra* note 9, s. 167(3)(c).

[30] The Constitution expressly declares itself to the "the supreme law of the Republic; law or conduct inconsistent with it is invalid, and the obligations imposed by it must be fulfilled." Ibid., s. 2.

[31] Compare *SA Const.*, ibid., s. 39(2) ("When interpreting any legislation, and when developing the common law or customary law, every court, tribunal or forum must promote the spirit, purport and objects of the Bill of Rights.").

call by the name of "that other law." That other law could be the one from which not only the Constitution but also the common law derives its force. That other law then would contain the recognition rules for both the Constitution and common law. Language in the Constitution stating that the Constitution is both pervasive and supreme vis-à-vis the common law then would "work" or not, depending entirely on the content of those recognition rules which are not in the Constitution but rather are in that law.

The key is the *content* of the recognition rules, not their notional location as between the Constitution and that other law. The recognition rules for the common law can be enacted outside the Constitution and the Constitution can still be pervasive and supreme with respect to the common law; those same recognition rules, wherever they may be sited, may make it so. So far as the latter result is concerned, there is no need that the common law be thought to derive its force from the Constitution.

The foregoing demonstration works smoothly with regard to the common law because "outside the Constitution" probably is where most jurists instinctively would place the recognition rules for the common law[32] (whence the rhetorical punch in *Pharmaceutical* from locating the recognition rules for the common law *inside* the Constitution). Not so for statutes. In any country having an enacted constitution that figures as supreme law, lawyers and others hardly can help thinking that statutes derive their force-of-law from that constitution. Unreflectively, we suppose that the enacted constitution sets an exclusive recognition rule for statutes. (Very likely, we suppose that a central part of the point of having introduced an enacted constitution into the system was to enable the authors of the constitution to shape and reshape the recognition rules for statutes to their liking, by the means and in the course of writing and amending the constitution.) Thinking thus that constitutions are basic laws vis-à-vis statutes, we may find perplexing the claim that you can, in even the most favorable weather (whatever "weather" may mean), achieve the same sorts of legal-systemic results via mere statutes that you can with a constitution. The rest of this chapter is devoted to an explanation and defense of the latter claim – in other words, Thesis 2 – ultimately in defense of Thesis 1.

IV. THESIS 2: THE CONSTITUTION AS STATUTOID

In order to set up the question addressed by Thesis 2, we have had to qualify the category "constitution" in a particular way. The constitution in our comparison has to be a legal object that both resembles mere statutes and differs from them, in ways that warrant treating the two classes as discrete subtypes under the more general type that we have dubbed "statutoid." Because the question here is about

[32] See, e.g., Joseph Raz, *Practical Reason and Norms* (Oxford: Oxford University Press, 1990) 130 [hereinafter *Practical Reason*]. ("In Britain, for example, the authority of Parliament is not derived from the Common Law, nor the authority of the Common Law from Parliament. Yet the Common Law confers in effect norm-making powers on the courts and these are not derived from parliamentary legislation.") Raz is concerned in this passage to show that the respective recognition rules for judicial and for parliamentary lawmaking constitute two distinct norms, according to the most apt criteria for the individuation of norms in a normative system. See also Joseph Raz, *The Authority of Law: Essays on Law and Morality* (Oxford: Clarendon Press, 1979) 95–6 [hereinafter *Authority of Law*]. I take no issue with that view, proposing only that both these two recognition rules (if two there be) may be located, conceptually, in what we see as a single body of underlying, recognitional law.

what category of law you must *write* or *enact* in order to achieve a desired sort of legal-systemic effect, the "constitution" we pose as one of the alternatives must be the kind of constitution that gets written and enacted. It must be the kind of constitution that is perceived to exist by virtue of having been duly enacted by authorities recognized (sooner or later[33]) as empowered so to enact it. Understanding that not all countries have constitutions of the enacted kind, we also can be clear that our ensuing discussions apply only to countries that do have them, or contemplate having them.

Our constitutional comparator, then, has to be an enacted constitution. Speaking strictly, it would not suffice to satisfy this condition that the constitution be written in the sense only that it have what Joseph Raz calls a "canonical formulation."[34] In order to bear the sort of comparison with mere statutes that concerns us here, the constitution in question must be a law whose existence as such is *owing to* enactment, just as is true by definition of every statute. Owing-existence-as-law-to-enactment is an attribute distinct from that of having a canonical formulation.[35]

A distinct but related point is this: We need not think of our enacted constitution as, or in its character of, a document (what Michael Perry call "Constitution$_1$"[36]). With greater suppleness, we may think of it as what Perry calls "Constitution$_2$,"[37] a set of norms composing our "supreme law,"[38] not to be equated with any document but nevertheless owing their recognition as supreme law to an occurrence, somewhere in their legal pedigree, of a duly connected performance of enactment.[39]

V. THESIS 2: STATUTOIDS AND "ULTIMATE RULES OF RECOGNITION"

From here on, the main drill is to sort through and reject sundry claims that may come to mind regarding legal-systemic effects that it takes *constitution* enactment,

[33] See *infra* Part VI.

[34] See Raz, *Authority of Constitutions, supra* note 1 at 153.

[35] Even if it would be a rare case in which a law would have the latter attribute but lack the former, such a case is not inconceivable. A case in point may be the view of some American jurists that the Declaration of Independence is a part of American constitutional law. See, e.g., Mark Tushnet, *Taking the Constitution Away from the Courts* (Princeton: Princeton University Press, 1999) at 11–14 (discussing also the views of Frederick Douglass and Abraham Lincoln). More generally: A piece of nonenacted verbiage – say, something from the work of a revered philosopher – might gain recognition as law gradually over time, in the manner of customary law. That portion of law then would have a canonical formulation but it would not owe its existence as law to enactment.

[36] See *What Is "the Constitution"?, supra* note 6.

[37] Ibid.

[38] See ibid. (internal quotation marks omitted).

[39] I understand Perry to include this "enactment" condition in his account of the mergence of transtextual, "bedrock" norms of the Constitution of the United States. See ibid. at 104–7. Perry says it can be legitimate for a current court to treat as valid constitutional law some norm that *it* does not believe is really contained in the enacted constitutional verbiage, correctly construed. But a condition for this possibility apparently is that the norm in question should present itself to the current court as one that some prior judgment, by a court duly empowered to set in motion a process of lawmaking via-precedent, had found, even if mistakenly, to be contained in the enacted text. Perry's bedrock constitutional norms become law through chains of enactment (or quasi-enactment) running back to a root of enactment. See ibid. at 105 ("If, over time, the practice or the premise decreed by the old, wrong (at the time) ruling has become . . . bedrock, then the premise has . . . become a part of our fundamental law. . . . ").

rather than mere statute enactment, to achieve. We start with a couple of easy put-aways, to get the juices flowing.

Enacted constitutions typically lay down second-order frameworks for further political decision making, as distinguished from purely first-order political decisions. True, but this will not in any deep way distinguish enacted constitutions from mere statutes. The decisive reason is not that constitutions sometimes contain strictly first-order material, for example, the U.S. Constitution's prohibition on certain acts of breaking and entering by government officers;[40] nor is it that the second-order/first-order distinction itself is problematic in ways that likely will make it impossible ever to say that a given constitution is second-order only.[41] Those facts would be harmless to a claim of special constitutional utility for establishing secondary norm structures, if *some* lawmaking of undoubted and major secondary character were, for more-or-less necessitating reason, accomplishable *only* by a constitution and not by mere statutes.

However, such does not appear to be the case. Major, basic, secondary-type statutes are cheap as sprats, as the Grand Inquisitor might have put it.[42] Just now, the U.K. Human Rights Act[43] looks to me like the all-time champion example of the breed, but consider the Continuity in Representation bill recently passed by the U.S. House of Representatives.[44] (If you are tempted to rejoin that the Human Rights Act, for example, is "really" a constitution or constitution making masquerading as a statute, consider what follows if you answer that way to every single instance I might give you of a statute doing something we think of as distinctively "constitutional." Would not that just be tantamount to conceding that enacted constitutions and statutes are not clearly demarcated subtypes? I have not, after all, suggested that secondary rule formation is not a distinct subtype of lawmaking, only that this subtype is not peculiar to constitutions as opposed to mere statutes.)

Well, you say, there are secondary legal norms, and then there are secondary legal norms. A legal system requires, for its very existence, a special class of secondary norms called rules of recognition and a constitution, you say, can supply these whereas a statute cannot. Again, apparently not so. Statutes are used to write rules of recognition all over the place. Consider, for example, the Acts of Congress that confer parcels of subject-matter jurisdiction, specifically defined and delimited, on various branches of the U.S. federal judiciary.[45]

40 See *Bivens v. Six Unknown Named Agents*, 403 U.S. 388 (1971); cf. *San Diego Gas & Elec. Co. v. San Diego*, 450 U.S. 621 (1981).

41 The first-order/second-order line is both substantively and analytically weak. *Substantive weakness*: Many lawmaking solutions that have an undoubted secondary aspect are also first-order insofar as they are contested on distributive or ideological grounds – the Connecticut Compromise, for example; see Melvin I. Urofsky and Paul Finkelman, *A March of Liberty: A Constitutional History of the United States* (New York: Oxford University Press, 2002) at 96–8. *Analytical weakness*: When the Constitution of the United States prohibits the State of Alabama from *making a law* that imposes civil liability for nonreckless defamation of a public official, see *New York Times Co. v. Sullivan*, 376 U.S. 254 (1969), or from *making a law* that enforces peonage contracts, see *Bailey v. Alabama*, 219 U.S. 219 (1911), are those effects first- or second-order?

42 See, e.g., Elizabeth Garrett, "Conditions for Framework Legislation," *infra* Chapter 14.

43 *Human Rights Act* (U.K.), 1998, c. 42.

44 H.R. 2844, 108th Cong., 1st Sess. (2003).

45 For a historical review of some important congressional enactments of this type, replete with citations, see Richard H. Fallon, Jr., Daniel J. Meltzer, and David L. Shapiro, *Hart and Wechsler's the Federal Courts and the Federal System*, 5th ed. (New York: Foundation Press, 2003) 826–31. These statutes confer on

Okay, you say, but *those* statutorily created rules of recognition owe their legal-systemic validity to a more basic rule of recognition found in the Constitution of the United States, Article III, section 1: "The judicial power of the United States shall be vested in one Supreme Court, and in such inferior courts as the Congress may from time to time ordain and establish." The regress of authorizations, you say, always has to stop somewhere. Every legal system, you say, must contain at least one "ultimate" rule (or rules) of recognition, whose recognized existence in the legal system rests on grounds that do *not* involve or presuppose any further rule of recognition.[46] Let us call this sort of rule an ultimate rule of recognition or "URR."[47] Every legal system, you say, absolutely has to contain at least one URR in order to exist as a legal system.[48] A statute, you say, cannot supply this rule: You would still need a recognition rule to explain the legal validity of the statute that fixed the rule, so the rule fixed by the statute could not be "ultimate."[49] That, you say, is how an enacted constitution differs critically from a statute. When we shape the URR to our preference by writing and enacting a constitution, the constitution we enact to that effect serves a unique function among statutoids. The enacted constitution then becomes the one statutoid containing a rule that needs to exist in order for the legal system to exist.

specifically designated classes of officers (i.e., duly appointed federal judges of various classes) in specified institutional circumstances (i.e., sitting in duly constituted federal courts) parcels of law-declaring authority that those officers otherwise would not have. Such enactments doubtless create or modify rules of recognition. (Remember, a rule of recognition is a norm in the legal system that "specif[ies] some feature or features possession of which by [some other alleged norm of the system] is taken as a conclusive affirmative indication that [the latter norm truly] is a rule of the [system] to be supported by the pressure [the system] exerts.") Hart, *supra* note 14 at 92.

46 You might cite Raz, *Authority of Law*, *supra* note 32 at 95 ("There must be in every system some criteria of validity that, although legally binding, are not legally valid, hence they must be set in the rule of recognition."), or Hart, *supra* note 14 at 104 (writing of the necessary rule for which "there is no rule providing criteria for the assessment of its own validity").

47 Hart calls such a nonlegally grounded norm of the legal system an "ultimate" rule of recognition. See ibid. at 102–7. It might also be called an axiom of the legal system, see *supra* note 28, reserving "ultimate rule of recognition" for the social fact that gives this rule authoritative effect. I explain below why I think we can safely ignore this refinement here, as long as we bear in mind that any alteration of the axiom strictly implies a corresponding alteration of its social-fact correlate. My usage in this chapter does not confine the class of "rules of recognition" to ultimate rules. Neither does Hart expressly do so, although he often does refer to "the rule of recognition" (sans further modification) when he plainly means an ultimate rule. See, e.g., ibid. at 102–5. I have found it clearer to speak of a plurality of rules of recognition in a legal system, some of which are not ultimate – for example, those jurisdiction-conferring Acts of Congress of which I have just spoken – and to speak explicitly of ultimate rules when those are what I have in mind.

Thus, if we follow my usage, when Joseph Raz declares, for example, the plain truth of the proposition that "every legal system has at least one rule of recognition" (see Raz, *Practical Reason*, *supra* note 32 at 146–7), he is referring to a URR.

48 See *supra* note 46. Raz maintains, contrary to Hart, that there is no reason why a legal system may not contain several rules of recognition on the "ultimate" level of systemically existent norms whose force-of-law rests on grounds not involving any more remote rule of recognition. See Raz, *Practical Reason*, *supra* note 32 at 147; Raz, *Authority of Law*, *supra* note 32 at 95. That dispute is beside the point of my argument in this chapter.

49 Hart puts the matter neatly:

> Even if [the rule that what the Queen in Parliament enacts is law] were enacted by statute, this would not reduce [that rule] to the level of a statute; for the legal status of such an enactment would necessarily depend on the fact that the rule existed antecedently to and independently of the enactment.

Hart, *supra* note 14 at 108.

This will not do. A *statutoid, enacted* constitution cannot do what you are talking about. The reason why it cannot is going to prove a big part of the story about why it may be possible, depending on the weather, to do anything you might be minded to do by writing a constitution by writing a mere statute instead. That reason is well known. In a system in which an enacted constitution is perceived to have the force of supreme law vis-à-vis mere statutes, or is perceived to be the law from which mere statutes derive their force of law, it seems there must be some *other*, legal-force-conferring source endowing the enacted constitution with these legal-systemic virtues. Okay, you might say, then it is that other legal source – the *really* basic legal source, the one from which *all* other laws in the system *do* derive their force, directly or mediately – for which we should be reserving the title "constitution."[50] Fine, as long as you recognize that this other legal source cannot be dependent on or given by enactment.[51] (If it were, the same need for a further legal source would arise all over again.) Thus, when it comes to URRs, enacted constitutions are impotent in just the way mere statutes are – like them, not different from them. It follows from what I have been saying that every country having statutes, including those that we would say have written constitutions, also has, by necessity, a nonenacted or "unwritten" constitution where is parked, if nothing else, its URR.[52] I assume it will be roughly evident what I mean by "non-enacted." I

50 Compare Charles Fried, "Foreword: Revolutions?" (1995) 109 *Harv. L. Rev.* 13 at 27 (remarking on the "temptation to fill the void – *natura non facit saltum* – by posing a 'constitution' behind" the visible Constitution).

51 See Hart, *supra* note 14 at 107 (asserting that "a rule of recognition is unlike other rules of the system" in the respect that "its existence is a matter of fact" independent of the application of any norm of the legal system). Raz, describing Hart's view, says that the (ultimate) rule of recognition "differs from other laws in that its existence is not determined by criteria laid down in other laws but by the fact that it is actually applied." See Joseph Raz, *The Concept of a Legal System: An Introduction to the Theory of the Legal System* (Oxford: Clarendon Press, 1970) at 198 [hereinafter *Legal System*]. Raz continues: "This seems to imply that the rule of recognition is always a customary and not a legislated rule." Ibid.

Raz himself disagrees with the view that a URR cannot be a legislated rule. He presents a case of a closed, circular chain of two or more enacted laws, each of which is validated by a chain of authorizations comprised by the rest (so that each "indirectly authorizes its own creation") and any one of which might be "presupposed" as valid. Raz concludes from this case that "it is not necessarily [true] . . . that every legal system includes a . . . non-positive [basic] norm." Raz, *Legal System*, ibid. at 139–40. I am going to disregard this possibility in what follows because (1) this is not the way in which systems with enacted constitutions typically are conceived, see *infra* Part VII, and (2) it is obvious – indeed, trivial – that in a system thus conceived my Thesis 2 would hold true; that is, there would be no way to maintain that you can wreak certain legal-system effects by some type of performance called constitution enactment that is categorically distinguishable from some other type of performance called statute enactment. (Would the enacted laws in Raz's circular chain properly be called "statutes"? Would they properly be called "constitution-parts"? Would one designation be more proper than the other? What sort of criterion possibly could provide the answer to such a question?)

52 Does Hart say differently? At one place he does remark as follows:

> If a [written] constitution specifying the various sources of law is a living reality in the sense that the courts and officials of the system actually identify the law in accordance with the criteria it provides, then . . . [it] seems a needless reduplication to suggest that there is a further rule to the effect that the constitution (or those who "laid it down") are to be obeyed.

Hart, *supra* note 14 at 246. (Charles Fried expressly invokes Ockham's razor against denials that a written constitution can "count as" the URR for its country's legal norms. Fried, *supra* note 50 at 25 n. 66.) Notice, however, that what Hart has done here is very far from posing a case in which the URR's existence is not strictly determined by "unwritten" social facts that cannot be equated or reduced to the existence of a written text. He has rather posed a case in which the determining social facts are

mean that the constitution, or this aspect of it, is law immanent in social practice – law directly referable, without the intermediation of any performative event, to a population's socially reciprocated understandings about structures and relations of legal authority, reflected in that population's more-or-less self-conscious, more-or-less cooperative, regulative conduct of social life.[53]

Now comes the tricky point that I would prefer to skip but feel that I had better not. My own view is that the nonenacted constitution that every legal system must have, not excepting countries possessed of what we would call full-scale enacted constitutions, must comprise a part of its country's *corpus juris*. It must be regarded as law in the fullest sense.[54] I say so having in mind a possible rival view, according to which the ultimate, secondary norms required to support exercises of legal authority within a country, including authority exercised by the writing of statutoids of whatever class (constitution or mere statute), can (or, indeed, must) be supplied from *outside* the corpus juris by a URR that is not a law – is not a recognized norm within the legal system – but rather is purely and simply a fact of social life lying beyond the provenance of law.[55]

The difference between these two views is not one that we have any need to resolve here.[56] We can elide it by terminological stipulation, as follows: (1) If you

so closely engaged with a certain text that the former is most efficiently described in terms that refer to the latter. Elsewhere, and more to the point, Hart wrote that reduction of a rule of recognition to writing

> is not itself [a] crucial step, though it is a very important one: what is crucial is the acknowledgement of reference to the writing . . . as *authoritative*, i.e., as the *proper* way of disposing of doubts as to the existence of the rule.

Hart, *supra* note 14 at 92. See also *supra* note 49.

53 Thus, my "unwritten constitution" is close kin to the "constitutional conventions" that Matthew Palmer finds indispensable from any complete constitution of a legal system. See *supra* Part I.

In *The Concept of Law*, Hart rejected use of the Diceyan term "convention" to encompass (ultimate) rules of recognition. See ibid. at 107–8. His view on that point may have softened, however. In a postscript to a subsequent edition of his book, Hart drew a distinction between a "consensus of independent convictions," where the concurrence of others is not a part of the reason each party has for concurring, and a "consensus of convention" where that is such a part. He then went on to assert that *The Concept of Law* treats the (ultimate) rule of recognition "as resting on a conventional form" of consensus. See H. L. A. Hart, *The Concept of Law*, 2nd ed., Penelope A. Bulloch and Joseph Raz, eds. (New York: Oxford University Press, 1997) at 266–7.

54 See Raz, *Legal System*, *supra* note 51 at 198 ("The rule of recognition is a legal rule and belongs to the legal system.") (describing the view of Hart); Hermann Heller, "The Essence and Structure of the State" in Arthur J. Jacobson and Bernhard Schlink, eds., *Weimar: A Jurisprudence of Crisis*, trans. by Belinda Cooper and Peter C. Caldwell (Berkeley: University of California Press, 2000) 265 at 277 (reprinting and translating *Wesen und Aufbau des Staates* ([Leiden: A. W. Sifthoff's Uigeversmaatschappij, 1934]). ("The [unwritten] constitution is not at all comprehensive as 'valid' if it is understood as a nonnormative, merely factually existing decision or plurality of such decisions.")

55 See Frederick Schauer, "Amending the Presuppositions of a Constitution" in Sanford Levinson, ed., *Responding to Imperfection: The Theory and Practice of Constitutional Amendment* (Princeton: Princeton University Press, 1995) 147 at 150–1. ("In referring to the ultimate rule of recognition as a *rule*, Hart has probably misled us.")

56 My guess is that the difference is not resolvable, because the URR is a transcendental concept fulfilling a need that demands its placement both inside and outside the category of legal norms. See Hart, *supra* note 14 at 108 (asserting needs for both ways of viewing the URR). Joseph Raz calls the URR "the point (one such point) at which – metaphorically speaking – the law ends and morality begins." Raz, *Authority of Constitutions*, *supra* note 1 at 161. "Being a social fact" is what allows the URR to provide us with a way "to identify the law without recourse to morality." Ibid. It is this social-factual existence that makes the URR "unlike any other legal rule," ibid. – Raz thus (it seems to me inevitably) covering the URR under the category of legal rules as well as under that of social facts.

picture the legal system in question, at any point in the discussion, as having its necessarily nonenacted, deepest recognition rules *inside* its corpus juris, those nonenacted rules of law will compose what I am calling an "unwritten constitution." You can then forget about any extralegal URR; it will be irrelevant to the concerns of this chapter. (2) If, to the contrary, you picture the legal system in question, at any point in the discussion, as one in which ordinary common law, statutes, and any enacted constitution there may be all ride on the bare back of an extralegal, purely social-factual URR, with no intermediating unwritten recognitional *law*, then read my term "unwritten constitution," wherever it appears, to refer to the URR.

I now stand ready to defend Thesis 2 on either set of understandings.

VI. THESIS 2: "I'VE BEEN WORKING ON THE URR"[57]

What reasons might a reformer of the legal system have for wishing to establish within the system a contained, identifiable body of enacted law that is uniquely *constitutional* in status, relative to all other law in the system? Inevitably, the answer will include the reformer's presumed wish to establish a body of enacted law that is supreme over other law. And now we may add, for the first time, that reformers who aim at establishing a special body of *supreme* law very likely also aim at having that body of law be relatively *entrenched* in the system, meaning (roughly) that its content is not alterable by the same institutional means by which actors in the system, choosing to do so, can alter the content of the system's ordinary statute law.[58]

Is the supremacy of a nonentrenched corpus of purportedly supreme law, then, completely fake? It is not. In order to alter ordinary laws in ways that would conflict with some part of such a corpus, ordinary lawmakers must first jump through the hoops of amending or repealing the obstreperous part, and politics or conscience might sometimes stop them from doing so.[59] But, of course, it is easily imagined that our legal-system reformers would count that sort of supremacy too diaphanous for

[57] The view I set forth in this part concurs with those of both Frederick Schauer and Joseph Raz, neither of whose treatments I can cite comprehensively here. For Schauer's view in a nutshell, see the article cited *supra* note 55. Schauer there summarizes as follows:

> Constitutions are . . . necessarily subject to amendment as their supporting presuppositions are amended, even though it cannot be the case that the amendment of those supporting presuppositions can be thought of in anything other than factual or other prelegal terms.

See Schauer, *supra* note 55 at 148.

Raz has written, just to take one example of his many pertinent discussions, that "the first constitution is the law because it belongs to an efficacious legal system (a fact which cannot be determined until some time after the first constitution is issued)." See Raz, *Legal System, supra* note 51 at 138. Not only does Raz accordingly reject as fallacious the view that "laws can[not] authorize their own creation," ibid., but he also holds that "the continuity of a legal system is not necessarily disrupted by the creation of new original laws. . . . The creation of a new original law disrupts the continuity of a legal system only if it is a constitutional law of great importance." Ibid. at 188. By "great importance," I take Raz to mean of sufficient importance to warrant an all-things-considered judgment that a break in legal-systemic continuity – and hence in political-systemic continuity – has occurred.

[58] To be exact, a relatively entrenched law is one that actors in the system cannot alter either by means that are "ordinary" – identical to the means by which they can alter ordinary law – or by means that are no more stringent than the ordinary means or no less likely than the latter to be practically within reach.

[59] My statement assumes that no contrary-tending doctrine of implied repeal is in effect.

their purposes. For perfectly good and understandable reasons, reformers sometimes will aim at establishing certain norms in the form of enacted law that is not only supreme but also is entrenched as such. (It is not an idle question why reformers should especially want an *enacted* law to have the properties of supremacy and entrenchment, but it is enough to say here – and I am confident readers easily will agree – that they could have their reasons. Think "democracy" or "government by the people." Think "rationality." Think "stability."[60])

In sum, we posit that law reformers may aptly perceive a need to secure the enactment of a selected body of norms as entrenched, supreme law. Eminent commentators have maintained that such a need can be served only by the availability and pursuit of processes of constitution enactment that stand securely distinct from processes of mere statute enactment.[61] I deny it. This part and the next show that anything along these lines you want to do you can do (weather permitting) by means that are perfectly well classifiable as enactment of a simple statute or Act of Parliament.[62]

We may as well move right to the hardest cases. Suppose you are the law reformer. Suppose your aim is to lay down for the future your legal system's secondary rules for enactment of statutes (and we can include your possible wish to establish bill-of-rights-type restrictions on valid statutory content). Maybe you want to alter the extant rule; maybe you want to establish a rule where none exists (Iraq, for example, on August 1, 2003). Try doing either of those by the ordinary means of mere statute enactment, you might say.

I say, why not? Let us first consider alteration, then fixation of a rule where none exists.

There is no conceptual barrier I know of to using a statute to write for the future a secondary rule for enactment of statutes that differs from the rule you are relying on to validate the statute you will use for this purpose. British constitutional history appears to be studded with events of this kind – the Human Rights Act being only the most recent of the series.[63] The truth appears to be that you can use a statute

[60] For a full survey of possible reasons, see Eric A. Posner and Adrian Vermeule, "Legislative Entrenchment: A Reappraisal" (2002) 111 *Yale L.J.* 1665 at 1670–3.

[61] See, e.g., the excerpts from Hans Kelsen's *Vom Wesen under Wert der Demokratie* (Tübingen: Mohr, 1929), reprinted in *Weimar: A Jurisprudence of Crisis, supra* note 54, 84 at 100 (footnote omitted):

> [A]s soon as administration and jurisdiction become possible only on the basis of specific legal authorization, and this principle of legality based on statute . . . becomes ever more conscious . . . the establishment of basic rights makes sense only if it unfolds in a specific *constitutional form*. This means that only a law created in a qualified, rather than a normal, procedure can protect the sphere composed of single basic rights against the executive and its restrictions. The typical form in which the constitution is qualified in comparison with ordinary statutes is a *heightened quorum and a special majority*.

[62] Kelsen (see ibid.) says that only a law "created in a qualified procedure" can protect the rights "against the executive." Unless Kelsen means "against the executive insofar as supported by a compliant legislature," his claim is mystifying. Therefore, I will take him to mean that. As I explain in the following text, I see no reason to accept the claim even as thus construed. Why should the fact that a law was *created* by a normal procedure necessarily mean that it can be *destroyed or gotten around* by a normal procedure?

[63] Consider, for example: "Parliament has changed the rules for the enactment of legislation [by itself, to wit] in the Parliament Acts 1911–49 by reducing the power of the House of Lords." Barendt, *supra* note 3 at 92. And what about, say, the series of Reform Acts extending the base of qualified electors of MPs? In the United States, it is thought seemly to make such changes via constitutional amendment. See U.S. Const. Amends. XV, XVII, XIX, and XXVI.

to write secondary rules for future statutes exactly as, and insofar as, the unwritten constitution – which, remember, either *is* the URR or directly reflects the content of the URR[64] – permits it to be done, and there is no logical reason why an unwritten constitution cannot provide an indefinitely wide berth for such legislative projects.

It is true that, in such a case, a sitting parliament will be trying to bind future parliaments. It may even be trying, in a significant sense, to abdicate its powers or to "commit suicide."[65] My point is that there are no logically deducible answers to questions, in the abstract, about whether your parliament is legally authorized to do this. In practice, the answer to the question will be self-validating; either the attempt "takes" or it does not. Once the answer is known, we can say – as a formal, expository matter – that the emergent answer all along was contained in the unwritten constitution, granting that we did not know the latter's tenor until the pudding did, or did not, get eaten, as the case may be. The point is that the answer can as easily be yes as no, so far as legal-systemic logic is concerned.

And what if the unwritten constitution is resistant, unaccommodating?[66] Then, no doubt, you will have to alter the unwritten constitution in order to get where you want to go. We can include here the Iraqlike case of apparent absence of an unwritten constitution, an apparent legal-systemic void. In this case, is your only hope for setting a new secondary rule for statutes to introduce an enacted constitution? I do not see why. Is that how the English Parliament was born? Suppose the Iraqi Governing Council set up for a time by the Occupying Power had just up and begun writing statutes by an ostensible rule requiring approval on each of two readings by a majority of a quorum defined as one-half or more of the full Council membership. Suppose they had used this rule to write statutes establishing a permanent parliament and the rules and arrangements for electing its membership from time to time. It might have worked (or "taken"); it might not. Only by knowing whether it did or not would we know the relevant content of Iraq's unwritten constitution over the relevant stretch of time.[67] It turns out, in other words, that the notion of Iraq lacking a constitution at that time is, in some contexts, virtually impossible to

[64] See *supra* Part V.

[65] Compare Bruce Ackerman, "Rooted Cosmopolitanism" (1994) 104 *Ethics* 516 at 522.

[66] A special case would be the situation where an enacted constitution holds sway and you want to revise for the future its expressly provided secondary rules for statutes. Even assuming – as maintained by Posner and Vermeule, *supra* note 60 – that there is no generally applicable reason of juridical or constitutional principle why a parliament today cannot, by enactment of a statute, set (and even entrench) new procedural rules to bind successor parliaments tomorrow and forever, surely it may not set procedures in contravention of express provisions in the extant, visible constitution? Surely, in that sense, enactment of the new rules in the form prescribed for constitutional amendment will be required? See ibid. at 1667, 1670, and 1680–1. Maybe; maybe not. What *finally* counts is not the *written* constitution but the unwritten one that appears to give the written one blocking force in this situation. It is quite conceivable that reformers can get their way by working on the unwritten constitution by, among other means, performances of statute-writing. Consider the partial replacement of treaties by executive agreements in American constitutional law. (See Bruce Ackerman and David Golove, "Is NAFTA Constitutional?" (1995) 108 *Harv. L. Rev.* 799.)

[67] See Raz, *Legal System*, *supra* note 51 at 171, where Raz speaks of valid acts of legislation that "were not guided by law, for their character as the exercise of legal powers is derived only from the fact that a subsequent [state of the legal system] contains laws enacted by them." Compare Frederick Schauer's hypothetical promulgation of a Constitution of the United States by himself. See Schauer, *supra* note 55 at 152–3.

maintain. We cannot think "Iraq," in the category of a free-standing country where valid law can be made, without attributing to it an unwritten constitution, content perhaps waiting to be discovered.

Discovered how? By the way we always discover such information: by observation, maybe participant observation. How does what I am imagining for Iraq differ essentially from what occurred in the United States in the 1780s? You want to set in motion a new or modified secondary-rule complex for statutes in the North American territory covered by the thirteen states? Writing and enacting a constitution – we well know – is a possible means for doing so, but it is not guaranteed. Every venture in constitution enactment is a bet. Whether the venture "takes" is entirely dependent on the contemporaneous state of the unwritten constitution. So enacted constitutions turn out once again to be not different from statutes but similar to them. It is true for both statutoid subtypes that an attempt to use them to alter or entrench the future secondary rules for statutes may or may not succeed, depending on the contemporaneous lay of the unwritten constitution ("the weather").

To turn the point around, it is identically true for projects in both constitution enactment and mere statute enactment that any given such project may or may not succeed in *dragging* the unwritten constitution along with it to some desired state.[68] In the United States in the 1780s, the Philadelphia Convention and the Congress-under-the-Articles conspired successfully to such an end by writing and securing the enactment of the Constitution.[69] What I am saying is that there is no reason of legal-systemic logic why Congress should not have succeeded as well by promulgating Articles I–VI (VII then could have been dispensed with) as a statute.

Situationally, contingently, it will often be the case that if you want to use some form of legal enactment in hopes either of revealing some desired state of the unwritten constitution or of dragging the unwritten constitution to the desired state, a performance of constitution enactment may be the advisable choice. Such quite clearly was the judgment of certain American reformers – of the persuasion that would come to be known as "Federalist" – around the time of the Annapolis and Philadelphia conventions.[70] But so may a performance of statute enactment sometimes be the advisable choice, as human rights-minded Britons of the 1990s apparently concluded – understandably, given the hard facts of British legal and political culture. Which is the better way to go will depend on contingencies of that sort.

No doubt the cultural contingencies may strongly advise resorting to a constitution-writing performance as a means of desired legal-systemic alteration. However true it may be that enacted "constitutions" and mere "statutes" are conceptually commingled categories in technical, positivist jurisprudence – and an intimation that they are has been a central tendency in my argument supporting Thesis 2 – the plain and important fact remains that constitution enactment and statute enactment can be qualitatively different kinds of performances from a political-cultural or (shall we say?) a political-theatrical standpoint. I take that to

[68] Compare Hart, *supra* note 14 at 149 ("all that succeeds is success").

[69] See, e.g., Bruce Ackerman, *We the People: Transformations* (Cambridge, Mass.: Belknap Press of Harvard University Press, 1998) 32–68.

[70] See *ibid.*

be a main point of Jon Elster's contribution to this collection.[71] The two kinds of performances thus remain quite distinct as instruments of statecraft.[72]

VII. THESIS 2: TWO-TIERED VERSUS THREE-TIERED CONSTRUCTIONS

Without a doubt, we can distinguish performances of constitution enactment (or amendment) from performances of statute enactment. We can also see easily how the choice of performance modes can, contingently, affect the chances of success of ventures in altering the legal system. What we still lack is any way to differentiate in general the kinds of alteration resulting from one mode or the other when successful. I now offer a last attempt.

We can think of a legal system as tiered, in a particular sense in which the number of tiers does not necessarily correspond to the number of degrees of hierarchy detectable within the system. In the conception I am posing, one tier of law lies just above another when the lower tier contains the immediate recognition rules for all the law on the higher tier. Thus, a system of the following description has two tiers only, although it contains at least three degrees of legal hierarchy. On what we may call a basement level is an unwritten constitution containing all (and only) the recognition rules for all the other law in the system, including both common law and statute law.[73] Just above, on what we may call the street level, are statutes and the common law. By force of the recognition-rule complex contained in the below-ground, unwritten constitution, the following hierarchies obtain: (1) later enacted ("junior") statute law prevails over prior, inconsistent, earlier enacted ("senior") statute law (i.e., no statute in conflict with a junior statute is law) and (2) statute law prevails over inconsistent common law (i.e., no common law norm in conflict with a statute is law).

As a result of the basement-level constitution's prioritizing recognition rules, the street level in this system contains at least three degrees of legal hierarchy: junior statutes, senior statutes, and common law. This system is two-tiered, nevertheless, because (as I am picturing it, and why may I not?) the same basement source, the unwritten constitution, supplies both statutes and common law with their recognition rules, including the shared subrules that junior statutes prevail over senior and all statutes prevail over common law.[74]

[71] See Jon Elster, "Legislatures as Constituent Assemblies," *supra* Chapter 9.

[72] Compare the case of the recent European constitutional proposal, as viewed by Joseph Weiler. In order to succeed with reform, the architects felt, they could not appear to be "simply redrafting Nice [a treaty]." Rather, they must appear to be "doing something far more transcendent. . . . [T]he treaty had to masquerade as a constitution in order to achieve [the] sought-after result." Theatrically, that meant presenting the matter as one to be put to "a European majoritarian constitutional will," as opposed to the treaty form of government-by-government acceptance or rejection. See J. H. H. Weiler, "On the Power of the Word: Europe's Constitutional Iconography" (2005) 3 *I-CON* 173 at 177, 182.

[73] Compare "that other, deeper law" of which I wrote in Part III.

[74] My analysis here follows that of Hart when he writes of the importance of distinguishing the relative *subordination* of one norm to another from the idea of the one's being *derived* from the other. Keeping these two notions distinct is required, Hart says, in order to avoid the false conclusion all law is, if only "tacitly," a "product of legislation." See Hart, *supra* note 14 at 98. Hart continues:

> In our own system, custom and precedent are subordinate to legislation since . . . common law rules may be deprived of their status as law by statute. Yet they owe their own status of law . . . not to a "tacit" exercise of legislative power but to the acceptance of a rule of recognition which accords them this independent though subordinate place.

Ibid.

We can also construct a three-tiered system. At street level lies an enacted constitution. Just above it, at (call it) a first-floor level, lie the system's statutes, senior and junior, and the common law. Just beneath it, at basement level, lies the unwritten constitution containing, now, *only* the recognition rule for the enacted constitution. Where, then, are the recognition rules (including any prioritizing subrules) for the law on the first floor, ordinary statute and common law? In a three-tiered construction or conception, those rules are found on the intermediate tier, that of the enacted constitution. The unwritten constitution's recognition rule for the enacted constitution contains a subrule that empowers the written constitution to set the recognition rules for statutes and the common law. I write here in terms of that being the way matters *are*, but of course what I really mean to posit is the possibility that such is how we might *see* matters, picture them, construe them.[75] A system we construe in the manner I have just described is a system we construe as three-tiered, inasmuch as law on each of the two lower tiers in the system is seen as carrying the requisite recognition rules for law on an adjacently higher tier.

The next point to notice – and here I simply am restating the central message of my argument in Part III – is that a two-tiered system easily can accommodate a body of enacted law that, for all practical purposes, functions in the legal system exactly as does an enacted constitution in a three-tiered construction.[76] Let us use the term "constitutional statute" to designate a body of enacted, supreme law in a two-tiered construction. A constitutional statute shares street-level space with other statutes and the common law, but it has hierarchical superiority over both of the latter, just as statutes have superiority over the common law. If the hierarchical relation of junior to senior statutes also obtains, then this will be a two-tiered system supporting at least four degrees of legal hierarchy at street level.

To speak of a supreme-law constitutional *statute* is to imply a two-tiered construction of the legal system. To speak of an enacted, supreme *constitution* is to imply a three-tiered construction. That is just a result of the way I have defined the terms. As a corollary, these two types of statutoids may be distinguished in the following way: *An enacted constitution is regarded as a basic law in its legal system; a constitutional statute is not.* An enacted constitution is understood to contain exclusive recognition rules for all other visible law in the system; a constitutional statute is not. In that respect (and that respect only), an enacted constitution lies categorically beyond the class of statutes but a constitutional statute does not.

Systems construed as relentlessly two-tiered certainly can be viable and workable, as witnessed by the United Kingdom and New Zealand. In the lifespan of a two-tiered system, a time may come when reformers will consider introducing into the picture an enacted constitution that will act as constructive carrier of the recognition rules for ordinary law, leaving the unwritten constitution to carry only the recognition rule for the enacted constitution. The reformers thus would be converting the system from a two-tiered to a three-tiered construction. By the same

[75] Construction of a legal system as two-tiered or three-tiered is like what Raz calls "principles of individuation" for laws in a legal system. Both are "determined by legal theory," as opposed to being given by the observable, empirical content of any extant system. See Raz, *Legal System, supra* note 51 at 141.

[76] Think, for example, of the Basic Laws in Israel. See *United Mzrahi Bank Ltd. v. Migdal Village,* C.A. 6821/93, 49(4) P.D. 221 (1995) (S. Ct. of Israel), excerpted, in English translation, in Norman Dorsen et al., *Comparative Constitutionalism* (St. Paul, Minn.: Thomson/West, 2003) 103–10.

token, they would be deciding to introduce an enacted constitution in preference to turning out a constitutional statute with identical substantive content.

We may now restate Thesis 2 as follows: ***Whatever of legal-systemic consequence can get done by working with a three-tiered construction of the legal system can also get done by working with a system construed as two-tiered.*** That is not a surprising claim, given that these alternatives are, after all, theoretical constructions of the local, social practice of legal ordering, not objectively observable properties thereof.

14 Conditions for Framework Legislation

Elizabeth Garrett

The United States Congress structures some of its deliberation and decision making through framework legislation. Framework laws establish internal procedures and rules that will shape legislative deliberation and voting with respect to a specific subset of laws or decisions in the future. They are laws about lawmaking in a particular arena.[1] They are related to the standing rules of the House or Senate, but unlike most of these rules, they are passed in statutes rather than through concurrent or simple resolutions. Some parts of the standing rules have also been passed initially as statutes, most notably, in the *Legislative Reorganization Acts* of 1946 and 1970.[2] These legislative reorganization laws are similar to framework laws in that they were first enacted in statutory form, but, unlike framework laws, their provisions changed congressional procedures and structures generally, not only for a subset of decisions.[3] Framework laws, by contrast, supplement, and sometimes supplant, ordinary rules of procedure only for a defined set of future decisions. Although framework laws are passed in statutory form, requiring concurrence of both houses and presentment to the president, the portions of the laws that set out internal frameworks are usually identified as exercises of the two houses' constitutional rule-making powers, and the right of either house to change the framework unilaterally is, in most cases, explicitly reserved.[4]

Framework laws are familiar, although little scholarly attention has been paid to them as a related legislative phenomenon in the United States. The congressional budget process is the most influential framework, and it has been amended with additional framework laws such as the *Unfunded Mandates Reform Act.* Some trade-implementing agreements are considered under a framework process called

[1] They are thus a paradigmatic example of secondary rules as defined by Hart. See H. L. A. Hart, *The Concept of Law* (New York: Oxford University Press, 1961), Chapter 5.

[2] Pub. L. No. 79–601, 60 Stat. 812 (1946); Pub. L. No. 91–510, 84 Stat. 1140 (1970).

[3] Bruhl calls the larger group of rules, including the *Legislative Reorganization Acts*, "statutized rules." See Aaron-Andrew P. Bruhl, "Using Statutes to Set Legislative Rules: Entrenchment, Separation of Powers, and the Rules of Proceedings Clause" (2003) 19 *J. L. & Pol.* 345 at 346. Some congressional analyses identify framework laws as "rulemaking statutes." See, e.g., Memorandum from Richard S. Beth, Congressional Research Service Specialist in the Legislative Process, *Statutory Procedures Limiting Debate* (June 3, 2003).

[4] See, e.g., *Budget Enforcement Act of 1990*, Pub. L. No. 101–508, §13305 (1990); *Omnibus Trade and Competitiveness Act of 1988*, Pub. L. No. 100–418, §1103(d) (1988). Congress has taken the position that reserve clauses are unnecessary because they "simply confirm what is the case" under the Constitution's rules of proceedings clause. See, e.g., S. Rep. No. 107–139, at 54 (2002) (in context of trade fast track bill); S. Rept. No. 104–2, at 15 (1995) (in context of *Unfunded Mandates Reform Act*).

fast track. The fast-track process in the trade arena was based on an earlier framework that accompanied the delegation of authority to the president to reorganize the executive branch. Congress uses a slightly different framework law to consider proposals to close or realign military bases sent to it by the president after he approves a package of recommendations from an independent base closure commission. Some foreign policy decisions are tied to framework laws; perhaps the most well-known of these is set up in the War Powers Resolution, but other arms sales laws and emergency legislation are also accompanied by internal congressional frameworks.[5]

In other work on framework laws,[6] I identified and described five purposes that framework legislation could serve: enacting a symbolic response to a problem salient to voters, providing neutral rules for future decision making, solving collective action problems in areas where they are particularly acute, entrenching certain macro-objectives so that future decisions are more likely to align with them, and changing the internal balance of power in Congress. A particular framework is likely to serve more than one of these purposes. Although the purposes may not be unique to framework laws, they address the objectives differently than substantive laws. For example, a procedural framework can symbolize that Congress is changing the way it does business in a certain area or can serve to link decisions made over time to one overriding objective. In some cases, only a framework can solve a particular problem, such as collective action challenges.

Because a framework law is not a necessary response to a certain kind of problem, the question arises: Why does Congress choose the tool of a framework rather than adopt a law that more directly pursues the desired objective? Or, to use Hart's formulation, why use secondary rules rather than primary rules in a particular instance? For example, if lawmakers wish to reduce federal spending, they can change the content of appropriations bills using the regular congressional rules. So why the use of budgetary framework laws? Even when a problem demands a framework solution – such as reducing collective action problems and facilitating the passage of certain legislation – why does Congress adopt special rules in some areas and rely on the ordinary rules of procedure in others? In short, under what conditions will Congress choose to adopt framework laws?

In this chapter, I begin to answer these questions by specifying some of the conditions that are necessary for the adoption of framework laws.[7] It is a preliminary analysis that will require further empirical research to test some of the hypotheses. Furthermore, it is a partial analysis because the conditions discussed here are those

5 For a relatively comprehensive listing of framework laws, see Constitution, Jefferson's Manual, and Rules of the House of Representatives, H.R. Doc. No. 107–284, at 1045–1200 (2002) (providing list and text of "Congressional Disapproval" provisions enacted by statute that apply in the House). For a list of some familiar and important framework laws, see at Table 14.1 (also providing citations for U.S. laws discussed in this chapter).

6 Elizabeth Garrett, "The Purposes of Framework Legislation" (2005) 14 *J. Contemp. Legal Issues* 717 [hereinafter Garrett, *Purposes*].

7 This chapter does not identify and analyze the reasons that particular members of Congress might vote for statutory frameworks or support retaining them once enacted. Such an inquiry requires a separate analysis of the varied and overlapping motivations of lawmakers in a system aptly described by Schickler as characterized by "disjointed pluralism." Eric Schickler, *Disjointed Pluralism: Institutional Innovation and the Development of the U.S. Congress* (Princeton, N.J.: Princeton University Press, 2001).

that are required before it is possible for Congress to consider enacting a framework law as a response to a problem. There will be different and additional conditions that lead Congress to prefer secondary to primary rules in particular instances, and those conditions are likely to differ according to the kind of framework under consideration. Because frameworks serve different purposes – for example, some facilitate enactment of certain laws, some entrench particular objectives, and some set out relatively neutral rules for decision making[8] – the conditions under which they are enacted are likely to be different as well. Isolating the larger context in which frameworks are an option for Congress will lay the groundwork for further analysis of additional conditions specific to the different types of frameworks.

In Part I, I present two necessary conditions that make it possible for Congress to use a framework law to deal with a set of particular decisions defined in the framework. Even when these conditions are present Congress may decline to use the option of a framework, but without the two conditions, a framework is not an option for lawmakers. First, Congress must be able to identify a concrete problem and describe it with specificity so that the framework can be triggered in appropriate circumstances. Second, the partisan configuration of Congress is significant in several ways to the adoption of framework laws, although further empirical work focused on each of the two houses is required to specify this condition more fully. Party cohesion plays a role in the decision to use this device, and the relative power of the majority and minority parties makes a difference in Congress' ability to enact frameworks that limit minority rights. I provide some hypotheses here with respect to the role of partisan configuration in enactment of frameworks and link the analysis to related literature studying parties and congressional procedures.

A second set of conditions relates to Congress' decision to enact frameworks as statutes, rather than as concurrent or simple resolutions, which do not require agreement of the president. There is no discussion in the political science and legal literature of reasons that impel Congress to use a statute to enact internal legislative rule changes. This silence in the literature is mystifying because two of the most important sweeping procedural changes in the modern Congress were adopted as statutes – the *Legislative Reorganization Acts* of 1946 and 1970.[9] Yet, none of the discussions of these rule changes includes analysis of the congressional decision to use a statute to effect internal procedural reform.[10] The puzzle of the choice of form used to enact new procedures is posed clearly by the study of framework

[8] In earlier work, I discussed conditions for the latter type of framework laws that establish relatively neutral rules of decision. Elizabeth Garrett, "The Impact of *Bush v. Gore* on Future Democratic Politics" in G. M. Pomper and M. D. Weiner, eds., *The Future of American Democratic Politics: Principles and Practices* (New Brunswick, N.J.: Rutgers University Press, 2003) at 141 (outlining conditions in the context of the *Electoral Count Act*).

[9] Although the *Legislative Reorganization Acts* are the most sweeping statutized rules, Bruhl writes that the first rule-making statute was passed in 1789 when the first Congress enacted a statute regulating the order of business at the start of a new session. See Bruhl, *supra* note 3 at 346.

[10] See, e.g., David C. King, *Turf Wars: How Congressional Committees Claim Jurisdiction* (Chicago: University of Chicago Press, 1997) at 35 (noting that detailed committee jurisdictions first appeared in a statute, the 1946 *Legislation Reorganization Act*, and then "statutory jurisdictions" were changed through resolutions, but not commenting on the significance, if any, of the form of the original enactment and of subsequent changes). Of course, scholars are aware that statutes are the source of some congressional rules: see, e.g., Walter J. Oleszek, *Congressional Procedures and the Policy Process*, 6th ed. (Washington, DC: CQ Press, 2004) at 6–7, but there is no discussion that I have found about why Congress may choose the statutory route rather than the more typical – and superficially more appropriate – routes of concurrent or simple resolutions, caucus rules, committee rules or norms.

laws because all of these special procedures are enacted as part of statutes rather than through purely internal processes. The conclusions drawn with respect to framework laws will shed light on the broader phenomenon of statutized legislative rules.

In Part II, I assess three conditions that could explain why Congress has chosen the statutory path with respect to framework laws. First, Congress may use a statute to signal that it is making a significant change in the way it does business and that it perceives the change as more durable than other rule changes. Second, and most importantly, Congress will use a statute when the internal procedural change is an integral part of a larger package that must be adopted simultaneously and contains some parts that must be enacted with legal effect. In many cases, the framework is part of a larger "interbranch treaty" that affects both houses of Congress and the executive branch, often with provisions delegating authority to the president. Because some of the package must be enacted as a statute, all parts are enacted in the same statutory vehicle. Finally, path dependency and institutional learning play a role, so that when an area like budgeting or trade begins to be characterized by rule-making statutes, then future changes also tend to be adopted by statute.

Although they are developed and examined in the context of framework laws, these conditions, particularly the second one, have broader significance, explaining why Congress would use a statute to adopt any internal rules and procedures. My hypothesis is that the second condition – the need to enact at one time an interbranch treaty or other integrated proposal with some legislative parts – is necessary for Congress to enact a framework law. The third factor of path dependency is a plausibility condition, not a necessary one, in that it only makes it more likely that Congress will choose the framework response. Finally, the signaling story has little explanatory power, although further testing is required to discard it entirely. None of these is a sufficient condition, however, because we observe arenas of congressional action that fit one or the other of these conditions, as well as both the conditions specified in Part I, and yet there is no framework to structure deliberation.

Put together with a better understanding of the purposes of framework laws and enhanced by further work on specific conditions that give rise to particular kinds of frameworks, this analysis can suggest when Congress is likely to consider adopting a framework. It provides a better sense of what is special about this "unorthodox" feature of the U.S. legislative landscape.[11] Furthermore, it draws attention to a largely overlooked aspect of legislative rulemaking: that the form in which rules are adopted – whether by statute, simple or concurrent resolution, or other internal vehicle – is not a matter of chance but a product of deliberate choice by political actors.

I. NECESSARY CONDITIONS FOR CONGRESS TO HAVE THE OPTION OF A FRAMEWORK LAW

Although frameworks serve different purposes and thus the different types may be used under different conditions, the similarities among frameworks are sufficient to allow identification of some common conditions. First, Congress must be able

[11] Barbara Sinclair, *Unorthodox Lawmaking: New Legislative Processes in the U.S. Congress*, 2nd ed. (Washington, DC: CQ Press, 2000) (considering framework laws as part of unorthodox lawmaking).

to describe a problem with relative specificity so that the framework can be triggered in appropriate circumstances. That requires a relatively concrete problem. Second, certain partisan configurations may be necessary for lawmakers to adopt frameworks. Relatively strong party cohesion is likely a condition for enactment of many frameworks that transfer power to centralizing entities like party leaders and organizations. Also, to the extent that a framework affects minority rights (for example, by eliminating the filibuster), then the relative strength of the minority and majority parties is relevant.

A. A concrete, well-defined problem

The concreteness of a problem is always relevant in lawmaking because it shapes the issue environment and the willingness of lawmakers to spend time addressing a problem. In discussing factors that affect issue definition, Cobb and Elder identify the dimension of "specificity" as relevant to the ability of policymakers to define an issue and shape the arena of conflict.[12] By that term they focus on how concrete or abstract a problem is. Concreteness is especially important in the framework context: Framework laws must include as part of their design a definition of the subset of decisions to which they will apply, and this specification is driven by the problems that the framework laws are intended to resolve. In order to specify the proposals that will trigger application of a framework law and limit the law's scope appropriately, the drafters must have a relatively clear idea of the problem they are addressing.

In some cases, a framework law's scope is primarily limited by its duration. The 1988 *Omnibus Trade and Competitiveness Act* allowed the application of fast-track procedures to implementing legislation for multilateral and bilateral trade agreements reducing tariff and nontariff barriers entered into before a certain date. The president had to consult with Congress during negotiations and notify lawmakers of his desire to use fast track procedures for particular legislation, but the set of bills eligible for the trade promotion fast track was defined primarily by a general subject matter and a time period.[13] Thus, the concrete problem was the need to empower the president to negotiate trade deals that all policymakers knew were likely in the near term and that addressed both tariff and nontariff barriers. The set of laws that would be eligible for fast track became better defined as the process went forward and the president gave Congress notice of his intent to use fast track. Congress then had another chance to consider whether to allow the use of the expedited procedures.

Many budget rules are triggered by the effect of provisions. For example, proposals that have certain effects on spending or revenues are subject to budget points of order. The scope of the budget process has been driven by the problem Congress sought to address after the mid-1980s: the worsening deficit and seemingly uncontrollable federal spending. The budget process also defines its scope by the type of bill, focusing on those that affect spending and revenues. Therefore, appropriations bills are within the universe of proposals shaped by spending targets, and

[12] Roger W. Cobb and Charles D. Elder, *Participation in American Politics: The Dynamics of Agenda-Building* (Washington, DC: CQ Press, 1983) at 96.

[13] See, e.g., *Omnibus Trade and Competitiveness Act of 1988*, Pub. L. No. 100–418, §1103(b) (1988).

budget reconciliation bills, which typically deal with changes in entitlement programs and tax laws, receive special treatment. Reconciliation vehicles are allowed expedited treatment in both houses, particularly the Senate. Because this legislation can most forcefully and comprehensively redefine spending and tax laws, budget rules also limit the kinds of provisions that can appear on a reconciliation bill so that they remain targeted to the concrete problem of deficits and federal spending. For example, lawmakers cannot add to a reconciliation bill an "extraneous" amendment, which is a provision that does not change revenues or outlays or affect current or future deficits.[14] Again, the scope of the budget rules is defined in terms of their effect on the concrete problem.

The more abstract the problem attacked by the framework law, the more difficult it is to define its scope. This can result in narrowing the law's objective to a more easily defined subset of the larger problem. Consider the *Unfunded Mandates Reform Act (UMRA). UMRA* purports to protect values of federalism, which are contested, poorly specified, and relatively abstract.[15] Accordingly, Congress decided to focus on one particular area of federal–state–local interaction: unfunded federal mandates that impose obligations on states or localities without providing federal resources to defray associated costs. Arguably, such mandates endanger federalism more than other laws because they may occur more frequently. Unfunded mandates are particularly tempting to federal legislators who can take the credit for popular programs but who can avoid the blame for the tax increases or service reductions required to pay for the programs.[16] So the limited focus of *UMRA* on a relatively concrete problem allowed for more precise specification – the problem of unfunded mandates is a more concrete one than the general problem of federal interventions that implicate the values of federalism.

One option for drafters struggling with definitions and coverage is to allow future Congresses to choose whether to use the framework law once a particular proposal is actually before a committee or a full house. The *Line Item Veto Act (LIVA)* used this technique with regard to targeted tax provisions, which were those that benefited 100 or fewer taxpayers. The definition of targeted tax provisions reflected lawmakers' belief that giveaways to small special interest groups were more likely to be undesirable "pork." But because that concept is not particularly concrete (one person's pork is another's worthwhile project), the definition was both under- and overinclusive. To further refine the Act's scope and also to limit the power delegated to the president, *LIVA* empowered the Joint Tax Committee to list all such targeted tax provisions subject to presidential cancellation contemporaneously with consideration of a revenue bill. The Joint Tax Committee limited its own discretion by

14 For a fuller specification of this rule, often called the Byrd Rule after its author, see Allen Schick, *The Federal Budget: Politics, Policy, Process*, rev. ed. (Washington, DC: Brookings Institution, 2000) at 128.

15 See Elizabeth Garrett, "Enhancing the Political Safeguards of Federalism? The Unfunded Mandates Reform Act of 1995" (1997) 45 *U. Kan. L. Rev.* 1113 at 1128–31 (discussing various ways that values of federalism could be understood).

16 See Evan H. Caminker, "State Sovereignty and Subordinacy: May Congress Commandeer State Officers to Implement Federal Law?" (1995) 95 *Colum. L. Rev.* 1001 at 1065 (calling this "liability shifting); see also Edward A. Zelinsky, "The Unsolved Problem of the Unfunded Mandate" (1997) 23 *Ohio N. U. L. Rev.* 741 (also discussing this problem of accountability). But see David A. Dana, "The Case for Unfunded Environmental Mandates" (1995) 69 *S. Cal. L. Rev.* 1 at 18–21 (disputing the intractability of the problem).

promulgating guidance about how it would classify tax provisions as targeted and therefore susceptible to inclusion on the list subject to cancellation.[17]

Similarly, framework laws of short duration, such as some trade fast-track laws or the base closure commission procedures, have a more definite scope because all participants are fairly sure about the precise laws that will be affected. Because such frameworks are drafted and adopted with nearly complete information about which bills will fall within their scope, these frameworks operate much like those that allow Congress or other political actors to trigger coverage, as in *LIVA*'s tax provisions. Moreover, in frameworks like trade fast track, further actions by the president or Congress can deny specific bills the advantage of the process. These techniques to define the framework laws' scope are problematic because they postpone specification to a time when Congress will have a much better idea of the content of specific proposals. The greater the knowledge of the proposals that will be considered under special procedures, the greater the chance for self-interested parties to use frameworks strategically, a prospect that many framework laws seek to minimize. At the least, there is often a tension between developing sufficient information to allow precise definition of the framework law's scope, and leaving enough uncertainty about the framework's future application to minimize that ability of strategic political actors to undermine its objectives and to pursue their narrow self-interest.[18]

B. Congressional parties and framework laws

The partisan configuration in Congress is relevant to framework laws in at least two ways. First, many aspects of frameworks tend to transfer power to party leaders and organizations, so members are likely to support such laws when they think their interests will be aligned with the congressional parties. In other words, the level of party cohesion is important. This analysis relates to literature in political science, most notably recent scholarship of Cox and McCubbins, that identifies agenda control as the most important power wielded by the majority party in Congress and that assesses the circumstances under which the agenda power will be largely negative, blocking disliked proposals, or largely positive, enabling passage of favored proposals.[19] Framework laws are mainly concerned with shaping the legislative agenda and changing the transaction costs of legislating, both of which are crucial aspects of the tools that party leaders wield to influence policy.

Second, frameworks often affect the balance of power between majority and minority parties in Congress. Thus, one would expect that frameworks are more likely under some distributions of power between the parties than others. Scholars have discussed related issues in the context of rule changes affecting the power wielded by the minority party, and those conclusions may apply here, although

[17] See Elizabeth Garrett, "Accountability and Restraint: The Federal Budget Process and the Line Item Veto Act" (1998) 20 *Cardozo L. Rev.* 871 at 906 (discussing this process).

[18] This implicates the information-neutrality trade-off most relevant to the formulation of neutral frameworks. See Garrett, *Purposes, supra* note 6 at 738–41 (discussing issue in context of framework laws); Adrian Vermeule, "Veil of Ignorance Rules in Constitutional Law" (2001) 111 *Yale L.J.* 399 at 428–9 (discussing in context of constitutional frameworks).

[19] Gary W. Cox and Mathew D. McCubbins, *Setting the Agenda: Responsible Party Government in the US House of Representatives* (New York: Cambridge University Press, 2005) [hereinafter Cox and McCubbins, *Setting the Agenda*].

framework laws present twists on the more general question of rules altering the balance of power between parties. The hypotheses I advance here are suggestive and draw on this literature dealing with different sorts of rule changes. Relating the study of framework laws to the larger study of congressional procedures indicates that further analysis of the partisan configuration in both houses at the time framework laws are passed or strengthened may shed light on the larger phenomenon of rule changes that affect the relative power of congressional parties, as well as answering questions about the adoption of frameworks.

1. **PARTY COHESION.** Framework laws generally are tools to centralize and organize congressional decision making. They frequently transfer power away from committees and toward entities that can take advantage of centralizing forces – party leaders and party organizations. To the extent that some committees are advantaged by frameworks, they are often committees that are closely associated with party leaders, such as the Budget Committees or the House Rules Committee.[20] Frameworks also tend to favor committees that are representative of Congress as a whole and thus more likely to report out bills that satisfy the party and to move power away from committees with outlying preferences. For example, frameworks often empower the tax-writing committees, with memberships that are microcosms of the floor; while one framework, the base closure process, transferred power away from the Armed Services Committees, comprised of members with atypical preferences, and to the floor and party leaders.[21] Although these observations are generally true of current framework laws, some older frameworks empowered particular committees, some of which were not representative of the body, because they included legislative vetoes that could be exercised by one or more committees.[22] Even with these frameworks, however, Congress had a choice in determining which entities would be given power to exercise legislative vetoes and could transfer power away from a committee to the full house or to both houses.[23]

Focusing on the shifts in the balance of power within Congress that can be caused by frameworks links the study of this legislation to work on the effect of other procedures on internal legislative dynamics. In their book on the role of parties in Congress and the use of procedures to achieve party objectives, Cox and McCubbins argue that the main power of the majority party in Congress lies in its

[20] See Roger H. Davidson, "The Emergence of the Postreform Congress" in R. H. Davidson, ed., *The Postreform Congress* (New York: St. Martin's Press, 1992) 21. For a discussion of the role of the budget process in empowering congressional parties, see Elizabeth Garrett, "The Congressional Budget Process: Strengthening the Party-in-Government" (2000) 100 *Colum. L. Rev.* 702 [hereinafter Garrett, *Party-in-Government*].

[21] See Garrett, *Purposes, supra* note 6 at 761–2.

[22] See Louis Fisher, *Constitutional Conflicts Between Congress and the President*, 3d ed. (Lawrence: Kansas University Press, 1991) at 140–2 (describing committee vetoes). Legislative vetoes were also constructed that could be exercised by both houses or sometimes by one house acting alone; indeed, these are often referred to as "legislative vetoes," whereas the vetoes exercised by one or more committees are called "committee vetoes." The defining characteristic of all such vetoes is that they allowed some part of Congress or both houses to act with legal effect without meeting the presentment clause of the Constitution.

[23] See Garrett, *Purposes, supra* note 6 at 759–62 (discussing base closure framework and Congress's decision to transfer power away from committees with outlying preferences to the party organization and the floor).

control of the agenda. They identify two types of agenda power. Positive agenda power allows party leaders to push their proposals through to enactment; negative agenda power allows party leaders to block bills they do not like from reaching final passage.[24] Frameworks are part of the majority party's tools of agenda control and can be used to enhance both types of power. Among other things, frameworks can allow party leaders to bypass committees; they can empower committees that are closely aligned with the congressional parties; they can enhance the importance of parliamentary tactics on the floor where party leaders excel; they can put in place supermajority voting requirements in the Senate or protective rules for omnibus packages to reduce the ability of members to change the terms of negotiated agreements; they can lead to deal-making in summits controlled by party leaders in the legislative and executive branches; and they can package provisions, putting them to legislators for one vote to make the deal more palatable to rank-and-file members.

Why would many lawmakers agree to frameworks that strengthen party leaders or support retaining frameworks that increase the power of congressional parties? Certainly, members serving in party leadership positions, or hoping to use those offices as a route to power and influence, would support centralizing reforms. But they will be a small minority in the final vote. Under some conditions, more powerful congressional parties also serve the interest of rank-and-file members, whose support is necessary to enact frameworks. Virtually all politicians affiliate with parties because the party cue is one of the strongest, if not the strongest, voting cues.[25] Recent evidence suggests that U.S. voters increasingly perceive the two parties as different with respect to their positions on important social and economic policy issues, making the party cue more meaningful.[26] In order to continue to provide candidates with an established brand name, parties need to demonstrate to voters that they can pursue and implement certain policies. Stronger parties-in-government enable members to overcome collective action problems, arguably made worse by the decentralizing reforms of the 1970s, in order to pass legislation advancing the parties' policy agendas.

Just how strong the individual members are willing to allow parties and their leaders to become depends on the amount of party cohesion. Recent Congresses have consisted of partisans with more homogenous ideological preferences, so giving up some individual autonomy has been relatively less costly for these members than it was for members of previous Congresses.[27] Nonetheless, members'

[24] See Cox and McCubbins, *Setting the Agenda, supra* note 19 at 20.

[25] See John H. Aldrich, *Why Parties? The Origin and Transformation of Political Parties in America* (Chicago: University of Chicago Press, 1995) at 205; Gary W. Cox and Mathew D. McCubbins, *Legislative Leviathan: Party Government in the House* (Berkeley: University of California Press, 1993) at 120–2; Cox and McCubbins, *Setting the Agenda, supra* note 19 at 18.

[26] See, e.g., Margaret Weir, "Political Parties and Social Policymaking" in M. Weir, ed., *Social Divide: Political Parties and the Future of Activist Government* (Washington, D.C. Brookings Institution Press, 1998) at 1, 8, 10–11; Michael J. Malbin, "Political Parties Under the Post-McConnell Bipartisan Campaign Reform Act" (2004) 3 *Election L.J.* 177 at 179. See also Keith Krehbiel, *Pivotal Politics: A Theory of U.S. Lawmaking* (Chicago: University of Chicago Press, 1998) at 200 (noting that budget issues, now structured by frameworks, are salient issues used by parties "to build and maintain their brand name").

[27] See John H. Aldrich, Mark M. Berger, and David W. Rohde, "The Historical Variability in Conditional Party Government, 1877–1994" in David W. Brady and Matthew D. McCubbins, eds., *Party, Process, and Political Change in Congress: New Perspectives on the History of Congress* (Stanford: Stanford University Press, 2002) 17 at 33–4 (describing resurgence of conditional party government).

willingness to adopt procedural frameworks to strengthen parties that at the same time reduce the influence of individual members will be tempered. Lawmakers value their autonomy to pursue constituent interests without the confines of party discipline.[28] Members will want to balance their interest in crisp political brand names provided by parties with clear-cut agendas on which action has been taken with their interest in sending particular benefits to constituents. These interests are not wholly unrelated, however. The ability to enact the laws that send benefits to those constituents depends on the ability to compromise and logroll – activities that parties facilitate.[29]

Interinstitutional dynamics also play a role in the willingness of rank-and-file members to empower congressional parties. Political parties can allow members of Congress to act together as a more potent force against a strong unitary presidency. Such coordination is desirable, even at the cost of individual autonomy, because members of a legislature dominated by the president, particularly one of a different party, share the same bleak fate in terms of their ability to shape and initiate policy. Not surprisingly, the period of the most frequent use of framework laws is also an era identified by many congressional scholars as a time Congress was working to "institutionalize its capacity to challenge the President" because the executive branch was particularly aggressive.[30] It is also a time of frequently divided government,[31] a fact of political life which increases congressional concern that a strong executive branch will usurp its prerogatives. In addition, during periods of divided government, the party in control of Congress wants to enhance its ability to formulate clear policy that contrasts with the president's agenda so that it has the chance of unified government after the next election.

Frameworks do not favor party organizations without exception; they are often blends of provisions, many of which centralize, but some of which continue to place power with committees, individual members, or floor majorities.[32] Framework laws

[28] See Lawrence C. Dodd, "Congress and the Quest for Power" in L. C. Dodd and B. I. Oppenheimer, eds., *Congress Reconsidered*, 1st ed. (New York: Praeger Publishers, 1977) at 269, 272, 281–2 (discussing this tension).

[29] Barbara Sinclair, *The Transformation of the U.S. Senate* (Baltimore: Johns Hopkins University Press, 1989) at 210.

[30] See Sarah A. Binder, *Stalemate: Causes and Consequences of Legislative Gridlock* (Washington, DC: Brookings Institution Press, 2003) at 51 (referring to characterizations by Sundquist and others) [hereinafter Binder, *Stalemate*].

[31] The effect of divided government on the quantity and substance of legislation is the subject of much debate. Compare James L. Sundquist, "Needed: A Political Theory for the New Era of Coalition Government in the United States" (1988) 103 *Pol. Sci. Q.* 613 (arguing that divided government is inefficient and unaccountable) with Morris Fiorina, *Divided Government*, 2nd ed. (Boston: Allyn and Bacon, 1996) (arguing that coalition governments, the situation with divided government, do not necessarily lead to negative consequences) and David R. Mayhew, *Divided We Govern: Party Control, Lawmaking, and Investigations, 1946–1990* (New Haven: Yale University Press, 1991) (finding no significant difference in legislative activity between areas of divided and unified government). That divided government would affect the use of framework laws and Congress's interest in establishing more effective ways to articulate distinct policies for electoral gain seems likely. Cf. Fiorina, *supra*, at 104 (noting that divided government may well produce "second-order" effects related to the ease of governing).

[32] See Christopher M. Davis, CRS, *Report to Congress, "Fast-Track" or Expedited Procedures: Their Purposes, Elements, and Implications* (July 21, 2003) (describing how many frameworks change the power of committees and party leaders). Although frameworks may take some flexibility away from party leaders because they provide certain laws privileged treatment on the floor or limit amendments or time for debate, some of these provisions may actually enhance the power of the majority party by protecting legislative vehicles from interference by either committees or members during floor deliberation. As

can be complex; although many of their provisions favor parties, some do not, for example, by guaranteeing certain bills privileged access to the floor regardless of the views of party leaders. This complexity is a result of the balance that members seek to reach vis-à-vis congressional parties, as they weigh their desire for autonomy against their interest in stronger party organizations. For example, in his study of the budget reconciliation process, Gilmour describes the realignment in power caused by this framework law as favoring congressional majorities, rather than congressional parties.[33]

Gilmour's conclusion slights the power shift to political parties in the budget framework, particularly through the reconciliation process. Certainly, it is the case that the majority parties in the House and Senate do not absolutely control budget outcomes, but they are stronger in this arena than they were before the adoption and evolution of the federal budget process. One would not expect that lawmakers, whose interest in stronger political parties competes with their interest in the unfettered ability to send particularized programs back to their districts, would accede to a procedural framework that would allow parties to completely dominate budgeting. Nevertheless, the majority party and the president, another party leader, exert greater control over the shape of the budget resolution and the fiscal policy agenda than any other entity. Many budget resolutions have been drafted almost entirely by party leaders, in consultation with the budget committees, and cannot be changed substantially on the floor because of restrictive rules. Other budget proposals emerge from summits that are orchestrated primarily by party leaders and frequently bypass committees entirely.[34] Nonetheless, Gilmour's emphasis on the shift of power to floor majorities, rather than solely to party leaders and organizations, underscores that the internal dynamics resulting from framework laws will often not entirely favor any one institution but may balance power among several competing players.

Cox and McCubbins argue that the mix of negative and positive agenda powers will change over time as the majority party becomes more or less homogenous.[35] Framework laws will provide an arena to test these conclusions because they can exhibit both negative and positive characteristics. The empirical work necessary to assess the importance of party cohesion on frameworks must consider the different types of frameworks separately, because each type has a different mix of positive and negative tools. For example, the frameworks that have enhanced the majority party's positive agenda powers – by facilitating consideration and passage of particular legislation on the floor and transferring positive power from committees to party leaders – have become more evident during the 1970s and 1990s as parties have become more cohesive and homogenous. Studies must also distinguish between the House and the Senate, because regular House procedures tend to benefit parties and thus framework laws may have less effect on internal dynamics there than in the Senate where party leaders lack the tools of the Rules Committee

long as party leaders have substantial influence over the details of the legislation considered under framework laws, such limitations do not necessarily reduce their power but may enhance it.

33 John B. Gilmour, *Reconcilable Differences? Congress, the Budget Process, and the Deficit* (Berkeley: University of California Press, 1990) at 134–7.

34 Garrett, *Party-in-Government, supra* note 20 at 724–9.

35 Cox and McCubbins, *Setting the Agenda, supra* note 19 at 223.

and special rules governing debate on the floor. Thus, although further empirical work is required to determine precisely how the mix of negative and positive agenda control in frameworks shifts according to the level of party homogeneity, partisan cohesion and the willingness to transfer power to leaders are necessary conditions for enactment of many provisions that comprise framework laws.

2. THE BALANCE OF POWER BETWEEN THE PARTIES. Many framework laws eliminate or weaken aspects of the legislative process that can be used by minorities in Congress to obstruct passage of bills or to force compromise. By eliminating the filibuster in the Senate, for example, frameworks avoid the need to put together large bipartisan coalitions; instead, they allow simple majorities to act.[36] One important framework, the congressional budget process, not only eliminates the filibuster, but it also includes several procedural points of order that require sixty votes to waive. Many of these points of order work to protect the legislative vehicle constructed by party leaders and their agents from attacks or change on the floor or preserve packages so that rank-and-file members are not put to difficult political votes. The framework shifts the effect of supermajority voting from a context that weakens the majority party in the Senate – the filibuster – to one that largely strengthens it – points of order. Thus, one question posed by the enactment of many frameworks is what conditions lead to the adoption of rule changes that reduce the power of congressional minorities.

Dion and Binder have reached apparently conflicting conclusions about the partisan balance most likely to lead to rules that limit minority rights.[37] Both scholars agree that it is the partisan dynamic that is most relevant to the development and maintenance of procedures affecting minorities. They both find that claims that such rules are driven by workload considerations or by desires to establish norms of reciprocity (so that today's majority is treated well when it is tomorrow's minority) do not withstand rigorous analysis. Although they agree on the relevant factor driving change, they seem to disagree on the details.

Dion concludes that "there is convincing evidence from a number of institutions [primarily the House of Representatives, but also the Senate and some comparative work] that it is small majorities that tend to adopt limitations on minority rights."[38] He argues that this occurs in part because small majorities are more cohesive than large ones and thus the party caucus of a small majority can agree on the procedural changes more easily. In addition, large minorities are most likely to obstruct successfully and thus there is more reason in these circumstances for the majority to attempt to change the rules. Although Dion's conclusion is superficially appealing because it is small majorities that have the most to fear from obstructionist tactics, it overlooks the difficulty of enacting rules that harm minorities, or repealing those that strengthen them, in a context where inherited rules already provide

[36] See Krehbiel, *supra* note 26 at 90–1 (discussing negotiating dynamics caused by filibuster pivot in Senate).

[37] See Sarah A. Binder, *Minority Rights, Majority Rule: Partisanship and the Development of Congress* (New York: Cambridge University Press, 1997) [hereinafter Binder, *Minority Rights*]; Douglas Dion, *Turning the Legislative Thumbscrew: Minority Rights and Procedural Change in Legislative Politics* (Ann Arbor: University of Michigan Press, 1997).

[38] Dion, ibid. at 246.

some protection for minorities. When the minority is relatively large and cohesive, it is in a better position to successfully resist change that weakens it.[39]

In her study of formal rule changes affecting minority rights, Binder comes to a different conclusion. Although Dion may describe the world in which the majority most wants to limit minority rights – when the majority is small and the relatively large minority aggressively exploits mechanisms for obstruction – Binder's work reveals that this is also the world in which limitations on minority rights are most difficult to pass.[40] A relatively strong minority party, which can appeal for support from some fraction of the majority party that expects to find its interests aligned in some cases against its own party, can resist unfavorable rule changes. It is usually only relatively powerful majority parties that can overcome the status quo bias of the legislative process and alter inherited rules in a way that decreases the ability of minorities to block and to force concessions. Thus, Binder agrees with Dion that the size of the party coalitions matters to the procedures that will be adopted, but she argues that change at the cost of minority rights is most likely to occur when the minority is weak and the majority particularly strong. She does not claim that this partisan configuration explains all such procedural change,[41] but she thinks it the best explanation given her thorough canvassing of the history of congressional reform.

Binder briefly mentions the statutory frameworks that have included restrictions on the filibuster in the Senate, noting that they are an exception to her larger finding that Senate majorities have not been generally successful in limiting the rights afforded minorities by the inherited rules.[42] She suggests that the policy and institutional concerns that motivate frameworks might convince senators who are traditionally protective of minority rights to water them down in limited circumstances. Further testing of the Dion and Binder hypotheses in the context of framework laws could reveal which vision of the role of parties more accurately depicts the conditions giving rise to frameworks. The partisan configuration in the House as well as the Senate should be considered when assessing the conditions under which framework laws are likely to pass. Even though senators may directly feel the effect of any weakening of the right of filibuster, such a rule change affects dynamics in both houses. Representatives who believe that their interests are likely to coincide with the obstructing minority in the Senate have an interest in retaining the filibuster and other protective rules. If Binder's analysis is a better explanation, we would expect that framework laws weakening protections provided to minorities to be passed when the majority parties in the Senate *and* House are relatively strong vis-à-vis the minority party. However, this condition may not be as strongly

[39] As Dion himself warns, his analysis is limited to the cases he studies and may not apply to "any and all attempts by the majority to limit any sort of minority rights." Ibid.

[40] Binder, *Minority Rights, supra* note 37 at 205.

[41] Ibid. at 207. Adrian Vermeule offers a different perspective on the relationship between Dion's and Binder's studies. "Sarah A. Binder . . . argues that small majorities must often make procedural concessions, as a few defections can turn the tables. Douglas Dion . . . argues that small majorities are more cohesive and thus more likely to curtail minorities' procedural rights. Binder is emphasizing a factor that reduces the capacity of small majorities to have their way, while Dion is emphasizing an offsetting factor that increases the same capacity. The net effect is unclear." Adrian Vermeule, "Submajority Rules: Forcing Accountability upon Majorities" (2005) 13 *J. Pol. Phil.* 74, 79 n. 17. Studying framework laws could help provide an answer to the question Vermeule raises, along with the questions discussed in the text.

[42] Binder, *Minority Rights, supra* note 37 at 200.

pronounced in the context of frameworks because the specific policy and other considerations that lead to the adoption of the framework may allow even a somewhat weaker majority party to amass enough support for the procedural change.

Particular framework laws are different in another key way from the usual context in which minority rights are weakened, that is, when the reduction in minority rights applies generally rather than to a defined set of legislative actions. Often, expedited procedures in frameworks that restrict committee influence and eliminate the filibuster and rights to amend on the floor are adopted as ways to more easily disapprove of the president's exercise of a particular delegated power. Before the Supreme Court ruled the legislative veto unconstitutional in *Immigration and Naturalization Service v. Chadha*,[43] many frameworks empowered a bare majority in one house or both houses to block the executive branch's decision. The president was not involved in the legislative veto process, which was ultimately part of the reason the Supreme Court found the procedure unconstitutional. When the legislative veto was a possibility, a minority might well support the adoption of the framework because it held out the chance that they could convince a few in the opposing party to join them and overturn future executive action. Without expedited procedures, they would need support from key committee members, a majority in the House, and a filibuster-proof majority in the Senate. In other words, when the framework acted as a mechanism to negate executive branch decisions without presidential involvement and often without bicameral requirements, it might actually empower a relatively strong minority because they would need to attract fewer supporters from across the aisle to undermine the use of power delegated to the executive by a congressional majority. The posture of the legislative veto therefore makes simple characterizations of the conditions for procedural changes difficult.

After *Chadha*, however, this description of the benefit of expedited procedures to a strong minority is no longer accurate. Now, although a bare majority may be able to pass a joint resolution of disapproval under certain framework laws, the president must sign the resolution. Presumably he is very unlikely to agree to undo the work of agencies or his own decisions, so resolutions of disapproval must effectively have the support of veto-proof supermajorities in both houses. Currently, expedited procedures have real bite in frameworks such as fast track for trade implementing agreements or budget reconciliation bills where they provide more favorable rules for passing these bills – and these are instances where the procedures do operate to limit minority rights to obstruct or to significantly change legislative proposals.

II. CONDITIONS LEADING TO ADOPTION OF FRAMEWORKS IN STATUTORY FORM

The U.S. Constitution provides that "[e]ach House may determine the Rules of its Proceedings."[44] The rule-making power is reserved to each house, which has

[43] 462 U.S. 919 (1983) [*Chadha*] (ruling that legislative veto violates bicameralism and presentment clauses). Before *Chadha*, many laws had included the legislative veto that was typically accompanied by a framework law and allowed both houses, one house, or sometimes just a committee to disapprove an executive branch action. For a discussion of the legislative veto, see Jessica Korn, *The Power of Separation: American Constitutionalism and the Myth of the Legislative Veto* (Princeton, N.J.: Princeton University Press, 1996).

[44] U.S. Const., Art. I, §5.

the power to unilaterally change its rules of proceedings, consistent with some minimal constitutional requirements, without the involvement of the other house or the president.[45] One would expect, that the House and Senate would adopt their rules primarily through internal vehicles such as simple resolutions when the procedures affect only one house or concurrent resolutions when coordinated action is required. Contrary to the internal character of congressional rules and procedures, however, framework laws are all contained in statutes. Furthermore, Congress has occasionally enacted sweeping rule changes as statutes, such as the *Legislative Reorganization Acts* of 1946 and 1970, so the conclusions reached about the statutory nature of framework laws will likely also shed light on this related phenomenon. Thus, we turn to a second question: Under what conditions might Congress use a statute for rule changes, such as those that comprise framework laws?

The choice of statutory form is not a costless one; it matters which route Congress uses to pursue internal change. First, as inclusion of boilerplate reserve clauses suggest, Congress understands that putting a provision in a statute might lead a court to believe that it has power to enforce those rules, whereas judges are more likely to refrain from interfering with the implementation of clearly internal rules. Although courts have not viewed these statutory provisions as different in a meaningful way from rules adopted in internal resolutions,[46] the statutory form could be seen as a signal that Congress is adopting something with legal effect to be treated by courts just like other laws. For example, Bruhl describes an argument that the trade fast track procedure has legislative effect because it affords the president "the right to implement a trade pact through the expedited process set forth in the statute."[47] Of course, whether the president has the right to fast track depends on whether the process is indeed legislative rather than an internal procedure wholly within the control of each house of Congress. Various aspects of fast-track demonstrate that Congress has not conferred any right on the executive. Reverse fast track provisions providing an internal process to revoke fast track if the president does not adequately consult with Congress during trade negotiations and the requirement for decisions by congressional entities to trigger the process for particular bills make it clear that no right has been conferred, as does the reserve clause. Nonetheless, by putting fast track in a statute, rather than by enacting it in a related concurrent resolution at the same time trade promotion authority is delegated to the president, Congress leaves open the possibility that some will consider it legislative and therefore capable of enforcement by third parties like courts.

Some scholars are now making constitutional arguments against framework laws based on the form of these rules. Kesavan argues that Congress cannot deploy its constitutional rule-making authority through statute because such a form is too

[45] See *Yellin v. United States*, 374 U.S. 109 (1963); *United States v. Ballin*, 144 U.S. 1 (1892). For discussions of the case law, see John C. Roberts, "Are Congressional Committees Constitutional? Radical Textualism, Separation of Powers, and the Enactment Process" (2001) 52 *Case W. Res. L. Rev.* 489 at 530–41; Bruhl, *supra* note 3 at 384–7.

[46] See, e.g., *Metzenbaum v. FERC*, 675 F.2d 1282 (D.C. Cir. 1982) (describing such rules in statutes as "binding upon [the House] only by its own choice" and holding their enforcement to be nonjusticiable political questions). See generally Michael B. Miller, "The Justiciability of Legislative Rules and the 'Political' Political Question Doctrine" (1990) 78 *Cal. L. Rev.* 1341.

[47] See Bruhl, *supra* note 3 at 392.

"binding" with respect to rules of proceedings.[48] The implication of this argument is unclear – perhaps such provisions should be viewed as ineffective, requiring readoption by simple or concurrent resolution, or perhaps the statutory form renders them into something more binding on Congress, although that could be inconsistent with the exclusive grant of rulemaking authority to each house. Bruhl rejects the entrenchment attack but raises separation of powers concerns if rules are adopted in a vehicle that demands presidential involvement in internal congressional matters.[49]

Regardless of the outcome of these constitutional questions, the point is that Congress should not be indifferent about the form it chooses to adopt new rules and procedures. Scholars and, more importantly to Congress, some judges could view the form as significant, either leading to nullification of the rule or inviting judicial interference in its enforcement and application. Past experience with some frameworks demonstrates that courts have been willing to disapprove of congressional innovations that are not seen as purely internal rules. In *Chadha*,[50] the Supreme Court invalidated the legislative veto, a key component of many framework laws before the mid-1980s. In *Bowsher v. Synar*,[51] the Court struck down the delegation of sequestration authority to the Comptroller of the General Accounting Office, although it did not consider any question of internal congressional procedure. In *Clinton v. City of New York*,[52] the cancellation authority delegated to the president was ruled unconstitutional. Although only *Chadha* dealt with the congressional procedure, and even that case implicated the framework law only indirectly, these cases certainly suggest to lawmakers that the Court may not stay on the sidelines forever, particularly when it comes to rule-making statutes.

Second, even if the fact of presidential approval raises no constitutional concerns, it is a significant aspect of the initial process to adopt frameworks. Using the statutory vehicle threatens the ability of Congress to adopt the rules quickly because a statute can be vetoed. Thus, even if the involvement of the president is not necessary, is not seen as changing the nature of the new rules, and does not alter the ability of either house to unilaterally change the rules, presentment is another step in the process that may lead to delay and the need for renegotiation and readoption, albeit in a resolution rather than a statute. Why should Congress choose to use a process with an additional vetogate – and one exercised by a different branch – when it has the constitutional authority to adopt the same rules without executive branch involvement?

To answer this question, we must analyze three possible conditions for statutized rules. First, Congress could view the statutory format as signaling that the procedural change is particularly important or substantial, and perhaps that it should be accorded greater durability. Although this condition surely plays some role in the choice of format, and it deserves further scrutiny particularly with respect to claims about durability, I argue that it is not a significant factor in the decision to

48 See, e.g., Vasan Kesavan, "Is the Electoral Count Act Unconstitutional?" (2002) 80 *N.C. L. Rev.* 1653 at 1779–87 (making argument with respect to some provisions of the *Electoral Count Act*).

49 See Bruhl, *supra* note 3 at 404–13.

50 *Supra* note 43.

51 478 U.S. 714 (1986).

52 524 U.S. 417 (1998).

use statutes to enact rules. Second, a statute is used when some parts of an interbranch treaty require legal changes and the dynamics of negotiation require that all parts of the agreement be enacted in the same vehicle. If some aspects of the treaty must be in statutory form, then the internal rules required to assemble majority support for the package must be enacted in the same vehicle. This condition is a necessary – and the key – condition in the use of statutory vehicles to enact frameworks. Third, there may be an element of path dependency, so that when an area has been characterized by statutory framework laws, subsequent changes tend to occur via statute. This condition is only a plausibility condition, making framework laws more likely in the context of interbranch negotiations or large packages with legislative components.

A. Statutes as signals of the extent of the change

Although no scholarship I have discovered focuses on why the *Legislative Reorganization Acts* were adopted as statutes, some do characterize them as relatively substantial changes in the internal dynamics of both houses of Congress. The far-reaching changes in committees made in 1946 still generally determine the organization of the House and Senate, and the 1970 Act worked to redistribute power away from committees and to open the legislative process to greater public scrutiny. Both acts are referred to as symbols communicating a message of change to those holding power under the status quo ante.[53] Some framework laws, such as the congressional budget process, the War Powers Resolution, the base closure process, and the fast track for trade implementing acts, are intended in part as a signal of renewed congressional resolve to address an issue or a signal of a change in the way Congress will make certain decisions. However, not all framework laws are intended to bring about sweeping change – indeed, some are obscure and little used – so this explanation for the use of the statutory form is only partly satisfying at best.

The symbolism of using a statute to establish a framework could be used to communicate one of several messages. First, Congress could be communicating the breadth of the change – that it intends reform to be substantial and comprehensive. However, some of the most significant rule changes in modern congressional history, the adoption of Reed's Rules of the 1880s, were not adopted by statute but by simple resolution changing the standing rules and by alterations in the rulings handed down by the Speaker.[54] Although statutized rules were rare at this time, they were not unknown. The *Electoral Count Act* of 1887 is an early example of a framework law.

Second, Congress uses framework statutes to make the change more salient to outside audiences – the executive branch or the public. This could explain the

[53] The 1946 Act was "the first attempt at comprehensive reform of the modern Congress," Thomas R. Wolanin, "A View from the Trench: Reforming Congressional Procedures" in D. Hale, ed., *United States Congress* (New Brunswick, N.J.: Transaction Books, 1983) 209 at 212, and was intended to signal the executive branch that Congress would no longer follow the submissive model it had adopted during the 1930s and World War II. Similarly, the 1970 Act was seen by some members as a "symbol to [primarily committee] leadership that they couldn't run over us like they used to." Norman J. Ornstein, "The Legislation Reorganization Act of 1970: First Year's Record" in N. J. Ornstein, ed., *Congress in Change: Evolution and Reform* (New York: Praeger, 1975) 187 at 200 (quoting Rep. Thomas M. Rees, D–Calif.).

[54] See Cox and McCubbins, *Setting the Agenda*, *supra* note 19 at 55–8.

choice of format for Reed's Rules, which were primarily directed at an internal audience. But other important changes that Congress has clearly seen as communicating messages to outside audiences – such as the changes made by the House of Representatives after the Republican takeover in the 104th Congress – were made through nonstatutory means.[55] In this case, although the House supported the changes, the Senate did not share the sense of urgency or the commitment to the reforms. Accordingly, a simple resolution that did not require bicameral action was used by House reformers to adopt the changes. So the political realities dictated the form of the rule changes. Similarly, if Congress is working to send the executive a signal that it plans to be more aggressive in the future, enacting that signal in a form that requires presidential involvement may be risky because the president can use the even more powerful signal of his constitutional veto. Presumably, for example, one reason Congress has been unwilling to change the concurrent budget resolution into a joint resolution, which is a legislative vehicle that requires presidential approval, is the desire to reduce the president's influence over this internal budget process. Thus, it seems puzzling that Congress would choose to send the president a chastening message using a statute, which requires his involvement to enact, unless circumstances suggest that he will have no choice but to accept.

Third, Congress might hope to signal that it expects a framework reform to be more durable than reforms adopted through internal vehicles. This signal is complicated because one reason Congress may use a framework law rather than a primary rule directed at the same objective is that secondary rules, whatever their format, are somewhat less durable. They can be changed unilaterally, and they can be waived or ignored in particular circumstances. However, statutized procedural rules may signal durability in a way that procedural rules adopted through internal vehicles do not; in other words, frameworks may have a sort of intermediate strength between substantive laws and internally adopted rules.

But the strength of this signal is undermined, at least with respect to sophisticated audiences, by the reserve clauses included in framework laws explicitly stating that they are exercises of rule-making authority and have no greater durability than any other internal rule. In addition, the House reenacts the rules adopted by statute each session when it passes its standing rules (which it does in the form of a simple resolution), suggesting that, just like other internal rules, statutized rules must be readopted each session to remain effective. Just as with the standing rules themselves, the House could adopt changes or modifications to the frameworks at this time, although it instead includes boilerplate language in the rules resolution keeping the framework procedures in place.[56] All Senate rules, whether or not contained in framework statutes, are relatively durable because, as a continuing body, its standing rules remain in effect from session to session, just as do

[55] See H. R. Res. 6, 104th Cong., 1st Sess. (1995). This internal resolution changed term limits for committee and subcommittee chairs to no more than three consecutive Congresses, prohibited voting by proxy, and required a three-fifths vote for any tax increase measures or amendments.

[56] See H. R. Res. 5, §1, 108th Cong., 1st Sess., 2003 (adopting all "applicable provisions of law . . . that constituted the rules of the House at the end of the One Hundred Seventh Congress"); H. R. Res. 5, House Rule XXVIII, 106th Cong., 1st Sess., 1999 (providing that the "provisions of law that constituted the Rules of the House at the end of the previous Congress shall govern the House in all cases to which they are applicable").

the procedures contained in statutory frameworks. Changes to Senate rules can be filibustered just like framework laws, but it is harder to cut off debate on changes to the standing rules because sixty-seven votes, not the usual sixty, are required to invoke cloture.[57] Moreover, to the extent that the standing rules have general applicability and therefore broader effects on future lawmaking, it could be the case that Congress considers internal changes made in these legislative vehicles more durable. Framework laws, on the other hand, affect certain policy arenas and thus may be viewed as more limited in their impact and easier to change without far-reaching effect.[58] In short, the signal of durability provided by a rule-making statute rather than a rule adopted by concurrent or simple resolution is ambiguous at best.

Enactment of a statute may show a greater commitment to a particular action because it requires the cooperation of both houses and the president – or, if he vetoes the framework, the agreement of supermajorities in Congress. That support may ensure durability for as long as the preferences of policymakers remain unchanged. But in that case, durability stems from acceptance of the practice by those who follow it, not from the form in which it was enacted. To determine whether the statutory form itself makes a different to the "stickiness" of the rule or procedure, further work is required to study the frequency and rate of change to rules adopted through statutes compared to those enacted in other forms. Changes to frameworks need not occur in subsequent statutes; one or both houses can formally change the rules through internal vehicles, or they can simply waive the procedures in particular cases. Thus, any study of the rate of change to statutory frameworks compared to similar nonstatutory procedures would need to include all sorts of methods of revision. I suspect that any difference in durability is insignificant. For example, even though the House readopts statutized rules each session with boilerplate language, it also leaves most of the other rules unchanged from session to session. Most alterations to House procedures occur through special rules promulgated by the Rules Committee that apply to a single bill.

Thus, none of the messages that might be communicated through the use of the statutory form seem to require this method of adoption for the signal to be expressed. There are other ways to make a framework salient to internal and external audiences. Although congressional insiders claim there is a perception of greater durability with respect to frameworks than to rules adopted in simple or concurrent resolutions, this statement is at least undermined by the reserve clause and may well turn out to be countered by the practice with the implementation of framework statutes. It is the second condition – that of enacting all parts of a comprehensive bargain simultaneously – that seems a more promising explanation.

B. Enacting bargains as a package

The key to understanding the use of statutes to enact frameworks lies in the most important difference between a statute and the various other legislative options available to Congress. Statutes are different from simple and concurrent resolutions

[57] Senate Rule XXII.

[58] Thanks to Sarah Binder for this speculation.

because they can be used to adopt reforms that have legal force and effect.[59] Thus, statutory frameworks (and other statutory rule changes) will be enacted under the following three related necessary conditions:

1. The congressional framework is related to other changes that require legal change, such as delegating authority to the president, changing legislative salaries, or modifying other aspects of the legislative process that have legal consequences, not just internal effects.
2. The entire package is negotiated as an integrated "treaty": Passage is possible only if all parts of the package are enacted, and contending forces demand simultaneous adoption to reduce the chances that the deal will unravel and only some parts will be enacted.
3. The negotiated package can obtain the support of both houses and the president – or it has two-thirds support in both houses that is sufficient to override a presidential veto.

My claim here is not that the framework laws are given legal force and effect because they are adopted in statutes; indeed, the reserve clauses explicitly deny frameworks status as legislation. Rather, frameworks passed as statutes are critical components of larger packages that include legal changes. If parties agreeing to the compromise insist that all parts of the package be enacted at the same time, then all must be adopted as a statute because some parts cannot be enacted as anything else. That necessity also means that all parts of the deal – internal changes as well as, say, delegation of authority to the president – must be able to pass the hurdles of bicameralism and presentment. If the president is unwilling to accept all parts of the deal – or the package cannot obtain supermajority legislative support sufficient to override a veto – then supporters of the package will have to decide if they will accept piecemeal passage of the deal or if the compromise will founder.

Simultaneous enactment of these packages is therefore a requirement of their negotiation, not a legal requirement. Of course, deals can be enacted in parts, with some in statutory form and some in the form of concurrent or simple resolutions. However, the 1921 *Budget Accounting Act* may be a cautionary tale for those considering passing the parts of a deal in different formats.[60] After Congress passed the first version of the Act in 1920, which primarily instituted an executive budget process and required the president to submit a budget each year, lawmakers then considered controversial rule changes that would alter the congressional appropriations process in response to the new executive branch apparatus. The new rules created one large appropriations committee in the House, thereby centralizing the legislative budget process in a move that mirrored the Act's centralization of the executive budget.[61] A divided House adopted the rule changes in a separate resolution, which served the strategy of the reformers who hoped to use the executive branch changes as leverage to force internal reform. Congress was then

[59] Joint resolutions are the same as statutes for these purposes – they have legal consequences and, accordingly, they must be signed by the president.

[60] See Charles H. Stewart, *Budget Reform Politics: The Design of the Appropriations Process in the House of Representatives 1865–1921* (New York: Cambridge University Press, 1989) at 204–11 (providing details of story).

[61] See ibid.

surprised, after it passed the internal restructuring, when Wilson vetoed the *Budget Accounting Act.* Ultimately, President Harding signed the bill and both parts of the compromise were enacted, but the episode highlights the danger posed to comprehensive reform by piecemeal enactment. Congress could have been left with a new internal appropriations process that a pivotal block of legislators had supported only in the context of executive branch reorganization. Although Congress could have repealed the internal reorganization, the status quo bias inherent in the legislative process would have made that somewhat difficult as long as the new structure retained some significant support. This episode demonstrates to lawmakers who view certain provisions as essential to their support that they should be sure to get their provisions at the same time as those supporting the other parts of the bill get theirs.

There are at least two related circumstances in which statutory frameworks are necessary to adopt larger packages of legal change. First, many framework laws are found in bills that delegate substantial authority to the president and executive branch.[62] Advocates are able to assemble majority support for the broad delegation only if it is accompanied by a framework law that enables Congress to more easily disapprove of the exercise of the delegated authority. This has been the case, for example, in laws delegating the power to reorganize the executive branch, empowering the executive to make certain arms sales, formally accepting the president's power to introduce the military into conflict in some cases without prior congressional approval, and dealing with particular emergencies.[63] Sometimes the internal structure merely guarantees consideration of a disapproval resolution on the floor, allowing a committee to be bypassed, or it can also provide privileged and expedited procedures for floor action. Sometimes, the framework moves the main locus of oversight from a committee seen as too closely allied with the executive branch to the floor or to party leaders, such as occurred in the base closure framework.[64] The heyday of framework laws, the 1970s and 1990s, have also been times of interbranch conflict, so it is not surprising that substantial delegations of authority came with changes designed to increase congressional capacity to check the use of that power.

Of course, not all – not even most – delegations of authority to the president are accompanied by framework laws. So although this aspect of frameworks is part of a necessary condition for their enactment as statutes, it is clearly not sufficient. It remains for further work to specify the conditions under which delegations are, or are likely to be, enacted with framework laws for disapproval resolutions or for approval of subsequent related legislation. It seems likely that, at the least, frameworks are used to enhance congressional oversight when ex ante specification of guidelines for the exercise of discretion is difficult and when oversight by third parties, such as courts, is rare or nonexistent. Many frameworks have been enacted

[62] See Garrett, *Purposes, supra* note 6 at 744–8.

[63] See, e.g., James L. Sundquist, *The Decline and Resurgence of Congress* (Washington, DC: Brookings Institution, 1981) at 349 (discussing demands by some in Congress for legislative vetoes, which were often accompanied by framework laws, before delegating substantial authority). Often the advantage of expedited procedures provided by framework laws is available only for a certain time after the president has exercised his delegated authority. See Christopher M. Davis, *CRS Report to Congress, Expedited Procedures in the House: Variations Enacted Into Law CRS-2* (July 21, 2003).

[64] The base closure process delegates most authority to make decisions about which bases to close or realign to an independent commission, with only limited involvement by the executive branch.

in areas where courts have declined to intervene, such as budgeting, foreign relations, trade, and emergencies.[65]

The coupling of framework laws with delegations of authority to the president reveals why Congress does not worry about obtaining presidential approval of some frameworks to enhance congressional oversight. If the president wants the delegated power, he must accept the bitter with the sweet. He may object to the framework, but his constitutional veto does not allow him to excise out the offending portions of a bill. In fact, after *Chadha*[66] declared the legislative veto unconstitutional, the president may not be particularly concerned about inclusion of framework provisions because any resolution of disapproval requires his signature and therefore effectively requires passage by veto-proof majorities. More problematic from the president's perspective are frameworks like trade fast-track procedures that require congressional approval before action can be taken. However, sometimes these frameworks actually serve the president's interest; for example, fast track protects his proposal for implementing legislation from amendment or delay once it is introduced in Congress. This framework benefits the president because it enhances his ability to make credibly binding deals in bilateral and multilateral negotiations. However, it also protects the congressional interest by requiring extensive consultation during negotiations, providing for a reverse fast-track process to withdraw the framework from a particular bill, and ensuring committee involvement in the drafting of the implementing legislation.[67]

Not all frameworks accompany laws that expand presidential power, however; the 1974 *Budget Act* constrained the president's impoundment power, the War Powers Resolution arguably constrained his military powers in some ways (while expanding it in others), and the base closure process delegates to an independent commission power that might have gone to the executive branch. In these cases, Congress must be certain either that the president has no choice but to accept the law in its entirety – perhaps because it provides sufficient goodies to entice him or because the president is relatively weak – or that it has the votes to override a veto. For example, the framework structuring consideration of rescissions proposals[68] sent by the president to Congress requires that lawmakers affirmatively accept the rescissions before they go into effect. President Nixon accepted this framework, and the larger congressional budget process, because he was at the brink of impeachment and knew that he could not successfully veto the *Budget Act* of 1974.[69]

A second sort of package also needs to be enacted as a statute. Some compromises require legal changes as well as internal ones to be entirely effective. For example, the *Legislative Reorganization Act* of 1946 – not a framework law but a sweeping and general internal change adopted through a statute – included a pay

[65] For preliminary analysis of these conditions, see Garrett, *Purposes, supra* note 6 at 745–6.

[66] *Supra* note 43.

[67] For a discussion of how fast track works to protect congressional interests, see Garrett, *Purposes, supra* note 6 at 757–9.

[68] A rescission is a proposal to refrain from spending, or to cancel, an appropriation previously enacted by Congress.

[69] See Allen Schick, *Congress and Money: Budgeting, Spending, and Taxing* (Washington, DC: Urban Institute, 1980).

raise for lawmakers and a new pension system, both provisions necessary to gain support for the entire package. Those who favored the legislative pay raise knew that it had to be passed together with internal reforms to make it more palatable to the press and the public.[70] The base closure process required that Congress establish an independent external commission to make closure and realignment recommendations because a majority trusted neither the Department of Defense nor the Armed Services Committees to make those decisions.[71] Such a commission could be set up only by passing a statute with legal force. Internal reform of the budget process would have been unlikely had it not been coupled with provisions to respond to the unprecedented policy impoundments by Nixon.[72] Later budget procedures contained both internal enforcement devices, which could have been passed by concurrent resolution, and also external enforcement of sequesters if spending exceeded predetermined caps. *UMRA* had a title applying to congressional deliberation, and a separate title applying to administrative agencies with respect to unfunded intergovernmental mandates. If one part of a legislative deal has to be enacted by statute to be effective, and parties to the compromise insist on simultaneous enactment, then all parts of the treaty must be enacted statutorily.

It is not necessary that all negotiated deals containing some legal aspects and some internal restructuring be enacted by one statute. Congress can always disaggregate the parts and enact the legal changes through statute and the rule changes through some sort of internal resolution. Indeed, both the House and Senate could use procedures to tie the enactment of two vehicles together so that they are both enacted at the same time. But the more coordination that is required, the more difficult it is to credibly commit to enactment of multiple parts. Particularly in the Senate where unanimous consent is required for many procedural moves, it is hard to credibly promise that separate bills will stay connected as consideration proceeds. In addition, there may be symbolic value to adoption in one package; that is, enacting pay increases along with internal reforms sends a different kind of message to voters than enacting each separately.

During negotiations on these legislative treaties and omnibus bills, those demanding procedural changes as the price for their support of the legal changes are surely aware that the former are less durable than the latter. The reserve clauses included with most framework laws make clear that each house reserves its right to change the rules included in the statute unilaterally without meeting the constitutional requirements for legislation of bicameralism and presentment. Nonetheless, there is a status quo bias inherent in all congressional action, and those who advocate frameworks know that once they are enacted, they will be relatively difficult to repeal. Although lawmakers may ignore or waive internal rules, there may be a political cost to be paid for that decision.[73] Frameworks are not illusory constraints, and legislators who demand them in return for their support of a larger package understand that. Moreover, there will be entities in Congress that become

[70] See Schickler, *supra* note 7 at 143 (also quoting La Follette that it all had to be "wrapped up in one package").

[71] See Garrett, *Purposes, supra* note 6 at 760.

[72] See Keith E. Whittington and Daniel P. Carpenter, "Executive Power in American Institutional Development" (2003) 1 *Persp. on Pol.* 495 at 508.

[73] See Frederick Schauer, "Legislators as Rule-Followers," Chapter 23 in this volume (discussing internal enforcement mechanisms for congressional rules and norms).

interested in retaining the frameworks once they begin to operate; for example, often the committee that has oversight responsibilities or party leaders who control the floor agenda work to protect a framework that has empowered them.

C. Path dependency

Finally, there is another practical reason that frameworks tend to be passed as statutes rather than through other mechanisms. Once an area of decision making is structured by rulemaking statutes, lawmakers may continue to adopt procedures through this mechanism. Moreover, problems that are similar to those that are governed by framework laws may also be the target of new frameworks. One can characterize this as path dependency or as a form of institutional learning. In other words, once members of Congress become familiar with a certain form of legislative process, they will often continue to use that form because it reduces transaction costs and poses less uncertainty. This condition is thus a plausibility condition, not a necessary one, making it more likely that Congress will respond to a problem with a framework.

Legislative entrepreneurs who champion framework legislation as a solution to a particular problem can reduce transaction costs by using familiar rules and procedures – it is more costly to invent a new wheel than to appropriate an old one and make it work with a few changes. Legislative entrepreneurs are vital to the adoption of framework legislation, as they are with respect to other legislative activity.[74] These actors will seek to minimize the costs of their entrepreneurial activity so that they can spend more time on constituent service, advertising, and other behavior vital to their reelection. They can save significant costs by using past frameworks as models for new proposals. Not only are costs of creation reduced, but it may also be easier to persuade others to join in the effort when the proposal borrows from other structures. Garnering majority – or sometimes supermajority – support for the adoption of a framework is more likely if lawmakers are comfortable with its familiar features and can better predict how they will be able to pursue their objectives within the new structures. The change can also be portrayed as less dramatic when it draws on or amends structures already in place rather than establishing entirely new arrangements. In short, there is institutional learning that takes place after experience with frameworks.

Thus, it should not be surprising that frameworks modifying the congressional budget process, enacted in statutory form because of the second condition, were also adopted as statutes. In some cases, a legal change was required so the statutory choice was dictated by the second condition relating to enactment of packages. In other cases, the choice of statute might be largely a matter of path dependency to decrease transaction costs associated with uncertainty (albeit at the price of the greater transaction costs of enacting a statute rather than an internal resolution). If the concurrence of both houses and the president are likely, then entrepreneurs may choose the familiar statutory form for framework laws to mute opposition. Of course, if one of the players in the Article I, Section 7 game[75] is unwilling to

[74] See generally Gregory Wawro, *Legislative Entrepreneurship in the U.S. House of Representatives* (Ann Arbor: University of Michigan Press, 2000).

[75] See William N. Eskridge, Jr., and John Ferejohn, "The Article I, Section 7 Game" (1992) 80 *Geo. L.J.* 523 (using this terminology to explain the interactions between legislative and executive branches in legislating).

Table 14.1. *Examples of Framework Laws*

Electoral Count Act[76] (1887) – procedures and default rules triggered by contested Electoral College votes.
Executive Reorganization Acts (first in 1939[77]) – expedited process to disapprove presidential reorganization plans formulated under power delegated by the Acts.
Various *Congressional Pay Acts* (first in 1967[78]) – expedited process first to disapprove of pay increases proposed by independent commission and then to approve the recommendations before they went into effect.
Congressional Budget and Impoundment Control Act[79] (first in 1974, with significant changes by *Gramm-Rudman-Hollings Act*,[80] 1985, and *Budget Enforcement Act*,[81] 1990) – provides complex structure for congressional budget process as well as setting up impoundment process.
Fast Track for Trade Implementing Agreements (first in 1974[82]) – expedited process for enacting president's proposed implementing laws for certain multilateral and bilateral trade agreements negotiated under trade promotion authority delegated to the president.
War Powers Resolution[83] (1974) – structures congressional involvement in declaring war and overseeing introduction of forces into military conflict.
Base Realignment and Closure Acts (first in 1988)[84] – expedited process to disapprove of recommendations to close and realign military bases that are put forward by an independent commission established in the Acts.
Unfunded Mandates Reform Act[85] (1995) – structures consideration of laws imposing intergovernmental mandates and makes it more difficult to enact them without also providing federal funding.
Line Item Veto Act[86] (1996) – expedited process to disapprove presidential cancellations and internal process to identify targeted tax provisions eligible for cancellation.
Congressional Review Act[87] (1996) – expedited process to disapprove major regulations.
Tax Complexity Analysis[88] (1998) – internal process to ensure that information about complexity of certain tax proposals is available to Congress.

play, then a different route may be taken, such as a concurrent resolution to ensure bicameral action or a simple resolution to effect intrachamber reorganization. For example, readoption of the budget pay-as-you-go rule in the tax and entitlement arena which was part of the 1990 *Budget Enforcement Act* was considered in 2004 during debate on a concurrent budget resolution – a vehicle that does not require presentment. Putting the rule in a budget law was not an option because President Bush supported pay-as-you-go only in the entitlement arena and not applied to tax bills.

[76] 24 Stat. 373 (1887).
[77] Pub. L. No. 76–19, 53 Stat. 561 (1939).
[78] Pub. L. No. 90–206, 81 Stat. 613 (1967).
[79] Pub. L. No. 93–344, 88 Stat. 297 (1974).
[80] Pub. L. No. 99–177, 99 Stat. 1037 (1985).
[81] Pub. L. No. 101–508, 104 Stat. 1388 (1990).
[82] Pub. L. No. 93–618, 88 Stat. 1978 (1974).
[83] Pub. L. No. 93–148, 87 Stat. 555 (1973).
[84] Pub. L. No. 100–526, 102 Stat. 2623 (1988).
[85] Pub. L. No. 104–4, 109 Stat. 98 (1995).
[86] Pub. L. No. 104–130, 110 Stat. 1200 (1996).
[87] Pub. L. No. 104–121, 110 Stat. 868 (1996).
[88] Pub. L. No. 105–206, §4022, 121 Stat. 685 (1998).

CONCLUSION

I have isolated several conditions relevant to the decision to enact framework laws. First, two conditions are relevant to the decision to attack a problem through a framework rather than through some other mechanism. The problem must be concrete enough to allow for the framework solution, with requires Congress to define ex ante when the framework will be triggered. Moreover, the partisan configuration of Congress doubtlessly figures prominently in the decision to use a framework response, but more empirical work is required to get a clearer sense of these partisan dynamics. Second, three conditions are relevant to the decision to use a statute to adopt internal congressional rules, with the most important necessary condition being that the rule changes are part of a deal that must be adopted as a package and that includes some provisions that must have the force of law.

ACKNOWLEDGMENTS

I appreciate very helpful comments by Stan Bach, Richard Beth, Sarah Binder, Aaron Bruhl, John Ferejohn, Louis Fisher, Andrei Marmor, Mat McCubbins, Eric Posner, Steve Smith, Adrian Vermeule, and Omri Yadlin, and research assistance from Robert Olson (USC '07) and Joanna Spilker (USC '05).

15 Super-Statutes: The New American Constitutionalism

William N. Eskridge, Jr., and John Ferejohn

Carolyn Aiello was caught in a constitutional transition. Living in the Bay Area of California, Aiello supported herself as a hairdresser. But her livelihood was (temporarily) cut off when complications associated with her pregnancy required her to take a medical leave on June 21, 1972. The doctors discovered that Aiello had an ectopic pregnancy and performed surgery to terminate her pregnancy. Although she would ultimately return to work on July 28, she could not afford the loss of even a month's income. Like millions of other Americans, Aiello applied for unemployment benefits on the basis of her physical disability – but, unlike most other applicants having serious even if temporary disabilities, her claim was denied. California's unemployment compensation program excluded from its coverage disability claims based on pregnancy.

This was a state discrimination affecting thousands of working women like Aiello. Represented by San Francisco civil rights attorney Wendy Webster Williams, Aiello and three other women sued the state to overturn this discrimination in its unemployment compensation law. Their argument was that the exclusion of pregnancy-based claims from the unemployment program violated the Equal Protection Clause. Speaking for a three-judge federal court, Judge Zirpoli ruled the exclusion unconstitutional – but the United States Supreme Court reversed. It held, in *Geduldig v. Aiello* (1974), that pregnancy-based exclusions are not subject to heightened equal protection scrutiny and that the California exclusion was a rational means for the state to tailor its program and, essentially, save money.[1]

Given this result, which the Supreme Court has never revisited, one might conclude that women have no fundamental right not to be discriminated against on the basis of their pregnancies. One would be wrong. The right of women to equal treatment is foundational in American society, and that foundational right entails the right not to be discriminated against on the basis of pregnancy. But the right has not been derived from the Constitution. It is embedded in a statute. A *super-statute.*[2]

[1] *Geduldig v. Aiello*, 417 U.S. 484 (1974).

[2] We first developed the notion of "super-statute" in William N. Eskridge, Jr., and John Ferejohn, "Super-Statutes" (2001) 50 *Duke Law Journal* 1215–76 ["Super-Statutes"]. Earlier writers have used this term to describe a constitution, see A. E. Dick Howard, *The Road from Runnymede: Magna Carta and Constitutionalism in America* (Charlottesville: University of Virginia Press, 1968) at 122, or as a big statute with no normative force outside its four corners. See Bruce Ackerman, "Constitutional Politics/Constitutional Law" (1989) 99 *Yale Law Journal* 522.

Just because Carolyn Aiello lost her constitutional case before the Supreme Court does not mean that she and her lawyers lost their normative campaign to establish pregnancy as a category that should, as a matter of fundamental right, not be the basis for state (or even private) discrimination. Our view is that fundamental rights are not exhausted by constitutional claims recognized by courts. Furthermore (and more iconoclastically), we maintain that fundamental rights at the dawn of the new millennium are more firmly and legitimately rooted in statutory claims recognized by legislatures and agencies as well as courts. The process by which fundamental norms stick in our society through statutory enactment, implementation, and interpretation is the heart of our project. Super-statutes have changed the way American public law evolves and ought to evolve.

What is this new constitutional form? This chapter will be occupied with elaborating as well as justifying it, but the idea itself can be stated simply: A super-statute is a law or series of laws that (1) seek to introduce or consolidate a norm or principle as fundamental in our polity, (2) over time do "stick" in the public culture even as the norm evolves through a series of debates and even conflicts about its elaboration or specification, (3) such that the super-statute and its normative principle have a broad effect on the law – including effects beyond the four corners of the statute. In American history, examples of such statutes include the *Sherman Act* of 1890, the *Civil Rights Act* of 1964, and (perhaps more tentatively) the *Endangered Species Act* of 1973. Each of these is concerned with defining and protecting certain substantive fundamental values or rights. Such laws not only reflect and help instantiate American public values, but those values also have driven American constitutional law, rather than vice versa. We would also include as super-statutes what Bruce Ackerman has called framework statutes that have the aim of establishing fundamental institutions within the federal system. Paradigmatic of these are the *Judiciary Acts* of 1789, 1891 and 1925, but one might well include the *Campaign Finance Act* of 1974 and subsequent amendments, and a number of other statutes as well such as those requiring that elections to the House be conducted in single-member districts or prescribing federal rules regulating the electoral college.

Super-statutes and related phenomena have given rise to what we call a *new American constitutionalism.* Unlike the standard account of American constitutionalism, this new constitutionalism maintains that changes in public norms and constitutional principles occur outside of the Article V process for changing the Constitution, are developed in legislatures and agencies as well as in courts, and are incremental and continuous rather than dramatic and episodic. We defend the normative superiority of the new American constitutionalism and explore some of its ramifications for the operation of public law in the new millennium.

I. THE STANDARD ACCOUNT OF AMERICAN CONSTITUTIONALISM

Wendy Webster Williams sought relief for Carolyn Aiello under the auspices of the standard account of American constitutionalism. The standard account was, and to some extent remains, the conventional wisdom of legal professionals, has long been thought to reflect the understanding of the framers of the U.S. Constitution and the Reconstruction Amendments (which added the Equal Protection Clause to the Constitution) and has enjoyed elaborate explanation by the leading academic theorists of the twentieth century – the likes of Alex Bickel, Charles Black, John Hart Ely, and (to a lesser extent) Bruce Ackerman. The standard account rests on three premises:

THE DOCUMENTARY PREMISE: THE CONSTITUTION IS A TEXT. Unlike British constitutionalism, American constitutionalism assumes a determinate document that has been formally adopted as a Constitution or as an amendment. The implications are that interpretation proceeds from within the language/structure/principles of the document; the "big changes" in constitutionalism come episodically, after a focused public deliberation aimed at changing the document (through Article V); and constitutionalism is stable for long periods of time. Aiello's lawsuit was filed right after Congress passed the Equal Rights Amendment by huge margins, with the expectation that thirty-eight states (the number required by Article V) would duly ratify. Under the ERA, or an ERA-influenced construction of the Equal Protection Clause, Williams believed that her client's pregnancy discrimination claim would prevail.

THE JUROCENTRIC PREMISE: COURTS ARE THE PRIMARY ARTICULATORS OF CONSTITUTIONAL VALUES. Aiello and her co-plaintiffs went to federal court – not the state or federal legislature – with their normative objections. Congress had spoken, and the job of the federal judges was to trump the legislative value of economy with the constitutional equality principle. Constitutional meaning/interpretation under the standard account is announced by judges; the model for proper constitutional analysis is the judicial opinion, and the model for constitutional stability is stare decisis. Lip-service is duly given to the role of the legislature, but the focus is on judges. To the extent the legislature is valorized, it is done so by representing it in judicialized terms: If a legislature follows proper procedures, assures everyone a fair hearing, and gives reasons – in other words, behaves like a court – it can play a modest supporting role in elaborating constitutional values.

THE COMMON-LAW PREMISE: DISTINCTION BETWEEN FUNDAMENTAL LAW AND STATUTES. Blackstone famously asserted that statutes should be construed to be consistent with the common law, and the framing generation extended his idea to maintain that statutes inconsistent with the Constitution are either invalid or should be narrowly construed.[3] The premise that statutes were essentially intrusions into fundamental law has been relaxed in the last 150 years, but American public law has never renounced the assumption that statutes create policy (not principle) and are subordinate to independently evolving constitutional principles. Accordingly, Williams maintained that California's stingy unemployment policy, excluding pregnancy-based claims, was not legally valid, on the ground that it was inconsistent with the underlying "fundamental" law of the Equal Protection Clause.

The standard account will no longer do. It has never completely described American constitutionalism, and its lack of descriptive power is now clear. As Larry

[3] William N. Eskridge, Jr., "All About Words: Original Understandings of the 'Judicial Power' in Statutory Interpretation" (2001) 101 *Columbia Law Review* 1002–70.

Kramer has shown, the documentary and jurocentric assumptions of the standard account were not ones actually held by the framers of the Constitution of 1787, nor were they consensus assumptions during Reconstruction.[4] The framers did distinguish between fundamental law and statutes, but they understood legislatures as important fora for articulating and elaborating fundamental law. Recall the famous debate in the cabinet and Congress regarding the federal power to establish a Bank of the United States. No less a judicialist than John Marshall considered the principle substantially settled by the political process by 1819.[5] Recall, too, the great debate over the *Sedition Act* of 1798. Presiding over trials of political critics of the Adams Administration, federal judges found no violation of the First Amendment. It was the legislatures of Virginia and Kentucky that announced important First Amendment problems with laws seeking to suppress political dissent. Their point of view prevailed in the critical election of 1800.[6]

Whatever ambiguities there were in the accuracy of the standard account during the late eighteenth and the nineteenth centuries, it has proven just as unreliable (but in different ways) as a description of the constitutionalism of the United States in the modern era. The conditions of American government and society have changed radically from the founding and even Reconstruction periods. On the one hand, these changes have made constitutionalism more important to Americans, for pervasive government pervasively threatens liberties and status. This has fueled demand for judicial review based on authoritative texts. On the other hand, these changes have paved the way for fundamental law to be articulated through statutory enactment, implementation, and interpretation. In short, the same general historical developments that have fueled the documentary and jurocentric assumptions of the standard account (assumptions that we believe are rhetorically attractive but oversold in practice) have undermined the common-law assumption.

The Constitution plus Reconstruction, as understood in the standard account, accommodated a constitutional law that strictly confined federal regulation to the movement of goods in interstate commerce and both state and federal regulation to common-law nuisances. This constitutional regime ensured that the common law would set the baseline for public as well as private rights. But common-law baselines were insufficient for the governance of an industrializing America, and those baselines were superseded by a series of statutory landmarks – the *Interstate Commerce Act* of 1887 and its periodic amendments, the *Sherman Act* of 1890 and the *Clayton Act* of 1914, the *Pure Food and Drug Act* of 1906, and so forth.

The modern regulatory state rejected the jurisdictional limits of the original Constitution – and it was the Constitution, even as interpreted by the Court, that acquiesced in a new order that accorded great power to Congress and rendered the states marginal players as to many policies. More radically, the modern state

[4] Larry Kramer, "The Supreme Court, 2000 Term: Foreword: We the Court" (2001) 115 *Harvard Law Review* 59 at 59–74, 116–22 ["We the Court"].

[5] On the Bank debate within the Washington Administration, see Paul Finkelman, "The Constitution and the Intentions of the Framers: The Limits of Historical Analysis" (1989) 50 *University of Pittsburgh Law Review* 358–71 ["Intentions of the Framers"].

[6] Akhil Amar, "Of Sovereignty and Federalism" (1987) 96 *Yale Law Journal* 1502. ("Although political agitation at the state level was unsuccessful in securing immediate repeal of the offensive legislation, it effectively transformed the national election of 1800 into a popular referendum on these bills.")

was administrative, and the agencies created throughout the twentieth century doomed original constitutional models of strict separation of powers, nondelegation of legislative authority, and even conceptions of procedural due process. All of these changes have been delivered through the mouths of Supreme Court Justices, even though they originated from and were powered by other sources. Constitutional meaning has proven highly dynamic, incremental but increasingly divorced from the document, and driven by social movements, shifting partisan balances in Congress, and legislative innovations. "Landmark" judicial opinions have either confirmed what has already occurred or yielded to popular responses or political fait accomplis. So the jurocentric and documentary assumptions have evanesced in practice.[7]

Indeed, they virtually disappeared in the wake of Earth Day 1970 and the environmental movement. Starting during the Nixon Administration, Congress enacted one landmark statute after another setting unprecedented restrictions on the freedom of businesses and private persons to dump chemicals in the nation's water, air, and landfills. The contours of those statutory schemes were set by Congress and the president, and their details carried out by the EPA and other agencies, with very little input by the judiciary. Even constitutional requirements, such as the jurisdictional limits on Congress directed by Article I and the just compensation requirements of the Takings Clause, retreated in the face of the national environmental crisis and green property.[8]

The big exception to the decline of jurocracy has, allegedly, been in the field of individual rights, epitomized by *Brown v. Board of Education* (1954) and the triumph of the anti-apartheid principle. We join those who consider *Brown* a great judicial achievement, but its elaboration and consolidation depended more on Congress, the president, and agencies (HEW as well as DOJ) than the Supreme Court. Indeed, the integration principle – the idea that the state is obliged to integrate and not just avoid explicit segregation – is more a product of Congress, Presidents Johnson and Nixon, and the EEOC than it is a product of judicial norm entrepreneurship.[9]

Stated at a more general level, we submit that the great identity-based social movements of the latter half of the twentieth century required this country to rethink its fundamental law to accommodate previously marginalized citizens. In this great rethinking, the Court has usually played the follower rather than leader role. For example, women's constitutional rights were all but ignored by the judiciary until the 1970s – long after President Kennedy's Commission on the Status of Women boldly endorsed the idea that "equality of rights under the law for all persons, male or female, is so basic to democracy and its commitment to the ultimate value of the individual that it must be reflected in the fundamental law of the land," and well after Congress assured women of equal treatment in the workplace

[7] See generally G. Edward White, *The Constitution and the New Deal* (Cambridge, Mass.: Harvard University Press, 2000).

[8] Cary Coglianese, "Social Movements, Law, and Society: The Institutionalization of the Environmental Movement" (2001) 150 *University of Pennsylvania Law Review* 114.

[9] See Hugh Davis Graham, *The Civil Rights Era: Origins and Development of National Policy 1960–1972* (New York: Oxford University Press, 1990); Gerald N. Rosenberg, *The Hollow Hope: Can Courts Bring About Social Change?* (Chicago: University of Chicago Press, 1991).

with the *Civil Rights Act* of 1964 and the *Equal Pay Act* of 1963. The Supreme Court announced heightened equal protection scrutiny of sex-based classifications only after Congress had passed the ERA, and most rights women have today are based on statutes and not the Constitution.[10]

Aiello's case illustrates that pattern. At the same time they were litigating *Geduldig*, feminist litigators were also arguing that the jobs title of the *Civil Rights Act* of 1964 bars employment discrimination based on pregnancy. Following the reasoning as well as the result of *Geduldig*, the Supreme Court rejected those statutory claims in *Gilbert v. General Electric Co.* (1976). Still confident of the validity of their norm, Ruth Weyand, Sue Ross, Wendy Williams, and a rainbow coalition of feminists and civil rights as well as religious groups turned to Congress and made a powerful case for the proposition that women's equal opportunities in the workplace are systematically and significantly compromised by pregnancy-based discriminations. Employers, insurance companies, and a few states made a rather half-hearted case for such exclusions. After an intense and public debate, Congress repudiated the Court's understanding of nondiscrimination and equal treatment, and amended the statute to include pregnancy-based discriminations as "sex discrimination." The *Pregnancy Discrimination Act* of 1978 (*PDA*) powerfully illustrates how even in the field of individual rights, where the Court does have some genuine advantages, the evolution of fundamental public norms has sometimes occurred more responsively as well as deeply in legislatures and agencies rather than in courts.[11]

Even if it better described the evolution of American public law, the standard account is bedeviled by normative problems. (The normative problems are probably related to the fact that the standard account does not provide a better positive description.) The normative problems arise out of the standard account's focus on judges interpreting constitutional texts to trim back legislative enactments. This focus invites difficulties of institutional legitimacy and competence.

PROBLEM 1: DEMOCRATIC LEGITIMACY. The standard account, especially as it has been articulated by law professors, places too much weight on judges and judicial appointments and too little emphasis on popular input into public norms. This has, misleadingly, been dubbed "the countermajoritarian difficulty." The legitimacy advantage that legislatures have over courts owes less to the supposition that legislatures better reflect majority desires than courts (although that is often the case), and more to the factors that render legislative value-elaboration as to fundamental norms more acceptable to We the People, including those in the minority.

(a) Accessibility. Courts are shrouded with technicalities and mysteries, and ordinary people do not think judges listen to them. So their decisions affecting ordinary people lack the perception that everybody has had a chance to be heard; legislatures, in contrast, are more open fora. Legislators acknowledge constituent letters and are more likely to be perceived as paying attention to them. The *PDA* hearings were a classic example of how a social group was able to present a compelling

[10] See Serena Mayeri, "Constitutional Choices, Legal Feminism, and the Historical Dynamics of Change" (2004) 92 *California Law Review* 755.

[11] *General Electric Co. v. Gilbert*, 429 U.S. 125 (1976), overridden by Public Law No. 95–555, 92 Stat. 2026 (1976), codified at 42 U.S.C. 2000e(k).

normative case, and legislators actually heard what women were saying. Contrast the Supreme Court's decision in *Geduldig*: It was widely perceived that the Justices had been unable to *comprehend* (or perhaps relate to) Wendy Williams's argument that pregnancy discrimination is both a formal sex discrimination (it targets only women) *and* a functional one (it has the effect of denying women equal workplace opportunities).

(b) Accountability. Legislators are distinctively accountable, not only because they are chosen by the people, but also because they are subject to removal or defeat if they fail to represent the people intelligently and sensitively. If working women believe they are being discriminated against because of pregnancy rules, they will petition legislators to enact a statutory response – and legislator failure to be responsive to reasonable demands will be met with electoral retribution. So even legislators interested only in reelection try to be responsive to genuine social needs. Representative Emmanuel Celler of New York learned this in 1970, when his sexist views, including his opposition to the ERA, cost him his longtime seat in the House; he was defeated by Liz Holtzman.[12]

(c) Diversity. Because of their larger size and less constraining membership rules (judges pretty much have to be lawyers), legislatures usually reflect the differing viewpoints in the community much better than courts do. Perspective makes a big difference in both the content and the legitimacy of public policy choices; a decision coming from a diverse group of decision makers is likely to be more legitimate than one coming from a more homogeneous group. The Supreme Court that decided *Geduldig* and *Gilbert* consisted of nine elderly men; that alone created a stench for their pregnancy decisions. In the debates leading up to the *PDA*, the Court's opinions carried no weight, and many witnesses even disrespected them as a matter of legal interpretation: Just a bunch of guys who do not understand and do not care. The internal records of the Justices' Conference, now available, provide unfortunate confirmation. The Chief Justice of the United States found no connection between sex and pregnancy. He found the exclusion easily justified on the ground that pregnancy is simply a "different kind of illness" than, say, "prostate problem," which is similar to "hysterectomy" but not pregnancy.[13]

PROBLEM 2: THE INSTITUTIONAL SUPERIORITY OF LEGISLATURES AND AGENCIES. The standard account, especially as it has been articulated by law professors, valorizes and even fetishizes judges way beyond what history or common sense supports. Apart from questions of legitimacy, norm-entrepreneurship by the judiciary has a problem of comparative institutional capacity and competence. Academics overstate judges' genuine advantages – their inability to control their own agendas, the requirement that they give reasons, and their relative insulation from normal politics. (Almost all legal academics worked for judges as law clerks; almost none have worked with legislators in drafting or enacting statutes.) Like

[12] See Jane S. Schacter, "Accounting for Accountability in Dynamic Statutory Interpretation and Beyond" in *Issues in Legal Scholarship: Dynamic Statutory Interpretation* (2002), available at http://www.bepress.com/ils/iss3/art5; Richard Lyons, "Former Rep. Emanuel Celler Dies; Civil Rights Champion," *Washington Post* (Jan. 16, 1981).

[13] The Justices' deliberations survive in notes taken by Justices Douglas, Brennan, and Blackmun. The papers for all three Justices are in the Manuscript Room of the Madison Building, Library of Congress.

judges, legislators are forced to grapple with issues thrust upon them by circumstances and are certainly required to advance reasons for laws they adopt. More important, legislatures have their own comparative advantages over courts in their deliberation about fundamental norms:

(a) Information and resources. It is commonplace to say that legislatures and agencies have greater access to resources and differing points of view than courts do – but most legal academics take positions that slight this universally conceded fact. (The fact is even more impressive if one includes the fact-finding efforts of agencies charged with implementing most statutory schemes.) In exploring normative debates, and especially in developing the contours of what Henry Richardson calls "deep compromises," information is key. A well-informed institution is better able to cut away issues that should not be a matter of dispute and to reconcile colliding norms.[14]

(b) Implementation flexibility. It has long been axiomatic that judges are not well-equipped to deal with polycentric problems, that is, problems with several interconnected dimensions and usually uncertainty about how changing one dimension will affect the others. Many normative debates have this feature, and in that event legislatures have further advantages over courts. Legislatures have greater freedom to address several features of a problem at once, or seriatim; have money to spend to fix a problem; or can turn over a problem or one dimension of it to agencies.

(c) Diversity. Like Jeremy Waldron, we believe that heterogeneity of viewpoint (diversity) is not only a legitimacy advantage of legislatures, but a functional advantage as well. To be sure, diversity of opinion often leads to impasse or raw unprincipled compromises – two of the admitted drawbacks of the legislative process when it comes to normative dialogue. But on issues where the public itself is engaged and the media watching attentively, legislators tend to step up to the plate and engage in a process that is more like Richardson's deep compromise, where difference of opinion is ameliorated by each side's normative evolution and is accommodated by mutual exploration of a principled resolution.[15]

PROBLEM 3: THE INADEQUACY OF THE WRITTEN CONSTITUTION. Let's face it, the standard account owes many of its problems to the document to which it is tethered. The U.S Constitution is both a wonderful document and an infuriating one, and for the same reason: It speaks in such generalities that almost anything can be teased (or tortured) out of it and almost nothing can be added to it. This has contributed to our current dilemma, where judges lacking both legitimacy and competence read their own political judgments into such open-textured provisions as the Speech Clause, the Equal Protection Clause, and the Due Process Clause – and We the People feel frustrated that We cannot correct the judges through constitutional revisions, given the now-impossible standards of Article V (two-thirds of each chamber of Congress and three-quarters of the state legislatures).

[14] Henry S. Richardson, *Democratic Autonomy: Public Reasoning about the Ends of Policy* (New York: Oxford University Press, 2002) at 146–57 [Richardson, *Democratic Autonomy*].

[15] Jeremy Waldron, *Law and Disagreement* (New York: Oxford University Press, 1999); Richardson, *Democratic Autonomy*, ibid. at 130–61.

So let us stop the charade that accompanies debates about the proper meaning judges should torture out of the Constitution. Let us return to first principles – not just those that were available to the framers but also those that we can see in other countries or even within individual states.

II. ALTERNATIVE PERSPECTIVES ABOUT CONSTITUTIONALISM

The standard account reflects the dominant tradition of American constitutional theory – Constitution as a Social Contract enforced by judicial review. The written Constitution created by superengaged popular majorities and enforced by judicial review has been America's great contribution to constitutional theory, but our own constitutionalism might be understood in a more sophisticated way if we expanded our focus to consider other perspectives. Do these other perspectives suggest solutions to some of the problems we have identified for the standard account of American constitutionalism?

ARISTOTELIAN PERSPECTIVE: CONSTITUTIONALISM AS EXPRESSION OF A POLITY'S FUNDAMENTAL COMMITMENTS. Aristotle would have been baffled by the notion of a written Constitution whose precise words act as constraints on the state. Aristotle, in the *Politics*, understood a constitution not as a set of limits or as a political straightjacket, but as a description of normal governmental practices. This is not to say that he refrained from normative judgments as to which kind of constitution would be best for a people. Indeed, he thought that a mixed or moderate constitution, which he called *politea*, was best for his audience of Greek polities. But for the most part he was concerned to describe the way a government functioned, that is, to describe the real constitution of a nation and not to focus on a document or collection of written texts.[16] What is important about the Aristotelian conception is its implied distinction between the constitution of a government and its written Constitution. Or, even better, the distinction between small *c* constitutionalism and large *C* Constitutionalism. Large *C* Constitutionalism might be identified with the official way that a people and their officials interpret and apply their Constitution. Small *c* constitutionalism is concerned with the actual arrangement of governmental institutions relative to each other and to the people whose government they form.

Aristotle's conception of constitutionalism has been pervasively important in Western history, influencing such thinkers as Polybius, Montesquieu, and many early Americans. Each of these writers thought, like Aristotle, that a good constitution would mix or balance popular and elite elements and that such a balanced constitution would be the best guarantee of liberty. The American colonists who declared their independence from Great Britain in 1775 acted in part on the ground that Parliament's claims on them were inconsistent with their fundamental rights as Englishmen. Some of the founding generation, including supporters of the Constitution like James Madison and James Wilson, were students of Montesquieu.

We are not interested in the precise descriptions found in Aristotle and Montesquieu, who believed that a good constitution would reflect the different

[16] Aristotle, *The Politics*, Bk. IV, ch. I (340 B.C.).

classes of society. What we like about their general conception is its openly normative aspiration: Rather than expressing a set of positive rules negotiated by long-deceased framers, the central metaphor of a large *C* Constitution as social contract, the Aristotelian small *c* constitution embodies fundamental values to which our polity is or ought to be committed. And constitutionalism is reasoning from those values to address new problems confronted by the nation.

Aristotle himself had a rather static understanding of the constitution, but a neo-Aristotelian perspective need not have that quality. America's unwritten constitution as well as the Constitution of 1787 acquiesced in the institution of slavery, as Aristotle himself did. The Supreme Court applied these commitments in *Dred Scott v. Sandford* (1856) to rule that African Americans could not be "citizens."[17] Chief Justice Taney's *Dred Scott* opinion appealed to both the original expectations of the framers of the Constitution of 1787 *and* to an Aristotelian understanding of natural law and social order. Set against this understanding, however, the abolitionists invoked what we see as neo-Aristotelian arguments for the proposition that America's most fundamental commitments were to universal human liberty and the idea that all men are created equal. Whereas Taney emphasized original expectations, texts, and norms of the founding generation, the abolitionists reasoned from the great principles of American constitutionalism. Of course, they replaced Aristotle's ideas about natural inequality with the equality notions celebrated not only in the Constitution but also in the Declaration of Independence and in features of America that made us a City upon a Hill. The danger of a static constitutionalism, therefore, may not be inevitable even under an Aristotelian point of view.

DELIBERATIVE PERSPECTIVES: CONSTITUTIONALISM AS DIALOGUES GENERATING OR ELABORATING ON NEW FUNDAMENTAL COMMITMENTS. Deliberative perspectives approach constitutionalism as a process by which our fundamental commitments are articulated and evolve. Examples include Aristotle's theory of practical reasoning as the way human societies address values and problems over time; the political theory of Edmund Burke, who saw the English constitution as rooted in an always-evolving tradition; hermeneutical approaches such as that of Hans-Georg Gadamer, who maintains that interpretation is a synthetic process reconciling past and present; and theories of direct democracy such as that of Mark Tushnet, where constitutional change is driven by popular discourse and initiatives elaborating on the grand norms of what Tushnet calls the "thin constitution." The virtue of these models is, for us, quite substantial. They are not only more dynamic than Aristotelian or social contract models, but they also insist on a process of publicly accountable reasoning to elaborate on the nation's values. Tushnet's theory has the added virtue of insisting that We the People be centrally involved in those debates.[18]

[17] *Dred Scott v. Sandford*, 60 U.S. (19 How) 393 (1856); see William E. Nelson, "The Impact of the Antislavery Movement Upon Styles of Judicial Reasoning in Nineteenth Century America" (1974) 87 *Harvard Law Review* 525.

[18] See Mark Tushnet, *The Constitution Outside the Courts* (Princeton, N.J.: Princeton University Press 1999); Ernest Young, "Rediscovering Conservatism: Burkean Political Theory and Constitutional Interpretation" (1994) 92 *North Carolina Law Review* 619.

Deliberative theories may be seen as functional theories. Constitutions, and constitutional practices that we call constitutionalism, have the effect of permitting the "people" to deliberate about shared values and rights. Whether they do this well or badly matters for how we evaluate them. So one way of justifying a constitutional practice is that it effectively brings We the People into a deliberative process in ways that recognize important ethical values. Our problem with the leading deliberative theories is they do not give enough attention to the legislature as a forum for deliberation. Philosophers Jeremy Waldron and Henry Richardson have begun to address this defect. Both authors maintain that legislatures should be the chief forums for norm elaboration in a democracy – yet neither relates legislative activities to constitutionalism (large *C* or small *c*).[19]

Nonetheless, Waldron's and Richardson's central argument relates very nicely to constitutional practices common in the West. The constitutions in Canada, several European countries, and some states in the United States give proper regard to the legislature as a forum for constitutional deliberation. Constitutions in these countries are more detailed than the U.S. Constitution but easier to change through legislation and/or popular vote.[20] In Hawaii, the state constitution can be changed through initiatives proposed by the legislature and then ratified by a majority of voters in the next general election. This is the process by which Hawaii rejected same-sex marriage: The legislature in 1997 created a new institution (reciprocal beneficiaries) for same-sex couples and proposed a constitutional amendment to override a trial judge's decision that the exclusion of same-sex couples from marriage violated the Hawaii Constitution; by a 70 to 29 percent margin, the voters approved the constitutional amendment in November 1998.[21]

The virtue of parliamentary models is that they engage both the legislature and the people in constitutional dialogue. (Nor does this approach render courts irrelevant. Their edicts are just not final.) Our concern here is that constitutional change comes too easily, and the advantages of deliberation *over time* are lost. The Hawaii same-sex marriage debate illustrates this problem. The quality of discourse was low, with opponents demonizing gay people as sexual predators and threats to the family. If the debate had been strung out, we believe the quality would have been higher, because people could have reflected on these charges.

The Constitutions of Vermont and Massachusetts are slightly different. To amend those constitutions, the legislature in two successive sessions must recommend a constitutional amendment, and then the voters must ratify it in the next general election. This kind of process has the advantages of popular as well as legislative involvement, without as many risks of speedy and perhaps ill-considered

[19] Thus, Waldron, *Law and Disagreement, supra* note 15, argues for the abolition of judicial review altogether, a radical precept (for this country) that causes him to neglect the important ways legislative deliberation contributes to constitutionalism already. He also ignores the administrative dimension emphasized by Richardson, *Democratic Autonomy, supra* note 14. But Richardson fails to relate his approach to constitutionalism in any sustained manner.

[20] Donald S. Lutz, "Toward a Theory of Constitutional Amendment" in *Responding to Imperfection: The Theory and Practice of Constitutional Amendment,* Sanford Levinson, ed., (Princeton, N.J.: Princeton University Press, 1995) 237 [*Imperfection*].

[21] For an account of the Hawaii same-sex marriage debate in the 1990s, see William N. Eskridge, Jr., *Equality Practice: Civil Unions and the Future of Gay Rights* (New York: Routledge, 2002), ch. 1 [*Equality Practice*].

amendment of the foundational document. We admire this most of all but admit that it, too, lacks a feature that the modern administrative state has taught us to valorize – the input of agency experts.

THE NEW DEAL PERSPECTIVE: POSITIVE AS WELL AS NEGATIVE FUNDAMENTAL COMMITMENTS. A social contract perspective emphasizes limits that a written Constitution places on the state. The standard account is most emphatic about this. It was willing to entertain (and reject) Carolyn Aiello's grievance only because she complained that the state unemployment plan discriminated against her without justification. American constitutionalism generally focuses on state action. Supreme Courts as diverse as the Marshall Court, the *Lochner* Court, the Warren Court, and the Rehnquist Court have been in agreement about that and have strictly limited constitutional doctrine and discourse to state action. If Aiello's pregnancy had been the occasion for her employer to fire her, for her landlord to evict her, or for a restaurant to refuse her service, the standard account does not consider her grief a Constitutional one. To the contrary, we do (but with a small *c*).

One lesson our nation has learned from the New Deal is that the state structures the economy, the environment, politics, and even the family. The state creates status as well as rules and crimes. In this process, it establishes duties and rights we all have vis-à-vis one another and the environment as well as vis-à-vis the state. Even during the minimalist state of the founding era, the common law – a form of state regulation – pervasively structured human affairs. It has never been the case in American history that the state has been anything but pervasive, but this fact was not widely recognized until after the New Deal replaced many of the common-law baselines with statutory ones.[22]

There is a second lesson of the New Deal: A political community might take on responsibility for helping its citizens achieve their goals and fulfilling their human potential. The modern regulatory state might contribute to human flourishing by assuring citizens security under circumstances of illness or decline, creating and conveying useful information and social knowledge, providing common experiences, and so forth. So in the modern regulatory state, we should want to assure citizens more than the protection of negative liberties; we should want to assure what Sir Isaiah Berlin called "positive liberties" as well – the ability to become the authors of their own life stories.

This has traditionally *not* been the project of American Constitutionalism. Even the occasional exception proves the rule. To remedy the ongoing effects of educational apartheid, federal courts required once-segregated school districts not only to desegregate (negative liberty), but also to restructure themselves in a way that assured integrated schools for all (positive liberty). For various reasons, this judicial experiment has been a failure in most school districts. After almost forty years of federal judicial remediation, school districts remain segregated; even the original *Brown* districts have resegregated.[23] Where there has been actual integration,

[22] Gary Peller, "The Metaphysics of American Law" (1985) 73 *California Law Review* 1201.

[23] Raymond Wolters, *The Burden of* Brown: *Thirty Years of Desegregation* (Knoxville: University of Tennessee Press, 1984), which documents the de facto (re)segregation of the school districts involved in the *Brown* litigation.

the agents of change have been Congress, the president and his cabinet, and local legislatures. Indeed, recent developments make this clear. As a matter of Constitutional doctrine, the U.S. Supreme Court has been encouraging federal trial judges to give up long-held jurisdiction over school districts, even when they remain actually segregated by race. In the teeth of this Constitutional development, enforced by federal judges, many communities have engaged in their own constitutional activism, creating interdistrict exchange programs that have modestly advanced the broader constitutional goals of actual integration and diversity. Surveys have suggested that students, parents, and teachers of all races positively value the experiences of these programs.[24]

A third lesson we derive from the New Deal era is enriched by comparative constitutionalism: A nation's fundamental commitments may be categorized and ordered. Inspired by the German *Grundgesetz*, or Basic Law, which openly announces a hierarchy of rights, we suggest that America's fundamental commitments entail the following:

Number 1: Dignitary Rights. Drawing from what Mark Tushnet calls the thin constitution, from the New Deal experience, and from various post–New Deal super-statutes, we should suggest that America's small *c* constitutionalism places individual dignity as our most fundamental commitment. Individual dignitary protections include positive as well as negative ones (in the Berlin sense) and can apply to private as well as state centers of authority.

Number 2: The Economy and Society. Small *c* constitutionalism is committed to the government's responsibility for managing the economy by generating conditions for a free market (and by correcting for market imperfections) and for assuring citizens of minimal securities and safety nets.

Number 3: The Environment. Although this is the newest commitment of small *c* constitutionalism, we believe there is enough social consensus to say that it is committed to protecting the environment itself. To be sure, this commitment is related to the first two: What meaning does individual dignity have if people are breathing dirty air? Doesn't the state's management of the economy entail some stewardship for preserving future economic viability by protecting the earth today?

The foregoing list brings us back full circle – to a neo-Aristotelian notion of fundamental commitments – and enables us now to announce our new American constitutionalism in some detail.

III. SUPER-STATUTES

If the United States were drafting a Constitution from scratch, there is much to recommend the German Constitution: It entails a sophisticated hierarchy of fundamental commitments and directs the parliament and its agents to carry forth these projects, with regular feedback from the citizenry. To be sure, Americans have never been attracted to the parliamentary model, and we certainly reject its (typical) assumption that the parliament rather than We the People constitute the legitimate

[24] See, e.g., Amy Stuart Wells and Robert Crain, *Stepping Over the Color Line: African American Students in White Suburban Schools* (New Haven, Conn.: Yale University Press, 1997).

sovereign. Given these objections, however, the legislature-plebiscite model found in the Massachusetts and Vermont Constitutions is an attractive option. It would produce an admirable Constitutionalism, in our view. Those states' deliberations on the topic of same-sex marriage have been of the highest quality – and that might suggest the virtues of their constitutionalism.[25]

At the national level, the prospects seem bleaker at first blush. The likelihood of a national Constitutional Convention seems low; the conditions which would call forth such a convention might or might not be those conducive to productive rethinking. So we assume, for the time being, that what we are calling small c constitutionalism will coexist with large *C* Constitutionalism. Many authors seem to assume that large *C* Constitutionalism is completely dominating small c constitutionalism. They and others bemoan the ascendancy of the Supreme Court as, effectively, sovereign. "We the Court," as Kramer acidly puts it.[26] We do not share their pessimism.

We think small c constitutionalism is alive and well in America and remains more important than the large *C* Constitutionalism that our academic colleagues find frightening. Upon reflection and study, and to our considerable surprise, it appears to us that the small *c* constitution of our nation has both diverged from and ultimately driven its large *C* Constitution. Small *c* constitutionalism is concerned with articulating and elaborating on our nation's fundamental commitments (including new commitments or revised versions of old ones). Those commitments include positive liberties for the people as well as negative ones. And the process by which fundamental commitments are named and elaborated is a dialogic one in which democratically accountable legislatures and agencies play a larger role than courts. The primary mechanism through which this all comes together is the *super-statute.*

Return to Carolyn Aiello's norm, that pregnancy should presumptively not be a basis for discrimination. This norm never got to Constitutional first base under the standard account; its current valence was not the product of a discourse where the Supreme Court interpreted the Equal Protection Clause. Rather, it was the product of a super-statute – the *Civil Rights Act* of 1964, as amended by the *PDA* in 1978.[27] The generation of the norm that pregnancy-based discrimination is wrong illustrates the three features we associate with super-statutes.

First, a super-statute seeks to introduce or consolidate a norm or principle as fundamental in our polity. The legislature does not enact such laws by accident or on the sly. Such laws are a response to a normative social movement or a popular demand for change, and the legislatures enacting them understand that they are propounding a fundamental normative commitment (often a new one) for the polity. The *PDA* illustrates this feature. In extensive committee hearings, Sue Ross, Wendy Williams, and their allies demonstrated to Congress the many ways

[25] On the Vermont deliberations, which created the compromise institution of "civil unions," see Eskridge, *Equality Practice, supra* note 21, ch. 2. The Massachusetts deliberations, responding to the state supreme court's same-sex marriage mandate, commenced in 2004 and are ongoing, with no final outcome at this point.

[26] Kramer, "We the Court," *supra* note 4.

[27] Our discussion of the legislative background of the *PDA* is informed by our reading of the legislative materials, which are usefully explored and analyzed in Kevin Schwartz, "Equalizing Pregnancy: Birth of a Super-Statute" (Yale Law School SAW, 2005) ["Birth of a Super-Statute"].

that pregnancy-based discriminations disadvantage women in the workplace and undermine their ability to have careers. Aware that the law would commit the country to significant changes in workplace rules, Congress enacted the law.

Not all statutes that propound fundamental normative commitments end up being super-statutes, for in many cases the statutory principles do not have legs. Agencies and judges might retreat from or even ignore the norm, and the legislature might allow it to languish as popular support for strengthening it does not materialize. Our second criterion, therefore, is whether the new statutory principle or norm "sticks" in the public culture in a deep way, becoming foundational or axiomatic to our thinking. The super-statute that emerges from Congress is not a completed product. Its norm requires specification and elaboration from administrators and judges, whose work is then subject to meaningful scrutiny and correction by the legislature and the citizenry. The process of elaboration will alter the norm, and may well strengthen it, as has occurred with the *PDA*. The EEOC and even conservative judges have given it a broad reading. Several dramatic Supreme Court decisions illustrate the mini-revolution effected by this statute.[28] Such a feedback loop is an essential feature of super-statutes, but its operation is variegated and impossible to predict. Each super-statute has a postenactment history that is as important as – and usually more important than – its enactment history.

Third, and finally, a successful super-statute will have an effect beyond its four corners – including an effect on large *C* Constitutionalism. The *PDA* by its terms is limited to workplace rules, but courts as well as agencies and lawyers have relied on its principle to argue against or head off pregnancy-based discriminations in other venues. After the *PDA*, California abandoned the pregnancy-based discrimination in its unemployment compensation program and later adopted rules providing extra state support for women needing workplace leaves for pregnancy and child-bearing reasons. The Chamber of Commerce and various employers challenged the statute's discrimination against men, for there was no paternity leave allowance. *California Federal Savings and Loan Association v. Guerra* (1987) required the EEOC and the Court to apply the nondiscrimination principle in a different context, and in the process these federal officials had to rethink the norm in a more complex way. Following the EEOC, the Rehnquist Court upheld the maternity-leave-only allowance, reasoning that the remedial need remained strongest for women bearing children than for men. Implicit in the Court's *Cal Fed* opinion was the assumption that the Equal Protection Clause permitted "special treatment" for women bearing children not afforded men fathering children.[29]

Many feminists, including those who were centrally involved in procuring the enactment of the *PDA*, believed that California's articulation of the *PDA* norm was too stingy. Certainly, California was correct to require employers to accommodate the pregnancy-related needs of working women – but not to limit that accommodation to working women. Why not working men? The state-imposed positive liberty enjoyed by workers ought to be one enjoyed by fathers as well as mothers, argued

[28] See, e.g., *Automobile Workers v. Johnson Controls, Inc.*, 499 U.S. 187 (1991); *California Federal Savings & Loan Association v. Guerra*, 479 U.S. 272 (1987); *Newport News Shipbldg. & Dry Dock Co. v. EEOC*, 462 U.S. 669, 684 (1983) ("The Pregnancy Discrimination Act has now made clear that, for all Title VII purposes, discrimination based on a woman's pregnancy is, on its face, discrimination because of her sex.").

[29] *Cal Fed*, 479 U.S. 272 (1987).

Williams and Ross. Although the Supreme Court gave California more leeway in *Cal Fed*, feminists and their allies in the labor movement worked for statutes authorizing or requiring *parental* (rather than just *maternal*) leave for employees having babies. Their great triumph was the federal *Family and Medical Leave Act* of 1993 (*FMLA*), which gives employees the right to take off as many as twelve weeks each year to care for a newborn child, parent, or loved one. The *FMLA* was more than an elaboration of the *PDA*'s principle, for Congress expanded it to include men as well as women and to embrace other caregiving options (such as an adult caring for his or her aging parent). The *FMLA* applied to the states as employers, a coverage that seemed inconsistent with Rehnquist Court decisions barring Congress from imposing new liabilities on the states. Yet in *Nevada Department of Human Resources v. Hibbs* (2003), the Court, in an opinion by Chief Justice Rehnquist himself, upheld the law on the ground that it was reasonably related to our nationwide campaign against sex discrimination in the workplace (the norm that *Geduldig* had slighted).[30]

As the evolution of the *PDA* and its principle illustrate, super-statutes contribute to American constitutionalism in multiple ways. One, they are foci for norm expression, articulation, and elaboration over time. Two, they are legally enforceable norms, and so they generate private as well as public conversations. Three, they have a gravitational force outside their own legal ambits. Super-statutes can and often do affect constitutional discourse and doctrine in courts as well as in legislatures. Perhaps surprisingly, this claim can also be illustrated with an example from the beginning of the American republic, an example we mentioned above.

The law creating the first Bank of the United States was adopted only after a great normative debate. Hamilton and his allies maintained that a federal bank was necessary for the orderly operation of the government and to foster commerce and industry in the new republic, while Jefferson and his allies maintained that the bank was ultra vires the national government and contrary to the arcadian republic of small farmers and shopkeepers that they envisioned. The arguments against the Bank's constitutionality were those of normal social contractarian interpretation. Because a federal bank would go well beyond the common law and would be inconsistent with state statutes, such a power needed to be explicitly named in Article I, Section 8's comprehensive listing of national powers, which of course it was not. Defending the Bank, Hamilton started from a different interpretive baseline: A fundamental project of American constitutionalism is to create institutions that facilitate the operation of national commerce, banking, and economy. In light of *that* fundamental commitment, the written Constitution should not be interpreted stingily or even literally to thwart the creation of a national bank. Hamilton persuaded the president that his vision was correct, and a similar debate in Congress culminated in the creation of the Bank of the United States in 1791.[31]

The Bank debate prefigured an enduring contrast between laws that have dramatically shifted national policy or norms and those which have followed or marginally altered common law and other well-trod furrows. Most proposals for

[30] *Nevada Department of Human Resources v. Hibbs*, 538 U.S. 721 (2003).

[31] Finkelman, "Intentions of the Framers," *supra* note 5 at 358–71. On the Hamiltonian vision that won out, see David McGowan, "Ethos in Law and History: Alexander Hamilton, *The Federalist*, and the Supreme Court" (2001) 85 *Minnesota Law Review* at 796.

dramatic shifts have in fact been defeated, but Hamilton persuaded the president and Congress to support his plan for the Bank of the United States, which operated successfully for more than two generations. The law met the first criterion for super-statutes in setting an important national policy and the second for enduring (albeit not for as long as most of the other super-statutes discussed in this book). The national bank policy stuck in public culture in ways other Hamiltonian policies did not. When the first bank act expired in 1815, Congress voted to renew the institution, but President Madison vetoed the law, for practical reasons; even though he had vigorously opposed the Bank for constitutional reasons in 1791, Madison in 1815 accepted its legitimacy but not its necessity. He reconsidered the latter conclusion in the next year, and the second Bank of the United States was created in 1816, at Madison's own urging. The most skeptical framer had become a convert to that part of the Hamiltonian program.[32]

Whereas Madison and Jefferson had maintained that the Bank idea must give way to the Constitution, it was ultimately the Constitution that gave way to the Bank. By the time the issue finally reached the U.S. Supreme Court, in *McCulloch v. Maryland* (1819), Chief Justice John Marshall was able to start his opinion with the observation that decades of experience with and acquiescence in the Bank of the United States gave it a heightened presumption of constitutionality. Not only did Marshall then proceed to sustain the Bank against constitutional objections, but he also set forth the most expansive theory for interpreting the Constitution ever penned by a U.S. Supreme Court Justice. After broadly construing Article I, Section 8, along the purposive and liberal lines originally suggested by Hamilton, Marshall then invalidated Maryland's effort to tax the bank as unconstitutional. Presumably, the latter holding represented a judgment that state taxation was inconsistent with the efficient operation of a federally chartered bank – but that was a judgment not made on the face of the statute and which Marshall teased out of the nature of things.[33]

In *Osborn v. Bank of the United States* (1824), Marshall created out of the Bank's authorizing statute an implied grant of federal jurisdiction over lawsuits in which the Bank was a party. This was not only a dynamic construction of the statute, which only said that the Bank could "sue or be sued" in state or federal circuit courts, but was also a preface to another breathtaking interpretation of the Constitution. Marshall construed Article III's "arising under" grant of jurisdiction to extend so far as to include cases where federal law is "an ingredient" of the cause of action. All of this was extraordinary and amounted to a dramatic judicial extension of both the statute and the Constitution. Yet, as Justice Johnson's (legally cogent) dissent wearily observed, "I have very little doubt that the public mind will be easily reconciled to the decision of the Court here rendered. . . . The Bank of the United States, is now identified with the administration of the national government. . . . [S]erious and very weighty doubts have been entertained of its constitutionality, but they have been abandoned."[34]

32 Finkelman, "Intentions of the Framers," ibid. at 467–8.

33 *McCulloch v. Maryland*, 17 U.S. 316 (1819).

34 Compare *Osburn v. Bank of the United States*, 22 U.S. 738 (1824) (Marshall, C.J., for the Court), with ibid., 871–2 (Johnson, J., dissenting).

Yet, in the next decade the Second Bank was dealt a fatal blow by the Jackson Administration. For some readers, including one of us, this might be evidence that the Bank Acts were, ultimately, a "failed super-statute," because their principle ultimately did not stick. There was no comparable federal management of national finance for the remainder of the nineteenth century. For other readers, including another of us, the super-statute status of those laws does not depend on their continuity. That the twentieth century retrieved the Bank Act's principle might suggest that this was a super-statute, even if an out-of-the-ordinary one. Both of us believe, and we hope thoughtful readers will agree, that most super-statutes have persevered without interruption, even as the precise contours of their central principles have evolved through public deliberation. The next section illustrates this point in more detail.

IV. SOME EXAMPLES: SUPER- AND NOT-SO-SUPER-STATUTES

The same impulse that created the Bank of the United States created more durable statutes of this sort as the modern regulatory state took shape in this country. Here we mention three super-statutes – the *Sherman Act* of 1890,[35] the *Civil Rights Act* of 1964,[36] and the *Endangered Species Act* of 1973.[37] Note that each super-statute reflects a kind of fundamental commitment instinct in our public life: individual dignity (the *Civil Rights Act*), structuring the economy (the *Sherman Act*), and the environment (the *Endangered Species Act*). And, although these commitments and their statutes may seem dissimilar, they share some common features that will help us to illustrate how super-statutes are created and maintained.[38]

NORMATIVE ORIGINS. Each super-statute originated in a popular normative movement seeking to create new fundamental legal baselines – competition and no monopolies (*Sherman Act*); nondiscrimination as regards race or sex (*Civil Rights Act*); biodiversity (*Endangered Species Act*). To gain enactment as legislation, the proponents of each super-statute had to persuade opponents that the old common-law baselines – freedom of contract and freedom to use property as one wishes – had to give way to a new regulatory baseline. The proponents also had to overcome the many legislative vetogates by making this normative case to an array of different representatives and interested groups. They accomplished these feats

[35] Public Law No. 51–649, 26 Stat. 209 (1890), codified as amended at 15 U.S.C. §1 et seq.

[36] Public Law No. 88–352, 78 Stat. 241 (1964), codified as amended in scattered sections of 5, 28, and 42 U.S.C. Title VII, barring employment discrimination, is codified at 42 U.S.C. §2000e et seq.

[37] Public Law No. 93–205, 87 Stat. 884 (1973), codified as amended in scattered sections of 16 U.S.C.

[38] The discussion that follows draws on the useful historical scholarship for each of our illustrative super-statutes. On the background and evolution of the *Sherman Act*, see Robert H. Bork, *The Antitrust Paradox: A Policy at War with Itself* (New York: Basic Books, 1977); Herbert Hovenkamp, *Federal Antitrust Policy: The Law of Competition and Its Practice* (St. Paul, Minn.: West Publishing Co., 1994); Hans B. Thorelli, *The Federal Antitrust Policy: Origination of an American Tradition* (Baltimore, Md.: Johns Hopkins University Press, 1955). For the Civil Rights Act, see Hugh D. Graham, *The Civil Rights Era, Origins and Development of National Policy, 1960–1972* (New York: Oxford University Press, 1990); Charles and Barbara Whalen, *The Longest Debate: A Legislative History of the 1964 Civil Rights Act* (Cabin John, Md.: Seven Locks Press, 1985). For the Endangered Species Act, see Tony A. Sullins, *Endangered Species Act* (Chicago, IL: Section of Environment, Energy, and Resources, American Bar Association, 2001).

through the force of their central ideas and the support those ideas had among voters and relevant interest groups, including some groups one would have expected to oppose such measures. (Big business, for example, supported the *Civil Rights Act*, which created new regulations pertaining to, and a new agency monitoring, private employment practices. Some farming and ranching interests supported the *Endangered Species Act*, which restricts land use.)

ONGOING CONFLICT AND POSITIVE POPULAR FEEDBACK. Once enacted, each super-statute continued to confront normative opposition and inertia. Opposition could come from the private sector, the states, the national judiciary, or even the executive branch – and the challenge posed by opponents could indeed reduce the putative super-statute to relative inefficacy. Thus, trusts continued to oppose the *Sherman Act*, and their judicial allies gave it a narrow reading – but the Act was rescued by popular support for its presidential fans in the 1904, 1908, and 1912 elections. Southerners set their sights on the *Civil Rights Act* – and were repudiated in the 1964 election; the Great Society's EEOC aggressively implemented the law's anti-race discrimination norm. Following the EEOC, the Supreme Court generally gave the Act a liberal interpretation. The Burger Court construed the Act narrowly in the pregnancy discrimination case, and Congress immediately overrode it with the *PDA*. When the Rehnquist Court sought to trim back the Act even more in 1989, it was immediately and intensely rebuffed by popular outrage and angry legislative overrides. Farmers, foresters, and ranchers have sought to nullify the ESA but have not yet been able to persuade either agencies or judges of their case.

THE PRINCIPLE BECOMES AXIOMATIC AND IMPERIAL. What was controversial in one generation became conventional wisdom in the next. The norms of business competition, nondiscrimination, and biodiversity became legally axiomatic because they became culturally unquestionable. That does not mean that the super-statute escaped debate and controversy, for settlement of its core normative claims invited debate and disagreement about what were the corollaries to those claims: Is market dominance automatically contrary to the competition norm? Does affirmative action violate the nondiscrimination norm? Is discrimination because of pregnancy sex discrimination? Does biodiversity justify closing down a $100 million dam to save a little snail darter from extinction?

In addition to becoming axiomatic, the super-statutory principle in each case has had an imperial quality, affecting other statutory schemes and even constitutional doctrine. Accordingly, the *Sherman Act* was the occasion for conservative Supreme Courts to go along with broad and aggressive Department of Justice assertions of Congress's regulatory authority under the Commerce Clause. The *Lochner*-era Court episodically struck down congressional enactments, as applied, as exceeding the Commerce Clause limit but uniformly upheld broad assertions of *Sherman Act* jurisdiction, even as to intrastate commercial activities.[39] Moreover,

[39] Compare *Hammer v. Dagenhart*, 247 U.S. 251 (1918) (invalidating statute prohibiting shipment of goods made with child labor in interstate commerce), with *United States v. Swift & Co.*, 196 U.S. 375 (1905) (upholding application of *Sherman Act* to intrastate price fixing conspiracy). One would have expected precisely the opposite results in these cases, under the plain meaning of the Commerce Clause.

the nation's commitment to the free-market principle of the *Sherman Act* has provided a coherent rationale for the Supreme Court's Dormant Commerce Clause jurisprudence, which strikes down state legislation that either discriminates against interstate commerce or imposes undue burdens on it.[40] Finally, the Court has generalized the *Sherman Act* principle into a general canon of statutory construction, that "exemptions from the antitrust laws are to be narrowly construed," and other regulatory schemes must usually accede to the demands of the *Sherman Act.*[41] *The Civil Rights Act* and the *Endangered Species Act* have had similar gravitational effects on both Constitutional law and other statutory schemes.[42]

It is important to stress that not all laws expressing fundamental commitments will become super-statutes. Recall the three criteria for distinguishing super from ordinary statutes. Super-statutes (1) establish fundamental values; (2) satisfy more process requirements than ordinary statutes (because of the serial deliberative processes by which agencies, courts, and the people themselves come to accept and rely upon them); and (3) are stable, especially if they establish a fundamental value that satisfies the process requirement in (2). So, we say that super-statutes are fundamental, extensively deliberative, and stable.

Seeing things this way allows us to speak to whether, for example, the first and second Bank Acts were a single super-statute. One can object that the Bank Acts (1) did not establish a fundamental value, or (2) did not derive popular support through a public deliberative process over time, or (3) ultimately proved not to be a robust contribution to small *c* constitutionalism. We are relatively agnostic as to whether the Bank Acts meet all three of these requirements, though on balance one of us does think that they do; the other is cagily hedging his bets. Consider the application of these criteria to other laws we do not consider to be super-statutes.

Most laws reported in the Statutes at Large are easy calls, because they represent policy decisions and compromises needed to keep the government operating in the normal way (especially appropriations measures) or to resolve local or short-term problems (most other statutes enacted by Congress). Thus, they do not meet our first, and most important, requirement of fundamental values. Some laws pretend to be fundamental normative realignments; their preambles bray their self-importance. But most of them remain ordinary laws reflecting ordinary policy choices; we call them *pseudo super-statutes.* Other statutes meet the first requirement of fundamental principle but do not stick, often because they meet resistance from judges or administrators and do not receive the popular reinforcement that saves super-statutes from such resistance. These *putative super-statutes* may be killed at birth (and so *stillborn*) or over time (and are *failed super-statutes*). Consider some examples of these statutes that are not super.

PSEUDO SUPER-STATUTE: THE ARBITRATION ACT? The *Federal Arbitration Act* of 1925 (*FAA*) trumped the common law procedural rule against enforcing compulsory arbitration clauses.[43] Its principle has stuck in our *legal* culture. Specifically,

[40] See, e.g., *West Lynn Creamery, Inc. v. Healy*, 512 U.S. 186 (1994).

[41] *Group Life & Health Ins. Co. v. Royal Drug Co.*, 440 U.S. 205, 231–2 (1979).

[42] Eskridge and Ferejohn, "Super-Statutes," *supra* note 2 at 1237–42 (Civil Rights Act), 1242–6 (Endangered Species Act).

[43] Public Law No. 68–101, 43 Stat. 883 (1925), codified as amended at 9 U.S.C. §§1–14.

the Burger and Rehnquist Courts treat the *FAA*'s deference to private dispute resolution principle as axiomatic.[44] But we are not sure that the *FAA*'s principle has been the situs of enough political conflict to have risen to the level of super-statutedom. The *Arbitration Act* might be a pseudo super-statute, because its principle has been pressed into it by unelected judges, without even the indirect popular feedback that has characterized the *Sherman Act* and our other super-statutes. Recent Supreme Court interpretations imposing arbitration on American citizens wanting their day in court may yet produce a political showdown where the statutory principle triumphs, but until that happens we are reluctant to find the *FAA* to be a super-statute. Many other popular – and less controversial – statutes fall into this category.

STILLBORN SUPER-STATUTE: NATIONAL RECOVERY ACT. An early New Deal measure, the *National Industrial Recovery Act* of 1934 (*NRA*) trumped the common-law freedom of contract with a principle of industry-developed regulatory norms.[45] The law was adopted with strong support from Congress and the president (himself elected by a large majority in a critical, realigning election). But the *NRA* was decidedly not a super-statute, because the Supreme Court killed it at birth, unanimously striking it down in *Schechter Poultry v. United States* (1935).[46] Unlike the phoenix and the national bank, this statutory idea never resurfaced. So this was a stillborn super-statute. A recent example of this phenomenon was the *Religious Freedom Restoration Act* of 1993, which sought to override the constitutional baseline that the state can adopt neutral rules having incidental and unintended burdens on religious free exercise.[47] The Supreme Court struck down the law on federalism grounds in *City of Boerne v. Flores* (1997), and its proponents have been unable to muster public excitement to override or resist the Court.[48]

FAILED SUPER-STATUTE: AMERICANS WITH DISABILITIES ACT? Adopted by lopsided bipartisan majorities and enthusiastically signed by the first President Bush, the *Americans with Disabilities Act* of 1990 (*ADA*) trumped the common law freedom of contract with a principle of nondiscrimination on the basis of disability.[49] More important, the *ADA* rested upon a reconception of the nondiscrimination idea, as entailing accommodation of disability. The judiciary has been exceedingly stingy in construing and applying this potentially revolutionary statute. Since 1991, a Supreme Court that has been liberal in applying Title VII's sex discrimination protections and new race discrimination rules, has been very conservative (often unanimously so) in applying the *ADA*. In *Board of Trustees v. Garrett* (2001), the Court struck down the *ADA*'s employment discrimination rules as applied to the states. Contrasting the constitutionally more serious kinds of discrimination (race and sex), Chief Justice Rehnquist's opinion for the Court denigrated the statute's

[44] For broad Supreme Court applications of the arbitration norm, see, e.g., *Southland v. Keating*, 465 U.S. 1 (1984); *Circuit City Stores, Inc. v. Adams*, 121 S.Ct. 1302 (2001).

[45] Public Law No. 73–67, 48 Stat. 195 (1933), codified at 15 U.S.C. §703 *et seq.* invalidated by *A.L.A. Schechter Poultry Co. v. United* States, 295 U.S. 495 (1935).

[46] Ibid.

[47] Public Law No. 103–141, 107 Stat. 1488 (1993), codified at 42 U.S.C. §§2000bb–2000bb-4.

[48] *City of Boerne v. Flores*, 521 U.S. 107 (1997).

[49] Public Law No. 101–336, 104 Stat. 327, codified in scattered parts of 42 U.S.C.

asserted public value.[50] Disability rights advocates have protested decisions like these, but without any significant political effect. The *ADA* is an important statute, but until it shows more normative legs it is far from being a super-statute. It may become an example of a "failed super-statute," one with a promising birth but unimpressive life cycle.

V. THE LIFE CYCLE OF A SUPER-STATUTE

It is a commonplace observation that statutes evolve over time, as they are applied to unforeseen circumstances and in new legal contexts. This feature gives most statutes a dynamic quality. Super-statutes evolve in a particularly dynamic way. Because they aim to displace old norms and create new principles, super-statutes open up a new discourse and invite elaboration and specification of their new norms. That process of elaboration and specification is bound to be controversial, further ensuring a dynamic evolution as administrators, judges, private groups, legislators, and citizens weigh in. Consider an example, after which we shall suggest a stylized model of the evolution of a super-statute.

Title VII of the *Civil Rights Act* of 1964 was bound to change as it was applied to issues such as pregnancy-based discrimination, which was not discussed in the elaborate legislative history of the law. Indeed, there was very little public discussion of Title VII's bar to employment discrimination "because of . . . sex," which had been added in an odd procedural gambit by a civil rights opponent in the House (Judge Smith of Virginia). It is not inevitable that discrimination because of sex includes pregnancy-based discrimination. A letter from the EEOC General Counsel opined on October 17, 1966, that employer exclusion of pregnancy from disability programs was not sex discrimination illegal under Title VII.

The Johnson Administration EEOC was notoriously uninterested in enforcing the sex discrimination bar, and that reluctance directly stimulated feminist political activism. The National Organization of Women (NOW) was formed in 1966 by feminists who walked out of a government-sponsored conference on employment discrimination to protest the EEOC's lack of receptivity to their concerns. NOW and other feminist groups insisted that open discrimination against women was only part of their problems in the workplace; structural barriers to women's employment opportunities were just as serious a problem. Feminists backed up their analysis with examples and studies – and once the agency started listening to women's stories of genuine employment disadvantage as a result of pregnancy rules, it rethought its interpretation. In 1972, the EEOC issued a guideline to employers which took the position that pregnancy-based workplace exclusions or discriminations violate Title VII.[51]

[50] Compare *Board of Trustees v. Garrett*, 531 U.S. 356 (2001), overriding Congress's effort to impose disability discrimination rules on state employers, with *Tennessee v. Lane*, 124 S.Ct. 1978 (2004), which upheld Congress's effort to impose public accommodation requirements on the states to benefit the disabled.

[51] The traditional judicial account of the EEOC's evolving policy on pregnancy discrimination is found in *General Electric Co. v. Gilbert*, 429 U.S. 125 (1976). That account is both incomplete and inaccurate, as demonstrated by Schwartz, "Birth of a Super-Statute," *supra* note 27.

The EEOC's 1972 guideline was an important elaboration of the statutory nondiscrimination principle – but it was much more than simply the application of a general principle to an unaddressed factual situation. The norm itself was in play. Clearly, a workplace nondiscrimination norm barred employers from refusing to hire women or hiring women and paying them much less than an equally qualified man. It might be inferred from the principle that an employer should not be able to justify lower pay on the ground that, "The female employee is more likely to take a lot of time off to deal with pregnancy." This inference might be contested on the ground that it is not an open *sex* discrimination; rather it is a *pregnancy* discrimination. But to use the possibility of pregnancy to deny all women equal pay would seem to violate the nondiscrimination principle. At the very least, women who do not become pregnant are treated unfairly. What if the employer simply said, "We shall pay women the same as men, but we won't give them any breaks if in fact they become pregnant." That is a harder case, because the discrimination is more tightly tied to pregnancy and is not generalized to all women – but the fact remains that the *only* employees penalized by the policy are female ones.

Viewed from the perspective of employers, the last-noted policy might be understood as a cost-effective measure formally unrelated to sex (it only applies to pregnant women, not all women). But viewed from the perspective of female employees, the policy not only has a discriminatory effect, but has that effect only on female employees – and the effect is significant and subjects many women to different workplace conditions than men enjoy. To follow this perspective, as the EEOC did in 1972, the agency was thinking more deeply about the 1964 norm: Sex discrimination entails policies that affect only women, even if they do not formally target women per se. The feminist position also rejected employer claims that disability or health insurance policies excluding pregnancy are not sex discrimination; feminists insisted that such policies are sex discriminations, even if the policies on the whole generate as many monetary benefits to women as they do to men. (This was the employer's main defense in *Gilbert*.)

These are all issues worth debating in a public manner – and the debate was more satisfyingly normative in the legislative process than in the judicial process. The Supreme Court in *Geduldig* and *Gilbert* agreed with the employer perspective, but with virtually no reasoning about the nondiscrimination norm and no apparent recognition that there were two ways of reading that norm. The Justices seemed to ignore feminist claims that pregnancy-based discrimination marginalized women in the workplace and impeded their integration. Between 1976 and 1978, Congress gave both perspectives full consideration and noticed that many public as well as private employers agreed with Williams and her allies. The *PDA* was the result. It not only confirmed the EEOC's 1972 guideline but also gave it much greater legitimacy because the American people and the media got involved and their elected representatives chose the feminist version of the norm after full debate.

At precisely the time the nondiscrimination norm was being elaborated in the *PDA*, Catharine MacKinnon was putting the finishing touches on her book, *Sexual Harassment of Working Women* (1979), where she argued that another way women are denied workplace opportunities was that they are pervasively harassed.[52] Although dismissed as too radical, MacKinnon's elaboration of the nondiscrimination norm had enormous resonance with people who were familiar with patterns of harassment when women entered workplaces, especially when they did so in token numbers. Sexual harassment was outrageous from a feminist point of view but also was indefensible from the point of view of the managerial workplace. In 1980, the EEOC adopted MacKinnon's framework as the basis of guidelines for employer liability under Title VII if supervisors or coworkers engage in sexual harassment or create a hostile workplace.[53]

The EEOC's sexual harassment guidelines were a different kind of norm elaboration than the *PDA* and the 1972 pregnancy discrimination guideline had been. As before, the core instances of discrimination were being expanded to consider the effect of workplace practices on women's opportunities. Unlike the earlier elaboration, the 1980 guidelines put employers on notice that their own inaction or lack of a policy could subject them to liability for acts of supervisors or coworkers. (The pregnancy cases involved affirmative employer policies or practices.) The 1980 guidelines also insisted that the nondiscrimination norm had to be concerned about the sexualized workplace. Like the pregnancy guideline, the sexual harassment guidelines revealed that women's physical differences from men, their great virtue from a traditionalist point of view, was a source of disadvantage and marginalization in the modern Weberian workplace. Both legal elaborations required that the nondiscrimination norm address issues of sexuality and gender role – and that dialectic committed the statutory principle to a fascinating political and normative evolution.

As before, these statutory interpretive issues went to the Supreme Court, which handled them with much greater normative awareness than it had shown in the pregnancy cases. In *Vinson v. Meritor* (1986), the Rehnquist Court unanimously upheld the EEOC's guidelines as a defensible application of Title VII.[54] Specifically, the Court held that quid pro quo harassment of a female employee by a male supervisor was a violation of the nondiscrimination norm. It is notable that a very conservative and text-oriented Supreme Court followed the liberal and dynamically interpreting EEOC when it ratified, at least in part, the 1980 guidelines. It is also notable that when Congress rebuffed the Court on its conservative interpretations of Title VII in race discrimination cases, both popular and legislative discussions supported the EEOC's and the Court's dynamicism in sexual harassment law. Not surprisingly, the agency and the courts continued the process.

In *Burlington Industries, Inc., v. Ellerth* (1998), the issue was what responsibility an employer has under Title VII for a supervisor's unwelcome sexual advances and threats of retaliation.[55] If Title VII were a criminal statute, the employer would not be liable for such advances absent a more specific scienter showing. If Title VII were an ordinary statute, it is not clear that courts should fashion detailed rules

[52] Catharine A. MacKinnon, *Sexual Harassment of Working Women: A Case of Sex Discrimination* (New Haven: Yale University Press, 1979); Vicki Schultz, "Reconceptualizing Sexual Harassment" (1998) 107 *Yale Law Journal* 1696.

[53] EEOC, "Guidelines on Discrimination Because of Sex," codified at 29 CFR ch. XIV §1604.45 *Federal Register* 25,024 (Apr. 11, 1980).

[54] *Meritor Savings Bank, FSB v. Vinson*, 477 U.S. 57 (1986).

[55] *Burlington Indus., Inc. v. Ellerth*, 524 U.S. 742 (1998).

for figuring out when supervisor advances (unknown to the employer) constitute "discrimination... because of... sex"; it would be well within our legal process tradition for the Court to insist that any such rules be fashioned by Congress. It is notable that no Justice in *Ellerth* took this position; all nine Justices – none of whom is an open activist – were willing to fashion specific rules, common-law style, to guide the agency, courts, and attorneys to determine when the employer should be liable. The debate within the Court was entirely over what detailed set of rules the judiciary should read into the open-textured statutory text. Justice Kennedy's opinion for the Court came up with some relatively tough rules: When the harassing supervisor visits a tangible employment action on the employee, both the policy of Title VII and principles of agency render the employer vicariously liable; when there is no tangible employment consequence, Title VII policies suggest there should sometimes be liability for the employer, subject to a defense that the employer took due care to prevent harassment (such as through an antiharassment policy and complaint procedure) and the employee failed to take advantage of the employer's internal protections.

Although the rules developed by Justice Kennedy are not the most liberal, pro-plaintiff rules the Court could have derived, choosing such rules is not entailed by our theory. Conservative judges and commentators are certainly correct to point out that no principle must be pursued at any cost and even the most important public policy runs up against others that set limits on it. These kinds of trade-offs and judgments have been the life of the common law. Thus, our super-statute rule of construction requires that interpreters develop the statute, common-law style, to carry out its robust principle and purposes, but cognizant of crosscutting costs and countervailing policies. *Ellerth* is a classic case for this kind of reasoning.

At this point, we should like to generalize our account of the *CRA*, the *Sherman Act*, and the *ESA*, as well as our more detailed account of Title VII's pregnancy and sexual harassment rules, by illustrating a "typical" life cycle. A stylized model in Figure 15.1 depicts the evolution of a super-statute and shows how its fundamental principle is refined and articulated over time. This is our standardized story for a typical successful super-statute. We are happy to acknowledge that actual super-statutes may deviate from this picture in various ways. There may be intertemporal gaps during which statutory development is sidetracked – as may have happened with the post–Civil War civil rights statutes. The fundamental principle may shift quite far from the one embodied in the original legislation, as probably occurred in the case of the *Sherman Act*. And a super-statute may after a period of time simply expire because its underlying principle no longer seems valuable, as with antebellum fugitive slave legislation.

VI. THE NEW AMERICAN CONSTITUTIONALISM

Super-statutes have reconfigured public law in the United States. This reconfiguration has been so pervasive as to justify our calling the resulting model, a *new American constitutionalism*. Although we call this conception of constitutionalism "new," it certainly has distinguished antecedents. Justice Harlan Fiske Stone and other early legal process thinkers understood statutes as potential sources of principle and public values. They did not, however, tie this idea to a robust

Responding to a normative social movement and after careful and public deliberation, Congress enacts a statute embodying a norm.

Statute is implemented by judges and/or agencies, with feedback from Congress. Implementation gives the norm specificity but also changes the norm.

Normative conflict, where one institution seeks to narrow the statute and compromise the norm:
• Legislature bows to pressure to create special interest exceptions.
• Court narrowly construes the statute.
• Agency is captured by the regulated group or a special interest.

Public debate about the attempted narrowing:
• Critical outrage, seeking to engage the public.
• Institutional opposition.
• Statutory narrowing may become an election issue.

Responsive to the normative debate, the legislature or agency reaffirms or adapts the core principle of the statute.

More crises, especially as statute is adapted to ever newer circumstances.

Figure 15.1. Life Cycle of a Super-Statute.

constitutionalism with institutional legitimacy and capacity advantages over the standard account. Political scientists and sociologists have demonstrated that social movements often, perhaps typically, seek statutory as well as judicial recognition of their norms. These lines of scholarship have suggested concrete ways in which legislatures can be not only sources of principle, but also fora for fundamental normative transformation. Professors Jerry Mashaw and Henry Richardson have suggested ways in which administrative agencies can and ought to be fora where important public values are not only applied to concrete issues and facts, but also where they are sharpened, refined, and even transformed.[56]

Our project is, in part, a drawing together of these different strands of thought to identify a new conception of constitutionalism. Under our account, super-statutes and debate about their values help to shape fundamental law. Legislators, executive officials, and popular social movements drive the evolution of public law more than judges do. Like the standard account, this new account is text-based and documentary, but the constitutional canon, the sacred text, is not limited to the Constitution. Instead, it includes statutes. The institutional focus of our new American constitutionalism is legislatures and agencies as well as courts.

There is a deeper relationship between super-statutory and Constitutional law in our country, and it has to do with the way the large *C* Constitution changes. Compared with the constitutions of other nations and of our own states, the U.S. Constitution is relatively short, old, and hard to change through the formal

[56] Jerry L. Mashaw and David L. Harfst, *The Struggle for Auto Safety* (Cambridge, Mass.: Harvard University Press, 1990); Richardson, *Democratic Autonomy, supra* note 14.

Article V process. These three facts about the Constitution have supported its updating through dynamic judicial interpretation of its provisions. This perception of judicial updating has called forth thousands of articles and books justifying or indicting or seeking to define the limits of judicial review. Professor James Bradley Thayer's classic criticism of judicial review is that it supplants or drains energy from popular (We the People) participation in governance.[57] This criticism continues to have bite, perhaps now more than before.

Many theorists have tackled the problem of reconciling the Constitution's meta-principle of popular sovereignty with the apparent reality of extensive and hard-to-check constitutional lawmaking by unelected judges who enjoy life tenure, but they have done so within the standard account, which has tended to defeat such projects. A few authors are breaking through the standard account to think more usefully about the relationship of constitutional norms and political mobilization.

In a series of books collectively entitled *We the People*, Bruce Ackerman maintains that Article V's rule of recognition is not necessary to change the Constitution even in a formal sense. Really fundamental constitutional enactments can occur outside the Article V procedures in special periods – *constitutional moments* – when the whole people are engaged and attentive to the establishment of a new constitutional ordering.[58] For Ackerman, what is crucial is not a detailed set of institutional requirements but the purpose served by such requirements: that the people, responding to a crisis pitting one institution against others, are engaged actively and purposively in reshaping the constitutional order. Whether or not they meet the Article V requirements, fundamental constitutional moments, according to Ackerman's theory, ought to attract great deference from courts because they effect a change in the constitutional text, guided by deeply held principles of political morality, and because they are put in place deliberately by an aroused and serious public. Note how Ackerman's theory is responsive to some of the problems we identified with the standard account's focus on constitutional text definitively interpreted by judges.

An extension of Ackerman's theory would be to understand some constitutional law to have been created by what one might, playfully, call *super-statutory moments*. Thus, the *Civil Rights Act* can be read as representing a showdown between a normatively engaged political coalition of civil rights reformers and their allies in Congress, versus the determined Southern Democrats in the Senate, who had repeatedly blocked strong civil rights legislation during the Eisenhower Administration. The election of 1960 offered proponents an opportunity to break this impasse, as it brought to power the Kennedy-Johnson Administration, which pushed hard for civil rights legislation. In 1963–1964, the debate over the civil rights bill engaged the entire country, with religious, business, and union groups joining civil rights groups in pressing for the adoption of this important legislation. The Southern opposition was decisively defeated by a coalition assembled by President Lyndon Johnson and Senate Majority Whip Hubert Humphrey. In the election that immediately

[57] James Bradley Thayer, *John Marshall* (Boston: Houghton Mifflin, 1901) at 103–7.

[58] Bruce Ackerman, *We the People: Foundations* (Cambridge, Mass.: Belknap Press of Harvard University Press, 1991) [*Foundations*], and *We the People: Transformations* (Cambridge, Mass.: Belknap Press of Harvard University Press, 1998).

followed in 1964, Johnson (with Humphrey as his running mate) won a great landslide over a Republican who had voted against the Act for reasons of "states' rights." This scenario roughly follows Ackerman's formula for *higher lawmaking*, whereby the people are engaged in constitutional moments.[59] We the People had arguably endorsed civil rights over states' rights – a principle that has altered policy as well as constitutional discourse ever since. 1964 might be regarded as a super-statutory moment permanently altering the normative foundations of public discourse.[60]

The idea of super-statutory moments along Ackermanian lines is a neat project, but it is not exactly our project. Our new American constitutionalism motored by super-statutes idea is broader. Descriptively, the main difference between a concept of super-statutory moments (our imaginative adaptation of Ackerman) and dynamically applied super-statutes (the approach we endorse) is that the latter acquire their normative force through a series of public confrontations and debates over time and not through a stylized dramatic confrontation. Thus, the *Civil Rights Act* of 1964, which was enacted in a particularly dramatic and publicly absorbing way, acquired only some of its normative force in 1964. The Act immediately transformed public culture in some ways but not in others. So there was indeed a great national debate in 1963–1964 that settled many issues of race discrimination – but the debate settled virtually no issues involving sex discrimination. Only Title VII prohibited sex discrimination, and then only by an adventitious confluence of interest between Southern opponents and feminist supporters of the civil rights bill. There was little public discussion as to what the prohibition would entail.

So the *Civil Rights Act* of 1964 did little to transform the workplace for women, in part because sex discrimination issues played almost no role in the great public debate surrounding that super-statutory moment of 1964. But the fact that Title VII did prohibit sex discrimination provided a focus and a legal forum for feminists to develop the contours of a robust norm of sex nondiscrimination. As we have already seen, feminists like Wendy Williams and Catharine MacKinnon, working within Title VII, opened a series of public debates and confrontations in the 1970s and 1980s. One might consider the *PDA* a super-statutory moment, but the 1980 Sexual Harassment Guidelines (perhaps the most important regulatory innovation of the last third of the twentieth century) were not such a moment. They were rather more consensual than conflictual: Informed by feminist work, the EEOC developed the guidelines; Congress was aware of them and left them alone with some degree of positive acquiescence or even approval; the Supreme Court endorsed them as law in 1986. All three branches of government were working together on this one. This is rather amazing in light of the way judges and policymakers dismissed women's concerns in the 1970s, and the major changes in American life that sexual harassment law has occasioned.

[59] Bruce Ackerman, "Higher Lawmaking," in *Imperfection, supra* note 20 at 63–88.

[60] Ackerman's formula for constitutional moments is this: Interbranch Impasse→Decisive Election→Reformist Challenge to Conservative Branch→Switch in Time. Ackerman, *Foundations, supra* note 58 at 49–50. The Civil Rights Act as a super-statutory moment might look like this: Interbranch Impasse on civil rights legislation during the Eisenhower Administration, with the Senate blocking it→Decisive Election of Kennedy–Johnson in 1960 →Kennedy–Johnson Reformist Challenge to Conservative Branch (Senate), with 1963–1964 civil rights bill, greeted by the public with strong and growing support→Switch in Time, when the Senate finally breaks the Southern filibuster in 1964.

In any event, the important point is not some stylized model that tries to parallel Article V. The important point is that serious feminist thinkers and their critics advanced ideas and norms as a framework for implementing the sex discrimination bar in Title VII. The EEOC and Congress were important fora for deliberation about these ideas, and We the People were continuously involved rather than mobilized only in one politically charged moment. The result was a public consensus that the antidiscrimination principle ought to have bite for women in the workplace – and that the bite entailed protections against discrimination on the basis of pregnancy or through sexual harassment in the workplace. The super-statute evolved through a series of debates and confrontations.

Like Ackerman, we understand lasting public norms to grow out of conflict (the 1978 *PDA*). Unlike Ackerman, we understand lasting public norms to form under conditions of consensus, too (the 1980 sexual harassment guidelines). Most unlike his theory, ours emphasizes evolution rather than revolution. A super-statute is not a moment, nor is it even a series of moments. Rather, it is an ongoing process of deliberation, consensus-building as to some issues, conflict as to other issues – and resolution of conflict by resort to popular feedback (again, often over time).

Most important, we think that this process of norm-elaboration, occurring outside the Article V framework, creates fundamental law. Return to Carolyn Aiello's case against Gilbert Geduldig. Long ago, California repealed the pregnancy discrimination in its unemployment compensation program, and the idea is so discredited that other states have followed suit, while none has accepted the Supreme Court's invitation to discriminate along these lines. But assume that the governor of State X proposes such a discrimination as part of a budget-balancing law. Legislators as well as citizens would inevitably, and we think quite properly, object that the discrimination violates fundamental public norms and is, in effect, unconstitutional. The governor might say that *Geduldig v. Aiello* upheld such a discrimination, but citizens would easily respond that the discrimination surely violates the state constitution. If they were advised by savvy law professors, they would also say, "In light of the *PDA* and the Court's aggressive sex discrimination jurisprudence after 1974, the Supreme Court would not follow *Geduldig* today." We think the Justices would not – they would overrule the 1974 precedent quicker than you can say "*Lawrence v. Texas*" (which overruled the notorious precedent, *Bowers v. Hardwick*).[61]

Indeed, if the Justices in our hypothetical (and most unlikely) scenario did *not* overrule *Geduldig v. Aiello*, there would be hell to pay (just as they learned after *Hardwick*). Just as gay rights advocates delivered a constant drumbeat of horror stories and criticisms to discredit *Hardwick*, feminists would pound away at any reaffirmance of *Geduldig*. And some of the most ardent critics would be middle-aged guys such as ourselves. The critics would make their case to an overwhelmingly receptive public audience. Most of the states would join them. Big business would applaud them and reject cost-benefit arguments for such policies. Social scientists would discredit the empirical bases for the policy. Virtually no major public figure would dare defend the Court. Many would complain that the Justices are not doing their job, are biased against women ("they just don't get it"), and so forth. Once

[61] *Lawrence v. Texas*, 539 U.S. (2003), overruling *Bowers v. Hardwick*, 478 U.S. 186 (1986).

fundamental law has shifted, even the Supreme Court must follow, or it risks strong criticism or, worse, ridicule.

VII. THE EVOLUTION OF MODERN CONSTITUTIONAL LAW

The new American constitutionalism has three big descriptive and three big prescriptive implications for constitutional law in the United States. The descriptive implications are that constitutional law is going to be driven by three phenomena:

THE MODERN ADMINISTRATIVE STATE AS THE CONTEXT. The big shift in constitutional law in the twentieth century is not the famous showdown between the New Deal and the Old Court. That was but a point in the more gradual replacement of the laissez-faire Watchman State by the Modern Administrative State. The normative baseline is no longer the old rights of contract and property; instead, the baseline is state or federal regulation in the public interest. The regulatory baseline is no longer judge-driven common law but is instead legislature-driven regulatory statutes. This has had and will continue to have implications for constitutional issues of federalism, separation of powers, the state action doctrine, and individual rights, especially procedural protections, free speech, and privacy rights.

SOCIAL MOVEMENTS AS THE ENGINE. As state regulation – rather than laissez-faire – has become the baseline, the motor for changing public norms has increasingly become social movements. Examples: populism and the progressive good government movement, the temperance movement, the civil rights movement, the old-age security movement, the birth control (and later the abortion) movement, the women's rights movement, the pro-life and anti-ERA movements, the environmental movement, the gay rights and traditional family values movements, and so forth. These large-scale social movements were strongly normative. Their focus was changing state policy, and their rhetoric was constitutional. The social movements in the early twentieth century sought to effectuate their normative programs through constitutional amendments; those in midcentury through judicial activism; those in the last third of the century through a combination of legislative, administrative, and judicial norm elaboration.

SUPER-STATUTES AS THE PRODUCT. As the previous point suggested, the goal of constitutional discourse is no longer to amend the Constitution or to create an Ackermanian constitutional moment, but to press for the adoption of super-statutes that change public norms through an ongoing administrative–judicial–legislative trialogue. Indeed, one might say that a great deal of constitutional discourse goes on within agencies and legislatures after a putative super-statute has been enacted.

Prescriptively, the new American constitutionalism ought to be guided by the following metaprinciples:

LEGISLATURES FOR POSITIVE GOALS, COURTS FOR NEGATIVE GOALS. The Supreme Court is hardly irrelevant or marginal in the new American constitutionalism, but its role is not nearly as glorious as the Warren Court's activism suggested it might be. The Warren Court and its successors have been most productive when they slow down or stop activist state regulation that unnecessarily encroaches on individual or group liberties. A rich and enduring part of the new American constitutionalism is the array of constitutional or statutory protections Americans have against state intrusions into private spaces, criminal proceedings and state incarcerations, state censorship, and so forth. The judiciary really is the least dangerous – and least potent – branch, and so affirmative agendas must be pursued through legislatures and agencies. Fundamental redistributions of property or even status entitlements will not effectively come anywhere but from the legislature.

AGENCIES AS WELL AS COURTS AS FORA FOR NORM ELABORATION. The *Sherman Act* essentially vested norm elaboration in federal judges, but the Department of Justice has in the last generation been the most productive force in thinking about the nation's anticompetition rules. The *Civil Rights Act* vested most norm elaboration in agencies. Even Title VII, which declined to give the EEOC substantive rule-making authority, has been dominated by the EEOC, with the Supreme Court playing the role of a near-sighted referee in an NFL football game – sometimes getting it right, but suffering the indignity of rebukes and legislative overrides when it has strayed from consensuses held by the EEOC, civil rights, and business groups. The *Endangered Species Act* gives almost all norm elaboration to agencies, with the Court episodically ratifying their decisions (so far). For all the criticisms heaped upon agencies as frequently captured, these have performed rather well, combining expertise and informed discourse with attentiveness to popular attitudes. As the issue of pregnancy-based discrimination suggests, the agencies have engaged in fundamental lawmaking more maturely than the Supreme Court has.

MANAGING PLURALISM. The United States has always been a pluralistic political regime, but America's pluralism is more complex and its management trickier than ever before. Issues that divide social or normative groups in the short term cannot and ought not be definitively resolved by the political or judicial process. The new American constitutionalism is not a discourse that creates a lot of losers, completely marginalized groups. The least that our government must do is to keep all social groups involved in the political process, but to insist that their actions and even rhetoric remain within the boundaries of public reason (understood roughly in the way articulated by John Rawls).

VIII. CONCLUSION: GAY RIGHTS AND THE NEW AMERICAN CONSTITUTIONALISM

We conclude by examining the recent evolution of gay rights in American public law. This story is, of course, incomplete and no one can know how precisely how it will play out, but it provides a powerful example of the challenges that this new constitutionalism faces in our heterogeneous new millennium.

At the national level, there is no fundamental law supporting gay rights, beyond the consensus view that the government ought not be able to outlaw people for their consensual sexual activities inside private spaces. This was the Supreme Court's holding in *Lawrence v. Texas* (2003). The Court was on safe ground. Even the solid

South fractured on the issue, with several states nullifying their own statutes as inconsistent with fundamental law. No major religion supported those criminal statutes, and some prominent religions filed *amicus* briefs against them. The Bush Administration, filled with fundamentalists and football-loving Texans, said not a word to support the statute. Texas itself declined to file a brief supporting its own law; poor Harris County carried the whole load, rather half-heartedly. All of this was plenty of evidence that fundamental law had already changed. The Supreme Court ratified that change, but a provocative dissenting opinion claimed that the country was on the brink of swallowing the entire "homosexual agenda," including same-sex marriage.[62]

Do not believe it. There is a putative super-statute to the contrary – the *Defense of Marriage Act* of 1996 (*DOMA*).[63] Supported by the Republican Party, most Democrats, and a centrist president, *DOMA* sailed through Congress with super-huge majorities. All but a handful of states have copied its norm, legislating that civil marriage can only exist between a man and a woman and that foreign same-sex marriages will not be recognized by their courts. The national consensus reflected in *DOMA* is not limited to same-sex marriage. (Three years before *DOMA*, Congress enacted a law excluding openly gay, lesbian, or bisexual Americans from serving in the military.) Any policy that is understood as "endorsing" homosexuality is suspect in America. For the time being, We the People are normatively engaged – and their engagement supports No Promo Homo, rather than Gay Is Good.

So super-statutes are not necessarily engines of social liberalism or progressivism. Gay people (like one of your authors) believe that *DOMA* is only a pseudo super-statute and that its principle will not prove robust over time, but that remains to be seen. The fate of *DOMA*'s no promo homo norm is in the hands of We the People, especially future generations. Although fraught with obvious constitutional problems, *DOMA* will be protected from Supreme Court invalidation until the nation's fundamental law changes. Is the nation at an impasse as to gay rights? We think not.

On matters of gay rights, the new American constitutionalism has been working assiduously at the state level. Indeed, state fundamental law relating to gay people is a work in progress exemplifying the desirability of our conception of constitutionalism, from the perspective of fundamentalists and gay people alike. Here's what is going on: Equality for gay people is not a boon that judges have the power to bestow, but it has come in many jurisdictions through the mechanisms we outline in this chapter. Consider the case of Vermont. This is a small tolerant state with a modest lesbian and gay population. Through grassroots organizing and proselytizing, gay people in 1991 persuaded voters and legislators to adopt a civil rights law protecting against sexual orientation discrimination in employment, public accommodations, housing, and education.[64] This (state) super-statute was gay

[62] *Lawrence*, 539 U.S. at 601 (Scalia, J., dissenting). ("This reasoning leaves on pretty shaky grounds state laws limiting marriage to opposite-sex couples.")

[63] Public Law No. 104–199, 110 Stat. 2419 (1996), codified at 1 U.S.C. §7 and 28 U.S.C. §1738C.

[64] The 1991 super-statute barred discrimination on the basis of sexual orientation in private as well as public employment, see 21 Vermont Statutes §495; housing, see 9 Vermont Statutes §4503; insurance, see 8 Vermont Statutes §4724; and public accommodations, see ibid., §4502.

people's version of the *Civil Rights Act* of 1964, but of course limited to Vermont. Like the national *Civil Rights Act*, Vermont's omnibus protection against sexual orientation discrimination announced an important principle that has stuck in that jurisdiction and has provided feedback to the state judiciary even in constitutional cases.

The super-statutory norm was acceptance of gay people as equal citizens in Vermont. That norm clearly made it wrong for state officers or even private persons to harass or commit violence against gay people; indeed, Vermont enacted a hate crime law along these lines.[65] A more difficult question, for Vermonters as for most Americans, was how this norm applied in the context of the family. Family issues required another learning campaign. Lesbians and gay men formed committed partnerships with the same meaning for the couples that marriage has for straight couples. Many of these couples were raising children. In 1993, the Vermont Supreme Court ruled that a lesbian could become the second legal parent of her partner's child – and the Vermont legislature ratified that ruling by codifying it.[66]

In 1997, three lesbian and gay couples petitioned the state courts to recognize their right to receive marriage licenses. In *Baker v. State* (1999), the Vermont Supreme Court ruled that the state owed these couples equal treatment.[67] In response to the attorney general's argument that the state could prefer nongay families, the court (unanimously) cited the 1991 super-statute, the hate crimes law, and the new adoption statutes. Although these sources supported a move toward equal treatment, the court was uncertain as to the most viable remedy and left to the legislature the decision as to what institutional form the equality move might take. In an amazing three months of deliberation and anguished discussion in early 2000, the legislature enacted a law creating civil unions for same-sex couples, with all the legal benefits and duties of the state's marriage law. This law was exemplary of the deep compromise. Each side of the debate really listened to the other and sought an institution that would meet the goals of the other. Although opposition was intense, moderate Republicans and Democrats came together in a normative way on this issue. Governor Howard Dean signed it into law, and civil unions have become a minor part of the culture of that state.[68]

By 2005 at least, it remains to be seen how many states will follow Vermont, whether the Massachusetts Supreme Court's ruling in favor of same-sex marriage will stick in that state, and whether President Bush will be successful in terminating both state experiments through a national constitutional amendment. What is predictable is that this important and ongoing debate about fundamental law in America will be conducted along the lines we have suggested: We the People will be centrally involved, and normative consensus will not be achieved without popular support. Legislatures rather than courts will be the primary governmental forum

[65] 13 Vermont Statutes §1455.

[66] 15A Vermont Statutes §1–102 and 1–112, codifying and expanding *In re B.L.V.B.*, 628 A.2d 1271 (Vt. 1993).

[67] *Baker v. State*, 744 A.2d 864 (Vt. 1999).

[68] Eskridge, *Equality Practice*, *supra* note 21 at ch. 2, which provides a detailed account of the *Baker* litigation and the Vermont legislature's deliberations that produced the *Civil Unions Act*.

for the normative debate, including the debate about what our fundamental law should be. And any norm that is adopted will itself be subject to ongoing debate and elaboration.

This is the new American constitutionalism in action.

ACKNOWLEDGMENTS

We appreciate the excellent research assistance of David Newman, Yale Law School, Class of 2006.

16 Interpretation in Legislatures and Courts: Incentives and Institutional Design

Mark Tushnet

Why should one be interested in the question of whether nonjudicial actors have incentives to interpret constitutions reasonably well? Primarily, because some answers to that question would alleviate some well-known tensions between constitutionalism and democratic self-governance. Constitutions deprive contemporary majorities of the power to do what they want to do and are, in that sense, antidemocratic.[1] Enforcement of constitutional restricts on self-governance by judges removed from direct democratic accountability poses the equally well-known countermajoritarian difficulty. The tension between constitutionalism and self-governance and the countermajoritarian difficulty would be substantially reduced if nonjudicial actors had incentives to interpret the constitution, and were at least as good as judges at doing so. We could get the benefits of constitutionalism *and* self-governance were the constitution's primary interpreters nonjudicial actors who did a reasonably good job of interpretation.

This chapter examines two questions that arise in considering the role of nonjudicial actors in constitutional interpretation, in nations with constitutional systems fairly characterized as having been democratic for some reasonable period.[2] First, what is the standard against which that role should be measured? Analyses typically examine how legislatures go about interpreting constitutions or measure how well they interpret, with reference to how courts interpret constitutions. I argue that a court-based standard is inappropriate, and offer a constitution-based standard instead. Second, what incentives do nonjudicial actors and judges have to engage in constitutional interpretation with reference to the constitution-based standard?[3]

[1] Of course, democratic constitutions create democratic governments in the first place and so make self-government possible. But, by removing issues that Frank Michelman refers to as the laws of lawmaking from democratic decision making, see Frank I. Michelman, *Brennan and Democracy* (Princeton: Princeton University Press, 1999) at 6, constitutions preclude democratic majorities from determining that their own understanding of what constitutes democracy is better than that of the constitution's authors.

[2] I have expanded my concerns beyond legislatures because considering the roles of executive officials and voters in constitutional interpretation sheds light on the role of legislators. For a useful recent introduction to the roles that different classes of nonjudicial actors play, see Bernard W. Bell, "Marbury v. Madison and the Madisonian Vision" (2003) 72 *Geo. Wash. L. Rev.* 197. To avoid formulations that would become stylistically tiresome, though, I usually refer only to legislators and legislatures. The analytic points apply to executive officials as well.

[3] Note that one could not ask this question about judges were one to use a court-based standard.

I argue that legislators have greater incentives than scholars typically assert and that judges have smaller ones than scholars typically assume. In making that argument, I develop a subsidiary argument about the institutions that legislatures might create to augment their capacity to engage in constitutional interpretation, and about the incentives legislatures have to do so.

I. A CONSTITUTION-BASED STANDARD OF EVALUATION

Many, perhaps most, scholars of constitutional law express deep skepticism about the ability of legislatures to perform the task of constitutional interpretation well. The rhetorical moves are familiar. Critics list statutes the courts have found unconstitutional; they identify enacted statutes that are, by their own criteria, clearly unconstitutional; they point to one or two particularly egregious examples of patently unconstitutional statutes that were nonetheless enacted.

These rhetorical moves do not really show that legislatures are incompetent at the job of constitutional interpretation. The lists of statutes found unconstitutional could show only that the courts and legislatures *disagree* about what the constitution means. Yet, often such disagreement rests on reasonable judgments made by both sides. Taking the lists of statutes held unconstitutional to reflect legislative incompetence is just to *assert* judicial superiority in constitutional interpretation, not to establish it.

Naming statutes the critic thinks unconstitutional does even less to establish that legislatures are incompetent at the job of constitutional interpretation. Sometimes the critic simply fails to make the necessary comparative judgment. The central issue in evaluating legislative performance is how well they perform relative to the courts. I might not think that some statute – a provision of the USA PATRIOT Act,[4] for example – is constitutional, but if the courts uphold it against constitutional challenge, my criticism should be just as much a criticism of the courts as the legislature. More important, as I discuss in more detail below, the premise of reasonable disagreement extends beyond reasonable disagreement over what the constitution means in connection with determining whether a particular statute is unconstitutional, to reasonable disagreement over how to determine what the constitution means. If my criticism of the USA PATRIOT Act rests on an originalist approach to constitutional interpretation, those who reasonably take a different interpretive approach need not be bothered by the fact that Congress enacted a statute inconsistent with original understanding.

Explaining why the examples of egregiously unconstitutional statutes do not establish legislative incompetence at constitutional interpretation is a bit more complicated, although the basic point is simple. Such statutes are unconstitutional no matter what interpretive approach one takes. I can identify only two pieces of U.S. national legislation enacted over the past few decades that were, in my view, not consistent with any reasonable interpretive theory. One was Congress's effort to ban

[4] Pub. L. 107–56, 115 Stat. 272 (Oct. 26, 2001), codified as amended in scattered sections of 5, 8, 18, & 42 U.S.C. Communications Decency Act: Pub. L. No. 104-104, title V, 110 Stat. 133 (codified as amended at scattered sections of 47 U.S.C.).

flag burning as a means of political protest.[5] The other was the Communications Decency Act, which would have had the effect of barring from the Internet and World Wide Web a large but vaguely defined category of "indecent" materials, a fair portion of which is plainly valuable when available to adults.[6]

Does the fact that Congress enacted these statutes, which for present purposes we can assume to be egregiously unconstitutional, show that it cannot be trusted to interpret the Constitution responsibly? The answer is, "No." The reason is that Congress enacted these statutes knowing that the Supreme Court was available to ensure that truly unconstitutional statutes would never go into effect. I have described this as the *judicial overhang* affecting how legislatures act in systems with judicial review.

The judicial overhang sometimes promotes legislative disregard of the constitution. Legislators may say to themselves, "Why bother to interpret the constitution at all, much less interpret it well, when the courts are going to end up offering the definitive interpretation anyway?" Political scientists include "position-taking" among the motivations legislators have, distinguishing it from "credit-claiming."[7] For a legislator to claim credit, something actually has to have happened, whereas legislators can take positions without being concerned about whether some policy gets implemented. Position-taking legislators may say to themselves, "I can get political mileage out of taking a position on this question, without worrying that anything actually will happen, because the courts will find the statute unconstitutional anyway."

Judicial review might encourage mere position-taking. Enacting statutes that are sure be to held unconstitutional – because they are inconsistent with any reasonable approach to constitutional interpretation – is position-taking. That legislators engage in this sort of position-taking does not show that they affirmatively desire to have obviously unconstitutional statutes go into effect. True, this kind of position-taking is a sort of legislative irresponsibility, but its existence flows from the existence of judicial review. In itself, it does not show that legislators are incompetent constitutional interpreters.

The easy arguments about legislative incompetence should be set to one side. How should we conduct a serious inquiry into the capacity of legislatures to engage in constitutional interpretation?[8] The easy arguments try to evaluate legislative

[5] Held unconstitutional in *United States v. Eichman*, 486 U.S. 310 (1990). I should note my uncertainty about whether even the anti-flag-burning legislation might be justified by a theory that allows for quite limited ad hoc departures from the conclusions compelled by all reasonable interpretive theories. For a brief discussion, see Mark Tushnet, "The Flagburning Episode: An Essay on the Constitution" (1990) 61 *Colorado L. Rev.* 39.

[6] The Act was held unconstitutional in *Reno v. ACLU*, 521 U.S. 844 (1997). Michael Bamberger uses the CDA as the focal point of his opening narrative to demonstrate legislative irresponsibility in *Reckless Legislation: How Legislators Ignore the Constitution* (New Brunswick, NJ: Rutgers University Press, 2000), which offers several additional case studies, supplemented by a survey of state legislators' and executive officials' attitudes toward constitutional interpretation.

[7] For position-taking, see David R. Mayhew, *Congress: The Electoral Connection* (New Haven: Yale University Press, 1975) at 61–73.

[8] For my earlier arguments on this question, see Mark Tushnet, "Evaluating Congressional Constitutional Interpretation: Some Criteria and Two Informal Cases Studies" (2001) 50 *Duke L.J.* 1395. Although I draw upon that article here, my thinking about the issues has evolved and I now believe that some of my earlier formulations were inaccurate.

performance by reference to how courts interpret constitutions.[9] Such a court-based standard is inappropriate. I think it helpful to begin the inquiry into the proper evaluative standard by noting that even in systems with robust judicial review, courts identify areas where legislative action is in fact regulated by the constitution but where the courts will not oversee legislative performance. The political questions doctrine in the United States, for example, marks out areas where the courts will not oversee legislative action to determine whether it is consistent with the limitations the Constitution places on Congress. The impeachment case of *Walter Nixon v. United States* provides a convenient illustration.[10] The House of Representatives impeached federal district judge Nixon after he was convicted of federal felonies. The case proceeded to the Senate for trial. Following rules it had adopted to impeachment trials of judges, the Senate convened a committee that heard testimony and reported to the entire Senate. Judge Nixon had no opportunity to present evidence to the Senate as a whole. The Constitution provides that the Senate has "the sole Power to try all Impeachments,"[11] and Judge Nixon contended that the Senate did not afford him a real "trial" as the Constitution required. In an analytically confused opinion, the Supreme Court held that Judge Nixon's claim presented a political question, meaning that the courts would not determine whether the procedure the Senate followed was a "trial" within the meaning the Constitution gave to that term.

The political questions doctrine does not mean that Congress is totally unconstrained by the Constitution in the areas it identifies. Rather, it means that Congress conclusively determines what the Constitution means in those areas. It follows that there are some areas in which the U.S. Congress does engage in constitutional interpretation. Yet, in the absence of judicial review, how can we evaluate Congress's performance? A court-based standard is plainly unavailable. That is, in examining the performance of nonjudicial actors in areas where there is no judicial review, we must develop some standard other than a court-based one. With such a standard in hand, we could identify the incentives legislators have *qua* legislators to interpret the constitution well or badly.

The most promising candidate for a non-court-based evaluative standard is, not surprisingly, the constitution itself. Saying that, however, is only the beginning of the analysis. Suppose first that a particular evaluator/critic has a preferred interpretive theory, such as textualism or originalism. Such a person can readily determine whether legislators (and courts) are properly interpreting the constitution, by measuring their performance against what the interpretive theory demands. Legislative and judicial decisions consistent with the text are good ones, for example, while those inconsistent with the text are bad ones. And, the evaluator can compare how well legislators do to how well judges do.[12]

[9] See, e.g., Bamberger, *supra* note 6. Bruce G. Peabody, "Congressional Constitutional Interpretation and the Courts: A Preliminary Inquiry into Legislative Attitudes, 1959–2001" (2004) 29 *Law & Soc. Inquiry* 127 (reporting a study that asked members of Congress whether they should defer to the Supreme Court on questions of constitutional interpretation), indicates that a majority of respondents believed that members had the duty to arrive at a judgment independent of the Supreme Court's views.

[10] *Walter Nixon v. United States*, 506 U.S. 224 (1993).

[11] "Sole power": U.S. Const., art. I, §3, cl. 6.

[12] My own judgment, for what it is worth, is that judges do badly according to a standard that requires originalist interpretation, and indeed according to any standard other than one that allows judges to choose eclectically among interpretive approaches.

The difficulty, as I have mentioned, is that there is reasonable disagreement about the proper interpretive theory. Some believe that textualism is correct, others that the constitution should be interpreted with reference to moral standards, yet others that decision makers should be eclectic and exercise good judgment in choosing which interpretive method to deploy when specific constitutional questions arise. Adrian Vermeule has pointed out that we have no way of ensuring that the judiciary, considered as a collection of individuals, will adhere to any prescribed interpretive theory,[13] and the point is clearly true of legislators as well.

This reasonable interpretive diversity forces us to modify the evaluative standard. We still want a constitution-based standard, but it cannot be one that rests on a controversial choice among interpretive theories. One possibility is that we should evaluate performance by asking how often courts and legislatures make decisions that are not consistent with *any* reasonable interpretive theory. This is obviously an extremely weak standard, in the sense that we should expect to find few decisions indeed, whether by judges or by legislators, that are consistent with no reasonable interpretive theory. And, even if the aggregate behavior of courts and legislators differs, we are likely to be dealing with small absolute differences. Courts may come out better than other decision makers, but the margin is likely to be small and probably not worth worrying about either way.

For purposes of analyzing incentives, another constitution-based standard might distinguish more effectively between courts and legislators. It begins by observing that interpretation is necessarily retrospective, and that nonjudicial policy making and some aspects of judicial decision making have important, perhaps dominating, forward-looking components. It is at least plausible to presume, pending empirical inquiry, that the mix of retrospective and prospective components differs as between courts and legislators: Courts might primarily look backward – engage in interpretation – and give forward-looking policy considerations a secondary role, whereas legislators might be primarily concerned about the future and only secondarily about the past. On this view, the constitution-based standard leads us to ask whether, to what extent, and why decision makers engage in the backward-looking exercise of interpretation.

Once again, we must be generous in assessing what counts as looking backward, in light of the reasonable diversity of interpretive methods. One obvious backward-looking approach focuses on the constitution's text. Another, almost equally obvious such approach attends to prior decisions – judicial or nonjudicial – about the constitution's meaning. Some nations, those whose nationhood is constituted by a constitution rather than by ethnicity or similar characteristics, have a third, somewhat less obvious backward-looking approach available. One would ask whether a proposal or practice is consistent with the aspirations of the nation's people as expressed in foundational documents.[14] These different approaches might

[13] Adrian Vermeule, "The Judiciary Is a They, Not an It: Interpretive Theory and the Fallacy of Division" (2004) 14 *J. Contemp. Leg. Issues* 549 (criticizing "the undefended assumption that sustained judicial coordination on a particular interpretive approach . . . is feasible").

[14] Those documents would, of course, include the nation's constitution, but, for the United States, could include the Declaration of Independence, Lincoln's Gettysburg Address and Second Inaugural Address, Franklin D. Roosevelt's "Four Freedoms" speech, and other similar documents. The French *Conseil Constitutionnel* has invoked the terse reference in the Preamble to the nation's 1946 Constitution, endorsed in the currently applicable Preamble to the Constitution adopted in 1958, to "the fundamental principles acknowledged in the laws of the Republic."

perhaps be captured in a more general formulation of a constitution-based standard: "To what extent do decision makers orient themselves toward a nation's constitutional tradition?" I think it worth observing that, like the standard "inconsistent with all reasonable interpretive theories," this standard too is unlikely to identify many examples of legislative incompetence or irresponsibility, because it seems to me nearly inevitable that a very large proportion of all decision makers will be socialized into accepting the proposition that their actions ought to be oriented to the nations constitutional tradition, at least in nation's whose democratic systems are reasonably long-lived.[15]

II. THE INCENTIVES OF NONJUDICIAL ACTORS

A. The individual level: legislators' motivations

We can begin by putting to one side what I believe is the most common, but erroneous, assumption about legislators' incentives. The point of a constitution is to place limits on legislators' natural inclinations to advance the interests of the majority at the expense of minority rights, and to adopt policies that give the decision makers short-term gains at the expense of long-term impairments of good government. I do not quarrel with this statement of the point of having a constitution, but it assumes, without independent support, that legislators have weak incentives to comply with the constitution's provisions.[16]

We must look more closely at constitutions themselves to see why this assumption is more questionable than proponents of the position I have described believe it to be. In the most general terms, constitutions contain two kinds of provisions, precise ones and abstract ones. The abstract provisions can be *specified* – that is, given meaning in real-world circumstances – in different ways, all compatible with the provisions' language and purposes. In addition, even precise constitutional provisions interact with each other. Specification and interaction mean that, more often than one might initially think, the constitution's meaning is underdetermined.

Sometimes a legislator uncontroversially violates the constitution's terms, and in these cases we can profitably examine what induced him or her to do so. But, notably, these cases are rare. As did Chief Justice John Marshall, we can describe a hypothetical case in which Congress enacts a statute violating the precise constitutional provision requiring testimony by two witnesses to the same overt act in treason prosecutions,[17] but we cannot overlook the fact that the example is hypothetical. Legislators do not violate precise constitutional provisions often enough for such violations to support a useful inquiry into their motivations. Further, legislators are likely to violate precise terms only when they believe the nation to be facing a real crisis – in which case constitutionalism more broadly is likely to come under pressure, in the courts as well as the legislature.

[15] I have considered limiting the suggestion to nonjudicial actors who broadly accept the premises of democratic self-governance, so as to eliminate from consideration people like military officers who participate in antidemocratic coups d'état. My sense, however, is that even such actors claim, and I think often not disingenuously, that they intervene so as to preserve rather than transform the nation's constitutional traditions.

[16] Put another way, the legislators' "natural inclinations" might themselves be weak.

[17] *Marbury v. Madison*, 5 U.S. (1 Cranch) 137, 179–80 (1803).

More often, and more interesting, legislators enact statutes that *arguably* are inconsistent with one or more specifications of the constitution's abstract provisions. But, in such cases the real issue is not *why* the legislature violated the constitution, but *whether* it did. The availability of different specifications of abstract provisions means that under some specifications a particular statute will be unconstitutional while under others it will be constitutional.

The problem of specification arises even when rights are not directly at stake. Consider, for example, the legislative veto controversy in U.S. constitutional law. That controversy involved statutory provisions that allowed one or both houses of Congress to block the implementation of actions by presidential officials, acting pursuant to a broad delegation of authority, if a majority of the House of Representatives or the Senate (sometimes, majorities in both houses) believed that the actions were inconsistent with the underlying statute. The advocate of the view that constitutions are designed to counter legislators' natural inclinations would be concerned that the legislature's disregard of the constitution's provisions (if there is such disregard) flows from its placing more value on short-term considerations than on ensuring that the long-term structure of government promotes good public policy. The alternative framing of the question is, however, obvious: Given the circumstances of modern government, is the legislative veto a component of a long-term structure of government that promotes good public policy? Here too, the constitutional controversy is *about* what best promotes constitutional values.[18]

The second characteristic of constitutions, the interaction among their provisions, raises the same question. Taken by themselves, two constitutional provisions might be clear or precise. But, taken together, they might generate ambiguity. Legislators can resolve that ambiguity by their decisions. And, in doing so, they do not disregard one or the other provision; they interpret the constitution as a whole.[19]

That alternative reasonable specifications of a constitution's provisions are available reproduces in the context of particular legislative decisions the problem posed by the availability of a range of reasonable interpretive methods. And, here as there, one cannot resolve the problem by stipulating what the constitution's abstract provisions mean and then examining the incentives that lead legislators to "violate" the constitution.

So far I have simply tried to clear away some confusions that often attend discussions of legislators' incentives to comply with the constitution. The main concern about legislators' incentives is simple: They are *elected*. Their primary incentive is to retain their jobs. They will have incentives to comply with the constitution – defined, as it should be, as orienting their actions to the nation's constitutional tradition – only if doing so will make it more likely that they will retain their jobs. Is there reason to think that it will?

[18] My understanding of these issues has been decisively affected by Frank I. Michelman, *Brennan and Democracy, supra* note 1.

[19] The recent controversy in the United States over the constitutionality of Senate filibusters of judicial nominations illustrates the problem identified here. There are two constitutional provisions. One would appear clearly to permit such filibusters when permitted by the Senate's rules. U.S. Const., art. I, §5, cl. 2. ("Each House may determine the Rules of its Proceedings. . . .") Another, however, makes it possible to argue that the Senate is required to vote on the merits of a nomination submitted by the president. U.S. Const., art. II, §2, cl. 2 (the president "shall nominate, and by and with the Advice and Consent of the Senate, shall appoint . . . Judges of the supreme Court, and all other Officers of the United States").

Bruce Peabody's recent survey of the views of members of the U.S. Congress indicates that its members do pay attention to the Constitution more often than academic skeptics think. And, interestingly, a fair number of Peabody's respondents take the view that Congress has the duty to arrive at a constitutional interpretation independent of the Supreme Court's interpretation.[20] That this view is so prevalent suggests that it would be profitable to speculate about why legislators might hold it, that is, why a person interested in retaining his or her job in an election might believe it proper to pay attention to the constitution.

From a purely self-interested point of view, legislators are interested in retaining their jobs until something better comes along. The latter qualification is important. Sometimes taking an action that is necessary if one is to retain one's job would make one worse off than leaving the job and going to the next best alternative. This constraint allows us to include in the analysis of incentives such things as the legislator's sense of himself or herself as a good person, or as a person making good public policy.[21]

Why might a legislator want to orient herself to the constitution? One answer is obvious: That might be what her constituents want. Of course we cannot rule out *a priori* the possibility that constituents will have such constitution-oriented preferences. Indeed, on some important issues it seems quite likely that constituent preference is based on views in the constituency about the constitution's meaning. In the United States, for example, constituent preferences about the proper public policy on abortion are, I believe, almost certainly based on judgments about the rights of women and the rights of fetuses, judgments that – whether pro-choice or pro-life – are well within the range of reasonable specifications of the Constitution's meaning. A legislator whose interest in reelection leads her to cater to constitution-oriented constituent preferences is (indirectly) orienting her legislative activity to the nation's constitutional traditions.[22]

Second, a legislator can "vote his or her conscience" on matters about which the constituency is indifferent. Some constitutional issues – ones that involve technical constitutional questions, for example – may have this characteristic. In essence, constituents delegate their own ability to make constitutional judgments to their representatives. A representative can act according to his or her own constitutional

[20] "[M]ore than 60% of the respondents refused to cede constitutional questions to the courts, believing instead that Congress should 'form its own considered judgment' on those issues." Peabody, *supra* note 9, at 146. The results of Peabody's survey are roughly consistent with others, such as Bamberger's and the survey reported in Donald G. Morgan, *Congress and the Constitution: A Study of Responsibility* (Cambridge: Belknap Press of Harvard University Press, 1966). In general, between two-thirds and three-quarters of respondents assert that legislators should form their own views on the constitutionality of legislation, that legislative discussions are reasonably well-informed about constitutional questions, and that discussions of constitutional questions influence legislators' votes.

[21] The important empirical study of members of the U.S. House of Representatives, Richard Fenno, *Home Style: House Members in Their Districts* (Boston: Little, Brown, 1978), demonstrated that these legislators were indeed motivated by their desire to make good public policy within the constraints of retaining their positions. We also must remain attentive to the fact that the judicial overhang affects the legislator's incentives.

[22] I believe it worth noting that standard examples of meanly self-interested constituent preferences, such as that of farmers for subsidies for their activity, involve legislation that, in the United States, receives rather limited substantive judicial review, and that aggressive judicial review occurs with respect to many issues, such as abortion, where constituent preferences seem to me likely to be constitution-oriented.

judgments (if the legislator has them – a question I discuss below) on these matters without fear of adverse electoral consequences – at least within broad limits.

Those limits are important in thinking about a final possibility. Even on matters as to which constituents are largely indifferent, a legislator runs some risk of getting too far out of line, that is, of taking a constitutional position that will lead constituents to vote against the legislator once the position is brought to their attention.[23] The obverse of this point is equally important. Sometimes a legislator will have substantial freedom to adopt constitutional positions at odds with the views of his or her constituents on a matter not central to the constituents' overall views. Consider, for example, a constituency in which most voters care a great deal about getting direct benefits from government expenditures ("pork," pejoratively), and care a bit, but not all that much, about allowing prayer in public schools. Such a constituency will cut their representative some slack on the constitutional issue if the representative is very good at bringing home the pork. Of course, the more important the constitutional issue is to the constituency, and the more uncertain the representative is about how important the constitutional issue is to voters, the less slack the representative will have.[24]

So far I have discussed electoral incentives for legislators to orient their action to the nation's constitutional traditions. Of course, those incentives will not always operate. Constituents may be hostile to the nation's constitutional traditions, for example.[25] More important, the presence of *other* decision makers with responsibility for constitutional interpretation may give nonjudicial actors incentives to ignore the constitution in their actions.[26] Here again, the judicial overhang plays a role, and I use it to illustrate the problem. But, the difficulty arises because responsibility for constitutional interpretation may be divided among various institutions, including the executive branch.

I have already mentioned the possibility of (mere) position-taking, which involves ignoring constitutional questions because the decision maker believes that some other actor will do so. A legislator may ignore constitutional questions because she believes the president will consider them in deciding whether to sign or veto legislation; a president may ignore constitutional questions because he believes that the courts will consider them in subsequent litigation. Mere position-taking can be particularly troublesome when the final mover takes the position that

[23] A complete analysis would therefore have to include some assessment of the circumstances under which legislators have varying degrees of risk aversion.

[24] Again, however, I emphasize that the most potent examples of cases in which constituents may be unwilling to cut a representative some slack are cases in which the constituents' views reflect reasonable judgments about what the constitution requires or permits.

[25] Given the breadth of the range of reasonable specifications of a constitution's meaning, however, this possibility seems remote as a practical matter in nations with well-established constitutional democracies.

[26] I develop the argument by considering the effect of the existence of judicial review, but I believe (at least for now) that the argument holds whenever there is some decision maker who is the last mover in a process of decision making. Here *last mover* means a decision maker whose actions cannot be overridden by ordinary majorities. In the United States, the president is the last mover with respect to ordinary legislation because his or her veto cannot be overridden without a supermajority vote, and the Supreme Court is the last mover with respect to constitutional decisions because its decisions cannot be overridden unless a supermajoritarian amendment process is carried through to a successful conclusion.

its decision should incorporate some degree of deference to prior actors, because the final mover may be deferring to a judgment that no one ever made in circumstances of mere position-taking.[27]

Mark Graber has identified another incentive that legislators and executive officials have for refusing to address constitutional questions.[28] Graber notes that dominant political coalitions sometimes face policy issues that might divide the coalition if its leaders are forced to take a stand on the policy questions. Coalition leaders would therefore like to find some way to avoid taking a stand. Passing the questions off to some other decision maker – notably, the courts – is an attractive strategy if the policy questions have constitutional overtones.[29] If the courts find constitutional impediments to adopting the policy, coalition leaders can assuage the policy's supporters by blaming the courts and can satisfy the policy's opponents by noting that the policy is in fact not going to take effect.[30]

Notably, these incentives to ignore constitutional questions exist because there is someone else to whom the buck can be passed.[31] That fact, in turn, might have some implications for designing institutions to make it less clear who the last mover actually is. Some forms of judicial review blur the line between the first and the last mover, perhaps to the point where the strategy of passing the buck will not be politically attractive. A Canadian legislator cannot hide behind that nation's Supreme Court, given the possibility of invoking the notwithstanding clause (or offering a stronger Section 1 defense of limitations on rights as demonstrably necessary).[32] That form of judicial review might *increase* the incentives legislators have to take their constitution seriously.[33]

[27] Justice Antonin Scalia rejects deference – at least when Congress has engaged in mere position-taking – in this statement: "My Court is fond of saying that acts of Congress come to the Court with the presumption of constitutionality. That presumption reflects Congress's status as a coequal branch of government with its own responsibilities to the Constitution. But if Congress is going to take the attitude that it will do anything it can get away with and let the Supreme Court worry about the Constitution . . . then perhaps that presumption is unwarranted." Quoted in Ruth Colker and James J. Brudney, "Dissing Congress" (2001) 100 *Mich. L. Rev.* 80 at 80 (quoting Antonin Scalia, U.S. Supreme Court, Address at the Telecommunications Law and Policy Symposium, Apr. 18, 2000).

[28] Mark A. Graber, "The Nonmajoritarian Difficulty: Legislative Deference to the Judiciary" (1993) 7 *Stud. in Am. Pol. Dev.* 35.

[29] Provisions for advisory opinions from a constitutional court, such as the so-called reference jurisdiction of the Supreme Court of Canada, provide a ready institutional form for implementing this strategy. See *Supreme Court Act*, R.S.C. 1985, c. S-26, ss. 36, 53, 54.

[30] There is an asymmetry in this strategy: The coalition leaders still face a political problem if the courts say that adopting the policy would be constitutionally permissible. Graber's central examples are the controversy over slavery in the U.S. territories in the late antebellum period and the controversy over abortion in the past thirty years; in both, the courts held that a policy that one part of the dominant coalition wanted to implement was unconstitutional.

[31] The reference jurisdiction of the Canadian Supreme Court, and provisions for advisory opinions in some U.S. state constitutions, formalize this strategy. See relevant sections of the *Supreme Court Act*, *supra* note 29. Notably, however, such mechanisms do not induce legislators to ignore the constitution in enacting statutes. Rather, they allow legislators to defer consideration of constitutional questions until after they receive advice from the judiciary.

[32] See the *Canadian Charter of Rights and Freedoms*, Part I of the *Constitution Act, 1982*, being Schedule B to the *Canada Act, 1982* (U.K.), 1982, c. 11, ss. 1 (the clause providing for reasonable limits on Charter rights if the reasonable limit is prescribed by law and can be "demonstrably justified in a free and democratic society"), 33 (the notwithstanding clause allowing Parliament or a provincial government to declare an Act or a provision thereof to operate notwithstanding certain sections of the Charter for a set period of time).

[33] Brief consideration of legislators' incentives in parliamentary systems is appropriate here. In parliamentary systems with strong parties, individual legislators must retain the confidence of the parties'

B. Courts and legislators

Evaluating legislative performance inevitably has a comparative component, which is sometimes submerged but deserves explicit attention, so I turn to comparing the capacities of legislators to those of courts. Constitution-based standards are retrospective. Legislation is largely forward-looking, putting in place policies that will guide the society in the future. Legislators enact forward-looking legislation to provide voters with a basis for assessing how much better the legislators have made the voters' lives. Put another way, legislators' incentives are not exclusively backward-looking.

Judges, in contrast, might be thought to look backward exclusively, examining the existing legal materials as a basis for determining what the law is. It might well be true that a large portion of judicial work is backward-looking, but it is not true that judges only look backward. And, their forward-looking work resembles the kind of policy analysis that a forward-looking legislator might do. Put in terms of incentives, the desire to perform the judicial job well gives a judge an incentive to look forward with an eye to making good law – just as a legislator has an incentive to look forward with an eye to enacting good laws.[34] Judges do two forms of forward-looking work, one inherent in the job of judging in a hierarchical judicial system and the other part of one prominent interpretive theory.

Judges articulate rules one of whose purposes is to guide behavior, sometimes by judges below them in the judicial hierarchy, sometimes by executive officials implementing the rules the judges articulate. As Richard Fallon has emphasized, that fact means that good judging means articulating implementable rules.[35] A

leaders if they are to remain in office. The majority party leadership is the nation's executive branch as long as it retains a majority, and – as a rule – only legislation supported by the party leadership will be enacted. Accordingly, attention should be focused on whether and why the majority party's leaders would follow the constitution. There are two qualifications. Party leaders may sometimes allow a free vote, that is, one in which members are allowed to vote their consciences without regard to the leadership's position. Free votes are rare in Canada and Great Britain, but they are said to occur on occasional "issues of conscience" that are not important to the majority party's platform. (Free votes have occurred in Great Britain and Canada on issues relating to abortion, capital punishment, televising parliamentary proceedings, and research on embryos.) Such matters are likely to be a (small) subset of constitutionally sensitive matters. Members of parliament casting free votes, voting their consciences, are in the same position as the legislators in separation-of-powers system whose incentives I have already discussed. In addition, the party leadership does not have complete control over whether a member remains in office. Some members have sufficiently strong support in the party, or in their constituencies, that they will remain on the party's election lists pretty much no matter what they do. These members too are like independently elected legislators in separation-of-powers systems.

[34] There is something of a play on words in this formulation. The laws a legislator has an incentive to make are good ones from the legislator's point of view because they increase the prospects of reelection by improving the lives of the legislator's constituents and thereby giving them reasons to reelect the legislator. The substantive goodness of the laws is only indirectly a matter of concern to the legislator. It is directly of concern to the judge seeking to do a good job. I should note that the literature on judges' incentives is extremely thin. The best of an unsatisfactory lot are Richard A. Posner, "What Do Judges Maximize? (The Same Thing Everybody Else Does)" (1993) 3 *S. Ct. Econ. Rev.* 1; Frederick Schauer, "Incentives, Reputation, and the Inglorious Determinants of Judicial Behavior" (The Robert Marx Lecture) (2000) 68 *U. Cin. L. Rev.* 215. I take these articles to argue that the only real incentives judges have are inner ones, such as the desire to do a good job, because, basically, there is nothing they could be asked to do that would make them worse off than they would be in their next best job. (Resignations of judges in the United States are rare, but sometimes occur because the judges find themselves unwilling to impose criminal sentences the law requires of them – and because such judges have decent alternative jobs available as practicing lawyers.)

[35] Richard H. Fallon, Jr., *Implementing the Constitution* (Cambridge, Mass.: Harvard University Press, 2001).

judge must look forward to determine whether a rule is implementable, anticipating how inferior judges and executive officials will respond to the rule. Concerned about implementation, judges will sometimes forgo articulating the rule that, in their judgment, best enforces the law in the backward-looking sense, because the second-best rule, when implemented by inferior judges and executive officials, will better achieve the goals revealed by an examination of the existing legal materials.[36] Being a good judge, that is, means looking forward as well as backward. The difference from legislators is one of degree, not of kind.

Implementability will be a concern no matter what the judge's interpretive theory is. Some interpretive theories are themselves quite forward-looking. The most obvious such theory is one that directs judges to interpret the constitution so as to balance rights appropriately against social goals.[37] General limitations clauses such as Section 1 of the Canadian Charter of Rights embed such an interpretive theory in constitutional language, but the impulse to balance is so strong that balancing is an attractive interpretive theory even without a limitations clause.[38]

Consider, for example, the standard formulation of the appropriate way to think about constitutional rights in connection with law enforcement: We are told that the constitution should be interpreted to reach the right balance between liberty and security.[39] Reaching that balance requires the judge to consider the consequences for liberty and security of adopting alternative rules – that is, to make judgments about the effects in the future of adopting one rather than another interpretation of the relevant constitutional provisions. Balancing, as has been widely observed, is the exercise by judges of the kinds of judgments legislators routinely make.[40] Again, a judge who adopts balancing as an interpretive theory will often be looking forward in much the way that a legislator does. To that extent, the judge will have incentives similar to those of a legislator.

Undoubtedly, the judge's incentive to do the judicial job well induces a higher ratio of backward- to forward-looking deliberation than does the legislator's incentive to retain office. I suggest, however, that the difference in the ratios is not as large as is typically assumed.

Courts have different institutional characteristics from legislatures, of course, going beyond the fact that the ratio of their backward-looking to forward-looking

[36] In using the word *goals*, I do not mean to endorse a purely instrumental view of "the law." Alternative phrasings, however, make the sentence unwieldy. (The best alternative is something like, "whatever it is that makes it good to follow the law.")

[37] I suppose the canonical text here is John Rawls's observation that a moral-political theory (and, inferentially, an interpretive theory) that does not take consequences into account is simply crazy. John Rawls, *A Theory of Justice* (Cambridge: Belknap Press of Harvard University Press, 1971) at 30. ("All ethical doctrines worth our attention take consequences into account in judging rightness. One which did not would simply be irrational, crazy.")

[38] For two complementary discussions, see David S. Law, "Generic Constitutional Law" (2005) 89 *Minnesota Law Review* 652 (discussing balancing as a general approach to constitutional interpretation); David M. Beatty, *The Ultimate Rule of Law* (Oxford and New York: Oxford University Press, 2004) (discussing proportionality review as a general approach to constitutional adjudication).

[39] See, e.g., David Cole, "Enemy Aliens" (2002) 54 *Stan. L. Rev.* 953 at 955 (a strong civil libertarian's endorsement of the standard formulation: "In the wake of September 11, we plainly need to rethink the balance between liberty and security.").

[40] See, e.g., T. Alexander Aleinikoff, "Constitutional Law in the Age of Balancing" (1987) 96 *Yale L.J.* 943; Gerald Gunther, "In Search of Judicial Quality on a Changing Court: The Case of Justice Powell" (1972) 24 *Stan. L. Rev.* 1001.

focus is somewhat higher than that of legislatures. Conventionally, it is said that courts have an obligation to hear claims and arguments offered them by anyone with a case to make, and to provide reasons for their action or inaction, whereas legislatures get to choose the issues they deal with and have no duty to provide reasons for what they do. Furthermore, the obligations to hear all cases and provide reasons are said to increase the likelihood that courts will reach correct results. These differences do exist, but, as with the issues I have already discussed, they are often described as larger than they really are.

The first point to note is that the conventional arguments rarely connect the normative claims about the duty to listen and provide reasons to descriptive claims explaining why judges have incentives to comply with the "duties," which are rarely if ever enforced by some other body that punishes judges who do not provide reasons for their decisions. I have suggested that the incentives lie in the judges' desire to do a good job, where what counts as a good job is defined by the conventions about what judges ought to do. But, as I also suggested, legislators also want to do a good job in addition to wanting to be reelected. And, there may well be conventions about what being a good legislator entails, conventions that I suspect include being willing to listen to complaints from constituents and to explain publicly, in newsletters, speeches, and the like, why the legislator does what he or she does.

True, legislatures as institutions have no duty to provide reasons for what they do. Sometimes there are committee reports and the like, but sometimes not. And even committee reports are not actions by the legislature as a body in the way that judicial opinions are the actions of a court. Legislators often give their reasons in debates leading up to a statute's enactment, or afterward in public discourse about what the legislature did or did not do. It is not clear to me why it should matter that the *institution* gives reasons as long as individual members – that is, individual legislators – do.

The importance of a distinctive judicial duty to listen can also be exaggerated. First, not all constitutional courts are designed to entertain individual claims. Some require that constitutional complaints be submitted by a designated institution, typically the president, premier, the majority party in the legislature, or a minority – of some stipulated size, such as 40 percent – of the legislature. Others allow individuals to raise claims in lower courts, but give those courts some discretion in deciding whether to dismiss the claims or to forward them to the nation's specialized constitutional court. The duty to listen, that is, is not a characteristic of judges as such, but rather of judges in constitutional systems designed in a particular way. The duty to listen may not sharply distinguish judges from legislators in systems with other designs.

Furthermore, systems where judges do have a duty to listen to all constitutional claims usually – and almost inevitably – give judges a variety of techniques to pay only the most cursory attention to those claims. In the United States, for example, the Supreme Court has nearly complete control over its docket, deciding in an entirely discretionary way which cases it wants to consider in detail. People say, "I'll take this to the Supreme Court," but if they do, there is no guarantee that the Supreme Court will listen. More formally, some courts, including those of the United States, have developed rules that screen out some cases as a matter of law. In 2004, for example, the U.S. Supreme Court invoked its doctrine of "standing" – the right to present a claim – to preclude Michael Newdow from continuing his case against the inclusion of the words "under God" in the Pledge of Allegiance.[41] The reason was that Newdow's right to bring the claim had to rest on the fact that his daughter was enrolled in a school where, state and local law said, the Pledge had to be recited every day. But, the Supreme Court held, Newdow could not bring the claim because as a noncustodial parent he had no legal right under state law to control the environment to which his daughter was exposed.

The real question about the duty to listen, in the present context, is once again comparative. Present the same claim to the courts and to the legislature, and then compare how seriously each one takes it. The example of Michael Newdow might be thought to show that courts will take claims more seriously. After all, he did get to the Supreme Court, where – before the Court dismissed his case – the Justices listened to his arguments against having the words "under God" in the Pledge of Allegiance. In contrast, we can be confident that no one in Congress would have listened seriously to Newdow's claim that, as enacted into law, the Pledge of Allegiance violated the Constitution's ban on establishments of religion. The reason, however, is that members of Congress would have thought that Newdow's claim was obviously wrong on the merits, not that they should not be bothered to think about his arguments. The Newdow example and similar ones that could be generated about constitutional claims raised by criminal defendants and other unpopular groups are sometimes offered to show that courts are better at listening than legislatures. Most of the examples do not show that, however. Instead, they show that sometimes courts and legislatures disagree about what the constitution means, to the point where legislatures sometimes treat as silly some constitutional claims that courts think substantial. As I have observed, that sort of disagreement does not count against the capacity of legislatures to listen to constitutional claims.

Taking all these items together, I think the fair conclusion is this: There are surely differences between the conventional norms defining what a good judge does and what a good legislator does, but they are probably not night-and-day ones.

Two concluding points arise from the constitution-based standard I have identified as the right one to use. The constitution-based standard raises a question about the connection between the purported duties of judges and the likelihood that they will come up with correct answers to constitutional questions. The duty to listen and give reasons might well increase the chance that judges will give a certain kind of answer – roughly, one that treats the constitution as a document embodying Reason. It is less clear, however, that the duty to give reasons in itself would increase the likelihood that a judge will correctly determine what the original understanding of a constitution's terms was. Put more generally, the claim about the relation between judges' duties and their ability to come up with correct answers must be that those duties will improve their ability to come up with the right answers, no matter what our criteria of rightness are. That claim seems to me quite implausible.

To see the next issue, consider a stipulated constitution-based standard, such as whether a decision maker adheres to originalist interpretation. What incentives do decision makers have to do so? Notably, we can ask that question about judges no less than about legislators. As far as I can tell, the only incentive a judge has to adopt

41 *Elk Grove Unified School Dist. v. Newdow*, 124 S.Ct. 2301 (2004).

any stipulated standard is internal to the judge; that is, judges are socialized into accepting that standard. Without detailed examination of socialization processes, I would not reject the possibility that legislators are similarly socialized.[42] A much more important conclusion suggests itself once we put stipulated standards to one side and consider the standard I have identified as the proper one, that is, whether the decision maker orients himself or herself to the nation's constitutional tradition. As I said earlier, in a reasonably stable democracy nearly everyone who becomes a legislator or a judge will almost surely have been socialized into doing so.

My conclusion from this comparison of judges and legislators is that there are indeed differences – hardly a surprising conclusion – but that the differences are probably not dramatic. If I am right, it might also well be that legislators can do a "good enough" job of constitutional interpretation – "good enough" relative to how well courts do the job.

III. THE INSTITUTIONAL LEVEL: EVALUATING LEGISLATIVE PERFORMANCE

Legislatures are different from legislators. The processes through which legislatures aggregate the positions of individual legislators might make legislative outcomes either more responsive to constitutional concerns or less so. Here I identify criteria we can use to evaluate legislative *outputs*, in contrast to the inputs I have dealt with in discussing legislators' incentives.

A modest way of beginning is this observation: Judges are (almost universally) lawyers. Legislators need not be.[43] Judges will have greater incentives to orient themselves to a nation's constitutional traditions to the extent that legal training is valuable in allowing someone to do so. The ordinary processes of socialization – growing up taking civics classes, studying a nation's history in school, and the like – may induce those who are not lawyers to have a properly constitutionalist orientation, but for present purposes I will assume that being a lawyer increases the chance that a person has such an orientation.

Of course, nonlawyers can obtain assistance from lawyers. In the United States, the chief executive need not be a lawyer, but the Department of Justice provides legal advice to the president, including advice on constitutional questions. Peabody's survey of members of the U.S. Congress indicates that a large proportion of them do rely on lawyers "for help with constitutional issues."[44]

What incentives do legislators have for seeking assistance from lawyers on constitutional matters?[45] One important reason arises from the fact that legislators are

[42] In particular, the lawyers among them seem to me likely to be exposed to roughly the same socialization institutions as judges are, and so might well accept internally the stipulated standard just as judges are said to do.

[43] For example, in Peabody's survey of members of the U.S. Congress, *supra* note 9, around half of the respondents were not lawyers. In the 108th Congress, 59% of the Senate and 40% of the House of Representatives are lawyers. See Mildred L. Amer, *Membership of the 108th Congress: A Profile*, CRS Report for Congress, at http://www.senate.gov/reference/resources/pdf/RS21379.pdf (last updated April 21, 2004). As of 2003, 61% of New York, 48% of California, and 30% of Missouri legislators were lawyers. See William M. Corrigan, Jr., "The Argument for Lawyers in the Legislature: A Proud History of Service" (2003) 59 *J. Mo. B.* 5, available online: http://www.mobar.org/journal/2003/sepoct/prezpage.htm .

[44] Peabody, *supra* note 9, at 151–3.

[45] I put aside the prudential concern for enacting legislation that will survive judicial review.

involved in making and implementing *law*. They will often find it helpful to have legal assistance if they are to do so effectively. A legislator will want help in drafting legislation that, if enacted, would actually accomplish what the legislator wants to accomplish; an executive official will want assistance in figuring out what the legislature has directed his or her agency to do. The legislator's incentive is provided by the job itself: Creating a legal staff will help a legislator do the job of being a legislator, and whatever motivates a legislator to take and seek to retain the job also motivates him or her to create a legal staff.

Drafting and interpreting legislation do not inevitably entail interpreting the constitution. A legal staff created to help legislators do the job might therefore not actually give advice on constitutional matters. Yet, the staff itself – by assumption, lawyers – may *want* to do so, and might even give it unsolicited, in the course of performing its other duties. Legislators might not have direct incentives to get advice on constitutional matters, but they do have incentives to create legal staffs to advise them on the law. Constitutional advice from these staffs might then be a by-product of their creation.[46]

Executive officials and legislators might also create legal staffs that specialize in constitutional law itself. The reason, at least in separation-of-powers systems, is the ambition that James Madison said should be set to counter ambition.[47] A chief executive or a legislature out to aggrandize power might offer constitution-based as well as policy-based justifications for its actions. Its opponents in the legislature or the executive branch would be well advised to have constitutional arguments at hand in the political combat that will ensue.[48] The dynamics are clear: Once one side offers a constitution-based argument,[49] the other side has an incentive to counter the argument. A good way of doing so is to develop a specialized staff.[50] And, once again, such a staff might take its professional mission to be attention to and advice about the constitution as a whole, not merely about separation-of-powers issues.[51]

The legal staff is an *institutional* feature of legislatures, created in response to individual legislators' incentives. Our criteria for evaluating legislative performance

[46] I draw the idea of a by-product from Jon Elster, *Sour Grapes: Studies in the Subversion of Rationality* (New York: Cambridge University Press, 1983) at 43, but do not contend that constitutional advice is an essential by-product of creating a legal staff, either in the usual sense that it inevitably occurs once a legal staff is created or in Elster's sense that it cannot occur by intentionally seeking to obtain it.

[47] The Federalist No. 51 (James Madison).

[48] Backbenchers, particularly permanent backbenchers, might be the moving force in parliamentary systems for the creation of this sort of legal staff. Mark Tushnet, "Weak-Form Judicial Review: Its Implications for Legislatures" (2004) 1 *N.Z. J. Pub. & Int'l L.* 7.

[49] Which, I emphasize, it need not always do. What matters is that the first step be taken.

[50] The Office of Legal Counsel in the U.S. Department of Justice historically has taken its primary role to be defending the constitutional prerogatives of the presidency against what its staff regards as congressional intrusions. That the Madisonian ambition only gives an incentive, but does not compel an outcome, is indicated by the fact that the U.S. Congress has not yet developed an equivalent specialized staff, although units like the counsel's offices in the House and Senate have the potential to become Congress's version. For a normative discussion, see Elizabeth Garrett and Adrian Vermeule, "Institutional Design of a Thayerian Congress" (2001) 50 *Duke L.J.* 1277.

[51] One implication of this argument is that constitutional deliberations that affect legislators might occur behind the scenes, as legal staffs give advice to those actors. The fact that legislators do not, or only rarely, mention constitutional matters in their public discussions would then not be evidence that they have not already engaged in deliberation about the constitution.

should focus similarly on the legislature as an institution – composed, of course, of individuals, but producing outcomes that might not be directly responsive to any individual legislator's incentives or interests. Paying attention to institutional action suggests a number of evaluative criteria.

First, evaluation should focus on institutional performance, not individual behavior. It is trivially easy to compile a list of constitutionally irresponsible or thoughtless proposals legislators make as they engage in position-taking. A member will shoot out a press release responding to some local outrage or put a bill in the hopper without taking any time to consider its constitutionality. Often these proposals result from the member's desire to grandstand, to do something that gets his or her name on the nightly news in the member's home district. They are not serious proposals for legislation, and the member has no real expectation that they would be enacted.

Noting grandstanding actions of this sort provides no basis for evaluating a legislature's performance of constitutional interpretation. What we need to examine are institutional actions, those that represent the outcome of a completed congressional process. Grandstanding proposals may count against assertions that members of Congress act in a constitutionally responsible manner, but the failure of such proposals to move through the legislative process should count in favor of such assertions. Institutional actions proceed through a complex set of organizational structures. Those structures, designed for other purposes, may sometimes serve (imperfectly and as a by-product) to screen out constitutionally irresponsible actions.[52]

Examining institutional actions, however, raises its own difficulties. Judges write opinions when they decide what the Constitution means. Legislatures usually do not. Enacted statutes typically become effective without an accompanying statement of the constitutional rationale on which the legislature relied.[53] Determining the constitutional basis for a completed action by a legislature requires us to examine a range of materials, such as committee reports, floor debate, and even newspaper stories, from which we can infer the constitutional basis on which the legislature acted. Such inferences will inevitably be open to question. The evaluation of a legislature's performance that results from such inferences will therefore often rest on a shaky foundation. Still, we should do the best we can.

In addition, legislators often might have varying rationales for their belief that a proposal is constitutional. Unlike judges, they need not sign an opinion giving

[52] Institutional actions can, of course, consist of inaction as well. Failures to enact legislation that the constitution requires are irresponsible. Some constitutions do impose substantial affirmative duties on legislatures, but the conventional wisdom is that the U.S. Constitution is not among them. For that reason, I focus on actions in what follows.

[53] One can design institutional mechanisms for supplying such rationales. For example, a "Committee on the Constitution" in each house could be given responsibility for preparing an authoritative statement on the constitutionality of every statute (or for stating that the Committee could come to no conclusion on constitutionality). Whether such mechanisms would counter the political processes that lead people to agree on specific proposals without agreeing on their constitutional rationales, and, perhaps more importantly, would overcome the pressure that time places on legislators who need to do something, seems to me quite questionable. And, of course, one would have to examine the incentives legislators have for creating such a committee.

a majority's position on the constitutional question.[54] Ultimately, each legislator must do no more than vote for the bill. But sometimes one constitutional rationale might be a good one and another bad. Imagine a statute adopted by a vote of 80–20. Sixty members of the majority may have thought about the constitutional questions the statute raised, and thought the statute justified by a rationale that, on detached reflection, one concludes was mistaken. But twenty members of the majority had a constitutionally good rationale for their votes. Without taking a position on the question, I simply observe that one reasonably could either challenge or defend the institutional action under these circumstances.

In addition to examining only completed actions, we should examine actions taken outside the shadow cast by courts. At this point, we can deepen the analysis of position-taking and grandstanding. Judicial review provides an opportunity for the legislature as a body, not just individual legislators, to engage in grandstanding by enacting statutes that the legislators can be confident will be held unconstitutional. Consider a situation in which legislators have a choice: They can enact a splashy statute that directly attacks a problem, albeit in a way that the courts will find unconstitutional, or they can enact a boring one, full of obscure details, that might be a bit less effective in achieving the majority's policy goals but that would be unquestionably constitutional. Presumably, enacting a statute that advances policy goals is attractive politically. Sometimes, however, enacting the splashy but unconstitutional statute may be even more politically attractive. Legislators then can take credit for trying to do something and blame the courts for the failure, even though the other statute might have been both constitutional and nearly as effective in achieving the legislators' policy goals.

This behavior, which we might call anticipatory disobedience, is pretty clearly undesirable (except to the extent that it may be valuable as a vehicle allowing representatives to blow off steam before they get down to the serious business of legislating). Even if rather common, however, anticipatory disobedience might shed little light on the question of legislative constitutional performance. People will overeat if someone gives them free candy, but that fact says little about their actual desires regarding nutrition. To determine those desires, one would have to take people away from the setting in which they have access to free candy. Analogously, we can get a better sense of a legislature's actual constitutional capacity if we examine only cases in which the legislature cannot engage in anticipatory disobedience. The fact that legislators behave badly when they know that someone is around to bail them out tells us little about how they would behave were they to have full responsibility for their actions. Such cases do exist: the "political questions" cases where there is no realistic prospect of judicial review, so that legislators know that they have full and exclusive responsibility for arriving at a conclusion that, according to their oaths of office, must be consistent with the constitution.

IV. EXECUTIVE OFFICIALS AND STATE AND LOCAL LEGISLATURES IN THE UNITED STATES

So far I have discussed legislators and legislatures and occasionally executive officials in quite general terms. But, of course, not all legislatures or officials are the

[54] I leave aside here the fact that the Supreme Court sometimes issues opinions in which only a plurality of the Justices accept a single rationale.

same. High-level executive officials can get advice, often in real time, from lawyers. Police officers on the beat cannot. National legislatures may have more time to consider constitutional questions than city councils and better advice when they do. It would be silly to contend that the incentives and institutional structures I have described affect *all* legislatures and executive officials to the same degree, and I do not. My focus is on national legislatures and high-level officials. There are reasons rooted in the structure of constitutional law for that focus. The most interesting questions of constitutional theory involve decisions by the highest law-making authorities in a nation. Nonconstitutional law can deal with actions by decision makers subordinate to those authorities.

A. Executive officials

The easiest place to begin is with low-level executive officials such as police officers or public social workers. Suppose a police officer beats a confession out of a suspect. Holding the officer liable for violating the constitution raises no issues of high constitutional theory.[55] Nations without judicially enforced constitutions, such as Great Britain before 2000 and the Netherlands today, find it easy to deal with such cases. They start with the observation that the police officer has the authority to detain and question the suspect only because some statute gives him or her that authority. They continue by finding that the legislature that enacted that statute surely did not intend to authorize police officers to engage in unconstitutional actions. Of course, they say – sometimes implicitly, sometimes explicitly – the legislature *might* have the power to authorize the action, but until the legislature does so quite clearly, the courts will not assume that the legislature did so.

British courts have been particularly vigorous in implementing this approach, known as the *ultra vires* (meaning, "beyond the power" granted) doctrine. A good example from another nation is the decision by the Supreme Court of Israel limiting the techniques the country's security service could use in interrogating prisoners suspected of aiding "terrorists."[56] The Court held that the nation's parliament had indeed authorized the security service to use normal investigative techniques, like those used by the ordinary police, but had not authorized them to use exceptional techniques such as sleep deprivation and extended periods in uncomfortable physical positions: "There is no statutory instruction endowing a GSS investigator with special interrogating powers that are either different or more serious than those given the police investigator."[57] The Court's opinion observed, "If it will nonetheless be decided that it is appropriate for Israel, in light of its security difficulties to sanction physical means in interrogations (and the scope of these means which deviate from the ordinary investigation rules), this is an issue that must be decided by the legislative branch which represents the people."[58]

[55] The point was made in the United States in Charles L. Black, Jr., *Structure and Relationship in Constitutional Law* (Baton Rouge: Louisiana State University Press, 1969) at 90 ("due process of law ought to be held to require that an active judgment by the legislative branch, rather than by the police chief, on how much of our personal liberty and security we must surrender in the interest of a practicable administration of justice.").

[56] It is hard to come up with neutral language to describe what are politically contested facts, but I have done the best I can.

[57] Judgment Concerning the Legality of the GSS Interrogation Methods, Supreme Court of Israel, Sept. 6, 1999, ¶ 32.

[58] Ibid. at ¶ 39.

Invoking the *ultra vires* doctrine allows the courts to question executive actions while leaving it open to legislatures to decide that the constitution is not in fact violated by those actions. It can be a quite powerful doctrine for keeping executive behavior within constitutional bounds. The U.S. Supreme Court invoked the *ultra vires* idea, without using the term, in its decision invalidating President George W. Bush's policy of detaining so-called enemy combatants without giving them access to the courts.[59] One of the people detained was a U.S. citizen, Yaser Hamdi. A statute enacted in 1991 provides that "[n]o citizen shall be imprisoned or otherwise detained by the United States except pursuant to an Act of Congress."[60] Forgoing analysis of the president's claim that he had inherent authority as commander-in-chief to detain citizens when he believed that such detentions would enhance the nation's military operations, four justices concluded that Congress had in fact authorized the detention of citizens found in Afghanistan, for purposes of ensuring that they would not return to combat against the United States, when it authorized military operations there after September 11, 2001. Justice Sandra Day O'Connor was careful to refer to the "narrow category" of citizen-detainees with which her analysis dealt, thereby suggesting that the authorization of action in Afghanistan might not extend to detention of other citizens seized elsewhere.

As the Hamdi decision suggests, the *ultra vires* doctrine does not raise serious questions of constitutional theory because the legislature can always enact a statute authorizing the action and thereby expressing its view on what the constitution permits – a view that is, technically, not in conflict with the courts' prior action. The *ultra vires* doctrine allows my analysis to focus on legislative capacity to interpret the constitution responsibly.[61]

B. Subordinate legislatures

A doctrine similar in structure to the *ultra vires* doctrine allows me to focus on *national* legislative capacity, particularly in federal nations. The *ultra vires* doctrine shifts attention from the executive official to the legislature that enacted the statute that was the source of the official's purported authority. A different doctrine, known as *preemption,* allows us to shift attention from a state or local legislature to the national legislature. The legislative authority of national governments and state or local governments often overlaps. The national government preempts state legislation when it enacts a statute that deals with some subject over which both levels have power, in a manner inconsistent with state-level legislation.[62]

Sometimes the national legislature will not have dealt with some subject over which both levels have power, but a state government will have done so, and in a constitutionally questionable manner. How could preemption doctrine come into play here? Courts could begin their analysis by noting that the national legislature had the power to deal with the subject. Its failure to do so, they could continue,

[59] *Hamdi v. Rumsfeld,* 124 S. Ct. 2633 (2004) [*Hamdi*].

[60] 18 U.S.C. §4001(a).

[61] Ordinary *ultra vires* doctrine controls what administrative agencies do. So, for example, the British Human Rights Act 1998 applies to acts of subordinate officials and lawmaking bodies but not to primary legislation, again reflecting the point that real questions about the relationship between judicial review and self-governance arise only in connection with primary legislation.

[62] Fully spelled out, preemption doctrine gets quite complicated, and I provide only the outlines here.

reflected its judgment that state legislatures would deal with it in a constitutionally responsible manner. So, the courts could conclude, the national legislature should be taken to have preempted the state-level statute – that is, to have foreclosed the state from enacting the statute.

This use of preemption is not at all theoretical. In 1956 the U.S. Supreme Court barred the states from enforcing their laws against seditious activity directed at the United States.[63] Such laws, which obviously raise serious free speech questions, were preempted by the existing federal antisedition statute, the Court held. In another constitutionally sensitive area, the Court invoked the preemption doctrine to bar states from enforcing their libel laws against statements made in political broadcasts, holding that federal regulation of broadcasting preempted state libel laws even though there was no provision in federal law saying anything one way or the other about libel.[64]

Another example is provided by the so-called dormant commerce clause. Dormant commerce clause doctrine is, at its base, a doctrine of implied preemption. A typical example of dormant commerce clause analysis involves a state statute that expressly discriminates against the sale within the state of some product made in another state.[65] The national courts routinely find such statutes "unconstitutional," invoking the national commerce clause. On its face, however, that clause simply gives Congress power to regulate interstate commerce, and says nothing – directly – about state powers. The best analysis of dormant commerce clause doctrine is that it is a version of implied preemption: Congress could certainly enact a statute requiring each state to accept the goods made in another state, but, believing that states would rarely do so, it gave the courts the power to overturn state laws inconsistent with the policy of free trade to which Congress was in fact committed.

A robust implied preemption doctrine could be quite important in federal nations where the national government has expansive powers even when those powers are not exercised. Courts could invoke the doctrine to overturn state and local legislation without raising questions about the ability of the nation's people to govern themselves by enacting national legislation on the very same subject. That point is driven home by another aspect of a well-designed preemption doctrine. Just as a legislature can expressly authorize an action that the courts find *ultra vires* because it is constitutionally questionable, so too the national legislature can expressly authorize a state legislature to adopt a law the courts find constitutionally questionable.[66] The courts need not be taken to be confronting "the people" in any dramatic way when they invoke the constitution against state legislatures in areas where the national government has the power to preempt or permit state-level action. All they are doing is insisting that the *nation's* people focus on what the courts regard as a constitutionally questionable action. The tensions of judicial review, constitutionalism, and democratic self-governance arise only if the

[63] *Pennsylvania v. Nelson*, 350 U.S. 497 (1956).

[64] *Farmers Educational & Cooperative Union v. WDAY, Inc.*, 360 U.S. 525 (1959).

[65] See, e.g., *Hunt v. Washington State Apple Advertising Comm'n*, 432 U.S. 333 (1997) (involving a statute that the Court found was intentionally designed to exclude Washington state apples from ready sale in North Carolina).

[66] For the United States, see *In re Rahrer*, 140 U.S. 545 (1891) (upholding as constitutional state legislation authorized by a congressional statute, after similar state legislation had been held unconstitutional).

courts disagree with what the national legislature does once it has focused on the action.

C. Two complicating factors

I must note two final complications. First, as to executive officials: The *ultra vires* doctrine is technically a doctrine of statutory interpretation: Courts should not construe statutes to authorize actions that the judges think are constitutionally questionable. Some constitutional courts lack the power to interpret statutes. Many European constitutional courts, for example, are supposed to do no more than interpret the constitution. Nearly every one, however, has developed some technique that allows it actually to interpret statutes. Some, for example, have taken upon themselves the power to say, "If this statute were interpreted thusly, it would be unconstitutional, and therefore we interpret it otherwise."[67] The U.S. Supreme Court is in a more difficult position with respect to actions by state executive officials, because the Court does not have the power, except in extraordinary cases, to interpret state law. If a state supreme court has said that its statutes authorize its police officers to act in a constitutionally questionable way, the U.S. Supreme Court is stuck with that interpretation and can only decide whether the action is in fact unconstitutional.[68] The *ultra vires* doctrine can help a great deal in alleviating confrontations between courts and legislatures, but it cannot do everything.

Second, as to preemption: Some federal systems simply deny the national government the power to preempt subnational legislation in some areas. The U.S. federal system does so in a quite small number of areas, the Canadian system in a larger number. In such systems, the question of legislative capacity to interpret the constitution in these nonpreemptible areas must be answered as to the state or provincial legislatures. My discussion of legislative incentives and structures would almost certainly need to be changed to address the modified question.[69]

V. CONCLUSION

I have argued that we should put stipulated constitution-based standards to one side and consider only whether a decision maker orients himself or herself to the nation's constitutional tradition. It seems to me nearly inevitable that a very large proportion of nonjudicial decision makers will have incentives to act in a constitutionally responsible manner, particularly to the (large) extent that incentives are provided by socialization. Those incentives are such that the margin in actual

[67] This technique has provoked some of the most persistent legal struggles in nations with specialized constitutional courts, that is, where one court is authorized to enforce the constitution while a different set of courts enforces ordinary law. The highest "ordinary" courts have not infrequently rejected the constitutional court's statutory interpretations on the ground that the constitutional court was not authorized to interpret statutes, but only to enforce the constitution. Most of these struggles have been resolved in favor of the constitutional courts' power, but some continue.

[68] Although some scholars contend that this limitation is rooted in the U.S. Constitution, the better analysis is that it arises because of the statutes Congress has enacted to regulate the Supreme Court's jurisdiction. Under that analysis, Congress *could* authorize the Court to interpret state law incidental to its power to consider the constitutionality of actions by state executive officials or by local governments.

[69] Because nonpreemptible areas in U.S. law are relatively small, it probably would not be either socially or constitutionally important were state legislatures to be constitutionally irresponsible in these areas.

performance between nonjudicial actors and judges is probably rather thin as a general matter. The basic question is empirical, and one on which we have relatively little systematic information. Systematic studies of nonjudicial decision makers are, in my view, more likely to be productive than additional conceptual inquiry.[70]

[70] For one study, see Janet L. Hiebert, *Charter Conflicts: What Is Parliament's Role?* (Montreal: McGill-Queen's University Press, 2002) at 7–18 (describing constitutional evaluation in Canada conducted by executive ministries and in Parliament). The present chapter will be included in modified form in a work-in-progress that will also include some case studies on the constitutional performance of nonjudicial decision makers.

17 Constitutional Engagement "Outside the Courts" (and "Inside the Legislature"): Reflections on Professional Expertise and the Ability to Engage in Constitutional Interpretation

Sanford Levinson

The topic of this section is "constitutional engagement by legislatures." This almost inevitably suggests that the legislature – although it is obviously a nonjudicial institution – can legitimately play a meaningful role in interpreting its particular national constitution. Should the legislature in question be a "parliament," then, of course, we need not speak of concomitant "executive" engagement because the executive, in a parliamentary system, is him- or herself a parliamentarian. In a "presidentialist" system like that of the United States, however, where a politically independent "chief executive" coexists with the legislature – and, of course, the judiciary – the question of nonjudicial "engagement" is necessarily broader. In any event, because of my own background as an American constitutional lawyer, I shall be discussing the extent to which *both* Congress and the executive can serve as independent constitutional interpreters. My major theoretical concerns, however, do not depend on the particularities (and peculiarities) of the American political system, and I certainly hope that my arguments will be relevant across national boundary lines and across political systems.

My focus in this brief chapter is the *capacity* of nonlawyer members of legislatures (or, for that matter, any other branch of government or, ultimately, ordinary citizens themselves) to engage in constitutional interpretation. Perhaps an even deeper question is whether constitutional interpretation requires *professional* training, which would, among other things, mark off the enterprise as significantly "esoteric," or is it indeed something that can be engaged in by ordinary, nonprofessionally trained men and women? Given that professionally trained lawyers are ubiquitous in all modern societies, not to mention the fact that a central role of lawyers in all such societies is to staff courts one of whose principal jobs is to interpret laws, including constitutions, the questions should have purchase on societies well beyond the borders of the United States.

These questions are well illustrated by one of the earliest episodes in American constitutional history, the bitter debate over the constitutional propriety of Congress's chartering a Bank of the United States. After all, a central mantra of the United States Constitution – and, one might suggest, of *any* "liberal" constitution – is that it established a *limited* government. Unlike the case with state constitutions, where governments were assumed to have plenary power in the absence of specific prohibitions set out in "bills of rights" and the like, the national constitution was "peculiar," as Madison put it,[1] in the assumption that the national government had only the powers assigned to it.

Perhaps the most important single feature of a casebook on constitutional law that I coedit[2] is that its first extended chapter begins not with a judicial opinion but, rather, with James Madison's speech before the House of Representatives condemning the proposed bill as beyond Congress's limited powers. What makes this of such importance is not simply the interesting arguments that Madison sets out but, rather, the fact that students are taught at the outset of the course that constitutional interpretation indeed takes place outside the courts and inside Congress. A serious embrace of the nonexclusivity of the courts as constitutional interpreters must necessarily have pedagogical implications, ranging from the construction of the casebooks we write to the organization of our courses, especially because students are almost inevitably predisposed to believe that courts have a monopoly on the enterprise of constitutional interpretation. Professors who take seriously the possibility of serious engagement by legislatures (or presidents) with constitutional issues must instantiate that perspective in their syllabi and class discussions.

Although Madison is sometimes described as "the Father of the Constitution," because of his important role in Philadelphia, his speech was to no avail. Not only did the House support the Bank by a 39 to 20 vote, but the Senate also gave its unanimous approval to the legislation. Of course, this was not sufficient to make it "law." The president also had to decide whether to approve it or to veto it and send it back to the legislature to see if it could attain the two-thirds support necessary to override a veto. (One will note that it was one vote short of that level of support in the House.)

President George Washington certainly did not appear to be casual in his decision-making process. He asked the three members of his cabinet, Secretary of State Thomas Jefferson, Attorney General Edmund Randolph, and Secretary of the Treasury Alexander Hamilton, to draft memoranda offering him their best judgment on the constitutionality of the bill. Unlike Madison, who had no legal training and who might well be described as a political scientist because of his deep interest in comparative government across both time and space, Jefferson, Randolph, and Hamilton were all lawyers. Moreover, Randolph's position as attorney general included the specific duty to "give his advice and opinion upon questions of law when requested by the President...."[3] Without going through all of the details, suffice it to say that both Jefferson and Randolph agreed with Madison that Congress lacked power to pass the legislation, whereas Hamilton vigorously disagreed. Washington, like Madison a nonlawyer – although, of course, he had been president of the Constitutional Convention in Philadelphia – signed the Act, which was ultimately upheld, in effect, by John Marshall's seminal opinion in *McCulloch v. Maryland*.[4]

[1] See Madison's speech to the House of Representatives, reprinted in Paul Brest et al., *Processes of Constitutional Decision-Making*, 4th ed. (Gaithersburg, Md.: Aspen Law & Business, 2000).

[2] Ibid.

[3] Quoted in Madison, ibid. at 11–12.

[4] 17 U.S. (4 Wheat.) 316 (1819). The "in effect" refers to the fact that the 1791 bill chartered the Bank for only a twenty-year term. It was not renewed when the charter expired (and when Madison was

This important episode in the early history of American constitutionalism amply illustrates what I am tempted to call the "paradox of nonprofessional lawyering." That is, what precisely empowered Madison and Washington – and, for that matter, the nonlawyer members of the House and Senate – to reach their own conclusions as to the constitutionality of the bill? There is, incidentally, no evidence that any legislator at the time argued that they should decide only whether the Bank was desirable as a policy matter and leave it up to the judiciary, presumably in later litigation, to decide whether it was constitutional as well as desirable.

It is worth emphasizing that the cabinet officer explicitly charged with the duty of giving "advice" to the president as to legal matters informed the president that the bill was unconstitutional. This might well be interpreted as meaning that Washington, who had taken an oath of office to "uphold" the Constitution, had a constitutional duty to veto it. Yet Washington apparently felt free to disregard this advice from his attorney general as well as the concurring memorandum from Jefferson; instead, he embraced the minority view, at least within the cabinet, expressed by Hamilton. By what right did he do so?

He might, of course, have simply said, "I defer to the judgment of the Congress, which debated the issue at length and decided by an overwhelming majority that the Constitution did indeed grant it the requisite power." But the very request for memoranda suggested that something more than institutional deference was involved. The only explanation for the request is that Washington believed that he had a duty to come his own independent conclusion about the constitutional merits of the legislation. So presumably Washington, if asked to defend his signing the legislation, would say (something like), "I read the various memoranda, and I was persuaded that Secretary Hamilton had better legal arguments than did Secretary Jefferson or Attorney General Randolph. What else could be expected of me?" Would anyone seriously argue that it should have been determinative that two of Washington's three cabinet officers, both of them well-trained lawyers, were unpersuaded by Hamilton? Should Washington have not been expected to "think for himself," as it were, as to what the Constitution required (or permitted)? If one treats this last question as "rhetorical," – *of course* the president should be allowed, indeed required, to "think for himself" – then one is necessarily saying that one does not in fact have to be a lawyer in order to resolve even the most basic disputes about constitutional meaning.

If one accepts this last proposition, then it should be clear that whatever else justifies deference to judicial decisions, it *cannot* be a simple claim of professional authority. It could, for example, involve a claim that the independence of judges from ordinary political exigencies is likely to make their judgments about constitutional norms better. But any such claim obviously does not rely on the fact that the judges in question are also professionally educated lawyers. Should professional

president). In 1816, however, Madison did in fact sign the bill establishing the Second Bank of the United States, which was at issue in *McCulloch*. Madison, incidentally, did not concede that he was mistaken in 1791. Rather, he "waiv[ed] the question of the constitutional authority of the Legislature to establish an incorporated bank, as being precluded, in my judgment, by the repeated recognition under varied circumstances of the validity of such an institution, in acts of the Legislature, Executive, and Judicial branches of the Government, accompanied by indications, in different modes, of a concurrence of the general will of the nation." Quoted in Brest et al., *supra* note 1 at 17.

training be of the essence, after all, one should expect that judges should exhibit greater deference to judgments made by legally trained legislators or by legally trained presidents (such as Richard Nixon or Bill Clinton) than to their nonprofessional counterparts; yet, I am unaware of any judicial opinions that refer to such professional backgrounds.

It should now be clear that any claim for the legitimacy of constitutional interpretation by (nonlawyer) legislators or presidents is linked with what has come to be called "popular constitutionalism" or, in a metaphor important to my own work, "protestant constitutionalism,"[5] which involves the rejection of a privileged institutional interpreter, analogous to the Vatican, in favor of the interpretive competence ultimately of the individual believer. Thus, the "priesthood of all believers" is mimicked by the notion of the "lawyerhood of all citizens," whether or not, of course, the believer has actually attended a seminary or the citizen a school of law.

One might try to resist the force of the "paradox of nonprofessionalism" by pointing to the myriad ways that lawyers are actively involved in legislatures and other branches of modern government. Even if we put to one side the near certainty that each legislator, even if not a lawyer him- or herself, will have lawyers on his or her staff, the Library of Congress has a justifiably highly esteemed cadre of lawyers in their Congressional Reference Service. Indeed, Louis Fisher, who was for many years the Service's Senior Specialist in Separation of Powers, is the author of many important books on his subject; he is at least as qualified to offer well-founded opinions as any judge in the land. Similarly, within the executive branch, the Office of Legal Counsel (OLC) within the Department of Justice often writes thoughtful opinions answering questions from the White House or one of the executive departments concerning the meaning of the Constitution. One need not believe in the least that it would be wise to "kill all the lawyers," who undoubtedly serve many useful roles in society. Rather, the question is only the ultimate *authority* of professionally trained lawyers.

Thus, the utility of having professionally trained lawyers to serve all sorts of social roles is ultimately beside the point with regard to the individual member of the legislature (or president) who, like George Washington, assesses the legal handiwork and comes to his or her own independent conclusion that may, by definition, involve the rejection of the ostensibly "authoritative" advice proffered by the Library of Congress or the OLC. At that point, we are forced to confront the brute fact that "expert" opinion takes second place to the views of the presumptively nonexpert decision maker.

But perhaps the real point is that we are confusing the notion of "expertise" with particular kinds of professional or institutional credentials, such as possession of a law degree or membership on a court. There are, after all, (at least) two forms of constitutional populism. The most extreme would say that the views of the populace (or any given member of the populace), whatever their basis, suffice to count as "constitutional interpretation" so long as one prefaces such "interpretation" with such "magic words" as "my view of freedom of speech is . . . " or "I think that 'equal protection' means. . . . " A less radical version of populism would argue that one need not go to law school in order to study, and therefore have informed opinions

[5] See Sanford Levinson, *Constitutional Faith* (Princeton, N.J.: Princeton University Press, 1988) at 37–46.

about, the meaning of the Constitution, but that it *is* necessary "to study," that is, to engage in some systematic inquiry. Indeed, Philip Bobbitt puts forth his famous notion of "modalities of interpretation"[6] precisely as an attempt to teach all of his readers, whether or not they are lawyers, what Jack Balkin and I have elsewhere termed the "grammar" of legal argument.[7]

Save in very rare instances, there are no "professional" speakers of English or French. There are only persons who have learned how to construct well-formed sentences in these languages. Just as Berlitz offers books and tapes to enable even isolated individuals to learn new languages, so does Bobbitt offer his own books as ways to learn what Balkin and I sometimes refer to as "lawtalk." "Lawtalk" is a highly structured mode of discourse, which means, among other things, that one is entitled to say of someone that he or she is simply not "speaking lawtalk" in the same way that we are able to say to someone that "whatever you are speaking, it is, alas, not French." From this latter perspective, law remains, in its own way, a "learned" language even if no longer a "learned profession." What remains "populist" – or "protestant" – about this understanding is the belief that almost anyone who makes some effort can learn "lawtalk" and thus feel entitled to engage in constitutional interpretation, including the rejection, as exemplified by George Washington, of more credentialed legal adepts.

Returning to the example of the Bank of the United States, one might be tempted to say that this presents a relatively small problem inasmuch as the judiciary had not yet spoken. That is, one cannot possibly describe Madison, Jefferson, Randolph, or Washington, or, for that matter, the Madison of 1816, as failing to demonstrate proper deference to the judiciary or, especially, the Supreme Court because it simply had not yet spoken to the point. The alternative to legislative and executive reflection on constitutional meaning in that instance would have been simply the throwing up of one's hands or reliance on later review by the judiciary (which, of course, presupposes the controversial practice of judicial review itself). Things get far more complicated, however, once courts do begin to speak. But here, too, the "case of the United States Banks" presents illuminating examples of "constitutional protestantism" in action.

Marshall, of course, upheld the Bank in *McCulloch,* in an opinion whose first paragraph thundered that "by this Court alone" can the Constitution's meaning be ascertained. But, as is well known, Andrew Jackson, who entered the White House ten years after Marshall's ostensibly authoritative construction of the Constitution, in fact paid the decision in that case relatively little heed. When his congressional opponents attempted in 1832 to recharter the Second Bank, which was due to expire in 1836, Jackson fearlessly vetoed the bill on constitutional grounds. "Mere precedent," he thundered in response to Marshall's own claims to authority in *McCulloch,* "is a dangerous source of authority and should not be regarded as deciding questions of constitutional power except where the acquiescence of the people and the States can be considered as well settled." Jackson concluded his discussion of the authority of precedent by stating that Congress and the president

[6] See Philip C. Bobbitt, *Constitutional Fate: Theory of the Constitution* (New York: Oxford University Press, 1984); Bobbitt, *Constitutional Interpretation* (Cambridge, Mass.: Blackwell, 1991).

[7] See J. M. Balkin and Sanford Levinson, "Constitutional Grammar" (1994) 72 *Tex. L. Rev.* 1771.

should grant to decisions of the Supreme Court "only such influence as the force of their reasoning may deserve."[8] It should be obvious that Jackson is rejecting the *doctrine* of precedent inasmuch as what gives it bite is precisely the belief that one should feel bound by earlier decisions even when they are regarded as seriously deficient in their reasoning. To follow an opinion because one respects it is really not to "follow" it at all, but to declare only that one has the capacity to distinguish good reasoning from bad and that the earlier decision is in fact an example of the former. "Authority" in this instance is held by the independent-minded legislator or president, most certainly not by the judge whose work is subject to independent evaluation and potential rejection. As a matter of fact, Jackson was a lawyer, although, to put it mildly, this was not his primary "professional" identity, which was that of a military hero.

It is at this point that some readers no doubt will find themselves being pulled in a more "catholic," that is, institutionalist, direction summarized in the contemporary term "judicial supremacy." It is well and good, they might concede, to have a flourishing conversation among all of the citizenry, professional and nonprofessional alike, about constitutional meaning when the issue is one of what lawyers call "first impression." But, they might go on to argue, *someone* must have the *last* word on constitutional meaning, and the usual candidate is the judiciary.[9] To dispute this, some would undoubtedly suggest, is to embrace a form of anarchy.

Of course, two quite different arguments are being conflated. One is derived from what might be termed the Hobbesian fear of multiple sources of legal definition. Sheldon Wolin has referred to Hobbes' "Sovereign Definer."[10] From this perspective, the important desideratum is to have someone who can quell interpretive disputes, and it really does not matter who that is, so long as there is someone (or, more to the point, some institution) that can play the role. The Hobbesian sovereign does not claim a particular "expertise" in defining words; rather, what it proclaims is an authority (or power) to make its definitions stick, as it were, and to quash any competitors. So if all we care about is finding a master definer of constitutional terms, there is no particular reason to choose a judge (or court) instead of a legislator (or legislature), save on prudential grounds.

The second argument is indeed based on expertise and views judges as uniquely equipped with the skills of defining. Obviously this rests not only on general assertions of professional skill, but also, more particularly, on the concept of a "legal science" whose methods are known only by well-educated and socialized adepts. As a matter of empirical fact, one can doubt whether this view has enough adherents any longer to provide the foundation for judicial (instead of legislative) supremacy. As suggested earlier, the rationale for such supremacy is far more likely to evoke a third argument predicated on the relationship between "independence" from political vagaries and what might be termed a kind of statecraft. Statecraft, however, cannot be a truly learned or "professional" skill, at least for judiciary buffs. It is obvious that legal education has precious little to do with educating people in

[8] Quoted in Brest et al., *supra* note 1 at 51–2.

[9] See, e.g., Larry Alexander and Frederick Schauer, "On Extrajudicial Constitutional Interpretation" (1997) 110 *Harv. L. Rev.* 1359.

[10] See Sheldon Wolin, *Politics and Vision: Continuity and Innovation in Western Political Thought*, rev. ed. (Princeton, N.J.: Princeton University Press, 2004).

any such skills, as contrasted, say, with graduates of the various schools of public policy or public affairs.[11]

So at the end of the day it appears difficult, if not impossible, for anyone who truly endorses any strong version of "the constitution outside the courts" to believe, at the same time, that (at least) constitutional law is an enterprise that requires much in the way of formal education and demonstrated professional skill. And, as much to the point, it seems impossible to limit a coherent notion of "the constitution outside the courts" only to institutions like Congress or the presidency unless one is an unabashed Hobbesian. Otherwise, one will ultimately find oneself, in the language of late eighteenth-century writers, "out of doors" listening to ordinary people discourse about basic constitutional issues. And, of course, one almost literally never knows what such people might "see" in a constitution that they are reading without the special glasses, rose-colored or otherwise, that are a concomitant of "disciplined" professional education.

[11] Though Bruce Ackerman, in what must certainly be his least persuasive book, offered a vision of legal education that would indeed make the American law school the incubator of skills in public policy construction. See Bruce A. Ackerman, *Reconstructing American Law* (Cambridge, Mass.: Harvard University Press, 1984).

18 Legislatures as Constitutional Interpretation: Another Dialogue

Andrée Lajoie, Cécile Bergada, and Éric Gélineau

I am especially grateful for this occasion to discuss the much overlooked role of the legislatures in the interpretation of the Canadian Constitution. Indeed, courts are seen as the main – if not the only – interpreters of the Constitution, and often criticized for what is seen as expanding their role into "lawmaking" at the expense of legislatures. However, the balance between the two institutions is more subtle and it is in that quite intricate web of interrelations that constitutional interpretation must be understood. I begin by briefly debunking a prevalent myth by showing both that the interpretive role of the courts has not increased as much as many claim since the entrenchment of the *Charter*, and that such a role is not now or ever has been exercised in a totally discretionary manner. I will then put the role of the legislatures in proper theoretical perspective by showing that far from only having the last word through the *notwithstanding clause*, they always have the first and most often the only word in a scenario where their interpretation prevails in the vast majority of instances, as they engage democratically in an altogether different dialogue than the institutional one.

DEBUNKING A MYTH

It is widely held, not only in the general public but unfortunately also in parts of the legal community, that the courts, and especially the Supreme Court of Canada, have dramatically increased and changed their role and their relationship to legislatures since the entrenchment of the *Charter* in 1982. Not to mention Morton, Manfredi, and consorts; even Peter Hogg has written that even if "Canadian courts have always had the power to review executive action, albeit on more limited grounds than are now available under the *Charter*. *What is new under the Charter*, and what tends to upset ardent supporters of parliamentary sovereignty, *is the power* of unelected judges *to interfere with the legislative decisions* of elected representatives."[1]

However, the role of the courts has been just as important for the division of powers since Confederation as it is now for the *Charter*, whereas the courts' legitimacy always rested and still rests on their interpretations being compatible with dominant values in the society where they adjudicate, a condition of both the legitimacy and the effectiveness of their pronouncements, of which courts are well aware.

[1] P. W. Hogg and A. A. Thornton, "Reply to 'Six Degrees of Dialogue'" (1999) 37 *Osgoode Hall L.J.* 529, 530. Italics added.

Invalidation: not a new role

A survey of division of powers cases between the end of the Second World War and the entrenchment of the *Charter*[2] shows that no less than twenty-six Supreme Court decisions rendered during that period resulted in complete or partial annulment of statutes (not counting bylaws, regulations, or common-law rules) for lack of constitutional jurisdiction under the division of powers.[3] In that light, it seems clear that interference with legislative decisions by the Court did not start with the *Charter*.

Granted, these invalidations are not only fewer in number (26), yearly average (0.7), and proportion of statutes enacted (0.083%)[4] than subsequent "affectations" of statutes under the *Charter* between 1983 and 2004 (numbering 48 for an average of 2.2 per year and a proportion of 0.36% of statutes enacted).[5] Moreover, post-*Charter* decisions involving statutes are reputed more invasive in some circles, as they have been implemented through new remedies, such as temporary validity, reading in, constitutional exemption, reconstruction, and even reporting orders.[6] Yet what these figures show is that even since the entrenchment of the *Charter*, the Supreme Court,[7] adding *Charter* and division-of-powers grounds,[8] has not invalidated more than 0.45 percent of public statutes enacted during the same period.[9]

So how can one explain that feeling of the legislatures' invasion when more than 99.5 percent of their enactments are left intact by the courts? And why the impression that it started with the *Charter*? It may be worth remembering that of the twenty-six decisions striking down statutes for lack of jurisdiction under the constitutional division of powers between the Second World War and the

2 *Canadian Charter of Rights and Freedoms*, Part I of the *Constitution Act, 1982* Schedule B to the *Canada Act, 1982* (U.K.) 1982, c. 11 [*Charter*].

3 See Appendix I.

4 Between 1945 and 1982, 31,089 public statutes have been enacted in Canada (excluding the Territories), which, divided by 26 invalidations on division-of-powers grounds, represent 0.083%.

5 Between 1983 and 2004, 13,074 statutes were enacted in Canada (excluding the Territories and the 2004 P.E.I. statutes, these lists being unavailable). That number has to be divided by the sum of invalidations on *Charter* grounds (48), which means a proportion of 0.36%. See Appendix II.

6 See Appendix II.

7 Only Supreme Court decisions have been taken into account, as well as those appellate courts' decisions for which a leave to appeal to the Supreme Court was lodged by the Government of the concerned legislature and has been refused, since the other appellate courts decisions either do not imply invalidation (when they relate to federal statutes, which are then only inoperative in the province concerned) or are kept invalid with the consent of the legislature when the invalidation of provincial statutes is not appealed to the Supreme Court by the concerned government, thus ending the "dialogue." We have excluded four Supreme Court decisions in which the invalidated statutes had already been abrogated by the concerned legislatures when the decisions were rendered: *R.* c. *Sieben* [1987] 1 S.C.R. 295; *R.* c. *Hamill* [1987] 1 S.C.R. 301; *Corporation Professionnelle des Médecins du Québec* c. *Thibault* [1988] 1 S.C.R. 1033; and *Schachter* c. *Canada* [1992] 2 S.C.R. 679. We have excluded two appellate court decisions for which appeals (both to the Supreme Court and the Court of Appeal) were lodged, but not by the government: *Badger et al.* c. *Attorney General of Manitoba* (1986), 30 D.L.R. (4th) 108 (Man. Q.B.), aff'd by (1986) 32 D.L.R. (4th) 310 (Man. C.A.), leave to appeal to S.C.C. refused: [1989] 1 S.C.R. v; *R.* c. *Budreo,* (1996) 104 C.C.C. (3d) 245 (Ont. Gen. Div.), aff'd by (2000) 142 C.C.C. (3d) 225 (Ont. C.A.), leave to appeal to S.C.C. refused: *News releases,* May 3, 2001, online: Supreme Court of Canada http://www.lexum.umontreal.ca/csc-scc/en/com/2001/html/01–05–03.3a.html.

8 See Appendix III.

9 The number of statutes enacted in Canada (excluding the Territories and the 2004 P.E.I. statutes) between 1983 and 2004 (13,074) has been divided by the sum (59) of invalidations on *Charter* grounds (48) and division-of-powers grounds (11), which comes to a proportion of 0.45%.

Charter, twenty-two resulted in centralization to the detriment of provincial legislatures, with a disproportionate number (four, or almost 20% of the total) issued in cases originating from Quebec, which is only one province in ten,[10] thus getting twice its share of invalidations.

Given the sensitivity of Quebeckers to issues of provincial legislative competence, could this factor explain why the Quebec Legislative Assembly, which knew what previously unlimited constitutional judicial control of its legislation meant, was less reluctant to use the notwithstanding clause? Could the same factor explain why in the rest of Canada striking down statutes on division-of-powers grounds would seem less serious than on *Charter* grounds, and account for why colleagues have been under the false impression that the courts' interference started with the *Charter*? Whatever the answer to these difficult questions, I will now turn our attention to the fact that even if constitutional control of the validity of statutes has somewhat quantitatively and qualitatively increased after the *Charter*, it is not and never has been exercised in a totally discretionary manner.

Invalidation: never discretionary

It is important to take note that the seemingly unfettered "power of unelected judges to interfere with the legislative decisions of elected representatives" is not and has never been really discretionary. It was always subjected to the weight of dominant values on the judges' interpretation of the Constitution and particularly of rights. In an in-depth analysis of minorities' fate in the Supreme Court between the inception of the *Charter* and 2002, I have shown that the claims of both social and political minorities have been integrated in Canadian law by the Court only insofar as they coincide, at least in part, and certainly do not collide, with dominant Canadian values and interests.[11]

Our results show that all minorities want their identity recognized and all obtain that recognition by the Court, except Quebeckers, when there appears to be a fear that granting such recognition will disrupt national unity. All also ask for indemnities to compensate inequalities; the Court will only award such monetary compensation to social minorities at the expense of private parties. It has never awarded them public funds, obtained through income taxes paid in greater proportion by the dominant minority of white heterosexual males. This latter kind of compensation it reserves, mostly in the form of access to resources, for political minorities as a quid pro quo for political power and control of the territory that they claim but never obtain, at least on the same object, this denial yet again being grounded in considerations of national unity.[12]

Another example of the effect of dominant values on judicial discourse can be found in the "evolving" interpretations that the Court gave to the expression

[10] See Appendix IV.

[11] See A. Lajoie, *Quand les minorités font la loi*, coll. "Les voies du droit," Paris, P.U.F., 2002; A. Lajoie, É. Gelineau, and R. Janda, "When Silence Is No Longer Acquiescence: Gays and Lesbians under Canadian Law" (1999) 13 *R.C.D.S.* 101; A. Lajoie, É. Gelineau, I. Duplessis, and G. Rocher, "L'intégration des valeurs et des intéréts autochtones dans le discours judiciaire et normatif canadien" (2000) 38 *Osgoode Hall L.J.* 143; A. Lajoie, É. Gelineau, M.-C. Gervais, and R. Janda, "La majorité marginalisée: Le trajet des valeurs des femmes vers le forum judiciaire et leur intégration dans le discours de la Cour supréme" (2000) 34(2) *R.J.T.* 1.

[12] A. Lajoie, *Quand les minorités font la loi*, ibid.

"free and democratic society," inscribed in section I of the *Charter* as a limitation on the legislative infringement of entrenched rights. Between 1985, when it heard the first case related to that definition,[13] and 1994, the Court has held three different definitions of that expression, each influenced by the successive dominant ideology at the time when they were coined: the first in the tradition of classic liberalism, the second in terms of communitarian pluralism, and the third grounded in neoliberalism.[14]

This influence of the dominant values on the judicial interpretation of laws, including constitutions, and the underlying dialogue of courts – this time not with the legislatures, but with citizens – is due to the fact that in contemporary times, the courts' legitimacy does not derive from their institutional status but from the coincidence of the values that they inscribe into the law with those of the addressees of the judicial discourse. Such concurrence is the price the courts must pay for the acceptance and effectiveness of their decisions.

LEGISLATIVE DIALOGUE ABOUT THE CONSTITUTION

I claim that dominant values also weigh on legislatures' constitutional interpretation, entail similiar relationships between the legislatures and the other institutions as well as the public, induce analogous dialogues, and can explain the legislative application/interpretation of the Constitution. A short account of hermeneutic theory and its application to what happens to the Constitution in the legislatures is provided as a useful background for understanding the specific and important role of legislatures in constitutional interpretation.

A theoretical approach to constitutional interpretation

Hermeneutics, which started with biblical interpretation in the eighteenth century and applies to many other disciplines, was later appropriated by the legal community, both in Europe, where it is associated with such names as Gadamer,[15] Ricoeur,[16] Perelman[17] and Timsit,[18] and in the United States, where its proponents include Dworkin,[19] Fish,[20] Rorty,[21] and Shusterman.[22]

[13] *Law Society of Upper Canada* c. *Skapinker* [1984] 1 S.C.R. 357.

[14] A. Lajoie et al., "Les repré sentations de 'société libre et démocratique' à la Cour Dickson, la rhétorique dans le discours judiciaire canadien" (1994) 32 *Osgoode Hall L.J.* 295.

[15] H. G. Gadamer, Philosophie herméneutique, coll. "Epinéthée," Paris, P.U.F., 1996.

[16] P. Ricoeur, "Le problème de la liberté de l'interprète en herméneutique géné rale et en herméneutique juridique," dans P. Amseleck (ed.), *Interprétation et droit* (Bruxelles/Aix-Marseilles: Editions Émile Bruylant/Presses Universitaires d'Aix-Marseilles, 1995).

[17] C. Perelman and P. Foriers, *La motivation des décisions de justice* (Bruxelles: Établissements Émile Bruylant, 1978).

[18] G. Timsit, "Sur l'engendrement du droit" (1988) *R.D.P.* 39.

[19] R. Dworkin, *Freedom's Law: The Moral Reading of the American Constitution* (Cambridge, Mass.: Harvard University Press, 1996); "Les contraintes argumentatives dans l'interprétation juridique" dans P. Amseleck (ed.), *supra* note 16; R. Dworkin, *Law's Empire* (Cambridge, Mass.: Belknap Press, 1986) at 77–8; R. Dworkin, *A Matter of Principle* (Cambridge, Mass.: Harvard University Press, 1985).

[20] S. Fish, *Respecter le sens commun* (Paris, L.G.D.J., coll. "La pensé e juridique moderne," 1995); *Is there a text in this class?* (Cambridge, Mass./London: Harvard University Press, 1980).

[21] R. Rorty, *Philosophy and the Mirror of Nature* (Princeton, N.J.: Princeton University Press, 1980).

[22] R. Shusterman, *Sous l'interprétation* (Paris: L'Éclat, 1994).

The easiest way to understand it is to represent it as a relationship between three poles: (1) first an object to be interpreted – be it a concerto, a sculpture or a text, here the Constitution; (2) then a subject, that is, the interpreter, who here can of course be the courts, but also the addressee of the constitutional norm; and (3) last but not least, their "horizon,"[23] that is, the societal context in which the norm is interpreted. Timsit[24] writes of three operations whereby the enunciator of the norm (here the constituent) *predetermines* it, while the interpreter (both the courts and the legislatures) *codetermines* it under the aegis of *overdetermination*, defined as the compelling effect of the range of dominant values in the society where the norm is enunciated and interpreted.

This range of dominant values, says Perelman, who writes in the context of judicial interpretation, relates to two audiences: (1) the "*auditoire particulier*," comprising the disciplinary community of the interpreter – for the courts: the legislator, the administration, the Bar, and the legal scholars, who expect consistency and continuity in legal interpretation; and (2) the "*auditoire universel*" comprising the litigants, their lawyers, the media, and the general public, who favor an equitable solution to the conflict affected by the interpretation. According to Perelman, what judges are trying to do is to reconcile the expectations of these two audiences to which the judicial interpreter is addressing its decision.[25] Mister Justice LeDain, who told me that he had not previously read Perelman, came to the same conclusion some years later when describing the role of judges.[26]

It is not disputed that the main concepts of this theory apply easily to judicial interpretations of our constitution, and, of course, in the relationship of the interpreter with its "*auditoire particulier*" you will have recognized the institutional dialogue between the courts and the legislatures that has been so well documented by Hogg and Bushell,[27] and Hiebert,[28] in their polemics with Manfredi and Kelly[29] and Morton.[30]

However, not one but four relationships can be deduced from this theoretical framework. The first has just been mentioned, while the second binds the judicial interpreter to the "*auditoire universel*" and implies the impact of dominant values on judicial interpretation, an impact that I have just outlined for the judicial interpretation of the division of powers,[31] minority rights under the *Charter*,[32] and

[23] H. G. Gadamer, *supra* note 15.

[24] G. Timsit, *supra* note 18.

[25] C. Perelman and P. Foriers, *supra* note 17.

[26] A. Lajoie and L. Rolland, "Gérald LeDain: sur la société libre et démocratique" (1993) 38 *McGill L. J.* 899.

[27] P. W. Hogg and A. A. Bushell, "The *Charter* Dialogue Between Courts and Legislatures (or Perhaps the *Charter Of Rights* Isn't Such a Bad Thing After All)" (1997) 35 *Osgoode Hall L.J.* 75; P. W. Hogg and A. A. Thornton, *supra* note 1.

[28] J. L. Hiebert, "Wrestling with Rights: Judges, Parliament and the Making of Social Policy" (1999) 5(3) *IRPP* Choices, on line: www.irpp.org/choices/archive/vol5no3.pdf; J. L. Hiebert, "A Relational Approach to Constitutional Interpretation: Shared Legislative and Judicial Responsibilities" (2001) 35(4) *Canadian Studies* 161.

[29] C. P. Manfredi and J. B. Kelly, "Six Degrees of Dialogue: A Response to Hogg and Bushell" (1999) 37 *Osgoode Hall L.J.* 513.

[30] F. L. Morton, "Dialogue or Monologue?" in P. Howe and P. H. Russell, eds., *Judicial Power and Canadian Democracy* (Montreal and Kingston: McGill-Queen's University Press, 2001) 111.

[31] A. Lajoie, *Jugements de valeurs*, coll. "Les voies du droit," Paris, P.U.F., 1997.

[32] A. Lajoie, *Quand les minorités font la loi, supra* note 11.

the definition of a "free and democratic society."[33] The third and fourth concern relationships of the legislatures as an interpreter of the Constitution with both its "*auditoire particulier*" (the institutional relationship with the courts, which is the counterpart of the first dialogue) and its "*auditoire universel*," the latter so obviously included in liberal democracy it has been overlooked so far. It is this last relationship and the dialogue it entails that I want to analyze more deeply now.

A ROLE FOR LEGISLATURES IN CONSTITUTIONAL INTERPRETATION. Up until now, the main role that has been recognized for legislatures in the interpretation of the Constitution is their usage of the notwithstanding clause to override judicial decisions regarding the application of the *Charter*. This power that gives them the last word on *Charter* issues is not an unimportant one, as evidenced by its more frequent usage in Quebec[34] than in other provinces, some of which have nevertheless used it.[35] But is this not the most important element of their role, which needs to be read in a much larger context involving not only redressing *Charter* cases, but also applying/interpreting the whole constitutional text through their daily legislative enactments.

To understand this larger role, one has to come back to the meaning of *codetermination* in Timsit's version of the hermeneutic theory: He states that *codetermination* is achieved both by interpreting and *applying* norms, because both operations give meaning to that norm. For instance, executive orders and administrative decisions count as *codetermination* just as much as court decisions. This is because application and interpretation are unseverable: It is impossible to apply a norm without first deciding what it means.

If this reasoning is transposed in the context of the enactment of statutes by both federal and provincial legislatures in Canada, it can be seen that in their daily enactments they are applying the constitutional norms that define both their jurisdiction and the limits within which they can affect rights. In relation to the Constitution, the legislature is in the same position as the executive when issuing orders-in-council in regard to the enabling statutes: It applies a norm within which its power is defined and must imperatively interpret it before applying it.

Indeed, any time the legislatures enact a statute, they at least implicitly decide that this legislation is within their jurisdiction and that it complies with other

[33] A. Lajoie et al., *supra* note 14.

[34] *Loi concernant la Loi constitutionnelle de 1982*, L.R.Q. 1982, c. 21; *Loi sur le régime de retraite de certains enseignants et modifiant diverses dispositions législatives concernant les ré gimes de retraite des secteurs public et parapublic*, L.R.Q. 1986, c. 44; *Loi modifiant la Loi sur la mise en valeur des exploitations agricoles*, L.R.Q. 1986, c. 54; *Loi modifiant de nouveau la Loi sur l'instruction publique et la Loi sur le Conseil supé rieur de l'éducation et modifiant la Loi sur le ministère de l'Éducation*, L.R.Q. 1986, c. 101; *Loi modifiant la Charte de la langue française*, L.R.Q. 1988, c. 54; *Loi sur l'instruction publique*, L.R.Q. 1988, c. 84; *Loi modifiant diverses dispositions législatives concernant les régimes de retraite des secteurs public et parapublic*, L.R.Q. 1991, c. 14; *Loi sur l'enseignement privé*, L.R.Q. 1992, c. 68; *Loi concernant certaines dispositions dérogatoires dans des lois relatives à l'éducation*, L.R.Q. 1994, c. 11; *Loi modifiant la Charte des droits et liberté s de la personne et d'autres dispositions législatives*, L.R.Q. 1996, c. 10; *Loi concernant certaines dispositions dérogatoires dans les lois relatives à l'éducation*, L.R.Q. 1999, c. 28; *Loi modifiant diverses dispositions législatives dans le secteur de l'éducation concernant la confessionnalité*, L.R.Q. 2000, c. 24; *Loi sur le régime de retraite du personnel d'encadrement*, L.R.Q. 2001, c. 31.

[35] *Land Planning and Development Act*, S.Y. 1982, c. 22 (this Act has never been enforced); *SGEU Dispute Stettlement Act*, S.S. 1984–85, c. 111; *Marriage Amendment Act*, S.A. 2000, c. 3.

constitutional norms, including the *Charter*. But such interpretations are sometimes quite explicit, as they are institutionalized in the bureaus entrusted in most if not all legislatures in Canada with reviewing legislation before it is brought to legislative debate in order to make sure that bills tabled are within the constitutional jurisdiction of the concerned legislature. As we well know, it even happens that the opinions of non-public service lawyers about the constitutionality of bills are sought in the process.

Furthermore, when they thus interpret and apply the Constitution, the legislatures engage in the second kind of dialogue already mentioned in the judicial context, that with the "*auditoire universel*," that is, the public and the media. That dialogue is not only a one-way virtual one resulting from members of the legislatures reading, hearing, and watching the media and the media reports prepared by their staff, but an interactive one, as happens in parliamentary committees and commissions, structured to receive input from the public.

Whether or not the legislatures take that input into account is another question, to be answered on a case-by-case basis, but they do not have much choice because their legitimacy is at stake – just as much if not much more than that of the courts – and this in the definitely impending threat of the next election. This feature of democratic practice is so obvious that it has been overlooked by most analysts, who consequently hold a reductive view of the constitutional role of the legislatures.

❧

In conclusion, it appears that the role of the legislatures in interpreting the Constitution is far wider than so far acknowledged, and far wider than that of the courts. If our analysis is accurate, all legislation that is not challenged in the courts is an interpretation/application of the Constitution by the particular legislature, which has both the first and the only word in the matter, in a process that involves two dialogues: one with the courts, exceptional and institutional; and the other with the constituent public, constant and universal. By this count, the federal and provincial legislatures in Canada have been the sole interpreters of the Constitution in 31,063 unchallenged statutes (or a proportion of 99.8% of the legislative production between the Second World War and the entrenchment of the *Charter*), and since the *Charter*, another 13,015 unchallenged statutes (or a proportion of 99.5% of the same between 1982 and 2004), not counting the 14 instances when a legislature resorted to the notwithstanding clause. Which leaves the courts with an average of approximately 0.2 percent of the interpretative field for the whole period since the Second World War, hardly a score to warrant accusations of judicial invasion of legislative territory, let alone the demise of democracy. In other words, much ado about nothing!

APPENDIX I. Supreme Court decisions rendered between 1945 and 1982 resulting in complete or partial invalidation of statutes

Winner c. *S.M.T. (Eastern Ltd.)* [1951] S.C.R. 887 (reading down).

Johannesson c. *Municipality of West Saint-Paul (Manitoba)* [1952] 1 S.C.R. 292 (striking down).

Johnson c. *Alberta (Attorney General)* [1954] S.C.R. 127 (striking down).

Campbell-Bennet Ltd. c. *Comstock Midwestern Ltd.* [1954] S.C.R. 207 (reading down).

Birks c. *Montreal (City)* [1955] S.C.R. 799 (striking down).

The Canadian Banker's Association c. *Saskatchewan (A.G.)* [1956] S.C.R. 31 (striking down).

Reference re: Farm Products Marketing Act (Ontario) [1957] S.C.R. 198 (severing).

Reference re: Orderly Payment of Debts Act, 1959 (Alta.) [1960] S.C.R. 571 (striking down).

Texada Mines Ltd. c. *British Columbia (A.G.)* [1960] S.C.R. 713 (striking down).

Esso Standard (Inter-America) Inc. c. *J.W. Enterprises* [1963] S.C.R. 144 (reading down).

Batary c. *Saskatchewan (A.G.)* [1965] S.C.R. 465 (striking down).

Quebec (Commission du Salaire Minimum) c. *Bell Telephone Co. of Canada* [1966] S.C.R. 767 (reading down).

A.G. Ontario c. *Policyholders of Wentworth Insurance Co.* [1969] S.C.R. 779 (severing).

Ontario (Registrar of Motor Vehicles) c. *Canadian American Transfer Ltd.* [1972] S.C.R. 811 (reading down).

Interprovincial Co-operatives Ltd. c. *Dryden Chemicals Ltd.* [1976] 1 S.C.R. 477 (striking down).

Quebec (Public Service Board) c. *Canada (Attorney General)* [1978] 2 S.C.R. 191 (reading down).

Canadian Industrial Gas & Oil Ltd. c. *Saskatchewan* [1978] 2 S.C.R. 545 (severing).

Reference re: Agricultural Products Marketing Act, 1970 (Canada) [1978] 2 S.C.R. 1198 (severing).

Central Canada Potash Co. c. Saskatchewan [1979] 1 S.C.R. 42 (striking down).

R. c. *Dominion Stores Ltd.* [1980] 1 S.C.R. 844 (reading down).

Labatt Brewing Co. c. *Canada* [1980] 1 S.C.R. 914 (severing).

R. c. *Fowler* [1980] 2 S.C.R. 213 (severing).

Manitoba c. *Air Canada* [1980] 2 S.C.R. 303 (reading down).

Quebec (Attorney General) c. *Lechasseur (Quebec Youth Court Judge)* [1981] 2 S.C.R. 253 (severing).

Reference re Family Relations Act (B.C.) [1982] 1 S.C.R. 62 (severing).

Peel (Regional Municipality) c. *MacKenzie* [1982] 2 S.C.R. 9 (severing).

APPENDIX II. Supreme Court decisions rendered between 1983 and 2003 resulting in complete or partial invalidation of statutes on *Charter* grounds

Regina c. *Rao*, S.C.C., no. 18832, 11 October 1984 refusing leave to appeal to S.C.C. against (1984) 46 O.R. (2d) 80 (Ont. C.A.) (reading down).

Quebec (A.G.) c. *Quebec Protestant School Board* [1984] 2 S.C.R. 66 (severing).

Hunter c. *Southam Inc.* [1984] 2 S.C.R. 145 (severing).

Singh c. *Canada (Minister of Employment and Immigration)* [1985] 1 S.C.R. 177 (severing).

R. c. *Big M Drug Mart Ltd.* [1985] 1 S.C.R. 295 (striking down).

Reference Re Section 94(2) of the B.C. Motor Vehicle Act [1985] 2 S.C.R. 486 (severing).

R. c. *Oakes* [1986] 1 S.C.R. 103 (severing).

Regina c. *Metro News Ltd., S.C.C. Weekly Bulletin*, 6 November 1986, p. 1371 refusing leave to appeal to S.C.C. against (1986) 29 C.C.C. (3d) 35 (Ont. C.A.) (severing).
Re Blainey and Ontario Hockey Association et al. (1986) 58 O.R. (2d) 274 (S.C.C.) (note) refusing leave to appeal to S.C.C. against (1986) 54 O.R. (2d) 513 (Ont. C.A.) (severing).
R. c. *Smith* [1987] 1 S.C.R. 1045 (severing).
R. c. *Vaillancourt* [1987] 2 S.C.R. 636 (severing).
R. c. *Morgentaler* [1988] 1 S.C.R. 30 (severing).
Ford c. *Quebec (A.G.)* [1988] 2 S.C.R. 712 (severing).
Andrews c. *Law Society of British Columbia* [1989] 1 S.C.R. 143 (severing).
Edmonton Journal c. *Alberta (A.G.)* [1989] 2 S.C.R. 1326 (severing).
R. c. *Hess*; *R.* c. *Nguyen* [1990] 2 S.C.R. 906 (severing).
R. c. *Swain* [1991] 1 S.C.R. 933 (severing).
R. c. *Seaboyer* [1991] 2 S.C.R. 577 (severing).
R. c. *Bain* [1992] 1 S.C.R. 91 (severing).
R. c. *Généreux* [1992] 1 S.C.R. 259 (severing).
R. c. *Zundel* [1992] 2 S.C.R. 731 (severing).
R. c. *Morales* [1992] 3 S.C.R. 711 (severing).
Baron c. *Canada* [1993] 1 S.C.R. 416 (severing).
Sauvé c. *Canada (Attorney General)* [1993] 2 S.C.R. 438; *Sauvé* c. *Canada (Chief Electoral Officer)* [2002] 3 S.C.R. 519 (severing).
R. c. *Grant* [1993] 3 S.C.R. 223; *R.* c. *Wiley* [1993] 3 S.C.R. 263; *R.* c. *Plant* [1993] 3 S.C.R. 281 (reading down).
R. c. *Fisher, S.C.C. Weekly Bulletin*, 2 February 1995, p. 245 refusing leave to appeal to S.C.C. against (1994) 111 D.L.R. (4th) 415 (Ont C.A.) (severing).
R. c. *Heywood* [1994] 3 S.C.R. 761 (severing).
R. c. *Laba* [1994] 3 S.C.R. 965 (severing and reading in).
Miron c. *Trudel* [1995] 2 S.C.R. 418 (reading in).
RJR-MacDonald Inc. c. *Canada (Attorney General)* [1995] 3 S.C.R. 199 (severing).
Benner c. *Canada (Secretary of State)* [1997] 1 S.C.R. 358 (severing).
Reference re Remuneration of Judges of the Provincial Court of Prince Edward Island; Reference re Independence and Impartiality of Judges of the Provincial Court of Prince Edward Island [1997] 3 S.C.R. 3 (severing).
Libman c. *Quebec (Attorney General)* [1997] 3 S.C.R. 569 (severing).
Vriend c. *Alberta* [1998] 1 S.C.R. 493 (reading in).
M. c. *H.* [1999] 2 S.C.R. 3 (severing).
Corbiere c. *Canada (Minister of Indian and Northern Affairs)* [1999] 2 S.C.R. 203 (severing).
United Food and Commercial Workers, Local 1518 (U.F.C.W.) c. *KMart Canada Ltd.* [1999] 2 S.C.R. 1083 (severing).
R. c. *Sharpe* [2001] 1 S.C.R. 45 (reading down).
R. c. *Ruzic* [2001] 1 S.C.R. 687 (severing).
Dunmore c. *Ontario (Attorney General)* [2001] 3 S.C.R. 1016 (severing and reading down).
Mackin c. *New Brunswick (Minister of Finance)*; *Rice* c. *New Brunswick* [2002] 1 S.C.R. 405 (striking down).
R. c. *Guignard* [2002] 1 S.C.R. 472 (severing).

R. c. *Hall* [2002] 3 S.C.R. 309 (severing).

Figueroa c. *Canada (Attorney General)* [2003] 1 S.C.R. 912 (severing).

Trociuk c. *British Columbia (Attorney General)* [2003] 1 S.C.R. 835 (severing).

Nova-Scotia (Workers' Compensation Board) c. *Martin* [2003] 2 S.C.R. 504 (severing).

R. c. *Demers* [2004] 2 R.C.S. 489 (severing).

Canadian Foundation for Children c. *Canada* [2004] 1 R.C.S. 76 (reading down).

APPENDIX III. Supreme Court decisions rendered between 1983 and 2003 resulting in complete or partial invalidation of statutes on division-of-powers grounds

Re Town of Summerside and Maritime Electric Co. Ltd. (1984) 55 N.R. 399 (S.C.C.) (note) refusing leave to appeal to S.C.C. against (1983) 3 D.L.R. (4th) 577 (P.E.I.C.A.) (reading down).

Canada (Labour Relations Board) c. *Paul l'Anglais Inc.* [1983] 1 S.C.R. 147 (reading down).

Canada (Attorney General) c. *St-Hubert Base Teachers' Association* [1983] 1 S.C.R. 498 (reading down).

Reference re: Upper Churchill Water Rights Reversion Act 1980 (Newfoundland) [1984] 1 S.C.R. 297 (striking down).

Bell Canada c. *Québec (C.S.S.T.)* [1988] 1 S.C.R. 749 (reading down).

Bank of Montreal c. *Hall* [1990] 1 S.C.R. 121 (reading down).

Shulman (Guardian at litem of) c. *McCallum* (1994) 111 D.L.R. (4th) vii (S.C.C.) refusing leave to appeal to S.C.C. against (1993) 105 D.L.R. (4th) 327 (B.C.C.A.) (reading down).

R. c. *Morgentaler* [1993] 3 S.C.R. 463 (striking down).

Hunt c. *T. & N. P.L.C.* [1993] 4 S.C.R. 289 (constitutional exemption).

Morgentaler c. *New Brunswick (Attorney General)* (1995) 124 D.L.R. (4th) vi (S.C.C.) refusing leave to appeal to S.C.C against (1995) 121 D.L.R. (4th) 431 (N.B.C.A.) (severing).

Husky Oil Operations Ltd. c. *Canada (Minister of National Revenue)* [1995] 3 S.C.R. 453 (reading down).

APPENDIX IV. Supreme Court decisions rendered between 1945 and 1982 striking down statutes and resulting in centralization at the detriment of the powers of provincial legislatures

Decisions originating from Quebec

Birks c. *Montreal (City)* [1955] S.C.R. 799.

Quebec (Commission du Salaire Minimum) c. *Bell Telephone Co. of Canada* [1966] S.C.R. 767.

Quebec (Public Service Board) c. *Canada (Attorney General)* [1978] 2 S.C.R. 191.

Quebec (Attorney General) c. *Lechasseur (Quebec Youth Court Judge)* [1981] 2 S.C.R. 253.

Decisions originating from other provinces

Winner c. S.M.T. (Eastern Ltd.) [1951] S.C.R. 887.

Johannesson c. Municipality of West Saint-Paul (Manitoba) [1952] 1 S.C.R. 292.

Johnson c. Alberta (Attorney General) [1954] S.C.R. 127.

Campbell-Bennet Ltd. c. Comstock Midwestern Ltd. [1954] S.C.R. 207.

The Canadian Banker's Association c. Saskatchewan (A.G.) [1956] S.C.R. 31.

Reference re: Farm Products Marketing Act (Ontario) [1957] S.C.R. 198.

Reference re: Orderly Payment of Debts Act, 1959 (Alta.) [1960] S.C.R. 571.

Texada Mines Ltd. c. British Columbia (A.G.) [1960] S.C.R. 713.

Esso Standard (Inter-America) Inc. c. J. W. Entreprises [1963] S.C.R. 144.

Batary c. Saskatchewan (A.G.) [1965] S.C.R. 465.

A.G. Ontario c. Policyholders of Wentworth Insurance Co. [1969] S.C.R. 779.

Ontario (Registrar of Motor Vehicles) c. Canadian American Transfer Ltd. [1972] S.C.R. 811.

Interprovincial Co-operatives Ltd. c. Dryden Chemicals Ltd. [1976] 1 S.C.R. 477.

Canadian Industrial Gas & Oil Ltd. c. Saskatchewan [1978] 2 S.C.R. 545.

Central Canada Potash Co. c. Saskatchewan [1979] 1 S.C.R. 42.

Manitoba c. Air Canada [1980] 2 S.C.R. 303.

Reference re Family Relations Act (B.C.) [1982] 1 S.C.R. 62.

Peel (Regional Municipality) c. MacKenzie [1982] 2 S.C.R. 9.

19 The Constitution and Congressional Committees: 1971–2000

Keith E. Whittington, Neal Devins, and Hutch Hicken

The United States Congress delegates a significant portion of its legislative work to its committees. Even though the power and independence of committees has varied over time,[1] the observation of a young Woodrow Wilson in the late nineteenth century remains largely true today: "The House sits, not for serious discussion, but to sanction the conclusions of its Committees as rapidly as possible. It legislates in its committee-rooms; . . . so that it is not far from the truth to say that Congress in session is Congress on public exhibition, whilst Congress in its committee-rooms is Congress at work." Congress both "deliberates and legislates" in committee.[2]

Congressional committees are nonetheless largely uncharted territory for constitutional scholars. The new scholarly interest in extrajudicial constitutional interpretation largely ignores the congressional committee system generally and its routine work. When it focuses on the legislature at all, this scholarship limits its sights to floor debates or committee activities of extraordinary interest, such as the Senate Judiciary Committee hearings on the nomination of Robert Bork to the Supreme Court. But, if committees are the primary sites in which Congress both deliberates and legislates, an adequate picture of congressional efforts to interpret and implement the Constitution will have to take into account the normal work of the committees.

Committee hearings provide a useful window into congressional deliberation. Hearings do not provide direct access to the investigation and negotiation that ultimately produces legislative action. But as staged events for public consumption, hearings do provide useful information. They are an important platform for members of Congress to win public notice, shape public opinion, and advance favored causes. Committee hearings are an important vehicle by which legislators seek to build a public record, communicating with legislative colleagues, executive branch officials, interested activists, and the general public. In hearings, legislators put political relationships and concerns on display and establish warrants of authority for legislative action. They serve as "rituals for legitimizing decisions," and it is precisely in those rituals of legitimization that we may expect the Constitution to be invoked.[3]

[1] See *infra* notes 14–15 (discussing how changes in the balance of power between party leaders and committee chairs impacts on congressional consideration of constitutional issues).

[2] Woodrow Wilson, *Congressional Government* (New York: Meridian Books, 1956) at 69, 62.

[3] John Mark Hansen, *Gaining Access* (Chicago: University of Chicago Press, 1991) at 23.

This chapter takes a bird's-eye view of congressional committee hearings raising constitutional issues. It maps the patterns of such hearing activity in Congress during the last three decades of the twentieth century. As such, it does not delve into what happens inside individual hearings or consider the quality of congressional deliberation on constitutional matters. Such tasks remain for the future. Instead, this chapter examines the quantity and location of constitutional discourse within Congress and the basic structure of constitutional deliberation in Congress, and it seeks to identify the determinants of legislative attention to constitutional subjects.

Such a perspective on congressional engagement with the Constitution reveals a surprising consistency in congressional hearing activity. While individual issues come and go and individual hearings respond to transitory and idiosyncratic forces, Congress maintains a fairly consistent and constant level of activity in discussing constitutional issues. Congressional engagement with the Constitution is not an exceptional and rare event, but rather is a routine feature of legislative business and politics. While dramatic high points of presidential impeachments or constitutional amendments grab our attention, such episodes occur against a background of more workmanlike and routine discussion of the goals and constraints of constitutional government. As this chapter will demonstrate, the number of constitutionally oriented hearings is not significantly affected by whether Democrats or Republicans control Congress or whether the White House and Congress are controlled by the same party. Likewise, external factors (the president's policy agenda, Supreme Court decision making) do not meaningfully influence congressional hearing activity on constitutional issues. The two parties have held hearings focused on somewhat different constitutional issues, however, and the Nixon Administration did provoke an unusual number of hearings called to respond to executive actions. In other words, constitutionally oriented hearings are largely driven by the general legislative calendar and reflect tendencies common to other hearings in Congress.

Congressional committees, like courts, regularly encounter the Constitution in the course of carrying out their normal responsibilities. Over time, however, the Judiciary Committees have come to dominate congressional consideration of constitutional issues. While other committees hold fewer and fewer hearings on constitutionally related issues, the Judiciary Committees continue to hold roughly the same number of constitutionally oriented hearings.[4] The continuing interest of the Judiciary Committees in constitutional issues is tied to the committee's mission and the interests of members who serve on these committees. The decline in the number of hearings held outside of the Judiciary Committees is harder to explain. Possible explanations include the ideological polarization in Congress, the increasing emphasis on constituent service by members, and the rise of position-taking legislation.

DATA AND APPROACH

The fact that committee hearings are generally public makes them a relatively accessible source of information about Congress. The fact that they are largely stage-managed raises questions about how that information can be leveraged so

[4] As discussed below, the mid-1990s is an exception to this general pattern.

as to gain a useful perspective on the reality of congressional deliberation and lawmaking. Political scientists have used witness appearances at hearings to provide insight into the relationship between Congress and interest groups, and the content of the discussions at legislative hearings has provided a wealth of information about what issues and people legislators takes seriously. The presence or absence of hearings on a given subject and their location within Congress can also provide useful information on change in the public agenda and jurisdictional control over issue areas.[5]

For this chapter, we collected data from committee hearings in the U.S. House of Representatives and U.S. Senate from January 1, 1971, through December 31, 2000. The Congressional Information Service (CIS) publishes an abstract and witness list for public hearings held by the committees and subcommittees of Congress. CIS also assigns multiple topic keywords to each hearing. Using an online version of the CIS database accessible through LexisNexis, we searched for every congressional hearing between 1971 and 2000 containing a variation on the word "constitutional" anywhere in the CIS entry, including the abstract, keywords, hearing title, or witness identifiers. We then examined each entry in order to exclude those that did not make substantive reference to the U.S. Constitution, such as hearings discussing the constitution of Russia or including constitutional law professors testifying on the assets of Holocaust victims. This left a data set of 1,152 congressional hearings. We then recorded subject matter, date, congressional session, committee, whether the hearing focused centrally on the constitutional issues it raised, and whether the hearing was responding to executive or judicial actions.

Our data set is undoubtedly underinclusive of the entire set of hearings that raised constitutional issues during the period. Hearing abstracts and keywords only capture issues that formed a substantial part of the witness testimony. Consequently, this search procedure leaves out hearings that included only relatively brief mentions of constitutional issues. This procedure is also dependent on CIS coding of hearings, and it is possible that some types of constitutional issues and discussions would not be reflected in the CIS entries. Moreover, CIS employs a number of keywords that are relevant to constitutionalism. Although such a procedure would pick up a central CIS keyword ("constitutional law"), it would not necessarily locate others (e.g., "civil liberties"). Nonetheless, there is substantial overlap in the CIS coding (e.g., hearings with the keyword "civil liberties" are often also given the keyword "constitutional law"), and many additional hearings were included based not on the keyword but on terms elsewhere in the CIS entry. In sum, these 1,152 hearings are a sample of the total universe of hearings raising constitutional issues during the period, but it is a sample that is likely to capture a large proportion of the relevant universe and that is broadly representative of the types of constitutional issues that come before Congress.

The data set as a whole includes 1,152 hearings, with 610 in the House, 528 in the Senate, and 14 in joint committees. The House held an average of twenty hearings per year, and the Senate held an average of eighteen per year. Half of all

[5] For a review of the literature making use of congressional hearings, see Keith E. Whittington, "Hearing about the Constitution in Congressional Committees" in Neal Devins and Keith E. Whittington, eds., *Congress and the Constitution* (Durham, N.C.: Duke University Press, 2005) at 87–109.

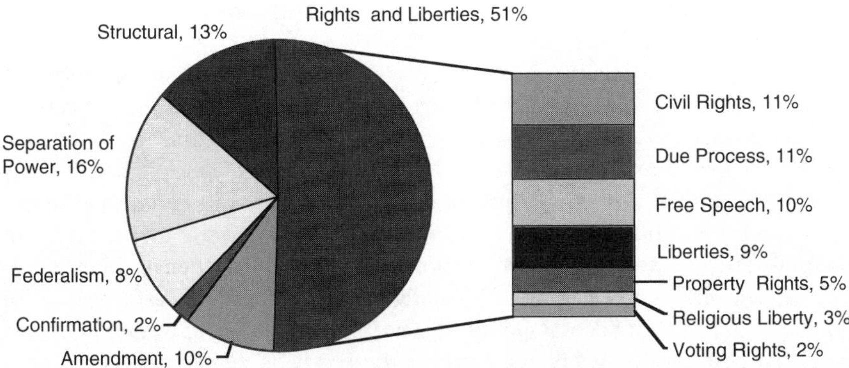

Figure 19.1. Subject Matter of Constitutional Hearings, 1971–2000.

the hearings in the sample addressed rights and liberties. The next most common subject of such hearings was the separation of powers at 16 percent, followed by issues of constitutional structure at 13 percent and constitutional amendment at 10 percent (see Figure 19.1).

Our data set allows us to examine how congressional committee hearings addressing constitutional issues are distributed across time, across the legislature, and across particular issue areas. We have three sorts of expectations as to how congressional attention to constitutional issues might be structured: those shaped by political parties, those shaped by internal institutions, and those shaped by external institutions.

We might expect the incidence of such hearings to respond to partisan pressures within Congress. The scheduling of committee hearings is a monopoly power held by the majority party in the congressional chamber, and so we might expect partisan factors to play a heavy role in determining whether constitutionally relevant hearings are scheduled. We consider three such possibilities. First, one party might be more prone to holding constitutionally oriented hearings than the other. We might imagine, for example, that one party has a greater ideological commitment to constitutionalism or includes more constituencies interested in constitutional issues than does the other party. The Republican Party, for example, is often identified with the "conservative social agenda." Party leaders have sought to countermand the Supreme Court for rulings on abortion, school busing, religion in the public schools, and gay rights. House Republicans have also championed numerous structural reforms as part of their Contract with America, including term limits, the item veto, and unfunded mandates.[6] On the other hand, it is a common perception that the Democratic Party is the more civil libertarian party, reflected in items ranging from 1988 Democratic presidential candidate Michael Dukakis's proud affirmation that he was a "card-carrying" member of the American Civil Liberties Union to the party's celebration of "activist" judicial decisions such as *Roe v. Wade*.[7] If true, we might expect the two chambers of Congress to hold more hearings raising

[6] In 1994, Republicans successfully sought majority control of the House by running on the so-called Contract with America. The Contract pledged a smaller federal government and a larger role for the states.

[7] 410 U.S. 113 (1973).

constitutional issues when they are held by the Democratic Party than when they are held by the Republican Party.

Second, constitutionally oriented hearings may spike when there is a turnover in partisan control of a chamber of Congress, but the number of such hearings may decay over subsequent sessions as a single party retains control of the chamber and the legislative agenda. We might imagine, for example, that both parties have constitutionally oriented agendas, but that the in-party monopolizes the legislative agenda and the control of committee hearings, frustrating the ability of the out-party to publicize its own agenda items. As a consequence, when partisan control turns over, a burst of legislative activity may result as a new set of policies and hearings become politically feasible. Once this pent-up demand for legislative hearings has been met, however, there may be a declining need to hold additional hearings over time as long as the same party continues to control the agenda.

Third, partisan polarization within Congress might affect the number of constitutionally oriented hearings. Ideological polarization might result in members placing more emphasis on validating their policy priorities than on exploring the constitutional soundness of their handiwork. As such, the growing ideological divide that separates the two parties might result in a decline in the number of constitutionally oriented hearings. Alternatively, by expanding the "gridlock interval," the range of status quo policies that cannot be displaced by an existing legislative majority, ideological polarization may reduce legislative productivity. Increased hearing activity on politically symbolic issues may compensate politically for the decreased legislative output, or the environment of heightened ideological conflict may encourage additional hearings on contested constitutional terrain.[8]

We might expect the incidence of such hearings to respond to internal institutional features of Congress. First, the general legislative and electoral calendar affects the pace and timing of hearings. Legislators may hold more constitutionally oriented hearings in even-numbered (i.e., election) years as they generate issues and a public record as they enter the campaign season. Alternatively, legislators may decrease hearing activity in even-numbered years as campaigns put pressure on the calendar and the legislative session winds to a close. Second, we would expect the House to hold more such hearings than the Senate. Because the full House faces reelection every other year, there may be more pressure on House members to hold hearings to highlight issues of public concern. Moreover, the greater size of the House may simply enable it to be more active in holding hearings without putting undue pressure on individual members. Third, if constitutional issues are routinely encountered as part of normal legislative business, we would expect the number of hearings involving constitutional issues to be a function of the number of hearings held generally in Congress. Fourth, we might expect committee expertise to affect the distribution of hearings touching on constitutional issues. Committees with established expertise and interest in constitutional issues should be disproportionately likely to schedule hearings addressing constitutional subject

[8] Keith Krehbiel, *Pivotal Politics* (Chicago: University of Chicago Press, 1998); Benjamin Ginsberg and Martin Shefter, *Politics by Other Means* (New York: Basic Books, 1990).

matter and more likely to recognize and hear testimony on constitutional issues that might be relevant to a given policy debate.[9]

Finally, we might expect the incidence of such hearings to respond to changes in the external environment of Congress. Bruce Ackerman has suggested that politicians may turn to constitutional deliberation out of frustration and in an effort to overcome some institutional obstacle to the realization of their policy preferences.[10] Two features of the external environment are particularly notable in this regard. First, the judiciary might push Congress into deliberating on constitutional issues. Left to their own devices, legislators may be content to ignore the Constitution and focus on more bread-and-butter issues in American politics. Increased judicial activity – most notably, the nullification of statutes by federal courts on constitutional grounds – may force legislators to turn their collective attention to constitutional matters and force increased constitutional deliberation. It has been cogently argued, for instance, that Congress has only deliberated on the scope of federal powers when the Supreme Court has aggressively enforced the boundaries of federalism.[11] This might be the case generally, and if so we might expect to see increased hearing activity in response to increased levels of judicial invalidation of statutes. Second, conflict with the executive branch may lead Congress into deliberating on constitutional meaning. During periods of divided partisan control of the government, Congress may be more likely to hold hearings exploring the limits of executive power or the scope of congressional power under the Constitution. The impeachment of Democratic President Bill Clinton and the later investigation of his use of the pardon power by the Republican-controlled Congress may illustrate a broader tendency of institutionally based partisan warfare to lead to constitutional challenges and argumentation.

PARTISAN FACTORS

We first consider the three expectations based on partisan considerations regarding the incidence of such hearings. We find limited support for any of the three party-based hypotheses. The first such hypothesis was that the number of hearings held in a legislative chamber would vary depending on which party controlled that chamber. It does not. In the thirty years between 1971 and 2000, the Democratic Party controlled the House for twenty-four years and the Senate for eighteen years. The Democratic Senate held an average of nineteen hearings per year; the Republican Senate held an average of sixteen hearings per year. The Democratic House held twenty hearings per year; the Republican House held twenty-two. The number of hearings held in Democratic-controlled years is not statistically distinguishable from the number of hearings held in Republican-controlled years. Although the two parties may have had somewhat different substantive commitments when it comes to constitutional issues, one party was not noticeably more likely to sponsor hearings raising constitutional issues than was the other. With this

[9] Frank R. Baumgartner and Bryan D. Jones, *Agendas and Instability in American Politics* (Chicago: University of Chicago Press, 1993).

[10] Bruce Ackerman, *We the People*, vol. 2 (Cambridge: Harvard University Press, 1998).

[11] J. Mitchell Pickerill, *Constitutional Deliberation in Congress* (Durham, N.C.: Duke University Press, 2004).

data, we cannot rule out the possibility that one party is uniformly more likely to raise constitutional issues but is able to raise those issues in hearings even when it is in a minority (because the minority party is granted the right to call witnesses at hearings), but we do not believe this to be the case given the subject matter of the hearings held under each party.

If we break down the hearings held by each party by subject matter, some partisan differences do emerge, however. When in Republican hands, Congress held approximately five additional hearings to discuss possible amendments to the Constitution (all results significant at the .05 level). Although it is somewhat ironic that the more conservative political party would give more attention to constitutional reform than would the more liberal party, a variety of constitutional amendment proposals have been a prominent part of Republican politics over the past two decades, including amendments relating to such items as a balanced budget, flag burning, and congressional term limits. Constitutional hearings addressing matters of federalism were also far more strongly associated with Congress under Republican control than under Democratic control, which is in keeping with the rhetoric of Republican presidents and party platforms during this period as well.[12] When in Democratic hands, Congress spent more time discussing separation-of-powers questions and constitutional rights and liberties. Congress held approximately five more hearings involving the separation of powers when Democrats were in the majority, a record that received a substantial boost from Nixon-era conflicts and their aftermath. A Democratic Congress held approximately seven additional hearings touching on constitutional rights and liberties compared with a Republican Congress. While most areas of constitutional rights and liberties drew the attention of both parties, Democrats scheduled far more hearings addressing due process and voting rights issues than did Republicans.

Our second party-based hypothesis suggested that hearings raising constitutional issues spiked when party control of a congressional chamber turned over. Congressional chambers changed hands four times during these three decades: in the Senate in 1981, 1987, and 1995, and in the House in 1995. We can compare the congressional sessions controlled by a new party with those controlled by a previously incumbent party. The average number of hearings held in the Senate in sessions controlled by a new party is statistically indistinguishable from the number held in incumbent-controlled sessions. At thirty-seven, the number of hearings held by the newly Republican House in the 104th Congress was significantly above the norm for the House during this period. Although turnover in party control does not appear normally to lead to more constitutionally oriented hearings, the "Gingrich Revolution" in the House following the 1994 elections was noticeably different in this regard. This deviation is not at all surprising. By running on a "Contract with America" that included the line-item veto, term limits, and federalism initiatives, House Republicans made constitutional reform a centerpiece of the 104th Congress.

Our final party-based hypothesis suggested that hearings raising constitutional issues would vary with the ideological polarization of Congress. To examine this

[12] J. Mitchell Pickerill and Cornell W. Clayton, "The Rehnquist Court and the Political Dynamics of Federalism" (2004) 2:2 *Perspectives on Politics* 33.

hypothesis, we turned to the difference in absolute party medians in each chamber as measured by DW-NOMINATE scores. NOMINATE scores are a now-standard measure of the location of legislators in ideological space (ranging from 1.000 to −1.000) based on their overall voting behavior, and the difference in absolute party medians captures the degree of party polarization in any given session as reflected in voting behavior on roll-call votes.[13] There is no statistically significant correlation between the degree of party polarization in a congressional chamber and the number of hearings involving constitutional issues.

INTERNAL INSTITUTIONAL FACTORS

We considered four expectations regarding the incidence of constitutionally oriented hearings and the internal institutional features of Congress. First, we expected that there would be variation across the legislative calendar of a two-year congressional session. There is indeed a robust relationship (at the .05 level) between the calendar and the number of hearings, with Congress holding an average of forty-seven hearings in odd-numbered years and thirty hearings in even-numbered years. Pending elections tend to crowd hearings off the legislative calendar, including those hearings that raise constitutional issues (see Figure 19.2).

We expected that the more populous and electorally pressured House would hold more hearings than the Senate. The House does hold a slight edge in the number of hearings raising constitutional issues, averaging twenty such hearings per year compared with the Senate's seventeen. This result is driven by the larger overall number of hearings held by the House, however. The number of hearings that raise constitutional issues in the Senate makes up a slightly higher percentage of that chamber's overall number of hearings than does that in the House. Hearings raising constitutional issues constituted 2.6 percent of the hearings held in the Senate during this period, but only 1.9 percent of those held in the House of Representatives. That percentage has also been much more stable in the Senate over these three decades than in the House. In the Senate, the number of hearings that raise constitutional issues is in part a function of the total number of hearings held (at the .05 level). Although the number of hearings raising constitutional issues in the Senate declined somewhat over this three-decade period, that decline tracks the reduced number of hearings held overall in the Senate. In the House, however, the number of constitutionally oriented hearings is independent of the total number of hearings held each year. The percentage of House hearings raising constitutional issues declined from a high in the early 1970s of over 4 percent to a low of under 1 percent in the mid-1980s before recovering somewhat in the late 1990s to levels that were comparable to the mid-1970s. Even as the House held more hearings overall in the late 1970s and 1980s, it held fewer addressing constitutional issues. The House began to hold more constitutionally oriented hearings in the 1990s, however, returning to the levels of the mid-1970s, even as the overall number of hearings declined.

Much of the upswing in House hearings, as already noted, is tied to the 1994 Republican takeover of Congress and, with it, the Contract with America's embrace of numerous constitutional reforms. In particular, the percentage of constitutional

[13] Keith T. Poole and Howard Rosenthal, *Congress* (New York: Oxford University Press, 1997).

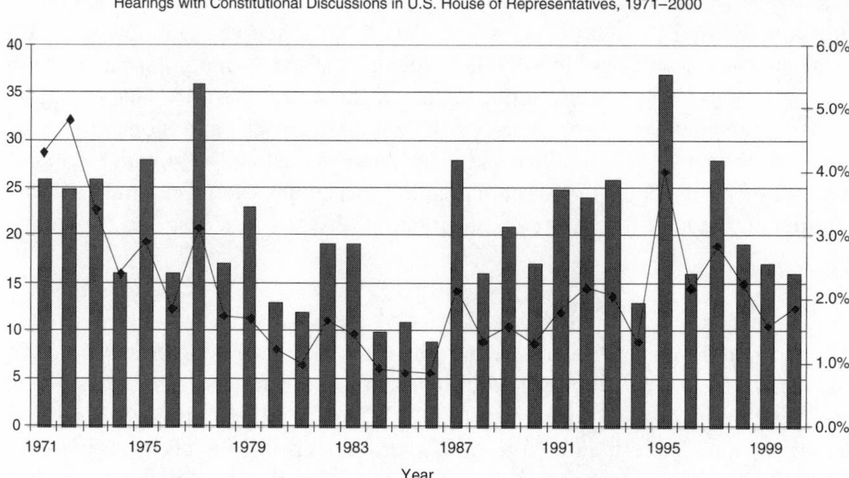

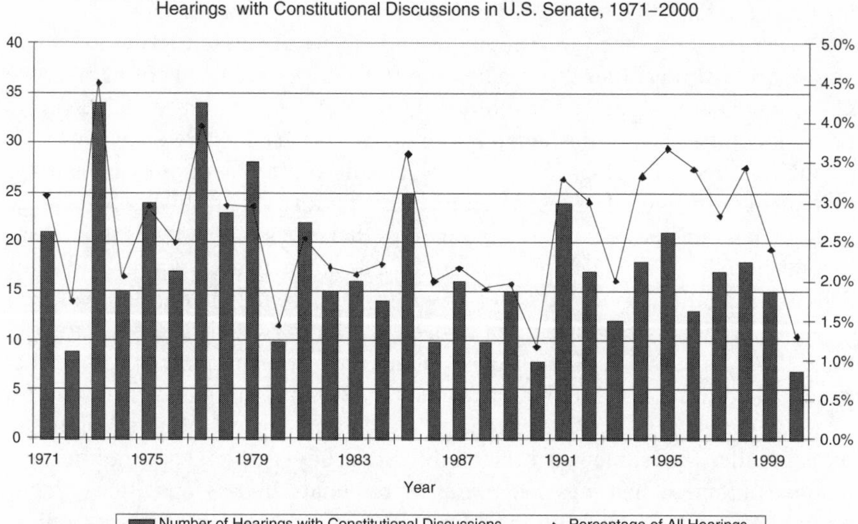

Figure 19.2. Hearings with Constitutional Discussions in U.S. House of Representatives and Senate, 1971–2000.

hearings from 1994 to 1997 matched the 1973 to 1977 period. More telling, by reforming the committee system in the House, the "Gingrich Revolution" shifted power away from the standing committees and toward majority party leadership.[14] During the mid-1990s, House leaders pursued constitutionally oriented reforms while reining in the committees. During the 1980s, however, committee chairs were

[14] See Steven S. Smith and Eric D. Lawrence, "Party Control of Committees in the Republican Congress" in Lawrence C. Dodd and Bruce I. Oppenheimer, eds., *Congress Reconsidered*, 6th ed.(Washington, DC: CQ Press, 1997) 163–92.

more autonomous and House leadership was less interested in advancing a constitutional agenda. In other words, the power of House leadership to exert control over committee priorities helps explain swings in the number of constitutionally oriented hearings held in the House.

Unlike the House, Senate leadership exerts less influence over the legislative process and work product. The fact that the percentage of constitutionally oriented hearings in the Senate has been much more stable than in the House reflects institutional differences in the two bodies. Majority leadership lacks the tools to push through a party-driven agenda. Relatedly, the need to build supermajority coalitions results in a lawmaking process that is more deliberate, more decentralized, and more accommodating to the preferences of individual Senators.[15]

THE JUDICIARY COMMITTEES

Committee expertise is clearly an important factor in determining whether that committee will hold hearings addressing constitutional issues. In each chamber, the Judiciary Committee dominates constitutional discussions, even though constitutional issues are occasionally raised in the hearings of most committees.[16] For the period as a whole, the House Judiciary Committee sponsored 43 percent of the hearings in the sample from that chamber. The Senate Judiciary Committee sponsored 55 percent. In both chambers, however, the Judiciary Committee has become more important as a site of constitutional discussion over the course of these three decades. From an average of 33 percent of the hearings in the first two Congresses in the sample, the House Judiciary Committee held an average of 66 percent in the last two Congresses. The story is not quite so dramatic in the Senate, but mostly because the Senate Judiciary Committee started at a much higher level. It held 46 percent of the hearings in the first two Congresses of the sample, but 62 percent in the last two Congresses (see Figure 19.3).

The Judiciary Committees did not become more active in holding such hearings; other committees became *less* active in deliberating on the Constitution. This partly reflects a fall-off from the widespread, although sporadic, consideration of constitutional issues in a large number of committees in the 1970s. But it also reflects the shrinking role of more regular participants in the constitutional dialogue. Committees such as the Government Affairs and Labor that once held multiple hearings raising constitutional issues every year averaged closer to one per year in the 1990s. Over the course of these three decades, the engagement with constitutional issues became a more specialized endeavor within Congress. At the same time, committees such as Foreign Relations and Education and Labor that once could plausibly claim to have an expertise of their own in addressing constitutional concerns as

[15] See ibid. (explaining why the Senate did not pursue structural reforms during the 104th Congress and, in so doing, distinguishing the two bodies); Barbara Sinclair, "Party Leaders and the New Legislative Process" in *Congress Reconsidered*, 229–45.

[16] The Judiciary Committees have jurisdiction over matters relating to the administration of justice in federal courts, administrative bodies, and law enforcement agencies. The committees also play an important role in impeachment proceedings. Through hearings and a committee vote, the Senate Judiciary Committee screens federal court nominees, including Supreme Court Justices. For additional discussion, see *infra* notes 17–18 and accompanying text.

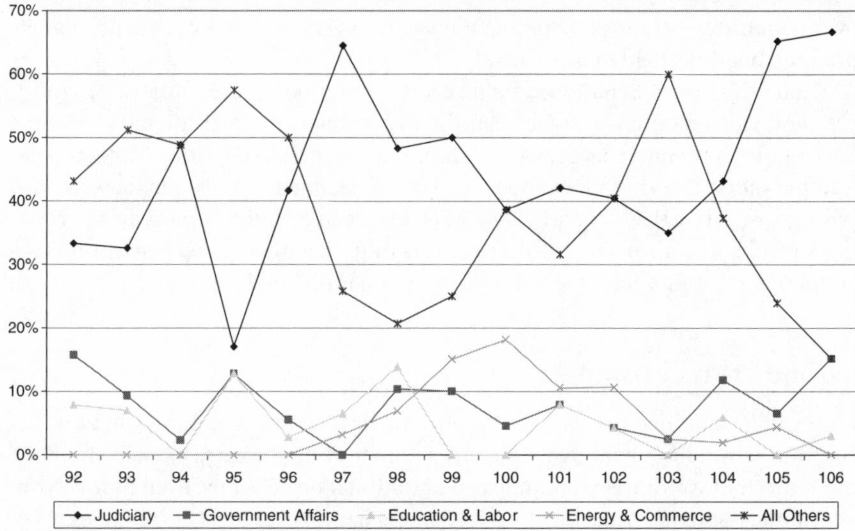

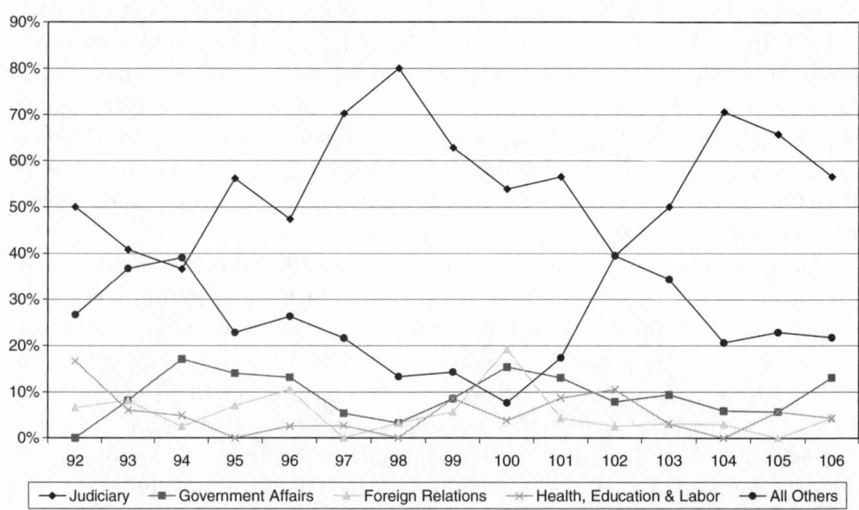

Figure 19.3. Percent of Constitutional Hearings by Committee, 92nd–106th Congress.

a result of their steady engagement with them, have largely ceded jurisdiction to the Judiciary Committees. Subject-specific concerns might still lead a committee into consideration of a constitutional topic to which they might bring substantive expertise or strong constituency interest, as when the Senate Committee on Indian Affairs turned its attention to religious liberty issues after the Supreme Court's 1990 *Smith*[17] decision or the House Energy and Commerce Committee contemplated

[17] In *Employment Division, Department of Human Resources v. Smith*, 494 U.S. 872 (1990), the Supreme Court upheld Oregon's power to deny unemployment benefits to drug counselors who lost their jobs

employee drug testing and tobacco advertising regulation in the mid-1980s, but such encounters are now likely to be fleeting.

Differences between the Judiciary Committees and other committees are to be expected. Judiciary Committee members are overwhelmingly policy-oriented lawyers. They are comfortable with, even relish, legalistic arguments. Also, because the Judiciary Committees often deal with highly divisive social issues (abortion, affirmative action, gun control), lawmakers who seek out these committees tend to be "true believers," individuals who do not feel the heat for taking a stand on contentious constitutional questions.[18] Moreover, Judiciary Committee members value a good legal argument, employ a "lawyer-like culture and deliberative style," and care a great deal about whether the Supreme Court will uphold their handiwork.[19] Given the skills, interests, and norms of the Judiciary Committees, it is hardly surprising that these committees regularly deliberate about constitutional matters. Relatedly, because Judiciary Committee members are genuinely interested in holding hearings on constitutional questions, the number of constitutional hearings held by the Judiciary Committees is fairly stable. Sometimes these hearings are extremely consequential (the confirmation of Supreme Court nominees, the impeachment of Presidents Nixon and Clinton) and other times they are largely symbolic; the overall number of hearings, however, seems more a function of staffing issues than of the saliency of issues before the Committee.

The steady decline in the number of constitutional hearings by other committees is harder to explain. What follows are some plausible explanations, although it is unclear how much impact, if any, these explanations have had in affecting committee practices. First, for some committees, the decline may be tied to changing norms. For example, Congress has ceded more and more of its war powers to the president during the past thirty years.[20] The drop in constitutional hearings by the Senate Foreign Relations and House Foreign Affairs Committees may reflect the changing balance of power between Congress and the president. Second, the decline may also be tied to a relative diminution in the importance of constitutional issues to the national policy agenda. In the early to mid-1970s, Watergate and civil rights were dominant issues. Likewise, when Republicans took over the House in 1994, the Contract with America promised numerous constitutional reforms. A third (and related) explanation for the decline is that today's lawmakers are not especially interested in defending Congress's turf as an independent interpreter of the Constitution. Through expedited Supreme Court review provisions, lawmakers

because they had used peyote as part of a Native American Church religious ceremony. In response to this decision, Congress enacted legislation legalizing "the use, possession, or transportation of peyote by an Indian for bona fide traditional ceremonial purposes." 108 Stat. 3125 (1994). Congress also enacted legislation providing broader protections of religious liberty, legislation invalidated by the Supreme Court in *City of Boerne v. Flores*, 521 U.S. 507 (1997).

[18] Christopher J. Deering and Steven S. Smith, *Committees in Congress*, 3rd ed. (Washington, DC: CQ Press, 1997); Mark C. Miller, "Congressional Committees and the Federal Courts": A Neo-Institutionalist Perspective" (1992) 45 *Western Political Quarterly* 949. For this very reason, most lawmakers do not want to serve on an ideologically polarized committee that deals with "no win" issues. Deering and Smith at 82.

[19] Miller *supra* note 18 at 961; Roger H. Davidson, "The Lawmaking Congress" (Autumn 1993) 56 *Law and Contemporary Problems* 99.

[20] Louis Fisher, *Congressional Abdication in War and Spending* (College Station: Texas A&M University Press, 2001).

sometimes delegate their power of constitutional review to the courts.[21] More telling, a recent survey of members of the 106th Congress (1999–2001) reveals that 71 percent of lawmakers adhere to a "joint constitutionalist" perspective whereby courts should give either "limited" or "no weight" to congressional assessments of the constitutionality of legislation.[22] Another related explanation for the decline in constitutionally oriented hearings is the ever-growing ideological polarization in Congress. More than ever before, lawmakers may have hard-and-fast views about the rightness of their policy agenda. The question of whether their policy agenda is constitutional may matter less to today's lawmakers. Correspondingly, Democratic and Republican leadership is increasingly is concerned with "message politics," that is, using the legislative process to make a symbolic statement to voters and other constituents. By focusing its efforts on the message its party is sending, lawmakers places less emphasis on whether a federal court will uphold legislation after it is enacted.[23] Likewise, through the growing use of position-taking legislation, today's lawmakers place greater emphasis on "making pleasing judgmental statements" than on making "pleasing things happen."[24]

EXTERNAL INSTITUTIONAL FACTORS

Two external institutional factors seem likely to affect the amount of constitutional deliberation that occurs in Congress: the constitutional activism of the judiciary and the partisan control of the presidency. In the aggregate, the number of hearings raising constitutional issues has little correlation with how active the Supreme Court might be in striking down federal or state legislation. Even the unprecedented levels of judicial nullification of congressional legislation in the late 1990s had little effect on the number of constitutionally oriented hearings scheduled in Congress. Even in the specific area where the Rehnquist Court's activism has been posited to increase congressional constitutional deliberation – federalism – Congress held nearly as many hearings in the 1970s as in the 1990s, and the hearings that it did hold in the 1990s were more associated with the newly empowered Republicans' celebration of federalism in 1995 than with the Supreme Court.[25] Throughout the period Congress scheduled hearings specifically to respond to particular judicial actions, but these were just over 10 percent of the total and displayed no particular pattern. If heightened judicial scrutiny of federal legislation spurs greater congressional attention to constitutional issues, it does not make itself evident in the number or subject matter of congressional hearings.

[21] See Neal Devins, "Congress as Culprit: How Lawmakers Spurred on the Court's Anti-Congress Crusade" (2001) 51 *Duke L.J.* 435 at 441–7.

[22] Bruce G. Peabody, "Congressional Attitudes Towards Constitutional Interpretation" in *Congress and the Constitution, supra* note 5 at 39–63.

[23] See C. Lawrence Evans, "Committees, Leaders, and Message Politics" in Lawrence C. Dodd and Bruce I. Oppenheimer, *Congress Reconsidered*, 7th ed. (Washington, DC: CQ Press, 2001) 217–39.

[24] David R. Mayhew, *Congress: The Electoral Connection* (New Haven: Yale University Press, 1974) 161. For a discussion of how Congress's use of position-taking statutes may be causally related to Rehnquist Court invalidations of federal statutes, see Keith E. Whittington, "Taking What They Give Us: Explaining the Court's Federalism Offensive" (2001) 51 *Duke L. J.* 477 at 511–15 ["Taking What They Give Us"].

[25] Cf. J. Mitchell Pickerill, "Congressional Responses to Judicial Review" in *Congress and the Constitution, supra* note 5 at 151–72.

This is not to say that courts play no role in setting the constitutional agenda as it appears in congressional hearings. The federalism decisions did not prompt a legislative response because they did not prevent lawmakers and interest groups from pursuing their policy agenda. The Court, while limiting Congress's power, had not sought a return to *Lochner*-era restrictions. Far from hampering the current Congress, the Court's federalism revival matched growing populist and lawmaker distrust of Congress and reinforced the ideological inclinations of House and Senate Republicans.[26] In contrast, were the Supreme Court to regularly undermine first-order policy preferences, Court decision making could become a focal point of the national political agenda. Absent something as stark as the *Lochner* era (where Court hostility to the New Deal undermined first-order priorities),[27] however, the constitutional agenda in Congress appears to be primarily set independently, by Congress itself, rather than being driven by judicial decision making.

Congressional deliberation on constitutional issues in hearings is also largely independent of the partisan control of the presidency. Throughout the period, Congress scheduled hearings specifically to respond to particular executive actions, but the number of such hearings dropped dramatically after the Nixon era and averaged only 7 percent of the hearings in the sample after 1974. Although the Nixon Administration provoked more such hearings (significant at the .05 level), divided government as such did not increase the number of hearings held to respond to particular executive actions or to address separation-of-powers questions generally. Divided government also did not affect the total number of hearings touching on constitutional issues. During the Reagan era, for example, Congress held fewer hearings than any other time in this study. It did not matter that Reagan explicitly campaigned against judicial activism, supported constitutional amendments on abortion and school prayer, opposed school busing, nominated Robert Bork and other conservatives to fill judicial vacancies, and much more. Congress, although taking the note of the "Reagan Revolution" in all sorts of ways, did not step up its hearings on constitutional issues in response to Reagan's efforts to reshape constitutional law.

CONCLUSION

There is more routine discussion of constitutional issues in congressional committee hearings than would have been expected given the state of the scholarly literature. Congressional scholars largely ignore the content of congressional hearings and certainly ignore constitutional discourse in Congress. Constitutional scholars are increasingly interested in extrajudicial constitutional interpretation, but they have only just begun to explore congressional efforts to interpret the Constitution and have not yet given sustained attention to the primary site of congressional deliberation, the committees.

In fact, Congress regularly hears testimony in committee hearings on constitutional issues. Although such hearings form only a small part of the overall

[26] See Keith E. Whittington, "Taking What They Give Us," *supra* note 24; Neal Devins, "The Judicial Safeguards of Federalism" (2004) 99 *Nw. U. L. Rev.* 1131.

[27] But see Keith E. Whittington, "Congress Before the Lochner Court" (2005) 85 *B. U. L. Rev.* 85.

congressional workload, they evidence a regularized mechanism for congressional constitutional deliberation and provide a useful window into the nature and extent of congressional engagement with constitutional issues. Congress engages a wide range of constitutional subjects. A surprising proportion of that legislative attention during these three decades was aimed at proposals to amend the Constitution, surprising given that no amendments were sent by Congress to the states for ratification during this period. Congress also gives regular consideration to the framework features of the constitutional system: federalism, separation of powers, and structural matters. The majority of its hearings, however, concerned matters of rights and liberties, although this broad category included a variety of more discrete issues.

Perhaps the most basic driving force behind congressional hearing activity involving the Constitution has been the internal demands of the legislature itself. In the Senate at least, hearings relating to constitutional issues are a partly a function of overall hearing activity. The legislative calendar imposes a rhythm on the hearing schedule, with most committee activity occurring in the year following an election. The Judiciary Committees have dominated congressional discussion of the Constitution throughout the last three decades of the twentieth century, but that dominance has become more pronounced in recent years as fewer committees engage in constitutional discussion and those that still do so less often. Unlike the Judiciary Committees, the power and prestige of other committees is not at all tied to their constitutional deliberations. For a variety of reasons, these committees have less and less reason to examine constitutional questions independently. Consequently, in comparison even to the 1970s, Congress is now far more dependent on the specialized expertise and interest of the Judiciary Committees to identify and vet constitutional issues.

In important ways, Congress appears to set its own constitutional agenda. Judicial activity factors into congressional discussions, but constitutional deliberation in committees does not require or follow obvious judicial spurs. Likewise, divided government exercised a surprisingly small force on congressional hearing activity. Although neither political party appears more inclined to consider constitutional issues in Congress, the two parties do differ somewhat in the types of issues that they have tended to raise for discussion. Whereas Republican majorities have tended to schedule hearings to consider proposals for constitutional reform, Democratic majorities have been more inclined to discuss separation-of-power issues and rights and liberties.

20 Democratic Decision Making as the First Principle of Contemporary Constitutionalism

Jeremy Webber

Most scholars treat "constitutionalism" as though it were entirely defined by conceptions of negative liberty. In their view, constitutionalism is about limits on government in the interest of human rights and constitutional order. Gordon Schochet's introduction to the 1979 Nomos volume on the subject is representative: The fundamental premises of constitutionalism are "limited government and the rule of law (that governments exist only to serve specified ends and properly function only according to specified rules)"; or again, "the hallmark of modern constitutionalism is its reliance upon formal limitations on political power that are directly tied to popular sovereignty."[1] Few political theorists today, few constitutional lawyers, would dissent from this definition. It shapes how we conceive of the domain of constitutional law, the internal values of that law, and the relationships between the various components of the state. Constitutional law is about constraining the state.

But constitutions are not primarily about limiting government. Their first role is to constitute government: to specify the processes by which public decisions are made. Any sensible approach to constitutionalism has to take seriously their role in defining the public voice – indeed in creating several complementary or competing public voices, for especially in a federal system, but also in nominally unitary systems, those institutional voices are plural. This is a positive role, a role that *enables* public action, not one that is adequately captured through the concept of limits. And in defining the public voice, democratic participation is fundamental. Indeed, it is the first principle of contemporary constitutionalism.

This chapter will explore that constitutive role, explaining why democratic decision making must be primary. It will also say something about what democracy must mean. To foreshadow an argument that will be developed at greater length, democratic participation must involve mechanisms through which real citizens can shape public decision making; it is not satisfied by ritualized appeals to an idealized "people" by decision makers over whom actual citizens have few practical means of influence (such as the courts). When one takes the principle seriously, it shapes in important ways how one addresses a host of constitutional questions, including the exercise of constitutional review by courts. At the most basic level, it

[1] Gordon J. Schochet, "Introduction: Constitutionalism, Liberalism, and the Study of Politics" in J. Roland Pennock and John W. Chapman, eds., *Nomos XX: Constitutionalism* (New York: New York University Press, 1979) 1 at 1 and 4.

forces one to see democratic institutions as the foundation of constitutionalism, not its enemy.

Now, there are others who have argued along similar lines. Jeremy Waldron's arguments are particularly germane, and I will refer to them often.[2] I should also note the work of John Hart Ely, Stephen Holmes, and others, who have argued forcefully that constitutions are about the definition of democratic institutions – about their formation, about their preconditions, not simply about their limitation.[3] At points my arguments will be particularly close to those of Stephen Holmes. But they differ from Ely's and Holmes's in one crucial respect. Those authors use the role of constitutions in constituting democratic institutions almost entirely as a way of justifying judicial review – as a way of justifying, for example, the judicial enforcement of rights of free speech. Their unique contribution lies in the argument that some forms of judicial review are fully consistent with, not antithetical to, democratic decision making.

This is true as far as it goes. But it is insufficient to acknowledge the importance of democratic participation only to encase it within the foundations of a theory of judicial review. The principle has to have some independent operation, constraining as well as justifying judicial decision making.[4] Otherwise one runs the risk of having the participation of citizens needlessly replaced, in important areas, by decisions taken in their name without any real popular participation, all justified on the basis of a democratic ethic that remains theoretical, never actual. Justifications for judicial review that are grounded in democracy have to keep constantly in mind the touchstone of democracy: the opportunity for real participation by the people themselves in the making of decisions. If that is done, some judicial review may well be desirable; indeed it will be essential. But the courts' role will be a distinctly limited one, always conditioned by the need to ensure popular participation.

I. THE ROLE OF THE COURTS

This chapter is primarily concerned with articulating that democratic principle. But it is useful to begin with a discussion of the role of the courts. My position is not resolutely anticourt. On the contrary, the judicial role is an essential component of a healthy constitutional system. This section sketches that role.

Many discussions of judicial review pose a simple contrast between judicial decision making and majoritarianism. People line up on one side or the other. They regard any decision of the courts as sacrosanct and any attempt to overturn it as tantamount to an attack on the independence of the judiciary; or they regard any decision of a simple majority of the legislators, on virtually any question, as unassailable. I argue for the primacy of democratic participation, but I do not

[2] Jeremy Waldron, *Law and Disagreement* (New York: Oxford University Press, 1999).

[3] John Hart Ely, *Democracy and Distrust: A Theory of Judicial Review* (Cambridge, Mass.: Harvard University Press, 1980); Stephen Holmes, *Passions and Constraint: On the Theory of Liberal Democracy* (Chicago: University of Chicago Press, 1995) especially Chapter 5.

[4] To be fair, there are elements of limitation in Ely's work, although his primary objective is to provide a foundation for what is, in the end, reasonably extensive judicial review. His disciples have often been less careful, emphasizing justification with little attention to limitation.

suggest the majority's opinion, on each and every question, should be considered conclusive, either in epistemological or in political terms.

First, I am acutely aware that all democratic institutions are artificial entities that create a collective voice that does not otherwise exist, at least not with the same level of clarity, consistency, and articulation. Indeed, the very voice of the "majority" will be different depending on how one defines the territorial scope of the society, the constituencies within which voting occurs, the electoral system, and the rules for representatives' deliberation and voting. The constructed character of the public voice is crucial to the analysis that follows – although, as I will insist, the fact that the voice is constructed does not mean that democratic participation is meaningless, inconsequential, or can be safely forgotten.

Second, there are, on any view, strong justifications for a significant judicial role in maintaining fundamental principles of the legal order – although, as will become clear, this role may take forms other than the judicial enforcement of constitutionally entrenched standards. So what are those justifications?

At the most basic level, the structure of democratic decision making itself has to be recognized and enforced. Courts must recognize – and, in doing so, inevitably help to define – the processes by which laws are made in the society. This is patent in countries marked by a federal division of powers, where each level of government has its own jurisdiction and the courts police the limits of each level's authority. But it is also true in societies like the United Kingdom, which have no written constitution and an all-powerful legislature. Even there, courts must have standards (albeit highly deferential) for recognizing when a valid law has been enacted. At the very least, the courts recognize Parliament as the oracle of that law. Indeed, they implicitly recognize the omnicompetence of that body through the doctrine of parliamentary sovereignty, and have more recently had to define the relationship between Parliament and the organs of the European Union.[5] Of course, these mechanisms have evolved through institutional interaction, contestation, and even a bloody civil war, not through a process of disembodied judicial rationality. It is a serious and naïve mistake to suggest that parliamentary power is the creature of the common law simply because that law has come to recognize legislative predominance.[6] Today's structure is a result of a dynamic equilibrium, in which the elected parliament has had, in recent centuries, by far the greatest weight in the process of definition. But nevertheless it is true that courts then proceed to act on presumptions about legal foundation and, in so doing, they confirm those presumptions, inscribing and reinscribing them in the law.

Some have argued that this role should be extended and that a number of preconditions for democratic participation, such as the apparatus of citizenship, constituencies, and electoral processes, or such fundamental political rights as freedom of speech, are properly the subject of judicial determination.[7]

[5] See especially *R. v. Secretary of State for Transport, ex parte Factortame Ltd (No. 2)* [1991] 1 A.C. 603 (H.L.).

[6] Hence the unreality, on this ground among others, of Trevor Allan's position: T. R. S. Allan, *Law, Liberty and Justice: The Legal Foundations of British Constitutionalism* (Oxford: Clarendon Press, 1993) especially at 10.

[7] This is a principal focus of Ely's argument: *supra* note 3, especially Chapter 5. Many others have argued along similar lines.

There is something to be said for this position, but, as we will see later in this chapter, not as much as is often assumed. In any ongoing democratic system, there are self-correcting mechanisms that form the principal buttress for democratic institutions. It is true that these mechanisms can be undermined or overpowered by the elected institutions themselves – but when that happens, it is doubtful whether review by the courts, without more, can stave off the collapse. There is no substitute for well-balanced, ongoing, participatory structures. There is no way of founding the system on bedrock outside political action. The courts themselves, after all, are not simply given but must be created, maintained, funded, and staffed. The value of judicial review of democratic preconditions therefore depends on a complex judgment about relative need and institutional capacity. In fact, in all societies, significant preconditions – such as the requirements for admission to citizenship, the mapping of constituencies, or the detail of the electoral process – are determined by means established under ordinary legislation, not constitutional prescription. Indeed, it is difficult to see how they could be determined by the text of the constitution without the system bogging down.

There is, however, another essential judicial role. Courts must maintain the rule of law, understood as procedural justice, including in particular the conscientious interpretation and (to the extent possible) impartial application of the law.

It has become common to read elaborate content into the rule of law, with fundamental rights imported into the very definition of law. Here I am adopting a narrower content to the principle, limited to processes for the public determination and public justification of the law, one dimension of which is fidelity to some reasonable reconstruction of the text when legislation is being interpreted and applied.[8]

This is an extension of the courts' role in recognizing the legislative process itself, for under a procedural conception of the rule of law, the courts are, above all, attempting to maintain the integrity of that law through to the point of implementation. The courts strive for an interpretation that is reasonably stable and that is consistent with the enactment (or, in the case of a common-law rule, that is consistent both with the body of the law generally as well as with norms taken to be implicit in a particular sphere of life).[9] Courts apply those rules in a manner sensitive to the specific situation at hand. A procedural conception of the rule of law therefore involves attention both to the general articulation of the law and to its instantiation in the particular case.

This dual obligation is, as Lon Fuller saw,[10] a necessary precondition to legislative efficacy. It permits legislatures to discuss and determine rules with reasonable confidence that the determinations will then be respected. It enables the orderly

[8] See Jeremy Webber, "The Foundation of the Rule of Law in the Public Justification of Governmental Action" (2002) 18 *Nanjing University Law Review (Nanjing Daxue Falu Pinlun)* 1. This article has been published only in Chinese. For an English version, please contact the author.

[9] This raises many complexities that cannot be resolved here. I addressed some of them in "A Judicial Ethic for a Pluralistic Age: Responding to Gender Bias, Class Bias, Cultural Bias in Adjudication" in Omid Payrow Shabani, ed. *Multiculturalism and the Law: A Critical Debate* (Cardiff: University of Wales Press, forthcoming, 2006).

[10] Lon L. Fuller, *The Morality of Law*, rev. ed. (New Haven: Yale University Press, 1969), especially at 33ff.

delegation of governmental authority. It allows for obedience on the part of citizens by ensuring that at least many aspects of the law are broadly determinate. It permits efficiency in social action by allowing some matters to be governed by authoritative determination, relieving citizens of the need to debate and decide each issue every time it arises. This rule of law is genuinely foundational, embedded in the very relationship among institutions of the state – indeed so foundational that its importance often disappears from view, hidden within the very idea of law.

It is also put to many subsidiary purposes, many profoundly important, which depend on the values of publicity and consistency fostered by the processes of legislative statement and judicial application. Above all, the mechanisms of the rule of law facilitate democratic responsibility by rendering norms and justifications express. It is these, for example, rather than constitutional stipulation, that have been the technique most used to increase the integrity of electoral processes: Legislation is employed to establish clear standards of electoral conduct, and these are then subjected to oversight or adjudicative assessment by electoral officers, commissions, or courts. This stabilizes the principles by which electoral conduct is governed, opens them to conscious debate, and demands a purposeful decision by the legislature before they can be dispensed with or contravened. The procedural conception of the rule of law serves as the essential precondition to democratic control and accountability. Throughout this chapter, we will see the use of similar mechanisms to address fundamental concerns.

This raises a further justification sometimes advanced for a strong judicial role: the countering of problems of agency inherent in representative democracy. Representative institutions act in the name of the society as a whole, but they are not that society. The interests of the representatives may diverge from those of the electorate. Constitutional provisions might therefore guard against representatives' self-interest coming in conflict with their duty of representation.

This is certainly true with respect to some fundamental aspects of the political structure. Different electoral systems, for example, can produce greater or lesser responsiveness, and it makes sense to take that into account in system design. Again, this does not necessarily require constitutional stipulation: Agency problems can be addressed through mechanisms instituted by ordinary legislation, such as ombudsmen or the office of the auditor-general.

Agency problems alone, however, will rarely be sufficient to justify substantive constitutional provisions such as balanced-budget amendments, requirements of a safe environment, or human rights protections. Agency problems are concerned with the divergence between representatives' personal interests and those of the population at large, a divergence produced by the autonomy with which representatives act between elections. But in the case of substantive guarantees, the relevant issues tend to be subject to genuine disagreement throughout the population, sometimes at the level of principle (as in balanced-budget amendments) and in any case at the level of application (as in rights guarantees). The aim of their proponents is not so much to make representatives more responsive as to put some matters beyond debate. There is little justification, on agency theory alone, for attempting to lock in substantive results and even less for conferring open-ended decision-making power on an even less representative agency, the courts.[11] Genuine issues of agency end up collapsing into questions of representation and mechanisms of administrative control, not substantive guarantees.

What about questions of minority rights, protecting individuals and groups who might otherwise be persecuted by the majority? This is, of course, the standard and most powerful justification for constitutional rights protections. It differs from the concern with problems of agency in that here, judicial review guards against dangers that lie within society itself – dangers that are not the result of the estrangement of the people's representatives but, on the contrary, a result of their very responsiveness to majority interests.

Again, there are many possible mechanisms for protecting rights. Some rely on the judicial review of constitutional provisions – although not all involve substantive rights protections: They may instead define the decision-making constituency so that the vulnerable minority itself has the power of decision (as in federal structures); they may institute voting rules that require the concurrence of members of the minority (as in requirements for special majorities or consociationalism); they may require processes that allow for nonbinding minority input (through consultation or joint deliberation). Some rely on the judicial review of standards established by ordinary legislation, thereby relying again on public decision making, public justification, and the rule of law. This is the case, for example, with bills of rights enshrined in statutory form or the use of human rights agencies or ombudsmen to promote respect for rights through legally sanctioned investigation and commentary. And, of course, there are options that do not involve the courts at all: participatory and deliberative processes that generate their own norms of mutual respect and self-limitation (these are most obvious in consociational processes but are common elsewhere; one could argue that such conditioning occurs in all forms of public deliberation[12]); the prior vetting of legislation by the executive or by a legislative committee to ensure respect for rights; and, above all, opportunities for public criticism and justification (and, of course, these may extend well beyond a country's boundaries, through the actions of international human rights agencies).[13]

11 Bruce Ackerman's justification for judicial review is essentially founded on problems of agency: Bruce A. Ackerman, *We the People: Foundations*, vol. 1 (Cambridge Mass.: Belknap Press of Harvard University Press, 1991). But he succeeds in making that argument only by postulating a stark contrast between "constitutional moments" in which the entire body of the people is engaged and ordinary politics in which political decisions are primarily in the hands of representatives. The courts defend the decisions of the former against the decisions of the latter. But note the burden imposed on the premise: There has to be stark difference in public engagement between the constitutional moments and ordinary politics; the former have to issue in outcomes that are highly determined, largely exempt from disagreement, and strongly consistent over time; and judges have to have privileged access to those transhistorical truths.

12 See, for example, Amartya Sen's argument that the defeat of the BJP in the 2004 Indian national election was caused by the population's revulsion at the complicity of the BJP's allies in sectarian violence against Muslims in Gujarat: Amartya Sen, "Passage to China," *The New York Review of Books* 51:19 (December 2, 2004) 61 at 65 n. 20.

13 See Jeremy Webber, "Institutional Dialogue between Courts and Legislatures in the Definition of Fundamental Rights: Lessons from Canada (and elsewhere)" [Webber, "Institutional Dialogue"] in Wojciech Sadurski, ed., *Constitutional Justice, East and West* (The Hague: Kluwer Law International, 2003) 61; Jeremy Webber, "A Modest (but Robust) Defence of Statutory Bills of Rights" (Paper presented to the workshop on "Protecting Human Rights in Australia: Past, Present and Future," Melbourne, Australia, December 10–12, 2003).

The choice among these devices again involves a complex judgment. It is not the case that because something involves the fundamental interests of a minority it should take judicially enforced constitutional form. After all, in instituting such a system one faces a paradox. The rights can only be established by political action – generally, in the established democracies, by democratic decision making. But if minority rights can be achieved by that means – if they enjoy sufficient popular support to be enacted – is it necessary that they be removed from democratic deliberation thereafter? One can imagine reasons why they might be. There may be considerable consensus on the importance of the rights in the abstract but real doubt as to whether the same consensus could exist in a particular case – because the majority may then be tempted to defect from the principle in order to derive an immediate advantage. Constitutionalization may forestall this problem by conferring the implementation of the rights on an independent entity. The adoption of the constitutional protections may be a condition precedent to the very formation of a community, with a potential minority declining to enter unless its fundamental interests are entrenched. (Indeed, the creation and stabilization of a democratic community raise a host of issues that fall beyond the scope of this chapter.) Or participants may simply worry that considerations that are very clear at one moment may be lost from view at some future time; judicial review may serve as one means of calling those considerations to mind.

There are potential reasons for constitutionalization. But there are also costs. If minority decision making is constitutionally entrenched – through autonomous self-government, guaranteed representation, or voting rules providing for a mutual veto – one had better be certain that the group's definition has staying power and that group differences are likely to remain acutely relevant to the issues to which the special provisions relate. Otherwise one skews the process of decision making unnecessarily. Constitutional limitations also pose important obstacles to governmental action, which can unnecessarily impede efficiency, generate expense, draw out the decision-making process, and in some cases prevent a decision altogether. They focus predominantly on the control of government, not its facilitation. They are structurally conservative, protecting what is, but doing little to transform. If one values collective decision making – if one believes that government action is positive, not merely a danger to be rigorously discouraged – one will want to be cautious in the enactment of constitutional safeguards.

But most importantly, constitutional provisions shift the locus of decision making from institutions that have real mechanisms for democratic participation (the legislatures) to structures that have few if any such mechanisms (the courts). That is their chief purpose. But as Jeremy Waldron has forcefully argued,[14] if the interpretation of rights remains subject to legitimate disagreement – especially if that disagreement is generalized within society and does not follow majority/minority lines – then the justification for removing the decision to the courts becomes much more problematic. These issues are often discussed as though they were simply about the protection of individual rights against majority power. Often in established democracies they are rather about the definition of rights: what rights are fundamental, what is the core purpose of the rights, how far the rights extend, and

[14] Waldron, *supra* note 2.

what should be the implication of the rights in a particular situation. The controversies are marked by disagreement over the very contours of the rights. Any justification for judicial review has to take that disagreement seriously. It must say why courts – of their nature unrepresentative and nonparticipatory – should have ultimate responsibility for making those decisions to the exclusion of more democratic processes.

This chapter argues that to resolve these issues of constitutional design at all adequately one has to take seriously the existence of disagreement within society. One returns to the fundamental problem of defining a public voice in the face of disagreement; and that challenge drives one back (as I will show) to the recognition of the fundamental importance of democratic participation. One may wish to define the public voice differently for different issues. Questions about the protection of rights might be transformed into questions of constituency, process, voting, and special majorities. Courts may play a crucial role in the outcome, recognizing it, enforcing it, and perhaps even making crucial substantive decisions within it. But note how that role is likely to be justified: as a means of facilitating democratic decision making or, perhaps, as a carefully framed surrogate for democratic decision making, but never as a mandate that can simply disregard the fundamental democratic principle of constitutionalism.

Finally, I should make clear that in arguing for a limited conception of judicial review, I am not suggesting that when one has entrenched a charter of rights one can justifiably ignore it. There are good reasons – tied to the fact that any viable public voice is constituted by rules – for working within the constitutional structures one has inherited, even if one's intention is to change them. If that structure contains a charter of rights, any interpretation has to be a plausible reading of that charter as a constitutionally entrenched instrument. But that said, a charter, like any legal instrument, has to be interpreted. It is perfectly legitimate – indeed, I will argue, mandatory – that judges give full weight to democratic principle in that act of interpretation.

II. THE FOUNDATIONAL PROBLEM OF DEFINING THE PUBLIC VOICE

This brings us to the heart of this chapter: the foundational challenge of defining a public voice. "Voice of the people," "will of the majority," "the views of society" – these are often naturalized, treated as though they simply exist. But they do not. They have to be consciously created through a rule-governed process of decision making. One of the principal functions of a constitution – indeed *the* principal function – is to fashion that public voice. Stephen Holmes says, quite rightly, that "It is meaningless to speak about popular government apart from some sort of legal framework which enables the electorate to express a coherent will."[15] Set procedures, set decision-making mechanisms are necessary to determine which position, among the welter of positions that actually exists in society, should be taken to express society's will. Those procedures define an authoritative voice, enabling the public to speak.

[15] Holmes, *supra* note 3 at 167.

I do not mean to denigrate political debate within society at large. That debate provides much of the content and texture of political interaction, identifying wrongs, formulating aspirations, consolidating positions, forming coalitions, producing leaders, and, through it all, building communities. Any adequate democratic theory has to be concerned with participation in society at large, and especially with the role of associational activity in promoting citizens' engagement. The design of democratic institutions should be adjusted to the contours of public debate, ensuring a broadly representative sample of opinion (associated with different geographical areas, ideological opinion, cultural and linguistic divisions) and when justified, providing for provincial autonomy or the self-government of national minorities.[16] But public institutions can never simply reflect public opinion for the simple reason that the public is never unanimous. Over a wide range of crucial issues – perhaps all issues of consequence – we disagree. Governmental structures have to provide means for aggregating opinion, producing determinate outcomes in the face of disagreement. Associational activity alone is insufficient for collective self-government. There also have to be ways to hammer out provisional solutions for the purposes of social action. Formal governmental structures permit this artificial, constructed position to be established.

Note that there is a range of means by which this position might be constructed, each potentially producing a different outcome and all compatible with democratic commitments broadly conceived. One might put every question to a referendum, so that each citizen has a direct say in what measure is adopted (at least ostensibly; this formulation ignores, of course, the means by which the question is determined, which can have significant influence over the outcome). One might elect representatives by a system of proportional representation, so that small parties have some chance of being elected, parties therefore represent relatively specific interests, and decision making occurs through a process of coalition-building within the legislature. One might use a first-past-the-post system, so that parties winning a plurality of the votes tend to get a majority of the seats, the parties themselves are coalitions, regional differences are exaggerated, and minority parties with national support are underrepresented. Each of these voting systems embodies core democratic values: structured opportunities for popular participation and rights of participation that are distributed essentially equally among all citizens. And yet the outcomes might well be very different. Moreover, this says nothing about the rules by which the representative assemblies, once formed, take their decisions (by consensus? by majority vote?), nor about the definition of the constituencies within which majorities are tabulated. Now, I am not suggesting that there are no grounds for judging among these various mechanisms. There clearly are. But although these grounds are related to core democratic values – one will want to draw on those values in arguing for one option over another – it would be difficult to claim that any one formula has a monopoly on democratic virtue or that any one system perfectly reflects the will of the people.[17]

[16] Jeremy Webber, *Reimagining Canada: Language, Culture, Community and the Canadian Constitution* (Montreal: McGill-Queen's University Press, 1994).

[17] Hence the wisdom of the Supreme Court of Canada's decision in *Reference re Prov. Electoral Boundaries (Sask.)*, [1991] 2 S.C.R. 158, which upheld an electoral map in which rural constituencies had systematically lower populations than urban ridings.

Any structure abstracts from the complexity on the ground. Any structure does some things better than others.

The fact that the public voice is artificial, is constructed in this way – that it does not reflect, in all their diversity, the views that exist within society – does not mean that it should be rejected as illegitimate. I will discuss the precise nature of democratic legitimacy in the next section of this chapter, but it is important to recognize the value of having *some* established mechanism for making authoritative public decisions, almost no matter what it is. This is the Hobbesian insight: the fact that orderly social life requires some mechanism for achieving political finality. It is a real benefit that such a mechanism exists, that it is knowable, and that it results in decisions that are then promulgated and consistently implemented. It means that issues are settled in an orderly and predictable fashion, without having every answer depend on who can marshal the most thugs on the day. Members know what the settled position is and can govern themselves accordingly. Moreover, any real form of citizens' participation – even in nondemocratic governments – is dependent on the existence of stable processes so that one knows when and where to make one's interventions.

This is why there is good reason to work through existing procedures: precisely because they exist, even if one would much prefer to have different processes. It is why, in the transition from communist to postcommunist societies in eastern Europe, democrats generally decided to work through the communist constitutional forms (or to subject them to distortions that were minor in scope, although important in effect), even though these forms were considered radically illegitimate, and even though their use meant that the apparatchiks had much more influence than any democrat would have liked them to have. Those societies had experienced genuinely revolutionary transformations, and they knew just how risky unmediated appeals to "popular will" might be.[18] It was much better to have the existing and imperfect institutions than to have none at all. There are times when wholesale rejection is appropriate – although even then, one will want to weigh the cost. And I will obviously argue for a higher standard of legitimacy in democratic institutions than mere existence! But the fact remains that one has to have *some* institutions if one wants to have the orderly formation of a public voice. That recognition creates a high threshold that any argument that one should simply ignore institutions – either because they are illegitimate or because they are worse than other institutions one might envisage – has to cross.

An essential role of constitutions is therefore to form this voice – to provide ways of overcoming the diverse and perhaps opaque interplay of actual voices within society in order to establish a public position. Note what is involved here. The "overcoming" does not do away with the disagreement. It does not eliminate plurality. Those disagreements persist in society and may provide the foundation for continued criticism of the outcome. That criticism may in the future win the day. Moreover, one can envisage situations in which a single position is not imposed – where members of society agree to disagree, defer matters to a future time, or

[18] A. Arato, "Dilemmas Arising from the Power to Create Constitutions in Eastern Europe" in M. Rosenfeld, ed., *Constitutionalism, Identity, Difference, and Legitimacy: Theoretical Perspectives* (Durham, N.C.: Duke University Press, 1994) 165, especially at 178–81.

recognize spheres of autonomous decision making in their midst. Having a single public position will sometimes be optional, and these considerations may have an impact on the voting practices one institutes (permitting subunits of the society to adopt different solutions, or requiring a higher degree of assent for certain kinds of decisions). But if one does wish to have a single public position on some matters – if one wants to have some rules that bind individuals who would rather flout those rules, if one wants to have means for achieving collective objectives across any segment of any conceivable society – that position will have the characteristics described here. It will be artificial and, in principle, provisional.

The public outcome should not be taken to be dispositive of the fundamental controversy. That controversy continues. One can strongly support the outcome without taking it to be epistemically correct. The majority position may have no better claim to truth than any other – or at least, its force does not depend on any such claim. It deserves respect not because it is true, but because it has the best warrant to be the position of society – because it is the product of the mechanism used to fashion a public position in that society. Its force is a function of the simple desire to live together in an ordered society, despite our disagreements.[19]

This theory of political decision making is nonfoundationalist. But it is not necessarily nonfoundationalist in an epistemological sense. It does not deny that there is truth. On the contrary, an individual citizen may very well recognize the force of a democratic outcome and yet believe that an entirely different position is true. Some citizens may accept a nonfoundational concept of truth; some may not. The theory is nonfoundationalist in a political sense.[20] It accepts the premise that for political purposes, in a society in which people fundamentally disagree, there has to be some mechanism for resolving disagreement – or there is no society.[21] That mechanism cannot entirely depend on the determination of what is true, for often what is true is precisely what is in dispute, and it remains in dispute throughout (although some winnowing out of the false, some consolidation of what one believes to be true,

[19] It is simplistic to found democratic legitimacy merely on the coincidence between governmental actions and our own preferences, supporting government only when it is in a better position to judge how to attain our objectives than we ourselves would be. See, for example, Joseph Raz, *Ethics in the Public Domain: Essays in the Morality of Law and Politics* (Oxford: Oxford University Press, 1994). These approaches neglect the extent to which living in society is itself a good, which requires the institution of public measures that we ourselves might not choose if left to our own devices. They may do so because they pay insufficient attention to what being left to our own devices means. They overestimate the extent to which we can attain our ends without the benefit of society.

[20] I accept Rawls's instinct that political legitimacy is founded on a basis that is more restricted than our normative arguments generally, and that that difference flows from the need to create common institutions among people who have different normative doctrines: John Rawls, *Political Liberalism* (New York: Columbia University Press, 1993). Unlike Rawls, however, I do not think that the basis is best understood as a "political conception of justice" that everyone shares and that is founded on overlapping consensus. Rawls's position puts the requirement of substantive agreement unrealistically and unnecessarily high. The basis is more rudimentary than that, consisting simply of the need to have a determinate solution if one wants to live in an ordered society. The position adopted may represent a rough aggregation of divergent views within society – indeed, this is highly desirable – but it is unlikely to amount to consensus or agreement.

[21] Compare Waldron, *supra* note 2 at 246–8, where he notes that Richard Wollheim's paradox – that there will often be conflict between our own sense of right and the outcome that emerges from any process of decision making – is general, affecting any process of decision making in a situation of disagreement. This is not problematic if we value a society in which people live together and yet remain free to come to their own ideas of right.

may be an extremely valuable part of the process; thus the hearing of evidence, the conducting of investigations, the attempt to marshal opinions, and deliberation are all important parts of good governmental practices). Rather, the legitimacy of the mechanism depends on the need for some way of artificially aggregating opinion, if in a given society one is going to have any public position at all.

Political decision making – and by extension political philosophy – therefore has two components. First, there is the set of questions about what is true, what is just, what is good, according to whatever lodestar particular members of society accept or can persuade others to accept. Those arguments explore the fundamental substance of political questions, with whatever insight and honesty the participants can muster. But there is a second set of questions that has to do with the hammering out of a common position: Given that we continue to disagree, what should we do? Should we decide this matter now or defer it to a later time? Should we count heads, so that whichever position has the most support becomes, for the moment, the position of our group? The two sets of questions each have their own integrity; they each have their own standards of justification. Both are necessary in any well-grounded society. They should not be collapsed into one another.[22]

Finally, note that this analysis is not limited to legislative or executive institutions. It is just as applicable to judicial institutions. Courts too have no direct claim on truth. They too have mechanisms for constructing an artificial position in situations of continuing disagreement. They aggregate what is often discordant opinion, attempting to generate agreement through processes of evidence-gathering and discussion but in the end relying on a show of hands to resolve the issue. This is the great truth in Jeremy Waldron's quip that courts too are majoritarian institutions; it is just that very few people get to vote.[23] Courts are constituted in unique ways and make their decisions through distinctive procedures. These characteristics make courts particularly good at certain roles and poor at others. But they too result in the artificial creation of a single public voice in the face of what is often continuing disagreement.

III. DEMOCRATIC DECISION MAKING AS THE FIRST PRINCIPLE OF CONTEMPORARY CONSTITUTIONALISM

To this point, I have explored the value of having some mechanism for generating an authoritative public voice, but of course there are good reasons for preferring certain mechanisms over others. This section argues that democratic participation must be the predominant principle.

There are many conceptions of democracy – some highly detailed in their prescriptions, others more schematic; some focusing on formal mechanisms for decision making, others requiring the engagement of society as a whole; some emphasizing representatives' choice of a particular option, others emphasizing the discussion that precedes a choice. These conceptions, and the debates that

[22] This too is a recurrent theme in Jeremy Waldron's work. See, for example, ibid. at 3, 213ff., and 245. Compare also Guido Calabresi's use of a comparable distinction: "The Supreme Court 1990 Term, Foreword: Antidiscrimination and Constitutional Accountability (What the Bork–Brennan Debate Ignores)" (1991) 105 *Harv. L. Rev.* 80.

[23] Waldron, *supra* note 2 at 15 and 306–7, and generally Chapter 8.

surround them, are immensely valuable. They have an important impact on the design of democratic structures and on the nature of representation. They certainly have an impact on the quality of decisions that result. But they all tend to be more demanding than is necessary for my purposes. In this context, I am interested in the most elementary grounds for preferring democratic participation – grounds that may be very broadly shared within society, grounds that do not presuppose too rich and therefore too contentious a theory of democracy, grounds that leave the choice among particular democratic structures open.

For these purposes, the central feature of democracies is the simple right of citizens to participate in public decision making on a basis of rough equality, where each citizen's voice counts (in principle if not always in practice) roughly the same as every other citizen's. The fundamental justification for this method of decision making is first, the inveterate existence of disagreement within society, and second, the lack of sufficient grounds for systematically preferring any one citizen's views over any other's in resolving that disagreement. Democracy entitles each citizen to have their own voice in public decision making (by some mechanism such as voting), and it does so on a basis of equality.[24]

The emphasis on equality perhaps requires more explanation, for as individuals we do not believe that all people are equally insightful or informed; we do prefer some views over others; and in all systems of democratic decision making, different people in fact have differential influence over the outcome. The emphasis on equality does not relate to our judgments as citizens on specific matters. In those judgments, we of course respect the views of some more than others and are willing to entrust our institutions to some people, not to others. We exercise our rights to participate and cast our ballots accordingly. The emphasis on equality relates instead to the structure of those participatory rights. There, in the formal mechanisms for producing provisional outcomes in the face of disagreement, we do observe a strict equality. We do this because there is insufficient basis for preferring, *a priori*, one person's voice over another. This is true in part because just as we disagree over substantive policies, we also disagree over the range of factors appropriate to deciding those policies.[25] If we based rights of participation on who was best qualified to decide, we would be forced into an infinite regress. We can, however, agree on our common identity as citizens and to the fact that we will all be affected to a roughly equivalent extent by the range of decisions made by government. This supports equality in rights of participation as the foundational element of any mechanism for resolving social disagreement.

This commitment can be buttressed by richer definitions of human equality, or by recognition of the fact that widely distributed rights of participation open public decision making to the full range of experience within society.[26] We can seek to improve our public culture by actively cultivating educated citizens and by fostering deeper engagement and deliberation within society at large. I favor

[24] Ibid. at 113–16.

[25] See Waldron's discussion of plural voting schemes, ibid. at 115–16, where he notes the difficulty in justifying differential voting rights without encountering precisely the intractable problems of disagreement that voting is intended to solve.

[26] See, for example, the truth-based defense of democracy in Cheryl Misak, *Truth, Politics, Morality: Pragmatism and Deliberation* (London: Routledge, 2000) especially at 96–7.

initiatives along all these lines. But I am reluctant to build my foundational defense of democratic decision making on them. As the democratic theory becomes richer, it also becomes more contentious and less widely shared. We lose sight of the compelling force of the foundational principle that political participation should be widely distributed on a basis of equality, because we overdefine the values that those institutions should express. I want to keep the focus squarely on the compelling force of that foundational principle, without cluttering it up with more tendentious content. A wide range of structures would be consistent with that principle. When making our decision within that range, we will discuss the relative merits of different procedures, but that should not obscure the fundamental touchstone of democratic legitimacy.

There is a second reason for focusing, in the first instance, only on the foundational principle. If we found our entire theory on a richer definition of democracy, we may be tempted to build extensive elements of that theory into the structure of the political order, beyond the reach of democratic deliberation and decision. Thus, we find ourselves in a variation of the problem noted above, attempting to set outside the system matters that are legitimately a matter of disagreement which should be debated and discussed within. We become seduced away from the foundational commitment, attempting to stack the deck in the very institutions that are designed to settle social disagreement.[27]

Now, the pared-down vision of democracy presented here strikes some people as unacceptably light on substantive content, especially people who fail to take disagreement seriously or who are so confident of their own wisdom that they do not see why they should have to take into account the views of the hoi polloi. Those people are especially prone to want to replace democracy's ostensibly uncritical aggregation of opinions with a self-consciously rationalistic process, generally that of the courts, at least in the case of certain important decisions. But that would come at a serious cost. It would foreclose the participation of most of society in the decision, removing those citizens from the formation of the public position. There would be no guarantee that the positions they would espouse, their interests, their opinions as to the just result, would be factored into the process. The number of actual decision makers would be reduced; there would be no concrete mechanism for assuring the accountability of those decision makers to a broader public; the number of people who could address the court would be limited; and the kinds of submissions that could be made would be limited. The inquiry as a whole would be constricted, and that constriction would exclude.

Recourse to such rationalistic processes is often justified by drawing attention to the defects of participatory processes, particularly the lack of power that many citizens feel, indeed often the lack of meaningful participation, in elections. These

[27] This is one of the dangers in approaches like those of Ely and Holmes, *supra* note 3, which invoke democracy only to focus primarily on judicial review. There is a similar danger in theories of democratic deliberation that issue in strong constitutional prescriptions, which try to set prior conditions that guarantee outcomes that the theorist finds acceptable, but which in the process foreclose much of the content of deliberation. See, for example, Joshua Cohen and Joel Rogers, *On Democracy: Toward a Transformation of American Society* (Harmondsworth, Middlesex: Penguin Books, 1983); Joshua Cohen, "Deliberation and Democratic Legitimacy" in Alan Hamlin and Philip Pettit, eds., *The Good Polity: Normative Analysis of the State* (Oxford: Blackwell, 1989) 17.

defects are profoundly important, deserve our attention, and justify active engagement in the reform of electoral and legislative processes. But they do not dislodge the fundamental justification for democratic decision making. Whatever the imperfections of those processes, they still involve more direct and equal means of influencing the outcome than are available to citizens-at-large before the courts. They afford a share in direct control over the identity of the decision makers, and they often provide, for the great run of citizens, an opportunity to speak that is not available before the courts. In fact, the sense of disempowerment and lack of meaningful participation that people feel in democratic institutions is often a direct result of the fact that in those forums, influence is distributed equally among a very large class of people. It is precisely the equality of access that makes citizens feel that they have little effective say. There may well be solutions to that problem, through decentralized decision making or through more carefully structured deliberation.[28] But I cannot see how that problem is resolved by foreclosing participation altogether – by having the decisions made by a small group of people, largely insulated from the rest of society. Those who most strongly favor the courts are often precisely the individuals who enjoy a disproportionate say in that forum: lawyers and legal academics – the privileged citizens of a rarefied and selective republic.

In fact, there is something disingenuous in the argument that decisions should be made by courts because of the defects in participation in the democratic organs of government when it is precisely the antimajoritarian nature of the courts that is their most notable (and lauded) feature. There may be reason to confer certain decisions on the courts, but we should be clear that by doing so we are restricting the range of participants, not extending it. If we care about the principles that justify democratic institutions – self-government; equality in the fashioning of a public voice – we must continue to care about the democratic elements of the state.

Nor should we uncritically accept that the courts make their decisions according to a pristine rationalism. Their procedures do include the systematic testing of claims, the probing of assertions, an aspiration to consistency, express justification, and focused attention to the facts of a particular case. Indeed, the insulation of the courts from the influence of citizens-at-large is designed precisely to foster these qualities, which are rightly considered to be essential to their core functions. But those procedures also limit the range of information that comes before them and shape the issues in ways that privilege certain outcomes and discourage others. To take one example, they tend to structure disputes as existing between two parties, the plaintiff and the defendant, and therefore tend to neglect the interests of individuals who are not parties to the action. Democratic institutions too have mechanisms for fact-finding and popular input. They extend the range of information available; in some respects they provide a stronger basis for deliberation and decision. Moreover, the fact that in courts only the judge makes the decision inevitably means that his or her views have disproportionate impact. The reason of the court is not a disembodied reason, but one marked by the processes and personages of the court.

[28] James Fishkin's experiments with deliberative polling are intriguing. See, for example, Bruce Ackerman and James Fishkin, *Deliberation Day* (New Haven: Yale University Press, 2004).

Turning now to participatory institutions, there is often a tendency to say that because they are founded on the equality of citizens, because they value effective participation and full deliberation, their outcomes should be controlled by some external agency (again the courts?) to ensure that they comply with our best understanding of those principles. Thus are born what Stéphane Perrault has called teleological approaches to democracy, where participation is judged by what are taken to be democracy's proper ends.[29] In some variants of this approach, participation itself tends to fall out of the picture. This is particularly so with theories that suggest that participation is not important as long as the outcomes are the same as those that participation would have produced – and thus it is acceptable to have deliberation by proxy, or to have levels of voter turnout that provide a representative sample of the population. This line of reasoning is seductive, for there is no doubt that the primacy accorded participation is justified by an appeal to broader values, such as the moral equality of persons, and one of the central roles of participation is to produce acceptable outcomes. But we should be careful, for this reasoning again has the potential to displace decision making from the citizens themselves to those who judge whether the processes have adequately fulfilled their promise. The fact of participation is downgraded, replaced by its idea. At the limit, the structure becomes a mere simulacrum of democracy, in which democracy is considered too important, too precious, perhaps even too fragile, to be entrusted to its citizens. For the principle of democratic participation to have reality, it has to operate at a broad level of generality, protecting actual citizen engagement but declining to direct how that engagement should be exercised. Otherwise, an ideal image of participation can cause us to neglect its reality.

The maintenance of practical, concrete mechanisms of participation – in which real, not just notional citizens have their say – is therefore indispensable. This implies substantial tolerance for imperfections of reasoning, engagement, and outcome.[30] Democracy is necessarily messy. It does not conform to an ideal set of principles precisely because it deals with real people, real processes, in all their imperfection and disaccord. Moreover, it implies substantial tolerance for different institutional structures, all within a very broad conception of citizen involvement and citizen equality: for different ways of blending direct and representative democracy, for different electoral systems, for different ways of defining constituencies, and for different voting rules. Democracy is justified as a response to social disagreement, and disagreement applies as much to the design of social institutions, to the detailed justification of decision-making procedures, as to substantive outcomes.

[29] Stéphane Perrault, *Le contrôle judiciare du droit de vote et d'éligibilité sous le régime de la Charte canadienne des droits et libertés: défis et limites de la légalité* (LL.D. thesis, Université de Montréal, 1997) [unpublished] at iv. For one example of a very large genus, which might also serve as an object lesson, see Samuel Freeman, "Constitutional Democracy and the Legitimacy of Judicial Review" (1990–1991) 9 *Law and Philosophy* 327.

[30] I do not accept the substantive limitations on justification that Rawls would require as part of his notion of "public reason": Rawls, *supra* note 20, at 212ff. It may well be wise for citizens to use arguments that appeal to people of differing beliefs, but to suppose that the nature of those arguments can be determined in advance and that nonconforming arguments can and should be screened out is to impose artificial and unnecessary restrictions on precisely the process that is intended to resolve disagreement. See Jennifer Nedelsky, "Legislative Judgment and the Enlarged Mentality: Taking Religious Perspectives," Chapter 5 in this volume.

One cannot escape disagreement by adopting a strict distinction between ends and means. The latter too are subject to vigorous debate.

This raises a potential problem of circularity. Democratic procedures are designed as a response to disagreement – as an acceptable way of fashioning a common public voice in the face of continuing dispute. But those procedures themselves embody very specific and controversial choices. How can they be justified without stepping outside the system or without making the outcome dependent on the very system that is in question? This problem has precise analogues in the day-to-day functioning of democratic states, where today's legislatures determine important aspects of the very makeup of the democratic process, even the structure of their own constituencies (through the process of revising electoral boundaries) or, in the case of the UK Parliament, the length of time between elections. Perrault has called this the problem of "auto-normativity."[31]

But there is no escape from this problem. No institution has absolute foundations beyond the reach of political disagreement. This is as true of the courts as it is of any other institution. The essential point is that auto-normativity necessarily applies to society as a whole: Society is in the business of regulating itself – of developing and then enforcing its own norms on itself.[32] The only way out of the circle is not to seek to eliminate political contention, but rather to exploit the potential for reflexivity within society itself. I believe this requires the simultaneous pursuit of two avenues.

First, one should reinforce – not eliminate – the impact of society-at-large on the institutions: One should actively foster the development of reflexive mechanisms within the system so that they can promote, over time, the very evolution of those institutions. In other words, one should support (to adopt Dicey's terminology[33]) the political sovereignty of the populace over the formal institutions of the state, subjecting institutions to democratic control. This is precisely what mechanisms for democratic participation do. And this approach is consistent with the justificatory language we commonly use to support social institutions. Virtually everyone appeals to "society" or to the people's "assent" to justify constitutional arrangements, including limitations on democratic institutions.[34] I simply suggest that we take that rhetoric seriously, refusing to reduce it to empty myth, but instead paying attention to the actual mechanisms available to real citizens to make their voices heard.[35]

That objective is consistent with a second avenue, which attends to the stability, transparency, and orderly nature of the edifice. We should never fall into the trap of thinking that the populace can, without the mediation of institutions, speak with a

31 See Perrault, *supra* note 29 at 77ff.

32 This point is made by Jon Elster, *Solomonic Judgements: Studies in the Limits of Rationality* (Cambridge: Cambridge University Press, 1989) at 196, and by Waldron, *supra* note 2 at 260–1.

33 A. V. Dicey, *Introduction to the Study of the Law of the Constitution*, 10th. ed. by E. C. S. Wade (London: Macmillan, 1959) at 73.

34 Cf. Holmes, *supra* note 3 at 172: "The constitutional 'limits' they [the Founding Fathers] imposed, of course, remain morally binding and factually in force only so long as citizens currently alive find them appealing and continue to impose them voluntarily upon themselves."

35 My gratitude to Kevin Tuffin for having repeatedly and successfully urged this position upon me. See Kevin Tuffin, *The Sovereignty of the People: A Political Interpretation of a Constitutional Principle* (Ph.D. thesis, University of Sydney, 2002) [unpublished].

coherent voice. Structures are necessary to construct a public position, and indeed the very efficacy and equality of citizens' participation depend on knowable and responsive institutional forms. Thus, elements discussed throughout this chapter, such as defined constituencies, electoral systems, voting rules, and the adoption by courts of a procedural conception of the rule of law, are all essential to meaningful and effectual participation. My argument is simply that these need to be justified always in relation to a fundamental principle of democratic decision making – and indeed generally achieved through democratic action. That principle will have an impact both on the extent of the measures adopted and on the constitutional form they take. Note, for example, that each of the elements listed above can be achieved – and in most countries is achieved – without constitutional entrenchment. Ordinary legislative action is a crucial contributor to the constitution of the public voice.

This approach does require substantial trust that reflexive structures will produce mechanisms of self-correction – that one will not be caught in a downward spiral of exclusion and constraint, driven by the self-interest of those who happen to hold the levers of power. Indeed, one can imagine that such a downward spiral might justify extraordinary constraints on new polities, where responsive institutions and a democratic ethic have yet to be established. But one should be careful even there not to impose constraint too readily. The limits have to be vested somewhere. Is the controlling institution any better? And will the imposition of external constraints promote the development of responsive institutions and a democratic ethic? Perhaps. But it is a delicate judgment.[36]

There is much less reason for constraint, much more reason for trust, in established democracies. After all, in many of those countries those very institutions were established through the progressive development of democratic mechanisms, driven by precisely the kind of responsive practices I describe. That was true, for example, of the extension of the franchise or of controls over electoral abuses – abuses, in other words, at the very heart of representatives' self-interest, precisely the kind of issue on which one would expect the interests of those already in office to diverge from those of the populace. Opinion in the population at large can play a real function in conditioning the attitudes of rulers, even before full institutional controls have been put in place. There are very significant self-correcting mechanisms.

Those mechanisms are driven by a dynamic roughly like this: Elections exist to establish the legitimacy of the government, so that it can depend to some degree on the willing acquiescence of the population. But elections can only have that legitimating function if representatives' conduct bears some tolerable relationship to their claims. As a result, there is inherent pressure (sometimes strong, sometimes attenuated, always present) pushing those in power to live up to their rhetoric. This is the truth behind Holmes's observation, drawn from Bodin, that self-binding can increase, not decrease, a monarch's power.[37] This points toward the reality of control exercised by a "political sovereign," even when the formal power of decision making is exercised through representative institutions. It is misleading to treat

[36] See Wojciech Sadurski, *Rights Before Courts: A Study of Constitutional Courts in Postcommunist States of Central and Eastern Europe* (Berlin: Springer, 2005).

[37] Holmes, *supra* note 3 at 113ff.

governmental structures as purely static and self-contained, only capable of virtue when subjected to formal, externally enforced controls.

And in any case, what choice do we have but to rely on self-correcting mechanisms? The hope of resorting to institutions founded on pure principle drawn from outside the realm of politics is a chimera. It is much better that we recognize the human character of our institutions, recognize that they depend on the ultimate support of their citizens, and seek to design and work with them accordingly.

IV. CONCLUSION

Democratic decision making is the first principle of contemporary constitutionalism. What difference does this make? I suggest three broad consequences.

First, the approach presented here reinforces the now common arguments that one should resist the constitutionalization of substantive ends, relying instead on legislative action to achieve those objectives. It builds this argument on the foundation identified by Waldron – the existence of deep-seated disagreement within society, and the good reasons for preferring democratic institutions as the primary means for resolving that disagreement. It differs from some criticisms of judicial review in that it does not spring from a generalized hostility to the courts. On the contrary, it recognizes that the courts have an essential role in enforcing the structure of democratic decision making and maintaining a procedural conception of the rule of law. These are fundamentally important tasks – tasks that we have tended to lose from view in our preoccupation with judicially enforced substantive guarantees. Taking democratic decision making seriously pushes us back toward more fine-grained responses to the challenges of rights and democratic participation, responses that are less dependent on entrenched guarantees and more attentive to the blending of different institutional forms.

Second, when constitutional rights do exist, this approach suggests an interpretive stance that is more cognizant of the prevalence of disagreement and more modest in its definition of the rights. It suggests, for example, an approach to rights that treats them as minimum guarantees, setting only the most egregious conduct beyond the judgment of the legislature. It suggests that courts should defer to legislative judgments when the latter are based on a complex balancing of considerations. And it supports practices for the drafting and interpretation of constitutional guarantees that do not seek to define the right exhaustively but instead leave the definition at a broad level of generality, so that the legislature can fashion its own solutions within those parameters.[38]

Finally, the approach sketched here encourages us to refocus on the design of representative institutions. If democratic decision making is indispensable, we should ensure that our structures embody a defensible theory of representation; that they are efficient and free from undue influence; that they foster broad participation, including among disadvantaged groups; and that they permit deliberation among a large portion of the citizenry, prompting the moral development that flows from the encounter with another's opinions and another's experience. There are no shortcuts. The promise of constitutionally entrenched standards – that we can

[38] Webber, "Institutional Dialogue," *supra* note 13 at 78–80.

reach directly for a perfect justice without having to engage our fellow citizens in debate – is false. In a diverse society – a society in which people disagree – we have no alternative but to take our compatriots' views seriously, seeking through persuasion and the aggregation of views by democratic means to fashion a workable, and perhaps even just, system of government.

ACKNOWLEDGMENTS

My thanks to Marcia Barry, Christina Godlewska, and Tony Price for their able research assistance and to Marcia Barry, Christina Godlewska, Tsvi Kahana, and Andrew Petter for their trenchant comments on earlier drafts of this chapter.

21 Legislative Constitutionalism in a System of Judicial Supremacy

Daniel A. Farber

To speak of legislative constitutionalism in the American context may seem paradoxical. After all, America famously provides the model of judicial supremacy.[1] Certainly, compared with the Westminster model in which the legislature has unlimited sovereignty, legislative constitutionalism seems far removed from the American scheme. Yet, a little reflection reveals that the American system actually contains important fragments of legislative constitutionalism. That is, Congress has a number of means for shaping, massaging, and sometimes even supplanting judicial doctrine, putting an important gloss on judicial supremacy.

Equally importantly, major parts of the fundamental structure of government are due to congressional action rather than constitutional text or judicial interpretation. Such legislation provides parts of the basic frame of government, and gain their stability (as in Westminster constitutionalism) from custom rather than judicial enforcement. In English usage, these structural rules would undoubtedly be called "constitutional." If these rules are not part of what Americans call constitutional law, they at least deserve to be called quasi-constitutional.

Paradoxically, judicial supremacy itself could be considered a matter of quasi-constitutional law, due in no small part to Congress's long-standing stance toward the federal courts. Congress created the lower federal courts, without which the Supreme Court would lack reliable enforcers of its decrees. In the first Judiciary Act, Congress authorized judicial review before John Marshall was even appointed to the Supreme Court. Congress has refrained from using the impeachment power to curb judicial activism, as it has largely refrained from using its control over Supreme Court jurisdiction to rein in the Court. By now, this convention of legislative non-interference may have risen to what would be considered the constitutional level under the Westminster model – in other words, it may be part of the unwritten American constitution.[2]

[1] For debate about the desirability of the American version of judicial supremacy – but no debate about its existence – see Larry Alexander and Frederick Schauer, "Defending Judicial Supremacy: A Reply" (2002) 17 *Const. Comm.* 455; Larry Kramer, "The Supreme Court 2000 Term: Foreword: We the Court" (2001) 115 *Harv. L. Rev.* 4; Jack Balkin and Sanford Levinson, "Understanding the Constitutional Revolution" (2001) 87 *Va. L. Rev.* 1045.

[2] Some thirty years ago, Tom Grey broached the possible existence of an unwritten U.S. constitution in Thomas C. Grey, "Do We Have an Unwritten Constitution?" (1975) 27 *Stan. L. Rev.* 703. His focus was on judicial protection for rights like abortion that are not specifically enumerated in the Constitution.

I. JUDICIAL VERSUS LEGISLATIVE SUPREMACY

The Supreme Court likes to proclaim itself as the definitive interpreter of the Constitution. In *Cooper v. Aaron*,[3] all nine Justices individually signed an opinion proclaiming that the Court's constitutional doctrines were the supreme law of the land. More recently, the joint opinion in *Planned Parenthood v. Casey*[4] emphasized the Court's role in settling national controversies, arguing that such decisions must receive extraordinary respect lest the Court's authority be undermined. Yet the Court's self-proclaimed supremacy has never been without its critics. For example, as early as 1819, Thomas Jefferson denounced what he viewed, even then, as the Court's pretensions to supremacy. Like later critics of the Court, he argued that if judges had the final word over the meaning of the Constitution, they could reshape the Constitution like wax to fit their own preferences.[5]

Despite continuing criticism, judicial supremacy is a basic fact about the American constitutional regime. Even its most stringent critics acknowledge that it reflects the popular understanding. Judicial supremacy has not, however, completely ousted Congress from constitutional matters. To understand the constitutional role of Congress today, we need to begin by examining why Congress failed to achieve a dominant role in constitutional interpretation despite the powerful example of English constitutionalism. We then need to understand the idea of judicial supremacy more clearly, in order to see why judicial supremacy does not fill all of the available space for constitutional interpretation. This will then set the stage for considering in detail the specific roles that Congress continues to play in American constitutionalism.

A. The Westminster model as nonstarter

When the Constitution of the United States went into effect in 1789, it was conceivable that American constitutional interpretation might take different turns. It might end up in the hands of the courts. Or it might have reposed entirely in Congress, or at least with Congress having the final word on constitutional issues. In effect, any real enforcement of constitutional limitations would be entirely political. It is this possibility that some current scholars seek to resurrect.[6] But in the antebellum era, this possibility lacked serious political support.

Strikingly, none of the major national figures in the early Republic believed that Congress was the sole judge of the constitutionality of its own actions. Even Jefferson, no friend of federal courts, did not give Congress the final word on constitutional issues. Instead, he believed that "each of the three departments has equally the right to decide for itself what is its duty under the constitution, without any regard to what the others may have decided for themselves under a similar

[3] 358 U.S. 1, 17–18 (1954). For background on the case, see Daniel A. Farber, "The Supreme Court and the Rule of Law: *Cooper v. Aaron* Revisited" [1982] *U. Ill. L. Rev.* 387.

[4] 505 U.S. 833 (1992).

[5] Letter from Thomas Jefferson to Judge Spencer Roane, September 6, 1819, in Thomas Jefferson, *Writings* (New York: Library of America, 1984) 1426–7.

[6] See Jeremy Waldron, *Law and Disagreement* (Oxford: Clarendon Press, 1999); Mark Tushnet, *Taking the Constitution Away From the Courts* (Princeton, N.J.: Princeton University Press, 1999).

question."[7] Thus, even the Court's opponents were not willing to give Congress the unlimited sovereignty ascribed to the English Parliament.

The Civil War changed a great deal in American constitutional thinking, but it did not pave the way for congressional hegemony. Even the Reconstruction Congress, as aggressive as it was in flexing its muscles in the aftermath of the Civil War, was unwilling to place all of its hopes in the hands of its own successors. In particular, the ultimate form of the Fourteenth Amendment seems to reflect a distrust of future legislation. Representative John Bingham's original draft of the Fourteenth Amendment simply empowered Congress to protect various individual rights against the states (like the current §5 of the Amendment). This draft was put on hold after the following comment by Representative Hotchkiss:

> Now, I desire that the very privileges for which the gentlemen [Bingham] is contending shall be secured to the citizens; but I want them secured by a constitutional amendment that legislation cannot override. Then if the gentleman wishes to go further, and provide by laws of Congress for the enforcement of these rights, I will go with him. . . .
>
> This amendment provides that Congress may pass laws to enforce these rights. Why not provide by an amendment to the Constitution that no State shall discriminate against any class of its citizens, and let that amendment stand as part of the organic law of the land, subject only to be defeated by another constitutional amendment. We may pass laws here to-day, and the next Congress may wipe them out.[8]

Bingham's next version of the Amendment followed this suggestion.[9] In his final attempt to explain the meaning of the Amendment, Bingham said that "protection by national law from unconstitutional State enactments" is "supplied by the first section of the amendment."[10] By imposing direct constitutional limitations on the states, the first section (which contains the due process and equal protection clauses) invited judicial enforcement. Congressional enforcement power was relegated to a separate section of the Amendment.

After the Civil War, the Court was faced again with threats to its independence. It dodged the most dangerous threats by ducking dangerous cases on jurisdictional grounds.[11] Nevertheless, the Court remained actively engaged in judicial review.[12] If the effort to impeach President Andrew Johnson had succeeded, and Congress had remained irate at the Court, perhaps the United States might have veered toward legislative supremacy. But as it was, judicial review survived the nation's greatest constitutional crisis and remained a fixture in the legal landscape.

The failure of congressional supremacy to thrive as a constitutional vision should not be surprising. Congressional supremacy would have faced an uphill battle, given the basic structure of American government. The use of a written constitution was not necessarily incompatible with congressional supremacy. Conceivably,

[7] Thomas Jefferson to Spencer Roane, September 6, 1819, in Jefferson, *Writings*, *supra* note 5 at 1427–8.

[8] Daniel Farber and Suzanna Sherry, *A History of the American Constitution* (St. Paul, Minn.: West Publishing Co., 1990) at 309.

[9] Ibid. at 310.

[10] Ibid. at 313.

[11] See *Mississippi v. Johnson*, 71 U.S. 475 (1867); *Georgia v. Stanton*, 73 U.S. 50 (1867); *Ex Parte McCardle*, 74 U.S. 506 (1869).

[12] See, e.g., *Ex Parte Garland*, 71 U.S. 333 (1866); *Cummings v. Missouri*, 72 U.S. 277 (1867); *Ex Parte Milligan*, 71 U.S. 2 (1866); *Ex Parte Klein*, 80 U.S. 128 (1871).

Congress could have been considered the final judge of any ambiguities in the constitutional text. But the existence of a written constitution, with specific procedures for amendment, did make it hard to maintain that Congress was the ultimate sovereign in the same sense that Parliament was sovereign in England.

Investing Congress with sovereignty was also difficult because of the way the constitutional system divided power. Congress could not make a convincing claim to be the embodiment of "We the People." With Senators allocated on the basis of states rather than population and selected by the state legislatures (until the Seventeenth Amendment), it was hard to view the Senate as somehow incarnating the popular will. Moreover, because the Framers created an independent chief executive, the president has at least as strong a claim to represent the American people as did Congress as a whole (or even just the House of Representatives).[13] State governments also shared in the claim to represent the people. Thus, Congress was simply one of several institutions for representing the popular will. For the Framers, as Stephen Gardbaum has said, Congress was "one among several organs of government . . . and in principle not less alien or more 'of us' – and probably more dangerous – than the executive branch, both of which are to be viewed with pragmatic suspicion and played off each other."[14] This political culture provided tenuous foothold for Westminster constitutionalism.

Other, more subtle barriers to congressional supremacy also exist. American culture has always had a strong strain of populism,[15] but this has never been the exclusive theme. James Madison (who took the lead in drafting the Constitution) believed that the majority was capable of posing a threat to liberty and that the Constitution needed to guard against this threat. Antebellum Southerners believed that the Northern majority was a threat to their interests. After the Civil War, the Reconstruction Congress feared that white Southerners might unite with Northern Democrats to repeal the rights of blacks. Today, libertarians on the right and civil rights advocates and civil libertarians on the left all fear abusive majority legislation. Finally, congressional supremacy is undercut by the longtime American distrust of politicians.[16] Given a choice between legislative and judicial supremacy, there seems little doubt of which would win a popular referendum – for all the distrust of judicial activism, distrust of politicians is even greater.

B. Supremacy versus hegemony

Judicial supremacy means that the courts have the final word on any constitutional issue that comes before them. In a formal sense, this is true in the United States,

[13] The president's claim to represent the people as a whole is discussed in Chief Justice Burger's opinion in *INS v. Chadha*, 462 U.S. 919 (1983).

[14] Stephen Gardbaum, "The New Commonwealth Model of Constitutionalism" (2001) 49 *Am. J. Comp. L.* 707 at 741.

[15] As recently and emphatically discussed in Larry Kramer, "Popular Constitutionalism, Circa 2004" (2004) 92 *Cal. L. Rev.* 959. A look at the daily newspapers confirms that this view is having something of a resurgence among conservatives as well.

[16] Nor is the unwillingness to repose final constitutional authority in the legislature unique to the United States. Notably, "all the newly emerging democracies of the late twentieth century have opted for some form of written constitution and adopted some form of constitutionally based judicial review." Samuel Issacharoff, "Constitutionalizing Democracy in Fractured Societies" (2004) 82 *Tex. L. Rev.* 1861 at 1863. Even Mark Tushnet admits that, "[f]or all practical purposes, the Westminster model has been withdrawn from sale." Mark Tushnet, "New Forms of Judicial Review and the Persistence of Rights- and Democracy-Based Worries" (2003) 38 *Wake Forest L. Rev.* 813.

with only a single narrow exception (the dormant commerce clause). Yet, judiciary supremacy should not be confused with judicial hegemony. Having the formal final word is not the same as autonomous control of the constitutional system.

Judicial hegemony would mean that the courts hear all constitutional issues, decide them without any reference to the views of the legislature, and foreclose any practical legislative response. The American constitutional regime, as we will discuss in more detail in Part II, falls short of judicial hegemony. Some constitutional issues are beyond judicial cognizance, and Congress may have the power to withdraw others from federal jurisdiction. Judicial supremacy cannot operate in the absence of judicial jurisdiction. Congressional actions may also influence the growth of doctrine. Established congressional traditions carry weight in separation-of-powers cases, and legislative precedents may also be heeded in other settings. In theory, Congress can neither extend the Court's vision of constitutional rights nor contract it. In reality, Congress has significant power to expand constitutional rights (correspondingly limiting the power of state governments). It also holds the critical role in the amendment process. The fact that this power has been seldom exercised in modern times does not make it insignificant, for the Court certainly is aware of its existence.

Congress also exercises authority over "constitutional" matters in a broader sense. Much of the basic structure of the U.S. government stems, not directly from the Constitution, but from congressional enactments. Congress could, for example, require some variant of proportional representation in House elections or change the operation of the Electoral College by prohibiting states from using winner-take-all voting systems. If it chose to take such actions, the effect on the political system would be profound. Congress has also created the modern federal bureaucracy and even the cabinet. These are matters one might well expect to be covered in a written constitution, and in the United States, Congress rather than the Court has filled in these gaps in the constitutional text.

One of the reasons the Supreme Court seems so dominant in American constitutional law is that Americans define constitutional law to involve only interpretation of the written Constitution and only the kinds of issues that are most likely to be decided by courts. On this understanding, how to interpret the constitutional restriction on retroactive changes in state contract law is an issue of constitutional law, but whether to use first-past-the-post or proportional representation in the House of Representatives is not. In a more realistic sense, the latter issue has much more to do with "constituting" the structure of government. Despite being a matter of legislation rather than judicial decree, it is as constitutional in nature as much of English constitutional law.

II. TRACES OF LEGISLATIVE CONSTITUTIONALISM IN THE AMERICAN LEGAL REGIME

When we list the elements of legislative constitutionalism in the American constitutional regime, they may seem individually insignificant. A mere collection of islands may not seem worthy of serious attention. Yet a collection of islands can add up to an important archipelago.

Two elements of legislative constitutionalism are considered by other contributors to this volume. As Bill Eskridge and John Ferejohn have observed, Congress passes super-statutes that dominate over ordinary statutes, even those enacted later.[17] Elizabeth Garrett also points out in her contribution to this volume that framework statutes have a channeling effect on later legislation.[18] This section adds another ten items, bringing the list to a dozen elements of legislative constitutionalism in American law. In the arena of constitutional interpretation, we will see that the Supreme Court formally has the final word, but Congress has several mechanisms for shaping, extending, and sometimes even overruling judicial doctrine. Congress also has independent interpretative authority over some important constitutional issues due to the political question doctrine. And it also has had much of the responsibility for creating the basic framework of government, a "constitutional" role in a broader sense.

A. Constitutional interpretation: shaping, extending, and overruling judicial doctrine

Complete judicial hegemony would leave no space for Congress to hold conflicting views of constitutional issues. No one thinks this is quite true: If Congress refuses to pass a statute because of constitutional doubts, it matters not that the Supreme Court would have cheerfully upheld the statute. As we will see, Congress's views of the Constitution interact with judicial doctrine in more subtle ways. In the area of federalism, Congress rather than the Court ultimately decides on the limits of state regulatory authority. In other areas, Congress's role is less decisive, but it does have some power to expand constitutional rights. Finally, in interpreting the Constitution, the Supreme Court does give some heed to past congressional practice. In this section, we consider the various means by which Congress's constitutional views have an impact on the law.

1. THE DORMANT COMMERCE CLAUSE. The commerce clause is by its terms a grant of authority to Congress to regulate interstate commerce. It does not purport to grant any authority over commerce issues to the federal courts. Nevertheless, since the early days of the Republic, the Supreme Court has invalidated state laws that interfere with interstate commerce, even in the absence of any congressional action.[19] In this situation, the commerce clause is "dormant," because Congress has not exercised its powers; thus, judicial oversight of state regulations in the absence of congressional action has become known as the "dormant commerce clause" doctrine. It is analogous to EU provisions guaranteeing the free movement of goods, except that it is a judicial construct rather than an explicit textual mandate.

Despite the growing mass of congressional legislation, the dormant commerce clause remains important today. For example, since the late 1970s, the Supreme Court has aggressively invalidated state laws governing the flow of solid waste. The Court began by invalidating laws that limited the import of solid waste or that taxed imported waste more heavily than local waste.[20] More recently, the Court

[17] William N. Eskridge, Jr., and John Ferejohn, "Super-Statutes: The New American Constitutionalism," Chapter 15 in this volume.

[18] Elizabeth Garrett, "Conditions for Framework Legislation," Chapter 14 in this volume.

[19] *Gibbons v. Ogden*, 22 U.S. (9 Wheat.) 1 (1824).

[20] See *City of Phildelphia v. New Jersey*, 437 U.S. 617 (1978); *Chemical Waste Management, Inc. v. Hunt*, 504 U.S. 334 (1992); *Oregon Waste Systems, Inc. v. Department of Environmental Quality*, 511 U.S. 93 (1994); *Fort Gratiot Sanitary Landfill, Inc., v. Michigan Dept. of Natural Resources*, 504 U.S. 353 (1992).

struck down efforts to ensure that a locality's wastes were treated locally rather than dumped elsewhere.[21] Even state laws that do not distinguish between local and interstate goods can be struck down if the Court decides that they "unduly burden" the flow of interstate commerce.[22] Although the dormant commerce clause doctrine has been harshly criticized because of its lack of textual warrant and its inherent bias in favor of laissez-faire economics,[23] it remains firmly embedded in American constitutional law.

What makes the dormant commerce clause relevant for our purposes is a twist in the doctrine. This is one area where judicial supremacy does not apply: When the Supreme Court holds a state law unconstitutional under this doctrine, Congress can override the decision and revalidate the state law. For example, in *Leisy v. Hardin*,[24] the Court held that states could not seize interstate shipments of alcohol in order to enforce their local regulations of alcohol. Congress immediately enacted a federal statute authorizing the states to regulate liquor once an interstate shipment had arrived within their borders, and the Supreme Court upheld this provision only a year after *Leisy* had held such state laws unconstitutional.[25] Congress's power to validate state legislation despite contrary Supreme Court rulings under the dormant commerce clause is now beyond question.[26]

Thus, when the Supreme Court strikes down a state law on federalism grounds, Congress can resurrect state regulation. Similarly, when the Supreme Court rejects a federalism attack on a state law, Congress can legislate in the area, overriding state law under the supremacy clause. Such preemption usually involves a conflict between federal regulation and state law, but not necessarily: Congress has the power to oust states out of regulating an entire field even when the state law does not conflict with any specific federal regulation.[27]

Because the Supreme Court's rulings on state regulatory authority are not the final word, Congress has ultimate control over how regulatory authority is allocated between state and federal governments. This control is bounded only by the limits of Congress's own regulatory authority. Despite a couple of Supreme Court decisions nibbling at the fringes of federal regulatory authority,[28] that authority remains exceedingly broad. Correspondingly, so is Congress's power to augment or limit state regulatory authority.

[21] See *C & A Carbone, Inc., v. Town of Clarkstown*, 511 U.S. 383 (1994).

[22] See, e.g., *Kassel v. Consolidated Freightways Corp.*, 450 U.S. 662 (1981).

[23] See, e.g., Julian Eule, "Laying the Dormant Commerce Clause to Rest" (1982) 91 *Yale L.J.* 425; Lisa Heinzerling, "The Commercial Constitution" [1995], *Sup. Ct. Rev.* 217.

[24] 135 U.S. 100 (1890).

[25] *Wilkinson v. Raher*, 140 U.S. 545 (1890).

[26] See William Cohen, "Congressional Power to Validate Unconstitutional State Laws: A Forgotten Solution to an Old Enigma" (1985) 35 *Stan. L. Rev.* 387.

[27] This doctrine has been most prominent in the field of labor relations, where states are barred from regulating union/employer relations. See, e.g., *Lodge 76, Int'l Ass'n of Machinists v. Wisconsin Employment Relations Comm'n*, 427 U.S. 132 (1976) (holding that the National Labor Relations Act preempted a state law barring a union ban on working overtime, because Congress intended to leave such union pressure unregulated, despite the absence of explicit federal protection for the overtime ban).

[28] The most notable is of course *United States v. Lopez*, 514 U.S. 549 (1995). The facts of *Lopez* show just how far away the Court is from invading the heartland of congressional authority – the statute in question prohibited possession of a firearm within 1,000 feet of a school, a matter on which the argument for uniform federal regulation is far from apparent.

The dormant commerce clause is not one of the more glamorous areas of constitutional law. Consequently, this may seem a marginally significant exception to the general rule of judicial supremacy. But, like the EU provisions on free movement of goods, NAFTA, and the WTO, the dormant commerce clause touches on key questions of social policy. The question of how much a political community should be constrained by the needs for economic integration has proven volatile enough to provoke large-scale riots against "globalization" and the WTO; the dormant commerce clause presents the same issues on a cross-continental rather than international scale. Here, it is Congress rather than the Court that is supreme.

2. EXECUTIVE AUTHORITY. One of the great constitutional issues is the extent of executive authority. The governing judicial approach today stems from Justice Jackson's concurring opinion in the *Steel Seizure* case.[29] Under Jackson's approach, the president's power is strongest when he acts with authority from Congress, weakest when Congress opposes him, and intermediate in strength in the gray area of congressional silence. Thus, Congress has great (though not complete) control over the breadth of executive authority.

The operation of the doctrine is illustrated in the Iranian hostages case.[30] In order to secure the release of American hostages, Presidents Carter and Reagan agreed to block pending lawsuits against Iran in U.S. courts. Only part of this executive action (lifting attachments of Iranian property) was expressly authorized by statute. Nevertheless, the Court upheld the entirety of the executive orders. The Court relied on a tradition of congressional approval for similar executive actions, under which the government had traditionally "espoused" claims of Americans harmed by foreign states, negotiating settlements in their favor in return for extinguishment of U.S. claims. The Court concluded that Congress had implicitly approved of a general executive power to suspend claims.

What is notable is that executive authority was validated by a custom of legislative approval rather than by any direct legislation applying to the case at hand. Thus, in effect, a presumptive role in favor of executive authority had become a matter of constitutional law because of a legislative custom. In theory, a course of congressional conduct has no power to change constitutional law. Yet, a presidential action that would have been ruled unconstitutional without such a legislative custom becomes constitutional when the custom is present. It is hard to avoid the conclusion that in such cases the legislative custom has attained some kind of constitutional status.

3. THE §5 POWER AND THE RATCHET. When the Supreme Court holds that a state law violates due process or equal protection, Congress has no power to validate the law. But the reverse is less clear. Congress clearly has some authority to invalidate state laws even when they would be held unconstitutional by the Supreme Court.

The most obvious source of congressional authority over civil rights is §5 of the Fourteenth Amendment. Section 5 gives Congress the authority to "enforce" the mandates of due process and equal protection found in section 1 of the Amendment. The §5 power is especially noteworthy because it allows Congress to override

[29] *Youngstown Sheet & Tube Co. v. Sawyer*, 343 U.S. 579 (1952).

[30] *Dames & Moore v. Regan*, 453 U.S. 654 (1981).

what would otherwise be a state's immunity to damage actions by private individuals. The question for our purposes is how far Congress can go beyond the judicial interpretation of due process and equal protection when it exercises this enforcement power. Can it invalidate state laws even though the courts would uphold those laws as constitutional?

In *Katzenbach v. Morgan*,[31] the Court suggested that Congress may simply adopt broader interpretations of the Fourteenth Amendment than the judiciary. Thus, constitutional arguments that had failed in court could win the day in Congress, providing a legitimate basis for legislation. (This is called the "ratchet" argument, because it applies only in one direction. Under this view, if the Court has struck down a state law, Congress cannot resurrect it, but if the Court upholds a state law as constitutional, Congress can adopt an alternative constitutional interpretation.)

It is plain that the current Court would not accept any power by Congress to independently interpret equal protection or due process. In *City of Bourne v. Flores*,[32] the Court rebuffed a congressional effort to broaden protection for minority religious practices beyond what the Court itself had provided. The Court seemed offended by the idea that Congress might question the correctness of its constitutional holdings. Thus, a federal statute that openly purports to correct a "mistaken" judicial interpretation of the Constitution seems doomed.

But this is not the end of the matter, because what Congress cannot do openly it may be able to achieve indirectly. The cases also provide Congress with the power to adopt prophylactic remedies for judicially recognized constitutional violations. This power can be quite sweeping. For example, in *City of Rome v. United States*,[33] the Court upheld stringent federal control of state electoral practices implicating race. The statute in question required prior approval by the attorney general of any new state or local electoral law in states with a history of racial discrimination (quite an extraordinary procedure with no explicit basis in the constitutional test). The attorney general was directed to approve a state law only if he found that it lacked both discriminatory purpose *and* discriminatory effect – even though the Supreme Court had ruled that discriminatory effect is not alone unconstitutional in the absence of discriminatory purpose. In effect, Congress had broadened the ban on discriminatory purpose into a ban on discriminatory effect.

As a practical matter, the question is how far Congress can push this prophylactic power. At what point will the Court decide that a statute cannot be considered remedial because it goes too far beyond the judicial understanding of the underlying constitutional right? *City of Rome* took a very generous view of remedial power, whereas *City of Boerne* was substantially more restrictive. An even more restrictive view was taken a few years later, which seemed to leave Congress with little room to expand the meaning of civil rights through "remedial" statutes.[34] These decisions were harshly criticized by some academic commentators.[35]

[31] 384 U.S. 641 (1966).

[32] 521 U.S. 507 (1997).

[33] 446 U.S. 156 (1980).

[34] *United States v. Morrison*, 529 U.S. 598 (2000) (striking down a federal statute creating a private cause of action for violence against women).

[35] See, e.g., Robert C. Post and Reva B. Siegel, "Protecting the Constitution from the People: Juricentric Restrictions on Section Five Power" (2003) 78 *Ind. L.J.* 34.

The most recent signs from the Court favor a broader understanding of congressional power. In *Nevada Department of Human Resources v. Hibbs*,[36] in an opinion by none other than Chief Justice Rehnquist, the Court upheld a federal statute requiring states to provide unpaid parental leave. The rationale for the statute was that female employees would otherwise be disadvantaged, which is certainly plausible. But there was little evidence that states had previously adopted restrictive leave policies with the intent of disadvantaging women, which would have been the necessary predicate for holding those prior leave policies unconstitutional. Realistically, Congress was much less worried about intentionally discriminatory leave policies than about achieving the laudable goal of creating more equal opportunities for women in the workplace. The reality was that Congress's understanding of gender equality was broader than anything the Court had been willing to read into the Constitution. Yet, the Court upheld the statute, and the following year, upheld a federal statute requiring handicap access on a similarly strained basis.[37]

The Court's view of §5 is obviously in flux. It is surely too soon to announce a return to the generous view of congressional power found in *City of Rome*, let alone a return to the even more generous view of *Katzenbach*'s ratchet theory. At least at present, however, Congress seems to have a reasonable amount of leeway in providing prophylactic remedies for rights, even when Congress is motivated by a different vision of discrimination than the Court's rather than a driving desire to stamp out possible violations of the Court's interpretation.

Congress can also go beyond the Court in banning discrimination by state governments through another route. Congress's §5 power is augmented by its power to regulate interstate commerce. That power has been extended to include the arena of civil rights. In 1985, the Court held that states enjoy no special immunity from the same regulations that apply to the private sector.[38] Perhaps surprisingly, given the Rehnquist Court's federalism revival, that decision has not been called into question in later rulings, and even the Court's most conservative members have evinced no interest in overruling it.

Thus, even outside of its §5 power, Congress enjoys broad authority to impose civil rights regulations on states. The commerce clause is a somewhat less appealing basis for action than §5 because it does not allow Congress to provide a damages remedy for injured citizens against state governments. Thus, it does not authorize Congress to provide equally strong judicial remedies. Nevertheless, substantive restrictions on states can still be enforced through injunctive relief (even in suits by private citizens) or through damage actions brought by the federal government. Admittedly, the commerce clause is not completely unlimited because in extreme cases the Court may find the statute to be too far removed from any economic transaction. Nevertheless, Congress clearly can use the commerce power to impose restrictions on state governments well beyond what the Court would be willing to impose as a matter of constitutional interpretation.

For example, under governing Supreme Court doctrine, the equal protection clause places little or no restriction on age discrimination by states. But the Court

[36] 538 U.S. 721 (2003).

[37] *Tennessee v. Lane*, 541 U.S. 509 (2004).

[38] *Garcia v. San Antonio Metropolitan Transit Authority*, 469 U.S. 528 (1985).

upheld a federal statute that prohibited age discrimination in employment by the states, on the theory that age discrimination affects interstate commerce.[39] In theory, there was no conflict between this statute and the Court's rulings – the statute involved a regulation of interstate commerce whereas the rulings involved the equal protection clause. But the reality is that Congress successfully outlawed a form of government discrimination that the Court had upheld as constitutional.

First-year law students are apt to view such legislation as "overruling" the Supreme Court. More sophisticated constitutional scholars know better: Technically, Congress is simply exercising independent regulatory authority rather than displacing the Court's role as final interpreter of the Constitution. Yet the naive view is not without truth: On some important matters, when Congress thinks the Supreme Court has read the Constitution too narrowly, it has the practical if not theoretical authority to implement its own constitutional vision.

4. LEGISLATIVE PRECEDENTS. On occasion, the Supreme Court has been known to give decisive effect to legislative precedents. Perhaps the most notable example is *Myers v. United States,*[40] which involved presidential authority to remove executive officers. The Constitution contains considerable detail about the appointment of executive officers but says nothing at all about their removal. Nevertheless, the Court held that the president has broad power to remove underlings (despite contrary legislation). The decision was primarily based on what the Court called the "Decision of 1789," which was not a judicial decision but rather a vote in the First Congress.

Legislative precedent has also been decisive in other cases. The Court upheld the practice of paying legislative chaplains, which seems at first blush to be a blatant violation of the establishment clause, because the practice had been in place since the First Congress.[41] Thus, a legislative tradition in effect controlled the interpretation of the Constitution. To similar effect, the Court upheld a restriction on electioneering within a certain radius of polling places largely because such legislation had become so universally well entrenched.[42]

Oddly enough, the strongest proponent of this form of customary constitutional law is Justice Scalia, who is also the Court's most outspoken believer in constitutional text. Nevertheless, Scalia has emphasized the entrenched constitutional traditions should serve as the fixed points of judicial constitutional interpretation.[43]

When American constitutional scholars think about this issue at all, they think of it as a question of how to interpret the Constitution; that is, they are primarily concerned with how much judicial interpretation should be influenced by deeply entrenched legislation. Such entrenched legislative positions are then seen as possible constraints on courts. But what constrains one side empowers on the other. Recognizing such traditions means that at least over the long haul, legislative views

[39] *EEOC v. Wyoming,* 460 U.S. 226 (1983). Note that this decision preceded that the Court more general approval of federal commerce regulations of states in the 1985 *Garcia* decision.

[40] 272 U.S. 52 (1926).

[41] *Marsh v. Chambers,* 463 U.S. 783 (1983).

[42] *Burson v. Freeman,* 504 U.S. 191 (1992).

[43] See, e.g., Scalia's dissent in *Board of County Commissioners v. Umbehr,* 116 S. Ct. 2361 (1996). For a critical discussion of Scalia's approach, see David Strauss, "Tradition, Precedent, and Justice Scalia" (1991) 12 *Cardozo L. Rev.* 1699.

of the Constitution acquire independent constitutional weight. As in other systems with "unwritten constitutions," legislation may acquire a kind of constitutional status over the passage of time.

5. JURISDICTION STRIPPING. Article III of the Constitution, which governs the judiciary, has two provisions that may allow Congress to prevent the federal courts from hearing an issue – thereby knocking the supposedly supreme interpreters of the Constitution out of the game.

The first provision giving Congress control of jurisdiction is Article III §1. It vests the judicial power in the Supreme Court and "in such inferior Courts as the congress may from time to time ordain and establish." This provision has long been understood to give Congress plenary control over the jurisdiction of the lower federal courts.

The second provision is Article III §2. It grants the Supreme Court appellate jurisdiction of cases involving federal questions (as well as some other cases) "with such Exceptions, and under such Regulations as the Congress shall make." On its face, this provision would seem to authorize Congress to oust the Supreme Court from any designated category of cases, such as abortion cases or cases involving the detention of terrorists.

Congress's power to restrict federal jurisdiction have seldom been exercised, with the notable exception of the post–Civil War period when Congress blocked the Court from reviewing critical aspects of Reconstruction.[44] Even where its exercise has only been threatened, however, the jurisdiction-stripping power has sometimes been potent. According to Lucas Powe, Congress successfully stopped the Warren Court in its tracks for several years through the threat of jurisdiction stripping.[45]

Scholars have ceaselessly debated whether there are implicit constitutional limitations on the congressional power to eliminate federal jurisdiction.[46] But the framing of the debate is significant. The Constitution plainly gives Congress some jurisdictional control, and the debatable question is whether this power has *any* limits. In a head-to-head confrontation with the courts, Congress might or might not prevail legally or politically. But there is no doubt that it has a potentially powerful weapon with which to restrain overly adventuresome judges. We will return in Part III to considering the constitutional significance of Congress's failure to exercise this power.

B. Independent interpretative authority

Judicial supremacy extends only so far as federal jurisdiction. Although the doctrinal categories have moved over time, the Supreme Court has always recognized

44 See *Ex parte McCardle*, 74 U.S. (7 Wall.) 506 (1869) (dismissing an appeal from a conviction by military tribunal under statute that eliminated the Court's appellate jurisdiction in habeas cases).

45 See Lucas A. Powe, Jr., *The Warren Court and American Politics* (Cambridge, Mass: Belknap Press of Harvard University Press, 2001).

46 See, e.g., Gerald Gunther, "Congressional Power to Curtail Federal Court Jurisdiction: An Opinionated Guide to the Ongoing Debate" (1984) 36 *Stan. L. Rev.* 894; Martin Redish, *Federal Jurisdiction: Tensions in the Allocation of Judicial Power*, 2nd ed. (Charlottesville Va.: Michie Co., 1990); Lawrence Sager, "Foreword: Constitutional Limits on Congress' Authority To Regulate the Jurisdiction of the Federal Courts" (1981) 95 *Harv. L. Rev.* 17; Leonard Ratner, "Congressional Power over the Appellate Jurisdiction of the Supreme Court" (1960) 109 *U. Pa. L. Rev.* 157.

that some constitutional issues are not appropriate for judicial resolution. The "political question" doctrine removes some constitutional questions from judicial cognizance for various reasons: (1) because a court could not fashion a meaningful remedy, (2) because the constitutional text commits the question to another branch, (3) because judicial intervention would be destructive of foreign policy, or (4) because there are no judicially ascertainable standards to govern the dispute. The modern leading case on the subject is *Baker v. Carr*.[47] That case narrowed the doctrine in certain respects but also established clearer guidelines about its applicability.

Where the political question doctrine holds sway, courts may not enter, leaving the field clear for other actors to interpret the Constitution without judicial oversight. In several key areas, Congress has final interpretative power or shares final interpretative power with the president. Because there are no cases on these subjects, they tend to be shortchanged in constitutional law classes, but they involve significant issues. In effect, as Mark Tushnet says, the political question doctrine "is commonly understood as a doctrine that identifies constitutional issues as to which political constraints on political actors are thought more likely to produce conformity to constitutional norms than would judicial review."[48] Thus, the political question doctrine marks the outer bounds of judicial supremacy, reserving some constitutional questions to other institutions such as Congress. The list of nonjusticiable legislative decisions is significant, as discussed below.

1. IMPEACHMENT. Article II §4 of the Constitution provides that the president, vice-president, and all civil officers can be removed from office on impeachment of "Treason, Bribery, or other high Crimes and Misdemeanors." Article I §2 grants the House of Representatives the "sole Power of Impeachment," and Article I §3 gives the Senate the "sole Power to try all Impeachments."

It has been generally assumed that impeachments present a nonjudiciable political question. The Supreme Court recently confirmed this understanding in *Nixon v. United States*.[49] Despite what one might assume from the name of the case, it involved a federal judge named Walter Nixon rather than the much better-known effort to impeach President Richard Nixon after the Watergate scandal. The Court held that the procedures used in an impeachment trial were not subject to judicial oversight. The Court also stressed that one key function of impeachment in the system of checks and balances was to restrain the judicial branch and that it would be unseemly for courts to engage in judicial review of such proceedings. This rationale seems to extend beyond the Senate's choice of procedures to include the interpretation of the phrase "high crimes and misdemeanors," although the Court's holding can be read more narrowly.

Impeachment provides Congress with what amounts to the ultimate weapon against the judiciary. Jefferson made an early effort to use impeachment to curb his ideological adversaries in the federal judiciary, and the action has not been

[47] 369 U.S. 186 (1962).

[48] Mark Tushnet, "Non-Judicial Review" (2003) 40 *Harv. J. on Legis.* 453 at 453.

[49] 506 U.S. 224 (1993).

repeated.[50] But if there is a constitutional limit on the use of impeachment for this purpose, it is evidently one that only Congress itself can ultimately enforce. Judicial impeachments have generally involved corruption, but there seems to be little restraint on broader use of the impeachment power except for what is now the long-standing legislative tradition against ideological impeachments.

2. FOREIGN AFFAIRS. Foreign affairs, and the use of the war power, are arenas in which the political question doctrine has held sway. For example, the Supreme Court consistently refused to rule on the constitutionality of the Vietnam War.[51] Presidents and Congresses have been tussling over the constitutional authority to control these issues for almost two centuries, with little judicial input.

The critical importance of these constitutional issues needs no explanation. Yet questions of war and peace and other international affairs are largely outside of the competence of the U.S. courts. This does not mean that constitutional interpretation has no role to play. What it means is that the constitutional issues are either decided by consensus among the president and Congress or become the occasion for political battle. Here is one area in which legislative constitutionalism has more application than any theory of judicial supremacy.

3. INTERNAL FUNCTIONING. Article I gives each house of Congress control of its own internal affairs. Under §5 of Article I, each house is the "Judge of the Elections, Returns and Qualifications of its own Members," and each house is empowered to "determine the Rules of its proceedings, punish its Members for disorderly Behavior, and, with the Concurrence of two thirds, expel a member." The Supreme Court has eschewed involvement in these issues except for holding that Congress lacks the power to add to the constitutional qualifications of age and residence for legislative office.[52]

These may seem to be merely housekeeping matters, but they potentially have wide significance. Congressional refusal to seat Southern delegations after the Civil War made Reconstruction possible, including some key constitutional amendments that otherwise would not have passed. Internal rules can change constitutional arrangements in more subtle ways. The Constitution guarantees each state equal representation in the Senate and creates supermajority requirements only for some limited types of actions such as impeachments. But the Senate has long required a supermajority to end debate and bring a measure to a vote, making the Senate notably nonmajoritarian in its operation. Use of the so-called filibuster allowed Southern minorities in the Senate to block federal civil rights legislation for decades. Today, it provides leverage to the minority Democratic party, which lacks majorities in either house.

Recently, there has been controversy about the imposition of supermajority requirements to bring measures in designated categories (such as tax increases) to a vote. Detractors argue that these provisions in effect amend the Constitution

[50] See, e.g., Thomas E. Mann, *Reining in a Runaway Federal Judiciary?*, The Brookings Institution, May 4, 2005, online: http://www.brookings.edu/views/op-ed/mann/20050504.htm.

[51] See, e.g., *Mora v. McNamara*, 389 U.S. 934 (1967) (denying certiorari over the dissents of Justices Douglas and Stewart).

[52] See *Powell v. McCormack*, 395 U.S. 486 (1969).

by disfavoring these categories of legislation; this is a particular concern regarding the Senate, where procedural rules remain in place indefinitely unless affirmatively amended (which could also itself potentially be the subject of a supermajority requirement).[53] Defenders argue that such supermajority requirements are a legitimate exercise of the rule-making authority of each house.[54] Whatever may be said about the merits of this constitutional issue, the one thing that is plain is that this is a constitutional dispute only Congress can decide. No court could order the House to enact a bill or to repeal a procedural rule because the Speech or Debate Clause immunizes members of Congress from any suit over their legislative acts.[55] Thus, as a practical matter, Congress could impose quasi-constitutional restraints on itself without going through the trouble of amending the Constitution.

4. GUARANTEE CLAUSE. Article IV §4 requires the United States to "guarantee to every State in this Union a Republican Form of Government." Early on, the Supreme Court ruled that defining a republican form of government was a nonjusticiable question, meaning that only Congress and the president could determine whether a particular state government was lawful.[56]

In the early twentieth century, the Court applied the political question doctrine to direct democracy. At issue was an Oregon procedure under which voters could directly enact legislation without the approval of the state legislature.[57] A plausible argument can be made that a "republican" government requires the popular views be filtered through deliberation by representatives. The Court held, however, that the question was nonjusticiable. In states like California, voter initiatives have become a major instrument of lawmaking (and in the eyes of some observers, a destructive one). Apparently, Congress could use its power under the guarantee clause to curtail this practice and to otherwise reform state governments in ways that a court could not entertain. Thus, it would appear important features of state government pass constitutional muster only at congressional sufferance.

C. Constitution making by Congress: constructing the structure of government

Courts engage in constitutional lawmaking through interpretation of the constitutional text. As we have seen, Congress also plays some role in constitutional interpretation. But as we will see in this section, Congress also engages in another form of legislative constitutionalism. It is Congress, rather than the constitutional text, that is responsible for many key features of the governmental structure. If these features are now too deeply embedded to be changed except under some

53 See, e.g., John C. Roberts and Erwin Chemerinsky, "Entrenchment of Ordinary Legislation: A Reply to Professors Posner and Vermeule" (2003) 91 *Calif. L. Rev.* 1773.

54 See, e.g., Eric A. Posner and Adrian Vermeule, "Legislative Entrenchment: A Reappraisal" (2002) 111 *Yale L.J.* 1665 at 1666.

55 U.S. Const. art. I, §6 ("The Senators and Representatives . . . shall in all Cases . . . be privileged from Arrest during their Attendance at the Session of their respective Houses, and in going to and returning from the same; and for any Speech or Debate in either House, they shall not be questioned in any other Place."). *Tenney v. Brandhove*, 341 U.S. 367, 376–7 (1951) "Legislators are immune from deterrents to the uninhibited discharge of their legislative duty. . . . "

56 See *Luther v. Borden*, 48 U.S. (7 How.) 1 (1849).

57 See *Pacific States Tel. & Tel. Co. v. Oregon*, 223 U.S. 118 (1912).

extraordinary pressure, they might be considered "constitutional" or at least quasi-constitutional. This is a form of constitution making that involves well-entrenched legislative enactments rather than formal textual amendment. It also should not be forgotten, however, that formal amendments are themselves largely within the control of Congress.

1. ESTABLISHING BASIC INSTITUTIONS. The Constitution establishes much of the basic framework of national government. Yet, it is striking how much of the basic structure is provided by later legislation. The Constitution does not provide for the existence of a cabinet, nor (unlike many state constitutions) does it establish any of the executive departments. The State Department, Treasury, the attorney general, and (under various guises) the Defense Department have existed since the nation's founding, but their charters come from Congress, not from the Constitution.[58] The Court has also declined to take on the question of when the president can unilaterally terminate a treaty.[59]

Another striking gap in the Constitution concerns political parties, which go completely unmentioned. Whatever legal status these parties enjoy, such as state-sponsored primaries or party listings on ballots, derives entirely from legislative acts by Congress and the states. Thus, the most important single feature of the modern political system gains legal recognition only through legislation.

As mentioned earlier, the Constitution does not speak directly to the question of removing federal officers. Beginning at least by the time of Andrew Jackson, partisan patronage became the fundamental feature of federal service. Congress eliminated most of the patronage system and created the modern civil service in the late nineteenth century.[60] It was only about a century later, in cases involving state patronage, that the Supreme Court held most of the patronage system unconstitutional under the First Amendment.[61] Thus, Congress, rather than the courts or the constitutional text, was the architect of the modern civil service.

In an earlier era, Congress was also responsible for the rules governing the vast territories held by the United States and for organizing those territories into states. It is due to Congress, not the Constitution, that today there are fifty states rather than thirteen. Congress's statehood decisions determined the basic geographic framework of government for most of the United States. With the exception of Texas (previously an independent nation) and the original thirteen colonies, the American states are the creation of Congress.

The era of territorial expansion is long past, but we may be early in a new era of globalization, in which important parts of the "constitutional" regime may be international. Here again, Congress has played a decisive role. Trade agreements such as the WTO gain their status (and funding) under U.S. law from congressional

[58] See Lawrence Lessig and Cass Sunstein, "The President and the Administration" (1994) 94 *Colum. L. Rev.* 1. The Constitution does of course speak of the Army and Navy, and designate the president as the commander-in-chief, but the secretary of defense is a congressional creation, as is the massive military force under his jurisdiction. The Framers were wary of "standing armies."

[59] See *Goldwater v. Carter*, 444 U.S. 996 (1979) (plurality applies political question doctrine; concurring Justice finds the case unripe).

[60] Sean M. Theriault, "Patronage, the Pendleton Act, and the Power of the People" (2003) 65 *Journal of Politics* 50 at 52. ("The Pendleton Act . . . implemented entrance exams for would-be bureaucrats. These exams replaced loyalty with merit as the medium of exchange in securing political appointments.")

[61] See *Burns v. Elrod*, 427 U.S. 347 (1976).

legislation. Congress is also responsible for funding international institutions such as the IMF and World Bank. To the extent that globalization is marking the beginning of a major shift in global governance, the U.S. part of this shift stems from Congress, not the courts or the constitutional text.

An example of the potential significance of this is provided by Chapter 11 of NAFTA, governing investor protection. An investor who is unsuccessful in obtaining a remedy from domestic courts may file an international claim for compensation for violation of NAFTA.[62] We may or may not ever see this, but it is at least a theoretical possibility that through this mechanism the U.S. Supreme Court could be "overruled" by an international tribunal. That surely would count as an event of constitutional dimensions.

2. ELECTORAL RULES. The Constitution gives Congress considerable authority over the conduct of elections. Some of the relevant provisions are as follows:

- Article I §4 provides that the "times, places, and manner" of electing members of Congress shall be prescribed by state legislatures "but the Congress may at any time by Law make or alter such Regulations, except as the Places of chusing Senators."
- Article II §1 gives Congress control over the date of presidential elections, which has allowed it to create a national election day.
- The Twelfth Amendment provides that electoral votes shall be opened "in the presence" of Congress and the "votes shall then be counted."
- Later amendments prohibit discrimination in voting on the basis of race (Fifteenth Amendment), sex (Nineteenth Amendment), ability to pay a poll tax (Twenty-Fourth Amendment), or age (Twenty-Sixth Amendment); each of these amendments gives Congress the power to enforce it by appropriate legislation.
- The Twenty-Third Amendment, which allows residents of the District of Columbia to vote for president, has similar enforcement language.

Congressional power under the antidiscrimination amendments has been the subject of considerable attention, particularly with reference to the Voting Rights Act (the subject of the *Katzenbach* and *City of Rome* cases discussed earlier).

The Article II provision for counting the presidential vote has served as the basis for legislation dealing with contested ballots – had it not been for the Supreme Court's intervention in *Bush v. Gore*, that legislation would probably have determined the outcome of the 2000 election. (The Article II provision governing the date of the selection of electors might also have proved significant if the Florida state legislature had carried through with threats to appoint electors directly when the popular vote was disputed, because that choice would have been made after the congressionally designated election date.) So far, however, these provisions have not been operative.

Article I §4 is important because one of the basic features of the American political system – first-past-the-post election of members of the House – exists only by congressional sufferance. Under its power to modify state regulations of

[62] For discussion of this provision of NAFTA, see Marc R. Poirier, "The NAFTA Chapter 11 Expropriation Debate Through the Eyes of a Property Theorist" (2003) 33 *Envtl. L.* 851.

the "manner" of election, Congress could modify this system at will. A number of scholars have called for some system of proportional representation, in part to combat the growing gerrymandering of congressional districts. This would be a radical change in American government and politics and surely should be considered constitutional in dimension, but it is a change that Congress could make by legislation.

3. INDEPENDENT AGENCIES. The Constitution creates three branches of government: the Congress, which creates binding law; the president, who executes these laws; and the federal courts, which adjudicate disputes involving federal law. But as every student of American government knows, there is now a fourth branch: the regulatory agency. These agencies make rules that have the force of law. The fiction is that they are merely filling in the details of congressional legislation, but everyone knows better. The same agency is in charge of granting permits, dispersing funds, filing enforcement actions, and other executive tasks. And the same agency generally adjudicates those same enforcement actions, with later review of the decision before the courts.

The disjunction between these agencies and the constitutional scheme is most obvious with respect to independent agencies. Unlike heads of ordinary executive departments, the members of these agencies serve fixed terms and can only be removed by the president for good cause. There has been much dispute among conservatives about the constitutionality of this arrangement, but both as a practical matter and as a legal matter,[63] the constitutionality of independent agencies seems beyond serious attack.

One would sometimes have the impression from discussions about this fourth branch that it somehow invented itself. This important constitutional innovation did not will itself into existence. It was a creation of Congress, which established independent agencies such as the Interstate Commerce Commission and the Securities and Exchange Commission in the first place.

4. CONGRESS AS CONSTITUTIONAL ASSEMBLY. The explicit role of Congress in constitutional change also bears remembering. Under Article V – which almost everyone agrees is the exclusive method for making formal amendments – there are two possible mechanisms for amendments. Under one mechanism, Congress drafts amendments that are then ratified by the states. Under the other mechanism, which has never been used, the states can demand that Congress call a constitutional convention to propose amendments. Even under this alternative mechanism, Congress would seem to have significant leverage through its control of the process for selecting delegates (and perhaps through its ability to narrow the convention's charge, although this is less clear).

The most noteworthy amendments were the Bill of Rights, adopted almost immediately after the Constitution went into effect, and the Thirteenth, Fourteenth,

[63] See *Morrison v. Olson*, 487 U.S. 654 (1988) (per Rehnquist, C.J.) (upholding congressional creation of an independent prosecutor immune from presidential control); *Humphrey's Executor v. United States*, 295 U.S. 602 (1935) (upholding limitation on president's power to remove members of the Federal Trade Commission).

and Fifteenth Amendments, adopted in the aftermath of the Civil War. (The post–Civil War amendments ended slavery, provided federal constitutional protection against state violations of civil liberties, and banned racial discrimination in voting laws.) But these were not the only significant amendments. By authorizing the income tax, the Sixteenth Amendment created the fiscal foundation for modern government. By giving women the vote, the Nineteenth Amendment took the first step toward gender equality. A series of other amendments have reinforced the democratic process by eliminating barriers to voting and requiring direct election of Senators (who were originally selected by state legislatures).

In practice, amending the Constitution has proved extremely difficult, perhaps more so than the Framers would have expected. It is more difficult to know whether the courts have been dissuaded from certain activities by the mere threat of amendment. Have there been so few amendments to overrule Supreme Court decisions because the amendment process is so cumbersome or because the Court knows the limits beyond which it would trigger an amendment?

III. IMPLICATIONS FOR CONSTITUTIONAL THEORY

There is an unfortunate element of circularity in first defining constitutional law to be composed of the kinds of issues decided by courts and then concluding that courts are the be-all-and-end-all of constitutional law. Yet that is the general impulse of American constitutional lawyers, who tend to identify constitutional law with the kind of work done by courts.

Discussions of legislative constitutionalism, such as those found in this volume, suggest a broader picture of constitutionalism. Actions can have constitutional stature in several significant ways: by interpreting a constitutional rule, by establishing basic government institutions and processes (rarely judicial), by formally creating new constitutional rules, or by creating entrenched understandings that are followed even without specific enforcement mechanisms. Judicial supremacy has great relevance in the United States to the first of these functions, but much less to the others. Even as to the first, interpretative function, there is room for congressional influence.

As it turns out, even in a purported system of judicial supremacy, the legislature continues to play a significant constitutional role. One of the more obvious lessons is the need for careful attention to institutional detail. It is easy to be distracted by seductive phrases such as judicial supremacy, or to take a legal system at its own word about the allocation of authority. The result can be to miss substantial deviations from the system's announced mode of operation. It is also easy to focus on the issues evoking the greatest controversy, without attending to the ways in which an institution such as Congress sets basic ground rules or establishes critical institutional structures.

This is not to deny the existence of judicial supremacy. One of the bedrock understandings of American law is that final judicial decrees must be obeyed by executive officers, even in the face of conflicting directives from the legislatures. A somewhat less fundamental, but nevertheless powerful, understanding is that other government actors should respect the Supreme Court's interpretation of the

Constitution regardless of any actual litigation. These norms are clearly part of U.S. political and legal culture. The important role of the federal courts in making constitutional law cannot be gainsaid.

We are apt to forget, however, how much of that judicial role has been underwritten by Congress. In the first Judiciary Act, well before *Marbury v. Madison*, Congress gave the Supreme Court jurisdiction to review lower courts' constitutional rulings. *Marbury* itself involved the rare case beyond the scope of that explicit authorization (because there was no lower court decision to review). Congress also established the lower federal courts and took specific steps to strengthen their ability to implement constitutional law. It authorized them to review state court convictions through habeas corpus and endowed them with jurisdiction over all cases raising federal questions, notably including constitutional cases. This has brought the full range of constitutional issues into the federal courts. Without the participation of the lower federal courts, the Supreme Court's control of unconstitutional state conduct would be limited to the few cases that the court itself can find time to review each year.

Congress has rarely attempted to use its powers over federal jurisdiction to limit judicial review of constitutional matters, nor has it used the impeachment power to discipline the courts. This does not even consider less direct measures such as court-packing, overloading the court's docket, budget cuts, or even the possibility of calling the Justices to testify at congressional hearings where they could be "raked over the coals." It is little wonder that a leading conservative legal scholar has bitterly denounced Congress for its implicit responsibility for the Supreme Court's activities: "[f]ar from being counter-majoritarian," he complains, "judicial activism is in fact the device that Congress relies on to make social policy for the nation, which Congress either approves or is at least unwilling to stop."[64]

This statement may exaggerate the scope of Congress's responsibility, but it remains true that over many decades Congress has acquiesced in broad judicial power. When inaction stretches over such long period of times, it hardens into the kind of custom that in other legal systems would be considered constitutional. American constitutional discourse does not provide a vocabulary for this phenomenon – an argument that a change of course by Congress was unconstitutional would be based on conventional sources such as text and precedent rather than on violation of constitutional custom. Still, a serious effort by Congress to use its powers against the Court would be seen as a stark departure and would require extraordinary justification.

We have all grown familiar with a simple picture of American constitutionalism: Congress makes constitutional rules only through the formal amendment process and leaves issues of interpretation to the Supreme Court. This picture is not so much false as incomplete. The reality is more complex. We have seen that Congress has significant power to shape, extend, or modify judicial interpretations. Congress also makes constitutional law – or at least quasi-constitutional law – in other ways. Congress is responsible for much of the fundamental framework of American government. Even in the field of what Americans consider to be constitutional law,

[64] Steven G. Calabresi, "The Congressional Roots of Judicial Activism" (2004) 20 *J. Law & Politics* 577.

Congress's influence is greater than is often appreciated. In the broader field of quasi-constitutional law, Congress plays a leading role. Indeed, as we have seen, even where the Supreme Court seems most supreme, its efforts take place against a background of congressional support for its authority. Considering that American constitutional law is notoriously oriented toward judicial supremacy, the remaining degree of legislative constitutionalism is all the more impressive.

22 Between Supremacy and Exclusivity

Owen Fiss

The Constitution of the United States is a broad charter that establishes the structure of government and identifies the values to which the country aspires. All Americans have the prerogative as well as the responsibility to give this charter meaning in our day-to-day lives. We live under the Constitution and must be faithful to its mandates. This duty of fidelity applies as forcefully to ordinary citizens as it does to public officials.

Throughout history, the Supreme Court has been depicted as the final arbiter of the meaning of the Constitution. Such a view does not deny the role that the other branches of government or, for that matter, the general citizenry have in interpreting the Constitution, but only posits a priority for the interpretations of the judicial branch. The governing assumption is that where there are conflicting interpretations, the Court's should prevail.

In our time, this assumption found powerful expression in *Brown v. Board of Education*[1] and in the struggles to make that decision a living reality. This assumption is now being challenged by a movement in the legal academy known as legislative constitutionalism, which claims a new and important role for Congress in the process of constitutional interpretation, but which, I am sad to say, is born of a misunderstanding of the role of the judiciary during the civil rights era and of a frustration with the Court ever since.

HISTORICAL ROOTS OF LEGISLATIVE CONSTITUTIONALISM

The Supreme Court's decision in *Brown v. Board of Education* declared the Jim Crow system of school segregation unconstitutional and in so doing set aside the laws of seventeen states and the District of Columbia. In the face of massive and forceful resistance, most notably to the desegregation of the Little Rock schools, President Dwight D. Eisenhower treated the Supreme Court's edict in *Brown* as authoritative – not necessarily right, but authoritative nevertheless – and used the military force at his disposal to ensure compliance. President John Kennedy did the same in 1962 when James Meredith sought to integrate the University of Mississippi.

[1] *Brown v. Bd. of Educ. (Brown I)*, 347 U.S. 483 (1954); *Brown v. Bd. of Educ. (Brown II)*, 349 U.S. 294 (1955).

Congress also treated the *Brown* decision as authoritative and, in a series of enactments that began in 1957 and continued through the 1960s, became an important participant in the project that came to be known as the Second Reconstruction. Some of these measures sought to enhance the enforcement of rights that had been declared by the Court. For example, Title IV of the *Civil Rights Act* of 1964 authorized the attorney general to commence school desegregation suits,[2] and Title VI of that same law commanded federal agencies not to fund programs that discriminated on the basis of race.[3] The *Voting Rights Act of* 1965 suspended literacy tests that, according to statistical indices devised by Congress, excluded blacks from the polls.[4] This act also authorized the appointment of federal officials to register voters.[5]

Other statutes were more ambitious and created rights not previously recognized by the Court. Title II of the *Civil Rights Act* of 1964, for example, prohibited racial discrimination in restaurants, hotels, and other privately owned public accommodations.[6] Similarly, Title VII prohibited discrimination by private employers.[7] Title VIII of the *Civil Rights Act* of 1968 prohibited racial discrimination in privately owned housing.[8] In creating these rights to be free from discrimination by private actors, Congress did not dispute the authority of the Court as the final arbiter of the Constitution. Rather, Congress viewed the Court's rulings on the scope of equal protection as a minimum or baseline and sought to build on it.

The Second Reconstruction was supported, maybe even inspired, by a broad-based organization of citizens, mostly black, led by Martin Luther King. Few of the achievements of the Second Reconstruction would have been realized without the courageous and noble protests of civil rights activists and the brutal sacrifices those protests entailed. A similar point must be made about the work of the executive branch and Congress. The Second Reconstruction should be viewed as a coordinated effort by all the branches of government, in which each branch used the powers at its disposal for a common purpose. Yet at the center of this extraordinary endeavor was the Supreme Court, then led by Earl Warren. The Court had issued the initial edict – the racial caste structure must be dismantled. The Court amplified that command at crucial junctures and went out of its way to protect the activities of the civil rights movement and to encourage the full participation of Congress and the president in the effort to achieve racial equality. The Second Reconstruction and its many achievements stand as a tribute to the Court and have greatly enhanced its claim to authority.

The Second Reconstruction is long over, as the proponents of legislative constitutionalism often remind us. The Second Reconstruction finally collapsed in

[2] Pub. L. No. 88-352, §§401–410, 78 Stat. 241at 246–49 (codified as amended at 42 U.S.C. §§2000c to 2000c-9 (2000)).

[3] §§601–605, 78 Stat. at 252–53 (codified as amended at 42 U.S.C. §§2000d to 2000d-4a (2000)).

[4] Pub. L. No. 89-110, 79 Stat. 437 (codified as amended at 42 U.S.C. §§1971 at 1973 to 1973bb-1 (2000)).

[5] Ibid.

[6] Pub. L. No. 88-352, §§201–207, 78 Stat. 241, 243–46 (codified as amended at 42 U.S.C. §§2000a to 2000a-6 (2000)).

[7] Civil Rights Act of 1964, §§701–716, 78 Stat. at 253–66 (codified as amended at 42 U.S.C. §§2000e to 2000e-17 (2000)).

[8] Pub. L. No. 90-284, §§801–819, 82 Stat. 73, 81–89 (codified as amended at 42 U.S.C. §§3601 to 3619 (2000)).

August 1996 when President Bill Clinton signed into law a welfare reform measure that divested the federal government of responsibility for America's poorest citizens,[9] a disproportionate number of whom are black.[10] Yet the decline had begun years earlier. Starting in 1966 fissures developed in the civil rights movement, some over the leadership of Martin Luther King, most over the demand by some factions of the movement for black separatism. In April 1968, King was assassinated, and the movement was left without a charismatic leader. By that time, President Lyndon Johnson had massively increased American military involvement in Vietnam, and public attention began to shift to the war. Protests against the war replaced marches for civil rights.

The impact of the war was soon felt in organized politics, most notably in the presidential election of 1968. Fearful of defeat because of the growing strength of antiwar sentiment, Johnson decided not to run for reelection. Robert Kennedy, then a senator from New York, who had served as attorney general in the early 1960s and in that capacity had emerged as a forceful advocate for civil rights, was a critic of the war and a popular contender for the Democratic nomination. He was assassinated in June 1968. Hubert Humphrey, Johnson's vice president, secured the Democratic nomination and faced Richard Nixon, the Republican candidate. Unlike Humphrey, Nixon was free of the onus of the war. He sought to broaden his appeal, especially in the South, by campaigning against the Warren Court and all that it stood for. He primarily attacked judicial decisions reforming criminal procedure, claiming that the Court was soft on crime, but also made it clear that he was opposed to the role the Court had played in launching and then directing the Second Reconstruction.[11]

Richard Nixon was elected president in November 1968. That event marked the end of one era of American law and the beginning of another – the one we must live with. Upon taking office, Nixon reversed the civil rights policies of his Democratic predecessors. From 1960 through 1968, the attorney general had been on the forefront of the effort to implement *Brown*, crafting and proposing new legislation and then using all the authority conferred by the civil rights statutes to enforce the decision.[12] Nixon's attorney general, John Mitchell, was of another inclination altogether, even asking for further delays in implementing *Brown*.[13] More significantly, during the six years that he was in office, President Nixon made a number of appointments to the Supreme Court – Warren Burger, William Rehnquist, Lewis Powell, and Harry Blackmun – that effectively changed the direction of the Court.

Throughout the 1970s and early 1980s, Warren Burger served as Chief Justice, but the intellectual and ideological leadership of the Court was provided by William Rehnquist.[14] When Burger retired in 1986, President Reagan conformed outward appearances to the inner reality by naming Rehnquist Chief Justice. Antonin Scalia

[9] Personal Responsibility and Work Opportunity Reconciliation Act of 1996, Pub. L. No. 104-193, 110 Stat. 2105 (codified as amended primarily in scattered sections of 42 U.S.C.); see Peter Edelman, "The Worst Thing Bill Clinton Has Done," *Atlantic Monthly*, Mar. 1997 at 43.

[10] See Jason DeParle, *American Dream: Three Women, Ten Kids, and a Nation's Drive to End Welfare* (New York: Viking, 2004).

[11] See Richard H. Rovere, "Letter from Miami Beach," *New Yorker*, Aug. 17, 1968, 93 at 93–4.

[12] See Brian K. Landsberg, *Enforcing Civil Rights: Race Discrimination and the Department of Justice* (Lawrence: University Press of Kansas, 1997).

[13] *Alexander v. Holmes County Bd. of Educ.*, 396 U.S. 19 (1969).

[14] See Owen Fiss and Charles Krauthammer, "The Rehnquist Court," *New Republic*, Mar. 10, 1982, at 14.

filled Burger's vacancy. The direction Rehnquist and Scalia charted for the Court was greatly aided by the appointment in 1991 of Clarence Thomas (to replace Thurgood Marshall) and, to a lesser extent, by the appointments of Anthony Kennedy and Sandra Day O'Connor. The latter two, on notable occasions, sided with the more liberal wing of the Court, especially once Stephen Breyer and Ruth Bader Ginsburg took their seats alongside John Paul Stevens (appointed by Ford to replace William Douglas) and David Souter (appointed by the first President Bush to replace William Brennan). Breyer and Ginsburg were appointed by President Bill Clinton and represent the only appointments by a Democratic president for more than thirty years.

In terms of personnel, the Rehnquist Court evolved out of the changes of the late 1960s and early 1970s. The Court's doctrine also has its roots in the program announced by Richard Nixon in the election of 1968. *Brown* remains on the books but has been drained of its generative force. Rights created by the Warren Court have either been diluted or, in some instances, repudiated. Of course, there are exceptions. In 1992, the Court reaffirmed the earlier decision in *Roe v. Wade* invalidating laws criminalizing abortion.[15] In 2003, the Court invalidated laws criminalizing sodomy[16] and upheld affirmative action in law school admissions.[17] In June 2004, the Court placed limits on the wartime detention policies of the second President Bush.[18] The importance of these decisions should not be minimized; yet, in truth, they were anomalies. They were the product of a sharply divided Court and were greeted with a sigh of relief and a measure of surprise. They were not new departures, but rather appeared almost as vestiges of another era.

For many in the academy, the jurisprudence of the Burger and Rehnquist Courts proved disheartening. It seemed to be a repudiation of the heroic idealism embodied in *Brown* and other decisions of the Warren Court. In earlier times this disenchantment with the Court found expression in a movement in the academy known as Critical Legal Studies (CLS). Although the proponents of CLS embraced the egalitarianism underlying *Brown*, they proclaimed the indeterminacy of all rules or principles and dismissed the objective aspirations of the law as a form of mystification. By their account, law is not law but simply politics in another guise.[19] Although CLS is now dead, the disenchantment that once gave it life has not disappeared but instead has become the lifeblood of legislative constitutionalism. As a movement of those who have soured on the Court, legislative constitutionalism has considerable sway in the academy today, especially among those committed to equality, and was abundantly represented at the conference out of which this book has grown. Interestingly, one of the leaders of CLS – Mark Tushnet – is at the vanguard of this movement, too.

Legislative constitutionalism seeks – in some ill-defined way – a greater role for the legislature in the process of constitutional interpretation. As a purely historical matter, it is understandable why those disenchanted with the Burger and Rehnquist

[15] *Planned Parenthood of Southeastern Pa. v. Casey*, 505 U.S. 833 (1992).

[16] *Lawrence v. Texas*, 539 U.S. 558 (2003).

[17] *Grutter v. Bollinger*, 539 U.S. 306 (2003). But see *Gratz v. Bollinger*, 539 U.S. 244 (2003) (finding an undergraduate admissions policy that granted points to applicants from underrepresented minority groups to be a violation of the Equal Protection Clause).

[18] *Rasul v. Bush*, 124 S. Ct. 2686 (2004); *Hamdi v. Rumsfeld*, 124 S. Ct. 2633 (2004).

[19] See "The Death of the Law?" in Owen Fiss, *The Law as It Could Be* (New York: New York University Press, 2003) 191.

Courts turned to Congress to redeem the promise of *Brown*. Although matters have changed since the arrival of the Newt Gingrich Congress in 1994, throughout the 1970s and 1980s and in the early 1990s, Congress defended rights against retrenchment by the judiciary.[20] In the *Pregnancy Discrimination Act* of 1978,[21] for example, Congress overturned *Geduldig v. Aiello*[22] and amended Title VII of the *Civil Rights Act* of 1964 to make discrimination on the basis of pregnancy unlawful, much like discrimination on the basis of sex. Congress could see, as the Court could not, that discrimination based on pregnancy was discrimination against women.

On numerous occasions Congress also responded to the Court's unwillingness to measure illegality in terms of social consequences. In 1982, when it came time to renew the *Voting Rights Act* of 1965, Congress took the bite out of the Court's decision in *City of Mobile v. Bolden* (1980)[23] by making seemingly innocent electoral practices (such as the use of multimembered districts or at-large elections) illegal if the effect is to disadvantage minorities.[24] In the *Civil Rights Act* of 1991, Congress made unlawful those employment practices that had the effect of disadvantaging blacks and did not serve a compelling purpose (or in technical jargon, were not justified by a business necessity).[25] As acknowledged in the preamble to the 1991 Act,[26] Congress wished to overturn the Court's grudging interpretation of Title VIII of the *Civil Rights Act* of 1964 in *Wards Cove Packing Co. v. Atonio* (1989)[27] and to restore in full the disparate impact principle previously announced by the Court in 1971 in *Griggs v. Duke Power Company*.[28]

When it enacted the 1991 Act, Congress built on the *Americans with Disabilities Act (ADA)* of 1990.[29] With the *ADA*, Congress extended the underlying principles of *Brown* to the disabled and, in requiring covered agencies to make reasonable accommodations for the special needs of the disabled, drew on the *Griggs* principle. Similarly, in the *Religious Freedom Restoration Act (RFRA)* of 1993,[30] Congress sought to provide the protection to religious liberty that the Court had refused to extend in *Employment Division v. Smith*.[31] *RFRA* prohibited the government from enacting measures that substantially burden religious exercise unless those

[20] William N. Eskridge, Jr., described the new role of Congress in his important article "Reneging on History? Playing the Court/Congress/President Civil Rights Game" (1991) 79 *Cal. L. Rev.* 613. His contribution to this volume, cowritten with John Ferejohn, "Super-Statutes: The New American Constitutionalism," Chapter 15, builds on that work, though the model he proposes, infected by the same disenchantment with the judiciary that belongs to the proponents of legislative constitutionalism, slights the role the Court played in the civil rights era – when it proclaimed rights and helped generate in an affirmative and positive way such fundamental legislation as the *Civil Rights Act* of 1964, the *Voting Rights Act* of 1965, and the *Civil Rights Act* of 1968.

[21] Pub. L. No. 95-555, 92 Stat. 2076 (1978) (codified as amended at 42 U.S.C. §2000e(k) (2000)).

[22] 417 U.S. 484 (1974).

[23] 446 U.S. 55 (1980).

[24] *Voting Rights Act Amendments of 1982*, Pub. L. No. 97-205, 96 Stat. 131 (codified as amended at 42 U.S.C. 1971, 1973–1973aa-6 (2000)). See generally James Forman, Jr., "Victory by Surrender: The Voting Rights Amendments of 1982 and the Civil Rights Act of 1991" (1992) 10 *Yale Pol'y Rev.* 133.

[25] Civil Rights Act of 1991, Pub. L. No. 102-166, 105 Stat. 1071 (codified as amended in scattered sections of 2 U.S.C., 29 U.S.C., and 42 U.S.C (2000)). See generally Forman, *supra* note 24.

[26] *Civil Rights Act of 1991*, §§2–3, 105 Stat. at 1071.

[27] 490 U.S. 642 (1989).

[28] 401 U.S. 424 (1971).

[29] Pub. L. No. 101-336, 104 Stat. 327 (codified as amended at 42 U.S.C. §§12101 to 12213).

[30] Pub. L. No. 103-141, 107 Stat. 1488 (codified as amended at 42 U.S.C. §§2000bb to 2000bb-4 (2000)).

[31] 494 U.S. 872 (1990).

measures serve some compelling state purpose and are narrowly tailored to achieve that purpose.

Given the scope and breadth of this legislative program, it was only natural that those disenchanted with the Court should exalt the authority of Congress. The Court itself also contributed, in an odd way, to the emphasis on legislation. Not content to do battle with the Warren Court, the Rehnquist Court took on Congress as well. Starting in the late 1990s, the Court embarked on a program of nullifying many of the congressional measures that sought to enhance rights, and this body of decisions further inflamed the proponents of legislative constitutionalism. The Court seemed to reserve for itself the role of deciding what rights citizens should enjoy.

Rights have often been enhanced by Congress through the exercise of the Commerce Power. The public accommodations provision of the *Civil Rights Act* of 1964 was sustained soon after its enactment as an appropriate regulation of commerce.[32] As a consequence, everyone assumed that the provisions of that Act barring employment discrimination were also valid as an appropriate exercise of the Commerce Power. The Supreme Court's decision in 2000 in *United States v. Morrison*[33] cast doubt on this assumption. In that case, the Court held unconstitutional a provision of the *Violence Against Women Act* (*VAWA*) that gave women a federal judicial remedy against gender-based violence inflicted by private actors. Such a measure, the Court declared, could not be sustained as an exercise of the Commerce Power.

An even more plausible source of authority for *VAWA* was Section 5 of the Fourteenth Amendment, but the Court held that Congress had exceeded the scope of that authority as well. Section 5 gives Congress the power to enforce the provisions of the Fourteenth Amendment, which, of course, includes the guarantee of equal protection. In 1966 in *Katzenbach v. Morgan*,[34] the Warren Court, anxious to facilitate congressional participation in the Second Reconstruction, gave new life and force to Section 5 and in that context adumbrated what later became known as the "ratchet theory."[35] One part of this theory proclaimed that Congress could not dilute or undermine the Court's interpretation of a constitutional provision – Congress could not, for example, limit *Brown* or interfere with the exercise of any other constitutional right that the Court had articulated in the process of interpreting a constitutional guarantee. The affirmative part of the theory acknowledged the power of Congress to proclaim and protect rights even where the Court had not done so. Such measures could provide remedies to implement rights that the Court had already articulated, but Congress was not confined to this task. It could also create rights.

In *Katzenbach v. Morgan* itself, the Court upheld, under Section 5, a provision of the *Voting Rights Act* of 1965 that banned the application of an English literacy test to students who had completed sixth grade in Puerto Rico. The Court had not yet

32 *Katzenbach v. McClung*, 379 U.S. 294 (1964); *Heart of Atlanta Motel, Inc. v. United States*, 379 U.S. 241 (1964).

33 529 U.S. 598 (2000).

34 384 U.S. 641 (1966).

35 See William Cohen, "Congressional Power to Interpret Due Process and Equal Protection" (1975) 27 *Stan. L. Rev.* 603 at 606.

ruled on this specific issue but had already upheld the application of an English literacy test in North Carolina.[36] The Court now proclaimed, however, that Congress was entitled to make its own judgment about the reach of equal protection and to prohibit the application of the English literacy test on the theory that such a test rendered a large portion of the Puerto Rican community in New York especially vulnerable to discrimination by local officials. The validity of the congressional action did not depend on the willingness of the Court to believe that it would have come to the same conclusion about the meaning of equal protection. Congress could prohibit conduct that the Court might not have, provided, of course, that the Court could perceive a basis on which Congress might think that the prohibited action would amount or lead to a denial of equal protection.

The scope of the *Katzenbach v. Morgan* principle was immediately recognized, first by commentators[37] and then by Congress itself when it enacted the *Civil Rights Act* of 1968, which prohibited race-based violence by private actors and racial discrimination in private housing. The Court limited the reach of *Katzenbach v. Morgan* in 1970 when it denied Congress the power to extend the right to vote to 18-year-olds,[38] but it continued to operate as an important font of congressional authority for the next thirty years – a period in which Congress resisted the Court's retrenchment on rights and crafted the legislative program that made legality turn more on the social consequences of a practice or law than on the motivation lying behind it.

A turning point came in 1997 in *City of Boerne v. Flores*.[39] In that case, the Court struck down *RFRA* as an inappropriate exercise of the Section 5 power. Although the enactment of *RFRA* could be understood to conform to the ratchet theory of *Katzenbach v. Morgan* – after all, Congress was not diluting any right that the Court had declared, but rather was adding to the rights that citizens enjoyed – the Court was of another opinion. It saw *RFRA* as an affront to its claim of supremacy.

Arguably, the Court was led to this view because of an expansive reading of *Smith*, the decision to which Congress was responding in *RFRA*. The Court understood *Smith* to define the bounds of the Free Exercise Clause and to declare that laws that are neutral and generally applicable do not interfere with the free exercise of religion. From that perspective, *RFRA* could not be defended as a measure to protect the religious liberty guaranteed by Section 1 of the Fourteenth Amendment and thus was beyond the powers of Congress under Section 5.

RFRA was an immediate and direct response to the Court's decision in *Smith*, and *Boerne* may have been colored by that particular dynamic, verging on confrontation, between the Court and the legislature. Soon, however, the assertion of judicial authority that was the essence of *Boerne* spread more broadly and extended to situations more similar to that of *Katzenbach v. Morgan*, in which there was no confrontation, but rather something closer to a lacuna. *Morrison* was such a case, though the Court primarily treated *VAWA* as an exercise of the Commerce Clause and only secondarily disposed of the Section 5 claim. However, in two decisions that

[36] *Lassiter v. Northampton County Bd. of Elections*, 360 U.S. 45 (1959).

[37] See, e.g., Archibald Cox, "The Supreme Court, 1965 Term – Foreword: Constitutional Adjudication and the Promotion of Human Rights" (1966) 80 *Harv. L. Rev.* 91.

[38] *Oregon v. Mitchell*, 400 U.S. 112 (1970).

[39] 521 U.S. 507 (1997).

soon followed – *Kimel v. Florida Board of Regents* (2000)[40] and *Board of Trustees of the University of Alabama v. Garrett* (2001)[41] – the Court confronted *Katzenbach v. Morgan* more directly and in effect overruled it. Section 5 was emptied of the meaning that *Katzenbach v. Morgan* had given it. As before, Congress had the power to provide remedies for well-established rights, but it no longer had the power to articulate rights under Section 1 of the Fourteenth Amendment that the Court itself was not prepared to recognize. The space that *Katzenbach v. Morgan* had opened for an independent role for Congress in the articulation of rights was now closed.

In *Kimel*, the Court held that Congress could not make states liable for damages when they discriminated against elderly employees. In *Garrett*, the Court denied that Congress had the power to make states liable for employment discrimination based on disability. In these two cases, Congress could not possibly be faulted for overruling a Court decision – a claim that might seem plausible in the context of *RFRA* – but the Court nonetheless concluded that Congress had exceeded the scope of its powers under Section 5. The Court accused Congress of altering the substantial meaning of equal protection, but what it meant was that Congress had deemed certain state practices a denial of equal protection in circumstances in which the Court itself was not prepared to do so.

In *Nevada Department of Human Resources v. Hibbs* (2003),[42] the Court upheld the *Family and Medical Leave Act* as a proper exercise of the Section 5 power. This decision was a surprise to many.[43] The Court reasoned that women were a protected group under Section 1, and that the leave provisions were an appropriate measure to allow them to participate fully in the economy and to do so on equal terms. The next year, in *Tennessee v. Lane*,[44] the Court upheld the obligation of states to make reasonable accommodation for the needs of the disabled in the context of guaranteeing access to courts. In these rulings, the Court did not revive *Katzenbach v. Morgan*, but rather indicated that it agreed with the congressional judgment about the rights declared and on that ground upheld the statutes. Thus, the shadow of *Boerne*, *Morrison*, *Kimel*, and *Garrett* remains and puts into question any effort by Congress to enhance rights. This shadow has only intensified the disenchantment with the Court and, as a purely historical matter, explains the ever-increasing popularity of legislative constitutionalism. It may also account for the especially strident form that this movement has taken in recent days – throwing out the good with the bad.

TWO FORMS OF LEGISLATIVE CONSTITUTIONALISM

One form of legislative constitutionalism – the more modest version – claims that the legislature has a role to play in constitutional interpretation. This branch of legislative constitutionalism denies the judiciary a monopoly on constitutional

[40] 528 U.S. 62 (2000).

[41] 531 U.S. 356 (2001).

[42] 538 U.S. 721 (2003).

[43] See, e.g., Robert C. Post, "The Supreme Court, 2002 Term – Foreword: Fashioning the Legal Constitution: Culture, Courts, and Law" (2003) 117 *Harv. L. Rev.* 4 at 9 (describing *Hibbs* as "a startling and fascinating decision").

[44] 541 U.S. 509 (2004).

interpretation; it simply rejects judicial exclusivity without questioning judicial supremacy and, as such, seems unobjectionable. It derives from a simple recognition of the universalism of the Constitution – that it is binding on us all. Every time the legislature acts, it must determine whether it has the constitutional authority to do so – for example, to decide whether a transaction it seeks to regulate affects interstate commerce or denies equal protection.

The proponents of legislative constitutionalism often present themselves as revisionists and in that posture criticize the role the Supreme Court assumed for itself during the civil rights era. The Warren Court is mocked as a hegemon. If we are speaking, however, of what I have called modest legislative constitutionalism, such claims seem entirely unfounded. The Warren Court went out of its way to encourage and facilitate congressional participation in the Second Reconstruction, both in the implementation and creation of rights. This is evident from the Court's holding in *Katzenbach v. Morgan*, from its decisions broadly and quickly sustaining the *Civil Rights Act* of 1964 and the *Voting Rights Act* of 1965, and also from the lengths to which it went to cast the mantle of validity on the fair housing provisions of the *Civil Rights Act* of 1968 almost immediately after that Act was passed. In June 1968, two months after the enactment of the *Civil Rights Act* of 1968, the Court transformed an ancient reconstruction statute into a fair housing law and upheld it under the Thirteenth Amendment.[45]

In recent decades, constitutionalism has become a global phenomenon. As Tsvi Kahana has suggested in conversation, this worldwide move toward constitutional governments may help explain the growth of legislative constitutionalism and has possibly contributed to its sense of newness. Thanks to the work of an ever-growing group of scholars (incidentally a group that includes Mark Tushnet), the comparative perspective of American lawyers has been enlarged.[46] We now have to consider the familiar American institution of judicial review within a global context that contains many constitutional governments founded on the principle of parliamentary supremacy. Granted, this comparative perspective has the inevitable effect of highlighting the manifold ways that legislatures can participate in the process of constitutional interpretation.[47] But these insights are not new and can easily be accommodated within the terms of the relationship that existed between the Court and Congress during the civil rights era.

What is truly new, and what I do contest, is a version of legislative constitutionalism that, much to my consternation, disputes not only judicial exclusivity but judicial supremacy as well, and thus strikes at the heart of *Brown* and the claim for authority upon which the Second Reconstruction was built. This form of legislative constitutionalism – the strong version – addresses a situation in which there are conflicting interpretations of the Constitution, one by the legislature and the other by the judiciary, and denies that the judicial interpretation should be authoritative.

[45] *Jones v. Alfred H. Mayer Co.*, 392 U.S. 409 (1968).

[46] See, e.g., Norman Dorsen et al., *Comparative Constitutionalism: Cases and Materials* (St. Paul, MN: Thomson/West, 2003); Vicki C. Jackson and Mark Tushnet, *Comparative Constitutional Law* (New York: Foundation Press, 1999).

[47] Janet L. Hiebert, "New Constitutional Ideas: Can New Parliamentary Models Resist Judicial Dominance When Interpreting Rights?" (2004) 82 *Tex. L. Rev.* 1963.

In the course of the conference out of which this book has grown, Professor Tushnet gave an example that might help us to understand strong legislative constitutionalism more fully. He asked us to imagine that the legislature is presently considering whether to enact a statute that proscribes the advocacy of violence – let us call it *USA Patriot Act II* – and there is a dispute over whether the First Amendment permits such a law. A majority of Congress is of the view that such a law should be governed by the so-called discounted clear and present danger test. Under this test, the advocacy of violence can be proscribed if such advocacy presents a clear and present danger, with the understanding that the greater the danger the less immediate or present it need be. Although the Supreme Court used this test in 1951 in *Dennis v. United States*[48] to sustain the convictions of the leaders of the Communist Party of the United States, it later repudiated the test in 1969 in *Brandenburg v. Ohio*.[49] Under prevailing doctrine, the Court would judge the Act's constitutionality under a more stringent test – one that would proscribe the advocacy of violence only when it constituted an incitement to imminent lawless action. An issue would thus arise as to which interpretation of the First Amendment should prevail: Should it be the Court's position or the legislature's? I understand strong legislative constitutionalism and Professor Tushnet's demand that we "take the Constitution away from the courts"[50] to mean that the legislative interpretation of the First Amendment should prevail and that there is no basis for the judiciary to impose its understanding of the First Amendment on Congress and declare the *USA Patriot Act II* unconstitutional.

Such a conclusion seems startling – not just at variance with *Brown*, but also *Marbury v. Madison*[51] and the 200-year history built on that precedent. Strong legislative constitutionalism does not purport to be an interpretation of our historical practice, but rather a critical revisionism driven by deep normative commitments, specifically an attachment to democracy and the system of governance that it implies. Admittedly, Congress is an imperfect institutional embodiment of this ideal, in part because of the inequalities in economic power that infect all elections but also because of the allocation of power in Congress (two Senators for each state, regardless of the number of people in the state). Yet Congress is a closer approximation of the democratic ideal than the judiciary, and this may lead some committed to democracy to embrace strong legislative constitutionalism and to insist on the supremacy of the legislature's interpretation.

Tushnet's example involves freedom of speech and thus the very integrity of the electoral process. Some may find in this fact the basis for resisting strong legislative constitutionalism and for subscribing to judicial supremacy on the ground that undemocratic means may sometimes be necessary to safeguard democracy. Such a view is not a logical necessity. As indicated by the chapters by Jeremy Webber[52]

48 341 U.S. 494 (1951).

49 395 U.S. 444 (1969). See generally Harry Kalven, Jr., *A Worthy Tradition: Freedom of Speech in America*, Jamie Kalven, ed. (New York: Harper and Row, 1988) at 125–236 (describing the Court's treatment of subversive advocacy prior to *Brandenburg v. Ohio*).

50 Mark Tushnet, *Taking the Constitution Away from the Courts* (Princeton, N.J.: Princeton University Press, 1999).

51 5 U.S. (1 Cranch) 137 (1803).

52 Jeremy Webber, "Democratic Decision Making as the First Principle of Contemporary Constitutionalism," Chapter 20 in this volume.

and Harry Arthurs[53] in this volume, a staunch democrat might go so far as to insist that the interpretation of the Constitution advanced by elected representatives should be supreme even when it comes to protecting the democratic process itself. Undemocratic means, so the argument goes, should not be used even to preserve democracy.

Believing, as I do, in the equality of all citizens – the moral foundation of democracy – I am as firm in my commitment to democracy as the next person. Yet, when used to provide the basis for legislative constitutionalism in its strong form, this invocation of democracy seems entirely overblown. The democratic ideal should be applied to the political system as a whole and should not be used to ascertain the legitimacy of each component within the system. As a test of the system, democracy requires only that each component be linked to public officials and institutions that are responsive to popular sentiment. Thus, although the judiciary may not be directly responsive to the people, as the legislature is, it is sufficiently embedded within a larger system of democratic governance to meet the objection that judicial review is undemocratic.

Although Justices of the Supreme Court are not elected, they are appointed by elected officials. The power also remains in the hands of the electorate to respond to the Court's decisions (as it did, for example, with the Sixteenth Amendment, removing the apportionment requirement for an income tax). True, the amendment process is cumbersome, requiring approval of both houses and three-quarters of the states, and life tenure of federal judges allows them to become entrenched and to exercise power long after the political regime that empowered them has disappeared. The test is not, however, whether the judiciary is empowered by, or accountable to, a current majority. Democracy requires only that the links between the judiciary and popular sentiment are sufficient to justify regarding the judiciary as part of a democratic system. That they are.

The existing links can, of course, be tightened to make a component – here the judiciary – more fully integrated into the democratic system. Having Justices of the Supreme Court serve for a fixed term of ten or twelve years, as is true of the constitutional courts of Europe, might be such a proposal. So might Section 33 of the *Canadian Charter of Rights and Freedoms*, which permits legislative override of a Supreme Court decision.[54] Such a provision seeks a fuller realization of the democratic ideal but at the same time avoids the extravagant claims of the more stringent form of legislative constitutionalism that disputes judicial supremacy. Although Canada is a parliamentary system and Section 33 may be

[53] Harry Arthurs, "Populism, the Legislative Process, and the Canadian Constitution," Chapter 8 in this volume.

[54] *Canadian Charter of Rights and Freedoms*, Part I of the *Constitution Act, 1982*, being Schedule B to the *Canada Act 1982* (U.K.), 1982, c. 11. S. 33 provides:

(1) Parliament or the legislature of a province may expressly declare in an Act of Parliament or of the legislature, as the case may be, that the Act or a provision thereof shall operate notwithstanding a provision included in section 2 or sections 7 to 15 of this Charter.

(2) An Act or a provision of an Act in respect of which a declaration made under this section is in effect shall have such operation as it would have but for the provision of this Charter referred to in the declaration.

(3) A declaration made under subsection (1) shall cease to have effect five years after it comes into force or on such earlier date as may be specified in the declaration.

(4) Parliament or the legislature of a province may re-enact a declaration made under subsection (1).

(5) Subsection (3) applies in respect of a re-enactment made under subsection (4).

regarded as a concession to that fact, the availability of the legislative override does not deny the supremacy of the Charter or the Supreme Court's interpretation of it.

Section 33 allows Parliament or a provincial legislature to declare that a measure shall "operate notwithstanding" a particular substantive provision of the Charter. Section 33 does not extend to all rights. Moreover, the legislative override permitted by Section 33 is only temporary, and thus does not reverse or abrogate a judicial determination that the measure is unconstitutional. Admittedly, Section 33 gives Parliament and the provincial legislatures the power to renew the temporary override, but even if that power to renew is exercised, the legislative declaration does not negate either the relevant substantive constitutional provision or the Court's interpretation of it. The provision and the Court's interpretation remain authoritative, though their operation is stayed.

Viewed as part of a larger political system, the judiciary's claim for authority, like that of any component, depends on its competency to perform its assigned task. In the constitutional context, the judiciary's task is not just to arrive at any interpretation, or even a reasonable interpretation – Congress or even the president can do that as well as the Court. Rather, the task is to arrive at a correct interpretation, and, in my view, the judiciary's authority and thus its claim to supremacy are derived from its special competence to arrive at a correct interpretation. By this I mean simply that in the generality of cases the judiciary is the branch most likely to arrive at a correct interpretation of the Constitution.[55]

The special competence of which I speak does not arise from the sagacity of those who happen to wear the robes. One of the most remarkable features of the American judicial system is the similarity, as a matter of personality and learning, of those who are judges and those who are political leaders or captains of industry. The competence of the judiciary derives not from the persons who are judges, but from the limitations on their exercise of power – limitations that commit the judiciary to what might be called public reason. Judges who fail to respect these limitations forfeit their authority and their claim to supremacy.

One limitation consists of a judge's obligation to listen to grievances that he or she might otherwise prefer to ignore. Another is the obligation of a judge to allow the parties to address the issues in open court with reasoned arguments and to inquire into the factual basis of the various contentions. Still another limitation arises from the requirement that the judge publicly justify his or her decision. To see a court work as it should is to see reason unfold.

Of course, sometimes a court does not work as it should. Precedents are ignored; arguments are misunderstood; too much emphasis is given to history as opposed to structure; the facts are not sufficiently developed. Mistakes will be made. This is only to acknowledge the fallibility of reason, not to deny the rationality of the process that is the basis for the judiciary's claim of authority. When we criticize a court and claim that is has erred in its interpretation of the Constitution, we seek to hold the court accountable to reason itself.

Admittedly, the criteria for deciding which interpretations are correct and which are mistaken – should the interpretation be governed by original intent or the

[55] See Fiss, *supra* note 19.

structure of the Constitution? – are often contested, as is the interpretation itself – the discounted clear and present danger test or incitement? Disagreement is, as Jeremy Waldron has reminded us,[56] a persistent and pervasive feature of interpretive practice, even interpretation of law. The presence of such disagreement does not, however, preclude the possibility of a correct interpretation. Nor does it alter the aim of the interpretive practice – to arrive at a correct interpretation – or mean that a correct interpretation is the one that most or all people agree with. A correct interpretation is one that is fully justified, not one that most accept.

Federal judges are insulated from political pressures because they are not elected but rather appointed. They serve for life and have protection against diminution in pay. This gives them a certain independence. This feature of the federal judiciary is frequently mentioned in debates about judicial supremacy. From my perspective, however, independence is not the source of judicial authority but rather a particular institutional arrangement that enables the judiciary to be faithful to its commitment to public reason, which I claim is the source of its authority. Appointment with fixed tenure is better than election at regular intervals, but even if judges are elected, as is true of some state judges, their obligation is the same. They are not the agents of the electorate, charged with enacting their will or promoting some public policy, but rather are obliged to give us an account of justice that is based on principle.

Reason does not belong to the judiciary alone. On the best of days, the legislature that decides to enact the *USA Patriot Act II*, on the theory that the discounted clear and present danger test is the proper standard for the First Amendment, presumably has made an attempt to arrive at a reasoned judgment comparable to that of the Court. But we do not allocate authority on the basis of what happens in any one instance. We must look at the generality of cases, and for that purpose, the limitations on the exercise of power are crucial. Although legislatures may sometimes reason in the same way as courts, their authority does not depend on it. Legislatures are not bound by the strictures of public reason. A statute is a statute even if – as in the case of the 9/11 Victims Compensation Fund[57] – its enactment is not preceded by hearings or meaningful deliberation and it does not contain within itself principled justification for all of its provisions. The authority of a statute does not depend on its rationality, or at least not on the rationality that would be conducive to arriving at a correct interpretation of the Constitution.[58]

Anyone with authority should listen. In deciding whether the *USA Patriot Act II* is constitutional, the Court certainly should take into account the position that the legislature has taken on the bounds of the First Amendment. The Court's authority rests on reason, and reason dictates that those seeking the right answer should listen to what others have to say. The Court's duty to listen also stems from structural

[56] Jeremy Waldron, *Law and Disagreement* (New York: Oxford University Press, 1999).

[57] See Elizabeth Berkowitz, *The Problematic Role of the Special Master: Undermining the Legitimacy of the September 11th Victim Compensation Fund* (2004) [unpublished, on file with author] (noting that the compensation fund was "proposed, debated, passed by the House, adopted by the Senate, and presented to the President all within eleven short days of the terrorist attacks"). See also Kenneth R. Feinberg, *What is Life Worth? The Unprecedented Effort to Compensate Victims of 9/11* (New York: Public Affairs, 2005).

[58] On the difficulties of interpretation by legislatures, see Tsvi Kahana, "Constitutional Cosiness and Legislative Activism" (2005) 55 *U. Toronto L.J.* 129 at 144–6.

features of Congress – from the fact that Congress is elected and accountable to the public and that it is a coordinate branch of government and as such is entitled, under the Constitution, to a measure of respect. In the end, however, after listening and listening carefully, the Court has the authority, indeed the obligation, to decide for itself whether the new *Patriot Act* is constitutional and, if necessary, to set the statute aside. Its judgment is supreme.

This appears to be settled doctrine when, in the example Professor Tushnet has given us, Congress takes a more limited view than the Court of the protection afforded by the Constitution. What happens, however, if the positions of the Court and Congress are reversed, and Congress takes a more robust view of rights than the Court? In some instances, Congress may decline to enact any law. For example, if Congress is of the view that any law that restricts speech other than incitement is barred by the First Amendment, Congress would simply not pass the law regulating subversive advocacy, and that would be the end of the matter. There would be no congressional regulation of speech and thus no federal statute for the Court to review. There is, however, another category of cases obscured by the Tushnet example, but sharply debated today, and highlighted by the controversy over *Boerne, Morrison, Kimel,* and *Garrett.* In such cases, Congress not only adopts a more robust understanding of rights than the Court, but also enacts a measure in furtherance of that view. An example is Title VIII of the *Civil Rights Act* of 1968, in which Congress, acting under Section 5 of the Fourteenth Amendment, sought to prohibit racial discrimination in privately owned housing as a way of providing equal protection. Congress might have been acting on the theory, not embraced by the Court, that ghettoization is likely to give rise to discrimination by the state in the provision of its services (police, schools, transportation, and the like) and that, therefore, the state action requirement of Section 1 of the Fourteenth Amendment was satisfied.

In passing on such rights-articulating measures, the Court has been especially jealous of its prerogatives, but such jealousy is unwarranted. The Court must decide for itself whether the measure falls within the powers granted to Congress – in this instance, whether it is a measure to enforce the Fourteenth Amendment. This much is required by the principal of judicial supremacy. But to insist on a higher standard – specifically, that the Court has embraced or is prepared to embrace the same views as Congress as to what rights the Fourteenth Amendment confers – is to confuse judicial supremacy with judicial exclusivity. Such a standard would deny Congress the deference that it rightly enjoys when a statute enhances citizens' rights.

The hypothetical proposed by Tushnet entails a rights-restricting measure and is predicated on a more grudging conception of rights than the Court's. Even in that context, Congress is entitled to a certain degree of respect. The Court must take seriously the congressional judgment implicit in the enactment, namely, that the measure is an appropriate exercise of an enumerated power and does not violate any rights conferred by the Constitution. In enacting the *USA Patriot Act II,* Congress would have to conclude that such a regulation of speech does not violate the First Amendment, and, in passing on that measure, the Court should take full account of Congress's judgment. As I said, this obligation to listen derives from the Court's commitment to public reason and from the respect that is due to Congress as an elected and coordinate branch of government. However, additional deference should be given to Congress when the Court reviews a rights-enhancing measure such as Title VIII of the *Civil Rights Act* of 1968. This added element of deference derives from the very fact that the statute enhances rather than restricts rights.

The distinction between rights-enhancing and rights-restricting measures is often hard to maintain, especially because it is always possible to transform interests into rights.[59] Although I see the fair housing provisions of the *Civil Rights Act* of 1968 as rights-enhancing, others might claim that they restrict not just an interest but a constitutionally guaranteed right of property owners to exclude anyone they wish. Cases such as this do not prove the impossibility of making a distinction between rights-enhancing and rights-restricting measures. They only underscore the challenge facing the Court. In applying the principle of *Katzenbach v. Morgan,* the Court must, in the first instance, decide whether the measure is rights-enhancing, and, in order to do this, the Court must determine whether the interests adversely affected by the statute are of constitutional proportions. The Court took up this challenge in *Kimel* and *Garrett.* The Court erred, however, as a matter of substantive law when it concluded that Congress had overstepped its bounds by providing the elderly and disabled with damage actions against the states for discrimination. The Court not only underestimated the import and scope of the equal protection guarantee but also misconstrued the principles of federalism. It exalted state sovereignty and endowed the state interests adversely affected by the congressional enactments with constitutional significance. By transforming rights-enhancing measures into rights-restricting ones in this way, the Court emptied *Katzenbach v. Morgan* of any significance.

Katzenbach v. Morgan also requires the Court to avoid too grandiose an understanding of its own interpretations of the guarantees of the Fourteenth Amendment that operate as the source of rights. If, as in *Boerne,* the Court takes the view that an earlier decision not only turned back a constitutional attack on a state statute but also propounded a full and complete understanding of the rights guaranteed by the Fourteenth Amendment, then the Court would have in effect denied Congress any space in which it might independently create rights under Section 5. Congress could only hope that the rights it confers coincide with the Court's own conception of Fourteenth Amendment rights. The genius of *Katzenbach v. Morgan* was to allow Congress to make a judgment about the meaning of equal protection (as it did in the *Civil Rights Act* of 1968) that the Court might not have made itself but which the Court could understand as having a plausible claim to being a true and correct interpretation of equal protection. Quite possibly, this is the *grundnorm* of the more modest and more appealing version of legislative constitutionalism that affirms judicial supremacy but denies judicial exclusivity.

In determining whether a statute is a proper exercise of an enumerated power, the Court must make a judgment about ends and means. When the Court concludes that a statute is rights-enhancing, then it has also made, at least in the context of Section 5, a judgment about the legitimacy of ends. The enhancement of rights is a permissible, indeed worthy, legislative end. A question remains, however, as to whether the statute is an appropriate means for enhancing rights, or in the terms

[59] See Robert A. Burt, "Miranda and Title II: A Morganatic Marriage" [1969] *Sup. Ct. Rev.* 81.

of the classic formula of *McCulloch v. Maryland* (1819),[60] whether the congressional intervention is "plainly adapted to that end." Because the statute is rights-enhancing, the Court should afford Congress a measure of deference in making this judgment over and above that derived from the dictates of public reason and from the fact that Congress is an elected and coordinate branch of government. This additional element of deference stems from the view – perhaps lying at the heart of *Katzenbach v. Morgan* – that the Bill of Rights and the Civil War amendments set forth the fundamental ideals of our nation, such as racial equality, freedom of speech, due process, and religious liberty, and that every measure that plausibly brings us closer to the realization of these ideals is, for that very reason, worthy of a special modicum of respect. More is better.

ACKNOWLEDGMENTS

With special thanks to David Harris, Michael Gerber, and Rebecca Charnas for their research assistance.

[60] 17 U.S. (4 Wheat.) 316, 421 (1819). The formula in full states: "Let the end be legitimate, let it be within the scope of the constitution, and all means which are appropriate, which are plainly adapted to that end, which are not prohibited, but consist with the letter and spirit of the constitution, are constitutional." Ibid.

23 Legislatures as Rule-Followers

Frederick Schauer

I

It is the signal achievement of *Magna Carta* to have established that even the king is subject to the law. Although a now-scorned account of law sees it as consisting in the commands from sovereign to subject,[1] after *Magna Carta* it is commonplace that the sovereign stands not above the law, but rather as part of it and under it. And now that the notion of a unitary sovereign has in most societies yielded to a more complex understanding of the role and status of government, the legacy of *Magna Carta* can be appreciated, in part, as the widely accepted proposition that no part of government – neither legislature nor executive nor judiciary nor bureaucracy nor military – is above the law.[2]

Yet although the proposition that government is not above the law will attract little dissent, the question of just what it means to say that government is not above the law is considerably more complex. Least controversially, the view that government is not above the law means that individuals who hold government positions are as subject as any other citizen to the laws of general application. Principles of diplomatic immunity may allow ambassadors to park with impunity in the vicinity of United Nations headquarters, but there exists no parallel principle of general governmental immunity that serves to immunize, except under rare circumstances, the actions of governmental officials from the ordinary application of ordinary law.

In the more important sense in which government can be said not to be above the law, however, government is expected to govern according to rules that organize, constitute, and constrain the process of governance. The legacy of *Magna Carta*, and in particular its Article 39, is centered around the idea that official power must

[1] The vertical command model is ordinarily associated with John Austin, H. L. A. Hart, ed., *The Province of Jurisprudence Determined and the Uses of the Study of Jurisprudence* (London: Weidenfeld & Nicolson, 1954). And the definitive critique of the vertical command model is H. L. A. Hart, *The Concept of Law*, 2nd ed. (Oxford: Clarendon Press, 1994) at 18–76. For a useful discussion distinguishing Austin from Bentham in their views about the role of commands in law, see Gerald J. Postema, *Bentham and the Common Law Tradition* (Oxford: Clarendon Press, 1986) at 324–8.

[2] Holding officials legally accountable is a conception of the rule of law commonly associated with A. V. Dicey, *Introduction to the Study of the Law of the Constitution*, 10th ed. (London: Macmillan, 1959) at 181–205. See also Richard H. Fallon, Jr., "'The Rule of Law' as a Concept in Constitutional Discourse" (1997) 97 *Colum. L. Rev.* 1.

be wielded only through the law and only according to the law.[3] Indeed, when we now speak of "the rule of law," we commonly mean, at the very least, that law stands above government, simultaneously both creating and constraining it.[4]

Yet although government is well understood to be subject to the law, government is also, in general, the maker of law. And if government, almost tautologically, possesses the lawmaking power, then it is initially curious, as it surely was to King John at the time of *Magna Carta*, that the same institution that makes the law is also bound by it. If the institution with the power to make law also holds the power to change it, then there appears little to prevent the lawmaking power, conceived broadly, from changing the law to suit its desires of the moment. And if this is so, then it is hard to see what constraint, if any, arises from the proposition that the lawmaking power is itself bound by the law. Out of this puzzle grew constitutionalism, but constitutionalism is but one corner of what turns out to be a considerably larger issue of legislative rule-following. To the extent that legislatures have the constitutional power to make the ordinary or subconstitutional rules that organize their own operation and constrain their own power, then how are we to conceptualize the status of such rules, and how are we to think about enforcement of the rules against the felt exigencies of the moment, exigencies that will frequently pull toward modification of the rules in order to allow what it seems now necessary simply to do? And to the extent that legislatures are understood as having significant powers of constitutional interpretation and constitutional enforcement,[5] then we confront the same issue at one remove, and ask what a constitution is, and what makes it so special, if it is capable of being changed by those it is designed to constrain in order to accommodate the felt necessities of the present.

II

The rules that constrain legislatures are, following John Searle, both constitutive and regulative.[6] Constitutive rules establish legislatures, grant them their powers, and structure their operation, just as the constitutive rules of chess create the game itself. And rules of a different sort – regulative rules – impose both procedural and substantive constraints on what legislatures may do and how they may do it. With

[3] We rarely find it necessary even to say this now, but for a rare and recent explicit acknowledgment of the same idea of legal supremacy that is embodied in Article 39, see Klaus Stern, "General Assessment of the Basic Law – A German View" in Paul Kirchhof and Donald P. Kommers, eds., *Germany and Its Basic Law* (Baden-Baden, Germany: Nomos Verlagsgesellschaft, 1993) at 17.

[4] This is implicit in the seventh of Lon Fuller's desiderata for the genuine operation of law, the requirement that there be "Congruence between Official Action and Declared Rule." Lon L. Fuller, *The Morality of Law*, rev. ed. (New Haven, Conn.: Yale University Press, 1969) at 81.

[5] As is now frequently urged in the United States. See, for example, Neal Devins and Louis Fisher, "Judicial Exclusivity and Political Instability" (1998) 84 *Va. L. Rev.* 83. Keith E. Whittington, "Extrajudicial Constitutional Interpretation: Three Objections and Responses" (2002) 80 *N. C. L. Rev.* 773. For a response, see Frederick Schauer, "Judicial Supremacy and the Modest Constitution" (2004) 92 *Cal. L. Rev.* 1045.

[6] John R. Searle, *Speech Acts: An Essay in the Philosophy of Language* (Cambridge: Cambridge University Press, 1969) at 33–42. Both Joseph Raz (*Practical Reason and Norms*, 2nd ed. [Princeton: Princeton University Press, 1990] at 108–13) and I (*Playing By the Rules: A Philosophical Examination of Rule-Based Decision-Making in Law and in Life* [Oxford: Clarendon Press, 1991] at 6–7) have questioned whether constitutive structures are best understood as rules but that issue is not germane here.

some frequency, however, a legislature's first-order policy preferences will come into conflict with the second-order rules that structure how those preferences may be effectuated and that at times constrain their substance.[7] When such conflicts arise, legislative majorities, usually for sound and well-meaning reasons, will be tempted to change or modify the second-order rules that constrain their first-order policy preferences, and it is under such circumstances that questions arise about the nature and effectiveness of the various mechanisms for the enforcement of these second-order rules.

A brief scan of some typical problems may clarify the issue. First, consider the question of legislative structure. Whether from extralegislative constitutional provisions or from rules designed by the legislature itself, legislatures establish the essential preconditions for the legal validity of their legislative actions. This will typically include the rules under which proposed legislation is taken up, the conditions for legislative deliberation (as with, for example, a requirement of discussion or deliberation at two distinct sessions, such as the "two session" rule for constitutional amendments in the Commonwealth of Massachusetts,[8] and as with the common "two meeting" rule adopted by many law faculties for the making of faculty appointments), the prerequisites for passage (including possible supermajorities for certain issues, and the relationship among the various components of a multi-institutional legislative process), and the formalities necessary for the legislative product to become valid law.

At times these preconditions, if made at much earlier times, will appear obsolete, and legislatures will think it important to circumvent them.[9] And at times, even if not obsolete, the various requirements will appear as impediments to important and pressing legislative action whose passage or effectiveness will be jeopardized by compliance with the governing rules. In such cases, legislatures, and not only (or even primarily) evil or corrupt ones but also well-meaning ones whose desires to implement important first-order policies will seem to them urgent, will, from their own lights, have good reasons to attempt to modify the constitutive constraints on the process of legislation.

Occasionally, these constraints will be less constitutive than procedural, even granting that the line between the constitutive and the procedural is an elusive one. But insofar as there are requirements for some form of due process in the legislative process itself[10] – insofar as there are requirements for publication of legislative history and for legislative actions to take place in public, for example – then

[7] On second-order constraints in general, see Joseph Raz, *Practical Reason and Norms*, 2nd ed. (Princeton: Princeton University Press, 1990) at 15–48; Joseph Raz, *The Authority of Law: Essays on Law and Morality* (Oxford: Clarendon Press, 1979) at 30–3; Cass R. Sunstein and Edna Ullman-Margalit, "Second-Order Decisions" (1999) 110 *Ethics* 5.

[8] Constitution of the Commonwealth of Massachusetts, Articles of Amendment, Article XVIII.

[9] Such was the case in *I.N.S. v. Chadha*, 462 U.S. 919 (1983), and *Bowsher v. Synar*, 478 U.S. 714 (1986), Supreme Court cases centered around the precise issue of whether in the good-faith desire to adapt two-centuries-old congressional procedures to modern needs Congress could bend what appeared to be moderately clear constitutional constraints. The answer in both cases was "No."

[10] As with, for example, requirements of public notice of proposed legislation. Insofar as administrative rule-making is in reality a form of legislation (itself a controversial proposition whose contours are not at issue here), then notice and comment requirements, and indeed much of the full *Administrative Procedure Act*, 5 U.S.C. §§101 *et seq.*, can in the United States be seen as just this kind of procedural constraint on governmental rule-making.

once again various second-order constraints on the process of implementing even wise and well-intentioned policy by way of legislation will often appear to legislators and to the public as imposing suboptimizing or delaying constraints on optimal legislative action. Here, too, both when such constraints are actually suboptimizing and when they are not, it will be tempting for those who made these rules to change them or for those who are constrained by them to avoid them.

Perhaps most importantly, it is often the case that the second-order constraints on legislation are substantive, particularly (but not necessarily) with respect to the domains we label "rights." Freedom of expression, freedom of religion, the rights of those charged with crimes, and the commands of equality, for example, are not only, and perhaps not even primarily, implemented to constrain tyrants, thugs, and despots. Nor are they now implemented primarily with respect to those official actions that are racially or religiously or otherwise intolerant. Rather, and with considerable frequency, these rights operate as side constraints (perhaps deontological and perhaps rule-consequentialist) on the pursuit of genuinely well-intentioned and often genuinely welfare (or efficiency, or happiness, or utility, or whatever) maximizing public policies. And it is with respect to such instances, far more common than is often appreciated, that even substantive constraints will be perceived by even well-intentioned and properly motivated legislatures as presenting unfortunately welfare impeding obstacles to wise public policies.[11]

III

It should be clear that such second-order constraints on first-order policymaking may have a variety of formal sources. The most obvious is a written constitution. Although some written constitutions, such as Australia's, may be largely concerned with the constitutive aspects of legislative constraint and not very much focused on rights or substantive constraint, much more common are written constitutions that establish the mechanisms and procedures for legislating and proceed also to impose various substantive side-constraints, usually through bills of rights, on the products of that legislation. But although rights and bills of rights are a common focus of constitutionally enshrined side constraints, other constraints may emanate from a desire to solve a variety of collective action problems. The constitutional constraints on state protectionism in the United States and the European Union, for example, exist not to enforce political or moral rights but rather in recognition of the way in which various state governments, in the hardly illegitimate pursuit of the economic welfare of their own citizens, may very well have good reason to engage in protectionist behavior that may at times be nationally optimal but supranationally suboptimal.

Yet although a written constitution is perhaps the most common source of second-order constraint on first-order legislative policymaking, it is far from the

[11] The problem is exacerbated insofar as the right-holders are systematically likely to have little political power or social resonance, as is prototypically case with respect to the rights of those charged with crimes. In the United States especially, the problem also arises with respect to the rights to freedom of speech, for in the United States more than in other countries free speech rights are especially likely to be championed by Nazis, Klansmen, child pornographers, and others whose moral standing and social acceptability is small and thus whose political resonance with legislators is small as well.

only source. Another type of source can be found in various quasi-constitutional enactments – occasionally called "organic" laws[12] – such as the New Zealand *Bill of Rights Act 1990*, the United Kingdom *Human Rights Act 1998*, and Israel's *Basic Law on Human Dignity and Liberty* (1992), all products of ordinary legislation, and all appearing in the statute books as ordinary legislation, but which by their terms have a status superior to that of ordinary legislation, and which by their terms can typically be amended or repealed only by extraordinary legislation.[13]

The third form of second-order constraint is found in those various legislative enactments and legislative rules that do not rise to quasi-constitutional status, but nevertheless purport to set the ground rules and procedures for legislation itself. Although the most basic outlines of the legislative process are set forth in Article I of the Constitution of the United States, most of the rules that establish what Congress does and how it does it come either from legislation enacted by Congress or by various rules – the rules regarding cloture of debate being among the most notorious, but there are thousands of others – made as legislative rules by the legislature itself. Some of these rules may specify the conditions for making of further rules, but in the final analysis the rules themselves are the products of the very legislature they attempt, in theory, to constrain and, more importantly, remain in the continuous control of that same legislature.

Finally, there are the unwritten constitutional and nonconstitutional norms to which legislatures understand themselves to be bound. British lawyers and British legislators have no trouble making sense of the idea of the British Constitution, because for these lawyers and legislators the constitution is a collection of various documents (*Magna Carta* and the *Bill of Rights of 1688*, for example), various understandings (sometimes called "custom" and sometimes called "convention," and including, for example, the understandings respecting the relative powers and responsibilities of the queen and Parliament), and various rights (freedom of speech, freedom of the press, freedom of religion, and the requirements of natural justice, for example) that have become historically and sociologically entrenched by virtue of some combination of customary and common law. So too in New Zealand, where much of the historical English Constitution has constitutional status, as do other documents, such as the treaty of Waitangi, establishing in 1840 the basic settlement between the English and the indigenous Maori.[14] And even where the source of the (more or less) unwritten constitution is not as clear, legislators often understand themselves to be organized according to a set of rules and bound to operate in accordance with a set of unwritten but still identifiable constitutive, procedural, and substantive rules.

IV

Because it bears emphasizing, let me repeat that an important part of the rules that constitute and regulate legislative action is the way in which such rules restrain

12 See O. Hood Phillips and Paul Jackson, *Constitutional and Administrative Law*, 6th ed. (London: Sweet & Maxwell, 1978) at 6.

13 Whether and how ordinary legislation can require extraordinary action for its repeal or modification is an interesting problem of self-reference, but is not especially germane here.

14 See Paul Rishworth, "The Treaty of Waitangi and Human Rights" [2003] *New Zealand L. Rev.* 381–5.

not only malintentioned official action, and not only well-intentioned but ill-functioning official action, but also, and most importantly, well-intentioned and actually wise first-order policymaking.[15] And the reason that this is important is that when we turn from the formal sources of legislative constraint to the mechanisms for their enforcement, we will see that it makes an enormous difference whether we are thinking of these mechanisms in terms of checking the abuses of self-serving and misguided (or even just mistaken) public legislators, on the one hand, or checking in the service of various second-order interests the public-interested and (first-order) optimizing acts, both well-intentioned and well-executed, in which our best legislators and legislatures engage.

Initially, however, it will be useful to offer an admittedly partial catalog of what appear to be the six most prominent forms of enforcement of legislative constraint. And first among these is what we can call *canonization*. Canonization, the creation of canonical texts, is a process that, tautologically, requires a text, and that, second, requires that a relevant community – the legislature, or the judiciary, or the population at large, most obviously – have a certain positive and reverential attitude toward that text such that it is largely unthinkable to imagine its modification or violation. So when the Congress of the United States consistently (but barely) refuses to amend the First Amendment to the Constitution in order to allow individuals to be prosecuted for desecrating the flag of the United States,[16] part of the explanation is that in the United States constitutional amendment itself is viewed as a form of tampering with the sacred, and amendment of the First Amendment even more so.[17] Much the same might be said about the status of the Canadian *Charter of Rights and Freedoms*, for the repeated unwillingness of legislative bodies to exercise their constitutionally explicit power to override judicial decisions interpreting the Charter[18] is likely explained, at least in part, by the canonical status that the Charter (and perhaps also the Supreme Court of Canada, about which much can be said, but not here) possesses.

[15] And this is not just because all rules are necessarily actually or potentially over- and underinclusive. See Frederick Schauer, *Playing By the Rules, supra* note 6. It is true that rules aimed at the evil and corrupt, just because they are rules, will at times constrain those who are neither. But my focus here is not merely on rules targeted at evil, and not even merely on rules targeted at innocent mistakes but also, and more importantly, on rules whose target is the good legislator who by virtue of her role and her constituencies is likely to underenforce the rules that constrain her own behavior in the service of larger and longer-term values.

[16] Constitutional amendment would be necessary because of several comparatively recent Supreme Court decisions holding that punishment for flag desecration is incompatible with the First Amendment's protection of freedom of speech. *United States v. Eichman*, 496 U.S. 310 (1990); *Texas v. Johnson*, 491 U.S. 397 (1989). With no prospects for judicial self-reversal on the horizon, those who feel strongly that these decisions are mistaken have had no choice but to press for a constitutional amendment.

[17] The reasons for the sacrosanct nature of the First Amendment are complex and include the enthusiastic support for the First Amendment by the institutional press, whose interests it generally serves, as well as a common public perception that something of importance attaches to the First Amendment because of its firstness. This perception is likely real, even though its premises are mistaken, the First Amendment having started out as the third amendment and rising to first only because the original first and second amendments failed to secure ratification. On the First Amendment's political salience and rhetorical power, see Frederick Schauer, "The Boundaries of the First Amendment: A Preliminary Exploration of Constitutional Salience" (2004) 117 *Harv. L. Rev.* 1765; Frederick Schauer, "First Amendment Opportunism" in Lee C. Bollinger and Geoffrey R. Stone, eds., *Eternally Vigilant: Free Speech in the Modern Era* (Chicago: University of Chicago Press, 2002) at 175–97.

[18] Canadian Charter of Rights and Freedoms, s. 33.

Second is *explicitness*. Consider so-called clear statement rules, for example, those rules that require legislatures, upon pain of invalidation of the legislation, to be more than normally explicit when they take certain actions.[19] Behind such rules is the view that when actions are taken explicitly, and when that explicitness makes it clear to the actor what is transpiring, then some number of actions are simply less likely to occur. The reasons why this is so are complex, and hardly invariant across time, place, and subject matter, but much of the effect is a function of the psychological phenomenon by which it is often harder to do hard things explicitly rather than implicitly, even assuming the absence of an external audience. The calorie counts on food packages and the warning labels on cigarette packets and alcohol containers provide examples of this phenomenon. The warning on a cigarette packet is surely not intended to provide information hitherto unknown to the cigarette smoker, at least not in this day and age. Rather, the warning by virtue of its explicitness makes it more difficult for people to refuse to face up to what they have known all along. So too with legislation, where clear statement rules are based on the premise that facing up to what is being done will make legislatures, at least some of the time, less likely to do it.

The third source of potential constraint is *publicity*, or *transparency*. Simply put, there are numerous actions that are easier to take in private than in public. Even assuming public agreement, being a first mover may involve risks and costs, which is why, for example, it is difficult for one member of a potential conspiracy to raise the possibility of conspiring, unless that member has firm evidence of the likely willingness of the other party.[20] Similarly, people who want to quit smoking or lose weight or take up jogging often act in concert with others, knowing that problems of weakness of the will may well be counteracted when the enterprise is joint rather than individual. Insofar as legislative violation or modification of a rule designed to constrain that legislature must be done in the glare of public and press attention, and insofar as it also attracts the attention of political opponents, what we know about individual behavior may suggest that for legislative behavior as well transparency and the consequent publicity may make rule-following easier, and rule-violation or rule-modification more difficult.

The fourth factor is *electoral accountability*. Insofar as the particular rules have public support, or insofar as the importance of following and not modifying the rules has electoral support,[21] then a legislator who is seen to be part of such rule-violation or rule-modification may do so at some risk of electoral defeat. In democratic countries with written constitutions but no or rarely exercised judicial

[19] See William N. Eskridge, Jr. and Philip P. Frickey, "Quasi-Constitutional Law: Clear Statement Rules as Constitutional Lawmaking" (1992) 45 *Vand. L. Rev.* 593. See also John Copeland Nagle, "Waiving Sovereign Immunity in an Age of Clear Statement Rules" (1995) 1995 *Wis. L. Rev.* 771; Note, "Clear Statement Rules, Federalism, and Congressional Regulation of the States" (1994) 107 *Harv. L. Rev.* 1959.

[20] The point has been made in the context of explaining why cheating is relatively rare in high-level contract bridge, despite the advantages cheating would bring. Because bridge is a partnership game, and because the most effective forms of cheating involve partnership agreements and signaling, engaging in cheating would require that one member of the partnership raise with the other the possibility that they should collectively cheat, an initial move that is likely very psychologically difficult. See Terence Reese, *Story of an Accusation*, rev. ed. (Toronto: Master Point Press, 2004).

[21] The subjunctive in the text is important. There may be little reason to believe that the electorate will punish legislators for violating legislature-constraining rules in the service of wise and popular first-order policies. See Frederick Schauer, "The Questions of Authority" (1992) 81 *Geo. L.J.* 95.

review (Belgium and Switzerland are common examples, and, with some complications, so too with the Netherlands, Norway, Denmark, and Sweden), for example, it is widely believed that constitutional enforcement takes place at the ballot box, and legislators who sought to violate the constitution would be checked by an electorate unwilling to reelect a person who does not take constitutional obligations seriously.

Fifth is *internalization*. Our value structures are complex, and I do not want to be understood as suggesting that the distinction between first-order and second-order values or reasons or considerations is in some deep way fixed or ontologically primary. Few (but, as we know, not none) people now would consider a restriction on torture a second-order constraint on what they would otherwise wish to do, for they have so internalized an aversion to torture that pursuit of that goal seems as much a primary goal of policymaking as does maximizing the general welfare. Other equally unpalatable examples (including some involving food) will occur to others, but the basic point is only that at some point some second-order constraints on first order-preferences begin to resemble first-order preferences, and so too with second-order constraints on first-order policies, and when this transformation occurs the phenomenology of constraint evaporates and the necessity of enforcement may, except to guard against outliers, disappear.[22]

Sixth, and finally, constraint may come from *external enforcement*. Police departments have divisions of internal affairs. Government agencies and the military have inspectors general. Workplaces often have ombudsmen. People who wish to exercise regularly often hire personal trainers not only for their expertise but also simply to authorize an external agent to nag them out of their lazier instincts. And although we can imagine legislative rules (and not just legislator misbehavior) being enforced by variously designed external institutions, the most common of these is the courts. From this vantage point, judicial enforcement of legislative rules, including but not limited to the rules that we call "constitutional," is a function not of some special capability, wisdom, insight, or probity of people with legal training and imposing outfits. Rather, the argument for judicial enforcement is largely a function of its externality, with the judiciary conceived, modestly, as an institution playing for the legislature a role not dissimilar to that played by external examiners in British universities.

V

All of these mechanisms have variants, and all often appear in combination with others. Yet when we focus on the particular issue of constraining the good legislator and the good legislature, the array of enforcement options appears to shrink. As those of us who have attended far too many faculty meetings well know, reposing

[22] This becomes obvious if we understand illegality and its consequent sanctions as a form of second-order constraint. Thus, the legal prohibition on cannibalism is aimed at a very small group of outliers, for all the rest of us would consider the practice unthinkable even absent legal sanctions. So too with child molestation, although the number of outliers is considerably greater. The issue is very different, however, with respect to tax avoidance and driving at a high rate of speed, for in these and many other instances the number (or proportion) of people who would engage in the practice were it legal is, to put it mildly, quite a bit higher.

the power to modify or avoid rules in the same body allegedly constrained by them is likely to produce far more frequent modification or avoidance than genuine constraint, and so too with legislatures. When what a rule prevents (or commands) is inconsistent with what well-meaning people now think is important to do, all things (except the rule) considered, then the likelihood that the rule will constrain is small. And even if we relax the "all things except the rule" constraint, and allow our first-order decision makers to simply make the best all-things-considered decision, including the virtues of the rule or the second-order constraint among the array of things to be considered,[23] the second-order values will often be undervalued. It is in theory possible to enforce rules on oneself, but in practice it is quite difficult.[24]

Part of this undervaluation is a product of role differentiation. Just as we expect (and train) police officers to be more concerned with apprehending criminals than with avoiding warrantless searches, then so too might we expect legislators, even conscientious ones, to be somewhat more focused on the desires of their constituents than they are with the second-order values that may at times prevent those constituent desires from being given effect.[25] Moreover, to the extent that a political system subjects legislators to frequent electoral accountability, it exacerbates the problem of role-based responsibilities, for it seems even less likely, as an empirical matter, that the very people whose welfare is to be maximized by good first-order policies will choose to detract from that welfare in the service of second-order procedural or substantive values. In addition, certain values are best appreciated over time and not in the heat of the moment, so the more we place second-order procedural and substantive values in the hands of institutions that are permitted for long periods of time to be nonresponsive to the desires of those who will benefit from policy maximization, the more we are likely to see effective enforcement of the full array of those second-order values whose benefits are especially likely to be temporally remote.

This perspective suggests a strong argument for external enforcement, and suggests as well the limitations of relying too heavily on explicitness, transparency, electoral accountability, or internalization as desirable institutional mechanisms for the enforcement of second-order constraints on legislative action. When a particular act of legislative policymaking is perceived by the population to be desirable in the short term, when that act is genuinely desirable in the short term, and when that act is the product of conscientious and public-spirited legislative

23 I have referred to this methodology as "rule-sensitive particularism." Frederick Schauer, *Playing By the Rules*, *supra* note 6 at 93–100. For critique, see Gerald J. Postema, "Positivism, I Presume? . . . Comments on Schauer's 'Rules and the Rule of Law'" (1991) 14 *Harv. J. L. & Pub. Pol'y* 797. For a response, see Frederick Schauer, "The Rules of Jurisprudence: A Reply" (1991) 14 *Harv. J. L. & Pub. Pol'y* 839 at 844–9. What I call "rule-sensitive particularism" has its origins in the more sophisticated versions of act-utilitarianism. See, for example, J. J. C. Smart, "Extreme and Restricted Utilitarianism" (1956) 6 *Philosophical Quarterly* 344.

24 See Thomas Schelling, "Enforcing Rules on Oneself" (1985) 1 *J. L. Econ. & Org.* 357.

25 A quite explicit version of this point was made by Franklin Roosevelt, who on several occasions in 1935 told Congress, in effect, that it was their job to make policy and not to be concerned with constitutionality, just as it was the Supreme Court's job, when necessary, to hold certain congressional policies unconstitutional. See Letter to Congressman Hill, July 6, 1935, and Proposed Speech on the Gold Clause Cases, February 1935, both excerpted from the Roosevelt papers in Kathleen M. Sullivan and Gerald Gunther, *Constitutional Law*, 15th ed. (New York: Foundation Press, 2004) at 24.

motivation, the likelihood that any of the mechanisms of explicitness, transparency, electoral accountability, or internalization will be effective in preserving long-run or second-order values is small. Such mechanisms are typically most effective when the proposed action has at least a bit of a bad odor around it, but when a proposed legislative act is genuinely popular, genuinely public-focused, and genuinely the product of conscientious legislative motivation, these particular mechanisms of constraint are likely to be least effective.

Thus, when legislative action is motivated by legislators thinking only (or at least largely) in terms of the welfare of their constituents, and when such legislative action in fact enhances the welfare of those constituents, the need for second-order constraint is no less, and indeed it may be more. As long as there are long-term institutional and process values that often require short-term welfare sacrifice, as long as there exist deontological side constraints on aggregate welfare maximization,[26] and as long as even conscientious public servants are likely to focus more on their geographically and temporally proximate constituencies than on those that are more remote in place or time, our need for durable second-order constraints is no less. In such circumstances, however, the various internal mechanisms for enforcing those constraints are likely to be especially ineffective, and thus the need for external constraint is largest.

Such external constraint need not be judicial review in the typical North American understanding of that practice. It might instead take the form of a moderately precise and widely respected document, sufficiently revered that plain departures would be thought unacceptable regardless of the benefits such departures would bring. Or it might be some legislative counterpart of an internal affairs division, authorized to monitor legislative compliance with the full array of legislative (including constitutional) rules, empowered to take action in the case of noncompliance, and immunized in some way from the consequences of taking legislatively and electorally unpopular actions.[27]

Yet although these and other external mechanisms are quite plausible, using the courts to perform this function is most common and most realistic. And this is not just a matter of a court enforcing the constitution and being treated as supreme when it does so. It is also a matter of courts being empowered to hold legislatures even to their own subconstitutional rules.[28] If the commands of *Magna Carta* and

[26] This has long been Ronald Dworkin's argument for judicial review. Ronald Dworkin, *Taking Rights Seriously* (London: Duckworth, 1977) at 190–4. As Dworkin himself acknowledges, there is an affinity between this argument and the classic principle of natural justice that no man should be judge of his own cause (*nemo debet esse judex in propria sua causa*).

[27] A good example is the legal chancellor in Estonia. The legal chancellor is appointed by the Parliament (*Riigikogu*) on proposal of the president, is constitutionally guaranteed a seven-year term, reports to no one, and can be removed from office only upon criminal conviction. The legal chancellor reviews all legislation for constitutional and legal conformity, and has the power to send legislation back for reconsideration and modification for failure to comply with constitutional or legal requirements. If the Parliament refuses to make the necessary modifications within twenty days, the Legal Chancellor is granted standing to challenge the laws directly and immediately in the Supreme Court. See Constitution of the Republic of Estonia, Chapter , §§139, 140, 142.

[28] How courts punish officials for violating the rules that constrain them is itself an important and not unrelated issue. Under current American law, for example, legislators (but not police officers or members of a town council) enjoy total immunity from being held personally liable for helping to enact even plainly unconstitutional legislation. A police officer who knowingly violates a clear constitutional command is personally liable for damages, but a legislator who does the same thing, apart from

the rule of law, inter alia, demand that legislation be made according to law, then the full range of laws that constitute and constrain the legislative function would be within the purview of a court operating in this fashion. Courts might plausibly, therefore, be understood not only as enforcers of the supralegislative rules we call constitutional, but also as enforcers of the process by which legislators are expected to follow their own rules until the point at which they decide to repeal or amend them.

VI

Much more could be said about the details of the various devices of external enforcement of second-order constraints on first-order legislative policymaking, but that would be a digression. Rather, the point of much of the foregoing is to establish that the argument for external constraint on legislatures, typically but not necessarily judicial constraint, is not an argument that requires either a dim view of legislators or a rosy view of the judiciary. It is undoubtedly true that many arguments for judicial authority in the United States, in Canada, and in South Africa, among other places, are arguments that unduly glorify the judiciary and equally unduly denigrate legislatures. When scholars such as Jeremy Waldron,[29] Richard Parker,[30] Larry Kramer,[31] and Mark Tushnet[32] chide legal academics for failing to appreciate the virtues of legislators (and the population at large) and for equally neglecting to perceive the failings of the courts, they are arguing against views not totally unknown in legal scholarship, in the faculty common rooms of North American law schools, or even in judicial chambers. Yet the stronger argument for judicial authority requires neither a low esteem for legislation nor especially high esteem for the courts. Under an alternative and better view, the virtue of the courts lies not in their wisdom, nor even in the supposed virtues of an allegedly distinctive form of judicial reasoning or judicial procedure. Rather, it lies simply in the courts' externality, in the way in which courts are the most obvious vehicle for imposing on wise and well-intentioned legislators those second-order constraints that even the best of legislators cannot be expected fully to enforce. First-order policies and preferences occupy the foreground of the consciousness of even the wisest of legislators, and the very nature of their role and their constituency reinforces this phenomenon. To suggest that legislators are in need of external constraint in order

the sanction of invalidity of the legislation, is accountable solely to the electorate. But because such unconstitutional legislative actions are usually in the service of, rather than contrary to, voter desires, what emerges is a situation in which legislators have few, if any, incentives to obey the Constitution or to obey governing case law when the law commands something that appears popular despite its unconstitutionality. On such "civil rights" actions and the various immunities, including legislative immunity, see Sheldon H. Nahmod, *Civil Rights and Civil Liberties Litigation: The Law of Section 1983*, 4th ed. (St. Paul, Minnesota: West Group, 1997).

29 Jeremy Waldron, *Law and Disagreement* (Princeton: Princeton University Press, 1999); Jeremy Waldron, *The Dignity of Legislation* (Princeton: Princeton University Press, 1999).

30 Richard D. Parker, *"Here, the People Rule": A Constitutional Populist Manifesto* (Cambridge, Mass.: Harvard University Press, 1994).

31 Larry D. Kramer, *The People Themselves: Popular Constitutionalism and Judicial Review* (New York: Oxford University Press, 2004).

32 Mark Tushnet, *Taking the Constitution Away from the Courts* (Princeton: Princeton University Press, 1999).

best to serve the collective and long-term values that second-order constraints on legislation bring us is not to look down on legislators, legislatures, or legislation. It is to conclude only that legislators are human, and like other humans they are often in need of external constraint even when their goals are wise and their motives pure.

ACKNOWLEDGMENTS

Research support was generously provided by the Joan Shorenstein Center on the Press, Politics and Public Policy, Harvard University.

24 Popular Revolution or Popular Constitutionalism? Reflections on the Constitutional Politics of Quebec Secession

Sujit Choudhry

A. TWO CONCEPTIONS OF CONSTITUTIONALISM

Constitutional theorists are in the midst of a debate over the appropriate institutional arrangements for the interpretation and enforcement of constitutional norms in a constitutional democracy – that is, a liberal democratic polity in which all exercises of public power must comply with some higher-order or basic law. In the United States, Larry Kramer has usefully described the two extreme positions in this debate as "legal constitutionalism" and "popular constitutionalism."[1] For legal constitutionalists, supreme authority to interpret and enforce the constitution rests with the courts. Because court judgments are regarded as authoritative by other government institutions and, indeed, by the public, these political actors defer to judicial pronouncements in the face of their own conflicting constitutional interpretations. Popular constitutionalists, by contrast, permit and even require that members of the executive and legislative branches independently interpret the constitution alongside the courts in the course of performing their functions. Moreover, these branches are ultimately subject to the "active and ongoing control over the interpretation and enforcement of constitutional law"[2] by the people themselves, "conceived as a collective body capable of independent action and expression."[3] Institutionally, although popular constitutionalists may accept the possibility of judicial review, they refuse to accept judicial supremacy.

As Frederick Schauer has insightfully suggested, it is possible to understand this debate over institutional design as turning on different underlying conceptions of the point and function of constitutions themselves. To popular constitutionalists, "a constitution . . . becomes both a statement of our most important values and the vehicle through which these values are created and crystallized."[4] On this conception, Schauer concedes that "it would indeed be a mistake to believe that the courts should have the pre-eminent responsibility for interpreting that constitution,"[5] as it

[1] Larry Kramer, "Popular Constitutionalism, circa 2004" (2004) 94 *Cal. L. Rev.* 959 at 959. See, more generally, Larry Kramer, *The People Themselves: Popular Constitutionalism and Judicial Review* (New York: Oxford University Press, 2004).

[2] Ibid.

[3] Ibid. at 962.

[4] Frederick Schauer, "Judicial Supremacy and the Modest Constitution" (2004) 92 *Cal. L. Rev.* 1045 at 1045.

[5] Ibid.

would eviscerate the fundamentally democratic function of constitutional charters. Legal constitutionalists, by contrast, subscribe to what Schauer variously describes as the "modest constitution" or the "negative constitution."[6] On this conception, a constitution serves to fetter majority decision making, especially when a majority is likely to disregard longer-term values to pursue short-term policy preferences. A constitution is therefore a precommitment device that "creates second-order constraints on wise and well-meaning first-order decisions."[7] For modest constitutionalists, interpretation and enforcement by an institution other than the ones that are bound by these precommitments – that is, the courts – is integrally tied to "the external nature of the constitutional norms themselves."[8]

In this chapter, I want to question Schauer's seemingly universal equation of constitutional strategies of precommitment with legal constitutionalism and judicial supremacy. I agree with Schauer that constitutions serve an important disabling function, in that they set up roadblocks in the way of political decision making. But it does not follow that external enforcement through judicial review is necessarily the sole institutional mechanism for enforcing those constitutional precommitments. Along with popular constitutionalists, I argue that it would be a mistake to infer that the boundaries of judicial decision making are coterminous with the limits of the constitution. The question in each case is whether institutional settlement – for example, through judicial review – can produce political settlement. Following Ronald Dworkin, we can usefully distinguish the justifications for constitutions from the practical question of what institutional mechanisms best enforce them.[9] Thus, even for the modest constitutionalist, the choice is not between legal constitutionalism and its populist alternative. Rather, the true choice is when and to what extent to opt for one or the other. Indeed, the challenge may be to design arrangements that permit the responsive and even tentative allocation of institutional responsibility for resolving constitutional questions.

B. CONSTITUTIONAL CRISES: SECESSIONS AND REVOLUTIONARY LEGALITY

I want to pursue this claim with respect to constitutional precommitments that are designed to prevent constitutional crises. A constitutional crisis is a term that constitutional theorists frequently deploy but rarely define. But one definition emerges from what I take to be the basic ambition of modest constitutionalism, one that Schauer would endorse: to channel political conflict that would otherwise spill into the streets, into institutions that operate peacefully according to law, and which reach decisions that members of a political community accept as authoritative. A constitutional crisis arises when some significant proportion of a political community refuses to accept as authoritative the decisions of its governing institutions, when defective constitutional design creates a constitutional blind alley which cannot be resolved from within the constitutional framework, or because of an

[6] Ibid. at 1065 and 1055.

[7] Ibid. at 1055–6.

[8] Ibid. at 1046.

[9] Ronald Dworkin, *Freedom's Law: The Moral Reading of the Constitution* (Cambridge, Mass.: Harvard University Press, 1997).

institutional stalemate created by the exercise of constitutionally assigned powers and which creates the political pressure to step outside the constitution.[10]

As a case study, I will focus on a recurrent Canadian constitutional crisis: the constitutional politics of Quebec secession. The relationship between Quebec and the rest of Canada has long been of interest to political theorists interested in how liberal democracies should address questions of ethnocultural difference. This is especially true in situations where there are national minorities who were collectively incorporated into the larger nation-state, who are territorially concentrated and linguistically distinct, and who demand powers of self-government – what Will Kymlicka and others have termed multinational federations.[11] But Quebec's place in Canada is also worthy of attention by constitutional theorists because it raises classic questions about revolutionary legality, and the relationship between legality and legitimacy. This issue has arisen in the context of whether Quebec could achieve independence as an independent state recognized in law as such through a unilateral declaration of independence (UDI) in contravention of the existing constitutional order.

For Commonwealth constitutional scholars, the central historical episode for raising and exploring this issue has been the Rhodesian constitutional crisis in the late 1960s, which prompted an extensive critical literature.[12] Rhodesia was a British colony that was governed by a white minority government. Rhodesia's black citizens did not enjoy political power, but Britain was moving toward universal suffrage and majority rule as a prelude to granting Rhodesia independence. Faced with the almost certain prospect of the loss of political power, the white minority government issued a UDI, with the objective of transforming Rhodesia's status from that of a British colony to an independent nation governed by a white majority, much as South Africa had done over a decade earlier.

Rhodesia's UDI raised important constitutional issues that quickly turned this political dispute into a legal dispute. Although a British colony, Rhodesia had exercised its powers under Rhodesia's colonial constitution, which was an enactment of the British Parliament. That constitution did not confer on Rhodesia a right to secede and declare its independence, which meant that the Rhodesian government had acted unconstitutionally. Rhodesia followed up its UDI with the enactment of a new constitution identical in most respects to its colonial constitution, and purported to govern under it. In response, the British government also turned to law. Within days of the UDI, Parliament enacted legislation that repealed Rhodesia's colonial constitution and assigned direct control over Rhodesian affairs to the British cabinet.

These conflicting assertions of legal authority by the Rhodesian and British governments set the stage for a series of challenges in the Rhodesian courts to the legality of the Rhodesian regime. The cases were brought by individuals who challenged

[10] For a similar list, see Keith Whittington, "Yet Another Constitutional Crisis?" (2002) 43 *Wm. & Mary L. Rev.* 209.

[11] Will Kymlicka, *Multicultural Citizenship* (Oxford: Oxford University Press, 1995).

[12] For example, A. M. Honoré, "Reflections on Revolutions" (1967) 2 *Irish Jurist* (NS) 268; R. W. M. Dias, "Legal Politics: Norms Behind the Grundnorm" [1968] *Cambridge L.J.* 233; J. Eekelaar, "Rhodesia: The Abdication of Constitutionalism" (1969) 32 *Modern L. Rev.* 34; F. M. Brookfield, "The Courts, Kelsen, and the Rhodesian Revolution" (1969) 19 *U.T.L.J.* 326.

the legality of their detentions, purportedly authorized by powers exercised under the new Rhodesian constitution. They argued that the Rhodesian authorities had acted unconstitutionally because the only legal sources of power were grants of authority ultimately traceable to the Imperial Parliament. The question for the courts was whether to accept this argument or to recognize and enforce the laws of the revolutionary regime. In Schauer's terms, these cases raised fundamental questions of constitutional theory, because they forced courts to grapple with the question "[w]hat makes a constitution constitutional?"[13]

The Rhodesian courts framed this legal question in positivist terms. There is a venerable tradition in constitutional theory that holds that the legal validity of the basic fact of political sovereignty within a nation-state is not subject to legal scrutiny in a court of law. Although Kelsen argued that the validity of the rule of recognition (his grundnorm) is presupposed, Hart rightly pointed out that validity is an internal statement about the relationship of rules within a legal system and the rule of recognition. The better view is that the rule of recognition merely exists, as a matter of sociological fact – defined by Hart as acceptance by the officials who govern themselves by it. Regardless of how this basic political fact arose – through legal mechanisms or a violent or velvet revolution – it nonetheless stands as the foundation of a valid constitutional order. Hart's rule of recognition incorporates this understanding of the relationship of law to basic political facts. The Rhodesian courts reasoned that because the existence of a constitutional regime was ultimately not a question susceptible to legal analysis but rather a matter of fact, so too was the issue of whether one constitutional regime had died and a new regime had taken its place. The test to be applied was one of effective control – that is, whether the facts on the ground gave rise to the conclusion that the Rhodesian regime had asserted a sufficient degree of control over the territory and people of Rhodesia for it to have replaced the prior colonial regime. If so, the court held, the rule of recognition in Rhodesia would have changed, shifting the title of Rhodesia's constitutional order away from imperial statute to its revolutionary constitution. Over a series of cases, the Rhodesian courts ultimately came to this view.

The two extreme positions in the Rhodesian debate framed the Canadian discussion prior to the Supreme Court of Canada's judgment in the *Quebec Secession Reference*,[14] which I discuss below. On the one hand was the view that Canadian constitutional law provided the relevant legal framework. Although the Canadian Constitution confers no right of unilateral secession on provinces, it is widely accepted that Quebec's independence could be achieved through constitutional amendment. Because the relevant amending procedures require federal and varying degrees of provincial consent, and provincial referenda carry no legal force, if Quebec were to secede unilaterally, even on the basis of an overwhelming referendum mandate, it would be acting unconstitutionally. Any commands issued by a Quebec government that had proclaimed independence to the citizens of

[13] Frederick Schauer, "Amending the Presuppositions of a Constitution" in Sanford Levinson, ed., *Responding to Imperfection: The Theory and Practice of Constitutional Amendment* (Chicago: University of Chicago Press, 1995) at 145 [*Amending Presuppositions*].

[14] *Reference re Secession of Quebec*, [1998] 2 S.C.R. 217 [*Secession Reference*]. For my earlier thoughts on the case, see S. Choudhry and R. Howse, "Constitutional Theory and the *Quebec Secession Reference*" (2000) 13:2 *Can. J.L. & Juris.* 143.

Quebec would be those of a revolutionary government attempting to usurp the lawful authority of the Canadian state. Legality is impervious to democratic legitimacy. Illegitimate or legitimate, the Canadian constitutional order would be in force in Quebec, and judges and governments would be duty-bound to obey it, unless it were withdrawn through normal constitutional procedures.

On the other hand was the view that at the end of the day, the law really did not matter at all. Sovereignist governments, and many of the Quebec élite, held that Quebec's accession to independence, and the termination of the sovereignty of the Canadian state over Quebec, would originate not from a war of independence but from the democratic will of Quebeckers as expressed in a majority vote in favor of independence in a referendum – an expression of political will that would operate to change the locus of sovereignty and to which the law would have to adapt. Legality would follow legitimacy. Quebec's 1995 referendum law, which explicitly contemplated the possibility of a UDI, was premised on this legal theory.

C. SECESSION CLAUSES AS CONSTITUTIONAL PRECOMMITMENTS TO AVOID CONSTITUTIONAL CRISES

The Canadian constitutional crisis thus presented the prospect of nothing less than the threat of a *popular revolution* in the event of a positive referendum result. And it would be a nonviolent revolution because, as good liberal democrats, all sides had eschewed resort to violence. The irreconcilable constitutional theories of the Quebec and federal governments set the stage for a disastrous struggle for legal supremacy. In the event of a positive referendum vote, the most likely response was for the federal government to insist that any change in Quebec's political status occur from within the Canadian constitutional framework, and for Quebec to simply reject this position. The result would likely have been a UDI, followed by federal attempts to assert control over the territory of Quebec, with the very real potential for a descent into legal chaos.

And so, not surprisingly, it has been suggested that the appropriate means, as a matter of constitutional design, to preempt and prevent the constitutional crisis that would be prompted by unilateral secession is to craft a constitutional right to secession which permits secession if certain procedures are followed. The goal is to discipline secessionist politics according to the rule of law. Such a secession clause, put in place in advance of an attempt to secede, would accordingly serve as a precommitment device to prevent the wholesale disintegration of the legal and political order during rounds of secessionist politics. A secession clause would serve as a constitutional safety valve, to channel political pressures that would otherwise lead actors to step outside the constitutional order through a set of institutional procedures operating under that order itself.

The most extended argument along these lines for a secession clause has been made by Daniel Weinstock.[15] Weinstock begins from the Madisonian premise that constitutional design not only institutionalizes our highest ideals, but must also address the probable, if not inevitable, political behavior that can threaten or destroy a constitutional order. Assuming that such behavior would likely occur even if it were unregulated, the Madisonian argument is that it may be better to

[15] Daniel Weinstock, "Constitutionalizing the Right to Secede" (2001) 9 *J. Pol. Phil.* 182.

permit and regulate such conduct rather than leave it uncontrolled. The thought is that the legal regulation of such conduct is warranted if, on balance, the consequences of legally regulated behavior are better than the consequences of legally unregulated behavior.

Applied to secession, Weinstock succinctly makes the case for a constitutional right to secede *not* on the basis of a moral right to self-determination, but rather on pragmatic grounds:[16]

> Proponents of the constitutional recognition of a right to secession believe that secessionist politics will occur anyway, regardless of legal silences and prohibitions, and that its occurring in a legal vacuum will be more harmful than were it to occur within well thought out legal and procedural parameters.

More specifically, Weinstock identifies two negative aspects to secessionist politics – namely, the strategic use of the threat of secession by a federal subunit "as a way of discouraging policies which run against their interests, rather than engaging in more arduous and demanding democratic deliberation with their fellow citizens" (termed the "blackmail threat"), and the responding attempts by the federal government "to nip any likelihood of autonomist stirring in the bud so as to diminish the likelihood of secession" (termed the "threat of oppression").[17] Channeling secessionist politics through a suitably designed secession clause, on Weinstock's view, would dampen both sets of behaviors. Procedural devices such as a supermajority requirement and a waiting period between referenda on secession would both make the threat of secessionist blackmail less credible and limit the frequency of occasions on which secessionist threats could be raised. The diminished threat of secession would in turn reduce the threat of oppression.

Although Weinstock makes a powerful argument, I think he is too narrow in his enumeration of the negative political consequences of secessionist politics that a secession clause would potentially combat. For alongside the damage that secessionist politics can cause to the functioning of multinational states *prior* to secession occurring, not subjecting the *process of secession itself* to legally constituted procedures could precipitate legal chaos and discontinuity. In particular, it places legal subjects who wish to act in good faith and obey the law in the impossible position of determining which sovereign's commands to obey. Allan Rock, Canada's former justice minister, put the point this way in a speech in the House of Commons:[18]

> A unilateral declaration of independence would create the most serious difficulties for ordinary Quebecers. There would be widespread uncertainty within Quebec about which legal regime was effectively in control.
>
> For the average citizen, business or institution in Quebec, there would be the greatest confusion. Individual Quebecers would be uncertain what laws applied, what courts and law officers to respect, to whom to pay their taxes. In such an environment, it is certain that Quebec society would be deeply divided over the course the provincial government would have adopted.

[16] Ibid. at 196.
[17] Ibid. at 195.
[18] *House of Commons Debates (Hansard)*, Vol. 134, Number 075 (September 26, 1996) at 4708, 35th Parliament, 2nd Session.

Conversely, if legal rules governing the process of secession itself were in place in advance, one might be able to lower these risks.

But my focus here is somewhat different. Weinstock is silent on the *institutional* question of whether a secession clause should be judicially enforced or left to constitutional politics. At one point, Weinstock rejects the idea of building into the terms of a right to secede substantive criteria, such as the imperiling of a group's fundamental interests, because it is difficult to imagine "[w]hat body could legitimately step in to determine what a group's fundamental interests are."[19] This passage suggests that Weinstock holds that a secession clause should not be judicially enforced. But more direct guidance can be gleaned from his characterization of the secession clause as a constitutional precommitment device, both in the *timing* of its entrenchment (i.e., at the founding of a multination state or at a moment of political calm when secession is not a real possibility) and in its *function* to protect political actors from their own destructive behaviors. As Weinstock writes:[20]

> Provisions such as the ones that I have described should be negotiated and drafted by willing partners looking down the road at temptations and grievances that might get the better of them when the political climate is more difficult. They may be tempted to protect themselves against destructive motives which they know they may come to have, but which they antecedently do not want it to be too easy to act on. They might therefore find it rational on such occasions to "bind themselves" in such a way as not to make it too easy to quit the association they are constituting on a whim.

On Schauer's logic, a secession clause definitely should be susceptible to adjudication because constitutional precommitments are precisely what legal constitutionalism and judicial supremacy are for. Indeed, this should be an easy case for Schauer and the legal constitution.

But this conclusion warrants further reflection in light of the *Secession Reference*, in which the Supreme Court of Canada seems to have crafted a secession clause that is *not* even subject to judicial interpretation, let alone judicial supremacy. A bit of background is in order. The federal government brought the *Secession Reference* by invoking the advisory jurisdiction of the Supreme Court of Canada. The Court was asked narrow questions – whether unilateral secession was legal under Canadian constitutional law and under international law – which it unsurprisingly answered in the negative. However, there were three highly unusual aspects to the judgment.

First, although submissions had focused almost entirely on the text of the constitutional provisions governing amendment, the Court's judgment was based on a set of *unwritten* constitutional principles: democracy, federalism, constitutionalism and the rule of law, and minority rights. In addition to functioning as interpretive aids, these principles are freestanding sources of binding constitutional obligations. The Court held that unilateral secession would be unconstitutional, not because the constitutional text did not permit it, but because the principle of democracy could not take priority over federalism and the rule of law.

Second, the Court held that even though a referendum vote for independence would not legally effect Quebec's secession, a "clear majority" voting in favor of a

[19] Weinstock, *supra* note 15 at 199.

[20] Ibid. at 198.

"clear question" in a referendum on secession would trigger a constitutional duty on the "political actors" to negotiate the terms of secession in good faith. The Court crafted this obligation from the unwritten constitutional principles. Moreover, these same principles had to be taken into account by the negotiating parties and properly balanced in the terms of any secession agreement. I refer to this set of obligations, collectively, as the Canadian secession clause. Any negotiated agreement for secession resulting from these constitutionally triggered and structured negotiations would also require a constitutional amendment.

Third, and perhaps most importantly for our purposes, the Court held that it would not enforce the terms of the Canadian secession clause in subsequent constitutional litigation. After setting out the constitutional duties flowing from the Canadian secession clause, the Court expressly limited its role "to the identification of the relevant aspects of the Constitution in their broadest sense," beyond which it had "no supervisory role."[21] Rather, as it said in its conclusion, it would "be for the political actors to determine what constitutes 'a clear majority on a clear question' in the circumstances under which a future referendum vote may be taken," in order to determine "the content and process of the negotiations."[22] The constitutional rules governing secession, in other words, are nonjusticiable. However, the Court took pains to explain that the nonjusticiability of these rules did not deprive them of their constitutionally binding status. As the Court said, these rules were "constitutional obligations."[23] This is a departure from normal Canadian constitutional practice, which categorizes those constitutional rules that are justiciable, and those that are not, into constitutional law and constitutional convention, respectively. Constitutional law is enforceable in the courts, whereas constitutional conventions "carry only political sanctions."[24] Set against this background, the Court could have been understood to be saying that the constitutional rules governing secession were constitutional conventions. However, it did not say that. Rather, it said that the duty to negotiate was an obligation arising under "the *law* of the Constitution."[25] And at the conclusion of its reasons, the Court could not have been clearer, when it stated that "[t]he obligations we have identified are binding obligations under the Constitution of Canada."[26]

This last point bears closer examination. The Court's refusal to exhaustively specify the contours of the requirements of a clear majority and a clear question was not unusual in itself. Although the lack of detail on the clarity requirements may arguably have impaired the ability of the Canadian secession clause to function effectively as a precommitment device, the Court could have justified its refusal to flesh out the terms of the Canadian secession clause on prudential grounds, declining to offer further guidance until such time as was strictly necessary to resolve a concrete case, on the basis of a calculation that the positive effects and unintended consequences of its judgment would be more readily apparent. But the Court went one step further and closed the door to further judicial intervention.

21 *Secession Reference, supra* note 14 at para. 100.
22 Ibid. at para. 153.
23 Ibid. at para. 102.
24 Ibid. at para. 98.
25 Ibid. [emphasis in original].
26 Ibid. at para. 153.

It explicitly rejected any future judicial role in interpreting the Canadian secession clause; it is implicit that judicial enforcement was off the table.

Thus, the Court held that the rules were both nonjusticiable and legally binding. But the Court left both the interpretation and enforcement of the Canadian secession clause – which imposes legal obligations – to constitutional politics. This is clearly inconsistent with a legalist conception of constitutionalism but is clearly consistent with populist constitutionalism. The question then becomes why the Court took the populist route. The Court did attempt to offer a justification for this unusual holding based on the comparative institutional advantage of the political actors in this area of constitutional adjudication, stating that the Court itself lacked the "requisite information and expertise."[27] Elaborating on the informational limitations of the litigation process, the Court explained that "the methods appropriate for the search for truth in a court of law are ill-suited to getting to the bottom of constitutional negotiations."[28] Moreover, the Court reasoned that "the strong defence of legitimate interests and the taking of positions which, in fact, ignore the legitimate interests of others is one that also defies legal analysis."[29] In other words, judicially manageable standards are absent. Unfortunately, this justification is weak. It is not at all clear, for example, that the Court is incapable of adjudicating upon both the preconditions to, and the process and outcome of, constitutional negotiations. The interpretation of the terms "clear majority" and "clear question," the enforcement of the obligation to negotiate in good faith, and even the compliance of the negotiated agreement with the unwritten constitutional principles are not totally beyond the realm of judicial competence.

So competence-based arguments based on a purported lack of judicial expertise cannot justify the Court's refusal to enforce the Canadian secession clause according to the tenets of legal constitutionalism. Before I offer an explanation for *why* the Court left the enforcement of the Canadian secession clause to constitutional politics, I want to briefly review how constitutional politics has gone thus far.

D. POPULAR CONSTITUTIONALISM AND CONSTITUTIONAL PRECOMMITMENTS: THE *CLARITY ACT* AND BILL 99

The *Secession Reference* was welcomed by the federal government because it won on the illegality of unilateral secession. But it was also welcomed by Quebec, which won judicial recognition of the legitimacy of the Quebec sovereignty movement, and the duty to negotiate on secession as opposed to renewed federalism. However, these important differences in interpretation paled in significance to the shared and immediate understanding among governments which had disagreed profoundly that the judgment provided an acceptable legal framework within which secession could occur. Matters were relatively stable for about a year after the *Secession Reference* was handed down, until Quebec reverted to its earlier position that, in Quebec's accession to statehood, legitimacy took priority over legality. The falling apart of this early consensus has produced two competing statutes.

[27] Ibid. at para. 100.
[28] Ibid. at para. 101.
[29] Ibid.

The federal government made the first move by enacting the *Clarity Act* in 2000.[30] The Act requires the House of Commons to determine whether the question Quebec has chosen and the level of support that that question obtains would trigger the federal government's constitutional duty to negotiate secession. The Act also limits how the House of Commons can make these determinations. At the federal level, the power to enter into constitutional negotiations, including negotiations for secession, is vested with the executive, meaning that without the Act, the federal executive would be charged with interpreting and complying with the Canadian secession clause. The Act, however, delegates to the House of Commons the power of the executive to frame interpretations of the clear majority and question requirements.

The clear question determination would be made by the House of Commons *ex ante*. Although the *Clarity Act* neither lays down the text of an acceptable question nor provides that the House of Commons could set out the text of a question that would meet the requirement of clarity, the Act sets out what would *not* constitute a clear question. In particular, it rules out the 1995 referendum question, which envisaged a positive referendum result as a mandate for Quebec to negotiate a new economic and political partnership with Canada, as opposed to outright independence. The thrust of the provision is that in order to trigger the duty to negotiate, whatever question Quebec poses must be a question on secession or independence.

In parallel to how it treats the clarity of a question, the *Clarity Act* does not define what could constitute a clear majority. But the Act takes a different approach to determining whether a majority vote in favor of secession is clear. It does not contain a numerical threshold for a clear majority (i.e., a negative definition of a clear majority, analogous to the negative restraints on the wording of the question). Nor does it delegate to the House of Commons the power to determine what a clear majority would constitute before the vote takes place. Rather, the Act leaves that assessment to *after* the vote has been held, based on factors including the size of the majority and voter turnout. The Act also affirms the unconstitutionality of a UDI and the need for a constitutional amendment.

Thus, under the *Clarity Act*, Quebec can hold whatever referendum it wants, but if the House of Commons were to determine the question to not be a clear question on secession or the resulting majority to not be clear, the federal government would be legally barred from entering into secession negotiations.

The *Clarity Act* reflects a number of critical interpretive choices concerning the scope of the Canadian secession clause. Perhaps most importantly, it does not attempt to use the *Secession Reference* as a jurisdictional basis for federal legislation on the rules for a provincial secession referendum, although one way of understanding the Canadian secession clause is as a subtraction from exclusive provincial jurisdiction over some of the procedures governing secession. The Act also reflects other important interpretive choices. It precommits the federal executive in advance of a future referendum to the procedures spelled out in the Act to determine both a clear question and a clear majority, as opposed to giving the federal executive a free hand. Indeed, it prohibits the federal government from

[30] *An Act to give effect to the requirement for clarity as set out in the opinion of the Supreme Court of Canada in the Quebec Secession Reference*, S.C. 2000, c. 26.

negotiating Quebec secession if the House of Commons determines that the question or the majority are not clear. Moreover, by choosing the House of Commons as the forum for determining the clarity of the question and the majority, the federal government has committed itself to a public process for examining these issues. The Act, however, treats the two assessments of clarity differently: although it requires the House of Commons to determine the clarity of the question before the referendum vote, the clarity of the majority is determined afterward in light of all the circumstances (e.g., turnout, votes of minority groups, etc.).

Quebec responded to the *Clarity Act* almost immediately with Bill 99, the *Fundamental Rights Act*, also enacted in 2000.[31] The key provisions of Bill 99 make a series of strong claims of exclusive provincial jurisdiction over the process surrounding a future referendum on Quebec secession. Bill 99 states that the people of Quebec have the right to freely decide its political regime and legal status. Bill 99 buttresses this provision by coupling it with a claim of *exclusive* provincial jurisdiction – that is, that the manner of exercising this right is a matter for Quebec alone to determine through its political institutions. The implication is that any attempts by the federal government to rely on the *Secession Reference* to regulate the referendum process would contravene Bill 99.

As I just mentioned, the *Clarity Act* does *not* purport to lay down federal rules for a Quebec referendum on secession; rather, it sets conditions for the federal recognition of such a referendum. Two further provisions of Bill 99 take direct aim at this aspect of the *Clarity Act.* One states that "[n]o condition or mode of exercise of that right, in particular the consultation of the Québec people by way of a referendum, shall have effect unless" accepted by the people of Quebec. Another states that "[n]o other parliament or government may reduce the powers, authority, sovereignty or legitimacy of the National Assembly, or impose constraint [*sic*] on the democratic will of the Québec people to determine its own future." Finally, Bill 99 affirms that a clear majority in a referendum is 50 percent plus one.

It would seem that the *Secession Reference*'s move to send the Canadian secession clause back to constitutional politics has failed. The Court likely contemplated that political actors would interpret the secession clause in the context of a future referendum. Although the Court was silent on how this would occur, its probable expectation was that the federal and Quebec governments would engage in negotiations, at an appropriate time and through mutually acceptable procedures, to arrive at a shared understanding of the wording of a referendum question and the level of majority required. This is the manner in which the federal and provincial governments interact routinely and, indeed, how the Court thinks secession should occur – that is, through a process of negotiation.

Instead, both levels of government have proceeded unilaterally. Moreover, the processes each Act creates or presupposes primarily or solely involve institutions within each level of government. At the federal level, the sole institution is the House of Commons, which determines the clarity of the question and the majority. Within Quebec, the National Assembly is the lead institution. Neither statute, for example, mandates that the resolutions or decisions of the other legislative body

[31] *An Act respecting the exercise of the fundamental rights and prerogatives of the Québec people and the Québec State*, S.Q. 2000, c. 46.

be taken into account or that there be consultation with the executive branch of the other level of government.

Proceeding unilaterally would not have posed difficulty had the Quebec and federal interpretations been compatible. But that has not happened either. Bill 99 defines a majority as 50 percent plus one. Although the *Clarity Act* deliberately does not lay down a numerical standard, the federal government took great pains during the debate over the *Clarity Act* to criticize the absolute majority standard, both as a misinterpretation of the *Secession Reference* – which always referred to a "clear" majority, never to an "absolute" or "simple" majority or just a "majority" – and also as a matter of constitutional design, reasoning that irreversible negotiations over secession should only be undertaken on the basis of a clear and stable majority, not a momentary and temporary majority of circumstance. The two bills therefore set the stage for a serious disagreement between the federal government and Quebec in the event of a future referendum vote, which many observers expect to be held in the next few years.

Moreover, if Quebec and the federal government do disagree on the level of support required, the divergent approaches taken by Bill 99 and the *Clarity Act* on *when* that numerical standard is to be set will exacerbate this disagreement. Bill 99 sets the threshold of 50 percent in advance of the next vote. The *Clarity Act*, by contrast, forestalls the House of Commons' assessment of whether there has been a clear majority vote until *after* the referendum. The accusation voiced by Quebec sovereignists is that such a process is inherently unfair because it would allow the House of Commons to set the standards for the federal government's response to the referendum result after the vote has occurred – judging the referendum by standards not known at the time of the campaign and vote. Moreover, it would allow the federal government to mask a political disagreement with the Quebec government over the merits of secession as a constitutional disagreement over whether the requirements of the Canadian secession clause had been met.

Finally, perhaps the most fundamental point is that the *Clarity Act* and Bill 99 conceptualize their relationship to the *Secession Reference* radically differently. The full title of the *Clarity Act* is "An Act to give effect to the requirement for clarity as set out in the opinion of the Supreme Court of Canada in the Quebec Secession Reference." Five clauses in the preamble summarize the salient points of the judgment, and the key provisions of the statute speak directly to the Canadian secession clause. Bill 99, by contrast, contains only one direct reference to the judgment in its preamble, noting its "political importance" and thus by implication denying it legal status. Bill 99 is not a direct attempt to engage and entrench Quebec's interpretation of the judgment; rather, it operates within an alternative constitutional vision that gives pride of place to the democratic will of Quebeckers. As a consequence, it deliberately does not match the federal response point for point.

E. FROM POPULAR REVOLUTION TO POPULAR CONSTITUTIONALISM?

At this point, it might seem that the *Secession Reference* got it terribly wrong in leaving the interpretation and enforcement of the Canadian secession clause to constitutional politics and the vagaries of popular constitutionalism. A legal constitutionalist could argue that if the constitutional strategy of precommitment is designed to regulate political decision making precisely because one cannot trust political actors to regulate their own conduct, then one cannot leave important interpretive issues to political actors to work out in advance of the event. The legal constitutionalist might suggest that the Court should have mandated intergovernmental negotiations over the Canadian secession clause, spelled out a decision-rule whereby divergent interpretations could be reconciled, and left open the door to judicial enforcement so the threat of future litigation could encourage a political settlement. Or, perhaps even more dramatically, the legal constitutionalist might argue that perhaps the Court should have eschewed constitutional politics entirely, and agreed to fully interpret and enforce the Canadian secession clause.

I think that this view is too simplistic. To understand why, let us return to the Rhodesian constitutional crisis. The Rhodesian courts had applied a test of effective control inspired by Kelsen to determine whether the old constitutional order had died and a new one had been born. This test conceptualized judges as passive observers of constitutional transitions, who would assess when one constitutional regime had been successfully replaced by another. But as critics of the Rhodesian courts persuasively argued, this way of structuring the question obfuscated and buried the true role played by the courts, which did not simply recognize, but actually consolidated, the new constitutional regime. Because the rule of recognition's existence flows from its acceptance, judges would presumably have to assess the attitudes and behaviors of other governmental actors and the public. However, as one of the principal organs of government, the courts' acceptance of the regime was not merely an inevitable consequence of constitutional regime change. Rather, it was in itself an element of effective control and, hence, part of the process of successful constitutional transition. So, under the guise of acting as external observers, judges were in fact exercising a choice whether to declare allegiance to the revolutionary regime.

Once the fact of judicial choice is brought to the surface, so are new questions about the nature of revolutionary legal change. In other writing, Schauer suggests an approach to tackling this issue. He has stated that the existence of a constitutional order depends on "presuppositions" which are "logically antecedent"[32] to the rule of recognition, and which give that rule its constitutional status. Schauer does not define what the presuppositions of a constitutional order consist of. But they appear to encompass the various reasons why a constitution is accepted as the highest law – a mix of historical, political, economic, moral, and cultural reasons that is highly contingent, potentially varying across political communities, and, indeed, potentially varying within a political community across time – perhaps even for constitutional regimes that are identical in both form and substance. Schauer explains extralegal change to constitutions in terms of, and as flowing from, changes to their presuppositions. As he writes, "because constitutions owe their 'constitutionality' to logically and politically antecedent conditions, the process of constitutional amendment may also take place at another level, when these logically and politically antecedent conditions are themselves amended."[33]

[32] Schauer, *Amending Presuppositions, supra* note 13 at 147.

[33] Schauer, ibid. at 160–1.

So two truly interesting questions raised by revolutionary legality are how to best understand the character of constitutional presuppositions that underlie the prior regime, and the reasons why those presuppositions might change. Moreover, in trying to understand shifts in constitutional presuppositions, it would be a mistake to focus exclusively on the courts. The literature generated in response to the Rhodesian constitutional crisis focussed narrowly on judicial decision making because the question of revolutionary legality arose as a legal issue for adjudication. However, this methodological choice should be understood as flowing from the facts of the Rhodesian case, as opposed to indicating the general way revolutionary legal change should be studied. Hart's rule of recognition turns on the fact of its acceptance by those officials who use it on a constant basis to frame and make their decisions, and as a lens through which to interpret, judge, and react to the decisions of others. Even on this narrow understanding of the range of acceptance required for a rule of recognition to exist, the question also arises of why nonjudicial officials in a constitutional regime accept a certain rule of recognition – that is, what the presuppositions are for their acceptance – and why those presuppositions might shift as well. Indeed, it is possible to push the point further and extend the scope of choice to citizens as well. In a liberal democratic political community that eschews the use of physical violence to settle political disputes, even over the basic question of the locus of political sovereignty, legal subjects must make the substantive choice of whether to accept the commands of the new regime. As John Finnis writes, "the problem of the jurist is the same as the problem . . . for the good man wondering where his allegiance and duty lie."[34]

It is this context, more than anything else, which explains why legal constitutionalism is not an option for the enforcement of a secession clause. The fact that citizens would be grappling with the fundamental question of whether Quebec should have its own independent constitutional order in the context of a referendum vote makes sense of the Court's decision to not enforce the terms of the Canadian secession clause itself and to instead rely on political actors to do so. As I explained earlier, a basic ambition of constitutionalism is to channel political conflict that would otherwise spill into the streets, into institutions that operate peacefully according to law, and which reach decisions that members of a political community accept as authoritative. In a constitutional state, institutional settlement translates into political settlement. A referendum vote understood as an exercise of popular will over the locus of sovereignty creates a context in which institutional settlement cannot easily, and perhaps even possibly, produce political settlement because what is at issue is the very source of the authority of those institutions.

So the wisdom of the *Secession Reference* lies in its recognition that in *this* kind of situation – an existential moment in the life cycle of a constitutional order – a court injunction against a Quebec UDI, even if issued by the Supreme Court of Canada, would have little or no effect. Legal constitutionalism is not an option. Popular will is necessarily, and unavoidably, engaged. The question then becomes what criteria should and will inform this choice by legal subjects. In a highly skeptical

[34] J. Finnis, "Revolutions and Continuity of Law" in A. W. B. Simpson, ed., *Oxford Essays in Jurisprudence: Second Series* (Oxford: Clarendon Press, 1973) 64 at 75.

review of Kramer's *The People Themselves,* Larry Alexander and Lawrence Solum suggest that whatever criteria these are, they are not constitutional, because the acceptance by legal subjects of the existence of a constitutional order as a matter of social practice would consist of no more than a thin "tacit endorsement."[35] Although this may constitute a form of popular constitutionalism, on their view, characterizing the attitude of legal subjects in this way would come at the cost of trivializing the concept. Their point may be that while a constitutional mindset involves "an interpretive act by the people themselves" that official conduct is consistent with the constitution, that attitude cannot be applied to the existence of the constitutional order itself.

Indeed, at times, the Court's discussion of revolutionary legality shows that it was working with this view of the status of the Canadian secession clause in constitutional politics. Revolutionary legality was considered by the Court in the context of a unilateral declaration of independence by Quebec, potentially after failed constitutional negotiations to achieve secession under the Canadian constitution. The Court first framed the issue of revolutionary legality much as the Rhodesian courts had: as an extralegal usurpation of the existing constitutional order, the success of which would be a question of political fact. Thus, the Court explained that "[a]lthough under the Constitution there is no right to pursue secession . . . this does not rule out the possibility of an unconstitutional declaration of secession leading to a *de facto* secession. The ultimate success of such a secession would be dependent on effective control of a territory and recognition by the international community."[36]

But this formulation of the problem of revolutionary legality repeats the conceptual mistake of the Rhodesian courts. And so it is significant that other parts of the judgment suggest that the ambition of the Canadian secession clause is to convert what would otherwise be a situation of popular revolution into popular constitutionalism, by providing a common framework within which constitutional politics can take place. Consider what the Court thought the role of political actors to be in the absence of judicial intervention. The Court was clear that it fell to political actors to enforce the Canadian secession clause. As the Court explained, "the conduct of the parties assumes primary constitutional significance. The negotiation process must be conducted with an eye to the constitutional principles we have outlined, which must inform the actions of *all* the participants in the negotiation process."[37] And the leverage parties would be able to deploy against each other would take the form of claims of legitimacy, with parties who act in accordance with the Canadian secession clause acting legitimately, and, conversely, the parties who act in contravention of the Canadian secession clause acting without legitimacy.

The Court's judgment should be read as advising an unspecified audience on the basis of which to make its choice of whether to recognize a UDI issued by Quebec. So who are these actors? The origins of the case can be traced to an intergovernmental dispute between Quebec and Canada over the legal framework governing secession.

[35] Larry Alexander and Lawrence B. Solum, "Popular? Constitutionalism?" (Review of *The People Themselves: Popular Constitutionalism and Judicial Review* by Larry Kramer) (2005) 118 *Harv. L. Rev.* 1594 at 1624.

[36] *Secession Reference, supra* note 14 at para. 106.

[37] Ibid. at para. 94 [emphasis in original].

As a consequence, the judgment is clearly directed at them. Indeed, the terms of the Canadian secession clause clearly govern the conduct of the federal and Quebec governments in the event of a referendum on sovereignty.[38]

But there is another audience for the Court's judgment: the citizens of Quebec and the rest of Canada. The context in which the Canadian secession clause would operate is a referendum, which is a particular kind of political decision-making procedure. Here, rather than acting through elected representatives, held accountable through periodic elections, the members of a political community act directly as political decision makers in an exercise of popular will. Although referenda are, strictly speaking, consultative political exercises without enacting or lawmaking authority, the perception during the Quebec referendum was rather different. All political actors accepted that Quebeckers were engaging in a collective political choice – in other words, that the referendum was an exercise in popular sovereignty.

The Court recognized the limitations of institutional settlement in producing political settlement and indicated that citizens would ultimately choose the constitutional regime to which they wished to declare allegiance. The Court's reasoning should thus be read as setting out the kinds of reasons on the basis of which citizens could assess the legitimacy of the differing positions of the parties. The Court imagined that the citizens of Quebec perceived themselves as legal subjects in a political community whose very self-description incorporates a commitment to the rule of law. These kinds of citizens would not want to act outside the law and would not wish to declare allegiance to a government that acted outside the law. This is true not only of normal periods in the operation of a constitutional regime, but even at the moment of existential crisis for the Canadian constitutional order, when the very survival of a positive legal framework would itself be in question. The Court conceptualized this moment as one of popular constitutionalism, not one of popular revolution.

This explains why, I think, the Court described the Canadian secession clause as giving rise to legal obligations that were binding on the parties, even in the absence of the prospect of judicial enforcement. As Mark Walters has explained, in light of the importance of legality to Canadian culture, the Canadian secession clause's status as law, as opposed to mere principles of political morality, would fundamentally change the politics of secession going forward. As he says, "[i]t would seem that the normative force of these legal arguments is felt by political actors on both sides in very different ways from the normative force of political and moral arguments, notwithstanding ... the absence of judicial sanction."[39] Political claims would become legal claims. Indeed, framing the Canadian secession clause as giving rise to legal obligations may have been designed to inject a sense of

[38] Yet another audience is the international community, because of its role in the recognition of an independent Quebec, should constitutional negotiations for secession fail. The Court suggests that in deciding whether to recognize an independent Quebec, foreign governments should determine whether parties had complied with the terms of the secession clause – relying on a normative vision of the international legal order in which states obtain international legal personality through their commitment to a core set of principles of political legitimacy.

[39] Mark D. Walters, "Nationalism and the Pathology of Legal Systems: Considering the *Quebec Secession Reference* and Its Lessons for the United Kingdom" (1999) 62 *Modern L. Rev.* 371 at 391.

constitutional obligation on all the actors involved, to distinguish the task at hand from ordinary politics, in which self-interest and partisanship are central.

Political actors seem to have understood the role of the *Clarity Act* and Bill 99 in this way as well, because they chose to respond to the judgment through enacting *statutes*. For example, as Quebec's Minister of Intergovernmental Affairs explained in the concluding debate surrounding Bill 99, Quebec felt compelled to respond to the *Clarity Act* with legislation of its own, as opposed to a resolution of the Quebec National Assembly, because, if it did not, "is there not a danger . . . that the Quebecois people, faced only with one law, the federal Parliament's law, come to believe that the only legitimate legal order is that of the federal Parliament, and that, if we are not in agreement with them, we are outside of the laws."[40]

F. CONCLUSION

The more general lesson is this: even if one accepts the legal constitutionalists' conception of constitutionalism and accordingly acknowledges the need for constitutional precommitments, it does not follow that one must necessarily adopt judicial supremacy as the appropriate institutional mechanism for enforcement. The institutional question is a separate matter altogether and must be sensitive to the nature of the issue at hand. When it comes to existential legal issues going to the very identity and existence of a constitutional order, judicial supremacy is unlikely to produce political settlement. However, it does not follow that the alternative is popular revolution. Popular constitutionalism may be able to prevail over popular revolution, against the backdrop of a liberal political culture whose subjects see themselves as legal subjects committed to the rule of law. So trusting the enforcement of constitutional precommitments to constitutional politics may be the best we can do.

There may be another lesson of somewhat broader significance. The *Quebec Secession Reference*, and the constitutional politics of secession, can be viewed not just through the lens of constitutional crises but also of federalism. In an important sense, the dispute between the federal government and the provincial government concerned which level of government was entitled to participate in the framing of the rules governing secession, including the manner in which a provincial population could express its views through a referendum. Prior to the *Quebec Secession Reference*, this process lay entirely within the control of the provincial government. Subsequent to that judgment, at least those aspects of that process that fall within the ambit of the Canadian secession clause arguably lie within both federal and provincial jurisdiction, as is reflected by the enactment of both the *Clarity Act* and Bill 99.

Under the Canadian constitution, the delineation of the respective scope of federal and provincial jurisdiction, and the resolution of conflicts between validly enacted legislation, have fallen to the courts. Indeed, leading students of comparative federalism have long assumed that judicial supremacy is an integral component of federal governance. K. C. Wheare famously argued that because the project of federalism is to set up two independent levels of government existing in a coordinate,

[40] Québec, Permanent Committee of Institutions, May 30, 2000 at 11 (translation).

not a subordinate, relationship, "it follows that the last word in settling disputes about the meaning of the division of powers must not rest either with the general government alone or the regional governments alone."[41] Rather, he continued, "[w]hat is essential for federal government is that some impartial body, independent of general and regional governments, should decide upon the meaning of the division of powers."[42] Wheare's preferred institution for this task was the courts. Indeed, if one understands a federal form of government as a pact between nations who have chosen to politically associate for some purposes while retaining the scope for independent action for others, written constitutions and judicial review are a form of constitutional precommitment to protect national minorities against breaches of the terms of the original federal bargain. Federalism, for these reasons, is an easy case for judicial supremacy.

The *Secession Reference* suggests that students of comparative federalism should revisit the view that federalism necessarily connotes legalism in every single case. Quite aside from the American literature on the "political safeguards" of federalism[43] – whose applicability to Canada and other federations, because of differences in the design of the federal legislature and the structure of the party system, is unclear – it may be that judicial enforcement of the division of powers should not be universal. Paul Weiler's argument that "[t]here is no logical necessity for judicial review in a federal system, even though that system by its very nature involves the creation of *limited* legislative powers," and that "the better technique for managing conflict is continual negotiation and political compromise,"[44] deserves closer consideration.

Let me conclude by tying the argument in this chapter to an argument I have made elsewhere that the birth and death of constitutional regimes are moments of what I term *constitutive constitutional politics*. At these moments, the rules governing constitutional change (i.e., the rules governing constitutional amendment) are incapable of constituting and regulating constitutional politics, and are instead drawn into it because they reflect one of the competing conceptions of political community on the table.[45] I have suggested that at these moments, we might reach the limits of constitutional design and constitutionalism itself. I may now need to qualify this conclusion. For if this conclusion were true, it would argue against the efficacy of a Canadian secession clause of any sort, as such a provision would be designed precisely to regulate the birth of a new constitutional order. The more accurate point may be this: for constitutionalism and legal continuity to prevail over legal discontinuity and revolution, the rules that regulate existential legal change (e.g., a secession clause) must be perceived as not being biased or

[41] K. C. Wheare, *Federal Government*, 3rd ed. (Oxford: Oxford University Press, 1953) at 60.

[42] Ibid. at 66.

[43] Herbert Wechsler, "The Political Safeguards of Federalism: The Role of the States in the Composition and Selection of the National Government" (1954) 54 *Colum. L. Rev.* 543; Larry D. Kramer, "Putting the Politics Back into the Political Safeguards of Federalism" (2000) 100 *Colum. L. Rev.* 215.

[44] Paul C. Weiler, *In the Last Resort: A Critical Study of the Supreme Court of Canada* (Toronto: Carswell, 1974) 165 and 175.

[45] S. Choudhry, "Ackerman's Higher Lawmaking in Comparative Constitutional Perspective: Constitutional Moments as Constitutional Failures?" (unpublished); S. Choudhry, "Old Imperial Dilemmas and the New Nation-Building: Constitutive Constitutional Politics in Multinational Polities" (2005) 37 *Conn. L. Rev.* 933.

unduly committed to the maintenance of the existing constitutional order. And, similarly, the choice of enforcement institution cannot be tied too closely to the constitutional regime whose survival is at issue – such as its courts.

ACKNOWLEDGMENTS

Thanks to Tsvi Kahana and Ira Parghi for helpful comments and Saad Ahmad for editorial assistance.

PART SEVEN. THE LEGISLATURE IN DIALOGUE: DOMESTIC AND INTERNATIONAL CONTEXTS

25 Disobeying Parliament? Privative Clauses and the Rule of Law

David Dyzenhaus

> Although in theory perhaps, it may be possible for Parliament to set up a tribunal which has full autonomous powers to fix its own area of operation, that, so far, has not been done in this country. The question, what is the tribunal's proper area, is one which it has always been permitted to ask and to answer, and it must follow that examination of its extent is not precluded by a clause conferring conclusiveness, finality, or unquestionability upon its decisions. . . . In each task [the courts] are carrying out the intention of the legislature, and it would be misdescription to state it in terms of a struggle between the courts and the executive. What would be the purpose of defining by statute the limit of the tribunal's powers, if, by means of a clause inserted in the instrument of definition, those limits could be safely passed?[1]

> The judges appreciate, much more than does Parliament, that to exempt any public authority from judicial control is to give it dictatorial power, and this is so fundamentally objectionable that Parliament cannot really intend it. . . . [C]lauses excluding the courts [are] left with no meaning at all and . . . judges will be unable to deny that they are flatly disobeying Parliament. . . . All law students are taught that Parliamentary sovereignty is absolute. But it is judges who have the last word. If they interpret an Act to mean the opposite of what it says, it is their view which represents the law. Parliament may of course retaliate.[2]

The privative clause is a statutory provision to which Commonwealth parliaments resort in order to protect public officials from judicial review. Judges find it difficult to make sense of these provisions, for they work within a tradition of public law in which two assumptions are taken for granted.

First, there is the assumption of legislative supremacy, or what Sir William Wade in the second epigraph to this chapter calls "absolute" "Parliamentary sovereignty." In the absence of an entrenched bill of rights Parliament is supreme, and if it expresses its intention in a statute with complete clarity on any topic, judges are bound to interpret the statute as it was in fact intended to be interpreted. A. V. Dicey's example was a statute which decreed that all blue-eyed babies should be put to death. He said that "legislators must go mad before they could pass such a law, and subjects be idiotic before they could submit to it." Thus, there are "internal"

[1] *Anisminic Ltd. v. Foreign Compensation Commission*, [1969] 2 A.C. 147 at 207–8 [*Anisminic*] per Lord Wilberforce.

[2] Sir William Wade, *Constitutional Fundamentals* (London: Stevens & Sons, 1989; The Hamlyn Lectures) at 82 [Wade].

and "external" limits on what Parliament can do, but a law that goes beyond those limits is still law.[3]

Second, there is the assumption that judges should have, as Wade says, the "last word" when it comes to interpretation of the law. Judges enforce law by ensuring that public officials stay within the limits of the law, where law means both the law of the statute that delegates authority to the officials and the common law. Both Dicey and Wade regard the influence of the common law in this process as morally beneficial. The common law contains moral principles, for example, presumptions about liberty and the principles of natural justice or fairness – the right to a hearing and the right to an unbiased adjudication. Judges are entitled to interpret the law of the constitutive statute as if the legislature intended its delegates to exercise their authority in compliance with these principles.

The privative clause subverts this conception of the rule of law by driving a wedge between the two assumptions. It goes further than telling judges that they do not enjoy the last word; it tells them that they have no say at all. For example, the privative clause in *Anisminic* provided that a determination by the Foreign Compensation Commission "shall not be called in question in any court of law." Moreover, the issue goes beyond the fact that the principles of the common law cannot play their allegedly beneficial role in disciplining official authority. The statute that delegates authority will prescribe the mandate the officials are to carry out. If that mandate is protected by a privative clause, it will seem that the officials may do as they please; they are a law unto themselves. So the problem can be seen as internal to the first assumption. A parliament is supreme only if its laws prescribe limits on the authority of public officials. Hence, a law that prescribes limits on authority and gives to officials the authority to decide on those limits sets up an internal contradiction.[4]

As the first epigraph tells us, judges can claim that the statute presents them with a puzzle which they are entitled to solve. They do so by subordinating Parliament's alleged intention to make the official a law unto himself through the privative clause to its abstract intention, contained in every statute, to prescribe a necessarily limited authority, the latter manifesting itself in the other provisions of the statute.

The tension between the privative clause and the other provisions of the statute, a clash between particular expressions of intent, can then be deployed by judges to infer a further component to the intention that officials have a legally limited authority. Legal limits can be claimed to include the limits set by common-law principles. Parliament is said to have the intention that officials should abide by the relevant principles of the common law as well as the terms of the statute. The difference is that although Parliament seems constitutionally disabled from contradicting the abstract intention to prescribe a limited authority in the sense of statutory limits on authority, it is hardly obvious that it cannot oust review on the basis of common-law principles by, for example, saying clearly that officials

[3] A. V. Dicey, *An Introduction to the Study of the Law of the Constitution*, 10th ed. (London: Macmillan, 1987) at 81–2 [Dicey].

[4] I am assuming here that enforceable limits means enforceable by judges. I concede that judges are not the only institution capable of enforcing limits. But if they are the only available institution as things stand in a legal order, the assumption is not controversial.

do not have to give the subjects of their decisions a hearing. Hence, if common-law principles operate as a kind of implied statutory condition on administrative authority, it might seem that all Parliament has to do to get rid of that condition is to remove its basis. Moreover, it might seem that all Parliament has to do to get rid of the problem of a tension between, on the one hand, the abstract intention to delegate a limited authority coupled with particular limiting provisions and, on the other, a privative clause, is to refrain from stating any limiting provisions. Parliament simply delegates an unfettered discretion.

However, if the principles of the common law are constitutional, and so operate directly on administrative authority without requiring the medium of intention, implied or express, it might seem that Parliament is disabled from contradicting the abstract intention that administrative authority be limited by the common law.[5] It might then also seem that we are stuck with the choice between "competing supremacies" – the supremacy of judges and the supremacy of Parliament, exactly the problem that Dicey bequeathed to the common law.[6]

This deep issue lies behind the disagreement between Wade and Wilberforce in the epigraphs. Wilberforce says of the judicial solution that "it would be misdescription to state it in terms of a struggle between the courts and the executive,"[7] whereas Wade sketches a struggle between judges and Parliament. Wade does propose that the judges are completely justified in resisting Parliament's attempt to create "pockets of uncontrollable power in violation of the rule of law."[8] But they are not justified in a "legal sense," only in a "distinct constitutional sense, "as for example is the case if Parliament were to legislate to establish one-party government, or a dictatorship, or in some other way to attack the fundamentals of democracy."[9] Indeed, Wade seems unsure of the import of his claim about constitutionality. He says that "judges have almost given us a constitution, establishing a kind of entrenched provision to the effect that even Parliament cannot deprive them of their proper function. They may be discovering a deeper constitutional logic than the crude absolute of statutory omnipotence."[10]

The difference between Wilberforce's confidence that all he is doing is applying the law and Wade's more nuanced and tentative account could be explained in terms of perspective. There is the judicial perspective – that of the engaged participant in legal practice who to preserve his sense of role has to claim that he is not engaged in a political battle. He is simply carrying out Parliament's intention. And there is the academic commentator who can give a realistic account of what the participant is up to. Wade's account is, however, no less engaged than Wilberforce's. He does not say that the judges had discretion and so had to take a stand determined by their political convictions and not by the law. He clearly supposes that the judges were doing their duty by preserving the rule of law, even

[5] These issues are at the heart of the "*ultra vires*" debate in the United Kingdom – see Christopher Forsyth, ed., *Judicial Review and the Constitution* (Oxford: Hart Publishing, 2000).

[6] See Murray Hunt, "Sovereignty's Blight: Why Contemporary Public Law Needs the Concept of 'Due Deference'" in Nicholas Bamforth and Peter Leyland, eds., *Public Law in a Multi-Layered Constitution* (Oxford: Hart Publishing, 2003) 337 at 339 [Hunt].

[7] *Anisminic, supra* note 1.

[8] Wade, *supra* note 2.

[9] Ibid. at 83.

[10] Ibid. at 87.

though he is unwilling to categorize that duty as legal, preferring to think of it as constitutional, or quasi-constitutional. I hope to show that Wilberforce's and Wade's disagreement provides insights into the content of the rule of law or legality, which help to grasp better the relationship between Parliament, the judiciary, and the executive.

I will discuss three approaches that Commonwealth judges have taken to the privative clause: the English or "evisceration" approach, one which empties the privative clause of all meaning, thus giving rise to Wade's charge of outright disobedience; the Australian or "reconciliation" approach, which seeks to give effect to Parliament's intention while preserving judicial control over the executive; and the Canadian or "deferential" approach, which understands the privative clause as one kind of signal Parliament can send judges about the appropriate standard for reviewing administrative decisions. But before I set out these approaches, it is important first to sketch different kinds of privative clauses.

KINDS OF PRIVATIVE CLAUSES

Recall the privative clause in *Anisminic*, which stated that no court could call "into question" a determination of the administrative body.[11] Such clauses are "finality clauses." They deem that an administrative decision is final by saying that or by declaring that the decision is not reviewable by a court. A second kind of privative clause – a "no jurisdictional review clause" – forbids the courts from granting the traditional remedies of judicial review for jurisdictional error. The court may not review even when the administration has done something outside of its authority. For example, in a case I will discuss later, the Australian High Court was faced with a provision of the *Migration Act* 1958 (Cth), which combined a finality clause and a jurisdictional review clause. There was no doubt about the authority of the Commonwealth Parliament to regulate immigration, as in Chapter I, Part V of the Constitution, "POWERS OF THE PARLIAMENT" section 51 says:

> The Parliament shall, subject to this Constitution, have power to make laws for the peace, order, and good government of the Commonwealth with respect to:- (xix) Naturalization and aliens.

And the privative clause in the *Migration Act*, section 474(1) stated:

> (1) A privative clause decision:
> (a) is final and conclusive; and
> (b) must not be challenged, appealed against, reviewed, quashed or called in question in any court; and
> (c) is not subject to prohibition, mandamus, injunction, declaration or certiorari in any court on any account.

Section 474(2) defined a "privative clause decision" as "a decision of an administrative character made, proposed to be made, or required to be made, as the case may

[11] Here I follow Mark Aronson, Bruce Dyer, and Matthew Groves, *Judicial Review of Administrative Action*, 3rd ed. (Sydney: Lawbook Co., 2004), ch. 17 [Aronson]. I do not deal within the text with clauses that deem a decision to have effect as if enacted by Parliament, clauses that vest "exclusive jurisdiction" in a body, evidentiary provisions that deem all things done by the body to have been validly done, or clauses that stipulate time limits for judicial review.

be, under this Act or under a regulation or other instrument made under this Act." The term "decision" is defined broadly in section 474(3) and includes a reference to the grant or refusal of a visa.

A third kind of privative clause states that judicial review lies only on the grounds the clause expressly stipulates and/or expressly excludes grounds of review that the courts would think are relevant. I will call this kind of privative clause a "substantive privative clause." Unlike the first two, which are general because they seem to oust altogether the guardianship role of judges over the rule-of-law, the substantive privative clause ousts the judicial role of guarding particular rule-of-law values, in particular the common-law values of natural justice or fairness.

For example, in a previous incarnation, the *Migration Act* 1958 (Cth) had provided in section 476 that the Federal Court of Australia has jurisdiction to review decisions made by immigration officials on very specific grounds, set out in subsection (1). Subsection (1)(f) said that the Court can review if "the decision was induced or affected by fraud or by actual bias." Subsection (1) was explicitly made subject to subsection (2), which says: "The following are not grounds upon which an application may be made under subsection (1): (a) that a breach of the rules of natural justice occurred in connection with the making of the decision; (b) that the decision involved an exercise of a power that is so unreasonable that no reasonable person could have so exercised the power." Subsections (3) and (4) sought to specify and narrow some of the grounds of review listed. Thus, (1)(d) permitted review for an "improper exercise of power" but (3)(f) said that this did not permit review for "an exercise of power in bad faith."

Another kind of statutory provision delegates authority in subjective terms by making the question of whether the facts exist which have to be in place before the official may act depend on the official's opinion that the facts exist and not on whether the facts actually do exist. For example, "if the minister is satisfied that X is a threat to national security, he may order that X be detained." Wade equates such subjectively framed discretions to privative clauses and suggests that the way in which judges have often required that such discretions be exercised objectively, that is, reasonably according to the judges, is akin to, although less dramatic than, their reaction to privative clauses.[12]

Like Wade, I am not that concerned with the question whether such "if satisfied" clauses are true privative clauses. Rather, I want to note that in common with privative clauses they seek to reduce the scope of judicial review. Furthermore, judges for a long time regarded such "if satisfied" clauses as protecting the official's decision against both any serious evaluation of its grounds and the requirements of natural justice and are still inclined to adopt this approach when the subject matter of the discretion is considered sensitive, for example, national security or immigration. In sum, "if satisfied" clauses were and often still are treated as a combination of the general and the substantive privative clause.

EVISCERATION, RECONCILIATION, AND DEFERENCE

Before discussing judicial approaches to privative clauses, I want to make two preliminary points. The first is about constitutional structure. Although Canada

[12] Wade, *supra* note 2 at 85–6.

and Australia inherited the common-law legal order of the United Kingdom, and thus its basic constitutional structure, they differed from the mother country in that they both had written constitutions. However, these constitutions are not what one might think of as a bill of rights constitution, by which I mean an entrenched set of rights and freedoms. Rather, they are federal constitutions because they confine themselves mainly to dividing power between the federal and the other, state or provincial, authorities.

In the Australian case, there is also strong implicit support for the separation of powers between the Commonwealth Parliament and executive, on the one hand, and the courts described in Chapter III of the Constitution, on the other. In addition, the High Court's jurisdiction is in certain matters guaranteed, including, by section 75(5): "In all matters ... [i]n which a writ of Mandamus or prohibition or an injunction is sought against an officer of the Commonwealth ... the High Court shall have original jurisdiction." In Canada, section 96 of *The Constitution Act, 1867*[13] simply says that "The Governor General shall appoint the Judges of the Superior, District, and County Courts." But this and the other sections on the judiciary have been interpreted by Canada's Supreme Court as entrenching the independence of judges. In contrast, the United Kingdom has a unitary constitution, often thought of as a common-law constitution.

The second point is about the kinds of legislation in which privative clauses first appeared. As we will see, in each of the classic cases in these jurisdictions, the decisions protected by a privative clause were the kinds of decisions that seem obviously better decided by expert officials than by generalist judges. However, the reason why the issue about privative clauses and the rule of law has recently attracted attention is that parliaments in the common-law world have recently resorted to privative clauses to protect decisions that impact on human rights, in particular in the immigration and national security areas, areas which as we know, especially since 9/11, often overlap.[14]

(i) Evisceration

Anisminic Ltd. was a British corporation that sought compensation for property damage caused to its mines in Egypt during the Suez crisis. The British government set up a fund for this purpose, administered by the Foreign Compensation Commission, in terms of the *Foreign Compensation Act*, 1950. Recall that section 4(4) of that Act provided that any "determination by the commission of any application made to them.... shall not be called into question in any court of law." The Commission largely rejected Anisminic's claim because it had sold its operation to the United Arab Republic before 1959, the date of the treaty establishing the Commission. The Commission thus held that Anisminic had not shown that in 1959 it or

[13] (U.K.), 30 & 31 Vict. c. 3, reprinted in RS.C. 1985. App. II, No. 5.

[14] See Mary Crock, "Privative Clauses and the Rule of Law: The Place of Judicial Review Within the Construct of Australian Democracy" in Susan Kneebone, ed., *Administrative Law and the Rule of Law: Still Part of the Same Package* (Canberra: Australian Institute of Administrative Law, 1999) at 57 and, more generally, both Crock, "Judging Refugees: The Clash of Power and Institutions in the Development of Australian Refugee Law" (2004) 26 *Sydney Law Review* 50 and Audrey Macklin, "Borderline Security" in Ronald J. Daniels, Patrick Macklem, and Kent Roach, eds., *The Security of Freedom: Essays on Canada's Anti-Terrorism Bill* (Toronto: University of Toronto Press, 2001) at 383.

its successors in title were British nationals, a requirement set out in an Order in Council, made under the Act. The House of Lords declared that the Commission's decision was void. It considered that the requirement about "successors in title" did not apply when the original owner was the claimant.

Wade argues that the important holding in the case is not that a privative clause cannot protect jurisdictional errors, but the Court's claim that the Commission's decision was a jurisdictional error, rather than an error of law within jurisdiction. While the judges in *Anisminic* purported to maintain the distinction between these two kinds of error, it is not clear that they provide any principled basis. And because subsequent decisions have explicitly confirmed that a privative clause does not protect errors of law of any kind, it might well seem that there is no such basis.[15] Put differently, once judges assert that they are still entitled to review for jurisdictional error in the face of a privative clause, there is no principled way of stopping them from eviscerating the privative clause to the point where they in effect read it out of the statute.

(ii) Reconciliation

In *R. v. Hickman; Ex parte Fox and Clinton*,[16] the Australian High Court interpreted regulation 17 of mining regulations made under the *National Security Act* 1939 (Cth). A Local Reference Board had a general power to settle disputes in the coal mining industry in any local matter likely to affect amicable relations between employers and employees. Regulation 17 provided that its decisions should "not be challenged, appealed against, quashed or called into question, or be subject to prohibition, mandamus or injunction, in any court whatever." The Board decided that lorry drivers, employed by independent hauling contractors and whose work was not confined to transporting coal, fell within their jurisdiction.

The High Court held that this decision was invalid. The privative clause could neither protect decisions that went beyond jurisdiction, which the Court concluded this decision did, nor decisions that violated constitutional requirements. Nevertheless, Dixon J.'s judgment for the High Court is considered to have put forward a reconciliation approach, one that tries to give genuine effect to the privative clause instead of reading it out of the statute. He said:

> [a privative clause] is interpreted as meaning that no decision which is in fact given by the body concerned shall be invalidated on the ground that it has not conformed to the requirements governing its proceedings or the exercise of its authority or has not confined its acts within the limits laid down by the instrument giving it authority, provided always that its decision is a bona fide attempt to exercise the power, that it relates to the subject-matter of the legislation, and that it is reasonably capable of reference to the power given to the body.[17]

The clauses that followed "provided" became known as the *Hickman* provisos. Although they were, of course, subject to the principle that no privative clause can be understood to transgress the Constitution, they were also understood to

[15] See H. W. R. Wade and C. F. Forsyth, *Administrative Law*, 7th ed. (Oxford: Oxford University Press, 1994) 735–6, 737–9. And see the discussion at 302–5.

[16] (1945) 70 C.L.R. 598 [*Hickman*].

[17] Ibid. at 615.

expand the jurisdiction of the tribunal or official by protecting a class of decisions that would otherwise be considered reviewable errors of law. In subsequent cases, Dixon J. complicated matters by adding one more proviso: No decision could be valid when it breached an "inviolable limit" – a statutory constraint so important that the legislature must have intended it to be supreme.[18]

Section 474, the provision in Australia's *Migration Act* used in the last section to illustrate a "no jurisdictional review" clause, was first tabled in Parliament in 1997, but was enacted finally together with various statutory measures in September 2001, as Australia reacted to the events of 9/11. In *Plaintiff S157 of 2002 v. Commonwealth,*[19] the plaintiff argued that section 474 of the *Migration Act* was invalid because it violated the separation of powers in Chapter III of the Constitution and section 75(5).[20] The plaintiff had been refused a protection visa and he claimed that this refusal had denied him natural justice, as the tribunal had taken into account material adverse to his claim for refugee status without giving him notice of the material or any opportunity to address it.

The Court rejected this challenge by finding that the section did not oust review for natural justice and so did not violate section 75(5) of the Constitution; that is, the High Court was not deprived of its jurisdiction to review for jurisdictional error. Gleeson C.J. and Callinan J.[21] gave separate reasons while Gaudron, McHugh, Gummow, Kirby, and Hayne J.J. delivered a joint judgment.

In his judgment, Gleeson C.J. said that "Parliament has legislated in the light" of its acceptance of *Hickman* and so section 474 could not be read literally as an attempted ouster of the Court's jurisdiction.[22] Parliament had accepted that a provision like section 474 had to be read so as to avoid violating not only the Constitution but also the judicial controls articulated in *Hickman,* including the added proviso about inviolable statutory limits. Understanding the section was then a matter of ordinary statutory interpretation, which meant that it had to be understood in a general context as part of a statute that "affects fundamental human rights and involves Australia's international obligations." This, he said, had the result of making certain "established principles" relevant.[23]

First, in the case of an ambiguity the Court should favor a construction that accords with Australia's obligations. Second, the Court should not "impute to the legislature an intention to abrogate or curtail fundamental rights or freedoms unless such an interest is clearly manifested by unmistakable and unambiguous language." Third, the Australian Constitution is "framed upon the assumption of the rule of law."[24] Fourth, and "as a specific application of the second and third principles," privative clauses are construed by reference to a presumption that the legislature does not intend to deprive the citizen of access to the

[18] See *Aronson, supra* note 11 at 853.

[19] (2003) 211 C.L.R. 476 [*S157*].

[20] The plaintiff also argued that section 486A – which sets a thirty-five-day time limit on application to the High Court for review of "privative clause" decisions – was invalid. I will not deal with this aspect of the case.

[21] Callinan J.'s reasons add little to those given by Gleeson C.J.

[22] *S157, supra* note 19 at para. 22.

[23] Ibid. at para. 27. The principles are set out, one per paragraph, in paragraphs 29–33.

[24] Ibid., citing as authority Dixon J.'s well-known dictum in *Australian Communist Party Case v. the Commonwealth* (1951) 83 C.L.R. 1 at 193.

courts, other than to the extent expressly stated or necessarily to be implied. Fifth,

> a principle of relevance to *Hickman* is that what is required is a consideration of the whole *Act*, and an attempt to achieve a reconciliation between the privative clause and the rest of the legislation.... There may not be a single answer to that question. But the task is not to be performed by reading the rest of the *Act* as subject to s 474, or by making s 474 the central and controlling provision of the *Act*.

Gleeson C.J. reasoned that the Commonwealth's argument was inconsistent with these principles, as it supposed that the effect of section 474 was to radically transform the preexisting conditions, so that they were no longer "imperative duties" or "inviolable limitations" on decision makers. It followed, the Commonwealth had concluded, that as long as a decision satisfies "*Hickman* conditions" in the sense that it is a bona fide decision about whether to grant a protection visa, it will then be valid.[25]

Gleeson C.J. responded that the principles of statutory construction did not lead to the conclusion that Parliament had evinced an intention that an unfair decision could stand as long as it was bona fide:

> People whose fundamental rights are at stake are ordinarily entitled to expect more than good faith. They are ordinarily entitled to expect fairness. If Parliament intends to provide that decisions of the Tribunal, although reached by an unfair procedure, are valid and binding, and that the law does not require fairness on the part of the Tribunal in order for its decisions to be effective under the Act, then s. 474 does not suffice to manifest such an intention.[26]

In evaluating Gleeson C.J.'s response, it is helpful to know that the Commonwealth also argued that Parliament could delegate to the minister "the power to exercise a totally open-ended discretion as to what aliens can and what aliens cannot come to and stay in Australia."[27] Alternatively, it argued that the statute could be redrafted so as to say in effect "[h]ere are some non-binding guidelines which should be applied" with the "guidelines" being the balance of the statute.[28] These arguments tell us that the Commonwealth did not so much ignore the proviso about inviolable limits, as take literally the thought that the issue was whether any particular statutory constraint was so important that the legislature must have intended it to be supreme.

Put differently, the Commonwealth's argument was that it is the task of the legislature to determine how to structure the discretionary authority of its delegates. It can choose to give them an unfettered discretion or a very narrowly confined discretion. It can thus also set out criteria for the exercise of discretion and make it clear that these criteria are not mandatory. Section 474 is then arguably consistent with *Hickman* in that it does not deprive the High Court of jurisdiction but simply makes it clear that the criteria set out in the statute are not mandatory.

25 *S157*, *supra* note 19 at paras. 34–5. Ibid. para. 27. The principles are set out, one per paragraph, in paragraphs 29–33.

26 Ibid. para. 37.

27 Subject only to the Court's jurisdiction to decide any dispute as to the "constitutional fact" of alien status; ibid. at para. 101.

28 Ibid.

Gleeson C.J. did not respond directly to the Commonwealth's claims that Parliament could delegate an unfettered discretion and so could also stipulate that statutory criteria are not mandatory. However, one can infer from his reasoning that his view was that if Parliament were clearly to exclude particular grounds of review, the High Court would have to defer to that exclusion, with the exception naturally that the officials would have to stay within limits set by the Constitution. This feature of Gleeson C.J.'s judgment, his adherence to a clear statement rule when it comes to an override of common-law principles, distinguishes his reasoning from that in the joint judgment.[29] For his reasoning does not rely on the division of powers in the Federal Constitution unless there is a clear violation of its provisions, and so it stakes its claim on a common-law doctrine of legislative intent.[30] Moreover, by treating the privative clause to the extent possible as expanding jurisdiction, but not to the point where the clause violates either the values of the common law or the Constitution, the stance avoids eviscerating the clause and thus avoids forcing Parliament to consider whether or not to challenge the judicial assertion of supremacy.

In contrast, the joint judgment adopts the evisceration approach while purporting to follow the reconciliation approach.[31] The judges deny that section 474 is a literal privative clause. But they are unprepared to find that any result follows from it, so that they read it not so much down as out of the statute, in effect invalidating it because it is a privative clause. In addition, the joint judges responded directly to the Commonwealth's claims about Parliament's authority either to delegate an unfettered discretion or to convert all the statutory provisions into permissive considerations. They suggested not only that they might find unconstitutional a grant of unfettered discretion, but also a grant that explicitly excludes grounds of review, for example, fairness, from consideration by the High Court.[32]

Here we should recall the previous incarnation of the *Immigration Act* that set out just such a "substantive" privative clause, one that seeks to remove particular grounds of review from the jurisdiction of the courts. The joint judgment suggests that at least some members of the High Court might invalidate such a clause, and they would do so on the basis of the way in which the text of their Constitution differs from that of both Canada and the United States of America.

The joint judgment is thus ambiguous between two positions, between a common-law constitutionalist one, which asserts that the common law contains fundamental constitutional values, and a kind of constitutional positivism, which asserts that the values of the constitution are only those values that have been explicitly stated in a constitutional text.

[29] See Sir Anthony Mason, "The Foundations and Limitations of Judicial Review" (2002) 31 *AIAL Forum* 1 at 17.

[30] In the Australian context such a stance has the advantage of including statutes enacted by the states within its scope. For a stance that roots itself wholly in the division of powers in the Federal Constitution can have the effect of permitting the states to do what is constitutionally barred to the federal parliament. For discussion of this issue, see Denise Myerson, "State and Federal Privative Clauses – Not so Different After All" (2005) 16 *Public Law Review* 39 and Enid Campbell and Matthew Groves, "Privative Clauses and the Australian Constitution" (2004) 4 *Oxford University Commonwealth Law Journal* 51.

[31] Contrast in this regard, *S157*, *supra* note 19 at paras. 76 and 77.

[32] Ibid. at para. 102.

Constitutional positivists are committed to a rigid doctrine of the separation of powers according to which the legislature has a monopoly on lawmaking and judges have a monopoly on interpretation of the law. A general privative clauses forces such positivist judges to choose between submitting to legislative supremacy or asserting their own. Because a legal order in which they have no interpretative role is unimaginable to them, they will pretend that a general privative clause was not intended to do what it states. However, a substantive privative clause is not as problematic for them, as it leaves them with a formal role in enforcing legal limits even though it removes from them the ability to enforce the values of the common-law constitution.

A substantive privative clause does, however, challenge judges who are common law constitutionalists, but who also adopt or purport to adopt the rigid doctrine of the separation of powers. Such a clause leaves them with their review authority but deprives them of its point – the substantive values developed by the common law. When such judges have a division-of-powers constitution, one which will almost of necessity protect to some extent their review jurisdiction or at the least contain provisions that can be so interpreted, they might be tempted to read into the text an intention to protect the substantive values. That allows them to pit text against text – the constitutional text against the text of the statute – and intention against intention – the intention of the founders of the constitution against the intention of the legislature. The text offers them the luxury of a prop to avoid the charge of judicial activism, while elevating rule-of-law values to a level where the values seem entrenched, and so not overridable even by the most determined legislature.

These judges then find themselves tempted in the direction of constitutional positivism, as long as they have a written constitution that is capable of being interpreted as preserving the separation of powers in a way that gives to them the role they want. They adopt the rigid doctrine of the separation of powers because it is convenient for them, but that creates tensions when they have to deal with situations in which all they have to rely on is the common law.

In contrast, Gleeson C.J. relies exclusively on a common-law method of interpretation because he is not as preoccupied by a rigid doctrine of the separation of powers. Thus, in *S157* he suggested that a privative clause protects errors of law that do not go to jurisdiction and, in this way, expands the jurisdiction of a tribunal beyond what it would have been had there been no privative clause. But he was well aware that it is very difficult to provide any successful test to distinguish between errors of law that go to jurisdiction and errors that do not. Indeed, he traced this difficulty back to the source of the reconciliation approach, the fact that in *Hickman* Dixon J. found a jurisdictional error when it was clearly arguable that at most the error was one of law.[33]

It is possible that the distinction between jurisdictional error and mere error of law is not that important to Gleeson C.J. As we have seen, he advocated interpretation of the alleged privative clause by placing it within the context of the statute as a whole, informed by presumptions of interpretation taken from both the Constitution and the common law. And he suggested at one point that the result of such a process is that the courts will review administrative decisions with different degrees of intensity, rather than by regarding some as totally protected by a privative

[33] Ibid. at para. 18.

clause.[34] It might then be the case that the reconciliation approach does not have to collapse into evisceration. Instead, it might collapse into the Canadian deferential approach. But, as I will now show, the deferential approach has a consequence that some judges might find unpalatable. It requires judges to accept that they do not have a monopoly on interpretation and thus to reject the rigid doctrine of the separation of powers.

(iii) Deference

The leading case on privative clauses in Canada is *CUPE*: *Canadian Union of Public Employees, local 963 v. New Brunswick Liquor Corporation.*[35] The tribunal was a Public Service Staff Relations Board, constituted by the *Public Service Labour Relations Act*,[36] whose decisions were protected by the following privative clauses:

> Section 101(1): "Except as provided in this Act, every order, award, direction, decision, declaration, or ruling of the Board, the Arbitration Tribunal or an adjudicator is final and shall not be questioned or reviewed in any court."
>
> Section 102(2): "No order shall be made or process entered, and no proceedings shall be taken in any court, whether by way of injunction, *certiorari*, prohibition, quo warranto, or otherwise, to question, review, prohibit or restrain the Board, the Arbitration Tribunal or an adjudicator in any of its or his proceedings."

The Board had to interpret a badly worded provision in its statute on which turned the issue whether management could do the work of employees during a strike. The New Brunswick Court of Appeal had held that the tribunal's expertise had to do with the application of the law to the particular facts of the dispute, so that the tribunal's interpretation of the provision had to be correct, that is, in accordance with the reviewing judge's understanding.

In the Supreme Court, Dickson J. was clear that judges had to take the privative clause seriously and hence should not use previously popular devices in an attempt to read it out of the statute. He emphasized that it was not only the formal expression of legislative intent in the privative clause that mattered but also the good reason for that formal expression: An administrative agency is expert within its area of law

> Section 101 constitutes a clear statutory direction on the part of the Legislature that public sector labour matters be promptly and finally decided by the Board. Privative clauses of this type are usually found in labour relations legislation. The rationale for protection of a labour board's decisions within jurisdiction is straightforward and compelling. The labour board is a specialized tribunal which administers a comprehensive statute regulating labour relations. In the administration of that regime, a board is called upon not only to find facts and decide questions of law, but also to exercise its understanding of the body of jurisprudence that has developed around the collective bargaining system, as understood in Canada, but

[34] Compare ibid. paras. 2 and 13. Sir Anthony Mason has suggested that the High Court together with the House of Lords rejects this deferential approach on the basis that it amounts to an "abdication of the judicial responsibility to declare and enforce the law." Sir Anthony Mason, "Judicial Review: A View From Constitutional and Other Perspectives" (2000) 28 *Federal Law Review* 331 at 339–40. See Aronson, *supra* note 11 at 840–60 for an extended discussion of the decision.

[35] [1979] 2 S.C.R 227 [*CUPE*].

[36] R.S.N.B. 1973, c. P-25.

also to exercise its understanding of the body of jurisprudence that has developed around the collective bargaining system, as understood in Canada, and its labour relations sense acquired from accumulated experience in the area.[37]

One way to understand Dickson J.'s judgment in *CUPE* is that it creates two standards for review, correctness for jurisdictional issues and patent unreasonableness for issues that fell within jurisdiction. And it seemed to follow from the Supreme Court's subsequent jurisprudence on section 96 of *The Constitution Act, 1867* that administrative decisions about the interpretation of the Constitution, the common law, statutes other than the tribunals' own statutes, as well as the jurisdictional limits on delegated authority would all count as constitutional.[38] The last category was to be determined by a "pragmatic and functional" approach to statutory interpretation, one that sought to reconcile the privative clause with the rest of the statute by working out which provisions went to jurisdiction. In short, it might seem the Canadian approach is reconciliation by another name, and, moreover, one might expect the same result – the collapse of reconciliation into evisceration.

As the Supreme Court developed its jurisprudence on deference, some of the judges made it clear that the collapse into evisceration was exactly their fear. They saw two causes for alarm. First, Dickson J. had warned that judges should be wary of characterizing an error as jurisdictional in order to make it reviewable on the correctness standard. But it seemed that this warning was not being heeded. Second, recall that on Dickson J.'s approach errors of law within jurisdiction are not deemed unreviewable: They will be reviewed if they are patently unreasonable. These judges thought that when a tribunal or official offered reasons for a decision, one should avoid the evaluation involved in asking whether the reasons supported the decision. The sole focus should be on whether an error jumps out. Their fear was that an exercise that focuses on the relationship between reasons and results inevitably draws judges to the point where the standard applied is whether they themselves would have made that decision.[39]

However, as other judges pointed out, it was difficult to understand how one could establish that a decision was reasonable without scrutinizing the reasons. They came to interpret Dickson J.'s judgment as staking the ground for a jurisprudence in which the privative clause is but one factor among those that a court must take into account in considering what standard of deference it owes to an agency. Put differently, it is now the case both that a privative clause is not necessary for deference and that the presence of such a clause is not always a sufficient basis on which to conclude that deference is due. At the same time, the Supreme Court developed the idea that the standard of deference could vary from patent unreasonableness through what was called "reasonableness *simpliciter*" to correctness, depending on the combination of factors in the particular context. A reasonableness standard demands evaluation of the reasons – a "somewhat probing examination" – as Iacobucci J. put it in the decision in which this standard was first properly articulated.[40]

[37] Ibid. at 235–6.

[38] See *Crevier v. Québec (AG)*, [1981] 2 S.C.R. 220.

[39] For example, Wilson J. in *National Corngrowers Association v. Canada (Import Tribunal)*, [1990] 2 S.C.R. 1324 and Cory J. dissenting in *Dayco (Canada) v. CAW-Canada*, [1993] 2 S.C.R. 230.

[40] *Canada (Director of Investigation and Research, Competition Act) v. Southam Inc.*, [1997] 1 S.C.R. 748.

I cannot here go into all the intricacies of the Canadian jurisprudence on deference. I must, however, note that its very sensitivity to issues such as the context in which the tribunal is operating, the kinds of interests that are affected by its decisions, as well as the variable standard of review creates a structure so complex and elaborate that it might look like judges will constantly be tempted into correctness review.[41] Even judges of the Supreme Court are now starting to worry openly about the way that their Court has developed the jurisprudence of deference.[42]

But I also want to point out that the deference approach, taken at face value, departs from the rigid doctrine of the separation of powers that underpins the evisceration approach. The deferential approach involves a judicial concession that the executive branch of government has authority to interpret the law. That concession is in a sense forced by the fact that the legislative branch of government has decided both to set up tribunals with the authority to interpret the law and to protect formally, via the privative clause, those interpretations from judicial review. However, *CUPE* involves more than concession. Right at the outset of the development of the idea of deference, it was clear that there was a judicial cession of interpretative authority to the tribunal, within the scope of its expertise – the area of jurisdiction protected by the privative clause. The cession was not total – the tribunal could not be patently unreasonable. But it was significant because it required that judges defer to the administration's interpretations of the law, except on jurisdictional, constitutional, or constitutionlike issues.

Moreover, it might be the case that the best interpretation of the Supreme Court's later jurisprudence is that the shift in focus from decision to reasons for decision, and the development of the third standard of review, shears the correctness standard off the continuum of standards of review. Even the most probing evaluation is to some extent deferential, as judges operate with a presumption that the reasons offered by the tribunal for its decision could justify a decision, which is not necessarily the decision that the court would have reached had it operated in a "vacuum."[43] So, for example, generally judges should conclude not only that the content of fairness will vary according to context but also that the legislature and the administrative decision maker are better equipped than they are to work out what is most appropriate to context. In other words, generally speaking judges should defer to legislative and administrative choice when it comes to institutional design, including the design of fair procedures. And in the case of deference to administrative choice, filling the vacuum is not desirable because of some natural

[41] Hunt, *supra* note 6 sets out at 353–4 the following list of factors: the nature of the right in question; the nature of the particular context (for example, fair trial rights where judges feel more comfortable in contrast with balancing interests where they do and should feel more diffidence); special expertise; relative institutional competence to conduct the type of decision making that preceded the primary decisionmaker's decision; the degree of democratic accountability of the primary decisionmaker as well as other mechanisms of accountability; the degree to which the primary decisionmaker has engaged with the question of compatibility of the decision with relevant legal values. For the Canadian Supreme Court's list, see *Baker v. Canada (Minister of Citizenship and Immigration)* [1999] 2 S.C.R. 817 at paras. 57–62. Compare the same kind of analysis when the question is the content of fairness; paras. 21–8.

[42] See LeBel J. in *Toronto (City) v. CUPE, Local 79*, [2003] 3 S.C.R. 77.

[43] As La Forest J. put it in the first decision in a trilogy of cases where the Supreme Court of Canada decided that a tribunal could entertain a Charter-based challenge to a provision in its statute – *Douglas/Kwantlen Faculty Association v. Douglas College* [1990] 3 S.C.R. 570 at 605.

abhorrence, but because what fills it is the expert understanding of the tribunal about how the law is to be interpreted in its specialized context. There is then no correctness review, only more or less intense scrutiny of reasons, whether tribunals are engaged in interpreting the law of their constitutive statute, or of another statute, or the common law, or the provisions of a written constitution, including, if there is one, their bill of rights. As a result, the deference approach does not so much read privative clauses out of the particular statutes in which they occur as render them redundant by reading them into every statute that delegates authority to public officials. However, they are read in a way that treats them as a legislative signal to judges to alert them to what is in any case their duty – to treat administrative interpretations of the law with respect, as long as these are serious attempts to carry on the rule of law project.

LEGALITY AND CONSTITUTIONALITY

Murray Hunt has recently argued that English law took a "false doctrinal step" when it introduced "spatial metaphors into the language of judicial review" by presupposing that there are certain areas within which public officials are "simply beyond the reach of judicial interference."[44] These metaphors express a vision of constitutionalism that embraces "competing" but irreconcilable "supremacies," the sovereign Parliament and the sovereign individual, whose guardian is the courts. One gets in the same package two "radically opposed narratives," constitutional positivism and liberal constitutionalism. To make things worse, one finds that adherents of this view tend to flip arbitrarily from one narrative to another.[45]

Sovereignty thus casts, according to Hunt, a "double blight" on the common-law grasp of constitutionalism. It hides the fact that Parliament is subject to constitutional constraints as well as the fact that Parliament "has an important role in both the definition and protection of fundamental rights and values." In addition, it obstructs the "proper articulation of what may be perfectly legitimate reasons for deferring" either to Parliament or to its delegates, "obscuring them behind a vocabulary of spaces and boundaries which are asserted as if the underlying assumptions about the constitutional division of powers were not contentious."[46]

In my view, it is the particular conception of sovereignty that is the problem, rather than the concept itself. It is important to know that Thomas Hobbes, who would ordinarily be considered one of the chief culprits for coining the vocabulary of sovereignty to which Hunt objects, and who, through John Austin, had an immense influence on Dicey, did not in fact conceive of sovereignty this way. Although Hobbes wanted lawmaking power located in one supreme body or person, the sovereign, he regarded the articulation of the content of any sovereign judgment as an exercise in which public officials, including judges, have a legitimate role. Moreover, in articulating the content of this judgment, the officials are under a duty to interpret the positive or civil law in the light of their understanding of the fundamental or constitutional values of legal order, the laws of nature, as the

44 Hunt, *supra* note 6 at 338.

45 Ibid. at 343–4.

46 Ibid. at 339.

sovereign's positive laws are to be understood as attempts to give concrete expression to the very same values.[47] Therefore, although Hobbes was opposed to the common-law tradition and its claims about judicial guardianship of the artificial reason of the law, he shared with it one crucial assumption – that the legislature, the executive, and the judges are best understood as engaged in a common legislative project that aspires to realize the fundamental values of legality. The same idea informs Hunt's argument, where he sketches in the English context an idea of law as promoting a culture of justification, informed by a "rich conception of legality and of the rule of law." Such a conception does not legitimate a role only for courts "in enforcing legal standards on public decision-makers." It also creates "space for a proper role for democratic considerations, including a role for the democratic branches in the definition and furtherance of fundamental values."[48]

The significance of this commonality between Hobbes and the common-law tradition resides in the fact that their aspirational view of the rule of law[49] can issue in different prescriptions about the institutional arrangements that will best implement its project. But whatever these different prescriptions, it is clear that those who have this view do not regard any particular arrangement of the separation of powers as fundamental; rather, they see such arrangements as instrumental to a larger purpose – the realization of value.

As Hunt rightly points out, this view requires that judges defer both to the legislature and the executive. Because the rule-of-law project is a common one, as long as the judgments of the legislature and the executive are either justifiable or justified as interpretations of the relevant values, judges should defer to these judgments. The kind of deference here is not deference in its primary meaning of submission to an order of a superior. Rather, it is deference as respect – respect for a successful attempt at justification.[50]

When a statute is challenged, it might contain a preamble that makes such an attempt, but often the justification will be offered only when a judge hears the challenge. With administrative decisions, often the very possibility of there being a challenge to a decision turns on whether reasons were offered justifying the decision; hence, the growing recognition in common-law countries of a duty on public officials to give reasons for their decisions. Imposing such a duty does, of course, have costs. But whatever the result of a cost-benefit analysis of a general imposition, it is important to see that its imposition may be understood as a kind of compliment to the administrative state, rather than as an intrusion performed in order to facilitate judicial colonization of the administration.

Consider, for example, the fact that until the 1960s and 1970s judges in the common-law world held the view that delegations of authority to officials that gave

[47] So much should be obvious from the Introduction to Hobbes's *Leviathan* (Richard Tuck, ed. (Cambridge: Cambridge University Press, 1991) 9–11), but Chapter 26, "Of Civill Lawes," should settle any doubts.

[48] Hunt, *supra* note 7 at 350. The term "culture of justification" was first used by Etienne Mureinik, a South African public lawyer, as Hunt acknowledges at 340.

[49] See Lon L. Fuller, *The Morality of Law*, rev. ed. (New Haven, Conn.: Yale University Press, 1969).

[50] For my most detailed attempt to elaborate this distinction, see my "The Politics of Deference: Judicial Review and Democracy" in Michael Taggart, ed., *The Province of Administrative Law* (Oxford: Hart Publishing, 1997) 279. For Hunt's account of what follows from the same distinction, see Hunt, *supra* note 6 at 351–4.

them "administrative" as opposed to "quasi-judicial" authority neither attracted the requirements of natural justice nor were subject to review on the basis of the content of the discretionary judgment, except in quite exceptional situations. In Hunt's terms, it was one of the areas treated as if it were "beyond the reach of legality, and within the realm of pure discretion in which remedies for wrongs are political only."[51] One of the indicia of a delegation of administrative authority was that the official was given authority to act by a subjective, "if satisfied" provision, instead of the more objective-sounding "if the minister has reasonable cause to believe." As suggested earlier, a subjective delegation of discretion was regarded as both a substantive and a general privative clause. And when common-law judges held that there is a general duty at common law for public officials to act fairly unless the statute expressly indicated otherwise, one reaction was that they were illegitimately usurping legislative authority.

But the thought that the administrative state is not lawless but subject to the rule of law, including the legal value of fairness, goes further than including the administrative state into the legal order in a way antithetical to the rigid doctrine of the separation of powers. It also supposes that the administrative state is legitimate because it is answerable to the fundamental values of legal order. And that goes beyond the claim that bodies that are not courts must make decisions in accordance with values that were previously thought to apply only to courts or courtlike – quasi-judicial – bodies. As indicated above, it should include the further claim that, generally speaking, judges should defer to legislative and administrative choice when it comes to institutional design, including the design of fair procedures.

My claim is not, however, that the rigid doctrine of the separation of powers precludes judges from developing a rich understanding of the values of legality, nor that they are unable to understand that there is reason to defer both to the legislative and the administrative branches. It is only that these understandings introduce serious instability into its theory of the rule of law, which then causes its adherents to flip between deference as submission and no deference at all.

There is, however, a rather large difference between, on the one hand, a genuine statutory or administrative attempt to design fair procedures and, on the other, a legislative or administrative declaration that no fairness is appropriate. Where it is the administration that refuses, clearly judges are entitled to review. But where the legislature puts in place a substantive privative clause, matters are more complicated.[52] Whether judges are entitled to react to a substantive privative clause by voiding it will depend largely on their understanding of their written constitution, if their legal order has one.

It might seem that I have just conceded that the question whether judges are entitled to enforce fundamental values of legality depends on whether there is a written constitution which permits them to do so, a concession which then undermines the claim that there are such values inherent in legal order. However, I have

[51] Ibid. at 339.

[52] Even more complex is the situation where the legislature stipulates some degree of fairness and is explicit that no more is appropriate, but the kind of decision seems to cry out for much more. The challenge to the legality of the military tribunals put in place after 9/11 in the United States is a challenge in this kind of situation. These tribunals do not operate in a legal black hole, but in space that is not adequately controlled by legality.

only conceded that there is such a question when the legislature very explicitly announces its intention to exclude such a value. That condition for excluding fairness is in itself a significant legal constraint because it requires a clear statement, as we saw Gleeson C.J. suggest, to override it. I would argue further that this constraint is constitutional, even though it might be the case that in the absence of a written constitutional protection of the judges' review authority over such matters, the judges cannot enforce the constraint in the face of a clear legislative statement. In fact, the idea that the nonenforceability of a norm by judges in the face of a clear legislative statement means that it lacks constitutional status is a product of the mind-set which includes the narratives of competing supremacies. The aspirational view of the rule of law, in contrast, recognizes that any of the branches of government may fail on occasion to live up to law's aspirations.

Two examples are helpful here. First, consider section 33 of the Canadian *Charter of Rights and Freedoms,*[53] which permits the federal and provincial legislatures to override by statute judicial determinations that their statutes violate certain *Charter*-protected rights and freedoms for a period of five years, after which the override must be legislatively renewed if it is not to lapse. The override does not render any of the overridable values unconstitutional. It merely gives to the legislature a limited opportunity to operate unconstitutionally for a period, but on condition that it owns up to that fact. Nor does it matter to the issue of constitutional status that there is a time limit on the operation of the statute. Thus, in the English context, the fact that a statute is not invalidated by a judicial declaration of incompatibility with the provisions of the *Human Rights Act* does not make those provisions any less constitutional in status than the provisions of the U.S. *Bill of Rights.* The differences between these constitutional documents resides in their mechanisms for enforcement, not in the status of their norms.

The second example is one I mentioned at the beginning – Dicey's example of the statute that orders that all blue-eyed babies be put to death. Recall that this example is meant to illustrate two things. First, the immorality of a statute does not suffice to make it illegal. Second, it is unlikely both that legislators would be inclined to enact such a statute and that their electorate would permit them to do so. I agree with Dicey but wish to point out that his example was a bad one, as a statute that orders the execution of any person or group is a bill of attainder. As the author of the 1962 Note in the *Yale Law Journal* explains, the term act or bill of attainder comes from the practice in sixteenth-, seventeenth-, and eighteenth-century England of using statutes to sentence "to death, without a conviction in the ordinary course of judicial trial, named or described persons or groups."[54] A bill of attainder is considered offensive to legality because it attempts to bypass the courts by establishing a system of either legislative or administrative conviction and punishment.[55] So the opposition to such a bill, within or without Parliament, would not be only that it was immoral, but also that it was illegal because it flouted the fundamental moral values of legality; just the sort of opposition that was incited recently in the

[53] Part I of the *Constitution Act, 1982* being Schedule B to the *Canada Act, 1982* (U.K.), 1982, c.11.

[54] "Note" (1962) 72 *Yale L.J.* 330.

[55] See T. R. S. Allan, *Constitutional Justice: A Liberal Theory of the Rule of Law* (Oxford: Oxford University Press, 2001).

United Kingdom by the government's proposal to protect immigration decisions by a draconian privative clause.

This still leaves open the question of what follows when the legislators do succumb to madness by going ahead with such a provision. Dicey supplies the answer in another context, that of *ex post* legislative validation of a government's illegal response to what it perceives to be an emergency situation. Dicey says that in this situation, the Parliament has "legalised illegality."[56] But he implies the wrong conclusion from this correct description when he goes on to say that Parliament thus manages to maintain law. For although Parliament can place officials in a zone uncontrolled by law, a legal black hole, this does not show that what they are doing or did is legal, only that political power can be exercised in a brute fashion, permitting those who wield it to break free of the constraints of constitutionality and legality.[57] Only in this situation, the situation where a space uncontrolled by law is deliberately created, do spatial metaphors become appropriate. But what those who wield such power cannot do, or more accurately should not be allowed to do, is have their cake and eat it too in claiming that because they can use law to break free of law, what they are doing is therefore legal. In this point lies the answer to the question of why judges are always legally entitled to read down a general privative clause, but may not be entitled to do the same with a substantive privative clause.

The answer depends on seeing that that privative clauses create problems at different levels. A general privative clause creates two different kinds of contradiction. It creates a contradiction within the statute between the positive injunction to courts not to review for jurisdictional error and the positive limits the statute sets out. It also creates a contradiction between the positive injunction and the limits set on the tribunal by the values of legality to be found in the common-law constitution. In creating the internal contradiction, the legislature sends a mixed message to judges which it is their constitutional responsibility to resolve by applying a presumption that the legislature must be taken to intend its statutes to be governed by legality. That presumption entitles the courts to interpret the privative clause as if the legislature intended it to work other than by excluding either positive or constitutional limits. Putting in place criteria and then saying government need not abide by them is an even worse kind of hypocrisy than that involved in ratifying a human rights convention and saying that it should have no effect internally. To think along these lines would be for judges to suppose that the legislature has removed itself from the common project of aspiring to the rule of law.

In contrast, a completely explicit substantive privative clause creates only the second kind of contradiction – one between the positive law of the statute and the values of legality. If the judge has no explicit constitutional basis for invalidating the provision, she can still point out its illegality in her judgment, in effect doing what Article 4 of the *Human Rights Act* requires judges to do in issuing a declaration of incompatibility. One should not underestimate the political clout that attaches even to such an informal declaration. The judges cannot be accused of judicial

56 Dicey, *supra* note 3 at 412–13.

57 Ibid. I say implies, because Dicey might mean only that without this illegal action the state might be overthrown.

activism. But they still send a signal to the public and the legislature that has to be taken seriously.

In sum, the difference between Gleeson C.J. and the joint judgment on the issue of whether the Constitution affords protection against a substantive privative clause is, from the perspective of legal theory, less important than their agreement, which they might of course deny, about the common-law constitution – the common law of legality.[58] But that agreement requires adopting a view of law unaffected by the spatial metaphors that follow from a rigid doctrine of the separation of powers. It might be that once this point is appreciated, so that judges see their role in review as protecting the values of legality, it is an easy step to read into a provision like section 75(5) protection of those values.[59] And that might raise the concern that the rather substantive account of the rule of law which informs the alternative, aspirational view of legal order invites judicial activism. Here is important to keep in mind that, on the contrary, the aspirational view requires a kind of deference to the legislature and the administration which is excluded by the rigid doctrine.

ACKNOWLEDGMENTS

I thank Emily Hammond for wonderful research assistance and comments and Geneviève Cartier for a very useful conversation.

[58] See, e.g., Murray Gleeson, "Courts and the Rule of Law" in Cheryl Saunders and Katherine Le Roy, eds., *The Rule of Law* (Sydney: The Federation Press, 2003) 178, which would seem to imply a rejection of this claim.

[59] In "Review of Executive Action and the Rule of Law under the Australian Constitution" (2003) 14 *Public Law Review* 219, Duncan Kerr and George Williams (who represented the plaintiff in *S157*) argue at 226 that the grounds of review are "necessarily contemplated" by section 75(5).

26 Look Who's Talking Now: Dialogue Theory and the Return to Democracy

Andrew Petter

What is the constitutional role of legislatures in a liberal democratic state? Authors in this volume provide a range of answers. Some depict legislatures as objects of constitutional decision making; for them, the primary role of legislatures is to be directed by constitutional norms.[1] Others represent legislatures as instruments of constitutional decision making; for them, legislatures play a significant role in fulfilling constitutional norms.[2] Still others characterize legislatures as sources of constitutional decision making; for them, legislatures play a key role in the generation of constitutional norms.[3]

Canadian adherents of "dialogue theory" go further. They portray legislatures as playing a crucial role in legitimizing constitutional norms, including norms articulated through judicial decision making. Advanced by leading constitutional scholars and embraced by the Supreme Court of Canada, this theory holds that the purpose of judicial review under the *Canadian Charter of Rights and Freedoms* is to augment democratic decision making. Dialogue theorists maintain that judicial decisions under the *Charter* are not conclusive but form part of a dialogue with legislatures in which the latter retain the final say. It is this capacity of legislatures to decide the outcome of *Charter* issues that, in the eyes of dialogue theorists, bestows democratic legitimacy on *Charter* decision making.

The notion that the legitimacy of constitutional decision making rests on the ability of legislatures to trump judicial decisions is replete with contradictions and ironies, and raises questions that have both promising and troubling dimensions. Chief among these is whether Canadian legislatures are capable of fulfilling the democratic mandate attributed to them by dialogue theorists. In my view, there are strong reasons for believing that they are not, and that dialogue theorists and others who regard democracy as a core constitutional value need to give more urgent attention to the democratic shortcomings of the Canadian state. Before addressing these and other issues, however, it might be helpful to review the developments that have given rise to dialogue theory and to consider some of its implications.[4]

[1] See, e.g., Frederick Schauer, "Legislatures as Rule-Followers," Chapter 23 in this volume.

[2] See, e.g., Jeremy Webber, "Democratic Decision Making as the First Principle of Contemporary Constitutionalism," Chapter 20 in this volume.

[3] See, e.g., William N. Eskridge, Jr., and John Ferejohn, "Super-Statutes: The New American Constitutionalism," Chapter 15 in this volume.

[4] The review that follows derives in part from Andrew Petter, "Twenty Years of *Charter* Justification: From Liberal Legalism to Dubious Dialogue" (2003) 52 *U.N.B.L.J.* 187.

I. THE DEMISE OF LEGISLATIVE SUPREMACY

The enactment of the Canadian *Charter of Rights and Freedoms* in 1982 was meant to mark the demise of legislative supremacy in Canada. According to its early adherents, the purpose of the *Charter* was to provide courts with a constitutional mandate to invalidate legislative and government actions that were inconsistent with the fundamental rights and freedoms that it guaranteed. As a consequence, the doctrine of legislative supremacy was to be replaced with a doctrine of constitutional supremacy. One problem with this view was that although supremacy of the constitution was largely uncontroversial, its meaning was not. The open-ended nature of *Charter* rights, combined with the qualification in section 1 subjecting these rights to "such reasonable limits prescribed by law as can be demonstrably justified in a free and democratic society," made the *Charter* more a forum for argument than a font for answers. This in turn begged the question as to who bore constitutional responsibility for resolving *Charter* arguments, many of which concerned highly charged and long-standing political issues such as abortion, commercial speech, and religious rights.

The conventional wisdom at the time of the *Charter*'s enactment was that final say over the meaning of constitutional rights and their limitations belonged to the courts.[5] But on what basis would courts exercise their interpretative powers, and how would they justify the legitimacy of their decisions? In a country like Canada, with a positivist legal tradition and a culture of judicial deference to legislatures, these questions were not easily answered. The initial response of the Supreme Court of Canada to these issues was to fall back on the familiar assumptions of liberal legalism. These assumptions, grounded in nineteenth-century legal traditions, hold that the role of the courts is to act as impartial arbiters whose responsibilities do not extend to policymaking, but are limited to unbiased adjudication of legal issues and objective interpretation of legal texts. Early *Charter* cases are steeped in language that reflects these assumptions. In *Reference Re Motor Vehicle Act (B.C.)*, for example, the Court maintained that, by subjecting the *Charter* to a "purposive analysis," it could derive "objective and manageable standards" for its operation, thereby "avoiding adjudication of the merits of public policy."[6] And while grappling with the thorny issue of abortion in *R. v. Morgentaler*, the Court insisted that its task was "not to solve nor seek to solve what might be called the abortion issue, but simply to measure the content of [legislation] against the *Charter*."[7]

These same assumptions were evident in the Court's approach to the "reasonable limits" clause in section 1. The amorphous standard created by this section appears to call upon courts to engage in interest balancing, an activity normally associated with political decision making. As such, it represents a threat to liberal legalism and its vision of judges as objective interpreters of the constitutional text. In *R. v.*

[5] One obvious qualification to this assumption was section 33, which gave legislatures the ability to override temporarily judicial decisions under the *Charter*, but this provision was seen as exceptional and was regarded with suspicion by *Charter* adherents, many of whom argued that it should never be used and ought to be repealed at the earliest opportunity.

[6] *Reference Re Motor Vehicle Act (B.C.)*, [1985] 2 S.C.R. 486 at 495–500.

[7] *R. v. Morgentaler*, [1988] 1 S.C.R. 30 at 46, 138.

Oakes, Supreme Court judges responded to this threat by setting out a two-stage "proportionality test."[8] By converting the section 1 inquiry from one focused on the "reasonableness" of legislation to one focused on the "proportionality" between legislative means and ends, and by stipulating specific criteria and a stringent standard for determining whether the requisite degree of "proportionality" had been met, the *Oakes* test diminished the subjective appearance of section 1 by providing an ostensibly neutral framework for judicial decision making.

The Court's resort to liberal legalism as the basis for understanding and explaining its new *Charter* role is also reflected in other aspects of its early *Charter* work. One example is the position it articulated in early *Charter* cases that the purpose of *Charter* rights is to constrain governmental action, not to authorize or compel it.[9] This precept is grounded in nineteenth-century liberal assumptions that the division between public and private spheres is clear and uncontested, and that state interference with private action represents the greatest threat to individual liberty. According to this view, the role of courts under the *Charter* is simply to police the boundary between these spheres so as to constrain the state from unduly interfering with individual freedoms. Thus, the Court in *R.W.D.S.U. v. Dolphin Delivery Ltd.* was able to refer to judges as "neutral arbiters" whose conduct (except when linked to legislative or executive actions) was nongovernmental and beyond the scope of *Charter* scrutiny.[10]

A related view embraced by the Court in early *Charter* cases was its insistence that because the role of judges is adjudicative rather than legislative, they were limited to striking down legislation inconsistent with the *Charter*, rather than repairing or extending it. In *Hunter v. Southam Inc.*, for example, the Court refused to read provisions into the *Combines Investigation Act*,[11] stating that it did "not fall to the courts to fill in the details that will render legislative lacunae constitutional."[12] Similarly, in *Singh v. Canada (Minister of Employment and Immigration)*, the Court declined to repair deficiencies in the *Immigration Act*,[13] noting that the *Charter* allowed the courts to perform "some relatively crude surgery on deficient legislative provisions, but not plastic or re-constructive surgery."[14]

II. THE REBIRTH OF LEGISLATIVE SUPREMACY

Drawing on the values of liberal legalism, the Court by the late 1980s had forged a seemingly coherent set of positions concerning the scope and nature of *Charter* rights and the role of judges in their enforcement. Yet, unhappily for the judges, these positions proved unsustainable. There are a number of reasons for this. First, the Court's attempts to portray *Charter* decision making as neutral and apolitical

[8] *R. v. Oakes*, [1986] 1 S.C.R. 103.

[9] See *Hunter v. Southam, Inc.* [1984] 2 S.C.R. 145 at 156 [*Hunter*].

[10] *R.W.D.S.U. v. Dolphin Delivery Ltd.* [1986] 2 S.C.R. 573 at 600–1. See A. C. Hutchinson and A. Petter, "Private Rights/Public Wrongs: The Liberal Lie of the Charter" (1988) 38 *U.T.L.J.* 278 [Hutchinson and Petter, "Private Rights/Public Wrongs"].

[11] *Combines Investigation Act*, R.S.C. 1970, c. C-23.

[12] *Hunter, supra* note 9 at 168–9.

[13] *Immigration Act*, 1976, S.C. 1976–77, c. 52.

[14] *Singh v. Canada (Minister of Employment and Immigration)* [1985] 1 S.C.R. 177 at 235–6.

were simply not credible in a postrealist age. Whatever the Court said, none but a few true believers were willing to accept that judges' interpretations of contested *Charter* rights, such as liberty and equality, were the objective outcome of "purposive reasoning," or that grappling with issues like abortion did not require judges to make subjective judgments based on their personal moral values. Second, the paradigm of liberal legalism, grounded as it was on nineteenth-century assumptions about the nature of the state, was out of sync with twentieth-century social norms and realities. The notion that *Charter* rights could constrain but not compel state action, that judges could strike down legislation but not repair or extend it, and that courts would apply a stringent standard against upholding legislation under section 1, gave the *Charter* an ideological slant that was at odds with, and at times hostile to, political expectations concerning the regulatory and redistributive functions of the modern state.[15] Third, as the Court was confronted with increasingly complex and difficult cases, splits started to emerge among judges, as some, feeling uncomfortable with the consequences of these assumptions, began to modify them or back away from them altogether. As a result, the number of Supreme Court *Charter* cases that were unanimously decided plummeted from over 85 percent in the first two years of *Charter* judgments (1984 and 1985) to about 60 percent in the next four years (1986 to 1989).[16] These growing divisions within the Court further undermined the appearance of judicial objectivity.

By the turn of the decade, some Supreme Court judges were openly admitting that the *Charter* imposed on them significant policymaking powers. The most candid acknowledgment of this came from Madam Justice McLachlin, who, in a lecture delivered in 1990, spoke of "the impossibility of avoiding value judgments in *Charter* decision-making," and referred to such value judgments as "essentially arbitrary."[17] As judges discarded the myth of judicial objectivity, they also dispensed with many of the trappings of liberal legalism associated with it. By the early 1990s, some judges were openly conceding that the *Oakes* test required them to make difficult policy decisions under section 1 and were arguing publicly about how those decisions should best be made.[18] The Court also started shifting ground on its approach to state action, acknowledging that judicial decisions should not be insulated from *Charter* norms[19] and accepting, in certain circumstances, that the *Charter* may require as well as constrain governmental action.[20] At the same time, the Court abandoned earlier claims that it was limited by its adjudicative role to striking down legislation, and began to embrace new *Charter* remedies – including

15 See A. Petter, "The Politics of the Charter" (1986) 8 *Supreme Court L. R.* 473; A. Petter, "Canada's Charter Flight: Soaring Backwards into the Future" (1989) 16 *Journal of Law and Society* 151; and Hutchinson and Petter, "Private Rights/Public Wrongs," *supra* note 10.

16 F. L. Morton, P. H. Russell, and M. J. Withey, "The Supreme Court's First One Hundred Charter of Rights Decisions: A Statistical Analysis" (1992) 30 *Osgoode Hall L.J.* 1 at 11.

17 Madame Justice B. M. McLachlin, "The Charter: A New Role for the Judiciary?" (1991) 29 *Alta L. Rev.* 540 at 545–6.

18 See, e.g., G. V. LaForest, "The Balancing of Interests Under the Charter" (1992) 2 *N.J.C.L.* 133 and Hon. B. Wilson, "Constitutional Advocacy" (1992) 24 *Ottawa L. Rev.* 265.

19 As Professor Peter W. Hogg has pointed out, the Court started shifting position on this in the late 1980s in cases like *B.C.G.E.U. v. B.C. (Attorney General)* [1988] 2 S.C.R 214: see P. W. Hogg, *Constitutional Law of Canada, Student Edition* (Scarborough: Carswell, 2000) at 706–9.

20 See *Dunmore v. Ontario (Attorney General)* [2001] 3 S.C.R. 1016 [*Dunmore*] at paras. 19–29.

severance,[21] declarations of temporary validity,[22] and reading in statutory extensions[23] and exclusions[24] – that allowed it to reshape legislation in creative ways.

The effect of these shifts was to destabilize the platform of liberal legalism upon which the Court had built and justified its *Charter* enterprise. This in turn raised a difficult question: If the Court could no longer justify its *Charter* role on the basis that judges' decisions were grounded in objective standards and purposive interpretations, what justification could it offer? Fortunately for the Court, an answer was in the making. While judges had been busy jettisoning key elements of their justificatory theory for judicial review, academic commentators sympathetic to the *Charter* enterprise had been laboring on alternative theories. In 1997, Peter Hogg and Allison Bushell published a paper defending the legitimacy of *Charter* review based on the claim that the *Charter* creates a dialogue between courts and legislatures.[25] According to the authors, *Charter* decisions were seldom determinative of issues but merely set the stage for legislative responses that, more often than not, achieved the same objective in a different way. Thus, the *Charter* did not undermine democratic decision making, but merely encouraged deliberation about rights issues as part of an interactive process – described by Hogg and Bushell as a "dialogue" – between courts and legislatures.

The radical nature of this theory is apparent from the fact that the authors proceeded from an assumption that judicial review is a highly subjective enterprise. Noting "judges have a great deal of discretion in 'interpreting' the law of the constitution," they conceded that "the process of interpretation inevitably remakes the constitution into the likeness favoured by judges."[26] This concession was important not only in accounting for the normative nature of judicial decision making, but also in explaining why legislatures, not courts, should serve as the final arbiters of constitutional norms. According to Hogg and Bushell, democracy alone provides the rationale for public policymaking, and *Charter* decisions are merely another contribution to a democratic dialogue in which legislatures, not courts, get the final say.

A related feature of the theory is the shift in attitude it marks toward key provisions of the *Charter*, most notably sections 1 and 33. Section 1, which previously had been viewed with suspicion by *Charter* enthusiasts because of its capacity to weaken the *Charter*'s commitment to liberal values, was now embraced for its tendency to strengthen the *Charter*'s commitment to democratic dialogue. This it does, according to Hogg and Bushell, not only by allowing governments to defend legislative provisions as being "reasonable limits" on *Charter* rights, but also by providing them opportunities to respond to adverse judicial decisions with legislative changes that propose alternative means to achieve the same objectives. Section 33, the override clause, which in earlier days had been shunned by *Charter* enthusiasts as a provision that undermined judicial authority to protect fundamental rights

[21] See *R. v. Hess*, [1990] 2 S.C.R. 906 and *Tétreault-Gadoury v. Canada*, [1991] 2 S.C.R. 22.

[22] See *Schachter v. Canada*, [1992] 2 S.C.R. 679 at 715–17.

[23] Ibid. at 695–702. See also *Miron v. Trudel*, [1995] 2 S.C.R 418 at para. 180.

[24] See *R. v. Sharpe*, [2001] 1 S.C.R. 45 at 111–27.

[25] P. W. Hogg and A. A. Bushell, "The *Charter* Dialogue Between Courts and Legislatures (or Perhaps the *Charter of Rights* Isn't Such a Bad Thing After All)" (1997) 35 *Osgoode Hall L.J.* 75.

[26] Ibid. at 77.

and freedoms, was now welcomed as a provision that, by allowing legislatures the final say, fortified the legitimacy of judicial decisions enforcing those rights and freedoms.

Supreme Court judges did not waste any time adopting dialogue theory as their own. Speaking for the majority in the 1998 *Vriend v. Alberta* decision, Mr. Justice Iacobucci embraced the concept of dialogue put forward by Hogg and Bushell, emphasizing that, "the final word in our constitutional structure is in fact left to the legislature and not the courts."[27] He went on to say:

> To my mind, a great value of judicial review and this dialogue among the branches is that each of the branches is made somewhat accountable to the other. The work of the legislature is reviewed by the courts and the work of the court in its decisions can be reacted to by the legislature in the passing of new legislation (or even overarching laws under s. 33 of the *Charter*). This dialogue between and accountability of each of the branches have the effect of enhancing the democratic process, not denying it.[28]

Given the tattered state of the Court's previous efforts to explain judicial review under the *Charter*, the readiness with which it seized upon dialogue theory is perhaps not surprising. The theory provided a convenient justification for their constitutional role and came with the added virtue of malleability. Unlike liberal legalism, which is animated by an established set of norms concerning the character of judicial decision making and the relationship between individuals and the state, dialogue theory is normatively agnostic. Thus, although judges can claim that their role in the dialogue is to make "reasoned and principled decisions,"[29] the theory does not dictate what the nature of those reasons and principles should be.

Where dialogue theory is not malleable, however, is in its claim that the legitimacy of *Charter* decision making is grounded in democracy and, in particular, in the ability of legislatures to exercise final say over judicial decisions. In this way, the Supreme Courts' embrace of dialogue theory represents a revival of the doctrine of legislative supremacy as much as it does a repudiation of liberal legalism. Moreover, this reborn version of the doctrine goes further than its predecessor in one important respect: It relies on the democratic character of legislatures to justify political decision making not only by elected governments but also by unelected courts.

III. DIALOGUE AND DEMOCRACY

Despite the support it has received from Canadian scholars and courts, dialogue theory does not in my view provide a compelling justification for judicial review under the *Charter*. First, the theory lacks normative content and provides no moral justification for judges' involvement in *Charter* decision making. Second, the theory is based on the erroneous proposition that a decision is legitimate simply because it is not conclusive. Third, the theory seriously understates the extent to which

[27] *Vriend v. Alberta*, [1998] 1 S.C.R. 493 at para. 137.
[28] Ibid. at para. 139.
[29] Ibid. at para. 136.

judicial decision making under the *Charter* drives public policy in Canada.[30] Beyond these objections, the theory suffers from a more fundamental weakness that supporters of *Charter* review have previously attributed to the arguments of *Charter* skeptics, namely, an uncritical acceptance of the democratic nature of political institutions. Dialogue theorists maintain that the *Charter* creates a "democratic dialogue" between legislatures and courts.[31] This dialogue is said to be democratic, and hence legitimate, insofar as legislatures rather than courts retain the final say. Yet this assumes that legislatures are themselves democratic. If not, dialogue theory is reduced to a proposition of two undemocratic wrongs making one democratic right.

There are many reasons to doubt the democratic character of Canadian political institutions. Such institutions remain horribly unrepresentative of the public. Women, for example, make up more than 50 percent of the Canadian population[32] but only 21 percent of members of Parliament.[33] Indigenous people, ethnic minorities, and the poor are similarly underrepresented in Parliament and in provincial legislatures. In addition, our "first-past-the-post" electoral system produces major distortions in translating voters' preferences into representation. Parties that attract support from a minority of voters regularly get to form majority governments. Voters in federal elections who support smaller parties that are regionally based, like the Bloc Quebecois, are generally overrepresented, whereas those who support smaller parties that are nationally based, like the New Democratic Party and the Green Party, are generally underrepresented or get no representation at all.

Federal and provincial governments also lack accountability to their citizens. Within these governments, power is concentrated in the hands of first ministers who, by virtue of their control over cabinet appointments, government perks and party structures, exercise enormous sway over elected members of their party, leaving legislatures with little or no capacity to influence government policy. The only significant qualification to this rule arises occasionally when there is a minority government. In this circumstance, opposition parties gain some influence from their power to defeat the government; though this influence is usually exercised by way of extralegislative bargaining and is tempered by the power of first ministers to announce policy, call elections, and otherwise control the levers of government.

At a more basic level, Canadian institutions of parliamentary democracy are artifacts of a nineteenth-century British system[34] that provide citizens with limited means to participate in public policymaking. Except when governments consider it in their interests to consult or otherwise engage the public, the only meaningful opportunity that citizens have to influence public policy is to vote in elections,

[30] For a fuller discussion of these objections, see Andrew Petter, "Rip Van Winkle in Charterland" (2005) 63:3 *Advocate* (B.C.) 337.

[31] Kent Roach, *The Supreme Court on Trial: Judicial Activism or Democratic Dialogue* (Toronto: Irwin Law, 2001).

[32] Statistics Canada, "Population by Sex and Age Group" (2003), online: Statistics Canada, http://www.statcan.ca/english/Pgdb/ demo10a.htm.

[33] Inter-Parliamentary Union, "Women in National Parliaments" (July 31, 2004), online: Inter-Parliamentary Union, http://www.ipu.org/wmn-e/ classif.htm.

[34] The British Parliamentary system dates back well before this, but the first serious effort to democratize the system by extending the franchise beyond a narrow set of elites did not occur until passage of the British Reform Act of 1832.

which may occur as infrequently as once every five years.[35] Even this opportunity, precious though it is, has become less relevant as governments have entered trade agreements ceding more and more of their regulatory capacity and transferring decision-making authority to unelected transnational organizations.

It is ironic that, in seeking to defend the legitimacy of judicial review, Canadian constitutional scholars and judges should turn from one set of nineteenth-century assumptions (those associated with liberal legalism) to another (those associated with parliamentary democracy). This irony is made more poignant by the fact that support for this form of democracy, at least as it is currently practiced, is on the wane in Canada. Voter participation rates in Canadian elections have been declining dramatically over the past twenty-five years, with turnout in the 2004 federal election the lowest in Canadian history.[36] A majority of Canadians attribute this decline to negative attitudes toward the performance of politicians and political institutions, and to an associated sense that political participation is meaningless.[37] The relationship between growing discontent with political institutions and declining voter turnout is confirmed by public opinion surveys conducted over the past twenty-five years. These surveys show that the number of Canadians with a great deal of confidence in the House of Commons fell 14 percentage points from 1979 to 2001,[38] while those with a great deal of confidence in political parties fell 17 percentage points.[39] In the same time frame, voter turnout declined 15 percentage points.[40]

IV. TAKING DEMOCRACY SERIOUSLY

The ascendancy of dialogue theory as the prevailing justification for judicial review under the *Charter*, ironic or not, carries with it some important messages. One is that, after two decades of experience with constitutional rights in Canada, democracy has reemerged as the dominant value relied upon to support Canadian constitutional structures. Another is that, the *Charter* notwithstanding, ultimate responsibility for giving expression to those rights has been recognized to rest with the people rather than with the courts. As a consequence, those who advocate judicial review based on dialogue theory join those who remain skeptical of judicial review based on democratic principles in having a significant investment in the democratic nature of the Canadian state.

35 As Rousseau observed, the English system of parliamentary democracy is free "only during the election of members of Parliament. As soon as they are elected, slavery overtakes it, and it is nothing": Jean-Jacques Rousseau, *The Social Contract*, trans. G. D. H. Code (New York: Everyman, 1950) at 94.

36 Voter turnout was 60.5 percent in 2004 compared to 76 percent in 1979: Canada 2004, "Voter Turnout 1867–2004," online: Canada 2004, http://www.nodice.ca/election2004/ voterturnout.html [Canada 2004].

37 Jon H. Pammett and Lawrence LeDuc, *Explaining the Turnout Decline in Canadian Federal Elections: A New Survey of Non-voters* (Ottawa, Elections Canada, March 2003) at 6–18, online: Elections Canada http://www.elections.ca/loi/tur/tud/TurnoutDecline.pdf.

38 From 38 percent in 1979 to 24 percent in 2001: Centre for Research and Information on Canada (CRIC), *Voter Participation in Canada: Is Canadian Democracy in Crisis?* (Montreal, October 2001) at 16, online: Centre for Research and Information on Canada, http://www.cric.ca/pdf/ cahiers/ cricpapers_nov2001.pdf.

39 From 30 percent in 1979 to 13 percent in 2001: ibid.

40 From 76 percent in 1979 to 61 percent in 2001: Canada 2004, *supra* note 36.

With this investment, however, comes responsibility. Against the backdrop of legislatures that are unrepresentative, governments that are unaccountable, and citizens who are losing faith in political institutions, there is a pressing need for *Charter* enthusiasts and *Charter* skeptics to give more urgent attention to the requirements of democracy. The goal of this enterprise should be to make Canadian political institutions as representative and responsive as possible, and to maximize opportunities for citizen participation and deliberation in relation to political decision making.

It is beyond the scope of this chapter to set out a detailed agenda of democratic reform, but let me highlight a few areas that deserve to be addressed. One obvious one is electoral reform. I have already described how our current "first-past-the-post" voting regime produces legislatures that do not represent the views of the electorate, diminishing or denying representation to smaller parties that are ideologically based, and conferring majority powers on parties that are supported by a minority of electors. This regime is an affront to basic principles of democracy and needs to be replaced with a proportional system aimed at producing legislatures that reflect the diversity of Canadian public opinion. Such a system should be accompanied by campaign finance laws that respect the equality of citizens and ensure that elections are not dominated by those who command money and power. In the context of a proportional system this means that, in addition to public election financing, campaign contribution limits (including prohibitions on corporate and union donations), disclosure requirements, and spending restrictions, election laws must be reworked to ensure that small parties get adequate funding and voice in the process.

Based on the experience of other countries, a proportional voting system supported by effective election finance laws is more likely to produce legislatures in which women, indigenous people, and ethnic minorities are better represented.[41] Such a system by itself, however, is unlikely to overcome the social and economic barriers that inhibit these groups from achieving their full measure of political representation. For this reason, further educational, fiscal, and structural measures aimed at countering these barriers and promoting equitable representation of these groups ought to be considered.[42]

Electoral reform would also go some distance to fostering parliamentary reform. A proportional voting system will tend to produce minority or coalition governments in which the power of first ministers is constrained by an ongoing need to accommodate the competing views of other parties. In such governments, issues are more likely to be fully and openly debated and decisions to reflect a broader range of interests. More, however, can and should be done. A range of institutional reforms is needed to give legislatures more sway over first ministers and their executives, to replace or do away with an unelected Senate, to give citizens greater opportunities for input into government decision making processes, and to ensure that such decision making is conducted in an open and accountable manner.

[41] Canada, Law Commission of Canada, *Voting Counts: Electoral Reform for Canada* (Ottawa, Law Commission of Canada, 2004) at 60–2.

[42] See, e.g., Melissa S. Williams, *Voice, Trust, and Memory: Marginalized Groups and the Failings of Liberal Representation* (Princeton: Princeton University Press, 1998).

The changes outlined above speak to the need for legislatures be more representative and responsive and to operate in a democratic manner. A meaningful commitment to democracy, however, should not be limited to representative institutions and certainly not to legislatures. Much has been written in recent years about the need to pursue new strategies to foster greater participation and deliberation on the part of citizens in relation to decisions that affect their lives.[43] There are a large number of such strategies that merit consideration. I will touch on three examples that I believe hold promise based on my experience in the Government of British Columbia.[44]

One such strategy is to devolve powers to local or regional governments. At a time when globalization has inhibited the ability of national and provincial governments to pursue social and economic innovations, local and regional governments may be better placed to advance the public interest in certain policy areas. Such governments enjoy the benefit of being closer to the people and farther from the reach of international capital. They also have greater capacity than national or provincial governments to be inclusive and responsive, and to tailor their strategies to citizens' needs.[45] To prevent national and provincial governments from using devolution as a means of shirking responsibilities or downloading costs, transfers of power must be accompanied by administrative, legislative and, possibly, constitutional guarantees, to ensure that local and regional governments gain the institutional and fiscal capacity required to discharge their enlarged responsibilities.

A recent example where this has occurred is in the context the Nisga'a Treaty in British Columbia. This treaty enables the Nisga'a people through their "Lisims Government" to exercise authority on matters of social policy and resource management, guarantees them fiscal transfers and taxation powers, and sets this out in a constitutionally recognized framework.[46] It is still early days, but few would deny that the Nisga'a government is in a better position to reflect and advance the needs of its citizens in these areas than was either the federal or provincial government. Thus, far from being a threat to democracy as some of its opponents have asserted, the Nisga'a treaty provides a model for democratic reform that might well be emulated in other indigenous and nonindigenous communities.

[43] See, e.g., Benjamin Barber, *Strong Democracy: Participatory Politics for a New Age* (Berkeley: University of California Press, 1984); James Fishkin, *The Voice of the People: Public Opinion and Democracy* (New Haven: Yale University Press, 1995); Amy Gutmann and Dennis Thompson, *Democracy and Disagreement* (Cambridge: Belknap Press of Harvard University Press, 1996); Joshua Cohen, "Deliberation and Democratic Legitimacy" in James Bohman and William Rehg, eds., *Deliberative Democracy: Essays on Reason and Politics* (Cambridge: MIT Press, 1997) 67–91; and Iris Marion Young, *Inclusion and Democracy* (Oxford: Oxford University Press, 2000).

[44] From 1991 to 2001, I served as an elected member of the British Columbia Legislature and, in that time, held numerous ministerial posts, including Aboriginal Affairs, Forests, Intergovernmental Affairs, Finance, and Attorney General.

[45] See Warren Magnusson, "Local Autonomy and Community Politics" in Warren Magnusson, Charles Doyle, R. B. J. Walker, and John De Marco, eds., *After Bennett: A New Politics for British Columbia* (Vancouver: New Star Books, 1986).

[46] For information on the treaty, implementing legislation and Nisga'a government, see "Nisga'a Lisims Government," online: Nisga'a Lisims Government, http://www.nisgaalisims.ca/home.html (date accessed: July 24, 2005).

Another devolutionary strategy, sometimes referred to as "associative democracy,"[47] would seek to close the gulf between government and civil society by assigning some matters of public policy to self-governing associations that can better represent the interests of those who are most affected. This strategy is nothing new in northern Italy where, in the city of Bologna, 85 percent of social services are delivered by cooperatives.[48] Similar initiatives have been tried in Canada on a more limited scale. In British Columbia, for example, experiments were undertaken in the 1970s and 1990s to give responsibilities as diverse as delivery of health services and management of forest resources to community-run boards. Initiatives of this kind could be employed on a more regular basis to allow citizens greater opportunity to influence social and economic policy at the local level. And parallel policies could be contemplated at the provincial or national level in relation to the governance of certain public utilities and crown corporations. Transforming such entities into consumer-run cooperatives would preserve their status as civic institutions while enhancing their accountability and providing greater opportunities for public participation in their governance.[49]

A third strategy that could be called "deliberative engagement" involves government charging representative groups of citizens with responsibility for recommending or deciding matters of public policy.[50] This strategy can be particularly productive in generating processes of public deliberation on issues that are polycentric or too complex for popular opinion to be gauged in conventional ways (by polling, for example). A process of this kind was used successfully in British Columbia in the 1990s by the Harcourt government to give representatives of communities and stakeholders responsibility for developing provincial and local land-use plans. By bringing these representatives into a structured process of public deliberation, deeply held differences were overcome and creative solutions were found to settle land-use conflicts that had previously defied resolution.

Another British Columbia experiment in "deliberative engagement" was launched by the Campbell government in 2003 to review British Columbia's electoral system. A Citizens Assembly of 161 people, composed of one man and one woman chosen by lot from each of the province's 79 constituencies, plus two Aboriginal members and an independent chair, was formed to study and recommend

[47] See Paul Hirst, *Associative Democracy: New Forms of Economic and Social Governance* (Amherst: University of Massachusetts Press, 1993).

[48] Robert Williams, "Bologna and Emilia Romagna – A Model for Economic Democracy" (Paper presented to the Annual Meeting of the Canadian Economics Association, Calgary, May/June 2002), online: B.C. Co-operative Association, http://www.bcca.coop/pdfs/ BolognaandEmilia.pdf. See generally Robert Putnam, *Making Democracy Work: Civic Traditions in Modern Italy* (Princeton: Princeton University Press, 1993).

[49] Transformations of this kind were proposed in British Columbia in the late 1990s in relation to the Insurance Corporation of British Columbia and British Columbia Hydro. Converting such entities into consumer-run cooperatives would have made them more directly accountable to the public they served, and provided a democratic alternative to privatization or turning them into not-for-profit corporations of the kind the federal government established to run its airports and harbors. These proposals did not proceed, however, when they proved too controversial to gain support within government.

[50] In this respect, the process might be thought of as an extension of what James Fishkin refers to as "deliberative polling": see Fishkin, *supra* note 43.

changes to the province's "first-past-the-post" electoral system. After months of study, public consultation, and deliberation, the Assembly recommended that the province adopt a "single transferable" voting system that would produce greater proportionality of representation based on multimember electoral districts.[51] This recommendation was put to voters in a referendum held in conjunction with the 2005 provincial election. In order for the proposal to proceed, the government stipulated that it had to gain the approval of 60 percent of those who voted, and a majority of those who voted in 60 percent of the province's seventy-nine electoral districts. In the result, the Assembly's recommendation received the support of over 57 percent of those who voted and of a majority in all but two electoral districts. While falling just short of the government's first threshold, the degree of support given to the recommendation sent a strong signal about the public's dissatisfaction with the status quo. This has left politicians in a quandary, and it is uncertain where the process will now lead. One thing that is clear, however, is that the process was highly successful in generating meaningful citizen engagement on a complex issue of public policy and in producing a recommendation that gained popular support. The process also broke new ground in ensuring equal representation of women in the deliberative process and in giving citizens direct power to decide the outcome, albeit based on a requirement of support from more than a simple majority of those who voted.

V. CONCLUSION

In the early 1980s, when I and other skeptics questioned the *Charter* and its implications for democracy, supporters of judicial review would often accuse us of romanticizing legislatures and their democratic role. Today, with the benefit of more than twenty years of hindsight, ten of them spent as a member of the British Columbia Legislature, I have come to accept that these accusations had merit. The early preoccupation of *Charter* skeptics with the shortcomings of judicial review diverted our attention from the deficiencies of parliamentary government and caused many of us to take Canadian democracy too much for granted.

In the period that my romance with legislatures has faded, however, many *Charter* enthusiasts have developed a passion for parliamentary government that makes my previous yearnings seem like mild infatuation. Whereas I and other *Charter* skeptics regarded legislatures as institutions whose democratic capacity was threatened by *Charter* review, today's dialogue theorists see legislatures as having sufficient democratic capacity not only to withstand *Charter* review, but also to legitimize its exercise. Now that is some democratic capacity!

The good news is that despite other disagreements, *Charter* enthusiasts and *Charter* skeptics now occupy the same boat in viewing democracy as Canada's core constitutional value. The bad news is that the ship is listing badly and taking on water at an alarming rate. Moreover, it is a ship that many Canadians have started to abandon. Rehabilitating this vessel will be no small challenge, but, thankfully,

[51] For a full account of this process, see Jack MacDonald, *Randomocracy – A Citizen's Guide to Electoral Reform in British Columbia* (Victoria: FCG Publications, 2005), online: http://209.200.81.6/BCEF/publication/Randomocracy.pdf.

work has already begun. Groups calling for changes to the "first-past-the-post" voting system are mobilizing across Canada, and electoral reform initiatives are under way in a number of provinces. Effective election spending laws have been put in place for national campaigns, parliamentary reforms have been adopted by the federal and some provincial governments, and a deliberative process requiring equal representation for women has been employed in British Columbia. Possibilities for democratizing political decision making through devolution, associative democracy and other deliberative means abound, and there is a growing body of academic literature on these and other strategies.

What remains is for constitutional scholars who are serious about their democratic commitments to join this enterprise and to direct their knowledge and intellectual energies to helping reclaim and reconstruct Canadian democracy. For those who maintain a skeptical outlook toward the *Charter*, this undertaking requires us to set aside our deconstructive tendencies and embrace a challenge that may seem as daunting as it does worthwhile. For those who subscribe to dialogue theory, however, there is additional motivation to partake in the endeavor. Unlike *Charter* skeptics who must be content with salvaging democracy for its own sake, this new brand of *Charter* enthusiasts can draw sustenance from their belief that, by salvaging democracy, they are also salvaging the legitimacy of *Charter* review.

27 An International Community of Legislatures?

Daphne Barak-Erez

A. LEGAL TRANSPLANTS AND LEGISLATION

Learning from other legal systems has always been a significant technique for developing law. Legal historian Alan Watson described this mode of development as "legal transplants,"[1] a term that he coined for this purpose. According to Watson, "at most times, in most places, borrowing from a different jurisdiction has been the principal way in which law has developed."[2] Instances of this mode of legal development can be found from the beginning of documented history, as evident in the presence of similar laws in various codes in use in the ancient Near East.[3]

Most of the literature dealing with the technique of legal transplants deals with the desirability of this practice. Some, like Watson, saw only the positive and useful aspects of learning from other countries. Others, like Otto Kahn-Freund,[4] have cautioned against the indiscriminate adoption of legal institutions or ideas that do not fit the conditions of the importing system.[5] Much earlier, Montesquieu had argued that the laws of a nation reflect its spirit and, therefore, cannot suit other communities.[6] This chapter pursues a different course. Rather than asking whether importing concepts from foreign law is a desirable practice, it looks more closely at the legal institutions and procedures involved in the implementation of such concepts. More specifically, this chapter focuses on the role of legislatures in the adoption of models and ideas from foreign statutes. The classic literature

[1] See Alan Watson, *Legal Transplants: An Approach to Comparative Law*, 2nd ed. (Athens: University of Georgia Press, 1993) [*Legal Transplants*].

[2] See Alan Watson, *Society and Legal Change*, 2nd ed. (Philadelphia: Temple University Press, 2001) at 98.

[3] For example, Watson points to the law of the goring ox, cited in the Code of Hammurabi, the book of Exodus, and many other ancient laws in force in this area. See Watson, *Legal Transplants, supra* note 1 at 22–4.

[4] Otto Kahn-Freund, "On Uses and Misuses of Comparative Law" (1974) 37 *Modern L. Rev.* 1.

[5] For further discussion of these contradicting views, see Eric Stein, "Uses, Misuses and Nonuses of Comparative Law" (1977–1978) 72 *Nw. U. L. Rev.* 198; Gunther Teubner, "Legal Irritants: Good Faith in British Law or How Unifying Law Ends Up in New Divergences" (1998) 61 *Modern L. Rev.* 11.

[6] Montesquieu *De L'Esprit Des Lois*, Livre Premier, Chapitre III ("Elles doivent être tellement propres au peuple pour lequel elles sont faites, que c'est un très grand hasard si celles d'une nation peuvent convener a une autre"). Kahn-Freund explains that his emphasis is different from that of Montesquieu. Montesquieu had referred to geographical, economic, sociological, and cultural differences between nations. Kahn-Freund argues that, in modern times, nations have become increasingly similar in these regards. Nevertheless, he points out that differences between the political conditions of various systems are important for evaluating the feasibility of legal transplants. See Kahn-Freund, *supra* note 4 at 8–13.

on legal transplants is concerned with the import of concepts from other legal systems in general, without paying much attention to the institutional aspects of the process. But the transplant of ideas developed in other countries can be achieved not only through legislation but also through judicial rulings, or even through administrative decisions in the context of existing law. This chapter focuses on the role that legislatures play in the adoption of this practice, and the question that will accompany us throughout the discussion is whether legislatures in various countries engage in a mutual dialogue in the course of the legislative process.

B. THE DIALOGUE DISCOURSE IN LEGAL SCHOLARSHIP

The background for the question concerning mutual influences between legislatures is the increasing awareness of ongoing institutional dialogues. The dialogue metaphor has been used to describe the complicated interrelations between courts and legislatures as, for instance, when court rulings serve as triggers for new legislation that, in turn, is interpreted, enforced, and reviewed by the courts, a process that has been described as "constitutional dialogue."[7] Legal scholarship has also traced the course of institutional dialogues in the international arena. Mutual influences between courts in different countries have been analyzed as judicial dialogues.[8] Transjudicial communication is found not only in the application of norms of international law but also in the growing recourse to comparative law, mainly in the area of constitutional law.[9] In addition, human rights activists from different countries tend to identify themselves as part of one international community that engages in a dialogue, this time mainly a dialogue of cooperation. Transnational issue networks and activists play a significant role in triggering the internalization process of international law.[10]

The purpose of this chapter is to focus on the possibilities for dialogue between legislatures of different states, mainly independent states but also legislatures of states belonging to one federal system.[11] In this sense, it joins the call for renewed and increased interest in the phenomenon of legislation, which for years failed

[7] See Louis Fisher, *Constitutional Dialogues: Interpretation as Political Process* (Princeton: Princeton University Press, 1988). The dialogue metaphor has been used extensively to describe various interactions between courts and legislatures. For example, see P. W. Hogg and A. A. Bushell, "The Charter Dialogue between Courts and Legislatures" (1997) 35 *Osgoode Hall L. J.* 75; Kent Roach, "Constitutional and Common Law Dialogues between the Supreme Court and Canadian Legislatures" (2001) 72 *Can. Bar Rev.* 481; Kent Roach, "The Uses and Audiences of Preambles in Legislation" (2001) 47 *McGill L. J.* 129 (analyzing legislative preambles as a form of dialogue between the legislature and the courts). For the virtues of "dialogic" judicial decisions, see Michael J. Perry, *The Constitution in the Courts: Law or Politics?* (New York: Oxford University Press, 1994) 99–101.

[8] Anne-Marie Slaughter, "A Typology of Transjudicial Communication" (1994) 29 *U. Rich. L. Rev.* 99; Laurence R. Helfer and Anne-Marie Slaughter, "Toward a Theory of Effective Supranational Adjudication" (1997) 107 *Yale L. J.* 273; Anne-Marie Slaughter, "A Global Community of Courts" (2003) 44 *Harv. Int'l L. J.* 191; Anne-Marie Slaughter, *A New World Order* (Princeton: Princeton University Press, 2004).

[9] For example, see Anthony Lester, "The Overseas Trade in the American Bill of Rights" (1988) 88 *Colum. L. Rev.* 537.

[10] Harold Hongju Koh, "Why Do Nations Obey International Law?" (1997) 106 *Yale L. J.* 2599; Harold Hongju Koh, "Bringing International Law Home" (1998) 35 *Hous. L. Rev.* 623.

[11] In a broader perspective, inspiration for legislative initiatives exists at the municipal level as well, when municipalities import ideas for local ordinances from other municipalities. See Stacy Laira Lozner, "Diffusion of Local Regulatory Innovations: The San Francisco CEDAW Ordinance and the New York City Human Rights Initiative" (2004) 104 *Colum. L. Rev.* 768.

to obtain the attention it deserves.[12] More specifically, it deals with the possibilities of legislation in one country providing inspiration for the national statutes of another. This is an issue I consider highly significant. The dialogue between courts or between human rights activists may indeed contribute to the development of law. Legislation, however, is still the main vehicle for introducing legal reforms and new legal concepts. Moreover, legislation is less constrained in adopting new concepts from other legal systems. Whereas courts can be inspired by foreign judicial rulings as far as these can be reconciled with domestic legislation, legislators are not bound to consider existing legislation as a constraint and can simply revise it.

Some areas of law can indeed develop even without intensive legislative activity, sometimes even without any legislative activity at all. Many human rights achievements, for instance, began as judicial interpretations of vague constitutional texts. But in other areas legislation is usually a precondition for reform, as is the case, for example, regarding corporate law or welfare law. In the area of welfare, reform must begin by defining detailed conditions of eligibility and establishing administrative agencies necessary for the operation of the welfare scheme. In this sense, the dialogue within the international community of judges is not an alternative for international inspiration in the sphere of legislation.

Discussing the influence of foreign legislation on domestic legislation becomes even more critical today, when our lives are characterized by a ceaseless flood of information. One can hardly assume that new options for accessing information about other countries will not be implemented in the sphere of legislation as well, and a more plausible assumption is that legislators will willingly rely on the experience of other countries, especially on issues not considered typically local or particularistic. The spirit of globalization is also expected to contribute to a growing openness to inspiration drawn from other legal systems.

C. LEGISLATION DURING TRANSITIONS

I begin with well-known historical examples of external influences on legislation in order to distinguish them from "ordinary" instances of legislation inspired by outside statutes. All these examples concentrate on transitional phases of national history in various settings.[13] At such times, legal systems undergo broad and at times revolutionary reforms, so that these examples do not represent "normal" legislative activity.[14] In addition, they usually concern newly emerging or developing countries

[12] See also William N. Eskridge and Philip P. Frickey, "Legislation Scholarship and Pedagogy in the Post-Legal Process Era" (1987) 48 *U. Pitt. L. Rev.* 691; Jeremy Waldron, *The Dignity of Legislation* (New York: Cambridge University Press, 1999).

[13] As Roscoe Pound wrote: "In legal history periods of growth and expansion call for and rely upon philosophy and comparative law. Periods of stability, striving for perfection of the form of law rather than for development of its substance, rely upon analysis and history." Roscoe Pound, "Foreword to 'The Valuation of Property in the Roman Law'" (1921) 34 *Harv. L. Rev.* 227 at 227.

[14] Borrowing from Ackerman's famous metaphor of "constitutional moments" (in Bruce Ackerman, *We the People: Foundations* [Cambridge: Belknap of Harvard University Press, 1991]), these are examples of legislation in "transitional moments." Schauer draws a similar distinction between microtransitions, involving changes of specific rules or even clusters of legal rules, and macrotransitions, which encompass the whole legal regime or significant parts of it. See Frederick Schauer, "Legal Development and the Problem of Systemic Transition" (2003) 13 *J. Contemp. Legal Issues* 261.

borrowing models from hegemonic states. Hence, although these examples merit scholarly attention, they cannot be a basis for answering the question as to whether legislators are engaged in an ongoing dialogue on a regular basis.

The perspective chosen here, emphasizing the transformative stage in the national history of the transplanting state, concentrates on the incentives to import foreign legislation. At the same time, it is important to bear in mind that exporting systems may also be interested in this process in order to promote the hegemony of their culture and ideology, to ease dealings for their own citizens in countries that adopt similar legislation, and even to strengthen the legitimacy of their national legislation by pointing to its reception beyond the national borders.[15]

(1) Colonialism

Inherent in colonialism was the idea of bringing Westernized ideas and culture to new areas that were considered "barbaric" or at least "underdeveloped."[16] As a result, colonial rulers enacted in their colonies laws that resembled those in their respective homelands or were at least inspired by them. The colonialist era was a time characterized by major legal transplants. And yet, although extremely important for the understanding of current problems and of prospects for change in countries liberated from colonial rule, the discussion of these transplants exceeds the scope of the present discussion because they were imposed by oppression and did not reflect the democratic choice of the colonized nations or their legislatures.

(2) Opening up to the west

Another form of transition characterizes countries that decided to replace their original national law in order to "open up" to the West, mainly to ease economic development. These legislative reforms are also not part of the "normal" operation of legislatures and actually mark the transition from one legal system to another, without this change being accompanied by a regime transition. An obvious instance of such a transition is the process of legislating new, Western-based laws in Japan during the last decade of the nineteenth century.[17] Another example is that of the new codes enacted in the Ottoman Empire between 1839 and 1881 in order to modernize a system that had previously been based on Islamic law.[18]

15 On the motivations of the exporting side, see also Frederick Schauer, "The Politics and Incentives of Legal Transplantation" in Joseph S. Nye and John D. Donahue, eds., *Governance in a Globalizing World*, (Cambridge: Brookings Institution Press, 2000) 253 at 261–3.

16 For example, see Jorg Fisch, "Law as a Means and as an End: Some Remarks on the Function of European and Non-European Law in the Process of European Expansion" in W. J. Mommsen and J. A. DeMoor, eds., *European Expansion and Law: The Encounter of European and Indigenous Law in the 19th- and 20th-Century Africa and Asia* (New York: St. Martin's Press, 1992) 15 at 33–5 [*European Expansion and Law*].

17 Japan adopted a constitution based on that of Prussia in 1889. In the decade that followed, the Japanese parliament enacted a series of statutes inspired by Western, mainly German, legislation. See Konrad Zweigert and Hein Kotz, *Introduction to Comparative Law*, 3rd rev. ed., trans. Tony Weir (Oxford: Clarendon Press, 1998) at 297–8; Eric Seizelet, "European Law and Tradition in Japan during the Meiji Era, 1868–1912" in *European Expansion and Law, supra* note 16, 59 at 67–72.

18 Esin Orucu, "The Impact of European Law on the Ottoman Empire and Turkey" in *European Expansion and Law, supra* note 16 at 44–51.

(3) Transitions of legal regimes

A special category of external influence includes legislation projects in newly emerging states or in states undergoing a regime transition.[19] This form of external influence relates to systems seeking new foundations rather than solutions for one or more specific problems. History shows that the standard choice in such systems was to import large sections of legal systems operating in countries that were considered close to their own culture and heritage or politically and economically hegemonic. There are several important examples of general transitions in legal systems based on the import of outside legislation:

(a) States liberated from colonialism: Many of these states wanted to celebrate their independence by establishing new legal systems, and used legislation imported from other countries for this purpose. One example of this pattern concerns the codes enacted in Latin America in the nineteenth century, based on the *Code Civil*.[20] The 1960s were marked by a tendency to offer models of legislation to countries liberated from colonialism (usually referred to as the "law and development movement of the 1960s"). At the time, this activity was considered a Western contribution to the successful development of the former colonies in Africa and Latin America. Today, however, these activities of the law and development movement are largely criticized as blind to the real problems of postcolonialist countries.[21]

(b) Germany and Japan after World War II: After the war, both Germany and Japan accepted new constitutions that were drafted with the assistance and under the influence of the winning powers, mainly the United States.[22]

(c) Post-Communism: After the collapse of the communist regimes in Eastern Europe, states in this block completely transformed their legal systems. Reforms responded both to the need for new constitutions and for new schemes of commercial law that could serve as the basis for market economies. The result was the acceptance of new constitutions based on Western models and drafted with the help of Western scholars, as well as of new commercial legislation influenced by Western paradigms, borrowed mainly from the United States.[23] In China too, a new

[19] Transition is a cardinal issue in current legal literature, and focuses on several issues. One that lies beyond the bounds of the present discussion relates to the challenge of correcting the wrongs of past regimes, including the problem of bringing to trial officials for their previous crimes. See Ruti G. Teitel, *Transitional Justice* (New York: Oxford University Press, 2000).

[20] See M. C. Mirow, "The Power of Codification in Latin America: Simon Bolivar and the Code Napoléon" (2000) 8 *Tul. J. Comp. & Int'l L.* 83; M. C. Mirow, "Borrowing Private Law in Latin America: Andrés Bello's Use of the Code Napoléon in Drafting the Chilean Civil Code" (2001) 61 *La. L. Rev.* 291.

[21] See David M. Trubek and Marc Galanter "Scholars in Self-Estrangement: Some Reflections on the Crisis in Law and Development Studies in the United States" [1974] *Wis. L. Rev.* No. 1062; James A. Gardner, *Legal Imperialism: American Lawyers and Foreign Aid in Latin America* (Madison: University of Wisconsin Press, 1980); Jorge L. Esquirol "Continuing Fictions of Latin American Law" (2003) 55 *Fla. L. Rev.* 41.

[22] See Sylvia Brown Hamano, "Incomplete Revolutions and Not So Alien Transplants: The Japanese Constitution and Human Rights" (1999) 1 *U. Pa. J. Const. L.* 415.

[23] See Joan Davidson, "America's Impact on Constitutional Change in Eastern Europe" (1992) 55 *Alb. L. Rev.* 793; Gianmaria Ajani, "By Chance and by Prestige: Legal Transplants in Russia and Eastern Europe" (1995) 43 *Am. J. Comp. L.* 93. Schauer argues that the tendency to adopt Westernized commercial laws was even greater, in comparison to the constutitutional domain, because they were perceived "as largely technical and nonideological, being largely instrumental to economic development." See Schauer, *supra* note 15 at 256–7.

wave of legislation was enacted aiming to develop appropriate tools for the country's developing economy, with significant influence of foreign experts (but with no equivalent constitutional reform).[24] These processes, often referred to as "the second law and development movement," have been criticized in terms similar to those condemning the first, namely, as imperialist and inattentive to the conditions of the receiving legal systems.[25]

D. THE INFLUENCE OF THE INTERNATIONAL AND INTERSTATE SPHERES

Another category of legislation with outside roots, to be distinguished from ordinary legislation inspired by statutes enacted in another state, is that of legislation enacted in the wake of international documents. In this case, inspiration is based on the hierarchy between the international and domestic spheres, although national legislatures are not always obliged to adopt the contents of international documents at hand, as explained below.

(1) Following binding conventions

The most obvious international impact on domestic legislation concerns international conventions that mandate, or at least encourage, the adoption of conforming laws by the contracting parties.[26] This dynamic may lead to similar laws in different countries. Yet, in this case, the legislatures that follow these conventions are not directly influenced by other legislatures. They abide by the relevant international conventions. At times, they do so due to pressures to adapt domestic legislation and practices to international standards.[27] The impact of international conventions is evident not only at the level of ordinary legislation, but also in the writing of national constitutions.[28]

(2) Following model laws

Another category of activities in the international sphere that have an impact on domestic legislation is that of model laws prepared by organs of the United Nations[29] or other international forums of cooperation, with recommendations for adoption by national legislatures.[30] These model laws are not binding international

[24] See Ann Seidman and Robert B. Seidman, "Drafting Legislation for Development: Lessons from a Chinese Project" (1996) 44 *Am. J. Comp. L.* 1.

[25] See Daniel Berkowitz, Katharina Pistor, and Jean-Francois Richard, "The Transplant Effect" (2003) 51 *Am. J. Comp. L.* 163. See also Jacques deLisle, "Lex Americana? United States Legal Assistance, American Legal Models and Legal Change in the Post-Communist World and Beyond" (1999) 20 *U. Pa. J. Int'l Econ. L.* 179.

[26] For examples in the context of English law, see Kahn-Freund, *supra* note 4 at 2–4.

[27] A prominent example is the battle to enforce "core" labor standards through the mechanisms of the World Trade Organization (WTO). For example, see Clyde Summers, "The Battle in Seattle: Free Trade, Labor Rights, and Societal Values" (2001) 22 *U. Pa. J. Int'l Econ. L.* 61.

[28] For example, see G. M. Danielko, "The New Russian Constitution and International Law" (1994) 88 *Am. J. Int'l L.* 451; Wiktor Osiatynski, "Rights in New Constitutions of East Central Europe" (1994) *26 Colum. H.R.L. Rev.* 111.

[29] An important international institution in this regard is the United Nations Commission on International Trade Law (UNCITRAL).

[30] Another important example is that of the International Institute for the Unification of Private Law (UNIDROIT), an independent intergovernmental organization which prepares uniform rules of private law in various fields. The UNIDROIT was established as an auxiliary organ of the League of Nations,

conventions, and therefore national legislatures are not legally compelled to follow them.[31]

Despite the absence of a formal legal obligation to follow the recommended model, political and economic pressures may be exerted in this direction. A good example in this context concerns the recommendations of the Financial Task Force on Money Laundering (FATF). The FATF is an intergovernmental body that sets standards and develops policies to combat money laundering and the financing of terrorism. To promote this goal, the FATF has formulated recommendations regarding legislation and enforcement at the national level. The FATF was originally established as an initiative of the G-7 states and the European Commission, and many countries are not members of it. Nevertheless, its recommendations are powerful and affect national legislation due to the economic and political influence of the countries behind the initiative.[32]

A similar phenomenon of legislation originating in model laws exists in the United States, where the American Law Institute (ALI) and the National Council of Commissioners for Uniform State Laws (NCCUSL) prepare model laws that can be adopted or rejected by the states.[33] This example is limited to the domestic sphere, but the process it relates to – preparing model laws that are not formally binding for the consideration of various legislatures – resembles the dynamics of international model laws.

E. THE IMPACT OF FOREIGN LEGISLATURES IN ORDINARY CIRCUMSTANCES

After dismissing transitional periods and international impact as special cases, I analyze in this section the circumstances in which one national legislature might be influenced by another. Scholars of comparative law do indeed widely agree that legislatures all over the world are inspired by other legislative bodies.[34] Beyond this

and later reestablished in 1940 on the basis of a multilateral agreement, the UNIDROIT statute (online: www.unidroit.org).

An example of a more preliminary project is that of the Commission on European Contract Law. The commission is a body of experts that outlines the unified Principles of European Contract Law. The actual prospects of this initiative to lead to future legislation are still not clear. See Klaus Peter Berger, "The Principles of European Contract Law and the Concept of the 'Creeping Codification' of Law" (2001) 9 *Eur. Rev. Private L.* 21; Christian V. Bar, "From Principles to Codification: Prospects for European Private Law" (2002) 8 *Colum. J. Eur. L.* 379.

[31] For instance, the General Assembly of the United Nations adopted a resolution approving the UNCITRAL Model Law on International Commercial Arbitration in 1985. This resolution only "recommends that all States give due consideration to the Model Law on International Commercial Arbitration, in view of the desirability of uniformity of the law of arbitral procedures and the specific needs of the international commercial arbitration practice." The model law was not adopted by important countries in the sphere of international arbitration, such as England, France, and Switzerland. For further elaboration on this model law and its drafting, see Howard M. Holtzman and Joseph E. Neuhaus, *A Guide to the UNCITRAL Model Law on International Commercial Arbitration: Legislative History and Commentary* (Boston: Kluwer Law and Taxation Publishers, 1989).

[32] For more information, see online: http://www.fatf-gafi.org/pages/0,2987,en_32250379_32235720_1_1_1_1_1,00.html.

[33] On this phenomenon, see Alan Schwartz and Robert E. Scott, "The Political Economy of Private Legislatures" (1995) 143 *U. Pa. L. Rev.* 595.

[34] According to Zweigert and Kotz: "Legislators all over the world have found that on many matters good laws cannot be produced without the assistance of comparative law." Zweigert and Kotz, *supra* note 17 at 16. As explained below, this description is too sweeping, in the sense that different countries are characterized by varying tendencies to look for legislative inspiration from outside. Grossfeld states

broad basis, however, the factors and processes leading to this outcome deserve closer scrutiny.

(1) Cultural tendencies favorable or adverse to external influences

Unquestionably, the dominant legal and political culture has a crucial impact on the tendency to learn from other legal systems. Some systems are relatively open to the idea of foreign influence, whereas others are characterized by animosity and suspicion toward this idea. These differences still prevail, despite growing openness worldwide to an international marketplace of ideas in an era of globalization.

The United States can generally be described as an almost "export only" legal-political culture.[35] Generally, bills drafted in the United States are not based on outside models or, at least, they do not usually rely on such knowledge deliberately. This pattern is related to a general trend prevalent in the American legal realm to refrain from reliance on comparative law, including in academia and in the courts. The American Supreme Court is famous for seldom, if ever, using comparative law,[36] and the same trend is dominant in the drafting of new legislation. This is also the case in the preparation of model legislation, such as the Uniform Commercial Code and the Model Penal Code.[37] Nevertheless, and contrary to their reluctance to draw from the experience of foreign legislation, state legislatures do consider legislation enacted by other state legislatures.[38]

By contrast, other countries show a proclivity for comparative law and legal transplants. This inclination is influenced by several factors. Germany, for instance, has a long history of basing legislation on research that includes a significant comparative component.[39] The English legal system is yet another case of a system with a tradition of learning from the outside.[40] The example of Israel is different.

regarding the use of foreign law in legislation that "legislators do indeed practice comparative law, if somewhat eclectically." See Bernard Grossfeld, *The Strength and Weakness of Comparative Law*, trans. Tony Weir (Oxford: Clarendon Press, 1990) 15. See also Peter de Cruz, *Comparative Law in a Changing World*, 2nd ed. (London: Cavendish Publishing Limited, 1999) at 20.

35 Note the correlation of this trend with the strong American tendency toward export at the material level of international trade.

36 See *Printz v. United States*, 521 U.S. 898 (1997); *Knight v. Florida*, 120 S. Ct. 459 (1999).

37 Stein states that the preparatory working papers of the American Law Institute contain only scattered references to foreign law, mostly English and Commonwealth laws. See Stein, *supra* note 5 at 211.

38 Ibid. at 212.

39 Zweigert and Kotz state in this context that "Ever since the second half of the nineteenth century, legislation in Germany has been preceded by extensive comparative legal research. This was true when commercial law was unified, first in Prussia and then in the German Empire, and also, after the Empire had acquired the necessary legislative powers, of the unification of private law, law of civil procedure, law of bankruptcy, law of judicature (courts system), and criminal law. Account was taken not only of the different laws then in force in Germany, including the French law in force in the Rhineland, but also of Dutch, Swiss and Austrian law. . . . As to the present, it can be said that no major legislation since the Second World War has been undertaken without more or less extensive research in comparative law." See Zweigert and Kotz, *supra* note 17 at 16. For concrete examples of incorporations of foreign models in German legislation, see Grossfeld, *supra* note 34 at 16–18.

40 This openness to outside inspiration is not always implemented with sufficient caution. A famous example of imported legislation failing to take into account the different conditions prevalent in the English system is that of the Industrial Relations Act 1971, which borrowed heavily from the American National Labor Relations Act originally enacted in 1935. See William B. Gould, "Taft-Hartley Comes to Great Britain: Observations on the Industrial Relations Act of 1971" (1971–1972) 81 *Yale L. J.* 1421. Eventually, it was repealed by the Trade Union and Labor Relations Act 1974. For more details on English

Historically, Israeli law was based on foreign transplants,[41] remnants of the Ottoman and British administrations that had ruled prior to the country's independence. The Israeli legal community was trained to accept, and even appreciate, the idea of foreign-inspired law, striving to use the best of models already tested elsewhere. In addition, when Israel was established in 1948, the leaders of its legal community were mainly Jews who had immigrated to Palestine after acquiring their legal education in other countries (mainly England and Germany).[42] Major legal reforms in Israel adopted through legislation have been based on foreign legislation. This is true regarding the so-called Israeli codification (the new Israeli contract laws), based on continental legislation, mainly the German B.G.B.,[43] and the *Basic Laws* on human rights enacted in 1992, heavily based on the text of the Canadian Charter.[44]

(2) Institutional capabilities for the study of comparative law

Learning from the legislation in other countries necessitates not only cultural openness but also institutional capabilities. Individual legislators are usually not equipped to engage in research of comparative law. Hence, only legislatures employing staff motivated and trained to learn from foreign legislation will eventually use this tool. In this respect as well, legislatures show significant differences. England is an example of a country that has enacted an institutional practice of learning from foreign legislation. The *Law Commission Act 1965* expressly provides for this by stating that one of the responsibilities of the Law Commission is "to obtain such information as to the legal systems of other countries as appears to the Commissioners likely to facilitate the performance of any of their functions."[45] American legislatures are not similarly equipped. In general, a comparison between these two countries shows that legislative processes in England are more professional and based on in-depth preparatory work.[46] In this case as well, we find

labor legislation based on American laws, see Lorraine M. McDonough, "The Transferability of Labor Law: Can an American Transplant Take Root in British Soil?" (1992) 13 *Comp. Lab. L.* 504.

41 Gad Tedeschi, one of the"founding fathers" of the Israeli academic legal community, wrote in this context: "In the law of the State of Israel the foreign elements predominate, and their foreign origin is obvious and unmistakable." See Guido (Gad) Tedeschi, "On Reception and the Legislative Policy of Israel" (1966) 16 *Scripta Hierosolomitana* 11 at 12. On the "mixed" nature of the Israeli legal system, see also Aharon Barak "The Tradition and Culture of the Israeli Legal System" in Alfredo M. Rabello, ed., *European Legal Traditions and Israel* (Jerusalem: Harry and Michael Sacher Institute for Legislative Research and Comparative Law, The Hebrew University of Jerusalem, 1994) 473.

42 The hegemonic view in Israel's legal community is that Jewish Law cannot be the basis for a modern secular state (aside from learning it for purposes of inspiration in specific areas). This assumption strengthens even further the inclination to learn from other legal systems.

43 For more details on the Israeli codification project, see Daphne Barak-Erez, "Codification and Legal Culture: In Comparative Perspective" (1998) 13 *Tul. Eur. & Civ. L. F.* 125.

44 Basic Law: Freedom of Occupation and Basic Law: Human Dignity and Liberty. The Canadian influence is most notable in two important provisions featuring in the new Basic Laws. First, the Basic Laws adopted the Canadian formula for reviewing legislation found to contradict rights enshrined in the Basic Laws. Second, one of them also adopts the quintessential Canadian "notwithstanding" clause, recognizing the possibility of legislation that infringes constitutional rights if it expressly declares awareness of this problem. On the Israeli Basic Laws, see Daphne Barak-Erez, "From an Unwritten to a Written Constitution: The Israeli Challenge in American Perspective" (1995) 26 *Colum. H. R. L. Rev.* 309 at 315–17.

45 *Law Commission Act 1965* (U.K.), s. 3(1) (f).

46 See P. S. Atiyah and Robert S. Summers, *Form and Substance in Anglo-American Law: A Comparative Study of Legal Reasoning, Legal Theory, and Legal Institutions* (New York: Clarendon Press, 1987) at 315–23; Stein, *supra* note 5 at 212.

nuances regarding the distinction between state and federal legislation, state legislators being less equipped and having less budget for comparative research.[47] The study of the institutional mechanisms that enable learning from the experience of other legislatures sheds further light on a question considered more thoroughly below: Do the members of various legislatures learn from each other, or is this learning confined to the professional and bureaucratic levels while the legislators themselves remain detached from it?

Another factor to bear in mind is language barriers. Legislation written in English is presently far more accessible than that written in other languages. Moreover, legislation in languages that are not used outside their national states is only rarely available to foreign legislators.

(3) Technological innovations and moral dilemmas

Areas where the legal system faces challenges on which no prior relevant experience is available are usually considered more susceptible to learning from foreign systems. This applies to innovations brought about by new technologies and to those resulting from social and cultural revolutions. Technological innovations that prompt legislators to search for models include computer issues and new reproduction technologies (such as surrogacy and human cloning). In an entirely different context but with similar results, legislatures usually need "precedents" when asked to affirm social behaviors previously deemed immoral and unacceptable. In the past, various countries adopted the no-fault divorce model by enacting legislation drawing on external inspiration.[48] A relatively new example in this context may be the inclination to review legal arrangements in other countries concerning acceptance of same-sex marriages or registered partnerships.[49] In a different direction, the new idea of covenant marriage, originating in a bill submitted in Florida, was eventually enacted in Louisiana, Arizona, and Arkansas.[50]

Often, new statutes confronting social revolutions are rights-enhancing laws. Successful legislation for the promotion of rights that had not been effectively protected in the past serves as a source of inspiration for other legislatures, due to the involvement of human rights activists in lobbying for the adoption of foreign models of rights enhancement. One of many examples in this context is the use of the *Americans with Disabilities Act 1990* as a model inspiring legislation in other countries.[51]

(4) Competition between states and economic incentives

Inspiration from foreign legislation can also be the result of competition, usually economic competition, between countries. States vie with one another for investments and new economic initiatives. Hence, lenient tax legislation or laws

[47] See also Alan Rosenthal, "The State of State Legislatures: An Overview" (1983) 11 *Hofstra L. Rev.* 1185. More information on state legislatures is provided by the National Conference of State Legislatures (NCSL) (online: www.ncsl.org).

[48] Kahn-Freund, *supra* note 4 at 14–15.

[49] On the use of comparative law for "overcoming 'taboo' subjects," see also Kai Schadbach "The Benefits of Comparative Law: A Continental European View" (1998) 16 *B. U. Int'l L. J.* 331 at 387–9.

[50] Katherine Shaw Spaht, "Revolution and Counter-Revolution: The Future of Marriage in the Law" (2003) 49 *Loy. L. Rev.* 1 at 49.

[51] See Neta Ziv, "Disability Law in Israel and the United States: A Comparative Perspective" (1999) 28 *Israel Yearbook on Human Rights* 171.

facilitating commercial activity and incremented profits are of immediate concern for competing countries.[52] The swift adoption of Westernized commercial laws in Eastern Europe should also be understood as influenced by economic incentives and competition, trying to capitalize on the preference of investors for familiar laws.[53] The dark side of this phenomenon is a race to the bottom with regard to welfare legislation and laws protecting employees' rights. In the United States, a well-known instance is the success of the corporate legislation enacted in Delaware to attract companies to register in that state. Nearly half of the corporations listed in the New York Stock Exchange are incorporated in Delaware,[54] and many other states have partially adopted the Delaware model of legislation.[55]

(5) Urgency

Countries confronting similar problems and challenges may not resort to inspiration from foreign legislation if the issues at stake need urgent solutions, especially when legislation procedures are advancing in all places simultaneously: "Anyone searching for instances of conscious transfers or transplants ought to keep in mind one caveat. A germ of a rule or of an institution may surface more or less simultaneously in widely divergent geographic areas in response to parallel social demands and without any evidence that the lawmakers concerned 'borrowed' or were even aware of the solution adopted elsewhere."[56] A recent example of statutes enacted at the same time without significant recourse to similar legislative initiatives elsewhere concerns the new antiterrorism laws enacted in several countries following the trauma of September 11, 2001. Western states aspiring to adapt their legal systems to the new war on terrorism formulated their own laws independently. Waiting for the experience of other countries was simply not possible. The *USA Patriot Act 2001* was tabled and enacted in October 2001. The United Kingdom's *Anti-Terrorism, Crime, and Security Act 2001* was introduced during November 2001 and became law by mid-December of the same year.[57]

(6) Legislation impinging on foreign states

A special case of foreign influence on domestic legislation is that of laws holding out incentives to countries which would follow their model. This may happen when the legislature of one country is interested in promoting similar legislation in other countries as well. For this purpose, it can choose to grant economic incentives to countries enacting similar legislation, or apply economic sanctions to countries

52 Reuven Avi-Yonah "Globalization, Tax Competition, and the Fiscal Crisis of the Welfare State" (2000) 113 *Harv. L. Rev.* 1573.

53 See also Schauer, *supra* note 14 at 274.

54 See Curtis Alva, "Delaware and the Market for Corporate Charters: History and Agency" (1990) 15 *Del. J. Corp. L.* 885 at 887.

55 Ibid. at 890.

56 Stein, *supra* note 5 at 206–7. The example that Stein uses to support this argument refers to the establishment of the American Securities and Exchange Commission in 1934 and the Belgian Commission Bancaire in 1935 under the impact of the worldwide crisis of the time in the trade of corporate securities.

57 For more details on these hasty legislative proceedings, see Philip A. Thomas, "Emergency and Anti-Terrorist Power: 9/11: USA and UK"(2003) 26 *Fordham Int'l L. J.* 1193 at 1209–10 and 1216–18. For a comparative discussion of the antiterrorism laws enacted in the United States, England, and Canada during the same year, see David Jenkins "In Support of Canada's Anti-Terrorism Act: A Comparison of Canadian, British, and American Anti-Terrorism Law" (2003) 66 *Sask. L. Rev.* 419.

refraining from doing so. This course of action is not common, for several reasons. First, most countries are not interested in acting in such direct ways to impose their legislative models outside. Second, most countries would not be inclined to legislate under such direct pressure. Third, the more common way of imposing legislative models on other countries is to sign international treaties whereby the contracting parties are obliged to enact certain arrangements. Fourth, incentives should be significant, making this model feasible only for a country that is particularly powerful, meaning the United States. Indeed, the classic example of the incentive model is the *American Victims of Trafficking and Violence Protection Act 2000,* aimed at combating human trafficking worldwide. This law mandates the preparation of reports regarding the state of compliance with the minimum standards set by the law for the elimination of trafficking in foreign countries. Needless to say, these measures include a prohibition on trafficking. The law states that it is the policy of the United States not to provide assistance to countries failing to comply with these minimum standards. Following that, per section 109 of the law, the president is authorized to provide assistance to foreign countries in order to help them meet minimum standards for the elimination of trafficking, including "the drafting of laws to prohibit and punish acts of trafficking."

F. THE CASE OF "FROM WELFARE TO WORK"

Let us consider a series of new laws enacted in several Western countries during the 1990s, intended to make welfare payments conditional on the recipients' willingness to seek work and remain employed. Although the idea of entwining welfare policy with incentives to work (hereinafter "workfare") is not new, it acquired much greater significance in the last decade of the twentieth century.[58] The shift in this direction in several countries is primarily a result of their need to confront the same problem, namely, the growing burden of welfare programs in Western economies. At the same time, policy decisions in some countries unquestionably influenced changes in others.

Most influential was the new U.S. legislation on workfare – the *Personal Responsibility and Work Opportunity Reconciliation Act* (PRWORA) enacted in 1996. This law required that states replace the traditional welfare programs based on unconditional cash assistance with assistance conditioned on work or participation in programs that develop potential employment skills, with only temporary and time-limited assistance to welfare recipients who are unemployed.[59] This legislation served as a model for other countries. More specifically, because the first state to introduce a new welfare regime based on this federal legislation was Wisconsin,

[58] An analysis of the changes introduced in the direction of workfare in Western countries is found in *"An Offer You Can't Refuse": Workfare in International Perspective,* Ivar Lodemel and Heather Trickey, eds. (Bristol, UK: Policy Press, 2000) [*An Offer You Can't Refuse*]. The book surveys the laws on this matter in France, Germany, the Netherlands, Norway, Denmark, Britain, and the United States. For a theoretical critique of the workfare trend, see Joel F. Handler, *Social Citizenship and Workfare in the United States and Western Europe: The Paradox of Inclusion* (Cambridge: Cambridge University Press, 2004).

[59] See: Michael Wiseman, "Making Work for Welfare in the United States" in *An Offer You Can't Refuse,* ibid. at 215. For criticism, see Kathleen A. Kost and Frank W. Munger, "Fooling All the People Some of the Time: 1990's Welfare Reform and the Exploitation of American Values" (1996) 4 *Va. J. Soc. Pol'y & L.* 3; Joel Handler, "The 'Third Way' or the Old Way?" (2000) 48 *Kan. L. Rev.* 765.

whenever the U.S. example serves as a source of inspiration the model most often cited is that of the so-called Wisconsin Program, or Wisconsin Works.[60]

The U.S. influence was most extensively discussed in the literature that focused on the operation of workfare programs in the United Kingdom.[61] A caveat, however, is in place here. The British statute on which the new workfare programs were based – the *Jobseekers Act 1995* – preceded the *Personal Responsibility and Work Opportunity Reconciliation Act,* enacted in 1996. The U.S. statute, then, did not affect the legislative sphere; rather, it left its mark on policy decisions and programs (known as the British "New Deal") accepted in the framework of existing law. Israeli law presents a "cleaner" example of adopting the American model on workfare through legislation. Following the report of a professional committee on the problem of welfare recipients unemployed for prolonged periods, which recommended the adoption of the U.S. model,[62] the government tabled a bill to that effect.[63] This bill was presented to the Israeli Knesset as an integral part of the government's economic budget and was therefore enacted into law without any significant changes.[64]

The British and Israeli cases may appear as two different examples of the impact that the new American welfare legislation had on other legal systems – one of influence on the bureaucracy and the other of influence on the legislature. On closer scrutiny, however, they emerge as very close to one another. In both of them, the U.S. inspiration operated at the bureaucratic level, with members of the legislature playing a marginal role. In the U.K., the government found that it could implement the U.S. model using existing legislation. In Israel, legislation was needed, but it was drafted and formulated by government officials. Although the legislature voted on it, its role was formal: The inspiration of the U.S. legislation was based on the initiative of government officials and mediated by them.

G. INSPIRATION WITHOUT A COMMUNITY

Having demonstrated that statutes have significant influence outside the borders of the territory to which they apply, the question is whether legislatures in different

[60] For the impact of the Wisconsin model of privatizing welfare, see Gillian E. Metzger, "Privatization as Delegation" (2003) 103 *Colum. L. Rev.* 1367 at 1385–6.

For the Wisconsin Model, see also Kelly S. Mikelson, "Wisconsin Works: Meeting the Need of Hard to Serve Participants" (2003) 8 *Geo. Public Pol'y Rev.* 65. For the New York experience, see Andrew Stettner, "A Dubious Future: The Challenge of Welfare Reform in New York City" (1999) 5 *Geo. Public Pol'y Rev.* 73.

[61] For the U.K. New Deal programs, see Heather Trickey and Robert Walker, "Steps to Compulsion within British Labour Market Policies" in *An Offer You Can't Refuse, supra* note 58 at 181. For U.S. influence on these programs, see Alan Deacon, "Learning from the US? The Influence of American Ideas Upon 'New Labour' Thinking on Welfare Reform" (2000) 28 *Policy & Politics* 5; Joseph P. Rompala, "'Once More Unto the Breach, Dear Friends': Recurring Themes in Welfare Reform in the United States and Great Britain and What the Principle of Subsidiarity Can Do to Break the Pattern" (2003) 29 *J. Legis.* 307. In his analysis of workfare regimes developed in Western countries, Joel Handler points to the development of a "US–UK model," with distinct features. Handler, *supra* note 58 at 15. At the same time, he adds: "Subject to the above caveats . . . there is substantial evidence that many of the negative practices found in the United States are also appearing in the administration of workfare in Western Europe." Ibid.

[62] *Interim Report of the Tamir Committee* (2001).

[63] Chapter F of the Economic Policy for the Budget Year 2004 (Legislation Amendments) Bill, 2003.

[64] Chapter G of the Economic Policy for the Budget Year 2004 (Legislation Amendments) Law, 2004.

countries can be regarded as constituting one international community, resembling the other international communities that legal scholarship has already traced (of judges and of activists). Although the above discussion showed that laws can exert significant influence beyond their country of origin, I propose to answer this question in the negative. The dynamics of legislation influencing foreign legislative initiatives should rather be described as based on inspiration without a community.

Judges and rights activists share a common background – either professional (in the case of judges) or ideological (in the case of human rights activists) – as well as similar value systems. By contrast, members of legislatures in different countries do not share a common background. At most, and only to a limited extent, members of parties with similar ideologies have a shared background (conservatives, socialists, "green" parties, and so forth). Moreover, members of legislative bodies feel accountable mostly to their constituents. This is their most significant link and the only one that can guarantee their professional future. Members of legislative bodies are also less exposed to their colleagues in other countries. Leading party members may take part in delegations visiting other legislatures, but most legislators stay at home. International institutions encouraging cooperation between legislatures for the purpose of mutual learning and experience sharing do not seem to be relevant to the daily work of ordinary legislators.[65]

Against this background, how can one account for the influence of foreign legislation on local statutes? One explanation ascribes it to professional involvement at the bill-drafting stage. This explanation applies to private bills submitted by individual legislators and prepared by their professional staff as well as to government bills drafted by legal advisors. The professionals working on the bills, be they legal advisors or other experts, do engage in dialogue with their foreign colleagues. The actual community behind the scenes therefore is a community of professionals. Learning from the legislative experience of other countries involves an economic dimension as well. It is a costly matter dependent on resources and on the ability to use professional assistance and is thus not available to the same extent in different countries.

In other cases, the network transferring ideas from one country to another is composed of activists in human rights groups and other nongovernmental organizations lobbying for the promotion of rights-enhancing laws and laws aimed at improving quality of life at large, such as environmental statutes. In these examples, the community behind the scenes is made up of activists and is not, once again, a community of legislatures as such.

Even in the process of drafting international agreements and model laws eventually affecting domestic legislation, the influential actors are professionals and interest groups. State delegates participating in the process of preparing international conventions and model laws are often not members of national legislatures but professionals – civil servants or academic experts. Other players in the international arena are interest groups seeking to influence the drafting of conventions so as to guarantee a favorable regime that will benefit them once these conventions

[65] Examples of interparliamentary activities or bodies include the International Organization of Parliaments of Sovereign States (IPU) (online: www.ipu.org); Commonwealth Parliamentary Association (CPA) (online: www.cpahq.org); Assemblée Parlementaire de la Francophonie (online: www.francophonie.org/apf/); Union Parlementaire Africaine (online: www.uafparl.org); Inter-Parliamentary Forum of the Americas (FIPA) (online: www.e-fipa.org), and others.

influence domestic legislation.[66] The same can be said of other bodies preparing model legislation, such as the American NCCUSL, which are based on the participation of professionals and susceptible to the influence of business interests.

In some instances, however, it is possible to trace direct influence of legislatures outside their countries. When the subject matter of the legislation is not strictly professional but rather a matter of public awareness, such as legislation on same-sex couples, the flow of information between countries provides members of legislative bodies with relevant, unmediated information, and they are influenced by it directly (whether they wish to adopt or oppose the foreign model). Also in this case, individual legislators who build their case on the experience of other countries probably do not feel part of an international community of legislatures either. Still, their argumentation could be viewed as the beginning of a dialogue between legislatures, even if limited in several regards. First, as noted, individual legislators are motivated to look for inspiration in foreign legislation mainly when the legislation touches on value issues, such as the recognition of same-sex marriages. In matters requiring expertise, the parties to the international dialogue are the professionals who draft the laws. Second, the so-called dialogue often assumes the form of a monologue, namely, countries adopting foreign models of legislation usually do not serve as legislation models for other countries. Eastern Europe adopted Western models of legislation but has never been viewed as a relevant source of legal inspiration by American lawyers or legislators. The judicial community, by contrast, is more egalitarian. Because this is a professional community, worthy precedents from small countries can be a source of inspiration also to judges active in countries that are politically and economically more powerful. Third, even when legislatures use the information regarding laws in other countries, they do not limit the scope of their learning to the legislative arena. A legal principle originally introduced in the exporting country by way of judicial interpretation will sometimes be adopted in the importing country by way of legislation.[67] In other words, legislators refer to any relevant source of inspiration, without granting priority to the principles created by their legislative counterparts.

ACKNOWLEDGMENTS

I thank Aeyal Gross, Tsvi Kahana, Gidon Sapir, and Roy Kreitner for their comments on earlier drafts. Additional thanks for useful comments go to Tania Groppi, Stephane Marsolais, Moin Yahya, and many other participants at the Conference on Legislatures and Constitutionalism, Banff, July 2004. I am also thankful to Batya Stein for the editing.

[66] See Eyal Benvenisti, "Exit and Voice in the Age of Globalization" (1999) 98 *Mich. L. Rev.* 167 at 200.

[67] For example, American sexual harassment law served as a source of inspiration for legislation in other countries, although in the United States itself this legal branch was developed by way of interpreting legislation on equality at work rather than through legislation.

28 Legislatures in Dialogue with One Another: Dissent, Decisions, and the Global Polity

Heather K. Gerken

Much academic work on legislative dialogue focuses on legislatures in conversation with other actors *within* the state. This chapter switches the focus to a different type of conversation: legislatures in dialogue with one another. Specifically, this chapter draws on a robust empirical literature suggesting that nation-states function like members of a "global polity," much as individuals are embedded in their own societies. They thus follow one another's lead just as individuals do. These empirical findings raise an intriguing policy question: Given the tendency of nation-states (and their legislatures) to engage in mimicry, how do we improve the quality of interlegislative dialogue?

This chapter offers an unusual response to that question. It argues that better decision making within legislatures may depend on variation among them. Drawing on a divergent set of literatures – global polity research, the democratic experimentalism literature, and Cass Sunstein's work on dissent – this chapter discusses a question relevant to any inquiry about improving legislative decision making: how to encourage productive dissent (at least under a Millian account) in the legislative process. The chapter is not intended to offer a fully developed set of answers to that question or even an in-depth analysis of the costs and benefits of the alternatives proposed here.[1] Offered in the spirit of a thought experiment, the chapter merely proposes a more precise set of analytic tools for considering it.

Specifically, this chapter offers a novel account of dissent that focuses on those instances where would-be dissenters have a chance to wield governmental authority and express their disagreement by rendering an outlier decision. The chapter argues that governance decisions by global minorities that enjoy a local majority can sometimes be understood as a variant of dissent. "Dissenting by deciding" is not a contradiction in terms but an unappreciated avenue for furthering the fundamental aims of dissent.[2] And it is one that may prove particularly useful for addressing the peculiar pathologies that can arise from interlegislative dialogue.

1 In this chapter, I merely try to sketch the best affirmative case that can be made in favor of decisional dissent, leaving a full analysis of its costs and benefits for another day.

2 For an in-depth exploration of these ideas as they relate to the three main categories of First Amendment scholarship (the marketplace of ideas, the role dissent plays in furthering the project of self-governance, and self-expression), see Heather K. Gerken, "Dissenting by Deciding" (2005) 56 *Stan. L. Rev.* 1745. Portions of this chapter draw from that article.

I. DISSENTING BY DECIDING

Everyone, it seems, believes in dissent. Our political mythology promotes a romantic vision: the solitary voice of reason, Holmes's prescient dissents, the lone juror in *Twelve Angry Men*. When talking about the role dissenters play in democratic governance, scholars offer a more workmanlike view. The conventional understanding of dissent as a practice recognizes that dissent is more than culturally resonant; it is a political strategy. Like any minority faction, dissenters can often get the majority to soften its views or at least obtain a concession or two. Scholars thus grasp that dissenters can wield power through participation or presence rather than persuasion.[3]

On this conventional understanding of dissent, dissenters have two choices with regard to governance: *act moderately* or *speak radically*.[4] To the extent that would-be dissenters want to govern – to engage in a public act, to wield the authority of the state[5] – they must try to influence the decision-making process. They will thus bargain with their votes and with the threat of public dissent to gain concessions from the majority. Would-be dissenters who deploy this strategy get to take part in an act of governance, but it is governance of a moderate sort. And even if the dissenter gets an opportunity to wield the authority of the state, dissent takes the form of an argument, one designed to persuade other members of the decision-making body to take a different stance. Dissenters speak truth *to* power – to those with a majority of the votes.

Alternatively, would-be dissenters on the conventional view can speak radically – that is, they can freely state the position they believe that the majority ought to take in a dissenting opinion or minority report. In doing so, dissenters sacrifice the chance to be part of the governing majority and thus to wield the authority of the state. When they speak, it is with a critical rather than authoritative voice; they speak on behalf of themselves, not the polity. Dissent, again, takes the form of an argument, speaking truth *to* power.

[3] The dictionary defines dissent simply as "withhold[ing] assent; not approv[ing]; object[ing]." *Webster's Third New International Dictionary of the English Language*, unabridged ed. (Springfield, Mass.: Merriam-Webster, 1993). This chapter uses the term *dissenter* in a more specific sense, to refer to someone who subscribes to an outlier view on an issue that she deems salient to her identity. A dissenter is someone whom we would naturally term an "electoral minority" because of the positions she holds. The arguments deployed here can be applied to many types of electoral minorities – racial, socioeconomic, political, religious – provided that the views of the population are divided along some axis of difference and the issue is one that individuals would deem germane to their political identity.

[4] They can, of course, do both at the same time – that is, speak radically first in the hope of getting more concessions when they are ready to act later. The trade-off with which this chapter is concerned, however, is between (1) these two variants of conventional dissent (acting moderately and speaking radically) singly or in combination, and (2) decisional dissent (acting radically).

[5] Throughout the chapter, I use variants of these terms – *public act, acting with the authority of the state, acting on behalf of the state, speaking truth with power* – to convey the notion that would-be dissenters wield state power; they render a decision on behalf of the government or some part of it. Although these terms come closest to conveying what is at stake in dissenting by deciding, they tread on certain terms of art deployed in other literatures. For instance, in describing the way dissenters issue a decision on behalf of the state, I do not mean to invoke the notion of *state action*, a term of art used in identifying a constitutional harm. Similarly, in some literatures, a *public* act refers not just to a governmental decision, but to anything done outside the privacy of one's home or in the presence of other members of one's community. Similarly, *speaking truth with power* here refers not to power in the most general of senses – that is, capable of having an effect – but *governmental* power.

What is missing from the usual account of dissent is a third possibility: that would-be dissenters could *act radically*. We have trouble envisioning dissent taking the form of state action. Our conventional intuition is that dissenters will try to change decision makers' minds, they may even moderate the decision rendered, but they will not – and ought not – determine the outcome of decision unless they can persuade the majority to alter its views.

The assumption underlying this conventional view of dissent is that dissent means speaking truth *to* power, not *with* it. That is, we assume that dissenters will be in the minority on any decision-making body. After all, we might think, if would-be dissenters had enough votes to control the outcome of the decision-making process, they would not be "dissenters" anymore. "Dissenting by deciding" seems like a contradiction in terms.

The main reason we overlook the possibility of dissenting by deciding is that we tend to conceive of democratic bodies as unitary – there is *one* legislature rendering *the* law, *one* populace voting on *the* initiative. It is thus quite difficult to discern what power an electoral minority ought to have in making *the* decision. Our intuitions about the legitimacy of majority rule lead us to resist proposals for minority rule, including those that would allow would-be dissenters to "take turns"[6] in exercising majority power or those creating a minority veto. We thus assume that the best – perhaps the only – model for distributing power fairly is to let electoral minorities influence a governmental decision or, failing that, to make their disagreement known publicly.

Where decision-making power is disaggregated – as with juries, school committees, local governments, even nation-states within a global polity – there are more options for thinking about how to allocate decision-making authority among members of the minority and majority. Disaggregated institutions create the opportunity for dissenters to decide, to *act* on behalf of the state. *Dissenting by deciding* thus occurs when would-be dissenters – individuals who hold a minority view within the polity as a whole – enjoy a local majority on a decision-making body and can thus dictate the outcome. Examples outside of the context discussed here – dialogue among national legislatures – could include a locality's decision to marry gays and lesbians, a school committee run by Christian fundamentalists deciding to teach creationism, or a jury dominated by libertarians engaging in nullification. In these circumstances, the notion of a "dissenting by deciding" is not a contradiction in terms. The decision makers in each instance subscribe to the same set of commitments held by individuals whom we would unthinkingly term "dissenters." But they express disagreement not through conventional means but by offering a real-life instantiation of their views. What is different in these instances is the *form* dissent takes.

Dissenting by deciding should be understood as an alternative strategy for institutionalizing channels for dissent within the democratic process. But because dissent has not been conceptualized in these terms, scholars have not given adequate thought to which form of dissent is preferable, and when.

In the remainder of the chapter, I suggest the salience of decisional dissent to interlegislative dialogue. This argument draws on the traditional Millian notion of

[6] See Lani Guinier, *The Tyranny of the Majority: Fundamental Fairness in Representative Democracy* (New York: Free Press, 1994) at 65–6.

the role dissent ought to play in a decision-making process – the idea that exposure to dissent improves the quality of our decisions. For dissent to play this productive role, it must be *visible*. And conventional dissent and decisional dissent make difference visible in quite different ways.

Specifically, Part II argues that those who have posed dissent as a solution to the problem of conformity have not given adequate consideration to the varied forms conformity can take. Conformity can take place *within* organizations and, as cutting-edge social science research reveals, it can take place *among* them. The notions of conventional and decisional dissent suggest that these phenomena may require different institutional cures. The taxonomy of dissent offered here thus provides a more precise set of analytic tools for implementing this functional account of dissent. Part III applies the insights derived from Part II to the question posed at the beginning of this chapter: how to institutionalize channels for dissent in a manner that improves the quality of interlegislative dialogue.

II. DISSENTING BY DECIDING AND THE MARKETPLACE OF IDEAS

Political theorists have long grasped the importance of dissent to sound decision making. Here I pull one analytic thread from this long line of analysis: the conventional Millian idea that dissent allows a society to test its views and positions, to assure itself of the accuracy of some views and to correct others. As Mill writes of the "peculiar evil of silencing the expression of [a dissenting] opinion," we should treasure dissenting opinions both because "[i]f the opinion is right, [we] are deprived of the opportunity of exchanging error for truth; if wrong, [we] lose, what is almost as great a benefit, the clearer perception and livelier impression of truth produced by its collision with error."[7] In legal circles, of course, this argument generally travels under the rubric of the "marketplace of ideas."[8]

In order for dissent to function in the manner Mill envisioned, it must be visible. If would-be dissenters keep their views to themselves, their ideas will never reach the marketplace of ideas. The crucial question here is whether conventional dissent

[7] John Stuart Mill, *On Liberty*, Elizabeth Rapaport, ed. (Indianapolis: Hackett Publishing Co., 1978) (1859) at 16. Mill was preceded, of course, by John Milton. See John Milton, *Areopagitica: A Speech for the Liberty of Unlicensed Printing* (1644) (Oxford: Clarendon Press, 1904) at 51–2.

[8] *Lamont v. Postmaster General of the U.S.*, 381 U.S. 301, 308 (1965); see also *Abrams v. United States*, 250 U.S. 616 at 630 (1919) (Holmes, J., dissenting) (describing the importance of "the competition of the market"). See also generally Thomas I. Emerson, "Toward a General Theory of the First Amendment" (1973) 72 *Yale L.J.* 877; Zechariah Chafee Jr., *Free Speech in the United States* (Cambridge, Mass.: Harvard University Press, 1967); William P. Marshall, "In Defense of the Search for Truth as a First Amendment Justification" (1995) 30 *Ga. L. Rev.* 1; George R. Wright, "A Rationale from J. S. Mill for the Free Speech Clause" [1985] *Sup. Ct. Rev.* 149. For the views of the skeptics, see, e.g., Frederick Schauer, *Free Speech: A Philosophical Enquiry* (New York: Cambridge University Press, 1982) at 19–29; Harry H. Wellington, "On Freedom of Expression" (1979) 88 *Yale L.J.* 1105; Jerome A. Barron, "Access to the Press – A New First Amendment Right" (1967) 80 *Harv. L. Rev.* 1641; C. Edwin Baker, "Scope of the First Amendment Freedom of Speech" (1978) 25 *U.C.L.A.L. Rev.* 964; Stanley Ingber, "The Marketplace of Ideas: A Legitimizing Myth" [1984] *Duke L.J.*; Owen M. Fiss, "Why the State?" (1987) 100 *Harv. L. Rev.* 781 at 787–8; Martin H. Redish, "The Value of Free Speech" (1982) 130 *U. Pa. L. Rev.* 591. For an effort to distinguish the search for truth from the marketplace of ideas, see generally Steven H. Shiffrin, *The First Amendment: Democracy and Romance* (Cambridge, Mass.: Harvard University Press, 1990); Steven H. Shiffrin, *Dissent, Injustice, and the Meanings of America* (Princeton, N.J.: Princeton University Press, 1999).

and dissenting by deciding produce different *kinds* of visibility for dissenting views. Below I explore that question, suggesting that they are different in Part II.A and speculating as to why this difference might matter to our thinking about how best to institutionalize dissent in Part II.B. I then turn to considering how these arguments play out in the context of interlegislative dialogue in Part III.

A. Decisional dissent and its role in making disagreement visible

If our goal is to make disagreement visible, the most salient difference between conventional dissent and dissenting by deciding is that the latter takes the form of a decision, not an argument.[9] As noted above, conventional dissenters have two choices: act moderately or speak radically. In either case, dissenters make arguments. Dissenters who act moderately try to persuade the majority on the decision-making body to soften its views. Dissenters who speak radically also make an argument, one directed both to majority of the decision-making body and to those outside of it.

Acting radically, in contrast, allows dissenters to express their disagreement through a decision. They are able to offer a concrete, real-world example of what their principles would look like in practice. It thus bears some resemblance to certain acts of civil disobedience.[10] Consider an example drawn from contemporary U.S. politics: San Francisco's decision to marry gays and lesbians. San Francisco officials surely understood that, with respect to the state population, theirs was the minority view. They surely understood their action to be a challenge of sorts to the prevailing view,[11] and that assessment was shared by others.[12] The principle embodied in San Francisco's decision was no different than the argument found in editorials, judicial dissents, and ongoing debates about the status of gays and lesbians in the United States.

What was different was the *form* dissent took. As a result of the city's decision, newspapers across the country carried stories about the marriages of elderly lesbian couples or gay lovers who had raised children together. San Francisco's decision gave us a concrete practice, not just an abstract issue, to debate. As *The New York Times* explained, "[t]he television images from San Francisco brought gay marriage

[9] I do not mean to suggest that acting radically precludes the use of argument or that acting moderately depends entirely on argument and thus does not leave room for the other activities, like bargaining. The point here is simply that conventional dissent is largely confined to argument – indeed, can be made visible only *through* argument – whereas decisional dissent (even if supported by argument) takes a concrete, instantiated form.

[10] Civil disobedience, like decisional dissent, can be understood as an act of partial disobedience, as I explore in Gerken, *supra* note 2. Indeed, as a conceptual matter, decisional dissent falls somewhere between civil disobedience and free speech, the two dominant strands of the dissent tradition. If one thinks of the free speech/free press tradition as *speaking with permission* (because the state recognizes the right of dissenters to speak against it) and civil disobedience as *acting without permission* (as it involves a deliberate violation of an existing law), dissenting by deciding represents an unusual fusion of the two. It involves acting (as with civil disobedience) with permission (like free speech). Ibid.; see also *infra* note 19 (drawing additional connections between decisional dissent and civil disobedience).

[11] Mayor Newsom, for instance, has invoked Martin Luther King's famous argument in favor of civil disobedience in justifying San Francisco's decision. http://www.gavinnewsom.com/index.php?id+47 (last visited Mar. 1, 2005) (reprinting transcript of an interview with Gavin Newsom where he invoked King's "Letter from a Birmingham Jail").

[12] See, e.g., Editorial, "The Road to Gay Marriage," *N.Y. Times* (March 7, 2004) A12 (arguing that San Francisco's mayor was engaged in a "civil rights tradition" akin to refusing to obey Jim Crow laws).

into America's living rooms in a way no court decision could."[13] One supporter of the decision sounded a similar theme, arguing that San Francisco's decision "put a face on discrimination."[14]

Consider also Ernest Young's claim about the relationship between federalism and political opposition. Young argues that opposition parties in federal systems are more successful than those, like the British Tories, in nonfederal systems because the former have a chance to govern in some subpart of the system. Both Tories and present-day Democrats are challenging the national dominance of another party. But contestation takes an intriguing form in the United States. In Young's view, "because the loyal opposition can not only oppose but actually govern at the state level" in federal systems, it can "develop a track record of success."[15] Thus, he argues, "the Democrats' control of so many statehouses" after losing the Senate in 2002 "'prepared the ground for a revival of their own party,'" whereas the Tories' electoral failures can be attributed at least in part to the fact that "'they lack a testing ground for their ideas.'"[16] According to Young, it is not a coincidence that "four of the last five presidents were former governors who developed a reputation for competence at the state level while the other party held the White House."[17]

1. ACTING MODERATELY VERSUS ACTING RADICALLY. It is not difficult to grasp the difference between dissenting by deciding (acting radically), on the one hand, and one variant of conventional dissent (acting moderately), on the other. Because dissenting by deciding takes the form of an outlier decision, not an argument, it is inherently visible to the polity.[18] When conventional dissenters use their votes to gain concessions from the majority, in contrast, dissent is confined *within* the decision-making body. It takes the form of an argument to the majority of decision makers. It is quite visible to members of the majority, those whom the dissenters are lobbying or trying to convince. But at the aggregate level, although we might see the *effects* of conventional dissent – a slightly less mainstream decision, a concession or two for the out-group – the substance of the dissenters' views is likely to remain opaque.

Consider, for instance, the difference between a verdict rendered by a jury with one juror who is suspicious of prosecutorial misconduct and a decision to nullify by a jury filled with such jurors. Or imagine the likelihood that the policies of a school committee that includes a member of a left-leaning minority will make the left's views visible compared to the likelihood that a committee dominated by left-leaning members will do so. To the extent that conventional dissenters choose to join the decision rather than distance themselves from it, policies may shift moderately, but dissent will be submerged at the politywide level.

[13] Ibid.

[14] Carla Marinucci, "Newsom in Spotlight – Even if Gay Marriage Issue Isn't," *S.F. Chron.* (July 28, 2004) A10 (quoting Pam Cooke).

[15] Ernest A. Young, "The Rehnquist Court's Two Federalisms" (2004) 83 *Tex. L. Rev.* 1 at 60–1.

[16] Ibid. (quoting "A Tale of Two Legacies," *Economist* [Dec. 19, 2002]).

[17] Ibid. at 59.

[18] Although the decision itself is public, the identity and commitments of the dissenters may not be. See Gerken, *supra* note 2.

2. ACTING RADICALLY VERSUS SPEAKING RADICALLY. The more interesting question is whether dissenting by deciding is different from publicizing a dissenting view, the other choice available to conventional dissenter. Is *acting* radically different from *speaking* radically? After all, there are many avenues for making disagreement public that do not involve rendering a decision. Much of the doctrine governing free speech is preoccupied with preserving such avenues. Nonetheless, dissenting by deciding provides a type of visibility that may be hard to reproduce by publishing a dissenting opinion, let alone writing an opinion editorial or answering a survey. Here again, there is a difference between dissent that takes the form of a decision and dissent that is expressed through argument.

To begin, dissenting by deciding may provide a more useful tool for agenda setting. Dissenting by deciding has a direct political consequence. That fact may ensure it receives attention that conventional dissent might not. To be sure, speaking radically – publicizing disagreement – can have political consequences; it may, for instance, shame the majority into changing its position. Because conventional dissent lacks a binding legal effect, however, under many circumstances it can simply be ignored.

Dissenting by deciding is harder to ignore because it takes the form of a decision rendered; getting rid of it generally means formally overruling it or persuading would-be dissenters to abandon it. Decisional dissent can thus force members of the majority to act, reevaluate, and engage with the decision and with those who made it.[19] It thereby allows electoral minorities to put an issue on the table and force a reluctant majority to engage in the conversation – precisely the type of agenda setting that is otherwise difficult for those outside the political mainstream.[20]

One might argue that dissenting decisions can be ignored as well, at least when they resolve a sufficiently trivial issue. To be sure, not all governance decisions are the stuff of national or international debate. The claim here, however, is only that an outlier decision about even a trivial issue is less likely to be ignored than a published dissent to the majority's preferred resolution of that trivial question.

3. REMAPPING THE POLITICS OF THE POSSIBLE. Even setting aside the possibility that a decision rather than an argument will lend more visibility to a dissenting view, there may be a difference in what precisely we end up seeing when dissent is couched in these competing forms. Dissent that takes the form of an argument takes on a distinctive, albeit familiar cast. When a minority caucus is formed or a dissenting view is published, conventional dissenters can only announce their

[19] Here again, dissenting by deciding bears some resemblance to civil disobedience. See, e.g., Martin Luther King, Jr., "Letter from a Birmingham Jail" (in James Melvin Washington, ed., 1991, *A Testament of Hope: The Essential Writing of Martin Luther King, Jr.*, p. 289; Apr. 16, 1963) (arguing that civil disobedience "seeks to create . . . a crisis and establish such creative tension that a community that has constantly refused to negotiate is forced to confront the issue. It seeks so to dramatize [an] issue so that it can no longer be ignored").

[20] On agenda setting generally, see, e.g., William Riker, *Liberalism Against Populism* (San Francisco: W. H. Freeman, 1982); John W. Kingdon, *Agendas, Alternatives and Public Policies* (Boston: Little, Brown, 1984); Roger W. Cobb and Charles E. Elder, *Participation in American Politics: The Dynamics of Agenda-Building* (Boston: Allyn & Bacon, 1972); Frank R. Baumgartner and Bryan Jones, *Agendas and Instability in American Politics* (Chicago: University of Chicago Press, 1993).

views in the abstract. All they can do is describe what members of their group would do *if* they had the power to decide.

Dissenting by deciding, in contrast, offers a real-life instantiation of an idea. It thus allows electoral minorities to remap the politics of the possible. When dissent takes the form of decision, electoral minorities have a chance to put their ideas into practice, to move from abstract principles to actual policy.[21] Decisional dissent gives us a concrete practice to examine, a real-world example to debate. We not only get to see whether the idea works, but how the new policy fits or clashes with existing institutional practices. *Speaking* radically thus looks different from *acting* radically.[22]

Even the mere fact that dissenters are, in effect, putting their money where their mouths are may lend the decision concreteness and weight in the eyes of the majority. Dissenters who decide take on not just the power associated with membership in the majority, but the responsibility. Dissenters no longer enjoy the luxury of the critic: inaction. They must figure out how to put their ideas into practice, negotiate a compromise, and, most importantly, live with the consequences of their critique. A jury filled with those who think our sentencing regime is unduly punitive must set a guilty defendant free in a case where the victim is more than a cipher. A zoning commission filled with pro-environmentalists will be forced to vote against worthy projects to protect the environment. A school committee that believes creationism should be taught in the school must choose a textbook, figure out precisely how to integrate those arguments with the school's science curriculum, and decide how to accommodate the views of those who think creationism does not belong in the school. Here again, dissenting by deciding makes difference visible differently than conventional dissent.

B. The dynamics of decision making – conformity, polarization, and cascades – and the appropriate institutional cure

Once we understand the difference between the type of visibility afforded by conventional dissent and dissenting by deciding, the question is when we would choose one strategy for institutionalizing dissent over another if we subscribe to Mill's view that dissent can improve our decision making. One useful way to ground

[21] This argument finds some support in the federalism literature, in which a number of scholars have argued that one of the strengths of a federal system is that it allows states to become what Justice Brandeis termed "laborator[ies]" of democracy. *New State Ice Co. v. Liebmann*, 285 U.S. 262, 311 (1932) (Brandeis, J., dissenting).

[22] These observations, of course, are consistent with some of the justifications offered for standing doctrine by courts and commentators. See, e.g., *Valley Forge Christian College v. Americans United for Separation of Church & State*, Inc., 454 U.S. 464, 472 (1982) ("[The specific injury requirement] tends to assure that the legal questions presented to the court will be resolved, not in the rarified atmosphere of a debating society, but in a concrete factual context conducive to a realistic appreciation of the consequences of judicial action."); Alexander M. Bickel, *The Least Dangerous Branch: The Supreme Court at the Bar of Politics*, 2nd ed. (New Haven: Yale University Press, 1986) at 115 ("there are sound reasons, grounded not only in theory, but in the judicial experience of centuries, here and elsewhere, for believing that the hard, confining, and yet enlarging context of a real controversy leads to sounder and more enduring judgments"); William A. Fletcher, "The Structure of Standing" (1998) 98 *Yale L.J.* 221 at 222 (one of the "stated purposes of standing" is "that a concrete case informs the court of the consequences of its decisions"); Richard H. Fallon, Jr., "Of Justiciability, Remedies, and Public Law Litigation: Notes on the Jurisprudence of Lyons" (1984) *N.Y.U. L. Rev.* 1 at 13–14 ("[a] specific and concrete injury helps frame issues in a factual context suitable for judicial resolution").

the analysis is to consider an alternative method for advancing the Millian aim of improving decision making: Cass Sunstein's recent work on the dynamics of dissent.[23] Because Sunstein's work draws on the Millian tradition and focuses on specifying mechanisms for institutionalizing dissent, it provides a useful example for thinking about the role dissenting by deciding might play in furthering the aims of dissent. It also provides an entrée into the question at the heart of this chapter: how to harness dissent in the service of healthy interlegislative dialogue.

1. DECISION-MAKING PATHOLOGIES AND THE NEED FOR DISSENT. Sunstein identifies three decision-making pathologies where dissent may provide a needed corrective: conformity, polarization, and cascades.[24] *Conformity* refers to the human tendency to do what everyone else is doing. The presence of a dissenter, say, on a corporate board or in an investment group can reduce the pressure to conform and thus free individuals on a decision-making body to share information or challenge the wisdom of a particular course of action. *Polarization* takes place when a group of people who agree upon an outcome reinforce each other's views during the decision-making process. As a result, the group takes a more extreme position than one would predict given its members' predeliberation tendencies.[25] *Cascades* involve conformity over time; a set of decision makers makes a choice and subsequent decision makers, influenced by the apparent agreement of the first movers, make the same choice even if they would have not reached such a decision independently.[26]

A recognition of the differences between conventional dissent and dissenting by deciding suggests that the pathologies Sunstein identifies may require different institutional cures. Conventional dissent – which is achieved by the presence of one or more potential dissenters on every decision-making body – seems the natural cure for conformity and polarization. The presence of one or more dissenters in every group seems likely to reduce the chances that the group will reach the "wrong" decision.

Dissenting by deciding, however, may be necessary to avoid cascades. If cascades stem from the unanimity among the decisions of first movers, an outlier decision seems like the most effective strategy for eliminating the appearance of consensus. It seems, in other words, to provide the right kind of visibility for the dissenters' view.

To put these concepts in more concrete terms, consider how these phenomena play out in the context of Sunstein's example of appellate panels. Sunstein argues that, given the important role dissent plays in helping people to get the right answer in a group decision-making process, each appellate panel would ideally include a judge who has been nominated by a different party than that which nominated the other judges sitting on the panel. His proposal would mean that each panel would contain either two judges nominated by Democrats and one nominated by a Republican, or two Republican nominees and one Democratic nominee. Sunstein, in other words, seeks conventional dissent on appellate panels.[27]

[23] Cass R. Sunstein, *Why Societies Need Dissent* (Cambridge, Mass.: Harvard University Press, 2003).
[24] Ibid. at 10–11 (defining all three terms).
[25] Ibid. at 11.
[26] Ibid. at 10–11.
[27] Ibid. at 166–93.

From the perspective of individual cases, one might think this proposal is all to the good. If we are worried about conformity or polarization, Sunstein's proposal is an excellent one. It would reduce the likelihood that group members would goad one another into a more extreme position than the group's members' predeliberation views would suggest.

If we are worried about *cascades*, however, we would probably want to encourage *decisions* that embody a dissenting view. If an outlier decision is our goal, it is not clear that we want a system in which each appellate panel includes someone from the other party. What we might lose under such a plan is dissent visible at the aggregate level – a decision that embodies the dissenting or outlier view – which could eliminate the appearance of consensus and short-circuit the cascade. If cascades are our biggest concern, it may be useful to have the perspective that an "ideologically amplified" decision made by an all-Democratic nominee or all-Republican nominee panel would provide.[28]

THE TRADE-OFF BETWEEN CONVENTIONAL AND DECISIONAL DISSENT. The notions of conventional dissent and dissenting by deciding also suggest a trade-off embedded in the choice we make about the appropriate mechanism for institutionalizing dissent. The two strategies can, of course, coexist – even complement one another – within a democratic scheme. Nonetheless, this framing device suggests that it may not always be possible to foster *both* types of dissent simultaneously within the same institution. At least within a given institution, there is a trade-off between conventional dissent and dissenting by deciding: Decisional dissent may reduce the risk of cascades but increase the risk of conformity or polarization, and conventional dissent may reduce the risk of conformity or polarization while increasing the risk of cascades.

Specifically, if we seek dissent on every decision-making body (to avoid the dangers of conformity or polarization), we must spread dissenters out across decision-making bodies rather than concentrating them in a few. These bodies are therefore likely to be roughly similar in their composition – and thus likely to render a roughly similar set of moderate decisions. Cascades, of course, occur precisely in such circumstances: when there appears to be an emerging consensus among the first movers.

If cascades are the concern, in contrast, we would want to give dissenters control over some decision-making bodies, reducing their numbers elsewhere but fostering occasional outlier decisions. That strategy, of course, precludes the presence of dissenters on every decision-making body and thus increases the likelihood that conformity or polarization will occur in some instances. Put differently, politically homogenous decision-making bodies – the ones most likely to be plagued by conformity or polarization – are likely to produce *visible* dissent in the system as a whole, and politically heterogeneous groupings submerge dissent at the aggregate level and thus create the risk of cascades.

Consider again Sunstein's proposal to ensure that every appellate panel contains at least one judge nominated by the other party. Consistent with the empirical evidence, we would expect the decisions those panels render to be relatively homogenous, as the presence of the Republican nominee would moderate the

28 Ibid. at 179.

decision rendered by the otherwise all-Democratic-nominated panel, and the presence of the Democratic nominee would moderate the decision rendered by an otherwise Republican-nominated panel.[29] Designing appellate panels to produce a more moderate set of decisions creates the risk of what Sunstein terms a "precedential cascade," where subsequent appellate panels follow the lead of the initial panels in ruling on a question.[30] Subsequent appellate panels – or the Supreme Court – might be less likely to depart from the "moderate" view than they would be if the set of appellate decisions on a given issue varied a bit. Dissenting by deciding (in the form of an "ideologically amplified" decision) would be useful to offset the precedential cascade that seems likely to take place were all appellate decisions to resemble one another.

In sum, the notion of dissenting by deciding suggests a trade-off embedded in the dynamics of dissent: Guaranteeing dissent within individual decision-making bodies may systematically submerge dissent within the system as a whole. It may be precisely when dissent flourishes at the intraorganizational level – when it takes the form of conventional dissent – that dissent visible at the interorganizational or aggregate level would be sorely missed.

The notions of conventional and decisional dissent thus provide a frame for connecting debates about institutionalizing dissent to a long-standing debate in election law circles – whether electoral minorities are better off exercising influence or control over the outcomes of a districted elections. Specifically, the question that is the focus of much districting scholarship concerns whether electoral minorities gain more legislative influence by "influencing" lots of votes at the legislative level or by "controlling" fewer legislative votes. The trade-off inherent in this choice has been thoroughly canvassed by scholars.[31] And it is fairly easy to conceptualize. Precisely because there is an easily identified mechanism for aggregating decisions (the legislature, which houses all of the candidates elected in a set of districts), we can see how concentrating one's votes to ensure control over some legislators precludes one from spreading out one's vote to influence many. To offer a rudimentary example, imagine a group large enough to constitute 50 percent or more in eight legislative districts. The question for the group would be whether it was better to create eight districts where the group controlled electoral outcomes or create sixteen districts where group members constituted 25 percent of the population (and thus could influence but not control elections).

The taxonomy of dissent offered here suggests that the same type of trade-off lurks beneath the surface when we make choices about the design of other disaggregated decision-making bodies, not just electoral districts. When viewed

[29] Sunstein terms this phenomenon "ideological dampening." Ibid. at 167.

[30] Ibid. at 59. Sunstein suggests that dissenting opinions may serve that role. In order to answer that question in this context, we would want to know whether dissents are more moderate when written for a mixed panel and whether, in the presence of significant agreement among two-judge panels, dissenting opinions will constitute *effective* dissents in light of the arguments sketched above.

[31] Much ink has been spilled over the relative merits of these two strategies. This question has been explored by political theorists, legal scholars, and empirically oriented political scientists. The political theorists have provided the terminology for the debate – descriptive versus substantive representation. See, e.g., Hanna Finechel Pitkin, *The Concept of Representation* (Berkeley: University of California Press, 1967), chs. 4 and 6. Descriptive representation is used to describe districts where racial minorities can elect a candidate of their own race. Substantive representation is used to refer districts where racial minorities can elect a candidate who will pursue policies favored by group members.

through this analytic frame, we can see that the main difference between these two sets of debates is simply that, in the districting context, there is a *formal* mechanism for aggregating decisions made on a district-by-district basis – the legislature – whereas "aggregation" in a context of cascades is a social phenomenon. Under certain conditions, when there are enough similar decisions by appellate panels or other decision-making bodies to reach a tipping point, those decisions, in the aggregate, set off a cascade.

This analysis suggests an interesting dilemma for electoral minorities: whether it is better to seek conventional or decisional dissent in situations where cascades are likely to occur. Conventional dissent among first-movers should increase the likelihood of a cascade. But it will also help *moderate* the set of decisions that triggers that cascade, so the uniform answer produced by the cascade will be a moderate one. Dissenting by deciding among first-movers may short-circuit or postpone a cascade. But if it fails to do so, electoral minorities may have lost the chance to moderate the decisions that ultimately become the consensus choice.[32]

Nor is this trade-off solely a concern for electoral minorities; it also matters for those seeking productive strategies for institutionalizing dissent and thereby improving democratic decision making more generally. After all, while we can imagine that some cascades are likely to be fruitful ones,[33] we can also assume that first-movers will not always reach the "right" answer (or at least not the "right" answer for subsequent adopters). Encouraging dissenting by deciding – differences in policy perspectives that are visible at the aggregate level – may serve an important purpose. It offers decision-making bodies a wider menu of models for appropriate choices, thereby allowing them to adopt a set of policies or principles that are tailored to their individual needs and forestalling or minimizing the harms potentially associated with a decision-making cascade.

III. INTERLEGISLATIVE DIALOGUE IN A GLOBAL ERA

Interlegislative dialogue offers an interesting arena in which to consider whether the notion of dissenting by deciding gives us any traction in making concrete policy choices about how best to institutionalize channels for dissent. Specifically, does

[32] For instance, imagine that environmentalists – aware of the emergency of a novel zoning question with serious environmental ramifications – were trying to decide whether to focus their resources and win a majority of seats on a zoning commission in one or two regions or to back a single candidate in each region to ensure the presence of at least one environmentalist on every zoning commission within the state. By spreading out their resources, environmentalists might be able to ensure that each commission to address the question during the early stages of the debate reached a slightly more favorable result. But that strategy would also generate a set of moderate decisions that might generate a cascade. Conversely, were environmentalists to concentrate their resources in one or two regions and garner majorities there, the decisions rendered by those environmentalist-dominated commissions might short-circuit a cascade by providing a visible, outlier decision (one highly favorable to environmentalists). But if the environmentalist-dominated commissions does not move first – so that their outlier decisions did not prevent a cascade – environmentalists will have lost a chance to seek a more moderate result elsewhere in the state.

[33] Ryan Goodman and Derek Jinks, for instance, have explored how to harness cascades in the service of promoting international human rights. See Ryan Goodman and Derek Jinks, "How to Influence States: Socialization and International Human Rights Law" (2005) 54 *Duke L.J.*, 983 ["Goodman and Jinks, *Influence*"]; Ryan Goodman and Derek Jinks, "Toward an Institutional Theory of Sovereignty" (2003) 55 *Stan. L. Rev.* 1749 ["Goodman and Jinks, *Sovereignty*"].

the taxonomy offered above – contrasting conventional and decisional dissent – suggests ways to structure international organizations in order to facilitate better decision making by nation-states? In the remaining part, I speculate as to possible applications of the theory offered here.

A. Dissent and the global polity

At first glance, one might think that worries about dissenting by deciding – dissent visible at the aggregate level – has little practical consequence for relations among national legislatures. Legislatures of nation-states, unlike appellate panels, are not embedded within the same governance system. Not only do they act independently of one another, but (unlike appellate panels) each must also deal with a different set of concerns and resource constraints. We would thus expect their decisions to bear no relation to one another. One might therefore think that if we seek sound policy outcomes, we ought to worry only about conventional dissent – dissent *within* national legislatures – not *among* them.

Recent empirical work, however, suggests that the cascades can affect the decisions of many institutions, including the governing structures of nation-states.[34] There is a robust set of empirical research suggesting that nation-states function like members of a "global polity,"[35] much as individuals are embedded in their own societies. They thus follow one another's lead just as individuals do. In the words of four leading scholars of the "global polity":

> Nation-state structures and policies are often expected to reflect the great diversity in resources and cultures behind these societies. But in fact, . . . studies show that striking similarities increasingly characterize nation-state structures and policies. Across many different domains, countries appear to be enacting common models or scripts of what a nation-state ought to be. This is true with respect to national constitutions and state bureaucracies (for example, statements of purposes and goals, cabinet and agency formation), socio-economic progress models (for example, emphases on economic growth and population control), and egalitarian citizenship models (for example, the rights of women and children).[36]

There is evidence that nation-state mimicry is pervasive. "Nation-states are remarkably uniform in defining their goals as the enhancement of collective progress (roughly gross domestic product per capita) and individual rights and development (roughly citizen enhancement and equality). This occurs in constitutions . . . in general statements on national education . . . in depictions of the

[34] For a helpful survey of this literature, see John W. Meyer et al., "World Society and the Nation-State" (1997) 103 *Amer. J. Soc.* 144; Martha Finnemore, "Norms, Culture, and World Politics: Insights from Sociology's Institutionalism" (1996) 50 *Int'l Org.* 325. For general introduction to the social science behind the global polity literature, see W. Richard Scott, *Institutions and Organizations*, 2nd ed. (Thousand Oaks, Calif.: Sage, 2001). Ryan Goodman and Derek Jinks have led the way in connecting this literature to legal scholarship and exploring its potential ramifications for international law, particularly human rights law. See Goodman and Jinks, *Sovereignty*, ibid.; Goodman and Jinks, *Influence*, ibid.

[35] The global polity "consists of much more than a 'system of states' or 'world economy' or 'international system.' Rather, the global environment is a sea teaming with a great variety of social units – states and their associated polities, military alliances, business enterprises, social movements, terrorists, political activists, nongovernmental organizations – all of which may be involved in relations with the polity." John Boli, "Sovereignty from a World Polity Perspective" in Stephen D. Krasner, ed., *Problematic Sovereignty* (New York: Columbia University Press, 2001) 53 at 59–60.

[36] Gili Drori et al., *Science in the Modern World Polity: Institutionalization and Globalization IX* (Stanford: Stanford University Press, 2003).

nation ... in educational curricula ... and in vast amounts of formal economic policy."[37] For instance, states deploy similar record-keeping systems,[38] and they mandate mass education in school systems with similar curricula and administrative structures.[39] Counterintuitively, we see mimesis even in areas where we might assume cultural differences would override it. The enrollment of women in institutions of higher education, for example, increased around the world at roughly the same rate and at about the same time in Western and non-Western countries.[40]

Scholars argue that membership in the "global polity" better explains the mimesis we see in nation-states than other competing theories, such as arguments about coercion or theories linking nation-state characteristics to a country's stage of development or internal needs.[41] As Ryan Goodman and Derek Jinks have noted:

> the empirical studies ... show that norm adoption does not correlate with the economic wealth or development of country.... [S]ubstantial evidence ... shows that isomorphism will frequently occur regardless of whether there is external political pressure to conform. For example, governments follow global scripts concerning the proper orientation of state policy toward children – even though powerful states do not have a strong interest in monitoring or forcing others to adopt such an ideology.[42]

Perhaps most remarkably, the isomorphism is "decoupled" from the on-the-ground needs of the country: "structural similarity does not reflect converging task demands, or, put differently, structures is not determined by function."[43]

The best explanation for nation-state mimicry, according to these scholars, is the existence of a global polity; international society constructs the identity of the nation-state by recognizing only those states that fit a particular model, leading other nation-states to reproduce the model.[44] Put differently, impulses toward conformity are not confined to individual actors but, at least in some contexts,

[37] Meyer et al., *supra* note 34 at 153.

[38] See Connie L. McNeely, *Constructing the Nation State: International Organization and Prescriptive Action* (Westport, Conn.: Greenwood Press, 1995).

[39] Isomorphism and decoupling have been found in "constitutional forms emphasizing both state power and individual rights, mass schooling systems organized around a fairly standard curriculum, rationalized economic and demographic record keeping and date systems, antinatalist population control policies intended to enhance national development, formally equalized female states and rights, expanded human rights in general, expansive environmental policies, development-oriented economic policy, universalistic welfare systems, standard definitions of disease and health care and even some basic demographic variables." See Meyer et al., *supra* note 34 at 152–3. See also David John Frank et al., "What Counts as History: A Cross-National and Longitudinal Study of University Curricula" (2000) 44 *Comp. Educ. Rev.* 29; John W. Meyer, "The Changing Cultural Content of World Society" 25–45, in George Steinmetz, ed., *State/Culture: State Formation After the Cultural Turn* (Ithaca, N.Y.: Cornell University Press, 1999).

[40] See Karen Bradley and Francisco O. Ramirez, "World Polity Promotion of Gender Parity: Women's Share of Higher Education 1965–1985" (1996) 11 *Res. in Sociology of Educ. and Socialization* 63.

[41] That is not to say that power relations do not matter. Wealthy and powerful states may play a greater role in determining which ideas and structures define the world conception of the nation-state, and thus which set off cascades that lead to worldwide conformity. See, e.g., John W. Meyer et al., *supra* note 34 at 167.

[42] Goodman and Jinks, *Influence, supra* note 33.

[43] Ibid. at 1759.

[44] For a skeptical view on whether an international community of legislatures exists, see Daphne Barak-Erez, *An International Community of Legislatures?*, Chapter 27 in this volume. Barak-Erez's discussion is primarily focused on exploring what she believes to be the institutional incentives (and disincentives) for mimicry; it does not, however, offer an empirical test for determining whether such mimicry takes place, nor does it take into account the findings of the global polity research.

seem to influence nation-states as well. Cascades can occur within the global community just as they occur in local ones. First-movers can thus have an unexpected influence on the decision making of other nation-states.

Given these counterintuitive similarities between models of individual and organizational decision making, these findings of nation-state mimesis raise several questions about the role of dissent in fostering productive interlegislative dialogue and may point to paths for future research. The data raise the intriguing possibility that good policymaking decisions *within* national legislatures may depend at least in part on fostering dissent *among* them. After all, athough mimesis may result in the adoption of policies most of us would laud – human rights being the most noteworthy example[45] – isomorphism can also be harmful. For instance, the global polity literature reveals that landlocked nations seem to follow global norms when designing their militaries, leaving them with navies without ports.[46] Similarly, countries where "scientists and engineers comprise less than 0.2 percent of the population, and research and development spending is infinitesimal" create science Policy Review Boards to issue ethics reports and give guidance to scientists.[47]

B. Practical policy implications for fostering productive interlegislative dialogue

It is this way in which the notion of dissenting by deciding – with its emphasis on fostering dissent at the *aggregate* level – may connect to efforts to improve interlegislative dialogue in the global era. Assuming we cannot pick and choose which norms and practices generate cascades and which do not, Mill teaches us that we ought to think of decisional dissent as a global good.

Consider one set of questions related to the problem of implementing dissent. Given the apparent prevalence of cascades, one might ask whether there are any mechanisms for fostering dissent at the aggregate level at a stage early enough to slow, halt, or redirect an unproductive cascade. Put differently, is there a way to foster a more diverse set of global scripts for countries embedded in the global polity – to engage in appropriate "norm management," to borrow one of Sunstein's phrases?[48]

Unfortunately, the mechanisms for generating or short-circuiting cascades are underspecified and understudied. Scholars have not yet provided a full account of what norms will seep into the global polity, which practices will generate cascades, and which will not. At this point, then, we can only speculate as to which strategies are likely to succeed in generating decisional dissent within the global polity.

One potentially fruitful area of inquiry stems from the work of sociologist Martha Finnemore.[49] Finnemore has documented the influential role that UN agencies

[45] Goodman and Jinks, for instance, have sought to harness cascades in the service of promoting international human rights. Goodman and Jinks, *Influence, supra* note 33.

[46] See Martha Finnemore, *supra* note 34 at 336–7.

[47] Goodman and Jinks, *Sovereignty, supra* note 33 at 1760; Martha Finnemore, "International Organizations as Teachers of Norms: The United Nations Educational, Scientific, and Cultural Organization and Science Policy" (1993) 47 *Int'l Org.* 567 at 593.

[48] Sunstein, *supra* note 23 at 44.

[49] Barak-Erez also speculates as to the institutional mechanisms that might foster legislative mimicry. See Barak-Erez, *supra* note 44.

and other intergovernmental organizations (IGOs) can play in encouraging the types of cascades that scholars of the global polity have documented. For instance, Finnemore shows that the United Nations Educational, Science, and Cultural Organization (UNESCO) and the Organization for Economic Cooperation and Development (OECD) actively promoted a set of best practices regarding the creation of science policy bureaucracies beginning in the 1950s.[50] She argues that their efforts to promote and assist in the implementation of science bureaucracies – efforts cast in explicitly normative terms – helped trigger a cascade. Finnemore thus concludes that nation-state mimesis "is a process, not a cause" and suggests that IGOs play an important role in building the norms that seem to trigger conformity among nation-states.[51]

If Finnemore is correct, then IGOs may also be able to play an active role in fostering dissenting by deciding. At least two strategies seem plausible: The first is *disaggregating* decision-making authority, and the second is *postponing* the aggregation of decisions.

To begin, IGOs might consider disaggregating their decision-making structures, as is the practice with juries, school committees, legislative committees, and the like. By varying the composition of decision-making bodies, we increase the chance that decisional dissent will emerge. For instance, one tool deployed by IGOs is to offer best practices guides, which may become, in effect, global "scripts" for nation-states. Rather than offering a single such guide, such institutions could divide themselves into committees that grant power to would-be dissenters that is, representatives from outlier states. IGOs could group national representatives by region, economic status, or some other relevant characteristics, as does the Interparliamentary Union. Individual committees could then generate separate best practices guides, thereby offering nation-states a menu of choices – a diverse range of "scripts" – when implementing a particular set of policies or practices.[52]

A second strategy IGOs could consider is to postpone the aggregation of decisions.[53] For instance, when international organizations like the UN begin to implement a program, they sometimes choose a small number of countries as initial

[50] Finnemore, *supra* note 47.

[51] Ibid.

[52] Needless to say, it is important that these disaggregated committees be able to issue competing and coequal best practices guides for the reasons noted above. If countries adopt best practices because they represent "scripts" for nation-states, labeling one of these scripts a "dissent" or "minority view" may undermine its value as such. Such a label might suggest that those countries seeking the indicia of nation-statehood ought to shy away from such practices rather than adopt them. For an in-depth analysis of the then-extant empirical work on minority influence (in both its public and private dimensions), see Wendy Wood et al., "Minority Influence: A Meta-Analytic Review of Social Influence Processes" (1994) 115 *Psych. Bulletin* 323.

[53] The idea of postponing the dissemination of information about the answers other nation-states have reached seems a bit counterintuitive given our common assumptions about the reasons favoring pooling information. But the empirical evidence on the prevalence of conformity suggests that such a step might be necessary to avoid having what *seems*, at first glance, like a safeguard against the problems associated with conformity – the existence of separate decision makers. To put this claim in more concrete terms, consider Cass Sunstein's speculation that federalism provides "circuit breakers" for cascades because even if several states reach one view, "the federal system ensures that other states might come to different views." Sunstein, *supra* note 23 at 154. If cascades can take place at the state level as well as at the individual level, then it is also possible that federalism will only serve as a circuit breaker if enough of the states that are early movers *disagree* on an issue.

implementation sites. IGOs then use the information generated from those implementation experiences to provide guidance to other countries. Rather than aggregate this information early on in the process, these groups could avoid publicizing the results of the implementation process until *after* a number of countries have independently reached a resolution, thereby reducing the chances of a precedential cascade taking place before at least some policy variation, or decisional dissent, has emerged.[54] Thus, rather than "benchmarking" a project immediately, to use a term deployed in the democratic experimentalism literature,[55] IGOs could postpone benchmarking until dissent of the decisional variety – local solutions, the implementation of the views of global dissenters – emerges.

Whatever choice we make, the key point of this chapter is simply that we ought to be more attentive to the varied forms dissent can take. The notions of conventional dissent and dissenting by deciding offer an analytic frame that allows us to think more carefully about the appropriate institutional cure for the decision-making dynamic we are trying to correct.

CONCLUSION

As noted above, this chapter is largely a thought experiment; its purpose is not to provide an answer to the problem of fostering productive dialogue among legislatures in a global era. It is merely to offer a new vocabulary for thinking about the problem and its potential solutions. The chapter nonetheless suggests several paths for future research.

First, the chapter raises questions about which design strategy electoral minorities ought to prefer in designing disaggregated decision-making bodies: one that fosters conventional or decisional dissent. As noted above, theorists and empiricists have long debated the relative merits of "influence" and "control" as strategies for maximizing political influence in legislatures whose representatives are elected on a district-by-district basis. The existence of the trade-off is obvious to us because the legislature provides a formal mechanism for aggregating the results of individual elections. Furthermore, as I have argued elsewhere,[56] districts may not be the only domestic institution where this trade-off is at stake. Juries, for instance, may offer a similar choice to electoral minorities.[57] One might think that juries are

54 Cass Sunstein proposes something similar with regard to doctors, noting that a person seeking a second opinion should never tell the second doctor what the first doctor thought. Ibid. at 60.

55 Democratic experimentalism is a design strategy for decentralized governance structures that empowers local authorities to experiment with solutions to ongoing governance problems while ensuring that information about the success or failure of these experiments is gathered by a central authority so it can be pooled and shared with others. The seminal articles articulating and developing the theory are Joshua Cohen and Charles F. Sabel, "Directly-Deliberative Polyarchy" (1997) 3 *Eur. L.J.* 313 and Michael C. Dorf and Charles F. Sabel, "A Constitution of Democratic Experimentalism" (1988) 98 *Colum. L. Rev.* 267. The theory is modeled on "benchmarking," a widely used corporate practice by which companies survey an industry in order to identify strategies for improving their own performance. Dorf and Sabel, ibid. at 287. The notion of dissenting by deciding may, in effect, offer a friendly amendment to this literature by sounding a cautionary note about the practice of benchmarking.

56 Heather Gerken, "Second-Order Diversity" (2005) 118 *Harv. L. Rev.* 1099.

57 One might think that these observations would not apply to institutions governed by a unanimity rule, such as the jury. On this view, the only person who matters is the fringe voter, who can "hold out" and force the other jurors to acquiesce to her more extreme position. Although voting rules plainly affect jury deliberations, group dynamics matter a great deal as well. Indeed, contrary to the intuition

independent decision makers because there is no formal mechanism akin to the legislature for "aggregating" the results of a jury's deliberation. If, however, prosecutors, public defenders, and civil litigants "bargain" in the shadow of the law – they choose to settle or go to trial based on their assessment of the range of possible verdicts – then there is a possibility that the trade-off exists here as well. The question for electoral minorities is whether they want to "influence" the decisions rendered by a lot of juries – for instance, soften the verdicts a bit – or "control" the decisions rendered by a few. Is one likely to achieve "better" results when bargaining takes place in the shadow of jury verdicts if the median of jury verdicts moves slightly in one's preferred direction (as we would expect to occur with a system fostering conventional dissent), or if the "ends" of the jury verdict spectrum embody dissenting views and are thus further from the median?

The arguments offered above suggest that, at least with regard to institutions and issues where cascades are possible, we see a variant of the same trade-off. Here, however, the "aggregation" takes place not through the formal mechanism of a legislature or the informal mechanism of plea bargaining and settlement. Instead, the "aggregation" is a social phenomenon: When there are enough similar decisions by nation-states to reach a tipping point, those decisions, in the aggregate, set off a cascade. And the question for electoral minorities, one requiring further empirical research, is whether it is better to seek conventional dissent among first-movers (perhaps increasing the likelihood of a cascade but moderating the set of decisions that triggers it) or decisional dissent among first-movers (which may either short-circuit or postpone a cascade, or conceivably set off subsidiary cascades along the lines that the electoral minority would prefer).

The second set of questions this chapter raises is whether the other values associated with dissenting by deciding on the domestic front – the expressive and participatory values associated with decisional dissent[58] – obtain in the international context. For instance, one might consider whether, in the context of development policy, the creation of a global polity may undermine the potential for meaningful democratic progress by creating what Thandika Mkandawire calls "choiceless democracies,"[59] and whether a possible cure is disaggregation of such

about holdouts, "strong social-psychological evidence [suggests] that the pressure to conform [is] nearly irresistible when a single person [is] faced with a unanimous majority." Phoebe C. Ellsworth, "One Inspiring Jury" (2003) 101 *Mich. L. Rev.* 1387 at 1396. Thus, the jurors most likely to determine the outcome of a case are those at the "tipping point" of the jury, not those who hold the most extreme position in the group. For a summary of the empirical evidence regarding the tipping point in jury decision making, identifying which jurors are likely to represent the counterpart to the swing voter, see, for example, Dennis J. Devine et al.,"Jury Decision Making: 45 Years of Empirical Research on Deliberating Groups" (2001) 7 *Psychol. Pub. Pol'y & L.* 622 at 692 (finding different thresholds for acquittal and conviction, and challenging the traditional hypothesis that the critical threshold is the two-thirds mark); Robert J. MacCoun and Norbert L. Kerr, "Asymmetric Influence in Mock Jury Deliberation: Jurors' Bias for Leniency" 54 *J. Personality & Soc. Psychol.* 21 (1988) (examining the "asymmetry effect" in mock jury settings where juries operated under different standards of proof). For some empirical evidence regarding the complexity of group dynamics on the jury, see Devine, *supra*. For a discussion of the effect of voting rules on jury deliberations and verdicts, see, for example, ibid. at 669; Douglas Gary Lichtman, "The Deliberative Lottery: A Thought Experiment in Jury Reform" (1996) 34 *Am. Crim. L. Rev.* 133; and Sunstein, *supra* note 23 at 164–5.

58 See Gerken, *supra* note 2; Gerken, *supra* note 56.

59 Thandika Mkandawire, "Crisis Management and the Making of 'Choiceless Democracies'" in Richard Joseph, ed., *The State, Conflict, and Democracy in Africa* (Boulder, Colo.: L. Rienner, 1999) at 119.

institutions – a set of regional banks like the African National Bank in place of the World Bank – that are more capable of granting meaningful decision-making authority to local actors.

ACKNOWLEDGMENTS

What follows draws inspiration from the work of Ryan Goodman, Derek Jinks, and Cass Sunstein and from conversations with Ryan Goodman, who provided invaluable guidance in connecting my own work to the topic of this panel. For helpful comments and suggestions, I also owe thanks to David Schleicher, the editors of this volume, and the participants in the Constitutionalism and Legislatures Symposium at the University of Alberta's Centre for Constitutional Studies. Excellent research was provided by Annette Demers, Monica Sekhon, Michael Thakur, and Andrew Werbrock.

Index